MW00535065

In this encyclopedic collection of everyday recipes—the first to cover the day-to-day home cooking of all twenty-one Latin American nations—Sandra A. Gutierrez, one of the most respected authorities on the foodways of the region, shares the dishes that you'll find bubbling on stovetops from Mexico to Argentina.

From Tortillas de Nixtamal (Fresh Masa Tortillas), Arroz con Pollo (Chicken and Rice), and Arepas Clásicas (Classic Arepas) to Solterito (Lima Bean, Corn, and Tomato Salad), Sopa Seca con Albahaca a la Chinchana (One-Pot Spaghetti with Achiote and Basil), and Pastel de Tres Leches (Tres Leches Cake), here are more than three hundred recipes—plus countless variations—that reflect the incredible breadth and richness of the culinary traditions of Latin America.

Sweeping in its scope, and filled with cultural history, personal stories, and handy cooking tips, *Latinísimo* is an essential resource for every kitchen.

ALSO BY SANDRA A. GUTIERREZ

The New Southern-Latino Table

Latin American Street Food

Empanadas

Beans and Field Peas

LATINÍSIMO

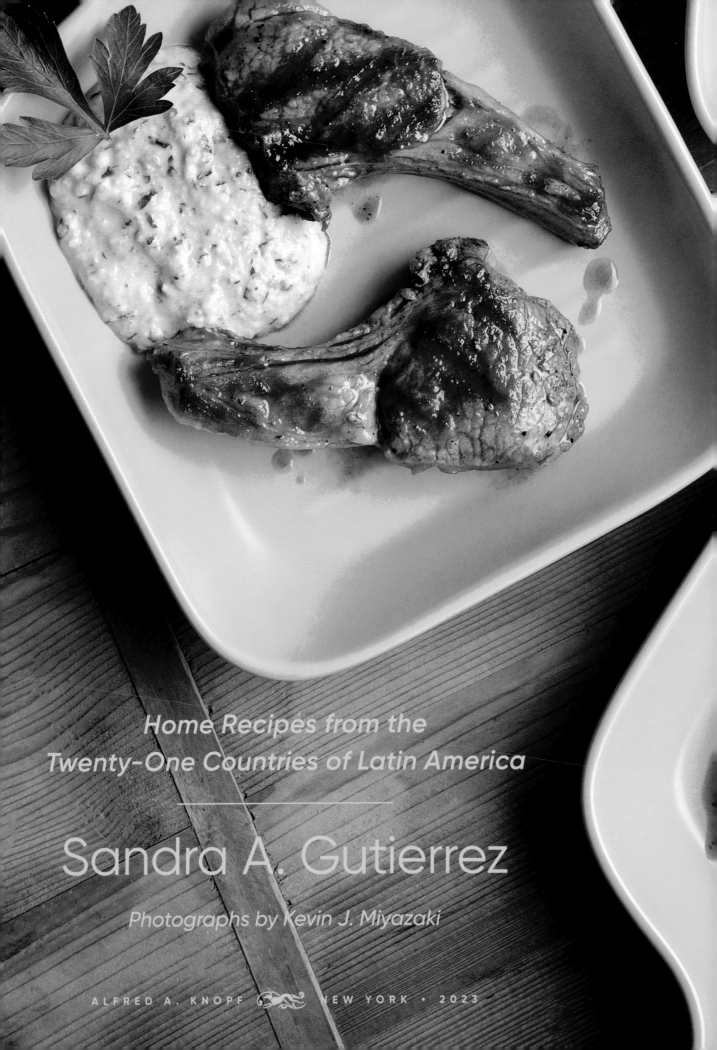

*Home Recipes from the
Twenty-One Countries of Latin America*

Sandra A. Gutierrez

Photographs by Kevin J. Miyazaki

ALFRED A. KNOPF · NEW YORK · 2023

LATINÍSIMO

THIS IS A BORZOI BOOK PUBLISHED BY ALFRED A. KNOPF

Copyright © 2023 by Sandra A. Gutierrez
Photographs copyright © 2023 by Kevin J. Miyazaki

All rights reserved. Published in the United States by Alfred A. Knopf,
a division of Penguin Random House LLC, New York, and distributed in
Canada by Penguin Random House Canada Limited, Toronto.

www.aaknopf.com

Knopf, Borzoi Books, and the colophon are registered
trademarks of Penguin Random House LLC.

Library of Congress Cataloging-in-Publication Data
Names: Gutierrez, Sandra A., author. | Miyazaki, Kevin J., photographer.
Title: Latinísimo: home recipes from the twenty-one countries of Latin America /
Sandra A. Gutierrez; photographs by Kevin J. Miyazaki.
Description: First edition. | New York: Alfred A. Knopf, 2023. |
Includes bibliographical references and index. |
Identifiers: LCCN 2022039482 (print) | LCCN 2022039483 (ebook) |
ISBN 9780525659259 (hardcover) | ISBN 9780525659266 (ebook)
Subjects: LCSH: Cooking, Latin American. | LCGFT: Cookbooks.
Classification: LCC TX716.A1 G8844 2023 (print) | LCC TX716.A1 (ebook) |
DDC 641.598—dc23/eng/20220821
LC record available at https://lccn.loc.gov/2022039482
LC ebook record available at https://lccn.loc.gov/2022039483

Some of the recipes in this book include raw eggs, meat, or fish. When these foods are consumed
raw, there is always the risk that bacteria, which is killed by proper cooking, may be present.
For this reason, when serving these foods raw, always buy certified salmonella-free eggs and
the freshest meat and fish available from a reliable grocer, storing them in the refrigerator until
they are served. Because of the health risks associated with the consumption of bacteria that
can be present in raw eggs, meat, and fish, these foods should not be consumed by infants,
small children, pregnant women, the elderly, or any persons who may be immunocompromised.
The author and publisher expressly disclaim responsibility for any adverse effects that may
result from the use or application of the recipes and information contained in this book.

Cover photograph by Kevin J. Miyazaki
Cover design by Emily Mahon

Manufactured in China
First Edition

To my husband, Luis, the love of my life

Latinísimo (*adj.*): very Latin American

Contents

Pork, Lamb, and Goat 405

Beef 441

Introduction

I often say that Latin American food is like a large house. The front door is Mexican food, because it is the most recognized of all Latin American cuisines; it welcomes cooks with familiar dishes like enchiladas, moles, and tacos. Yes, Mexican food is great. I love it, too. And I cook it often.

However, step further into the house, and ah . . . ! There are twenty other kitchens inside. Each one is as delicious as the next, and each one is different from the rest. Join me as we walk across the threshold.

Starting from the north, directly adjacent south of the United States, Mexico heads the geographic area known as Latin America. Mexico, together with the seven countries that form Central America—Guatemala, Belize, El Salvador, Honduras, Nicaragua, Costa Rica, and Panama—is known historically as Mesoamerica, and is the de facto bridge between North and South America, which is made up of Colombia, Venezuela, Ecuador, Peru, Chile, Paraguay, Uruguay, Argentina, Bolivia, and Brazil. The Spanish-speaking island nations of Cuba, Puerto Rico, and the Dominican Republic, located directly above Central America, compose the rest of the Latin territory.

I have so much to share with you, and the three-hundred-plus recipes you hold in your hands are only the beginning of what you will find in the homes and on the stovetops of cooks from the twenty-one countries that make up Latin America. This book is a collection of recipes from home cooks who, like you and me, have to decide what is for dinner when the family is hungry or time is short. Cooks who spend their days at work,

keeping homes and children, and yet put food on the table and gather communally to break bread, or tortillas, or arepas together each and every day. I have tried my best to represent each country in this book, because each has its own flavors, its own culinary roots, its own cultural amalgamations that have shaped the foods eaten there. And because each cuisine is as delectable, exciting, and vibrant as all the others.

First, a caveat: As you read and cook through this book, keep in mind that I have only touched on the smallest fraction of the recipes found across Latin America. You see, Latin food is like a Horn of Plenty, a never-ending parade of dishes, regional twists on recipes, and generational renditions that have evolved from a base history but continue to change as you read these words today.

I have spent my entire life studying, cooking, writing, and teaching about Latin American foodways. I've written cookbooks and taught cooking classes and traveled the world giving lectures to offer my food the recognition it deserves. My first tortilla press and comal are even on exhibition at the Smithsonian National Museum of American History. Yet my deepest wish has always been to bring my knowledge into the kitchens of everyday cooks.

Born in the United States, I grew up in Guatemala learning about Latin America's many food traditions through happenstance, without giving a thought to the fact that my palate was being educated a bite at a time. I was born into a family of global travelers who felt as comfortable eating in a Parisian bistro as they did in a Mexican cantina. There were unspoken rules: to taste everything at least once, and if the meal was in someone's home—considered the ultimate gift of hospitality—to eat whatever I was served, without question.

Many of the recipes in this book come from family members and friends, because much of my culinary knowledge has been gained at their tables or while cooking alongside them in their kitchens. It helped that my parents (my dad, a world-famous oral surgeon, and my mom, an economist) were social butterflies. Their social lives and professional networks were richly diverse; they hobnobbed with educators, scientists, artists, diplomats, and ambassadors stationed in Guatemala City, where we lived. In a country where people open their homes regularly, birthdays, international holidays, diplomatic soirées, educational and political lectures, and social gatherings frequently offered us opportunities to partake around a table.

I moved back to the U.S. at a time when French food was considered the only elegant "ethnic" cuisine. I was perplexed to discover that unlike Latin Americans, North Americans were not (yet) particularly proud of their own foods.

I come from a culture rich with recipes that have survived the test of time, through conquests, mass immigration, industrialization, modernization, totalitarian dictatorships, dispersions, and globalization. The culinary techniques that shaped the food of Latin America all the way into the twenty-first century make it ideal for the modern kitchen because they are familiar methods to most cooks or are very easy to learn. These are procedures that have been passed down the generations through oral history and practice. Although written recipes have been chronicled in many forms—books, notecards, handwritten notebooks, and so on—over the centuries, most Latin cooks have learned to cook things until they just look, smell, sound, or feel ready. Exact formulas or recipes for the home cook are still very vague, precisely because the methods needed to cook them were straightforward for the average cook.

However, today's cooks are busier with careers or other responsibilities, and are less likely to have learned cooking at the side of their moms or grandmothers.

Showcasing how to toast rice to release the aroma of the grains, to "fry" sauces in order to deepen their color, to sauté aromatic bases to give a recipe a regional flair, or to roast vegetables to produce sweeter stews enables busy cooks to make full-bodied meals without spending hours in the kitchen. That is the soul of this book.

Each country is represented with recipes that are based in its individual history but have survived through time. Some of these recipes have origins that can be traced back centuries; all are beloved dishes still cooked in people's homes today. Most have been popularized and widely adopted around the globe: tacos, ceviches, arroces, arepas, picadillos, and milanesas are just the beginning. Think one-pot pasta dishes are a modern invention? Ask Mexican and Peruvian home cooks how long pastas secas (such as uncooked fideos, which are simmered in rich sauces until tender) have been part of their everyday menus (answer: for more than a century).

In these pages, you'll find recipes that Latin American people are actually cooking at home. You won't find many recipes with complicated preparations—those have a place in the cuisines of Latin America but aren't often served on family tables day in and day out. Missing, too, are special-occasion recipes that are only enjoyed once a year during religious or national holidays. Nor will you only find dishes from only a particular period in time (the colonial, Republican, or ancient periods, for example), because the recipes in this book are representative of what Latin American home cooks are making today.

Some of these recipes are still prepared pretty much the way they were before Europeans arrived in the Americas, some have resulted from the maridaje (blending) of world cultures through the centuries, and some are still evolving today. This is not a book to relegate to your bookcase for instruction or research alone. It is a book to cook from. Because as much as I have tried to pepper them with history, trivia, and culinary tips, these are pages meant to be splattered with food.

Some recipes are quick and easy because the thirty-minute cooking craze also took hold of busy Latin American cooks and because this is the way Latin America eats today. Then there are those recipes for cooks who rarely spend time in the kitchen but who enjoy playing top chef on weekends—recipes that are hands-on intensive and require the constant stirring and shaking of pans. And there are a good dose of dishes that are lazily assembled and will cook on their own with just a little bit of effort from the cook while laundry is folded or books are read.

So join me on a journey of the cuisine of the twenty-one Latin American countries, to learn why pasta laden in tomato sauce (called tuco) is popular in Argentina, but pasta dressed in avocado and nut sauce is more likely the choice in Chile, its neighbor. Or why stir-fries are popular in the day-to-day cuisine of Peru, while almost nonexistent in El Salvadorian homes; or why every single Latin American country offers dishes similar to Spain's paella.

Eating through Latin America is akin to tasting world history. Every cuisine is a result of the melding of cultures, an ode to globalization on every plate. It's impossible to eat rice and beans in Nicaragua or Belize and not taste the African influence; it is equally impossible to bite into a dish of shredded beef in Venezuela or Cuba and not taste the legacy of the Spanish colonizers. None of the cuisines in vibrant contemporary Latin cities or the tiniest pueblos throughout the continent can escape this connection with the past.

Culinary knowledge is power; it destroys stereotypes, helps to build understanding, makes the unknown relatable, and opens borders. Cookbooks preserve cultures and build peace and understanding between strangers. By using this cookbook, you can help me desegregate Latin cuisines and open them up for the rest of the world.

I want to dare you to feel comfortable finding the differences between each cuisine, not just the similarities. Because as Latin Americans we celebrate diversity: each of our foods is as different from the other's as is our music, our histories, our language, our stories, and, of course, our countries. We are all one people, but we come from many. We are all Latin Americans, but we're not the same. That's how we want it. Argentinean food remains distinct from Peruvian food, Cuban specialties are unlike those from Mexico, Nicaraguan dishes are dissimilar from those in Chile. Belizeans, Colombians, and Brazilians all use coconut in their dishes, but each cuisine is still distinct and has its own characteristics. In a world where sameness seems to be a goal, Latin Americans still celebrate individuality; that, friends, is to truly love diversity. It's not to destroy differences but to accept and celebrate them, and to build bridges between us that can ultimately form a colorful, multicultural, and equitable quilt of humanity—a true melting pot. Not by making us all the same but by giving us all, different as we may be, equal rights, respect, and value.

Deciding on the recipes to put together into this book, restricted as I am by finite space, was a difficult task, not only because the job is a gargantuan one but also because there is no way to encompass all of Latin America in a single tome. There are thousands upon thousands of additional recipes that didn't make it into this book. (Perhaps another book is in my future, or maybe other Latin American authors will follow suit and fill the voids.)

Nonetheless, I believe that the recipes I have selected for you will give you an idea of the many voices of true Latin American cooks.

The front door is open wide: Pasen adelante.

Where Is the Latin Caribbean? · When I refer to the "Latin Caribbean," I mean the countries in the area of water south of Florida and above Central America that divides the North and South American continents. These are nations that embrace Latin, African (particularly Garifuna), Indo, and Caribbean cultures in a bundle, and where Spanish is the main language. This includes Puerto Rico, Cuba, the Dominican Republic, and the coastal towns on the Caribbean side of Guatemala, Honduras, Nicaragua, Panama, Costa Rica, Colombia, Belize, and the Gulf of Mexico. Although there are other countries in the Caribbean, such as Haiti, Jamaica, the Greater and Lesser Antilles, Guyana, Barbados, Curaçao, and others, there is great debate as to whether or not they also form part of the Latin Caribbean. I don't include them when I use that term and choose only to include those countries in which Spanish is spoken (with the exception of Brazil, where Portuguese is spoken), because so many people from those nations do not consider themselves Latino, but rather Caribbean or Afro-Caribbean.

A Short History of Latin American Cuisine

Once upon a time, the world was flat. People on one side ate things that those on the other side had never tasted or even heard of. The Old World had ingredients such as rice, citrus, beef, poultry, onions, cilantro, pork, wheat, butter, lard, milk, and sugar. The New World had chocolate, chiles, tomatoes, potatoes, peanuts, turkeys, squashes, beans, and corn.

The colonization of the Americas was the result of greed: for spices, for power, and for riches. For years, Spain had wanted to traverse the world via the Atlantic, in order to reach Asia, which would have allowed them to control the spice trade. Back in the fifteenth century, spices were very expensive; controlling the market meant great economic power that could fuel the expansion of empires. But by the time the Spanish turned their attention away from persecuting Jews and re-conquering the territory that the Ottoman Empire had taken from them, the Portuguese had already dominated the spice trade. The rivalry between the Spanish and the Portuguese fueled a new competition: to see who would control the lucrative market for sugar, which had become the most expensive commodity in the Old World.

In 1492, a Genovese navigator named Christopher Columbus presented several European kingdoms with a plan to circumnavigate the globe. After several rejections, Columbus convinced Spain to pay for his voyage. Aided by funds provided by Queen Isabel de Castilla and King Fernando de Aragón, he took off on his first voyage to "discover" what lay on the other side of the ocean. His goal was to reach Asia through waters that were not under Portuguese control. Not only did he disprove

the popular theory that the world was flat, he found a world filled with new flora, fauna, and Indigenous peoples with great civilizations. An unintended result was that he opened the doorway into a shared, global culinary exchange that made the world turn round and round. It has not stopped since.

When the ingredients and cooking techniques of Europe, Asia, Africa, and the Middle East met those found in the Americas, it was akin to a gastronomic tsunami. A fusion of flavors began to take place—not like the kind carefully orchestrated by restaurant chefs today, but one that has naturally evolved from the mixing and matching of ingredients within the kitchens of everyday cooks, like you and me. That was the start of culinary globalization.

Italians gained access to tomatoes, for use in their sauces; the Swiss built a whole industry around chocolate; the French (or Belgians, depending on whom you ask) came up with a recipe for fried potatoes; the Italians learned to turn corn into polenta; the people of India incorporated chiles into their curries; and so the story continues.

But changes took place in the New World, too, as Americans as a whole learned to use novel ingredients to produce food and entire industries. Latin Americans learned to bake breads with more than just corn or yuca flour; Argentineans built an entire cuisine around beef; Brazilians learned to fry food from the Portuguese, and then Afro-Latinos helped to spread the technique to their neighbors. Every Latin country inherited a love for rice and chicken dishes, meat stews and soups, and handheld pies. As sugarcane continued to grow well in the region, aided in the process by countless enslaved Africans who worked the plantations (called ingenios), the New World inhabitants also learned the craft of making sweets.

The foodways of Latin America are poisoned by the stain of enslavement, just as they are in the countries to the north. People from Africa were forcefully transported to every single region of La Nueva España in order to "replace" the millions of Indigenous Amerindians who had already succumbed to disease, wars, and inhumane treatment at the hands of Europeans. Portugal and Spain started the transatlantic slave trade in South America by the sixteenth century in order to enable them to fulfill their quotas of sugar and silver, which were declining due to the high mortality rates of Amerindians and indentured servants. Every Latin American country was tarnished by the slave trade, starting with Mexico, Brazil, and Peru. During the seventeenth and eighteenth centuries, the British, French, and other Europeans brought ships of enslaved people into the Caribbean and South America. The degree to which each country participated, offered sanctuary, encouraged interracial marriages (mestizaje), and freed Black individuals was different. The culinary imprint of Africa on the cuisines of Latin America was swift and everlasting. Latin American cooks quickly adopted African yams (ñame), plantains, and coffee. Gradually the culinary exchanges caused transformations to the native cuisines of every country in the world.

At the end of the nineteenth century, after wars and conquests had taken their toll, and after many of the giant empires had collapsed, the Old World was struggling to feed its people. Masses of immigrants turned to the promise of a better life that the Americas offered. Not only did waves of immigrants arrive in North America through Ellis Island, they also made it to the south and inland into the Latin American continent. By this time, swaths of land in the New World stood uninhabited, most of their original peoples having perished due to war and germs. Smallpox alone, brought over by conquistadores, killed millions; other diseases killed millions more. Slavery and exploitation took care of the rest. The newly formed republics (now independent of their European conquistadores) were desperate for people who could come and work the land (and defend them from possible conquest by neighboring countries), and they began to offer visas and parcels of land to new immigrants who were willing to "come to make the Americas" and work.

Different groups gravitated to different parts of Latin America. Italians found that Argentina reminded them of home, with terroir similarly suitable for growing grapes for wine. The British fell in love with the pampas deep in Argentina, as well as with Belize, "on loan" from the Guatemalan government, which they made part of their territory (just as they did with the Falkland Islands, "loaned" from Argentina). Neither territory was ever returned; instead, both were eventually granted independence.

Immigrants from the Philippines, China, and Japan settled in large numbers in Mexico, throughout Central America, and in Peru, Venezuela, Colombia, and Brazil. In fact, in the 1800s, Chinese nationals had begun to settle in Peru, where they worked to build railroads (just as they did in California). Lebanese immigrants settled in Brazil, Ecuador, and Colombia, and then went westward into the continent and all the way up to Mexico. Eastern Europeans found a home in Chile and Uruguay; later, during and after World War II, Germans settled throughout the continent, some escaping horrors and others running from justice. In the nineteenth century, droves of Jewish immigrants also moved to the continent, forming settlements throughout, with the greatest numbers moving to Argentina, Brazil, and Uruguay.

All of these immigrants brought with them culinary traditions, techniques, and ingredients that were quickly adapted and adopted by those already living in the Americas. The exchange continued.

Still, throughout Latin America a culinary common denominator remained: Spanish culinary traditions, which permeated through every culture that had once been part of their empire. (Except for Brazil, where Portuguese culinary traditions prevailed.)

At the base of each Latin American

cuisine, the remnants of their individual native heritages also remained intact; the flavors and customs of the Aztec, Maya, Inca, Olmec, Toltec, Taino, Quechua, and myriad other Indigenous peoples left their culinary imprint. Throughout all of Latin America, too, an African culinary heritage from the enslaved peoples forced to move to the Americas became an integral part of the gastronomic heartbeat of the New World.

This story continues to this very day. That is what this book is about: cuisines that have always been and continue to be in flux, changing and adapting to the many cultures that blend together in each region, city, town, and country in Latin America. The term *fusion food* may be a relatively new one (circa 1990s, coined by my friend Chef Norman Van Aken), but blended cuisines have always been a part of Latin America.

You will find Lebanese, Jewish, Italian, British, Asian, Indian, African, eastern European, French, Middle Eastern, and North American influences in the food of the twenty-one countries of Latin America. Kibbeh (quipe) found in the streets of Brazil and in the Dominican Republic have roots in Lebanese culinary traditions, as do the tacos árabes found in Mexico. Chinese recipes for chow mein have been adapted in the state of Jutiapa, on the eastern coast of Guatemala, and wontons filled with duck (wantanes de pato with tamarind sauce) are served all over Lima, Peru.

One doesn't have to look far to find the Italian influence in Argentine cookery. There, pasta dishes and grilled meats reign supreme. Tomato sauce, known as sugo in Italy, becomes Tuco (page 165), and Ñoquis de La Nona con Mantequilla Negra (page 296) and Berenjenas Empanizadas al Horno (page 242) all represent Italo-centric cuisine in the Americas. Mexicans also enjoy pasta in their sopas secas (literally, "dry soups"), in which noodles are cooked directly in sauce (this was popular in Mexico way before one-pot pasta became a trend elsewhere). The Italian influence is found all over the American continent, in fact. Chilean pesto is made with avocado; Guatemalan spinach, egg, and cheese crostini, called Tostaditas

con Espinaca (page 248), are similar to those found in Abruzzo, Italy.

French culinary influences abound in recipes such as Lomito en Trozo con Salsa de Chiles Secos y Cognac (page 472) and Arroz con Vino (page 333).

Likewise, Asian flavors can be found all over Latin America, especially in Peru, with its stir-fries, the most famous of which is the national beef dish, Lomo Saltado (page 470). The everyday cuisine of Peru features recipes similar to Japanese sushi and sashimi, as well as others that are very much influenced by Chinese cuisine, including dumplings and wantanes (fried wontons stuffed with different fillings), all sorts of fried rice concoctions called chaufas, and oodles of noodles like the Sopa Seca con Albahaca a la Chinchana on page 201.

Eastern European patisserie is found all over Latin America—particularly in Argentina, Uruguay, and Chile. You'll also find strong undercurrents of German and French baking on the table in many Latin homes. Recipes that reflect these currents include the Latin pound cake called magdalena (after the madeleines of France) found all over Latin America; Chilean sugary puff pastry cookies called orejas de burro or palmiers, and German apple cake (Kuchen de Manzana, page 529); and several other desserts, such as the famous Argentinean Pionono de Dulce de Leche (page 520) and Tarta Frola de Dulce de Leche (page 523).

Similarly, the food of the Middle East has had a profound impact on Latin American cuisines. Most rice dishes in the New World use the "pilaf" technique (in which grains or pasta are toasted in fat before any liquid is added), such as Argentinean Arroz con Fideos (page 329), as do the many versions of rice dishes called arroces that include different versions of Arroz con Pollo (page 332) and Arroz con Coco (page 501).

African culinary influences are obvious in such dishes as Cuba's Fufú (page 304); curries like Pollo en Coco (page 393), and stews like the Tapado or Seafood Stew on page 369. Not to mention the many dishes that use okra, peas, coffee, and other ingredients native to Africa. Africans in America also disseminated the cooking technique of battering and frying that they learned from the Portuguese.

Of course, the undeniable Spanish culinary roots that shaped many of these cuisines is a reminder of the past and evoked in dishes such as Carne Mechada (page 461), Cocido (page 462), and Flan (page 512).

By now, each country in Latin America has adapted and adopted different aspects of all of these immigrant cuisines. To this day, modern-day Latin American food is global and flavorful. This is not a cuisine that can be easily deciphered by exploring only one country's culinary heritage, because Latin American food is a virtual quilt made up of countless different global movements.

Learn to make a pilaf, and you'll have a base for most of the rice dishes in the Latin repertoire. If you can make custard, you can make flan. While each cuisine is different, cooking techniques and ingredients reverberate throughout the entirety of the Latin territories.

By understanding the common denominators that join together this vast culinary landscape, you will discover the distinctions that make each Latin American cuisine unique.

Some of the Indigenous Groups of Latin America · The Aztec, Maya, and Inca civilizations are the most recognized Indigenous cultures of Latin America—they are the ones who left large cities and impressive written accounts (and hieroglyphs) that showcased scientific, architectural, and mathematical advances. And yet, there were many other Indigenous groups that populated the original Latin American territories that simply disappeared without historical accounts to mark their time on Earth. These are the ancestors of the Americas; some were completely exterminated (by humans or disease) after the Columbian exchange; others disappeared during modern wars and famines. But some groups managed to survive and still exist and thrive today. We are indebted to them for the domestication of ingredients, flora, and fauna that formed the basis of each and every Latin American cuisine. We owe it to them to remember and celebrate their contributions. And we owe them a place in history. Here is a short list of some of the original Americans.

- Aztec (Mexico)
- Mexica/Nahuatl (Mexico)
- Olmec (Mexico)
- Chichimeca (Mexico)
- Toltec (Mexico)
- Mixtec (Mexico)
- Zapotec (Guatemala and Mexico)
- Tlaxcala (Mexico)
- Tzotzil (Mexico)
- Totonac (Mexico)
- Nahoa (Guatemala and Mexico)
- Maya (Yucatan Pensinsula, mostly Guatemala)

- K'iche' (Guatemala)
- Kaqchikel (Guatemala)
- Q'eqchi' or Kekchi (Guatemala)
- Garifuna (Guatemala)
- Mam (Guatemala)
- Matan (Guatemala)
- Inca (Peru)
- Sirionó (El Beni, Bolivia)
- Guaraní (Paraguay)
- Asunceno (Paraguay)
- Mojo (Bolivia)
- Bauré (Bolivia)
- Taino (Latin Caribbean, mostly the Dominican Republic and Puerto Rico)

- Wari (Peru)
- Tiwanaku (Peru)
- Chanka (Peru)
- Chincha (Peru)
- Wauka (Peru)
- Xauxa (Peru)
- Moche (Peru)
- Yanomamo (Brazil)
- Ka'apor (Brazil)
- Nasca (Peru)
- Chavín (Peru)
- Chimor (Peru)

Notes on Ingredients

- Eggs are always large.
- Black pepper is always freshly ground.
- Salt is always fine sea salt.
- Sometimes recipes call for ingredients to be "divided." This means that a recipe will use the same ingredient in different steps—so don't add it all at once.
- Always read the recipes first to make sure that you have all ingredients and equipment necessary and to understand the steps that will follow. There's nothing worse than finding out in the middle of the instructions that you're missing an important ingredient!
- Vegetable oil may be substituted with your favorite unflavored oil such as avocado, grapeseed, corn, or peanut. Flavored oils such as olive or walnut are not recommended as a substitute.
- When it comes to parsley and cilantro, do not play the "he loves me, he loves me not" game with the leaves. Include the stems, except the tough ends at the bottom. The stems have delicious flavor, and it will save you time in the kitchen.
- Ground beef can be lean or not, depending on your preference and health requirements, but should always be finely ground, unless otherwise specified.
- Coconut milk cans contain roughly 13.5 ounces, 403 ml, or 1⅔ cups.
- 1 large garlic clove yields 1 teaspoon of finely chopped garlic.
- Sugar is always white granulated sugar, unless otherwise specified.
- Milk is always whole cow's milk, although most recipes are suited for replacing with milk substitutes (rice, coconut, etc.) or even with goat milk, as long as it's whole.
- Heavy whipping cream is cream with 36 percent milk fat. It may be known as crema dulce, sweet cream, whipping cream, or heavy cream, depending on where you live. I refer to it as heavy whipping cream throughout.
- Shredded coconut is the same as flaked coconut. Unless specified otherwise, the coconut will be unsweetened.
- I tested all the recipes in this book using organic chickens weighing anywhere from 3½ to 4½ pounds (1.6 to 2 kilograms) because I find smaller chickens to be less expensive, much more flavorful, and just the right size to feed a small family. Today, many mass-produced chickens are colossal and filled with salted water to plump up their flesh. My advice is to use what you can find and adapt the cooking time accordingly. A chicken is done when its flesh, both white and dark, can be pierced with a fork and only clear juices run out (none of that pink juice, please).

LATINÍSIMO

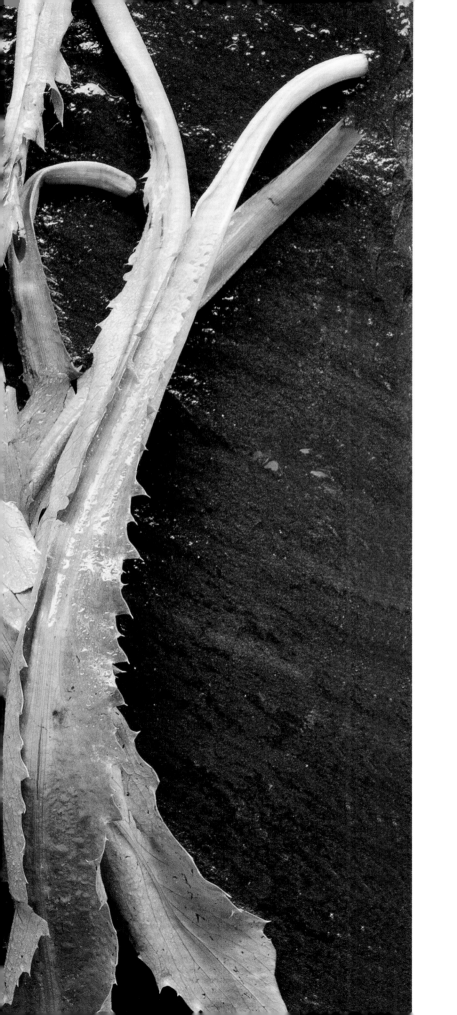

ESSENTIALS

Each and every world cuisine rests on basic culinary tenets that serve as the starting points upon which its recipes are built. You couldn't begin to tackle French cuisine without an idea of how to make a good mirepoix (a mix of carrots, onions, and celery) and at least a few of the famous "mother sauces" that serve as a base to so many of that country's national dishes.

Likewise, you cannot possibly begin to understand any Latin cuisine (let alone all twenty-one of them) without first learning some of the basic recipes, spice mixes, and flavorings that are fundamental to many (if not most) of its dishes.

This chapter will help to guide you through some of the most essential sauces, sofritos, pastes, vinaigrettes, and flavored oils that are important to the success of the recipes in this book. Learning even one new cuisine may seem a daunting prospect, and the thought of learning so many new cuisines at the same time may, naturally, feel even more intimidating. However, if you can understand the basic recipes that tie the entire region together, you can then understand what sets each country apart. This chapter includes both recipes that are widely shared by different countries and others that are strictly used in only one cuisine.

For example, all Latin American cuisines include a kind of sofrito that begins with a mixture of oil, garlic, and onions, inherited from the Spanish culinary tradition. However, there are many different types of sofritos; what sets them apart is the other ingredients that are added to the basic formula. For example, while Mexicans add hot chiles, Cubans prefer to include achiotes and no chiles whatsoever. And while Argentineans keep their sofrito very simple (resembling European flavor bases such as mirepoix), Puerto Ricans will most always add long-leaf culantro (*Eryngium foetidum*, an herb with long, serrated leaves grown in Central America and the Caribbean with a similar but much stronger flavor profile than cilantro) to theirs. Those different ingredients change the flavor completely. The same goes for spice mixes used to season meats or avocado mashes that serve different purposes, which at first glance may look the same but are, in fact, different from each other.

A great exercise is to make several pots of rice, and start each one with a different flavor base so you can taste the world of difference those ingredients can make to the same simple dish. Try it—it's an eye-opening and delicious way to taste the nuanced differences between one country and another.

Here are some of the most elemental recipes that will serve as a starting step to most of the dishes in this book. You'll want to come back to this chapter often. Consider it the key that unlocks the front door of Latin American cuisines.

Adobo de Casa

Everyday Spice Mix

Puerto Rico | Yield: Makes ½ cup (85 grams) | Difficulty Level: Easy | Total Cooking Time: 5 minutes

I am a faithful witness to my Puerto Rican friends' love for this savory spice mix. Most of them use a store-bought version. Violi Casellas, one of my dearest girlfriends from my days at Smith College, used to bring her own bottle to all of her meals so she could add a little bit of flavor from home. The bottle would make its way around the table so we could all add some to our plates—it elevated even the blandest dishes to new heights. Suffice it to say that I became addicted to its garlicky flavor. I've been making my own rendition at home for years so as to avoid the MSG in premade versions. Use this to season Puerto Rican dishes or as a dry rub for meats, poultry, pork, or seafood.

3 tablespoons (55 grams) garlic powder

2 tablespoons fine sea salt

2 teaspoons dried Mexican oregano

2 teaspoons white pepper

1 teaspoon ground cumin

1 teaspoon turmeric (optional)

Combine all ingredients in a jar and shake well; store at room temperature for up to 6 months. Always shake well before using.

Adobo para Carnes Asadas

Dry Rub for Grilled Meats

Central America | Yield: Makes ½ cup (85 grams) | Difficulty Level: Easy | Total Cooking Time: 5 minutes

This is a dry rub my grandmother used to make. Cumin imparts a grassy, lemony flavor, and dried chiles add fruity, sweet, and spicy elements. There are herbal and salty undertones, too; she'd rub it all over beef, lamb, goat, or chicken before she grilled it perfectly over a coal fire. Today, I use this spice mix whenever I wish to enliven quickly cooked meats. Since it keeps well in an airtight container for up to six months, I have a jar at the ready at all times in my kitchen.

2 tablespoons fine sea salt

2 tablespoons ground cumin

1 tablespoon ground ancho chile powder

2 teaspoons garlic powder

2 teaspoons ground coriander seeds

1 teaspoon dried thyme

1 teaspoon paprika

1 teaspoon freshly ground black pepper

Place all ingredients in a glass jar with a tight-fitting lid; shake well. Always shake again before using.

Adobo Uruguayo

Uruguayan Dry Rub

Uruguay | Yield: Makes ½ cup (85 grams) | Difficulty Level: Easy | Total Cooking Time: 5 minutes

This is my rendition of the spice mix used in Uruguay to season red meats, pork, poultry, or vegetables before grilling. My Uruguayan friends each have their own secret formulas, so I made my own. I like to make a batch at the start of summer and keep a jar in my pantry for those times when I get the urge to grill something for dinner. It lasts up to six months if sealed properly. Similar adobos used for cooking in Brazil are known as temperos da carne or tempero da essencia.

¼ cup (5 grams) dried parsley

2 tablespoons fine sea salt

1 tablespoon ground cumin

1 tablespoon paprika

2 teaspoons aji powder (see Sources)

1 teaspoon dried oregano (preferably Mexican)

½ teaspoon freshly ground black pepper

Combine all the ingredients in a bowl and stir together well; transfer to a jar with a tight-fitting lid. Store for up to 6 months in a cool, dark place. Always shake again before using.

Aliño Completo

Dry Spice Mix

Chile | Yield: Makes ⅓ cup (45 grams) | Difficulty Level: Easy | Total Cooking Time: 15 minutes

This is the ubiquitous flavor profile in many Chilean dishes—a simple spice mix that is available in most supermarkets there, but also easily made at home. Its sweet and smoky flavor complements almost any savory dish. I love to add it to stews and salad dressings.

2 tablespoons whole coriander seeds

2 tablespoons cumin seeds

1 tablespoon fennel seeds

1 teaspoon whole black peppercorns

1 tablespoon sweet paprika

1 teaspoon garlic powder

Place the coriander, cumin, and fennel seeds in a small nonstick pan set over medium-low heat and toast them until fragrant, about 2 to 3 minutes. Transfer the toasted spices to a plate and cool for 10 minutes. Place them in a spice grinder along with the peppercorns and pulse until finely ground, about 8 one-second pulses. Stir in the paprika and garlic powder and pulse until mixed well, about 2 one-second pulses. Transfer to a jar with a tight lid. This keeps well for up to 3 months, at room temperature. Shake before using.

Aderezo

Seasoned Oil

Peru | Yield: Makes ¾ cup (180 ml) | Difficulty Level: Easy | Total Cooking Time: 5 minutes

This is the secret ingredient that Peruvian cooks use to deepen the flavor of many of their dishes. Aderezo is made at the very last minute and must be added while still pilpileando—sizzling hot. It contains a mixture of ingredients, starting with onions but also including different herbs and chiles, all fried in oil until creamy. The point is to add the hot, flavored oil to food that is of a different temperature (from slightly cooler to entirely cold) right before serving. The sizzle is immediate, and the flavor is "sealed" into the dish, in a technique similar to what Indian cooks call tempering. This recipe for aderezo can be added at the last minute to any Peruvian rice or bean dish, or stew. Some cooks vary the type of chile used: ají amarillo is preferred in some homes; other cooks always use rocoto chiles; while those who live in the Sierra (the mountainous area of Peru also known as the Cordillera de los Andes, where the historical cities of Quito, Riobamba, and Cuenca are located) prefer to use ají panca. For this reason, I'm giving you a basic formula that you can play with to make your own. To adjust the level of heat, add extra chile paste.

3 tablespoons (45 ml) olive oil

1½ cups (170 grams) very finely chopped red onions

6 garlic cloves, finely chopped

2 tablespoons ají amarillo, panca, or rocoto paste (see Sources)

1 teaspoon fine sea salt, or to taste

½ cup (30 grams) finely chopped fresh long-leaf culantro (or double the amount of regular cilantro) (optional)

In a medium skillet, heat the oil over medium-high heat; add the onions, garlic, chile paste, salt, and culantro (or cilantro). Cook, while stirring, for 2 to 3 minutes or until the mixture is soft and has thickened slightly. Add immediately to the dish you wish to flavor and serve.

Aji-li-mójili

Puerto Rican Garlic Sauce

Puerto Rico | Yield: Makes 2 cups (480 ml) | Difficulty Level: Easy | Total Cooking Time: 10 minutes

This is an acidic, herbaceous, very garlicky, and distinctly Puerto Rican dip. Back in my college days, my Boricua friend Mari Carmen Schell introduced me to aji-li-mójili (pronounced *ah-hee-lee-moh-jee-lee*) and crispy tostones. Ajicitos dulces, also known as ají cachucha or ají gustoso, may look exactly like habaneros but have none of the heat that the latter are known for; they're a bit hard to find, unless you have a Latin American market that caters to Caribbean customers. Substitute sweet wax peppers in this recipe or habanadas, an habanero hybrid without heat. Mari Carmen blends this sauce until smooth and uses it as a marinade, or leaves it chunky to use as a dipping sauce, depending on what mood she's in. I offer you both renditions. Keep in the refrigerator, well sealed, for up to two weeks; shake well before using.

6 large garlic cloves

4 jalapeños or 8–10 ajicitos dulces, seeded and deveined

½ cup (30 grams) fresh long-leaf culantro (or double the amount of regular cilantro)

⅓ cup (75 ml) white vinegar

⅓ cup (75 ml) freshly squeezed lime juice

1 tablespoon fine sea salt

2 teaspoons freshly ground black pepper

1 cup (240 ml) extra-virgin olive oil

To use as a marinade: Place all the ingredients in the jar of a blender. Blend on high until smooth.

To use as a dipping sauce: Finely chop the garlic, jalapeños or ajicitos, and culantro by hand. Place them in a jar with a tight-fitting lid, add the rest of the ingredients, and shake until combined.

Aliño

Vinegary Marinade

Ecuador | Yield: Makes about 1¾ cups (450 ml) | Difficulty Level: Easy | Total Cooking Time: 10 minutes

This is an uncooked liquid flavor base that is added to many Ecuadorian dishes at the start of a recipe. Be aware that it's very strong. Serve it on the side of Ecuadorian recipes that can use a bit of acidity.

½ cup (115 grams) very roughly chopped red onions

½ cup (115 grams) very roughly chopped white onions

½ cup (120 grams) very roughly chopped celery

10 garlic cloves

2 teaspoons ground cumin

2 teaspoons ground oregano

1–2 tablespoons white vinegar, to taste

½ cup (120 ml) boiling water

Place all the ingredients in a blender and blend until very smooth. The aliño will be quite liquid. Store it in a tightly covered jar (or nonreactive container) for up to 1 week in the refrigerator.

Note: I freeze this in ice cube trays; once frozen solid, I transfer to ziplock bags to use as needed (they will keep for up to 4 months). Always bring back to room temperature before using.

Mojito Isleño

Herb and Garlic Sauce

Cuba and Puerto Rico | Yield: Makes 1½ cups (360 ml) | Difficulty Level: Easy | Total Cooking Time: 10 minutes

This is the garlic-citrus-spice-rich sauce that often accompanies plates of Latin Caribbean dishes. It will keep for up to four days if properly covered and refrigerated, but it's easy enough to make to order whenever you crave a taste of the islands. If you can't find long-leaf culantro, which makes the mojito a vibrant green color and amps up the flavor, use twice the amount of regular cilantro instead. Use this as a dip for fried foods.

1 small (4 ounces/115 grams) white onion, roughly chopped

3 large garlic cloves, roughly chopped

1 cup (170 grams) roughly chopped fresh long-leaf culantro (or double the amount of regular cilantro)

⅓ cup (75 ml) freshly squeezed lime juice

1 teaspoon dried oregano

½ teaspoon ground cumin

1 teaspoon fine sea salt

1 teaspoon freshly ground black pepper

1 cup (240 ml) extra-virgin olive oil

Place all the ingredients in a blender and blend until smooth; set aside.

VARIATION: A great way to use mojito is as a dipping sauce for chicken chicharrones, a typical Creole food in both Puerto Rico and Cuba. To make the chicharrones, cube 2 pounds (910 grams) of boneless chicken thighs (skins on) into bite-sized pieces. Season them generously with Adobo de Casa (page 6), then dredge them in flour, shaking off any excess. Shallow-fry in very hot vegetable oil (360°F/180°C) until crispy and cooked through. Serve with mojito on the side, as a starter or appetizer. Add a side of white rice and a salad for a whole meal.

Mojo Cubano

Citrus and Garlic Marinade

Cuba | Yield: Makes 1 cup (240 ml) | Difficulty Level: Easy | Total Cooking Time: 15 minutes

My son-in-law's family is Cuban, and I've made it my mission to perfect as many of the recipes of his beloved heritage as possible. Mojo is a pungent and garlicky sauce with many uses. You'll find it sold in large jars at most grocery stores, but it's so easy to make at home and it tastes much better. It can be served as a dip for fried plantains, as a topping for fried pork bits, or as a sauce for boiled yuca. It also makes a magnificent marinade for chicken, pork, and shrimp. Mojo will last in the refrigerator for up to twenty-four hours. If serving on the side, let it come back to room temperature. Sour orange (naranja agria) is usually used to make mojo; if you can find it, by all means use it. If not, I find that the combination of lemon and orange juices mimics the taste almost exactly.

⅓ cup (75 ml) extra-virgin olive oil

⅓ cup (75 ml) freshly squeezed lemon juice

⅓ cup (75 ml) freshly squeezed orange juice

6 large garlic cloves, minced

1 teaspoon fine sea salt

½ teaspoon ground cumin

½ teaspoon freshly ground black pepper

Place the olive oil in a medium pot set over medium heat. In a small bowl, combine the lemon and orange juice and set aside. When the oil is hot, add the garlic and cook for 20 seconds. Stand back and quickly add the citrus juices (be careful, it will splatter); lower the heat to low and add the salt, cumin, and pepper. Bring up to a low simmer, then immediately remove from the heat. Cool completely before using.

VARIATION: Marinate a cut-up whole chicken in the mojo for 8 hours in the refrigerator; preheat the oven to 400°F (200°C). Place the chicken pieces and marinade in a roasting pan, season with salt, and roast for 45 to 60 minutes or until juices run clear when pierced with a fork.

Pasta de Ajo

Garlic Paste

Peru | Yield: Makes ¾ cup (180 ml) | Difficulty Level: Easy | Total Cooking Time: 10 minutes

Many Peruvian recipes begin with this paste, particularly all sorts of saltados (stir-fried dishes). You'll find jars of garlic paste in Peruvian supermarkets, but it's so easy to make that I keep it around all the time; if stored in a glass jar, it lasts two weeks in the refrigerator. I add it to any recipe that uses garlic (Peruvian or not)—always as the last ingredient so it won't burn. It's fabulous in pasta sauces, bean pots, stews, or in any soup that can benefit from an extra kick of garlic. The acidity in the lime juice will prevent the mixture from oxidizing and turning an ugly shade of black; it will also help to preserve the garlic longer.

30–35 large garlic cloves (about 3 heads, weighing a total of 5 ounces/145 grams), roughly chopped

4 tablespoons (60 ml) vegetable oil
1 teaspoon fine sea salt
Juice of ½ lime (about 1 tablespoon)

Place the garlic, oil, and salt in a blender. Blend by pulsing until smooth; add lime juice and blend again to combine. To freeze individual portions, line a baking sheet with parchment paper and drop dollops (about 2 teaspoons each) of the paste, separated by a couple of inches, onto it; freeze them until solid and transfer them to a freezer-safe container or ziplock bag; they will last up to 4 months.

Pasta de Chipotle

Chipotle Chile Paste

Mexico | Yield: Varies | Difficulty Level: Easy | Total Cooking Time: 5 minutes

More than a recipe, this is an easy formula that my grandmother learned to make when she lived in Mexico City. Use two teaspoons of this paste every time a recipe calls for one canned chipotle chile with adobo sauce. I keep it in a jar in the back of my refrigerator, where it lives comfortably for four to six months. If you intend to store it any longer, I suggest you freeze it in portions: lay spoonfuls on a baking sheet lined with parchment paper, freeze them until solid, and then transfer to a freezer-safe container or ziplock bag. Kept frozen, they will last indefinitely.

1 can (any size) chipotle peppers in adobo sauce

2–3 tablespoons white vinegar

Place the entire contents of the can in a blender; blend until completely smooth. It will turn into a dark, brick-colored paste. Add the vinegar (begin with a tablespoon and then adjust to taste) and blend quickly to combine. Store in a jar or freeze for later, as noted above.

Note: An authentically Mexican way to use this is in creamy chipotle spaghetti. Combine a couple of dollops of this chile paste with Mexican crema, stir it into hot, buttered spaghetti, and top with grated Parmesan cheese and chopped fresh cilantro.

Pasta de Ají Colorado

Red Chile Paste

Various Countries | Yield: Makes ½ cup (120 ml) | Difficulty Level: Easy | Total Cooking Time: 35 minutes

You can purchase many chile pastes today, especially online. However, this is the easiest way to process dried chiles into a smooth paste yourself. You can use this method to work any type of dried chile into a puree. If you want a truly spicy-hot mix, then use the smaller dried chiles de árbol, chipotle chiles, or chiles de Cobán. If using sweet chiles, you can add this paste to moles, stews, rice, and soups (such as pozole). However, if you use very spicy chiles, it's best to offer it on the side. My favorite chiles to use here are ancho, guajillo, morita, cascabel, New Mexico, Anaheim, mulato, California, chocolate, or a mixture of them all.

8 dried chiles (see headnote), seeded and deveined

½ cup (120 ml) boiling water

Place the chiles in a blender and pour the boiling water over them; cover the blender and let them sit for 30 minutes. Blend until smooth, then press through a sieve into a bowl to remove any solids. Cover and refrigerate for up to 2 weeks (or freeze for up to 1 month).

Chimichurri al Cuchillo

Classic Chimichurri

Argentina | Yield: Makes 1 cup (240 ml) | Difficulty Level: Easy | Total Cooking Time: 35 minutes

There are many recipes for this famous Argentinean herb mélange. For this chimichurri, the ingredients are quickly chopped with a knife (cuchillo) and stirred together into a sauce, giving it a toothsome texture and making it my condiment of choice for any good piece of grilled steak or as a dipping sauce for yuca fries and French fries.

1 cup (40 grams) finely chopped fresh Italian parsley (leaves and tender stems)

⅓ cup (40 grams) finely chopped white onions

4 large garlic cloves, minced

1–2 tablespoons red wine vinegar, or to taste

½ teaspoon fine sea salt

¼ teaspoon red pepper flakes

¼ teaspoon freshly ground black pepper

½ cup (120 ml) extra-virgin olive oil

In a medium bowl, combine the parsley, onions, garlic, vinegar, salt, red pepper flakes, and pepper. Whisk in the olive oil, in a drizzle, until combined. Cover and let the chimichurri sit at room temperature for 30 minutes before serving. If not using it immediately, refrigerate it for up to 2 days; bring it back to room temperature before serving.

Chimichurri de Cilantro

Cilantro Chimichurri

Central America | Yield: Makes 1¼ cups (360 ml) | Difficulty Level: Easy | Total Cooking Time: 5 minutes

Chimichurri can be used as a vinaigrette, a marinade, or a sauce. It is made by pounding green herbs and garlic into a paste, similar to pesto, but instead of cheese and nuts, it's flavored with herbs and spices. There are as many renditions as there are cooks, and although traditional chimichurri is made with parsley in Argentina, Nicaraguans use a variety of herbs. In South America, some traditional chimichurris include carrots and celery; others peppers (pimentón); and yet others tomatoes. But this version integrates cilantro, in the tradition of one most often found in Central America.

1½ cups (120 grams) chopped fresh cilantro (leaves and tender stems)

1½ cups (120 grams) chopped fresh flat-leaf parsley (leaves and tender stems)

1 cup (115 grams) roughly chopped white onions

3 garlic cloves, finely chopped

3 tablespoons (45 ml) white wine vinegar, or to taste

½ teaspoon dried oregano

½ teaspoon red pepper flakes

½ cup (120 ml) extra-virgin olive oil

1 teaspoon fine sea salt, or more to taste

¼ teaspoon freshly ground black pepper, or more to taste

In the bowl of a food processor (or in a blender with a good motor), combine the cilantro, parsley, onions, garlic, vinegar, oregano, and red pepper flakes; pulse for 10 to 20 seconds or until finely chopped. Add the olive oil in a thin stream through the feeding tube while pulsing until the chimichurri is completely smooth; season with salt and pepper to taste. Keep chimichurri covered and refrigerated for up to 1 week, or freeze for up to 2 months.

Garnitura Criolla

Tomato Garnish

Bolivia | Yield: Makes 3½–4 cups (600–685 grams) | Difficulty Level: Easy | Total Cooking Time: 15 minutes

Here is the basic topping that Bolivians turn to when they want a refreshing and crispy garnish for their spicy-hot stews, called sajtas, which are made with chicken and beef. It is also used as a condiment for grilled meats, as well as with chicken, pork, and goat dishes. I use it on Falso Conejo (page 469). If you cannot find long-leaf culantro, use double the amount of regular cilantro instead. This is usually made only minutes before serving so it retains all of its crunch.

1½ cups (175 grams) white onions, sliced thinly on a bias

1 cup (225 grams) seeded and thinly sliced plum tomatoes

1 cup (175 grams) stemmed, seeded, and thinly sliced green bell peppers

Juice of 1 lime (about 2 tablespoons), or to taste

¼ packed cup (10 grams) finely chopped fresh long-leaf culantro (or double the amount of regular cilantro)

¼ teaspoon freshly ground black pepper

In a bowl, combine all ingredients; marinate for 5 to 15 minutes and serve.

Note: If you need to make this ahead of time or have leftovers, know that it keeps, if covered and refrigerated, for up to 2 days, but will lose a little bit of its crunch.

Garnitura Simple

Onion Salad

Bolivia and Ecuador | Yield: Makes 1¼ cups (280 grams) | Difficulty Level: Easy | Total Cooking Time: 15 minutes

This refreshing and crunchy onion salad—similar to (but not the same as) Garnitura Criolla (page 15)—is ever-present as both a side salad and a garnish in the city of Cochabamba, which sits directly in the middle of Bolivia, and it is also found in the depths of Ecuador (where it is also known as ensalada de cebolla). Some cooks chop the ingredients finely, while others leave them in large wedges—I fall somewhere in the middle. Like many dishes of the region, this salad is meant to be spicy, but if you want less heat, omit the serranos altogether. If you're making this like they do in Guayaquil, Ecuador, chop everything finely.

¾ cup (115 grams) chopped yellow onions

2 cups (340 grams) chopped plum tomatoes

1–2 serrano peppers, finely chopped

1 cup (170 grams) stemmed, seeded, and chopped green bell peppers

2 tablespoons red wine vinegar

2 tablespoons freshly squeezed lime juice

1 teaspoon fine sea salt

½ teaspoon freshly ground black pepper

1 tablespoon vegetable oil

In a medium bowl, combine the onions, tomatoes, serranos, and bell peppers. In a small bowl whisk together the vinegar, lime juice, salt, and pepper; slowly drizzle in the oil while stirring with a whisk or a fork and pour it over the vegetables. Let marinade until ready to serve.

Note: This garnish can sit at room temperature for up to 6 hours (refrigerate after that). It will keep, refrigerated, for up to 3 days.

Harissa de Santo Domingo

Dominican Harissa

Dominican Republic | Yield: Makes 1 cup (240 ml) | Difficulty Level: Easy | Total Cooking Time: 5 minutes

This is a spicy-hot marinade used to flavor red meats (particularly lamb and goat)—although it is also delicious on chicken—prior to grilling, broiling, or cooking on a griddle. The Arab influence in some Latin American cultures goes way beyond the recipes brought over by the Spaniards. A second wave of Middle Eastern peoples emigrated to the Dominican Republic after World War II. Along with the many Lebanese, Syrians, Egyptians, Tunisians, Moroccans, and Palestinians who arrived came many culinary traditions, including recipes for harissa. These were quickly adapted and adopted into the Latin American cooking lexicon. This is my version. I purchase chile powders in bulk online (see Sources).

1 cup (240 ml) extra-virgin olive oil

2 garlic cloves, finely chopped

½ cup (115 grams) ancho chile powder

½ cup (115 grams) pasilla chile powder

2 tablespoons cayenne pepper

1 teaspoon ground coriander

1 teaspoon ground cumin

Heat the oil in a small saucepan set over medium heat, about 3 minutes or until warm. Place the garlic, ancho and pasilla chile powders, cayenne pepper, coriander, and cumin in a nonreactive bowl. Pour the hot oil over the spice mixture and stir with a wooden spoon until it forms a smooth paste; allow it to cool completely before transferring to a storage container.

Note: Harissa lasts in the refrigerator, in a nonreactive container and well covered, for up to 2 weeks.

Recado Verde

Garlic and Herb Flavor Base

Panama | Yield: Makes 1½ cups (360 ml) | Difficulty Level: Easy | Total Cooking Time: 40 minutes

This olive-green "sofrito," redolent with the aroma of garlic and herbs, will impart a taste of Panama to your cooking. It is usually added at the beginning of a recipe and sautéed in oil before aromatics such as onions and leeks are added. Or it is used at the very end, swirled into soups, for instance, to impart a rich culantro flavor. Either way, I make this in one batch, divide it by two tablespoonfuls in an ice cube tray, and freeze it, storing the frozen cubes in a freezer-safe ziplock bag. They will keep for up to six months.

12 garlic cloves, peeled and left whole

1 cup (240 ml) vegetable oil

2 packed cups (140 grams) fresh long-leaf culantro (or double the amount of cilantro)

2 packed cups (140 grams) fresh Italian parsley

¼ cup (60 ml) water

1 teaspoon freshly squeezed lime juice

1 teaspoon fine sea salt

In a small pot over medium heat, combine the garlic and the oil. Bring the oil to a simmer (it will take about 2 minutes). Lower the heat and keep the oil at a slow simmer until the garlic has turned a light golden color, about 4 minutes (being careful not to let it burn). Immediately remove it from the heat and let it cool for 20 minutes (the garlic will continue to deepen in color as it cools). In a blender, combine the culantro (or cilantro), parsley, water, lime juice, and salt; with a slotted spoon, remove the garlic from the oil and add it to the blender. Blend everything; if you need to add more water to help the motor run, do it one tablespoon at a time, until the mixture starts to blend. Turn the motor on high and slowly add the oil until it all comes together. Refrigerated, recado verde lasts for 4 days; it lasts frozen for up to 6 months.

VARIATION: Fried whole fish is common throughout the coastal areas of Latin America. For a Panamanian version, select one cleaned and gutted red snapper per person. Season with salt and pepper, then place a tablespoon of this recado inside the cavity of each fish. Dredge the fish in flour and fry in hot oil (360°F/182°C) until crispy and cooked through (the flesh should flake easily with a fork). Serve with more of the recado on the side and lots of lime wedges.

Sofritos · Sofritos are the flavor bases for many savory dishes throughout the Latin American territories. They originated in Europe as an onion sauce, fried in olive oil; later, garlic was added. The oldest recipe for sofrito (sofregit) is found in the medieval *Book of Sent Soví*, from Catalonia, Spain.

As defined by that recipe, the main ingredient for all sofritos is onions. I mention this because when you cross oceans (of both time and space), you will find a plethora of sofrito recipes—so many that it's very hard to keep up with them! Yet the one ingredient that is ever present is the onion. Considering that onions were brought to the New World by colonizers, you can be sure that sofritos as we know them today in the different countries represented in this book did not exist in their present form until after Europeans came to the Americas. Once onions arrived, the simple recipe went through many transformations. Instead of solely using olive oil as the chosen medium for frying, lard, butter, red palm (dendê) oil, suet, and other vegetable oils were incorporated (and still are used today).

The two most important ingredients that the Americas imparted to sofritos were chiles (both sweet and spicy) and tomatoes. Additionally, pigments were added, to change the color of these mixtures. The first of the two favored colorants is paprika, also known as pimentón, ají molido dulce, or ají molido picante. Paprika is preferred by many cooks who want to impart a sweetish flavor and a reddish color, and is particularly beloved by those in the southernmost tip of South America, including Chile and Argentina. The second, and my personal favorite, is achiote or annatto (the seed of the plant *Bixa orellana*) (see the chapter dedicated to this ingredient, beginning on page 189). Achiote imparts a deep golden, yellow, or orange tone to food depending on how much you add. The flavor is hard to describe, but I find it "rusty" and a bit acrid in combination—albeit very subtle. It is also known as bija, bijol, color, urucu, and achuete. In places like Central America, the Latin Caribbean, and the northern countries of South America, achiote has long been part of the different versions of sofritos. Herbs also add color and taste: long-leaf coriander (culantro), cilantro, parsley, mint (hierbabuena), thyme, and bay leaves make up an important flavor component in some sofritos. Depending on the country (or even the region within each country), sofritos will be called by different names: recado, salsa frita, and salsa refrita in Mexico and Central America; sazón, hogáo, hogado, ahogao, ahogado, guiso, refrito, aliño, aliño rojo, and rehogado in South America; refogado in Brazil; and recado and recao criollo in the Latin Caribbean.

Some sofritos are smooth and velvety; others are chunky and textured. However, the basic technique remains the same:

1. Heat the oil.
2. Add a colorant to stain the oil, if using.
3. Add onions and garlic; sauté until softened.
4. Add tomatoes and peppers, if using.
5. Add herbs and spices.

Throughout this book, you will find different sofritos; each one is identified by the region or country in which it is most commonly used. Whenever you wish to re-create the flavors of an area of Latin America, a sofrito is your best bet. Cook a pot of beans or rice with a little bit of one of these bases, and you'll produce the flavor of a particular locale with very little effort. Sofrito is a vehicle for exploring the taste of the Americas—use it often and travel freely through its many iterations.

Sofrito de Ana Raquel

Green Pepper, Culantro, and Garlic Paste

Puerto Rico | Yield: Makes 3¾ cups (840 ml) | Difficulty Level: Easy | Total Cooking Time: 15 minutes

No Puerto Rican cook would be caught without at least a few tablespoons of this basic condiment in their kitchens—whether it's homemade or store-bought (it's so popular that you'll find it both jarred and frozen in many grocery stores around the world). Although many varieties of sofritos abound in Latin America, this Boricua version is rich in garlic and has sour undertones; it's made green and remarkably piquant by long-leaf culantro (also known as recao). I reached out to my friend Ana Raquel Morales, a cooking instructor and nutritionist living in Atlanta, for her own recipe. Once you try it, you'll want to use it often to experience the herbal aroma of the Isla del Encanto.

2 cups (285 grams) stemmed, seeded, and chopped green bell peppers

3 cups (455 grams) chopped white onions

20–25 large garlic cloves (about 2 heads weighing a total of 3 ounces/85 grams)

1¼ packed cups (85 grams) fresh long-leaf culantro (leaves and stems) (or double the amount of cilantro)

4 tablespoons (60 ml) white wine vinegar

Place all of the ingredients in the bowl of a food processor fitted with a metal blade (or in a blender). Process until the mixture has the consistency of a puree. Freeze in ice cube trays (about 2 tablespoonfuls each) until solid; transfer to freezer-safe containers. Keeps for up to 2 weeks if refrigerated; 8 months, if frozen.

Sofrito Rojo

Red Sofrito

Central America | Yield: Makes 3 cups (720 ml) | Difficulty Level: Easy | Total Cooking Time: 30 minutes

This is the flavor base for many of the Central American dishes found in this book. For this reason, I always keep some frozen into portions so I can reach for it whenever I need to add sazón hogareño (homemade flavor) to my everyday dishes. If you don't have a food processor, finely chop everything by hand.

1 pound (455 grams) plum tomatoes, very roughly chopped

2 cups (280 grams) roughly chopped white onions

½ cup (115 grams) stemmed, seeded, and roughly chopped red bell peppers

5 garlic cloves

¼ cup (60 ml) vegetable oil

1 teaspoon dried thyme

1 large bay leaf

1 teaspoon fine sea salt

¼ teaspoon freshly ground black pepper

Place the tomatoes, onions, peppers, and garlic in the bowl of a food processor fitted with a metal blade; pulse until finely chopped (about 10 to 15 one-second pulses), stopping occasionally to scrape down the sides of the bowl. Heat the oil in a large skillet set over medium-high heat; add the thyme and bay leaf and cook for 30 seconds. Add the processed ingredients, salt, and pepper. Stir and cook over medium-high heat for 4 minutes; lower the heat to low and continue cooking, stirring occasionally, for about 10 minutes or until the mixture is thickened. Remove from the heat; discard the bay leaf. Use at once or freeze in ice cube trays (about 2 tablespoonfuls each) until solid and then transfer to freezer-safe containers. Keeps for up to 1 week if refrigerated, 8 months if frozen.

Refrito

Achiote and Aromatics Base

Ecuador | Yield: Makes 2 cups (480 grams) | Difficulty Level: Easy | Total Cooking Time: 10 minutes

Refrito, meaning refried, is the flavor base for this Ecuadorian version of sofrito. My recipe resembles those found in the Manabí and Guayaquil coastal regions, and distinguishes itself from others by the addition of aceite de achiote (achiote oil) and a mixture of cumin and oregano. Like many sofritos, this amalgamation of flavors is a direct result of the African influence on the cuisine of South America. Refrito is at the base of the many Ecuadorian coconut-based stews (encocados), peanut-based dishes (biches), and stewed plantains (zangos).

1½ cups (170 grams) very roughly chopped white onions

1½ cups (170 grams) very roughly chopped red onions

1 cup (170 grams) stemmed, seeded, and roughly chopped green bell peppers

5 garlic cloves

¼ cup (60 ml) Aceite de Achiote (page 194)

2 teaspoons ground cumin

2 teaspoons dried oregano

Place the white onions, red onions, bell peppers, and garlic in the bowl of a food processor fitted with a metal blade (or in the jar of a blender); pulse, stopping to scrape down the sides of the bowl occasionally, until the mixture is smooth (it will be watery). Heat the oil in a medium skillet set over medium-high heat and add the blended mixture, the cumin, and the oregano; cook until fragrant and slightly thickened, about 4 minutes. Cool completely before storing. The sofrito keeps well in the refrigerator if tightly covered for up to 1 week, or can be frozen in a container for up to 3 months. (See the recipe for Sofrito de Ana Raquel on page 21 to see how I divide this for storage in the freezer, in individual portions.)

Crema

Crème Fraiche

Various Countries | Yield: Makes 1½ cups (360 ml) | Difficulty Level: Easy | Total Cooking Time: There is no cooking required for this recipe, but you'll need to start it a couple of days before you intend to use it, as it needs to thicken.

Crema is the Latin American version of crème fraiche—a velvety cream that can be used in cold or hot recipes. Each country has its own variation; some are saltier than others, while some are thinner than others. Whenever I can't find authentic Latin American cremas, I use this most basic recipe to make my own. It couldn't be easier: the combination of both creams makes the mixture thicken and sour while it sits. Make sure to start this recipe two days before using it.

1 cup (235 ml) sour cream

1 cup (235 ml) heavy whipping cream or buttermilk

In a large, nonreactive bowl, whisk together both creams; cover with plastic wrap and let sit at room temperature for 12 hours. Uncover, whisk again, cover, and refrigerate for 24 hours before using (it will keep in the refrigerator for up to 1 week).

> **Crema** · Mexican crema is similar in texture to heavy whipping cream, but a bit thicker. Guatemalan crema is saltier and more yellow in color. Honduran and Salvadorean cremas are tangier and thicker than their Mexican cousin. Every country has its own formula, but they are all delicious, and I encourage you to find your favorite, as they can be used interchangeably in recipes. Find them fresh in Latin American stores. If you can't find crema, and you don't want to make your own, substitute with crème fraiche.

Tres Salsas Blancas

Three White Sauces

Various Countries | Difficulty Level: Intermediate | Total Cooking Time: 20 minutes

Salsa blanca is a béchamel sauce. There are the three basic white sauces that most Latin American cooks rely on: Salsa Blanca Sencilla (below), Salsa Blanca Espesa (page 25), and Salsa Blanca con Cebolla (page 26). They are all made in the same manner but with a different ratio of ingredients. If you're not using them immediately, they will last for twenty-four hours if refrigerated, as long as plastic film is placed directly on the surface (otherwise, a skin will form on top).

Salsa Blanca Sencilla

Simple White Sauce

Yield: Makes 2 cups (240 ml)

This lighter béchamel is used to thicken soups such as the Geo's Crema de Chile Poblano (page 185) and to dress Canelones de Espinaca con Queso (on page 247), to dress pasta dishes, and to turn vegetables into creamy concoctions. It is the ideal sauce with which to make gratins.

4 tablespoons (60 grams) unsalted butter

¼ cup (35 grams) all-purpose flour

2 cups (480 ml) whole milk

½ teaspoon fine sea salt

Pinch of ground nutmeg

In a medium saucepan set over low heat, melt the butter. Add the flour and stir well to combine. Cook for 1 to 2 minutes, stirring constantly so the flour doesn't brown. Remove from the heat; add the milk, salt, and nutmeg. Whisk well until the mixture is smooth and free of lumps. Return to the heat and continue cooking until the sauce comes to a boil and thickens to the consistency of heavy cream, about 10 to 12 minutes. Remove from the heat promptly.

Note: If not using immediately, place a piece of parchment paper directly onto the sauce, to prevent it from forming a skin.

VARIATION: Make Costa Rican palmitos gratinados by slicing 16 jarred hearts of palm (drain them well) and place them in a small casserole dish. Pour enough of this sauce to cover and sprinkle with Parmesan cheese, to taste. Bake in a 400°F (200°C) oven for 15 to 20 minutes or until bubbly and slightly golden on top. →

Salsa Blanca Espesa

Thick White Sauce

Yield: Makes 1¼ cups (300 ml)

This is the thick version of salsa blanca and is preferred to help bind together ingredients to make croquettes and casseroles.

6 tablespoons (90 grams) unsalted butter

1 cup (120 grams) finely chopped white onions

⅔ cup (90 grams) all-purpose flour

1 cup (240 ml) whole milk

½ teaspoon fine sea salt

Pinch of ground white pepper

Pinch of ground nutmeg

In a medium saucepan set over low heat, melt the butter. Add the onions and cook for 3 to 4 minutes or until softened (but don't let them take any color). Add the flour and whisk well; cook for 1 to 2 minutes, stirring constantly so the flour doesn't brown. Remove from the heat; add the milk, salt, pepper, and nutmeg. Whisk well and return to the heat; continue cooking for 2 minutes or until the sauce comes together with the consistency of thick mashed potatoes. Remove from the heat; cool until ready to use.

Note: If not using immediately, place a piece of parchment paper directly onto the sauce, to prevent it from forming a skin.

VARIATION: To make Cuban croquetas de Jamón, stir in 1 pound (455 grams) finely chopped cooked ham into the warm sauce; cover and refrigerate for 4 hours. Line a baking sheet with parchment paper. Divide the ham mixture into 16 to 20 equal parts and shape each into a cylinder about 1 inch (2.5 cm) in diameter. Place ½–¾ cup (70-100 grams) of flour in a dish, 3 beaten eggs in a bowl, and 2 cups (240 grams) of bread crumbs in another bowl. Dust each cylinder in flour, then roll in the beaten eggs and coat in the bread crumbs. Heat 2 inches (5 cm) vegetable oil over medium heat and fry the croquetas until they are golden and crispy on all sides. Drain them over a metal rack set over a baking sheet and serve hot or at room temperature. →

Salsa Blanca con Cebolla

White Sauce with Onions

Yield: Makes 2½ cups (600 ml)

The onion version of salsa blanca is the preferred one for use in tart fillings and to bind ingredients used inside empanadas.

6 tablespoons (90 grams) unsalted butter, sliced

1 cup (115 grams) finely chopped yellow onions

⅔ cup (185 grams) all-purpose flour

3 cups (720 ml) warm milk (110°F/43°C)

1 teaspoon fine sea salt

½ teaspoon white pepper

¼ teaspoon freshly grated nutmeg

In a medium saucepan set over low heat, melt the butter. Add the onions and cook for 3 to 4 minutes or until softened (but don't let them take any color). Add the flour and whisk well; cook for 1 to 2 minutes, stirring constantly so the flour doesn't brown. Remove from the heat; add the milk, salt, pepper, and nutmeg. Whisk well and return to the heat; continue cooking for 2 minutes or until the sauce comes together with the consistency of heavy cream (about 10 minutes). Remove from the heat; cool until ready to use.

Note: If not using immediately, place a piece of parchment paper directly onto the sauce, to prevent it from forming a skin.

VARIATION: Make empanadas de espinaca by combining 1 pound (455 grams) frozen spinach, thawed and squeezed dry, with 1¼ cups (115 grams) shredded mozzarella cheese in a bowl; stir in the onion béchamel and stir to combine. Preheat the oven to 400°F (200°C) and line two baking sheets with parchment paper. Beat 1 large egg with 1 tablespoon cold water in a bowl and set aside. Thaw 2 ready-to-bake puff pastry sheets (1.1 pound/485 gram package) according to package directions. On a clean floured surface, roll out each puff pastry sheet to form a 12 x 12 inch (30 x 30 cm) square; using a sharp knife, cut each sheet into nine 4 x 4 inch (10 x 10 cm) squares. Line a baking sheet with parchment paper and divide the spinach mixture into 18 equal portions about 3-4 tablespoons (50-65 grams). Working with one square at a time, place a portion of the spinach mixture on the center of each square, brush the edges of the pastry with egg and fold the pastry over the filling to form a triangle. Use the tines of a fork to crimp the edges shut. Transfer the pastry onto the parchment-lined sheets, brush the tops of the empanadas with egg, and bake until golden, about 15 to 20 minutes. Serve warm or at room temperature.

Caldo de Pollo y Pollo Cocido

Chicken Broth and Poached Chicken

Various Countries | Yield: Makes 2 quarts (2 liters) stock and about 1 pound (455 grams/4 cups) cooked white meat and ½ pound (225 grams/2 cups) cooked dark meat | Difficulty Level: Easy | Total Cooking Time: 2½ hours

Knowing how to properly poach chicken and make a quality stock is a basic skill all cooks should learn, in my opinion. In Latin American cooking, poached chicken is used in soups and as a filling for tacos, enchiladas, casseroles, pies, cannelloni, and many other dishes. I encourage you to use organic, local chickens whenever you can. I select birds that include the neck and giblets so I can benefit from their great flavor. Chicken livers cause stock to become murky, so I never use them as part of my poached recipes (discard them or use for other dishes). If you can get your hands on chicken feet, by all means add them—your stock will be even richer. It takes some time to cook chicken well, but the effort is minimal. It is important to keep the liquid at a bare simmer while the chicken poaches so the flesh remains moist and does not become stringy. You can use rotisserie chicken in place of poached chicken for any recipe in this book. However, if you cook your own, you'll find yourself armed with luscious stock that can be used for preparing many other dishes.

One 4½–5 pound (2–2.3 kilogram) chicken, preferably with giblets and neck

½ pound (255 grams) chicken feet (optional)

1 tablespoon fine sea salt

1 small (about 4 ounces/120 grams) white or yellow onion, left whole and unpeeled

1–2 medium leeks, washed and trimmed of tough leaves

1 carrot (about 6 ounces/170 grams)

1 large head garlic, unpeeled

2 bay leaves

1 teaspoon whole black peppercorns

Remove the giblets and neck from the cavity of the bird; discard the liver (or reserve for another use). Place the chicken, giblets, and feet, if using, in a large stockpot containing enough cold water to cover. Add the salt and bring the pot slowly to a boil over medium-high heat, spooning off any foam that rises to the surface. When foam no longer rises, reduce the heat to low or just so that the liquid barely simmers. Add the onions, leeks, carrot, garlic, bay leaves, and peppercorns. Adjust the heat so the liquid continues to simmer very gently (you should see only a very few bubbles) and cook for about an hour (more for a larger chicken), uncovered, turning the chicken over once so both sides poach uniformly. Test for doneness by piercing one of the thighs with a fork. If the juices run clear, the chicken is done; if not, continue barely simmering and check every 10 to 15 minutes. Once the chicken is done, remove from the stock and allow to cool slightly, about 30 minutes, before deboning and shredding or dicing. Strain the stock into a large bowl and discard the chicken feet, vegetables, and aromatics. Cool the stock and divide it into containers. If refrigerated, it will last, covered, for up to 2 days; it will keep frozen for up to 2 months. Degrease it after it has chilled (a layer of fat will solidify on top, making it a cinch to remove).

Note: Cool any leftover chicken and cover it with its own broth. Freeze it for up to 2 months. To thaw it, leave it in the refrigerator overnight; transfer it to a pot and heat it through at a low simmer. If you use chicken feet, make sure to chop off the toenails before using.

A Busy Cook's Secret Weapon: Rotisserie Chicken! · Not only are store-bought rotisserie chickens time savers in the kitchen, but they are also extremely versatile. You can use the flesh in all of the recipes that call for cooked chicken in this book. Do not throw out the carcass! I place the skins, any leftover bones, and wings in a pot and cover them with water. Sometimes, I'll add an onion. Let it simmer for 1 to 2 hours, until the liquid is dark, golden, and thick. Then strain it and press all the juices out of the bones. This bone broth gelatinizes when it is refrigerated and is a fabulous base for soups or sauces. It's like pure gold in the kitchen.

Caldo de Res

Beef Bone Broth

Various Countries | Yield: Makes 3 quarts (2.8 liters) | Difficulty Level: Easy | Total Cooking Time: 4 hours of very easy work (don't let the time intimidate you—this can be cooked while you do something else)

Basic bone broth is a must in recipes that call for a richly flavored base, such as soups and stews. Many cooks today rely on store-bought beef base, bouillon, or canned broth, which is perfectly fine for everyday cooking, but I assure you that nothing elevates simple soups like properly made broth. Considering that soups frequently make up an entire meal in Latin America, it's understandable why many cooks will keep lots of this precious amber liquid, portioned out and frozen, for those times when they want quick results. This recipe will not disappoint. Make it on days when you are home; it takes time but very little effort. You will want this broth to have a lot of flavor, but remember that it is best to avoid oversalting it, as you'll want to retain control of the flavor in the final dish you use it in.

3 pounds (1.4 kilograms) beef bones with meat attached (such as neck or oxtail)

1 large white onion (8 ounces/230 grams), cut into 3 inch (9 cm) chunks

2 medium carrots (10 ounces/280 grams), unpeeled and cut into 3 inch (9 cm) chunks

1 small (about 5 ounces/140 grams) leek, washed, green leaves trimmed, and left whole

2 celery stalks, preferably with leaves

2 tablespoons vegetable oil

1 tablespoon fine sea salt, or more to taste

6 whole black peppercorns

1 small bunch fresh parsley (about 3 ounces/85 grams), with stems

Preheat the oven to 450°F (230°C). Place the bones, onion, carrots, leek, and celery in a large, deep metal roasting pan, without crowding them; toss with the oil. Roast until the bones and vegetables are nicely browned (about 45 to 50 minutes), tossing once or twice during this time. Transfer the browned bones and vegetables to a large stockpot. Pour 1 quart (960 ml) water into the roasting pan to deglaze (scraping the brown bits stuck to the bottom of the pan) and then pour it into the stockpot. Add enough water to the stockpot to cover the bones; bring to a simmer over medium heat. Do not boil. Lower the heat to medium-low (or low, if your stove runs hot) after it reaches a simmer. It is essential to maintain only a slight simmer so the stock will remain clear. Constantly skim any foam that rises up to the top (during the first 10 to 15 minutes), with a skimming spoon. Add the salt, peppercorns, and parsley. Keep the stock simmering for 2 to 3 hours or until the meat falls off the bones (adding more hot water to keep the bones covered as needed). Taste for salt and adjust to your liking. Cool the stock in the pot for 30 minutes. Strain through a sieve that has been lined with cheesecloth; chill stock overnight. With a spoon remove the solidified fat that has risen to the top of the pot and discard; use the bone broth immediately.

Note: If you wish, divide and portion the broth into freezer-safe containers and freeze for up to 4 months (or refrigerate for up to 2 days).

Carne Cocida

Boiled Flank Steak

Various Countries | Yield: Makes about 1 quart (960 ml) stock, 4 cups (910 grams) boiled beef | Difficulty Level: Easy | Total Cooking Time: 1½ hours

This simple way to boil beef forms the base of some of the most delicious dishes in the Latin American repertoire. Boiled beef is usually shredded and stirred into sauces for simple everyday stews. This recipe also makes a broth that I use as a base for soups or as a cooking liquid for rice dishes. As with cooked chicken, I freeze leftovers of this boiled beef, submerged in some of its broth (it keeps for three months frozen) and use it as needed.

1–2 pounds (455–980 grams) flank steak

1 small (about 2 ounces/60 grams) white onion, peeled and halved

1 celery stalk, preferably with leaves

1 large or 2 small bay leaves

2 sprigs fresh thyme

1 garlic clove

1 teaspoon fine sea salt

¼ teaspoon freshly ground black pepper

Place the flank steak in a large pot. Pour in enough water to cover by about 1½ inches (4 cm). Add the onions, celery, bay leaf or leaves, thyme, garlic, salt, and pepper. Bring to a boil over medium-high heat; cover, lower the heat to low, and simmer for 1½ hours or until the beef is easily shredded with a fork. Remove the beef from the pot; strain the liquid through a sieve and reserve it for other uses (such as for soup bases) and set both aside to cool. When the beef is cool enough to handle, remove any fat or sinew and slice it across in half. Use your fingers to shred it into thin strands or chop it with a knife into fine dice, as required; chill, covered, until ready to use (up to 2 days). Both the meat (covered with its broth) and the liquid can be frozen in containers for up to 2 months.

Caldo de Pescado

Fish Stock

Various Countries | Yield: Makes 4 quarts (3.8 liters) | Difficulty Level: Easy | Total Cooking Time: 1 hour

This is my basic fish stock, used to start seafood soups such as Biche (Viche) de Pescado (page 364). It is also delicious when used to flavor rice or Moqueca do Peixe (page 367). Ask your fishmonger to save you some good fish bones—most of them will charge you very little for these parts, which they otherwise discard. Fatty fish such as sea bass are particularly good for making stock.

1½ pounds (680 grams) fish heads and bones or 1 whole fish with bones, gutted, scaled, and cut into large pieces

1 large white onion (about 10 ounces/280 grams), peeled and quartered

1 large green bell pepper (about 6½ ounces/185 grams), stemmed, seeded, and quartered

6 garlic cloves, peeled and smashed

1 handful (about 2 ounces/60 grams) fresh cilantro, left whole, including stems and leaves

2 teaspoons fine sea salt

Place the fish bones and heads (or whole fish), 5 quarts (4.7 liters) water (enough to cover the fish), onions, green bell peppers, garlic, cilantro, and salt in a large pot set over high heat, and bring to a boil. Lower the heat and simmer, uncovered, for 30 minutes. Let cool for 20 minutes, then strain the broth; discard all of the solids. Cool, cover, and refrigerate until ready to use.

Note: Fish stock can be cooled completely, covered, and stored in jars in the refrigerator for 24 hours or in freezer containers and frozen for up to 2 months.

Salsa de Country Club

Pink Mayonnaise

Various Countries | Yield: Makes 1⅓ cups (315 ml) | Difficulty Level: Easy | Total Cooking Time: 5 minutes

This all-purpose dipping sauce, also known as salsa rosada, could be found in most Latin American country clubs back in the 1950s, and is a mixture between a Thousand Island dressing and cocktail sauce, if you will. It's easy to make and has saved many cooks when impromptu visitors call unannounced, because it's even delicious when served as a dip for potato chips. And yet, it's fabulously elegant for dipping cooked artichokes in, or to drizzle on grilled seafood. Puerto Ricans make a similar condiment that they call "mayo-ketchup." You can now find bottled versions in most grocery stores, but making your own is still better. Put this sauce on avocados, French fries, yuca fries, tostones, or other fried foods or use it as a dressing for hearts of palm or salads.

¾ cup (180 ml) mayonnaise

½ cup (120 ml) ketchup

1 tablespoon Worcestershire sauce

2 teaspoons yellow mustard

2 teaspoons brandy (optional)

¼ teaspoon fine sea salt, or to taste

Pinch of white pepper

In a small bowl, whisk together the mayonnaise, ketchup, Worcestershire sauce, mustard, and brandy (if using); stir in the salt and pepper. Cover and chill until ready to use (up to 4 days, if stored properly in the refrigerator).

Vinagreta Básica

Everyday Vinaigrette

Various Countries | Yield: Makes ¾ cup (180 ml) | Difficulty Level: Easy | Total Cooking Time: 5 minutes

Every cook should learn to make a vinaigrette instead of purchasing bottled versions full of unpronounceable ingredients meant to keep them shelf-stable. At its most basic, it must always be made with a ratio of one part acid to three parts oil. It is important to whisk the dry ingredients (salt, pepper, or dried spices) into the vinegar before adding the oil so they dissolve completely—otherwise, the vinaigrette will end up with a gritty texture. If you vary the kind of vinegar or oil used, you'll vary the entire flavor of the vinaigrette. For this reason, I keep a shelf of different vinegars (such as balsamic, sherry, white and red wine, champagne, rice, malt, and white) and another with oils (like olive, nut, sesame, and avocado). This is my basic version, which I also use as a marinade for pork, lamb, and chicken. I grow my own herbs and sometimes add chervil, parsley, cilantro, or tarragon to this vinaigrette—but you can play with herbs and make it your own.

¼ cup (60 ml) sherry vinegar

1 tablespoon Dijon mustard

1 shallot, finely minced

1 teaspoon fine sea salt

¼ teaspoon white granulated sugar

Freshly ground black pepper, to taste

¾ cup (180 ml) extra-virgin olive oil

2½ tablespoons minced fresh chives

1½ tablespoons minced fresh thyme

In a large mixing bowl, whisk together the vinegar, mustard, shallots, salt, sugar, and pepper. Slowly whisk in the oil until the mixture has emulsified. Stir in the fresh herbs.

Note: This vinaigrette stores well at room temperature for up to 2 days, or refrigerate for up to 1 week.

Vinagreta de Albahaca

My Basil Vinaigrette

Argentina | Yield: Makes 1½ cups (360 ml) | Difficulty Level: Easy | Total Cooking Time: 10 minutes

This dressing is tangy, sweet, and tasty. Basil has been adopted into the cuisines of many countries where Italians settled. My Argentinean friends have different iterations: some add parsley, others add sweet onion in place of shallots, and yet others use different kinds of vinegar. This became my own rendition, and today this dressing is one of the most requested recipes by the students who take my cooking classes. If you happen to have abundant basil to use during the summer, double or triple this recipe, which lasts, if properly covered and refrigerated, for up to two weeks. It's good on lettuce, over sliced tomatoes and mozzarella, and in my favorite salpicón made with jícama (Salpicón de Jícama, Pepino y Aguacate, page 232). It's also my go-to dressing for quick pasta salads (no mayonnaise needed) or spooned over grilled fish, boiled shrimp, or seared scallops. Try it as a dip for any fried food (from potato and yuca fries to eggplant coins to patacones). It's a winner, through and through—or, as they would say in Argentina, "Es un manjar": It's a delicacy.

2 cups (40 grams) fresh basil leaves

½ cup (120 ml) white balsamic vinegar

½ cup (120 ml) avocado or olive oil

½ cup (85 grams) finely sliced shallots

1 garlic clove

1–2 tablespoons honey, or to taste

Small handful fresh chives (optional)

1½ teaspoons fine sea salt, or more to taste

½ teaspoon freshly ground black pepper, or more to taste

Place all ingredients in a blender. Blend until smooth.

La Pasta Básica de Huevo

My Egg Pasta Dough

Argentina and Uruguay | Yield: Makes 28 ounces (800 grams) (serves 6–8) |
Difficulty Level: Intermediate | Total Cooking Time: 2 hours (including resting period)

Even before scores of Italian immigrants descended on the New World during the late 1800s, their culinary influences were palpable throughout the continent. Copies of *The Art of Cooking* by Maestro Martino de Como, written in the mid-fifteenth century, were found in many convents in the Americas by the start of the sixteenth century. Each Latin American culture has since adopted and adapted favorite ways to cook pasta. Although most Latin Americans cook dried pasta, those who have Italian roots still make fresh pasta by hand. Growing up in Guatemala City, I ate in the homes of countless friends of Italian heritage, enjoying all sorts of pasta dishes. When in the mid-1980s I moved to Canada, the first winter proved brutal for a Latin American girl. I was expecting my second child, had constant cravings for Italian food, knew not a soul, and was lonely. Italian markets offered me a respite: opportunities to meet warmhearted cooks who would start conversations as we waited to pay, who loved to offer advice on raising bambini, and who were willing to share myriad recipes. It was in those years that I learned to make pasta from Italian *nonne* (grandmothers) willing to teach me; they'd come to my kitchen to play with eggs and flour, while my girls napped. At first, I learned to mix pasta by hand, but dear Argentinean friends taught me to use the food processor to save time without hurting the results.

3 cups (540 grams) pasta flour

3 large eggs plus 1 egg yolk

¼ teaspoon fine sea salt

½ cup (55 grams) all-purpose flour, for rolling the pasta

Combine the pasta flour, eggs, yolk, and salt in the bowl of a food processor fitted with the metal blade. Begin processing the dough, slowly adding 7 to 8 tablespoons (about 120 ml) water, one tablespoon at a time, until the dough comes together. Turn out the dough onto a clean and lightly floured surface and knead it for 5 minutes or until smooth. Wrap the dough tightly in plastic wrap and let it rest at room temperature for 30 minutes. Roll and cut the pasta according to the directions of your pasta maker, using extra flour to make sure it doesn't stick to the rollers. Place the cut pasta on a lightly floured surface until ready to cook. Cook the pasta in plenty of salted, boiling water, until done (about 3 to 4 minutes for strands, and 6 to 7 minutes for large squares, as for cannelloni or lasagna).

Note: You can let fresh pasta air-dry for up to 24 hours before putting it away in containers; stored this way, it will last 1 month.

A note on pasta flour: I learned to make pasta with a mixture of durum wheat, semolina, and all-purpose flour. Today, you can find plenty of flour mixes called "pasta flour" or "00 flour." However, all-purpose flour alone and even bread flour will also work (as long as you add eggs to the equation). I suggest you find pasta flour in your grocery store or look for it online (see Sources for some of my favorite purveyors). Still, don't let the kind of flour you have on hand stop you from making pasta at home—it's inexpensive and tastier than anything you can buy.

Masa Básica para Pies y Tartas

Classic Pie and Tart Shell

Various Countries | Yield: Makes one 10 inch tart, 2 single-crust pies (tarts), 1 double-crust pie, 24 single-crust mini tarts, or 16 mini double-crust pies | Difficulty Level: Intermediate | Total Cooking Time: 2 hours (including chilling)

This is a basic tart pastry that every cook should have in their baking arsenal. To "blind bake" means to prebake the pastry without any filling, until golden.

1½ cup (170 grams) all-purpose flour

¼ teaspoon fine sea salt

9 tablespoons (130 grams) unsalted butter, cut into ¼ inch (12 mm) cubes, chilled

1 large egg

3–4 tablespoons iced water, divided

In the bowl of a food processor, combine the flour and salt; pulse for 10 seconds to combine. Add the cubed butter; pulse the motor on and off until the butter forms pea-sized lumps. Beat the egg together with 1 tablespoon of iced water and add it to the pastry dough all at once, pulsing until combined. Add more water, a tablespoon at a time, through the feeding tube, all the while pulsing until the pastry comes together into a ball (you may or may not need the full amount of water). Carefully turn the pastry onto a sheet of plastic wrap, flatten into a disc, and chill for 30 minutes before using.

(Note: If you wish to store pastry longer, you may keep it chilled for up to 8 hours or freeze it for up to 2 months—thaw it in the refrigerator overnight before using.)

When ready to use, unwrap the dough and lightly flour a clean surface; place the dough onto the floured surface—keep in mind that too much flour will cause the pastry to toughen—and give it a couple of whacks with a rolling pin to flatten further. If it cracks, it is too cold; let it sit at room temperature for 5 to 10 minutes and try again.

- If making a 10 inch tart: Roll into a 13 inch (33 cm) circle (the dough should be about ¼ inch/6 mm thick). Line a 10 inch (25 cm) tart pan with a removable bottom with the pastry. Remove excess pastry around edges and chill tart pan until oven is preheated (no more than 4 hours).
- If making 2 single-crust pies (tarts): Cut the disc in half and roll each piece into an 11 inch (28 cm) circle.
- If making single-crust mini tarts in ½ cup (2¾ x ½ inch/7 x 12 mm) muffin tins: Roll out the dough into a 13 inch (33 cm) circle, about ¼ inch (6 mm) thick. Cut out 24 rounds with a 4½ inch (11 cm) round cookie cutter. If needed, reroll the scraps, chill the dough for 20 minutes, and roll and cut again, until you have all 24 rounds.
- If making mini double-crust pies: Cut out 16 rounds for the bottom with a 4½ inch (11 cm) round cookie cutter and 16 rounds for the tops with a 3 inch (7.5 cm) cookie cutter. If needed, reroll the scraps, chill the dough for 20 minutes, and roll and cut again until you have all 32 rounds.

To Blind-Bake   Preheat oven to 425°F (220°C). Using a fork, punch tiny holes all over the tart base—these prevent the pastry from getting puffy. Line pastry with parchment paper, leaving an overhang to help you remove it later, and weigh it with baking weights (or old beans used only for blind-baking).

For a large tart: Bake the shell for 10 to 12 minutes (the pastry will begin to take on a little color; take it out if it's getting too dark, as ovens vary). Remove the shell from the oven, and remove the parchment paper and weights or beans (carefully, as they will be hot). Bake the pastry for 10 more minutes, or until it begins to turn golden; remove from the heat and let cool at room temperature. →

For two 9 inch pie or tart shells: Blind-bake for 10 minutes (the pastry will begin to take on a little color; take it out if it's getting too dark, as ovens vary). Remove the pie shells from the oven; remove the parchment and weights or beans (carefully, as they will be hot). Bake the pastry for 8 more minutes or until it begins to turn golden.

For mini tarts: Blind-bake for 5 minutes (the pastry will begin to take on a little color; take them out if they're getting too dark, as ovens vary). Remove the pie shells from the oven; remove the parchment and weights or beans (carefully, as they will be hot). Bake the pastry for 5 to 6 more minutes or until beginning to turn golden.

Your pastry is now partially cooked and ready to fill with quiche, custard, tart, and pie toppings.

To Fill with Unbaked Fillings   Finish cooking the tart shell as follows: Add 10 to 12 more minutes of baking time to the shell (5 to 8 more minutes for two 9 inch pies; 2 to 3 more minutes for mini tarts) or until golden; cool completely. Then fill.

Pasta Frola

Egg Pastry for Sweet Tarts

Argentina and Uruguay | Yield: Makes enough for 2 singe-crust tarts or 1 double-crust tart |
Difficulty Level: Easy | Total Cooking Time: 2 hours (including chilling time)

This egg-based pastry dough is a sweet tradition brought by Italian immigrants to South America. It's my preferred dough for any tart, whether savory or sweet, that requires a sturdy pastry that will hold its shape while baking; it's strong enough to contain heavy fillings. The addition of egg yolks adds both color and richness. As many Argentinean bakers do, I favor white leaf lard (known also as tallow) in place of butter because it makes the flakiest pastry; since lard takes longer to melt than butter, more steam is released as the dough bakes, producing more layers. However, there is a luxurious taste that only butter can lend to pastry, so I often use a mixture of the two (shortening also works in place of lard). I always use any leftover trimmings to cut out pretty shapes to top other pastries, or I bake them in my toaster oven, sprinkled with cheese, and nibble on them as I wait for the tart to cool. The dough keeps in the refrigerator for two days (any longer and it will turn gray) but may be frozen for up to four months. To thaw it, simply put it in the refrigerator overnight.

2½ cups (350 grams) all-purpose flour

Pinch of fine sea salt

3 tablespoons (40 grams) white granulated sugar

10 tablespoons (150 grams) leaf lard or unsalted butter (or half of each), chilled and diced

3 egg yolks

1 teaspoon pure vanilla extract

6–8 tablespoons (90–120 ml) iced water, divided

Place the flour, salt, and sugar in the bowl of a food processor fitted with a metal blade; pulse until just combined. Add the diced lard or butter and pulse for fifteen 1-second intervals or until the texture resembles sand; add the egg yolks and vanilla and pulse for five 1-second intervals. While pulsing, add the iced water through the feeding tube, one tablespoon at a time, until the dough comes together into a ball. Carefully remove the dough onto a lightly floured surface; divide it into two pieces. Place each half on a large strip of plastic wrap and flatten them into a disc; wrap each tightly and refrigerate for at least 30 minutes (up to 2 days). Follow each recipe's directions as to how to roll out and bake.

Note: Chilling the pastry will allow the gluten in the flour to rest so it's easier to roll and shape. If your dough is too cold to roll, you'll know it because it'll crack around the edges. Simply let it sit at room temperature for 10 minutes and try rolling it again; repeat if necessary. Pasta frola withstands baking at a range of temperatures, from 350°F to 425°F (175°C to 220°C), so follow each recipe's instructions. Also, some recipes call for painting the pastry with cream or egg wash before baking to give it a shiny finish; others bake it as is.

Pasta para Tarta Salada

Savory Tart Dough

Various Countries | Yield: Makes enough for 2 single-crust tarts or 1 double-crust tart | Difficulty Level: Easy | Total Cooking Time: 2 hours (including chilling time)

This is a basic dough recipe for pies and pastries that I have been using for as long as I can remember, and it is my preferred dough for any tart that has a savory filling. It is simple to make in a food processor or by hand, and ideal for everything from empanadas to the ultimate double-crusted Pascualina (page 251), a giant pie that hides a generous filling of chards and cheese. If you don't have a food processor, make this dough by hand, using a pastry cutter to cut the fat into the flour and then switching to your hands to mix until it comes together. Don't forget to chill this dough for at least thirty minutes (and up to two days) before you roll it out; this allows the gluten to relax and makes it easy to roll out to the desired thickness and size, without fear of shrinkage.

3½ cups (455 grams) all-purpose flour, plus more for dusting

1 teaspoon fine sea salt

11 tablespoons (155 grams) butter, lard, or shortening, chilled and diced

1 whole egg

8–10 tablespoons (120–150 ml) iced water, divided, plus more as needed

Place the flour and salt in the bowl of a food processor fitted with a metal blade; pulse until just combined. Add the butter and pulse for 15 one-second intervals or until the texture resembles sand; add the whole egg and pulse for 5 one-second intervals. While pulsing, add the iced water through the feeding tube, one tablespoon at a time, until the dough comes together into a ball. Carefully remove the dough onto a lightly floured surface; divide it in two. Place each half on a large strip of plastic wrap and flatten each into a disc; wrap them tightly and refrigerate for at least 30 minutes (and up to 2 days). Follow each recipe's directions as to how to roll out and bake.

Note: If making it for a Pascualina (page 251) or for Pie de Pollo para Onces (page 399), divide the dough into two pieces. Use two-thirds of the dough to make one disc and the remaining third for the top crust.

How to Roll Out Pie and Tart Dough • Always work on a well-floured surface (or over a lightly floured piece of parchment paper) to prevent the dough from sticking and tearing. Pound down the dough to soften it, using your rolling pin. If the edges crack, it's too cold to roll; let it sit at room temperature for 10 minutes and try again. Lightly flour the top of the dough.

To roll out perfect circles: Start with the dough shaped as a flat disk. I always roll the dough starting from the middle and then outward to the edges. Imagine a line running across the diameter of the dough. Place the rolling pin on the imaginary line and roll toward one edge; turn the dough one quarter; imagine another line across the diameter and place the rolling pin back on the imaginary line, rolling it toward the edge. Keep on turning and rolling the dough in this manner (it will form a perfect circle) until it's the desired size. Keep the surface lightly floured at all times so the dough doesn't stick.

Masa para Pizzas, Fougazza y Fougazettas

Pizza Dough

Argentina and Uruguay | Yield: Makes 2 large pizzas, 1 large fougazza, or 12 small fougazettas |
Difficulty Level: Intermediate | Total Cooking Time: 4 hours

Pizza and focaccia are as familiar to South Americans as they are to Italians, but with their own slight twists. For instance, in Argentina, empanadas can be made with pizza dough, filled with cheese and other ingredients like calzones; but while calzones are baked, empanadas are deep-fried. Focaccia—that soft, dimpled bread often topped with herbs and oil—is transformed into fougazza by topping it amply with caramelized onions; when made into individual portions, they are called fougazettas. To make all of these delicacies, you'll need a good dough, and this is the one I've been making in my home for decades. It takes a while, but it's worth every single minute.

2¼ teaspoons (9 grams) instant yeast

1 tablespoon white granulated sugar

1⅓ cups (315 ml) warm water (100°F/38°C)

3½ cups (455 grams) all-purpose flour, plus more for dusting

1 teaspoon fine sea salt

2 tablespoons olive oil, plus more for greasing

Lightly grease a large bowl with oil (or cooking spray); set it aside for later. In a medium bowl, stir together the yeast, sugar, and water; set it aside for 5 minutes. When it foams up, it's ready to use. In a large bowl, whisk together the flour and salt; add the warm yeast mixture and the 2 tablespoons of olive oil. Stir the dough together, using a spatula. Transfer the dough onto a clean, floured surface and knead it for 2 minutes or until it is smooth and comes together into a ball. If it's too sticky, add just a tad more flour but resist the urge to add too much or the dough will be tough. Place the dough in the greased bowl; grease a large piece of plastic wrap with cooking spray or oil and use it to cover the bowl so the dough won't stick. Place the bowl in a warm spot (I use my oven turned off but with the light on; on top of a refrigerator also works). Let it rise for 80 to 90 minutes or until doubled in bulk. At this point you can use it as is, wrap it in plastic and refrigerate it overnight, or freeze it for up to 2 months (defrost it at room temperature before using it).

Note: Gluten is the protein content in flour that makes it gluey. How do you feel on a Friday after a week's worth of work? Tired, stressed, and tense? That's what gluten feels like after it's been kneaded. When you let dough rest after kneading, you give it a break and let it relax (in the same way a weekend does). That is why when you try to shape or roll out newly kneaded dough, it will shrink back to its original size. Therefore, let dough rest for a few minutes (yes, step away from the dough!) before you try to shape or roll it out into the desired size. You'll be rewarded with yielding dough that will stretch as you like it.

Note: Yeast is a live organism. If it doesn't "bloom" or foam up when combined with water and food (sugar), give it another 5 minutes. If it still refuses, your yeast is probably old (dead)—toss it, get new yeast, and start again.

VARIATION: To make any pizza: Roll out the dough to the desired thickness and transfer it to a baking sheet; top with tomato sauce, melting cheese, and any toppings you like. Bake in an oven preheated to 450°F (230°C) until the cheese has melted and the top begins to turn golden.

Crepas Basicas

Basic Crêpes

Argentina and Uruguay | Yield: Makes 20 crêpes | Difficulty Level: Intermediate |
Total Cooking Time: 1½ hours (includes resting time)

Making crepas (crêpes) can be time consuming, but my method is simple. Just blend the ingredients in a blender, chill, and cook. I make loads of crêpes and stack them, divided with parchment paper; then I freeze them in batches in ziplock bags and use them whenever I need to put together a quick dinner. The batter does best if left to rest in the refrigerator for an hour before they are made; this allows the flour to absorb all of the liquid, creating soft and lump free crêpes. You can make this batter ahead and keep it refrigerated overnight, if you desire; just let it sit at room temperature for 10 minutes before using, as the long chilling process will make the butter solidify. A 10-inch (25 cm.) crêpe pan is ideal but any non-stick pan will work. The easiest way to spread the batter is to pour it into the middle of the pan; lift the pan and slowly rotate your wrist until the batter covers the pan's surface. The first one will probably be a loss (eat it while nobody is watching), but with practice making perfectly shaped crêpes will become second nature.

1½ cups (180 grams) all-purpose flour	¼ teaspoon salt	6 tablespoons (90 ml) melted butter, plus more for cooking the crêpes
1½ cup (360ml) whole milk	3 eggs	

In a blender, blend together the flour, milk, salt, and eggs until smooth. Blend in the butter; strain the crêpe batter through a sieve and into a bowl. Chill the batter for 1 hour before using. Brush a non-stick pan, heated over medium-high heat, with melted butter, and pour in ¼ cup (60 ml) batter, swirling the pan to coat the bottom with the batter. Cook the crêpe for one minute on the first side; turn carefully and cook for 30 seconds on the second side. Don't let it brown, just a tinge of golden should be visible on the bottom and around the edges. Stack the crêpes, divided with parchment paper, until ready to use.

Crepas de Hierbas

Herbed Crêpes

Argentina and Uruguay | Yield: Serves 4–6 (makes 20 crêpes) | Difficulty Level: Intermediate | Total Cooking Time: 1½ hours (includes resting time)

Parsley, basil, dill, thyme, marjoram, oregano, and chives all work well in these herb-flecked crêpes. I prefer to combine two or three herbs at a time for more robust flavor. Fillings are only limited by your imagination—creamed spinach, seafood, ricotta cheese, etc. Sauce them up if you want, with tomato based or cream based sauces; heat through and enjoy. This is my favorite crêpe batter—the perfect substitution for pasta sheets whenever I want to make quick cannelloni.

1½ cups (180 grams) all-purpose flour

1½ cup (360ml) whole milk

¼ teaspoon salt

3 eggs

6 tablespoons (90 ml) melted butter, plus more for cooking the crêpes

¼ cup (20 grams) mixed, chopped herbs (see headnote)

In a blender, blend together the flour, milk, salt, and eggs until smooth. Blend in the butter; strain the crêpe batter through a sieve and into a bowl. Stir in the herbs and chill the batter for 1 hour before using. Brush a non-stick pan, heated over medium-high heat, with melted butter, and pour in ¼ cup (60 ml) batter, swirling the pan to coat bottom with the batter. Cook each crêpe for one minute on the first side; turn carefully and cook for 30 seconds on the second side. Don't let it brown, just a tinge of golden should be visible on the bottom and around the edges. Stack the crêpes, divided with parchment paper, until ready to use.

Milanesas

Every country in Latin America has at least one version of breaded cutlets, called "milanesas." Thinly slicing meats, poultry, fish, or vegetables allows them to be stretched further, making more portions out of a single piece. The cutlet is then dredged in flour and dipped in egg. Only then is it coated in bread crumbs and fried. This technique—brought over by Italians—offers families a great way to make less feel like more. Latin Americans ran with it, making milanesas out of veal, pork, chicken, turkey, liver, goat, lamb, fish, and all sorts of vegetables, such as zucchini, eggplant, and peppers. Therefore, more than a recipe, this is a formula. It will come in handy no matter what you're using. My method involves sautéing the cutlets briefly until the coating is golden and then baking them just until cooked through. This ensures that the coating always remains crispy and the interior stays tender. (See the recipe for Berenjenas Empanizadas al Horno on page 242 for step-by-step photos for how to make Milanesas.)

6 large beef, veal, lamb, chicken, or pork cutlets (about 1–1 ½ pounds/ 455–680 grams in total)

1–2 teaspoons fine sea salt, or more to taste

Freshly ground black pepper, to taste

Flour for dredging (about ½ cup/55 grams)

1–1¼ cups (65–85 grams) dry bread crumbs

2 large eggs, lightly beaten with 1 tablespoon water

¼ cup (120 ml) melted unsalted butter

½ cup (120 ml) vegetable oil

Lime or lemon wedges

Pound the meat to ¼ inch (1.5 cm) thick. Preheat the oven to 300°F (150°C). Line a large baking pan with a metal rack. Season the cutlets with salt and pepper on both sides. Place the flour and bread crumbs in 2 separate shallow pans. (For easy clean-up, I spread out a clean paper bag on the counter and mound the flour directly on one side of the bag and the crumbs on the other). Place the bowl of beaten eggs in the center. Working with one cutlet at a time: dredge it in the flour, shaking off the excess; coat completely with the egg, and transfer to the bread crumbs, pressing the cutlets into the crumbs so they'll adhere completely. Let the cutlets sit at room temperature for at least 10 minutes and up to 20 minutes so they dry a little bit. In a heavy 12-inch skillet, melt the butter and oil over medium-high heat. Working in batches, sauté the cutlets on both sides until they are golden brown, about 2 to 3 minutes per side (reduce the heat if they're browning too quickly). Place the cutlets on the prepared pan and bake until cooked through, about 12 to 15 minutes. Serve with lemon or lime wedges, on the side.

Note: Vegetables such as eggplant, zucchini, chayote squash, and large mushrooms that can be sliced into large slices can also be made into milanesas.

Milanesa Tips

- 1½ pounds (680 grams) of thinly cut beef, veal, chicken, liver, or pork should yield about 6 cutlets.
- If making vegetable milanesas, do not preheat the oven. There is no need to pound vegetables; simply slice them thinly. Bread in the same manner and sauté them until they're golden brown, about 2 minutes per side (reduce the heat if they're browning too quickly). Serve immediately.
- Combining equal parts butter and oil guarantees the flavor of the former but the high smoking point of the latter, which prevents the fat from burning as the food fries.
- If using meat or any other kind of protein, it is important that it be cooked through. This is why it's pounded thinly. You fry the cutlets to make a crispy crust. Baking in the oven completes the cooking process.
- Add flavor to the flour, eggs, or bread crumbs. For instance, my Argentinean friend Hugo Gimeno seasons them with garlic and herbs, further infusing the cutlets with flavor. Add spices or dried herbs to the flour and bread crumbs as you wish.
- Milanesas make the absolute best sandwiches; simply select your favorite bread, slather it with mayonnaise, then top it with Milanesas, and any toppings of your choice such as lettuces, onions, tomatoes, etc.
- For a magnificent Mexican torta, make a sandwich using a bolillo roll and slather it with refried beans, guacamole, and hot sauce. Set a Milanese in the middle and dig in.
- Fried Milanesas freeze beautifully. I will make several batches and freeze them in a single layer; once solid I transfer them to ziploc bags and remove them as I need them. They go straight from freezer to hot oven; bake until hot.
- Fish Milanesas are delicious; however, I don't recommend freezing and reheating them. Cook them right before you serve them. Choose thin filets of white fish such as grouper, flounder, red sea bass, etc. Bread in the same fashion and sauté until golden brown, about 3 minutes per side or until the fish flakes easily with a fork. Serve with lemon.

CORN

n the beginning there was corn. Maize, or maíz, is the gold of the Americas—perhaps not the one that convinced greedy men looking for riches to leave their side of the globe for unknown lands across the sea, but one that ultimately fed (and still feeds) millions around the world. Corn is so important to the evolution of human civilization that it is still considered a sacred food by most of the Indigenous cultures that survive throughout the American continents.

Native to Mesoamerica—which encompasses Mexico, Guatemala, Belize, El Salvador, Honduras, Nicaragua, Costa Rica, and Panama—corn's actual birthplace is a matter of disagreement and a lot of mystery. Who discovered it? Who first planted it? Who first learned to cross-pollinate its female and male flowers—the only way to produce the grains?

All we know for sure is that it has been cultivated since the year 3000 BC. According to Jan de Vos, a Belgian historian, the earliest remnants of corn, in the form of both fossils and seed, were found at the edge of Lake Petenxil in Petén, northern Guatemala. Mexicans claim that they domesticated corn first, but so do other Central Americans.

Few staple ingredients have been claimed by as many cultures, or gone by as many names. It was first called "Roman wheat," before it became "Turkish wheat" (although the Turkish actually called it "foreign grain"). It was called "Asian wheat" or "Indian grain" by European merchants seeking to make corn more marketable by giving it an aura of sophistication to make it more desirable to eat (and, therefore, to sell). Finally, the British coined the term *corn*, which was actually the same name they gave barley and wheat—in other words: grain. Even so, it took Europeans hundreds of years to truly accept corn as food for humans. With the exception of Italian and Russian peasants and very poor people, who ate it because they would have starved

otherwise, Europeans believed it to be animal fodder—and some still do today!

In the meantime, the Indigenous societies of the Americas were already enjoying corn preparations in the form of fermented drinks, such as atoles and inoles; stews like puli'kes and sub'anikes; nixtamal in the form of masa for tortillas, tamales, boxboles, xep'es, and tayuyos; and all sorts of other delicacies.

By the time that Fray Bernardino de Sahagún, the Franciscan friar turned missionary and food historian, documented Latin American traditions in his book *General History of the Things of New Spain* (published in 1577, and also called *The Florentine Codex*), the Aztecs already grew eight different varieties of maize.

According to the Popol Vuh, the ancient Mayan story of creation (believed to be one of the oldest creation stories there is, communicated for centuries in the oral tradition and only written down in the 1550s, where it was discovered in the highlands of Guatemala), the gods first made men of mud, but they couldn't speak and couldn't see. For their second attempt the gods made men out of wood, but these were coldhearted and lacked a soul to praise their makers. According to legend, on their third attempt, the gods created men from white corn, with bodies and muscles built of cornmeal that made them strong. These men of corn were intelligent and could speak and see everything on Earth and in the heavens. The gods then decided to take some of their power away so they wouldn't be as mighty as the deities themselves. It wasn't until the gods perfected the first four men that they were satisfied with their creation. Then they crafted women from yellow corn, so mankind could reproduce. Since then, Maya have called themselves "hombres de maíz"—men of maize.

Think what you may of the story (the Spaniards destroyed the original manuscript in fear that it would interfere with their efforts to convert the Maya to Christianity, which was the religious excuse used to conquer new territories), what is categorically true is that the genetic roots of corn (*Zea mays ssp.*, *Zea mays L.*) are found in Mesoamerica, where it was first domesticated.

So why did it take so long for the rest of the world to come to value corn? Well, because in its natural state, ancient corn varieties (unlike the hybrids found today) were not nutritionally adequate for human consumption. Raw, untreated corn doesn't provide the body with niacin and protein, needed for proper nutrition. When Europeans first took corn back to the Old World, sailors who depended on it as a source of food on their journeys contracted pellagra, a disease that causes skin discoloration, stomach disorders, and dementia. The Indigenous peoples of the Americas, whose diet was entirely corn based, didn't suffer from pellagra; they knew that for the niacin in corn to be activated it needs to be combined with an alkaline, that is, nixtamalized. The process of nixtamalization was discovered by the Maya (although many say the Aztecs did it first) and involves soaking the kernels in water that contains high levels of alkaline in the form of crushed seashells, or culinary lime (also known as cal or calcium hydroxide), or in combination with sodium carbonate provided by ashes. This nixtamal is what, once ground into dough, is called masa and is used to make tamales, pupusas, and tortillas, and to thicken sauces and stews; masa is also the base of very thick drinks called atoles. Many people in the Americas still eat a corn-based diet; however, they also include beans, vegetables, and meats, which in combination with corn provide a wholesome vitamin and nutrient base.

Today, Indigenous ecologists, home gardeners, and agronomists intent on saving lost seeds are eager to rescue the hundreds and hundreds of corn varieties from yesteryear, long-lost crops that have been victims of single-grain agriculture. Thanks to their efforts, we can once again plant corn that comes in different colors: purple, red, blue, orange, and yellow, as well as glass-gem corn, which contains kernels in all the colors of the rainbow in a single cob. Now, children in Guatemala, Chile, Paraguay, Mexico, and everywhere else can once more eat corn grown on stalks that were planted with seed from their grandmother's land, like I did many years ago.

What do you first envision when you think of corn? Perhaps a boiled cob, drenched in butter. In Latin America, preparations include corn cooked and slightly charred over coals or wood fires—"asados"—sprinkled with salt and sometimes with citrus, cremas, and chile. Or corn ground into powders and toasted, used to make pinolillos or pinoles that are derived from the food of the ancient Nahuatl from Mexico; mixed with water (or in modern times, with milk), these drinks are sweetened with ground, raw sugar called piloncillo and with Ceylon cinnamon. Or the creamy atoles of Nicaragua, flavored with cacao and allspice, and in Guatemala, with achiote seeds. In other Mesoamerican countries, ground beans, chia seeds, and spices are added for more protein.

To the peoples of Venezuela and Colombia, the word *corn* elicits images of plump arepas, some stuffed with eggs, others sandwiched around fillings such as beans and cheese, or chicken and avocado salad; while to others, arepas are flat and sometimes sweetened with sugar. To the descendants of the Garifuna (Afro-Caribbean peoples) in Belize, Colombia, and Honduras, corn can invoke golden slices of corncobs floating above coconut chowders.

To most of us throughout Latin America, corn reminds us of the hominy that our ancestors left us, a legacy of the land that we use to make stews, breakfast hashes with eggs, salads, flatbreads, dumplings, and soups. For me, corn means freshly ground masa, steaming hot tamales filled with either savory or sweet fillings (and sometimes both). It means tortillas, pupusas, molotes, and tostadas; thickened moles and pepianes. Whatever your vision of corn is, I hope this chapter helps you discover ways of tasting it anew.

The Three Sisters · Long before European colonizers arrived, the Indigenous peoples of the Americas ate a diet based on beans, squash, and corn. Latin American cuisines were built on the backbone of corn stalks, on which beans could wind up and reach to the skies, and under which squashes could spread out and conquer the land with cover, in order to provide protection and soil rich in humus (what we call compost today, the dark organic material that forms in soil when organic matter decays). Ancient Americans called these three plants "the Three Sisters." Planted together, they are called "milpa." Beans contribute the amino acids necessary to make the protein in the corn complete, while squash provides additional vitamins. In combination, these three ingredients provide a complete meal: corn provides amino acids, cysteine, and B vitamins, magnesium, zinc, and fiber; beans provide tryptophans and amino acids called lysines, loads of protein, and iron; and squashes are rich in vitamins, particularly C and beta carotene. In ancient America, the Three Sisters, chiles, grains (such as chia seeds and amaranth), and avocados made for a well-rounded, protein- and fat-rich diet. I keep a bed in my potager garden dedicated strictly to growing milpa, so that I may never forget where I came from and I can provide both food and tradition to my family.

Canchita

Andean Corn Nuts

Peru | Yield: Serves 4–6 | Difficulty Level: Easy | Total Cooking Time: 5 minutes

Cancha corn is a large-kernel popping corn from Peru. It is usually served as a topping for ceviches, but many of my Peruvian friends (and many restaurant chefs) also use it to add crunch to soups or salads. It's even delicious on its own. This corn doesn't pop like the popcorn offered in movie theaters; rather, it puffs up and retains its shape, developing a crispy and starchy texture that is easy to chew on. If you find it as addictive as I do, you'll want to season it with spices of your choice (like cumin, dried ají amarillo powder, and so on) while still hot, and serve as an appetizer with a drink, just as you would serve peanuts. You can purchase cancha corn in Latin American stores or online (see Sources). I can eat it by the handful, so I recommend making extra; once popped, it will keep fresh in an airtight container for up to two weeks.

2 tablespoons vegetable oil

1 cup (140 grams) cancha corn (Peruvian large-kernel popping corn)

Fine sea salt, to taste

Heat the oil in a medium pot over medium heat; add the corn and stir to coat with the oil. Partially cover the pot with a lid. As soon as you can hear the corn popping, shake the pot. Continue shaking over the heat for 1 to 1½ minutes or until the kernels are toasted, being careful not to burn the corn. Transfer the corn onto a plate and season with salt.

Elotes con Rajas

Creamy Corn and Poblano Pepper Toss

Mexico | Yield: Serves 4–6 | Difficulty Level: Easy | Total Cooking Time: 20 minutes

Rajas are strips of roasted chiles, such as poblanos, mixed with onions, and this is a contemporary, creamy version of the spicy dish that has graced the tables of Mexican homes for centuries. Myriad recipes combining chiles and corn that were developed before the Europeans arrived in the Americas still exist today. I gravitate toward this version, which adds a touch of tanginess from cream cheese. Crema is the crème fraiche of Latin America, a beloved ingredient that varies in tanginess, consistency, and saltiness. If you can't find it, make your own (see page 23) or use crème fraiche, in a pinch. I often enjoy this simply wrapped in a warm corn tortilla or as a side to scrambled eggs.

2 tablespoons unsalted butter

½ cup (60 grams) finely chopped white onions

4 cups (510 grams) fresh corn kernels (or frozen and thawed)

2–3 poblano peppers, roasted, stemmed, seeded, deveined, and cut into strips (about 1 cup)

2 garlic cloves, finely chopped

½ cup (120 grams) softened cream cheese

½ cup (120 ml) Crema (page 23) (or crème fraiche)

½ teaspoon fine sea salt, or more to taste

½ teaspoon ancho or guajillo chile powder (or black pepper)

½ cup (60 grams) Cotija cheese (or grated Parmesan cheese)

Melt the butter in a large skillet set over medium-high heat. Add the onions and cook for 1 minute or until translucent. Add the corn, poblanos, and garlic; cook, tossing well for 2 minutes or until hot. Add the cream cheese, crema, salt, and chile powder, stirring for 2 to 3 minutes or until the cream cheese has melted into the cream and the corn is tender. Stir in the cheese and serve immediately. If the sauce is too thick, loosen it up by adding a little bit of water, until it's of your desired texture.

Note: See page 185 for details on how to roast peppers.

Solterito

Lima Bean, Corn, and Tomato Salad

Peru | Yield: Serves 4–6 | Difficulty Level: Easy |
Total Cooking Time: 2 hours if using dried beans, 30 minutes if using cooked beans

This invigorating salad is creamy, juicy, and crunchy all in one bite, packed with flavor and vibrantly colorful. *Soltero* means "single," and this mélange is a loving play on the word. Some say it was so named because it's such an easy salad that anyone—even a single man—can prepare it; others say the salad is so healthy that it helps a single man keep in shape until he is married. Any type of corn kernel will work, but try to find the giant, toothsome, white-kerneled corn of the Inca called "choclo desgranado," if you can. Similar in appearance to hominy, it is chunky, with unevenly sized and starchy kernels, but hasn't been treated with culinary lime (also known as cal or calcium hydroxide). Found frozen or canned in Latin American stores (see Sources), it only needs to be rinsed under running water and requires no cooking. Or use canned hominy in its place. If you wish, add black olives, cooked quinoa, and grilled chicken to transform this salad into a main dish. Cook lima beans as you would any other bean, by boiling them in water until fork tender. This recipe keeps, refrigerated, for up to a week and doubles beautifully for a crowd.

4 cups (455 grams) Peruvian giant corn kernels

2 cups (170 grams) cooked and rinsed lima beans

2 cups (285 grams) grape or cherry tomatoes, sliced in half

1 cup (170 grams) crumbled queso fresco (or feta)

½ cup (60 grams) finely chopped red onions

2 green onions (white and green parts), thinly sliced (about ¼ cup)

½ cup (120 ml) red wine vinegar

2 teaspoons rocoto paste, or more to taste (optional)

1½ teaspoons fine sea salt, or more to taste

½ teaspoon freshly ground black pepper, or more to taste

½ cup (120 ml) vegetable oil

Finely chopped fresh parsley, for garnish (optional)

In a large bowl, combine the corn, lima beans, tomatoes, queso fresco, and onions. In a small bowl, whisk together the vinegar, rocoto paste, salt, pepper, and oil; pour the dressing onto the salad and stir well to combine. Chill salad for at least 20 minutes (or overnight); sprinkle with parsley, if using, and serve.

Ensalada de Esquites

Creamy Corn Salad with Cheese

Mexico | Yield: Serves 4–6 | Difficulty Level: Easy | Total Cooking Time: 30 minutes

Esquites are bowls of steaming corn broth, topped with cream and cheese, sold in the streets of Mexico. Over the decades, this favorite dish has moved indoors into people's kitchens, where it has gone through several transformations. This is a cold version—a salad that juxtaposes the sweet taste of fresh corn with the saltiness and tangy tones of the other ingredients. I'm particularly fond of the smokiness lent by grilled corn; however, if you prefer, use frozen and thawed corn kernels or raw kernels scraped off very fresh corn, instead. When my kids were teens, they loved stuffing this salad into hollowed-out tomatoes and packing them in their lunch boxes.

¼ cup (60 ml) Crema (page 23) or sour cream

½ cup (118 ml) mayonnaise

2 tablespoons freshly squeezed lime juice or more to taste (about 1 lime)

1 jalapeño pepper (½ ounce/15 grams) stemmed and finely chopped (seeded and deveined if less heat is desired)

½ teaspoon fine sea salt, or more to taste

¼ teaspoon freshly ground black pepper, or more to taste

4 cups (680 grams) grilled or raw corn kernels (about 6 large ears) (see Note)

½ cup (60 grams) ground Cotija or Parmesan cheese

Pinch of chipotle chile powder (or Tajín), or more to taste

In a large bowl, whisk together the crema, mayonnaise, lime juice, jalapeños, salt, and pepper; stir in the corn kernels and mix until combined. Sprinkle with the cheese; stir to combine and chill, until ready to serve (up to two days). Right before serving, sprinkle with the chile powder.

Note: To grill corn: Place the peeled ears directly onto a grill pan or outdoor grill and cook them on all sides for about 5 to 6 minutes in total, rotating them, until you get a slight char; slice the kernels off the cob.

VARIATIONS: For a one-bowl meal, add 8 ounces (225 grams) of shredded surimi (imitation crabmeat) or chopped cooked shrimp.

Pastel de Choclo

Corn-Crusted Beef and Chicken Casserole

Chile | Yield: Serves 6–8 | Difficulty Level: Intermediate | Total Cooking Time: 2 hours and 15 minutes

This casserole is a fabulous example of the intertwining of world ingredients that happened following the Columbian exchange. The Arab-inspired beef picadillo, called pino in Chile, already popular in Europe, was married to the flavors of corn—the gold of the Americas. I adapted this recipe from one my friend Elizabeth Donoso makes. The amount of milk you will need to add to the corn will depend entirely on how moist or dry the corn is to begin with—the point is to make a creamy topping the consistency of soft mashed potatoes.

FOR THE FILLING

2 tablespoons vegetable oil

¾ cup (115 grams) finely chopped white onions

2 garlic cloves, finely chopped

1½ pound (680 grams) ground beef

2 tablespoons sweet paprika (or pimentón dulce)

1½ teaspoons ground cumin

1 teaspoon ground oregano

2 teaspoons fine sea salt, divided

½ teaspoon freshly ground black pepper

1 cup (240 ml) beef broth or water

⅓ cup (60 grams) raisins (golden or "sultanas" preferred)

⅓ cup (55 grams) pitted and sliced green olives

2 hard-boiled eggs, peeled and sliced

3 cups (345 grams) cooked, shredded, and cooled chicken

FOR THE TOPPING

6 cups (795 grams) corn kernels (see Note)

2 cups (480 ml) whole milk

2 tablespoons unsalted butter, diced

¼ cup (40 grams) white granulated sugar, for sprinkling on top

2–4 tablespoons stone-ground cornmeal (optional) (see Note)

Grease a 9 x 13 inch baking pan (23 x 33 cm) and set aside. Heat the oil in a large skillet set over medium-high heat and add the onions, cooking until transparent, about 1 minute. Add the garlic and cook for 30 seconds. Add the beef, paprika, cumin, oregano, 1½ teaspoons salt, and pepper; stir well and cook, while breaking up the beef with the back of a spoon, until it's no longer pink, about 3 to 4 minutes. Add the broth and stir well; lower the heat to medium-low and cook, uncovered, until the broth has reduced by half but the mixture is still juicy, about 8 to 10 minutes. Transfer the beef mixture to the prepared pan and spread it all over the bottom. Sprinkle the beef evenly with the raisins and olives; layer the egg slices on top. Place the chicken in a layer, on top of the eggs; set aside and make the topping. Place the corn kernels and the milk in a blender (or food processor) and blend until pureed (you may have to do this in batches). Transfer the corn mush into a large pot set over medium heat, stirring for 8 to 12 minutes or until the corn has changed to the consistency of soft mashed potatoes (if it's too thin, keep adding cornmeal; if too thick, add a little bit more milk at a time, until it reaches the desired consistency. It should separate from the sides of the pot when you stir it). Pour the corn over the top of the eggs in the baking dish and level it so it's evenly spread. Preheat the oven to 375°F (190°C). Dot the top of the casserole with the butter and sprinkle evenly with the sugar. Bake for 60 to 75 minutes or until the top is golden and the casserole is hot. Serve immediately.

Note: For this recipe, try to find choclo granado, a large, flat, white corn kernel, usually found frozen in Latin American stores; it is starchier and thicker when pureed than other corn varieties.

How to Make Hard-Boiled Eggs · Place 4 to 8 eggs in a small pot and cover with cold water; bring to a boil over high heat. Fill a bowl with iced water and set aside. As soon as the water boils, cover the pot and remove it from the heat. Allow the eggs to sit in the covered pot for 14 minutes. Drain the eggs and add them immediately to the bowl of iced water; once cold, refrigerate the unpeeled eggs for up to 5 days or peel and use immediately.

Bori-Bori

Corn Dumpling Soup

Paraguay | Yield: Serves 4–6 | Level of Difficulty: Intermediate | Total Cooking Time: 1 hour and 45 minutes

Here light broth is filled with cubes of orange squash and tender shredded chicken; as if that weren't enough, this soup of the Guaraní people is filled with tiny corn dumplings. Known in Spanish as bolitas, because of their round shape, the name evolved to boris or voris in the Tupi-Guaraní language (which is why sometimes you'll find this soup called vori-vori instead). Paraguay is one of the only countries in all of Latin America that has one ancient Indigenous language—jointly with Spanish—as its official language (some others have more than one); thus, the soup and its name have gone unchanged over generations. There are many dumpling soups around the world, such as Jewish matzo ball soup, German kluten, Chinese wonton soup, and Thai kiao nam gai; if you like any of those, you'll want to add this one, very popular with children, to your cooking repertoire.

FOR THE SOUP

1½ pounds (680 grams) bone-in chicken breasts

1½ teaspoons fine sea salt, or more to taste

1 small (about 4 ounces/115 grams) yellow onion, peeled and left whole

One 4 ounce (115 grams) carrot, peeled

2 ounces (60 grams) celery stalk

1 garlic clove

5 cups (680 grams) peeled and seeded butternut squash, diced into ½ inch (12 mm) cubes

FOR THE DUMPLINGS

1 cup (140 grams) stone-ground white or yellow cornmeal

1 egg plus 1 yolk

¼ cup (55 grams) grated white onions

2 tablespoons clarified butter, ghee, or unsalted butter, at room temperature

1 cup (105 grams) grated queso blanco (or ricotta salata)

⅓ cup (30 grams) chopped fresh parsley, for garnish (optional)

To make the soup: In a medium soup pot (at least 5 quarts/4.7 liters), place the chicken, salt, onion, carrot, celery, and garlic; cover with cold water and bring to a boil over medium-high heat; immediately lower the heat and simmer for 30 to 35 minutes or until the chicken is cooked through (its juices should run clear when pierced with a fork). Use a spoon to remove any foam that floats to the top of the simmering broth during the first 10 minutes. Allow the chicken to cool in the broth for 10 minutes. Remove the chicken to a plate until it's cool enough to handle. Strain the vegetables and aromatics from the broth and discard them. Measure out the broth (you should have about 6 cups); add enough chicken broth (or water) to make 8 cups and return to the pot. Cover and set aside while you make the dumplings.

To make the dumplings: Place the cornmeal in a large bowl. In a separate bowl, whisk together the egg, egg yolk, and onions; add this to the cornmeal and stir to combine (the mixture will look crumbly). Work the clarified butter in with your fingers, breaking it up and combining it with the dough; knead in the cheese until you have a smooth dough, the consistency of play dough (at first, it will still look crumbly, but it will come together as you knead it). Cover and let it rest for 10 minutes. Shape the dough into 16 (about 1 inch/2.5 cm) balls. Fill a medium soup pot (at least 3 quarts) with water and bring it to a boil; lower the heat to a soft simmer. Working in batches, carefully lower a few dumplings at a time and let them cook until they rise to the surface, about 4 minutes; let them continue simmering for 5 minutes. Use a slotted spoon to remove them from the water and place them on a large plate until all are cooked; set aside while you finish the soup.

Add the butternut squash to the soup pot and set it over medium-high heat. Bring it to a boil; cover, lower the heat, and simmer, covered, for 10 to 15 minutes or until the squash can be easily pierced with a fork. Shred the chicken into large pieces and add back into the pot, along with the corn dumplings. Simmer for 5 minutes, just enough to warm the chicken and the dumplings through. Divide the soup into 4 to 6 large bowls. Serve, sprinkled with fresh parsley, if using.

Polenta Rellena

Savory Polenta Cake

Argentina and Uruguay | Yield: Serves 4–6 | Difficulty Level: Intermediate | Total Cooking Time: 1½ hours

This layered and savory corn pie has a crispy exterior and a highly satisfying soft interior. During the height of the Roman Empire, polenta (grain mush, also called pulmentum) was made out of ancient grains such as farro, buckwheat, and spelt, and even with legumes such as chickpeas. Italians were introduced to corn or maize, native to the Americas, somewhere at the end of the sixteenth century, when it became part of what is now known as cucina povera (or food for the poor). Italians, in turn, brought polenta back with them to South America when they emigrated in force at the start of the nineteenth century. Nowhere else in the Americas are polenta dishes more popular than in Uruguay and Argentina, where they abound. This is one of my favorite comfort foods, simpler to make than lasagna and yet similarly layered. I like to serve it with tomato sauce on the side, but it's good all on its own. If you are able to find "Reggianito" cheese, a Parmesan-type cheese from Uruguay, use it here (sheep's-milk Pecorino Romano also works well).

Butter, for greasing the baking dish

2 teaspoons vegetable oil

½ cup (115 grams) diced uncured pancetta

1 teaspoon fine sea salt

2 cups (480 ml) whole milk

1 cup (200 grams) uncooked polenta (cornmeal)

½ cup (60 grams) finely grated Parmesan cheese

½ cup (120 ml) heavy whipping cream

Preheat the oven to 350°F (180°C). Butter an 8 x 8 inch (20 x 20 cm) baking dish and set aside. Heat the oil in a medium skillet set over medium-high heat. Add the pancetta and cook, stirring often, until nicely browned but not yet crisp, about 4 minutes. Remove the pancetta to a plate lined with paper towels to drain and set aside. Place 2 cups (480 ml) water in a large pot set over medium-high heat; as soon as it comes to a boil, add the salt and the milk. Reduce the heat to low and add the polenta, making sure to whisk it well so it doesn't clump. (It isn't necessary to do this in a slow stream as many recipe books tell you; just plop it in there and whisk!) Increase the heat to medium. Switch to a wooden spoon and keep on stirring until the polenta has thickened and just begins to simmer, about 5 minutes. Turn the heat to low and continue cooking until the polenta pulls away from the sides of the pot and has thickened to the consistency of mashed potatoes (depending on how coarse the polenta is, this can take anywhere from 12 to 16 minutes). Working quickly (to prevent the polenta from solidifying), spread half of the polenta into the bottom of the prepared baking dish and level it out. Top it with the pancetta and sprinkle with Parmesan. Place the remaining half of the polenta over the filling, spreading it evenly. Drizzle the top with the heavy cream and bake for 50 to 55 minutes or until the top is slightly golden. Let it rest for 10 minutes before cutting into squares.

VARIATIONS

- Instead of pancetta, layer slices of ham and a good melting cheese in the middle.
- Make it vegetarian by substituting sautéed mushrooms for the filling.
- Make it vegan by substituting the filling with roasted vegetables and Tuco (page 165).
- Gild the lily by topping it all with the Salsa Blanca Sencilla (page 24); add more cheese and broil until golden.
- Have a jar of roasted peppers? Drain and slice them, and place them in the middle layer with sliced provolone cheese and a sprinkle of dried oregano.
- Or try my husband's favorite variation, stuffed with cooked and crumbled Italian sausage, pesto, and mozzarella cheese.

Torta de Elote

Sweet Corn and Cheese Pudding

Central America | Yield: Serves 6–8 | Difficulty Level: Easy | Total Cooking Time: 90 minutes

This kind of corn pudding has been enjoyed since the early 1500s and is just as popular today as it was then. A simple, sweet ending to any meal during the height of corn season, this is the type of dessert that is offered for a light merienda or refacción (snack) in the middle of the afternoon. The cheese adds a bit of saltiness to what would otherwise be a very sweet recipe.

3 cups (370 grams) raw corn kernels (from about 6 cobs)

1½ cups (360 ml) whole milk

½ cup (115 grams) melted unsalted butter, plus more for greasing baking dish

¼ cup (30 grams) Cotija cheese, grated queso seco, or ground Parmesan cheese

1 cup (215 grams) white granulated sugar

4 eggs

Preheat the oven to 350°F (180°C). Grease a 9 x 13 inch (23 x 33 cm) baking dish and set aside. Place the corn and the milk in a blender; puree on high speed, until smooth, about 1 minute. Add the butter, cheese, sugar, and eggs and blend until it's all combined and the sugar has dissolved, about 1 minute. Pour into the prepared pan and bake for 1 to 1½ hours or until the custard is barely set in the middle and the top is a light golden brown. Allow it to rest at room temperature for 30 minutes before cutting.

nixtamal

The many innovations of ancient American civilizations include the Mayan invention of the number zero, the 365-day Aztec calendar, and the monumental architectural wonders of the Inca such as those found in the city of Machu Picchu. Yet one of the most important discoveries was that of nixtamal, or hominy, which converts corn into a nutritious powerhouse that has since fed the world.

The term *nixtamal* (pronounced *neex-tah-mahl*) derives from the Nahuatl words *nixtli*, which means "ashes," and *tamalli*, which translates into "masa" or "dough." In its natural state, ancient corn was not nutritionally adequate for human consumption. Raw, untreated corn couldn't provide the body with the niacin needed for it to properly absorb any of the other nutrients from corn.

That is why when the first colonizers returned in ships filled with corn to their European countries, they arrived sickened, thin, and malnourished with pellagra, a horrible disease that caused them to become weak and disoriented and that led to a painful death. Who, exactly, discovered nixtamalization—and how—is still a matter of contention, but it is generally agreed that Mesoamerican Indigenous peoples were the first to use the technique. These ancient civilizations realized that hard corn kernels could be softened with the use of ashes from their cooking pits, broken shells from their oceans, and (much later) culinary lime (also known as cal or calcium hydroxide) from their land. In ancient times, both Aztecs and Maya used nixtamalized maize to make tortillas, tamales, atoles, and pozoles. Furthermore, unlike any other grains, corn needed the intervention of humans to reproduce; it is a species that must be sown and hand pollinated in order to become food. This meant that Maya, Aztec, Olmec, and other ancient pre-Columbian civilizations had the scientific and anthropological know-how to transform one ingredient into another by forcing a chemical reaction (something often forgotten by modern-day historians who have ignored all of the incredible contributions made by ancient cultures long before Europeans ever arrived to colonize the Americas).

Nixtamal can be made with all types of native American corn. Armed with my recipe for masa, the supple corn dough used as the base for so many Mesoamerican dishes, you can create tortillas and pupusas of different colors. Follow the recipe for the most basic of tamales found here, and you'll open a window to myriad possibilities; fill them with moles, shredded meats, cooked mushrooms, chopped herbs, and sautéed greens and make your own variations.

Use whole nixtamalized corn kernels to craft rich soups, hefty stews, and delicious breakfasts. Mix hot milk into cooked hominy and season it with sugar and cinnamon for a cereal that far surpasses any that comes in a box. These only scratch the surface of the many applications of nixtamal, but they'll bring you closer to realizing the flavors of long ago.

Masa Harina Versus Masarepa

Masa Harina In 1949, Roberto Gonzáles Barrera founded the first masa harina factory in Mexico, called Maseca. He is credited with creating the process by which the wet dough or masa used to craft tortillas could be dried into a powder called masa harina. Today, Maseca is still the most popular brand of masa harina (the name derives from the words *masa* and *seca*, which means "dry masa"). Masa harina is the dried corn flour that you'll use to make many of the tortillas in this book. The corn is treated with calcium hydroxide (known as cal in Spanish), has its hulls slipped, and is then dried. The dried corn, also known as hominy, is then ground into a meal. You can now find a plethora of brands of masa harina, including some made in small batches by specialty companies and organic entrepreneurs and sold under different labels. There are many brands of masa harina out there, but I recommend using the two most popular: Maseca or Torti Masa, which can be found worldwide, or my absolute favorite (albeit more expensive) small-batch masa harina sold within the United States, under the label Masienda. Some bags of masa harina sometimes say "Instant Corn Masa Flour." This dry corn flour only needs to be reconstituted with water in order to become masa once again. You can find masa harina of different colors in some specialty food markets, particularly in the Southwest (blue corn and red corn varieties are most popular, but the white one is traditional).

Masarepa (Also Known as Harina Pan) Masarepa is a type of dehydrated precooked cornmeal invented in 1957 by Luis Caballero Mejías, a Venezuelan engineer, in order to make the crafting of arepas easier for everyday cooks. The process requires the corn to be cooked, ground, and then dried into a very fine powder. (You'll notice that the technique for making masa for tortillas requires the corn to be dried and then ground.) Masarepa is used in Colombia and Venezuela. The resulting meal is used to make arepas and cachapas (sweet corn pancakes that can be filled like tortillas). Masarepa can be reconstituted with the addition of any warm liquid—sometimes water; other times milk or broths. It comes in two colors, white and yellow. Either one will work for the recipes in this book. Two very popular brands are Goya and P.A.N.

Note: Regular cornmeal or polenta cannot be substituted for either masa harina or masarepa, since it has not been treated in the same way. For the same reason, masa harina and masarepa are not interchangeable, but both types of dehydrated cornmeal are widely available around the globe.

Masa Nixtamalizada

Homemade Corn Masa

Central America and Mexico | Yield: Makes 2½ pounds (1.2 kilograms), enough for 2 dozen tortillas |
Difficulty Level: Advanced | Total Cooking Time: 10–16 hours (if left overnight)

"A true tortilla contains only three ingredients: corn, water, and either finely powdered calcium hydroxide or wood ash," my friend and Mexican food expert Cristina Potters wrote to me, when I first starting making my own masa. In Spanish, *masa* means "dough," but in Mesoamerica, it almost always denotes the corn mush made after cooking alkalinized corn or nixtamal (known also as pozole, posol, mote, moti, or flint corn) used for the creation of tortillas, tamales, pupusas, and other delicacies that derive from the ancient Aztec and Mayan culinary traditions prior to the conquista. The process of nixtamalization is simple but time consuming; it requires soaking the corn overnight in water mixed with culinary lime (also known as cal or calcium hydroxide) and then grinding it until smooth. Masa is traditionally ground by hand in a three-legged, volcanic stone (the three legs are said to represent childhood, youth, and old age by the Maya) called a metate (from the Náhuatl word *metatl*) with a long conical stone called a mano or a metlapil. In latter centuries, home cooks could take nixtamalized corn to nearby mills to have it ground into masa. The twentieth century saw the invention of a mill that home cooks could use for making nixtamalized masa themselves.

In truth, even in Mexico, most people have become accustomed to eating factory-made tortillas, crafted with dehydrated corn flour and seldom, if ever, make their own masa. But the flavor of even the best of these mass-produced tortillas cannot compete with those made with fresh nixtamal. A simple tortilla made with dried flour is good—don't get me wrong—but one made with homemade masa, with its meaty, creamy, and toothsome texture, is sublime and, in my opinion, should be experienced at least once in a lifetime. Most modern cooks, however, don't have the time for this process and instead purchase instant, dehydrated masa, called masa harina, that only requires the addition of water and is what I recommend for your daily use (see page 83 for the recipe). The most common brand is Maseca, but there are dozens available worldwide.

I grew up making tortillas from fresh masa in my grandmother's house in Guatemala, where I was constantly recruited to shape tiny ones to serve as appetizers. A book on the food of Latin America would not be complete without the recipe for proper nixtamal, so I include it for those of you who are inclined try it—first, perhaps, as a weekend project, but as you gain practice (and if you use my food processor method) as something you make frequently. For the best masa, you will need a home grain mill for wet corn and some strong arm muscles. I find that grinding is not enough to get the supple texture that helps masa become creamy and smooth, so I always finish mine by processing it in the food processor with a bit of water. This step makes the difference between good tortillas and great ones. Masa is ready when it holds an indentation when pressed down on and doesn't crack when shaped into a disc. If it cracks, knead in more boiling water, one tablespoon at a time. (See Sources for purchasing hominy.) →

The Grain Mill Method for Masa Nixtamalizada

Central America and Mexico | Yield: 2½ pounds (1.2 kilograms), enough for 2 dozen tortillas |
Difficulty Level: Advanced | Total Cooking Time: 10–16 hours (if left overnight)

Making masa with hominy and culinary lime (also known as cal or calcium hydroxide), requires a corn grinder that can handle wet ingredients. The twentieth century saw the invention of a grain mill fit for homes, which many still use today. After reaching out to my Latin American colleagues and after much comparison between hand-cranked, inexpensive machines and motorized grinders that ran into thousands of dollars, I invested in one commonly used in Mexico, which my friend Maricel Presilla, a renowned author and food historian, calls "a true classic." It sells under the Victoria brand (made in Colombia) and can be used to grind everything from dried beans to yuca to, of course, grains. (See Sources.)

4 cups (680 grams) dried white, yellow, red, or blue hominy corn	2 tablespoons culinary lime (see Sources)	Boiling water

Wash the dried corn under running water to remove any grit or dirt. Combine the corn, 8 cups (2 quarts) water, and the culinary lime in a large nonreactive pot and set it over high heat; bring it to a boil and immediately cover, then lower the heat to low and keep at a simmer for 1 hour. Remove from the heat and let sit, covered and at room temperature, for 10 to 12 hours (ideally overnight). Drain the hominy in a colander, place the colander in a bowl, and wash the grains in three or four changes of cold water, rubbing them between your hands to remove as much of the skin as possible (and to remove all of the culinary lime), until the water runs clear. If the tip carp—the sharp and hard point found at the end of each kernel—is still attached, remove it from the individual grains by pinching the edges, and discard. (I don't always bother when I'm grinding masa in a mill but always do it when using the food processor method, see page 67.)

To grind the corn into masa, follow the directions of your grain mill. Grind the hominy two times through the mill, then transfer it to a food processor in batches, and pulse it, while adding boiling water, one tablespoon at a time, until you end up with dough the consistency of soft plasticine or mashed potatoes. Repeat until all of the masa is ground and processed. Keep it covered as you work; when done, let it rest in a bowl, covered, for 5 minutes.

The Food Processor Method for Masa Nixtamalizada

Central America and Mexico | Yield: 2½ pounds (1.2 kilograms), enough for 2 dozen tortillas |
Difficulty Level: Advanced | Total Cooking Time: 10–16 hours (if left overnight)

I've been intent on finding the perfect method for making easier homemade masa any day of the week for years—a method with less effort, and little mess to clean up. My Instagram friend Vero Albin was born in Mexico and lives in Houston, Texas, where she has studied nixtamal for years and where she works to preserve the technique by teaching free workshops. (You can find her @albinvero.) She inspired me to try grinding masa entirely in a food processor. She suggested that I air-dry the nixtamalized kernels in a single layer on a clean kitchen towel before processing, with a small amount of hot water. After much trial and error, I found that the best results came from making sure to remove the tip carps from the nixtamalized hominy. Not doing so changes the color of the masa, speckling it with black and keeping it very coarse, since tip carps won't grind easily. I also found that boiling water worked best in the food processor, as it helped the masa plump up faster and thus required less effort from the motor. I am happy to report that, finally, making masa is doable every day of the week!

4 cups (680 grams) dried white, yellow, red, or blue hominy corn	2 tablespoons culinary lime (see Sources)	Boiling water

Wash the dried hominy under running water to remove any grit or dirt. Combine the hominy, 8 cups (2 quarts) water, and culinary lime in a large nonreactive pot and set it over high heat; bring it to a boil and immediately cover it; lower the heat to low and keep at a simmer for 1 hour. Remove from the heat and let sit, covered and at room temperature, for 10 to 12 hours (or overnight). Drain the hominy in a colander; place the colander in a bowl and wash the grains in three or four changes of cold water, rubbing them between your hands to remove as much of the skin as possible (and to remove all of the culinary lime), until the water runs clear. If the tip carp—the sharp and hard point found at the end of each kernel—is still attached to the tip of the kernels, remove it by pinching the edges, and discard. Do not skip this step when using this food processor method.

After removing the tip carp, rinse and drain the kernels one more time, then lay them in a single layer on a clean kitchen towel to air-dry for 30 to 40 minutes. Working with 2 cups of nixtamalized corn at a time, place in a food processor fitted with the metal (chopping) blade. Pulse for 60 one-second pulses or until the corn resembles fine cornmeal (open the processor periodically to scrape down the sides of the bowl). Add ¼ cup (60 ml) boiling water and pulse for 30 one-second pulses. Add another 2 tablespoons of boiling water and turn the processor on continuously for 2 to 3 minutes or until the masa comes together to form a ball with the consistency of plasticine or mashed potatoes; stop to scrape the sides of the bowl periodically. The masa should hold together when pressed between your fingers. If it doesn't, then keep on processing and adding boiling water one tablespoon at a time, until it does. Remove the masa from the food processor (be careful not to cut yourself with the blade) and shape it into a ball; repeat with the rest of the masa until all of it is processed. Keep it covered as you work; when done, let it rest in a bowl, covered, for 5 minutes.

About Hominy · Dried hominy corn is found in most Latin American stores and also easily sourced online (see Sources). I have found that although many varieties of corn work for making nixtamal, the one that produces the softest and easiest masa to grind, shape, and cook is South American mote pelado, which results in the creamiest masa and is guaranteed to help tortillas puff as they cook (a sign of the perfect tortilla). Plus, most of the time it's been rid of the tip carp, removing a crucial step. However, most Latin tiendas (stores) will sell corn under the names maíz pozolero, maíz para nixtamal, or dried flint corn. I tend to select larger, white kernels, as I find that the smaller ones are harder to grind. Don't worry if you can't grind your corn all the way until it's completely smooth; depending on what variety you use, ground corn will always retain some of its texture, which won't affect most dishes. Even if you're using it to make tortillas, those made with masa that is a bit granular are still succulent; however, the smoother the masa, the easier it will be to fold and roll the tortillas. Hominy also comes in blue, yellow, and red kernels, which produce masa of different colors.

Mote/Maíz para Pozole/Posol

Hominy

Various Countries | Yield: Serves 4–6 | Difficulty Level: Easy |
Total Cooking Time: 10–16 hours (must be prepared a day before you intend to use it)

Plump, toothsome, and nutty, hominy is truly one of the most important gifts that Indigenous Americans have given the world. There is no exact data on who the first person to discover that soaking corn in lye or covering it in ashes made it digestible. However, we have many clues that the Maya and the Aztecs were the first to discern this chemical process, called nixtamalization, that makes corn edible. While historians from both Mexico and Guatemala go back and forth vying for discovery rights, I simply invite you to discover the ancient taste of corn still valued in quotidian cooking all over the Americas today. Purchase dried hominy corn (also called mote pelado or maíz pozolero) with the tip carps (the tiny sharp bottom ends that attach to the cob) removed, as it is much easier to cook and doesn't require cleaning (see Sources). Cooking it with culinary lime (also known as cal or calcium hydroxide) (which is also used to pickle cucumbers) causes the endosperm or outer skins of the kernels to separate from the inner corn grains. You will notice that the usually white (or very light yellow) dried hominy turns a dark yellow color (blue and red hominy will turn darker too) when it comes into contact with the calcium hydroxide—this is the chemical reaction you want to see. As the corn cooks, it will lose its endocarp, revealing plump, soft kernels: pozole.

1½ cups (230 grams) dried
hominy corn (maíz pozolero)

1 tablespoon culinary
lime (see Sources)

Wash the dried hominy under running water to remove any grit or dirt. Combine the hominy, lime, and 2 quarts (2 liters/8 cups) water in a large nonreactive pot and set it over high heat; bring it to a boil and immediately cover it; lower the heat to low and keep at a simmer for 1 hour. Remove from the heat and let sit, covered and at room temperature, for 10 to 12 hours (or overnight). Drain the hominy in a colander; place the colander in a bowl, and wash the grains in three or four changes of cold water, rubbing them between your hands to remove as much of the skin as possible (and to remove all of the culinary lime), until the water runs clear. (If the tip carp, the sharp and hard point found at the end of each kernel, is still attached to the tip of the kernels, you can remove it from the individual grains, but I don't always bother.) Drain one more time. Store the cooked hominy, well covered, in the refrigerator for up to 24 hours before using.

Note: You can substitute this recipe with one 29 ounce (822 gram) can of cooked hominy, drained well.

A word on canned hominy: I prefer to make my own hominy but am aware that it may take more time than most modern cooks have. For this reason, I am not opposed to the use of canned hominy in everyday dishes that are meant to be stewed or cooked further. Never use canned hominy to make masa, though. And purchase only the best canned hominy you can find. (I'm partial to Mexican brands such as Juanita's Foods that retain their bite and nutty flavor.) Avoid overly processed white hominy.

Mote Pillo
Hominy with Eggs

Ecuador | Yield: Serves 4 | Difficulty Level: Easy | Total Cooking Time: 15 minutes

This hearty breakfast, common in the Andean region of Ecuador, where nixtamalized corn is called mote (pronounced *móh-teh*), tastes like Novo America (the name given to Latin America shortly after the colonization) through and through. The ancient flavors of nutty corn meet the comforting taste of eggs (from chickens, brought over by the Spaniards). Natilla (the crème fraiche or crema of South America) is the matchmaker that creates a creamy emulsion of the elements. Tinted with the golden color of achiote, the finished dish makes me think of a plate full of gold coins.

2 tablespoons Aceite de Achiote (page 194)

2 cups (280 grams) cooked hominy (Mote/Maíz para Pozole/Posol, page 69) (or use canned hominy, well rinsed and drained)

5 eggs, lightly beaten

½ cup (120 ml) natilla or any other type of crema (or substitute crème fraiche or heavy whipping cream), plus more for garnish

¼ teaspoon fine sea salt, or more to taste

Heat the oil in a nonstick skillet set over medium-high heat; add the hominy and cook, while stirring, for 2 minutes or until the hominy has taken on a golden color and has a toasty aroma. Add the beaten eggs and half of the crema, stirring well, until the eggs are scrambled (but still creamy) and all of the hominy is coated with the eggs. Serve immediately, topped with more crema.

Mote Sucio
Hominy with Pork Renderings

Ecuador | Yield: Serves 4 | Difficulty Level: Easy | Total Cooking Time: 15 minutes

Nutty and toothsome nixtamalized corn is traditionally cooked in the rendered fat left after making Fritanga (page 409), the national pork dish of Ecuador. When cooked in this rich and tasty lard, called mantequilla negra (literally, "black butter"), the hominy becomes dirty (or sucio). The mantequilla negra is the essential ingredient without which you cannot make this seemingly simple dish, because it is what gives it a complex flavor and distinctive color. I save portioned-out mantequilla negra in the freezer to use for just this purpose.

2 tablespoons mantequilla negra (see Fritanga, page 409)

4 cups (570 grams) cooked hominy (Mote/Maíz para Pozole/Posol, page 69) (or use canned hominy, well rinsed and drained)

½ teaspoon fine sea salt, or more to taste

¾ cup (50 grams) sliced green onions

Heat the mantequilla negra in a large nonstick pan set over medium-high heat; as soon as it melts, add the hominy and toss, while cooking, for 3 to 4 minutes or until the hominy is heated through and begins to crisp slightly. Transfer to a serving platter, toss with the salt, and sprinkle with the green onions.

Pozole Rojo de Pollo

Red Chile Pozole

Mexico | Yield: Serves 4–6 | Difficulty Level: Easy | Total Cooking Time: 2 hours

The word *pozolli* derives from the Nahuatl word for "boiled." Although pozoles are traditional fare for Mexican Independence Day in September, they're frequently enjoyed in homes all year round. Based on one of the oldest Aztec meals, pozole has undergone a few changes, for which we are undoubtedly grateful. When Fray Bernardino de Sahagún first chronicled this dish in his 1577 work *General History of the Things of New Spain* (also called *The Florentine Codex*), he was horrified to recount that the flesh of captured warriors was one of the main ingredients! These days, pork, turkey, or chicken are the meats used. Pozole comes in three colors, representing the Mexican flag: this red version, as well as white and green variations (see Note). Pozole is traditionally enjoyed with rolled-up corn tortillas.

1 whole chicken (about 4 pounds/ 1.8 kilograms), cut up into 8 pieces

3 tablespoons (45 ml) vegetable oil

2 cups (285 grams) chopped white onions, divided

3 ounces (85 grams) carrot, peeled and left whole

1 bay leaf

1 teaspoon Mexican oregano, plus more for garnish

1 teaspoon dried thyme

1 recipe cooked hominy (Mote/ Maíz para Pozole/Posol, page 69) (or use 29 ounces/822 grams of canned hominy, well rinsed)

3 guajillo chiles

3 ancho chiles

3 cups (720 ml) boiling water

2 large garlic cloves, roughly chopped

2 teaspoons fine sea salt, or more to taste

½ teaspoon freshly ground black pepper

GARNISHES

About 2 cups shredded romaine lettuce

4–6 radishes, thinly sliced (about 1 cup)

1 Hass avocado, halved, seeded, peeled, and cubed (optional)

2 limes, quartered into wedges

Pat the chicken pieces dry with paper towels. In a large Dutch oven, heat half of the oil over medium-high heat until it shimmers; sauté half of the chicken pieces until browned on all sides, about 6 to 8 minutes. Remove the browned chicken to a bowl and repeat with the remaining oil and chicken, setting the browned pieces aside as they are ready. Remove all but 1 tablespoon of fat from the pot (discard the rest). Reduce the heat to medium and add half of the onions; sauté until slightly golden, about 2 minutes. Add the carrot, bay leaf, oregano, and thyme. Return the chicken to the pot, along with any juices collected in the bowl, cover with water by 2 inches (about 1.5 liters/6–7 cups), and stir to incorporate the browned bits at the bottom of the pot. Add the hominy and bring the liquid to a boil; cover, reduce the heat, and simmer until the chicken is tender, about 30 minutes. In the meantime, place the chiles in a large bowl and cover with 3 cups of boiling water. Place a heavy plate on top of the chiles to keep them submerged and soak them for 10 minutes. Drain the chiles over a bowl; reserve the soaking liquid. Remove the stems, seeds, and veins of the chiles and discard, and place the chiles in a blender. Add half of the soaking liquid, the remaining onions, and the garlic, and blend until smooth. Remove the carrot and the bay leaf from the Dutch oven; discard. Strain the red chile mixture through a sieve into a bowl, pressing down firmly to remove all solids. Return the solids to the blender and add the remaining soaking liquid; repeat the process, discarding any leftover chile solids. Add the strained chile mixture to the simmering pot. Season the pozole with salt and pepper and simmer for an additional 20 minutes. To serve, ladle the pozole into bowls and garnish with the lettuce, radishes, avocado, and lime wedges; sprinkle with more oregano.

White pozole: Sauté all of the onions and garlic after browning the chicken and omit the blended chile mixture. You'll have to cook the posole for 50 minutes total. The broth will be clear, but just as delicious.

Green pozole: Instead of using dried chiles, blend 6 medium tomatillos (husks removed), ½ cup (80 grams) hulled and toasted pumpkin seeds (pepitas), and 1 small bunch fresh cilantro with the onions and garlic, adding 1 cup (240 ml) water to help the motor start. Heat 1 tablespoon of vegetable oil in a medium pot with high sides, set over medium-high heat, and add the sauce, making sure to step back, as it will splatter for the first 30 seconds; reduce the heat and simmer for 5 minutes. Stir it into the soup (without straining it) in place of the blended chile mixture, and continue with the recipe as directed above.

Tamalitos Blancos

Everyday Tamales

Mesoamerica | Yield: Makes 12 tamales | Difficulty Level: Easy |
Total Cooking Time: 2 hours total (30 minutes active cooking time)

These are the simplest tamales you can make, and the ones chosen to accompany stews and soups native to Mexico and Central America. During the rainy season in Guatemala, you'll find these tamales served in place of tortillas—not only are they more filling, but they hold on to the heat longer, while you eat. The two-hour cooking time is deceptive. A large part of the time is to allow the husks to rehydrate; another significant chunk of time is given over to steaming the tamales; but the actual active time for this recipe is only about 30 minutes. Since there is no filling, the dumplings are simply formed into balls and wrapped in the corn husks. Once cooked, they can be frozen for up to four months, and steamed to order whenever you crave them. Trust me when I say that as simple as these are to make, these tamales are always a showstopper at the table.

FOR THE HUSKS

35 large dried corn husks (see Note)

6 cups (1.4 liters) hot but not boiling water (150°F/60°C)

FOR THE TAMALES

2 cups (455 grams) dried masa harina (see Sources)

2 teaspoons fine sea salt

3 cups (720 ml) warm water (120°F/48°C)

3 tablespoons (45 ml) vegetable oil

Place the corn husks in a very large bowl; cover with the hot water and let them soak for 20 minutes. In a separate large bowl, whisk together the masa harina and salt until combined. In a small bowl, combine the water and oil. Slowly, add the warm water mixture to the dry ingredients, kneading as you do so, and continuing to knead until the dough has the consistency of plasticine or mashed potatoes. Cover and let rest for 5 minutes. Turn dough onto a clean surface and knead for 1 minute. (See the box on page 75 to tell when your dough is ready.) Take five corn husks and tear them into 24 long, thin strips to tie the tamales (pull following the natural ridges of the husks and they'll break into strips); set aside. With the remaining, whole husks, working with one corn husk at a time, place it on a clean surface and wipe it dry. Divide the dough into 12 pieces, approximately 3 ounces (85 grams or a generous ⅓ cup each). Shape each piece roughly into a ball and, working with one at a time, place each in the center of a husk. Roll the left side of the husk lengthwise over the dough to cover it, flattening the dough slightly. Fold the right side so it overlaps the other side of the husk, encasing the dough completely. Twist the ends of the corn husk (like a candy wrapper) and tie both ends with the prepared corn husk strips. Repeat with the rest of the masa. Fit a large pot with a steamer basket and line the basket with a few corn husks; fill the pot with 2 to 3 inches (5 to 7.5 cm) of water. Layer the tamales flat in the basket. Cover the pot and bring the water to a boil over high heat; reduce the heat to a simmer and steam the tamales for 45 minutes (replenishing the water as needed with more boiling water). Turn off the heat and let cool in the pot for 30 minutes. To serve, remove the ties and slide each tamale out of its husk; discard the husks.

Note: Dried corn husks are widely available in grocery stores and online, sold in 1 pound (455 gram) bags. For the purpose of this recipe, use the largest husks in the package. If the package of husks only has smaller corn husks, overlap one over another to make the wrapper larger. To store these tamales: cool completely and place them in a covered container (or ziplock bag). Refrigerate for up to 48 hours or freeze them for up to 4 months. Steam them again, until heated through.

VARIATION: If you feel adventurous, mix in a handful of loroco buds or ½ cup (40 grams) of queso seco (or both) to your masa and proceed.

Want to know if your masa is the right consistency? Do the masa test: Shape some masa into a ball and press it down between the palms of your hands to form a disc. If the edges break, knead in more water a tablespoon at a time until it can be shaped without breaking. If the masa is too loose, add more masa harina a tablespoon at a time, until it can be pressed into a disc with smooth edges.

Tortillas

Picture a perfect disc of corn masa cooking on a hot comal, its moist dough developing beautifully charred flecks of golden browns and black on the side that sits directly on the hot surface, while the top remains untouched. Flip it over and let it develop brown flecks on that side. Flip it over once more—any craftsman will tell you that a tortilla has three sides—and cook it for a few seconds. It will puff up like a balloon, just momentarily (a good sign), and you'll begin to smell the earthy aroma of roasted corn, before resting it in a basket lined with a moist towel. Let the tortilla steam for just a moment so it will soften; remove it from the basket, sprinkle some coarse salt on its surface, and roll it up like a cigar. You should taste the nuttiness of the nixtamalized corn, the earthiness of the hearth, and the crunchiness of the savory salt. This is true of tortillas throughout all of Mesoamerica. But the similarities end there.

Different Definitions of Tortilla Tortillas are the most famous flatbreads in Latin America, without a doubt. However, not all Latin Americans eat them, delicious as they may be. Nor does the term *tortilla* mean the same thing in every Spanish-speaking country. From Mexico to Panama, it means a flatbread made with corn that has been soaked in alkaline, peeled, and ground finely. The fresh, wet dough (masa) is then used to make tortillas. What few people realize is that the corn tortilla goes through a visible transformation throughout the Mesoamerican territory, depending on the country.

Different Sizes The Mexican tortilla is, by definition, very thin, anywhere between 5 inches (13 cm) and 12 inches (30.5 cm) in diameter. However, once the tortilla crosses into Guatemalan territory, it's transformed into a meatier, thicker, and smaller disc of about 4 inches (10 cm) in diameter and triple the thickness of its Mexican counterpart. Keep on traveling into El Salvador, and the tortilla keeps on getting thicker, and is now often stuffed before going onto the griddle, producing pupusas. As you move into Nicaragua, Costa Rica, and Panama, the tortilla becomes even thicker—almost like a bun—and gets smaller in diameter, as small as 2 inches wide. And once you cross over into South America, the term comes to denote its original Spanish form—that of an egg omelet that no longer has anything to do with flatbreads or corn.

As different as they are in size and thickness, corn tortillas from Mexico to Guatemala and all the way to Costa Rica are used as a bread, to accompany any meal—from breakfast to an after-dinner snack—and are often filled, rolled, stuffed, or topped with different delicacies.

Tortillas are traditionally cooked on a comal—a round clay or cast-iron griddle that is set directly over a flame—but they can be cooked on modern-day griddles perfectly well. Use a nonstick pan or an electric skillet with a nonstick finish if you have one; or simply use a well-seasoned cast-iron skillet.

The Formula Not a recipe but a formula, my way of making tortillas calls for more water than most you'll find in books and online; that's because I believe that masa must be moist enough to retain enough water to help the tortilla puff as it cooks. Additionally, you'll end up with tortillas that have smooth edges that won't break or crack when shaped. Once the masa harina is properly hydrated, it can be enhanced by adding color (from achiote or chile pastes to make it red; blanched and pureed spinach or herbs like cilantro to make it green; or pureed beets or carrots for hues of purple and orange).

Tortilla Presses I own several kinds of tortilla presses: square, round, large, small—in fact, my oldest tortilla press is now on exhibit at the Smithsonian Museum in Washington, D.C.—but my consentida, or favorite, comes from Masienda (see Sources), is square, and is perfectly weighted to produce even tortillas. Although a tortilla press comes in handy, shaping tortillas with a rolling pin or flattening them down with a plate or skillet also works.

On Water Content   When making tortillas, keep your hands moistened so the masa doesn't stick to them. Also, keep the masa covered so that it doesn't dehydrate (it happens quickly). If the masa starts cracking when shaped, simply knead in a tablespoon or two of water.

On Preventing a Mess   Use a plastic bag, cut open on three sides, to encase the masa as you shape it; this will prevent it from sticking to the press. Moistening the exterior of the bag with a little water helps it stick to the press, making it easier to work.

On Flipping Tortillas Over   This takes practice, but you'll get the hang of it. Like pancakes, tortillas release from the cooking surface only when their exteriors are fully cooked. Fight the urge to flip them until they're ready, or you'll destroy their shape. Tortillas are always flipped three times, and if you're lucky, they'll puff up beautifully on the griddle—the sign of the perfect tortilla (but they'll taste just as delicious if they don't). Sometimes pressing them down slightly with a spatula at the last minute helps them to inflate.

On Steaming Them Again   At first, tortillas will seem tough ("cardboardy"), but if you stack and wrap them in moist towels immediately after cooking them and let them rest, their own steam will make them pliable.

On Keeping Them Warm   Make sure your tortillas are still warm when you use them for any of the recipes in this book; they can be reheated wrapped in a damp towel in the microwave for a minute or two or wrapped in aluminum foil and baked in a 350°F (180°C) oven for 10 to 12 minutes. The best way to reheat a tortilla, though, is to place it on a griddle or directly on a gas flame for a few seconds on each side, until pliable once more.

On Flour Tortillas   In addition to the original Mesoamerican nixtamalized corn cakes, the arrival of European wheat led to the crafting of wheat or flour tortillas. These, too, have their own culinary uses, although not as many as corn tortillas. Flour tortillas are beloved in northern Mexico, in some areas of Guatemala, and especially in Honduras (where they serve to make the most mouthwatering breakfast wraps, called baleadas) and in Costa Rica, where they are made with coconut milk.

The array of recipes that use tortillas within the territory that spreads from Mexico all the way to Panama is enormous. There, the tortilla as we know it suddenly disappears. You won't find them (or tacos) once you set foot in South America.

Tortillas de Nixtamal

Fresh Masa Tortillas

Mesoamerica | Yield: 2 dozen tortillas | Difficulty Level: Intermediate |
Total Cooking Time: 30 minutes (with nixtamal already prepared)

Chances are that most of the tortillas you have come across have been made with masa harina (or prepared cornmeal flour). However, if you want to taste ancestral America, try a homemade tortilla made with fresh nixtamalized masa; only then will you experience the nutty, smoky flavor of real hominy that the flour version can't equal. Once you have mastered nixtamal (or masa) you can prepare delicate tortillas that puff up as they cook and result in fluffy, soft, and aromatic flatbreads rich with history. People often ask me why I love food so much. Food is what gives us a sense of cultural and personal identity, and no matter the historical elements that helped shape it—whether joyful or full of strife—food is our bridge to both our past and our future. As long as people keep making nixtamal, as long as we keep the art of crafting tortillas alive, our ancestors will remain part of our heritage, and will continue to usher us into the future. If you want to taste history, eat simply, but eat well.

1 recipe Masa Nixtamalizada
(page 65)

With moistened hands, divide the masa into 24 equal portions (about ¼ cup/2 ounces/ 60 grams each). Roll each into a ball, keeping them covered with a damp towel as you work. Heat a nonstick griddle or cast-iron skillet over medium-high heat (or heat an electric griddle to 375-400°F/190-200°C). Keep a bowl of water nearby to moisten your hands as you shape the masa. Working quickly so the masa doesn't dry out, place a ball of masa in the center of a tortilla press lined with plastic (a bag or plastic wrap); cover it with the top of the plastic, and flatten it into a 5-6 inch (12-15 cm) disk, ⅛ inch (3 mm) thick. If the edges break, wet your hands, roll the dough into a ball again to moisten it, and press it again. Pull back the plastic from one side of the tortilla (to loosen it), cover it again, then flip the tortilla (still inside the plastic) and pull the plastic off that side. Lay the side of the tortilla without plastic gently on the extended (and moist) fingers of your dominant hand. Pull off the plastic completely and flip the tortilla directly onto the center of the griddle. If it folds, flatten it with wet fingers (it won't stick if you work quickly and your fingers are moist). Cook the tortilla on the first side until it has golden flecks, about 2 to 2½ minutes. Flip the tortilla over with a spatula and cook until it also has golden flecks on the other side, about 2 to 2½ minutes. Flip the tortilla again and cook it for 30 seconds to 1 minute, pressing on it gently with a spatula or your fingers (if it's moist, it should inflate—this will happen as you get more practice). Wrap the tortillas in a moist kitchen towel, making sure to stack one over the other as you finish the rest.

Note: Don't own a tortilla press? No worries: Use a heavy plate or skillet. As long as the masa is inside the plastic, it will work just the same.

Tortillas de Masa Harina

Corn Tortillas Made with Masa Harina

Mesoamerica | Yield: 12 tortillas | Difficulty Level: Easy | Total Cooking Time: 45 minutes

This is it: my recipe for fluffy, handmade tortillas that you'll be pressed to make often (pun intended!). Try different brands and colors of masa harina: blue, yellow, and white corn are all fun to play with. Just keep in mind that different brands will absorb different amounts of liquid, so always be prepared to stir a bit more masa harina (or water) into the formula until you obtain the right texture. Once made, tortillas freeze, if well wrapped, for up to two months. To reheat them, let them thaw at room temperature and cook them lightly on a griddle until hot. Eating a steaming-hot tortilla after spreading it with butter (or mashed avocado) and a sprinkling of salt is an almost religious experience in its own right.

3 cups (400 grams) masa harina

3¼–3½ cups (800–840 ml) warm water (110°F/40°C)

In a large bowl, combine the masa harina with 3¼ cups (800 ml) of the water and knead with your hands until you have a soft dough with the consistency of thick mashed potatoes (add more water, one tablespoon at a time, if needed); cover with plastic wrap or a damp kitchen towel and let rest for 10 minutes. (The masa will continue to absorb the liquid as it sits.) In the meantime, line a tortilla press with a plastic bag cut open along the sides (so the bag opens like a book). With moistened hands, divide the dough into 12 equal portions (about ¼ cup/2 ounces/60 ml each). Roll each into a ball, keeping them covered with a damp towel as you work. Heat a nonstick griddle or skillet over medium-high heat (or heat an electric griddle to 375°-400°F/190-200°C). Keep a bowl of water nearby to moisten your hands as you shape the masa. Working quickly so the dough doesn't dry out, place a ball of masa in the center of the tortilla press lined with plastic; cover it with the top of the plastic and flatten it into a 5-6 inch (12-15 cm), disk, ⅛ inch (3 mm) thick. If the edges break, wet your hands, roll the dough into a ball again to moisten it, and press it again. Pull back the plastic from one side of the tortilla (to loosen the plastic), cover it again, then flip the tortilla (still using the plastic) and pull the plastic off that side. Lay the side of the tortilla without plastic gently on the extended (and moist) fingers of your dominant hand. Pull off the plastic completely and flip the tortilla directly onto the center of the griddle. If it folds, flatten it with wet fingers (it won't stick to your fingers if they're wet). Cook the first side until it has golden flecks, about 2 to 2½ minutes. Flip the tortilla over with a spatula, and cook until it also has golden flecks, about 2 to 2½ minutes. Flip the tortilla again and cook it for 30 seconds to 1 minute. Wrap the tortillas in a moist kitchen towel, making sure to stack one on top of the other as you finish the rest.

Note: The plastic bags that I use when making tortillas are years old; simply wipe them and dry them well between uses and sandwich them between your tortilla press until you need them again. Use them only when working with masa.

How to Craft the Perfect Taco in Three Steps · In Mexico and in parts of Central America, a taco (from the Náhuatl language, in which it means "half") is a filled corn or flour tortilla folded over delicious fillings. However, in other Latin American countries, taco can mean the heel of a shoe, a plug, a thick piece of wood, or a short, stocky person (among other things!). As long as you follow these simple guidelines, you too can make the perfect edible Mexican-style taco.

- Select the right tortilla: Whether it is made of nixtamalized corn masa or wheat flour, the tortilla is the base upon which tacos are built. Choose a flimsy one, and your taco will disintegrate in your hand before it makes it to your lips. Therefore, use quality tortillas that are thick enough to withstand all of your favorite toppings—or use two stacked together. If you can't make your own tortillas, purchase quality handcrafted ones. Keep them warm at all times so they're supple and can fold around any filling.
- Select your filling: grilled beef, battered and fried fish, pulled pork carnitas, picadillo, and sautéed vegetables all belong in a taco. So do chorizo and potatoes cooked into a hash, or beans with chicharrones, poblano rajas with melting cheese and corn, chapulines (tiny grasshoppers) and lime, nopales (cactus paddles) salad, stewed beef tongue (lengua), and sausages. And remember that even a simple grilled chicken breast can become a building block for a great taco. Whatever you choose, make sure it's packed with flavor—this is the treasure that hides within each taco. The secret to a good taco, in my opinion, is to keep the filling simple and to let it shine.
- Now, for the most fun part: Select your toppings! From guacamole to pico de gallo, here is where you can set your taco apart from any other. Hot sauces and any of the hundreds of salsas—including sweet fruit salsas—available are just the start (try the salsas in this book). Chopped chiles, cilantro, onions, and tomatoes are good choices. So are crema, myriad kinds of cheese (crumbly or creamy), chile powders, and lime juice.

How to Heat Corn Tortillas

- Heat them directly over the flame of a gas stove for 20 seconds per side or until hot and pliable—my favorite way.
- Heat them directly on a hot griddle for 30 seconds per side or until hot and pliable.
- Wrap eight stacked tortillas in foil and heat them in a 400°F (200°C) oven for 8 to 10 minutes or until hot and pliable.
- Working with eight tortillas at a time, wrap them in lightly dampened paper towels and microwave for 1 minute or until hot and pliable.

What to Look for When Purchasing Corn Tortillas

- Look for transparent packages, instead of paper, so you can see the product inside. Avoid any tortillas that are broken or dry.
- Use the thickest factory-made tortillas (especially if you're a beginner) because they're a bit sturdier.
- If you're looking for crunch, beware of flour tortillas or those that combine flour with corn, as these don't crisp well (they are flaky, instead), plus they contain gluten and absorb more oil.
- White and yellow tortillas are widely available. If you're lucky, you'll find blue corn tortillas. Any of these work well.
- Corn tortillas must be hot before they can be filled and rolled (otherwise, they will break).

Molotes

Picadillo-Stuffed Masa

El Salvador, Guatemala, Honduras, and Mexico | Yield: Serves 4–6 | Difficulty Level: Easy | Total Cooking Time: 1 hour

Shaped like torpedoes, these small masa buns hail back to pre-Columbian days, when they were stuffed with wild greens, duck, and beans. Today, you'll also find them filled with chicken, cheese, or a hefty amount of beef, as in this recipe. They are then fried to form a crispy exterior, while maintaining a softer texture within. Molotes are served as an informal lunch or light dinner, with plenty of toppings, such as tomato salsas, avocados, or crema, and a salad. You can make one of the picadillo recipes in this book, or simply use your favorite ground beef recipe. It is important to keep both the masa and the uncooked molotes covered with a damp towel as you shape them, so they don't dry out in the process and crack.

2¾ cups (340 grams) masa harina, plus more as needed

1 teaspoon fine sea salt

2¼–2½ cups (540–600 ml) warm water (110°F/40°C), plus more as needed

Half recipe Picadillo Sencillo (page 449) or El Picadillo de Nikki (page 450)

Vegetable oil, for frying

TOPPINGS

1 recipe Curtido de Repollo (page 227)

Salsa de Tomate Preparada (page 161), to taste

Crema or sour cream, to taste

Shredded iceberg lettuce, to taste

Ground queso seco or Parmesan cheese, to taste

In a large bowl, whisk together the masa harina and salt. Gradually add 2¼ cups (540 ml) of the water, kneading the mixture with your hands until it comes together into a ball with the consistency of plasticine or mashed potatoes. (If the dough is too dry, add a few more tablespoons of water at a time; if it's too wet, add a few tablespoons of the masa harina at a time.) Turn the dough onto a clean surface and knead it until smooth, about 1 minute. Return it to the bowl, cover it with a damp kitchen towel, and let it rest for 10 minutes so all of the liquid can be fully absorbed. To determine whether the dough is of the correct consistency, shape a bit of masa into a ball and press it flat into a disc. If the edges crack when shaped, add a bit more water, a few tablespoons at a time; if the dough is too soft, add a bit more masa harina, a few tablespoons at a time. Divide the dough into 14 equal portions, about 2 ounces (60 grams) each, and roll into balls. Press the balls into 5 inch (12 cm) discs that are ¼ inch (6 mm) thick. Place 1½–2 tablespoons of the picadillo filling in the center of each disc, fold the edges over the filling, and seal well. Roll each into a torpedo (quenelle) shape. Line a baking sheet with a metal cooling rack and set aside. Heat 1 inch of oil in a skillet with high sides, over medium-high heat. The oil will be ready when it reaches 350°F (180°C) on a thermometer or when the end of a wooden spoon sizzles when it comes into contact with the oil. Working in batches, lower the molotes into the oil and cook until they are golden and crisp. If they are browning too quickly, lower the heat and wait for the oil to cool slightly before continuing to fry. Using two forks (I prefer these to tongs, which can tear the molotes), turn them over and continue cooking and turning until they are crisp and golden all over, about 4 to 5 minutes. Place the molotes on the prepared cooling rack to drain until they're all cooked. Serve them with plenty of toppings.

Note: To keep them warm, place the molotes in an oven preheated to 250°F (120°C) for up to 1 hour. Cooked molotes freeze beautifully: simply place them in one layer on parchment paper-lined baking sheets and freeze until solid. Transfer them to freezer-safe containers and keep them for up to 4 months. When ready to use, bake them directly from the freezer at 400°F (200°C) until hot, about 8 to 10 minutes.

VARIATIONS: Fill molotes with cooked and shredded chicken (rotisserie chicken works great here), with a good melting cheese that has been grated and mixed with green onions and cilantro, or with leftover refried beans.

Pupusas de Queso y Loroco

Cheese and Loroco Bud Pupusas

El Salvador | Yield: Serves 4–6 | Difficulty Level: Intermediate | Total Cooking Time: 1 hour

Pupusas are the plump, stuffed, and griddled Salvadorian masa cakes beloved by multitudes around the world. They can be filled with beans, cheese, pork, or a combination of the three, called revueltas. But my preferred pupusas are stuffed with a mix of both creamy and melting cheeses that serve as a canvas to the delicate flavor of loroco buds, from the vine that grows in the wild throughout Central America. Loroco is easy to come by in Latin American stores, where you'll find it either frozen or packed in jars, but if you can't find it, substitute your favorite green (such as kale or collards) or chopped asparagus.

3 cups (400 grams) masa harina

3¼–3½ cups (800–840 ml) warm water (110°–120°F/40°–50°C)

1½ cups (115 grams) shredded queso blanco, Muenster, or other melting cheese

½ cup (115 grams) soft goat cheese

½ cup (60 grams) chopped loroco buds

½ cup (120 ml) vegetable oil

1 recipe Curtido de Repollo (page 227)

1 recipe Salsa de Tomate Preparada (page 161) or Salsa Santa Rosa (page 163)

In a large bowl, combine the masa harina with 3¼ cups (800 ml) of the water and knead with your hands until you have a soft dough with the consistency of playdough or mashed potatoes (add more water, one tablespoon at a time, if needed). Cover with plastic wrap or a kitchen towel and let the dough rest for 10 minutes. To determine whether it is of the correct consistency, shape a bit of masa into a ball and press it flat into a disc. If the edges of the masa crack when shaped, add a bit more water, a few tablespoons at a time; if the dough is too soft, add a bit more masa harina, a few tablespoons at a time. In the meantime, in a medium bowl, stir together the cheeses and loroco buds until the mixture comes together into a ball. Line a baking pan with a damp kitchen towel. Heat a nonstick griddle or skillet over medium-high heat (or heat an electric griddle to 375°-400°F (190°C-200°C). Moisten your hands with a little bit of the oil and divide the masa into 12 equal portions of about ⅓ cup (3 ounces/85 grams each); pat each into a ½ inch (12 mm) thick disk. Keep them covered with a damp towel so they don't dry out. Working with one disk at a time, place 2 heaping tablespoons of the cheese filling in the center; bring the outer edges of the dough up and together over the filling to enclose it. With oiled hands, roll the pupusa into a ball and then pat it again into a ½ inch thick (12 mm) disk between the palms of your hands (or press it down with a tortilla press lined with plastic), making sure that the filling does not escape. Repeat with the remaining dough and filling. Place the pupusas on the griddle and cook until they are golden, with brown flecks, about 4 to 5 minutes per side. (If the griddle is too hot, the exterior of the pupusas will burn before they're cooked through. If you see black rather than brown flecks forming as they cook, reduce the heat of your griddle.) Transfer the finished pupusas to the prepared baking pan, covering them with the damp towel (this allows them to steam and become tender). Serve the pupusas topped with the slaw and a generous spoonful of the tomato sauce or salsa.

VARIATIONS
- To make pupusas de queso, replace the loroco buds with more melting cheese.
- To make pupusas de chicharrón, replace the cheese and loroco with 8 ounces (225 grams) of cooked ground pork (or shredded carnitas).
- To make pupusas revueltas, mix cheese, loroco, and cooked pork in a food processor until it forms a paste with the texture of thick mashed potatoes (it should hold its shape when pressed together), then use it to stuff the pupusas.

Tortillas Aliñadas

The Creamiest Tortillas

Costa Rica | Yield: Makes 12 tortillas | Difficulty Level: Intermediate | Total Cooking Time: 35 minutes

These may look like regular tortillas, but you will be surprised by their creamier texture. This is a recipe that hails back to the Costa Rica of the early 1900s, when women in train stations carried these tortillas in baskets into the train cars to sell them to hungry customers as they waited for their journey to continue. Since they have crema in them, these tortillas will stick to the griddle (or skillet) unless you add a layer of fat to it. Lard used to be traditional, but today, home cooks use oil. I've seen these tortillas the size of large plates (people break off pieces in a communal way) or on the smaller side, individually portioned, as they are here. Have plenty of melting cheese, such as a buttery queso blanco or chihuaha (Muenster or mozzarella work too), and extra natilla (or crème fraiche) on hand to spread over these before folding them. Some refried beans wouldn't hurt either.

2¼ cups (270 grams) masa harina

1¾ cups (420 ml) warm water (100°F/40°C), plus more if needed

½ cup (120 ml) natilla, crema, or crème fraiche, plus more for serving

2 tablespoons melted lard or oil, plus more if needed

In a medium bowl, combine the masa harina and water. With your hands, mix to form a lump-free dough with the consistency of thick mashed potatoes. Knead in the crema with your hands, until the dough is smooth and the texture is like that of soft mashed potatoes. Do a test by pressing a small ball of dough between your palms—if the edges crack, add a bit more water (a tablespoon at a time). If the dough is too wet and it won't form a ball, then add a bit more masa harina (a tablespoon at a time) until it does. When the dough has reached the desired consistency, cover the bowl with plastic wrap and let rest for 10 minutes (the masa will continue to absorb the liquid as it sits). In the meantime, line a tortilla press with a plastic bag cut open along the sides (so the bag opens like a book). With moistened hands, divide the dough into 12 equal portions of about ¼ cup (2 ounces/60 grams) each. Roll each into a ball, keeping the balls covered with a towel as you work. Heat a nonstick griddle or skillet over medium-high heat and brush it with lard or oil. Working quickly so the dough doesn't dry out, place a ball of masa in the center of the tortilla press, cover it with the top of the plastic, and flatten it into a 5 inch (12 cm) disk, ⅛ inch (3 mm) thick. If the edges break, wet your hands, roll the dough into a ball again to moisten it, and press it again. Pull back the plastic from one side of the tortilla (to loosen the plastic), cover it again, then flip the tortilla (still using the plastic) and pull the plastic off the other side. Lay the side of the tortilla without plastic gently on the extended fingers of your dominant hand. Pull off the plastic completely and flip the tortilla directly onto the skillet. If it folds, flatten it with wet fingers (it won't stick to your fingers if they're wet). Cook the first side until it has golden flecks, about 2 to 3 minutes. Flip the tortilla over with a spatula (they are a bit fragile, so take your time until you get really good at it) and cook until it also has golden flecks, about 2 to 3 minutes. Brush the skillet with lard or oil between cooking each tortilla. Place the tortillas in a kitchen towel and fold the towel over them, making sure to stack one on top of the other as you finish the rest.

Note: These tortillas will continue softening when wrapped, and their own steam will keep them pliable.

Tostadas

Tostadas

Mesoamerica | Yield: Makes 24 tostadas | Difficulty Level: Easy | Total Cooking Time: 15 minutes

In Spanish, *tostada* means "toast." These crispy corn tortillas can be topped with infinitesimal toppings and used for Garnaches (see page 93). I'm giving you two different ways of making them: fried and baked. I recommend that you air-dry the tortillas for at least one hour (preferably overnight) before preparing them so they have less water in them; this will help minimize splattering when frying. This is one recipe in which store-bought corn tortillas work best because they are very thin and produce delicately crispy bases that shatter upon biting. However, either the Tortillas de Nixtamal (page 83) or the Tortillas de Masa Harina (page 84) will work too.

Vegetable oil, for frying (or brushing)   24 corn tortillas (6 inches/15 cm in diameter)

For fried tostadas: Fit a baking pan with a metal rack and set aside. Add 1 inch (2.5 cm) of oil to a medium pot or skillet with high sides. Set it over medium-high heat. Dip the end of a wooden spoon into the oil; if it sizzles on contact, the oil is hot enough (it should register 360°F/180°C on a thermometer). Working one at a time, carefully slide a tortilla into the oil and fry on each side for 30 to 35 seconds or until golden. Transfer the tortilla to the prepared rack using tongs while you finish frying the rest (this helps them drain).

For oven-baked tostadas: Preheat the oven to 360°F (180°C). Fit two baking pans with oven-safe metal racks. Working in four batches (of six tortillas each), brush each tortilla with vegetable oil, coating well on both sides. Place them on the prepared racks, then bake them for 4 minutes or until they begin to turn golden. Turn them over to the other side and bake for 4 to 5 minutes or until they are golden and crisp. Cool slightly before placing them on a platter. Repeat with the rest of the tortillas until all are done.

Note: Once baked or fried, these tostadas will keep well, if stored in a tin, for up to 1 week at room temperature. If they lose their crispness, simply bake them in a 360°F (180°C) oven for 2 to 3 minutes or until they are warmed through.

VARIATIONS: Single-ingredient tostadas are a favorite snack in Central America. Refried beans, any kind of salsa, guacamol (or guacamole), ceviches, and escabeches can all be used to top them. Or you can build a salad on top of a tostada, sprinkle it with cheese, and call it a meal! Just keep in mind that the heavier the filling, the sturdier the tostada must be. Reserve those tostadas made with the thinnest store-bought tortillas for single toppings. Use tostadas made with the Tortillas de Nixtamal (page 83) or the Tortillas de Masa Harina (page 84) for heavy toppings.

Garnaches

Corn Tostadas with Beans and Cabbage

Belize | Yield: Serves 4–6 | Difficulty Level: Easy | Total Cooking Time: 30 minutes

Garnaches are the Belizean variation on bean tostadas, topped with crisp cabbage, and the kind of food that I can't stop munching on after I start. Hot and cold and crunchy and creamy textures create a collision for the senses that's very hard to resist. Perhaps this is why they are so beloved, and why you'll find them as often served at home as they are on the street and in restaurants. The refried beans are as important to this recipe as the crispy corn tortilla. You can purchase tostadas in many Latin American stores, but they're easy to make (see page 91).

In Guatemala, these are known as garnachas and are topped with a tomato salsa (like the Chirmol de la Mari on page 152). Before Belize became a Commonwealth country in 1862, and way before it gained independence in 1981, it was part of Guatemala. I was a little girl when Guatemala was on the brink of war with England, ready to fight for the Belizean territory; thankfully, it didn't come to that. Garnaches are a testimony to the history Guatemala and Belize still share on the plate. You will need half of a small cabbage for this recipe; use the rest to make the other curtido (or cabbage slaw) recipes throughout the book, such as the Curtido de Repollo on page 227.

5½ cups (680 grams) finely chopped green cabbage

¾ cup (115 grams) finely chopped white onions

¼ cup (60 ml) distilled white vinegar, or more to taste

1½ teaspoons fine sea salt, or more to taste

½ teaspoon freshly ground black pepper, or more to taste

1 recipe Tostadas (page 91)

1 recipe Frijoles Fritos (page 131), ideally fried in coconut oil and heated through

Hot sauce, to taste

In a large nonreactive bowl, combine the cabbage, onions, vinegar, salt, and pepper; let sit at room temperature for 15 minutes (or cover and refrigerate for up to 1 week). Smear a good amount of frijoles fritos all over the top of each tostada, top with the cabbage, and serve with hot sauce.

Note: Belizean cooks refry their beans using coconut oil, which imparts a coastal taste; you may substitute any fat you have on hand.

MY VARIATION ON REFRIED BEANS: For the quickest refried beans, drain two 15 ounce (425 gram) cans of red or black beans, reserving some of the canned liquid, and place them in a blender. Blend them until smooth, adding enough of the reserved liquid to help the beans blend. Heat 2 tablespoons of fat (coconut oil for Belizean beans; lard or vegetable oil for all others) in a nonstick pan set over medium-high heat. Add the beans and start stirring; when they begin to bubble, lower the heat slightly (to medium) and continue cooking, while stirring, until the beans are thickened to your desired consistency. Season liberally with salt and serve.

Chilaquiles Caseros con Huevo Estilo Michoacán

Egg Chilaquiles

Mexico | Yield: Serves 4 | Difficulty Level: Easy | Total Cooking Time: 30 minutes

One of my dearest friends, Cristina Potters, a well-respected authority on the food of Mexico, is an American expat living in Morelia, on the west coast of Mexico. She is the author of the award-winning blog "Mexico Cooks!" and an extraordinary cook. This is her recipe for a breakfast dish made with leftover, stale tortillas and lots of eggs. Most people assume that all chilaquiles (pronounced *chee-lah-keel-ehs*) are drenched in sauce (like Salsa de Tomate Preparada on page 161). However, in Michoacán, where Cristina lives, this is the preferred way of eating them—perfectly scrambled with eggs and aromatics and served with toppings. Cooks in parts of northern Mexico and in Texas call these migas, because they resemble the dish of the same name found in Spanish and Portuguese cuisines made by mixing stale bread with eggs. Cristina recommends serving these with refried beans, avocados, crema, and a great cup of hot chocolate or coffee. When I don't have stale corn tortillas, I leave fresh ones in one layer on cooling racks and let them sit at room temperature for a day or two. After tasting this hearty dish, you may just find yourself purchasing or making extra tortillas to ensure that you've always got plenty for chilaquiles. These make a delicious lunch when paired with a simple salad.

10 eggs

¼ cup (60 ml) whole milk

½ teaspoon fine sea salt

1–2 teaspoons (5–10 ml) red hot sauce (any sort will do, so use your favorite), to taste

¼ cup (60 ml) vegetable oil

1⅓ cups (170 grams) chopped white onions

1–2 fresh serrano peppers, finely chopped (seeded and deveined for less heat)

Twenty stale 6 inch (15 cm) corn tortillas (the staler the better), cut into 1½ inch (4 cm) squares

1 cup (240 ml) Mexican crema (or sour cream)

1 Hass avocado, peeled, seeded, and cubed

Break the eggs into a large mixing bowl; add milk, salt, and hot sauce. Whisk until all of the ingredients are mixed and set aside. Heat the oil in a large nonstick skillet set over medium-high heat. Add the onions and the serranos, cooking, while stirring, for 3 minutes or until the onions are translucent but not browned. Add the tortilla pieces to the skillet and continue cooking, stirring often, until they are browned and moderately crunchy, about 4 to 5 minutes (the onions will take on a golden color during this process and begin to caramelize). As soon as the tortillas begin to turn crispy (but not as crispy as packaged chips), add the beaten egg mixture—you'll notice the tortillas turning shiny with egg. Lower the heat to medium and cook, while stirring, until the eggs are set and the tortillas are no longer shiny. Divide the chilaquiles onto four plates and top each with a dollop of crema and a quarter of the avocado cubes. Serve immediately.

Sopa de Tortilla de Todos los Días

Quick and Easy Tortilla Soup

Mexico | Yield: Serves 6–8 | Difficulty Level: Easy | Total Cooking Time: 50 minutes

What could be better than deeply flavored chicken broth that invites you to top it with as many ingredients as your heart desires? That's why tortilla soups are so beloved all over the world. This is a very simple recipe, but one that showcases many of the ingredients that most of us have come to expect from Mexican recipes: fruity dried chiles, tangy tomato sofrito, creamy cheese that melts deliciously, and, of course, crispy tortilla chips that provide texture and, most importantly, an element of fun! Be generous with the toppings, because chances are that your family will enjoy eating them in copious amounts. I give you no quantities here, simply fill bowls and offer them at the table for everyone to indulge. In my home, this soup makes up an entire meal; sometimes, to make it more filling, I'll add shredded, cooked chicken (leftover rotisserie chicken is great here) or some cooked chickpeas.

FOR THE SOUP

4 large garlic cloves, unpeeled and left whole

1 small (about 4 ounces/115 grams) yellow onion, peeled and halved

2 pounds (910 grams) plum tomatoes

1 tablespoon ancho chile powder

8 cups (2 liters) chicken broth

2 tablespoons vegetable oil

Salt, to taste (see Note)

Pinch of freshly ground black pepper, or more to taste

FOR THE TOPPINGS

2–4 pasilla chiles, stemmed, seeded, deveined, sliced into rings, and fried (see box on page 182)

2 Hass avocados, halved, seeded, peeled, chopped, and tossed with lemon juice

Queso fresco, crumbled (feta may be substituted in a pinch)

Mexican crema (or sour cream)

Chopped fresh cilantro

Fried tortilla strips (see box on page 95)

Heat a griddle over medium-high heat, add the garlic cloves, onion halves, and tomatoes and roast them for 5 to 6 minutes, turning them as they char. Remove them from the griddle to a cutting board; roughly chop the onions and tomatoes and place them into the jar of a blender. Peel the garlic cloves (discard the skins) and add them to the blender; add the ancho chile powder. Blend until smooth (use a bit of the broth to get the motor started, if needed). Heat the oil in a large pot, set over medium-high heat. Standing at a distance, add the blended vegetables (careful, it will splatter for a few seconds) and stir with a long spatula. Cook for 1 minute; lower the heat to medium and continue cooking for 5 minutes or until it begins to thicken. Add the broth, increase the heat, and bring it up to a boil. Lower the heat to medium and simmer, uncovered, for 20 to 30 minutes (the longer it simmers, the more the flavors will concentrate as the broth reduces). Season with salt and pepper to taste. Serve this soup piping hot with plenty of the toppings suggested.

Note: The amount of salt needed will depend on how much sodium is in the broth you're using. For this reason, taste it first, and add salt at the end, to adjust.

To fry corn tortillas · Use scissors to cut the tortillas into strips. Heat 2 inches (5 cm) oil in a pot set over medium-high heat until it reaches 350°F (180°C) or until a wooden spoon inserted into the oil begins to sizzle. Add the tortilla strips in batches, frying them for 30 seconds to 1 minute or until crisp and golden (do not let them brown, as they will continue to darken as they cool). Remove them with tongs and let them drain on a cooling rack. Repeat until all tortillas are fried.

Sopa Seca de Tortilla o Chilaquiles

Tortilla Casserole

Mexico | Yield: Serves 6–8 | Difficulty Level: Easy | Total Cooking Time: 1 hour

I tasted my very first chilaquiles in a Mexican tianguis (pronounced *tee-ahn-geese*) or flea market, when I was six years old. It was one of the very first recipes I ever asked for. The señora making them just said, "Salsa, totopos, y lo que le quieras ponerles encima." ("Sauce, chips, and whatever toppings you want.") She invited me to stand next to her stove to watch her make a few more. She heated a portion of sauce in one of several small, rickety saucepans, added fried tortilla strips, and coated them with the sauce with a spoon. She'd soften them to taste, like pasta for customers who wanted them aguadas (soft) and crispy for those who didn't; adding more sauce to some and leaving them secas (dry) for others. She alternated the sauces (I only tasted the red one, but she had green and deep rust-colored versions, too). She'd then serve them on paper plates and hand them out for her daughter to top with crema, cheese, chile strips, avocado, herbs (cilantro and what I now think must have been epazote), and a variety of hot sauces. Some plates got topped with a fried egg, others with shredded chicken or other meats. Over the years, I've found them cooked in casserole dishes (such as this one) and like pasta, in large pots. If you enjoy dishes such as lasagna or moussaka, you'll love this—and it's fabulous for a crowd.

2–3 cups (480–720 ml) vegetable oil, for frying

Twenty 8 inch (20 cm) corn tortillas, sliced into strips and air-dried overnight

4 pasilla chiles (1 ounce/30 grams), seeded, stemmed, and cut into thin strips

Cooking spray, for greasing the pan

1 recipe of Salsa de Tomate Preparada (page 161)

3 cups (720 ml) Mexican crema

4 cups (400 grams) shredded quesadilla cheese (Muenster or Monterey Jack or other melting cheese)

2 Hass avocados

Fit a pan with a metal cooling rack and set aside. Heat the oil in a Dutch oven or a large skillet with high sides and set over medium-high heat. Working in batches, fry the tortilla strips until they're crispy, 30 seconds to 1 minute (don't let them get too brown—they will continue to deepen in color as they cool). Drain the tortillas on the prepared rack and set aside. Fry the chile strips for 10 to 20 seconds in the oil; drain on paper towels and set aside. Spray a 9 x 13 inch (23 x 33 cm) baking casserole with cooking spray. Place a bit of tomato sauce in the bottom of the pan; top with a layer of the fried tortillas, a layer of crema, and a layer of cheese. Repeat the layers one or two more times, ending with cheese. Preheat the oven to 400°F (200°C). Bake the casserole for 20 to 25 minutes or until it's bubbly. Remove from the oven and let cool slightly for 5 to 8 minutes. In the meantime, halve and pit the avocados. Scoop out the flesh onto a board and chop into cubes. Top the casserole with avocado and the chile strips. Serve immediately.

Note: I treat leftover oil that I use for fried foods much in the same manner that most Latin cooks still do today: I let it cool completely; strain it through a fine mesh into a jar, and reuse it in other recipes. You'll know when the oil is too old when a foam begins to form on the surface when you fry (usually after 3 or 4 uses); it is then time to ditch it and start another batch. The only oil I will not reuse for frying is that used for fish or seafood, which will impart an unpleasant taste and aroma to the food; discard after using.

Tacos de Pollo o de Carne Deshebrada

Rolled Chicken or Beef Tacos

Guatemala and Mexico | Yield: Serves 4–6 | Difficulty Level: Intermediate | Total Cooking Time: 45 minutes

They say that the way to a man's heart is through his stomach, and this was certainly true with my husband, Luis, who loved these crunchy tacos from the very first bite. These thin and perfectly rolled parcels are fried until crispy. Growing up, we drowned them in simple tomato sauce (ahogados), sprinkled them with queso seco (similar to feta), and topped them with thinly sliced onion rings and parsley. The colorful presentation alone is enough to make mouths water. Properly made, they'll elicit ecstatic sighs followed by almost reverent silence. The idea is to smother the taquitos with sauce across the middle, leaving the edges clean so they can be held without staining your fingers. The first bite of these taquitos is always crunchy, but as you nibble into the sauced center, the texture changes—the crunch returning only on your last mouthful. Although you can fill these with any leftover meats, rotisserie chicken is perfect for a fast meal. It can be quickly shredded and rolled into store-bought corn tortillas, making what used to take hours to prepare a very easy weekday meal.

3 cups (400 grams) shredded rotisserie chicken or Carne Cocida (page 30)

16 corn tortillas (5–6 in/12–15 cm in diameter)

Vegetable oil, for frying

Salsa de Tomate Preparada (page 161)

Crumbled queso seco, to taste

¼ cup (55 grams) very thinly sliced white onions

Finely chopped fresh Italian parsley, to taste

Line a baking sheet with parchment or waxed paper and set aside. Line a second baking sheet with a cooling rack and set aside. Divide the shredded chicken (or shredded flank steak) into 16 portions (about 2 generous tablespoons each), placing each mound of filling onto the baking sheet lined with paper; set aside. Heat the tortillas directly over a gas flame until pliable and warm, about 20 seconds per side; keep them wrapped in a lightly damped kitchen towel. Place one portion of the filling on one side of a tortilla and mound it slightly. Roll the tortilla starting on the side with the filling, moving upward to form a cigar, and secure the seam with a toothpick. As you work, place the rolled taquitos on a plate; cover them with plastic wrap (or use a plastic bag cut and opened up like a book) and place a clean kitchen towel over them. By keeping them warm this way, you can stop the tortillas from flaking before they're fried. Heat 1 inch of oil in a skillet with high sides over medium-high heat. The oil will be ready when it reaches 360°F (180°C) on a thermometer or when the end of a wooden spoon sizzles when it comes into contact with the oil. Lower the taquitos (seam side down; the toothpick should be holding the seam together—by doing this, you'll prevent the taquitos from unfurling) into the oil and cook until the seam side is golden and crisp (at this point, they will not unfurl anymore). If they are browning too quickly, lower the heat and wait for the oil to cool slightly before continuing to fry. Using two forks (I prefer these to tongs, which can tear the uncooked side of the tortillas), turn them over to the other side and continue cooking and turning until they are crisp and golden all over, about 4 to 5 minutes total. Place the finished taquitos on the cooling rack until you finish cooking them all. →

Pull out the toothpicks, and place the taquitos side by side on a long platter. Coat with as much tomato sauce as you want (making sure to leave at least one end of the taquitos unsauced, to allow you to hold them easily). Sprinkle with cheese, onions, and parsley, and serve.

VARIATION: To make flautas, a northern Mexican variation, use flour tortillas instead of corn tortillas. Cook them the same way. They'll be flakier than those made with corn tortillas. Serve them with tomatillo salsas, shredded lettuce, and crema. (The Crema Fría de Chile Poblano on page 175 is particularly delicious as a dip.)

Arepas

As soon as you cross over from Panama into South American territory, specifically into Venezuela and Colombia, the tortilla goes through yet another transition. It is no longer made of corn that has been nixtamalized in the traditional way. This alternate process for making dough from corn—called maíz pilado or maíz pelao—follows the same steps of soaking in alkaline, but the corn isn't cooked; rather, it is mashed in a pilón (a conical African contraption or basin made out of wood in which grains can be ground with the help of a giant mortar), which separates the endosperm from the germ of the kernel, peeling it. Only the clean kernels are cooked, then ground in a mill to produce dough. This is the corn used to make arepas.

The word *arepa* derives from *erepa*, which means "corn" in the Wayuu language. Arepas are South American cornbreads. According to historians, their round shape honors the sun and the moon. The first arepas were very thin. Today, arepas vary greatly in thickness, depending on the region where they are made. They can be as thin as pita breads or as thick as British scones; they can be large in diameter, or tiny. Some are teeny and thick, like little buns, and are used to soak up sauces and the juices of grilled meats. Others are so thin that they will remind you of Central American tortillas (especially the arepas of Colombia), but their flavor is sweeter. The texture of arepas is also dissimilar to that of tortillas in that they're denser and have an almost creamy center, like very thick polenta. The nutty and earthy flavor of tortillas is replaced by the sweeter flavor of fresh corn, reminiscent of the hoecakes made by Native Americans. Yellow corn was preferred in ancient times, but today, both white and yellow varieties are used.

Both arepas and tortillas can be grilled, sautéed, griddled, or fried. They are also gluten free. Broadly speaking, there are many differences between tortillas and arepas: while tortillas may be wrapped around a filling, arepas function more like bread, on which toppings are placed on or stuffed into, or served on the side. While tortillas are always savory, arepas can be savory or sweet.

The process for preparing these flatbreads used to be arduous and very time consuming (not so in modern times, as you'll see on page 104). Here I offer you just a handful of arepa recipes—enough to get you started falling in love with them. Enjoy the many recipes for fillings that you'll find here—most of which can be prepared with leftovers of other dishes found in this book.

An arepa is as delicious eaten when it's hot, topped with sweet butter and perhaps some molasses, as it is when it's topped with thinly sliced melting cheese and some natilla (South American crema). Basically, if you can put it on bread or stuff it into a sandwich, you can put it into or onto an arepa.

Arepas Clásicas

Classic Arepas

Colombia and Venezuela | Yield: Makes 6 arepas | Difficulty Level: Easy | Total Cooking Time: 25 minutes

This is the simplest recipe you'll find for arepas; it will yield buns that are thick enough to slice in half and stuff with whatever filling you like. In Venezuela, you'll find them stuffed modestly with ham and cheese (my favorite!), with chicken and avocado salad, and with the ingredients that make up pabellón, their national dish: shredded beef, plantains, and rice. In Colombia, arepas are shaped a bit thinner (some quite thin) and either served as bread on the side or topped with melted cheese and other humble delicacies, from suero (similar to crème fraiche) and jams and jellies to tomato sauce-laden shrimp or fried eggs. There are many wonderful ways to eat them, but you'll need a great recipe to start with, and here it is.

2 cups (170 grams) white or yellow arepa flour (also known as masarepa or harina pan)

1 teaspoon fine sea salt

2⅓–2½ cups (550–600 ml) warm water (120°F/48°C)

Vegetable oil, for coating griddle or nonstick skillet

Set aside a baking sheet with high rims. In a large bowl, mix the arepa flour and salt together. Slowly, add the water in a thin stream as you begin to knead the dough, breaking up all the clumps of flour as you knead, until it is of a consistency similar to mashed potatoes (this should take about 2 minutes). Cover and let it sit for 10 minutes at room temperature. With moistened hands, divide the dough into six equal pieces (about 4 ounces/115 grams each) or about ½ cup of dough at a time and shape them into patties that are about 3¼ inches (8 cm) wide and about ½ inch (12 mm) thick. Preheat a griddle over medium heat to about 375°F (190°C). Brush the griddle generously with vegetable oil. Place the arepas directly on the griddle (working in batches, if needed) and cook for 4 to 5 minutes per side or until golden specks are visible on the bottom. Place the baking sheet directly over the arepas and cook for 2 to 3 more minutes (or bake in a 350°F/190°C oven for 5 to 6 minutes) or until slightly puffed. Serve hot.

Note: If you desire them a bit sweet, stir a couple of tablespoons of unrefined sugar (panela or papelón) to the water until dissolved.

Arepas de Queso

Cheese Arepas

Colombia and Venezuela | Yield: Makes 6 arepas | Difficulty Level: Easy |
Total Cooking Time: 35–40 minutes (includes resting time)

A few years back, I organized a panel for a food conference in New York City and invited several women, all experts on Latin American foodways, to join me. We presented to a "who's who" of international culinary authorities, among them editors, publishers, and authors. Our goal was to break as many as possible of the stereotypes that tied our Pan Latin cuisines together in less than two hours. We began with this: Not all Latinos eat tortillas. To illustrate, we served arepas, the traditional flatbreads of both Colombia and Venezuela. The audience was instantly enamored, surprised by the warm, cheesy bread, crispy on the outside and creamy in the middle. Today, of course, restaurants that specialize in arepas have taken the world by storm, feeding diners as far away as Australia and England. Arepa precooked corn flour (not to be confused with cornmeal) is easy to source in most grocery stores and online; it only needs to be mixed with warm liquid to produce the malleable dough necessary to craft arepas. There are many recipes for arepas; I can't possibly include them all, but this is a version of the ones we served back in New York City. Hopefully, we opened the minds of some of those people in the food industry, moving them beyond the taco.

2½ cups (340 grams) arepa flour (also known as masarepa or harina pan)

1 teaspoon fine sea salt

2½ cups (600 ml) warm water (about 115°F/50°C)

1 cup (115 grams) shredded good melting cheese (llanero, mozzarella, or queso blanco)

2 tablespoons unsalted butter

2 tablespoons vegetable oil

Preheat the oven to 350°F (180°C). Line a baking sheet with parchment paper and set aside. In a large bowl, mix the arepa flour and salt together. Slowly, add the water in a thin stream as you begin to knead the dough, breaking up all the clumps of flour as you knead, until it is of a consistency similar to mashed potatoes (this should take about 2 minutes). Knead the cheese into the dough until well combined; cover and let sit for 10 minutes at room temperature. With moistened hands, take 6 ounces (170 grams/about ¾ cup) of dough at a time and shape into patties that are about 3 inches (7.5 cm) wide and about ¾ inch (2 cm) thick. In a large skillet, heat the butter and oil over medium heat. Carefully slide the arepas into the pan (working in batches, if needed) and cook for 4 to 5 minutes per side or until golden specks are visible on the bottom. Transfer to the prepared baking sheet and bake in the oven for 8 to 10 minutes or until slightly puffed. Serve hot.

Note: Because arepa flours vary in water content and respond to the humidity in the atmosphere, follow these tips: If, when you begin to shape the arepas, the dough cracks around the edges, add more water, 1 tablespoon at a time, until the dough holds together without cracking. If the arepas don't hold their shape and are too mushy, add more arepa flour, 1 tablespoon at a time, until the dough holds together without cracking. Allow it to rest for 5 minutes, and proceed.

Arepitas con Guasacaca de Comino

Mini Arepas with Avocado-Cumin Sauce

Venezuela | Yield: Makes 24 mini arepas | Difficulty Level: Easy | Cooking Time: 35 minutes

Here tiny corn cakes are topped with the Venezuelan avocado sauce, guasacaca. These are dainty—you can actually make them any size you want, but I love to serve them as appetizers during my cooking classes and parties. They're always among the first food to disappear from the table, so make plenty.

FOR THE AREPITAS

2 cups (170 grams) yellow or white arepa flour (also known as masarepa or harina pan)

1 teaspoon fine sea salt

2⅓–2½ cups (550–600 ml) warm water (120°F/48°C)

Vegetable oil, for coating the griddle or nonstick skillet

FOR THE GUASACACA

2 Hass avocados, pitted and peeled

Juice of 1 lemon

1 teaspoon red wine vinegar

¼ cup (70 grams) very finely chopped white onions

½ teaspoon ground cumin

Salt, to taste

Freshly ground black pepper, to taste

Grape tomatoes (red and/or yellow), halved (optional)

Fresh flat Italian parsley, leaves only (optional)

To make the arepitas, set aside a baking sheet with high rims. In a large bowl, mix the arepa flour and salt together. Slowly, add the water in a thin stream as you begin to knead the dough, breaking up all the clumps of flour as you knead, until it is of a consistency similar to mashed potatoes (this should take about 2 minutes). Cover and let sit for 10 minutes at room temperature. With moistened hands, divide the dough into twenty-four equal pieces (about 1 ounce/30 grams) each or about 2 tablespoons of dough at a time and shape them into patties that are about 1 inch (2.5 cm) wide and about ½ inch (12 mm) thick. Preheat a griddle over medium heat to about 375°F (190°C). Brush the griddle generously with vegetable oil and place the arepas directly on the griddle (working in batches, if needed) and cook for 2 to 3 minutes per side or until golden specks are visible on the bottom. Place the baking sheet directly over the arepas and cook for 1 to 2 more minutes (or transfer the arepitas to the baking sheet and bake in a 350°F/180°C oven for 5 minutes) or until slightly puffed. To make the guasacaca, mash the avocados with the lemon juice and vinegar in a medium bowl. Stir in the onions, salt, and pepper. Top each arepita with the avocado mixture, then a tomato half and a parsley leaf, if desired. Set them all on a large platter and serve.

VARIATION: For a quicker appetizer, serve the arepitas with a slice of queso llanero or any good melting cheese, and a dollop of honey.

Arepas Dominó

Bean and Cheese Stuffed Arepas

Venezuela | Yield: Makes 6 arepas | Difficulty Level: Easy | Total Cooking Time: 25 minutes

Black beans and fresh, white cheese are the colors of a domino—thus the name for this popular sandwich. This is only one version of black bean–stuffed arepas that you'll find served in homes in Venezuela. To embellish, top with sliced red onions, avocados, or a combination of both. There are no strict rules on what you can stuff into an arepa, as long as the fillings are so delicious that when they're combined with the corn cake they enhance each other.

1 recipe Arepas Clásicas (page 104)

2 tablespoons vegetable oil

½ cup (115 grams) finely chopped white onions

½ cup (170 grams) seeded and finely chopped plum tomatoes

1 teaspoon ground cumin

½ teaspoon garlic powder

Two 15 ounce (425 gram) cans whole black beans, drained

½ teaspoon fine sea salt

¼ teaspoon freshly ground black pepper

2 cups (340 grams) shredded melting cheese (such as queso blanco or mozzarella)

Keep the arepas warm in a 250°F (120°C) oven. Heat the oil in a medium pan over medium-high heat. Add the onions, tomatoes, cumin, and garlic powder; sauté for 3 minutes or until the onions are softened. Add the beans, ½ cup (120 ml) water, salt, and pepper. Bring to a simmer and cook uncovered for 10 minutes or until thickened; keep warm. Split each arepa in half through the middle, leaving a piece still attached at the end. Fill each arepa with some beans, and top with cheese. Serve immediately.

Arepas Pabellón

Beef, Bean, Plantain, and Cheese Arepas

Venezuela | Yield: Makes 6 arepas | Difficulty Level: Easy |
Total Cooking Time: 30 minutes (if constituent parts are already prepared)

Pabellón is the name given to a dish of shredded beef, plantains, beans, and rice, served all over Venezuela. In Caracas, these traditional ingredients have been transformed into a filling for arepas. This is a classic arepa, ideal for making with leftovers. Use either the recipe for Carne Cocida (page 30) or the sauced-up Carne Mechada (page 461) for the best results. Fried plantains offer a sweet contrast to the salty beef; melded with beans and cheese, the mainstay of most meals in Venezuela, they result in an explosion of comforting flavors.

1 recipe Arepas Clásicas (page 104)

1 recipe Carne Cocida (page 30) or Carne Mechada (page 461), reheated

1 recipe Frijoles Exprés (page 119), reheated

1 recipe Platanitos Fritos (page 307)

1¾ cups (280 grams) salty, crumbly cheese such as llanero, fresco, or feta

Keep the arepas warm in a 250°F (120°C) oven. Split each arepa in half through the middle, leaving a piece still attached at the end. Fill each arepa with some beef and some beans, and top with a couple of slices of fried plantains. Top liberally with cheese. Serve immediately.

Arepas de Pollo a la Catira

Arepas with Shredded Chicken

Venezuela | Yield: Makes 6 arepas | Difficulty Level: Easy | Total Cooking Time: 30 minutes

Long before hamburguesas (hamburgers) made it into the Latin American lexicon, chicken sandwiches were already popular among the working class in Latin America. One such example is this arepa version made with rotisserie chicken and sautéed vegetables. It may look simple, but it's one of the most popular dishes in Venezuela.

1 recipe Arepas Clásicas (page 104)

1 small (3 pound/1.4 kilogram) rotisserie chicken

2 tablespoons vegetable oil

2 cups (280 grams) thinly sliced white onions

1 cup (185 grams) stemmed, seeded, and thinly sliced red bell peppers

2 cups (455 grams) shredded melting cheese such as queso blanco

Keep the arepas warm on a baking sheet in a 250°F (120°C) oven. Shred the chicken and place it in a bowl (you should have about 8 cups). Heat the oil in a medium pan over medium-high heat. Add the onions and peppers, stirring while you cook for 4 minutes or until just softened; stir in the chicken and warm through. Remove the arepas from the oven and increase the heat to 400°F (200°C). Split each arepa in half through the middle, leaving a piece still attached at the end. Fill the arepas with the chicken mixture and top with a very generous amount of cheese. Place the arepas back on the baking sheet and into the warm oven; heat until the cheese is melted, about 5 to 8 minutes. Serve immediately.

Arepas de Huevo

Egg-Stuffed Fried Arepas

Colombia | Yield: Makes 6 arepas | Difficulty Level: Advanced | Total Cooking Time: 30 minutes

These crispy corn cakes, which burst with runny egg when they're cut, are my favorite treat for breakfast in Colombia. This is not an easy recipe to make, but once you've done it a few times, you'll get the gist of it. Here are a few tips to help you out: Work with only one arepa at a time. Shape and flatten the dough to the exact measurements I offer here, then fry in hot oil, ideally to 360°F (180°C). Too cold, and the arepas will just absorb the oil and remain flat; too hot, and they will burn on the first fry. At first, the arepas will sink to the bottom of the pot; a few seconds later they should rise to the top. This is when hot oil must be spooned over the top of the arepa so it can inflate, like a balloon—don't skip this step. They must be cooled enough for handling. This is where it gets interesting: you'll use the back of a spoon to open a hole into the puffiest side of the arepa and slide a raw egg into the hole (it's easiest to do so using a cup that has a spout and small eggs). Then the arepa is placed in the hot oil to fry a second time, this time to cook the egg inside. Ready to try it?

1¼ cups (170 grams) arepa flour (also known as masarepa or harina pan)

1 teaspoon fine sea salt

½ teaspoon ground achiote (optional)

1¼ cups (300 ml) hot tap water (about 100°F/40°C)

Oil, for frying (about 6 cups)

6 small eggs

1 cup (240 ml) crema or crème fraiche, for garnish

1 recipe Luisa's Aliño Crudo (page 158), for garnish

2 Hass avocados, halved, pitted, scooped out, sliced, and brushed with 1 tablespoon lime juice (to prevent discoloration), for garnish

Combine the arepa flour, salt, and achiote in a medium bowl; add the water and use a spoon to mix together. Switch to your hands and knead for 1 to 2 minutes or until the dough is smooth and free of lumps (the texture of mashed potatoes). Cover the dough and let it rest at room temperature for 10 minutes (this will allow it to absorb all of the water). In the meantime, line a tortilla press with a plastic bag cut open along the sides (so the bag opens like a book). Line a large baking pan with a metal cooling rack and set aside. With moistened hands, divide the dough into six equal pieces (about 2½ ounces/70 grams/¼ cup each). Roll each piece into a ball; keep them covered with a clean, damp towel while you work. Working quickly so the dough doesn't dry out, place a ball of cornmeal in the center of the tortilla press lined with plastic; cover it with the top of the plastic, and flatten it into a 5½ inch (14 cm) disk, ¼ inch (6 mm) thick. Fill a medium pot with oil and heat it to 360°F (182°C). Working with one arepa at a time, slide it into the oil; as soon as it rises to the top, spoon oil over it—you should see it inflate. Don't stop spooning oil! Fry for 60 seconds. Turn the arepa over carefully and cook for 30 seconds on the second side (again, keep spooning oil over the top). Use a slotted spoon to transfer it to the cooling rack; continue until all of the arepas are fried. Break 1 egg into a cup with a spouted end. Working with one arepa at a time (if necessary, hold it using a napkin so you don't burn your fingers), use the back of a wooden spoon to open a small (1 inch/2.5 cm) slit on one side of the arepa (not the top). Gently slide the egg into the hole and immediately put the arepa back into the oil (slit side up) to fry for 40 to 45 seconds, while spooning oil over it. Carefully flip the arepa over to its other side and fry for another 40 seconds, while spooning oil over it. Remove with a slotted spoon and place on the rack. Continue until all of the arepas are filled and fried. Serve immediately with the crema, aliño, and avocado as garnishes.

Note: In lieu of a tortilla press, use a heavy skillet to shape the dough into discs (make sure to place the dough between sheets of plastic so it doesn't stick to the skillet). You can place the finished arepas in a warm oven (250°F/120°C) for up to 20 minutes or until all of the arepas are fully cooked. To do this, fit a metal rack into a baking pan and place the cooked arepas on top of the rack. This will help drain off the oil while keeping the arepas crispy.

BEANS

Frijolitos pintos, claveles morados, ay, cómo sufren los enamorados!
(Little red beans, purple carnations, oh, how lovers suffer!)

—Children's folk song by Linda Escobar, 1965

Beans, the bejeweled, multicolored little beads of the Phaseolus family, have fed us since ancient times and are the darlings of the Americas. Grown alongside corn and squash, they comprise the trinity that we call "the Three Sisters." According to Bernardino de Sahagún in his book *General History of the Things of New Spain* (also called *The Florentine Codex*), published in 1577, there were twelve kinds of beans grown in Mexico when Hernán Cortés arrived. Hundreds of bean varieties (more than four hundred, to be exact) found in the rest of the Americas were not included in this calculation. Many, unknown to the majority of cooks worldwide, are still being rescued from extinction every day by legions of bioethicists and farmers. If you want to see Latin American diversity, collect a basket of beans. Together they put even a rainbow to shame with their different hues of red, black, white, pinto, brown, golden, purple, orange, yellow, blue, and green.

There are thousands of recipes for beans in the Latin culinary repertoire: boiled, stewed, mashed, fried, and refried. They are used in not just savory recipes but also sweet ones (usually with sugar, cinnamon, and cacao). We eat them all by themselves or combined with other ingredients like in the Chilean stew Porotos Granados (page 122), which incorporates all of the Three Sisters.

You may be most familiar with refried pinto beans or Mexican frijoles refritos, fried in lard and mashed but still deliciously lumpy, but all beans, no matter their color, can be refried. Some preparations are totally smooth, like Guatemalan frijoles volteados (or "overturned beans," see page 131), because they're flipped over in the pan to form a loaf, called a maleta. In others—called frijoles colados—blended beans are strained to remove any skins. In Peru, different shades of cooked beans (which Peruvians call frejoles) are semi-mashed and refried; then they're mixed with spices, rice, or quinoa, seasoned with an ají paste, and formed into torpedo-shaped quenelles, called tacu-tacu.

Then there is the marriage between America's native beans and the rice brought by the Spaniards, best symbolized by the Cuban dish moros y cristianos ("Moors and Christians"), made by cooking white rice and black beans together in a pot (and similar dishes, called congrís, that use different colors of beans), and the gallo pinto of Nicaragua and Costa Rica, a mixture of rice and red beans, cooked with seasoned sofrito.

When I was growing up in Guatemala it was customary to find pots of beans bubbling on most stoves. This long-held tradition continues in many households today, although sadly less often than when cooking at home was more popular. Like everywhere else, canned beans have become a mainstay of busy cooks in Latin America, but most still cook them from scratch.

Beans can be simply seasoned with a chunk of onion and a few garlic cloves; but in Latin America they often get flavored with meats (bacon, ribs, sausages, chorizo, pig ears and tails, and so on); herbs such as epazote or long-leaf culantro; aromatics such as leeks and shallots; a single bay leaf; and sometimes with a fresh or dried chile to add a kick of heat. Cooking them in water alone suffices, but when you add seasonings to a pot of beans, great things happen. As the popular saying goes, "No hay buena olla con agua sola"—"Water alone does not a good pot make."

A Bean Primer

A la hora de freír frijoles, manteca es lo que hace falta.
[When frying beans, lard is necessary.]

—Old Mexican saying

How do I know how many beans to cook?   My formula for a family of four to six is to start with
1 pound (455 grams/16 ounces) of dried beans, which will produce about 6 cups of cooked beans.

Can I use canned beans instead?   Yes! Substitute one 15-ounce can of beans for ¾ cup/125 grams
dried beans.

How long does it take to cook beans?   Beans will take anywhere from 30 minutes (for tender beans)
to 3 hours (particularly if they are old). As a rule of thumb, check for softness around the 1 hour
mark. If they mash easily, they're done; if not, cook them a little longer and check again. Larger
beans will take longer to cook. If you purchase dried beans from a source such as Rancho Gordo
(see Sources) or from your local farmers' markets, or if you grow your own, they will cook faster than
those purchased at a large grocery store.

Do I have to soak beans?   Soaking is not necessary (oh, heresy!), and in fact, I avoid it completely
when it comes to dark-colored beans. They will lose much of their hue in the soaking liquid, which
will leave you with lackluster, grayish beans (called rubios or canches). Plus, dark beans make a
flavorful, dark broth that can be used as a base for soups or enjoyed all by itself. Why waste it by
throwing it down the drain? Soaking is meant to soften the outer layer of the beans so they'll cook
faster. Red, white, navy, kidney, black-eyed peas (caritas negras), pigeon peas (guandú, gandú, or
gandúles), and chickpeas (garbanzos) can benefit from soaking, and since none of them lose their
color, like dark beans do, I will soak them if time allows (anywhere from 8 to 12 hours).

How much water do I need to soak and cook beans in?   As a rule, cover beans with water by at least
3 inches (7.5 cm); add water to replenish, as it evaporates while cooking. Wider and taller pots
require more water. What matters is to keep the beans submerged in enough water to allow them
to double or triple in size as they cook.

Is salt good or bad for beans?   My grandmother taught me that beans only attain proper flavor—
"la sazón correcta"—if they are salted right from the start. In the 1990s, a new theory suggested
that adding salt before they softened turned beans hard. I soon became disillusioned by flavorless
beans and returned to my old habit of salting the liquid from the beginning. Based on hundreds
of conversations with Latin American cooks who salt their beans, I have found consensus: salting
delays softening of the beans by only minutes. My advice is to add salt at the start.

When do I add tomatoes or vinegar to beans?   I add them after the beans are fork tender. Many
Latin recipes call for an onion, garlic, pepper, and tomato mélange (such as sofrito, hogáo,
hogado, guiso, or guiso rojo) for flavor; these are always stirred into the recipe last.

Are all Latin American bean recipes filled with spices and hot chiles? Hardly! Most Latin Americans include an onion and some garlic. Although some cooks will add a hot chile (dry or fresh), sweet varieties are often preferred (for example, chile pimiento or ají dulce). Finishing the beans with a touch of a grassy herb is more common, usually mint, long-leaf culantro, or epazote.

What is the best method to cook beans?

a. Stovetop: This is my preferred way to cook beans and the way I was taught to do it as a little girl. Simply place the beans in a large pot, cover with water by 3 inches (7.5 cm), add seasonings or aromatics, and let come to a boil. Then lower the heat, partially cover, and cook the beans until softened (adding more liquid as needed to keep at least 3 inches of liquid above the beans).

b. Pressure cooker: I will confess to never having learned to use a traditional pressure cooker—an explosion in my grandma's house that sent hot beans flying all over the kitchen and screaming people running from them traumatized me for life! However, I am told that new versions of pressure cookers are a lot safer. My Cuban son-in-law swears by this method. He is able to have beans ready in less than an hour, and always produces rich, thick, flavorful broth.

c. Instant Pot: This is where I learned to use the pressure-cooking technique, free of any fear of exploding pots. I use my Instant Pot as often as I can for the sole purpose of cooking beans. My formula is very easy: For 1 cup of dried beans I use 3 cups of liquid. I add my usual aromatics and use the pressure-cooking setting for 30 minutes. I let it release pressure naturally, which takes about 20 extra minutes. This yields 3 beautiful cups of cooked beans every time. Sometimes, I'll make a double batch, but I never make more than that.

How do I store cooked beans? Once cooled, transfer them with their cooking liquid to a plastic or glass container with a tight-fitting lid and refrigerate for up to a week or freeze for up to 1 month.

My only two unbreakable rules about cooking beans are: (1) never undercook them and (2) I never burn them. The former can break a tooth and aren't fully digestible; the latter are worse than raw.

My grandmother swore that a combination of epazote and garlic offset the gaseous side effect of beans and that if beans are cooked until very soft, and eaten often, the bloating effect could be counteracted completely. I never questioned her wisdom.

Frijoles de Olla

A Basic Pot of Beans

Various Countries | Yield: Serves 4–6 | Difficulty Level: Easy | Total Cooking Time: 1 to 3 hours

Here is your master recipe for beans of any shape or color. If the beans are light in color, peel the onion. If they are dark, don't bother, as the onion skin will add flavor and deeper color to the broth.

1 pound (455 grams/2 cups) dried beans, picked over and rinsed

1 medium (6 ounces/170 grams) yellow, white, or red onion, cut in half

4–6 garlic cloves, peeled and left whole

1 bay leaf

1 tablespoon fine sea salt, or more to taste

Place the beans, onion halves, garlic cloves, bay leaf, 2 teaspoons of salt, and enough water to cover the beans by at least 3 inches, in a large (6-8 quart/5.7-7.5 liter) Dutch oven set over medium-high heat. Bring to a boil; cover, lower the heat to low, and simmer until the beans are tender (about 1 hour, but check, because older beans will take longer). During the first minutes of cooking all beans, foam will rise to the surface; skim it off with a slotted spoon and discard it. When you can easily mash a few beans between your fingertips (just make sure they're cool enough to touch), the beans are ready. Strain over a large bowl, in order to collect the broth; remove the onions, garlic, and bay leaf and discard. Add the rest of the salt and stir well. The beans are now ready to use for any recipe, and the broth can be saved to use for other recipes.

Note: I cook beans on low, but stoves vary, so make sure to keep them at a constant simmer. The foam doesn't affect the flavor of finished dishes but will make the liquid cloudy. I care when cooking black beans, since I use the broth in stews or soups and thus prefer to remove it. However, you may omit doing this step if you're in a hurry. To make a wonderful and easy starter soup with black beans, season the resulting broth with salt to taste and serve topped with croutons and chopped parsley.

Frijoles Exprés

Pressure Cooker Black Beans

Guatemala and Mexico | Yield: Serves 4–6 | Difficulty Level: Easy | Total Cooking Time: 1½ hours

My grandmother used a pressure cooker to cook black beans every day. This is her recipe, which I've adapted for use with one of the electric multipurpose cookers that feature a setting for pressure cooking. The result are tender beans with great sazón (seasoning) and a velvety sauce. If you own a traditional pressure cooker, follow the instructions of your model—the ingredients and ratios remain the same. Remember that no matter which you use, it takes a few minutes for the pressure to build up and seal the valve and a few more to release the pressure at the end. In reality, this recipe involves only three minutes of active cooking time and produces some of the most delicious beans I've ever had.

2 cups (400 grams) dried beans, picked over, and rinsed

1 medium (6 ounces/170 grams) yellow, white, or red onion, peeled and cut in half

4–6 garlic cloves, peeled and left whole

2 tablespoons finely chopped fresh epazote (or long-leaf culantro), or more to taste

1 tablespoon fine sea salt

6 cups (960 ml) water

Place all of the ingredients in a multipurpose cooker. Close the vent and set it manually to Pressure Cook on HIGH for 1 hour. Allow the valve to release the pressure on its own (it'll take between 20 to 30 minutes). When the pressure valve releases, remove the lid carefully. Serve hot.

Note: A Latinismo is a word in another language that has been adopted and adapted to Spanish. Exprés is one such instance, where the English term "express" is changed to represent the Latin American spelling and pronunciation. Other examples include: bistec (beefsteak), bol (bowl), and sanguiche (sandwich).

Cebiche de Cho Chos

Lupini Bean Salad

Ecuador and Peru | Yield: Serves 4 | Difficulty Level: Easy | Total Cooking Time: 20 minutes

Here is a vegan recipe that is by definition both a salad and a ceviche, emblematic of the mountainous city of Pomabamba, in the Ancash region of Peru, known as the Cordillera de los Andes—"the Mountain Range of the Andes"—which is famously surrounded by snow-capped volcanoes. The dish's sour, herbal, and spicy vinaigrette seduces the palate, and the heat lent by red ají limo can be adapted to your taste. It features the lupini beans of South America (*Lupinus mutabilis*, similar but not to be confused with the Old World *Lupinus albus*, which were native to Egypt and spread by the Roman Empire), known as chocho or tarwi and popular since pre-Hispanic times. These beans tend to be bitter; in order to reduce their harshness, they must be soaked, cooked, rinsed thoroughly several times over, and then peeled. Luckily for us, chochos are widely available already processed in jars or canned, and need only a light rinse under cold water, saving hours of preparation (see Sources). I love to serve this on its own, topped with plantain chips, Canchita (page 50), or popcorn, or as a side dish to simple grilled fish.

Two 15 ounce (425 gram) cans or jars lupini beans, rinsed well under cold water

¾ cup (85 grams) thin strips red onions

1¼ cup (85 grams) thinly sliced celery

2 tablespoons finely chopped fresh long-leaf culantro (see Note)

1 red ají limo or serrano pepper, seeded, deveined, and finely chopped (about 1 teaspoon)

1 teaspoon finely chopped huacatay, huacatay paste (see Note), or fresh mint

⅔ cup (165 ml) freshly squeezed lime juice, or more to taste

½ cup (120 ml) freshly squeezed orange juice

1 teaspoon fine sea salt, or more to taste

½ teaspoon ground cumin

Pinch of freshly ground black pepper, or more to taste

Combine all of the ingredients in a bowl; allow the salad to marinate for at least 20 minutes before serving chilled or at room temperature.

Note: If you can't find long-leaf culantro, use double the amount of regular cilantro instead. Huacatay is a type of South American mint that adds a depth of grassiness to this recipe, but you can use any kind of mint you like or omit it altogether. You can find huacatay chopped and frozen or as a paste in jars. Ají limo can be found frozen, canned, or jarred. See Sources for my favorites.

Tip: Bean salads such as this one taste even better after they are allowed to marinate overnight. It'll keep for up to 3 days if properly covered and refrigerated.

Elizabeth's Porotos Granados con Mazamorra

Corn, Squash, and Cranberry Bean Chowder

Chile | Yield: Serves 4–6 | Difficulty Level: Easy | Total Cooking Time: 1 hour

This thick, stick-to-your-ribs stew made with corn, squash, and creamy cranberry beans is smoky-sweet and just what I crave when it's rainy outside. *Purutu* is the Quechua word for "bean," and has morphed into *poroto* in modern-day Chile, Peru, and Argentina. I got this iconic recipe from Elizabeth Donoso, whom I met in Guatemala City, where we both attended the same elementary school. It combines the three most Indigenous American elements in a single pot. Known as "the Three Sisters," beans, squash, and corn are native to the New World and were always planted together. This is a summer dish in Chile. The corn, called mazamorra, is a large cob with tiny white kernels; substitute any fresh (or frozen and thawed) white corn you can find. Some cooks make a hot oil to pour over the top (a technique known as tempering, see Note), which sizzles on contact with the hot soup; I offer you that option here.

1 cup (170 grams) cranberry beans, picked over and soaked overnight

1 pound (455 grams) butternut squash, peeled and seeded

1 tablespoon vegetable oil

1 cup (114 grams) finely chopped white onions

1 garlic clove, finely chopped

2 teaspoons fine sea salt

1 teaspoon dry chicken consommé or buillion (optional)

1 teaspoon Aliño Completo (page 7)

1 pound (455 grams) fresh white corn kernels (or frozen and thawed) (about 3 cups)

10 large fresh basil leaves, torn

Drain the cranberry beans and place them in a small pot; cover with cold water by 2 inches (5 cm) and bring to a boil over medium-high heat; reduce the heat and simmer for 30 minutes or until tender. Set them aside, reserving the cooking liquid. Cut the butternut squash into ½ inch (12 mm) cubes and set aside. Heat the oil in a medium Dutch oven set over medium-high heat until it shimmers. Add the onions and garlic; sauté just until fragrant, about 1 minute. Add the cranberry beans (with their cooking liquid), salt, dry consommé (if using), the aliño completo, and the butternut squash, stirring well. Cover and lower the heat; simmer for 15 minutes or until the squash is fork tender. In the meantime, place the corn, basil, and ½ cup (120 ml) water in a blender; blend until you have a mixture that resembles cooked oatmeal, pausing periodically to stir it; add more water if the motor needs it (a couple of tablespoons/30 ml at a time). Add the blended corn to the pot and increase the heat slightly, just to bring it back to a boil; cover, lower the heat, and continue simmering for 15 minutes, stirring occasionally. The corn will turn a darker color as it cooks. Serve hot.

Note: The process of heating oil with spices, herbs, and sometimes chiles is known as tempering. Adding the hot, tempered oil to dishes infuses beans and legumes with rich flavor. If you wish to finish this chowder with tempered oil, in the Chilean style, heat 2 tablespoons of vegetable oil in a pan over medium-low heat. As soon as it shimmers, add 2 teaspoons of sweet paprika (ají dulce or pimentón), stir gently, and remove from heat. Drizzle this hot oil over the pot of chowder (it should sizzle on contact), and serve immediately.

Frejoles con Aderezo de Rocoto

Spicy Canary Bean Stew

Peru | Yield: Serves 4–6 | Difficulty Level: Easy | Total Cooking Time: 1½–2 hours

I thought I knew beans. After all, I have enjoyed them practically since the crib. Then, one day, my family stopped at a pollería—a Peruvian restaurant where chickens roasting on a spit baste each other with flavor—and I tasted creamy canary beans for the first time. Also known as canarios, mayocobas, or frejoles (pronounced *fréh-hoh-lehs*, and spelled with an *e* instead of an *i*), the beans themselves, golden to begin with, turn light tan once cooked and produce an amber-colored broth that can be used as a base for soups and rice dishes (make sure to save it for that purpose). In Peru, canary beans are daily fare, sometimes stirred in with leftover rice, in soups, or as a side dish for secos. By far my favorite way to eat them is in this spicy stew, richly flavored with a punch of heat that wakes up the palate.

FOR THE BEANS

1 pound (455 grams/2 cups) dried canary beans, picked over and rinsed

FOR THE ADEREZO

3 tablespoons (45 ml) olive oil

¾ cup (115 grams) very finely chopped red onions

6 garlic cloves, finely chopped

1 tablespoon rocoto paste, or more to taste (see Sources)

1½ teaspoons fine sea salt, or more to taste

1 tablespoon red wine vinegar, or more to taste

Place the beans in a large (6-8 quart/5.7-7.5 liter) Dutch oven and cover with water by at least 3 inches. Set over medium-high heat. Bring to a boil; cover, lower the heat to low, and simmer until the beans are tender (about 1½ hours, but check because older beans will take longer). I cook them on low, but stoves vary, so make sure you keep a simmer going all the time. When you can easily mash a few beans between your fingertips (just make sure they're cool enough to touch), the beans are ready. Strain them over a large bowl in order to collect the broth. Return the beans and 2 cups (480 ml) of the broth to the cooking pot (save the rest for another use) and keep warm over medium-low heat. As soon as you return the broth to the pot, I suggest you remove a cup of cooked beans and mash them well, then add them back to the pot, to create a creamy texture.

In a small skillet, heat the oil over medium-high heat; add the onions, garlic, and rocoto paste and cook, while stirring, for 2 to 3 minutes or until the mixture is soft and has thickened slightly. Add this to the hot beans (it will sizzle); add salt and vinegar to taste, stir, and serve.

Note: Cooked canary beans can be stored, well sealed, in their broth in the refrigerator for up to 1 week. Beans are also great frozen (in the same manner) for up to 1 month.

Feijoada Todo Dia do Janine

Everyday Feijoada

Brazil | Yield: Serves 4–6 | Difficulty Level: Easy | Total Cooking Time: 35 minutes

If upon the mention of feijoada, a complicated bean stew that includes all parts of the pig (including tails and ears) and takes hours and hours to make is what springs to mind, you'll be pleased to know that that incarnation is only made for special occasions. The everyday version is most like this aromatic recipe, an adaptation of one given to me by Janine Hertzog Santos, who hails from Porto Alegre, in the state of Rio Grande do Sul, in Brazil. I knew I had to include this recipe in this book the evening her kids, Valentina and Lorenzo, showed up at my door with a steaming bowl for me to sample. They are particularly proud—as they should be—of their beloved family recipe, a staple in the south of Brazil. Their favorite way to eat it is "a la minuta" with steamed white rice, eggs sunny-side up, a simple salad of lettuce with tomatoes, and French fries. Sometimes, Brazilians will add a scoop of potato salad and a thin slice of steak (known as bife) or with a milanesa (see page 42). Between the border of the largest Brazilian states, Rio Grande do Sul and Santa Caterina, there's a gas station that serves only this dish—so popular, Janine tells me, that whenever she and her family stop there on the way to their beach house it usually means waiting for a parking spot. Now that her family lives in the United States, she makes this comforting dish as often as she can. It's a good thing that I live next door and can walk over without having to worry about where to park.

2 teaspoons vegetable oil

2 ounces (55 grams) bacon, finely chopped

1¼ cups (170 grams) finely chopped white onions

3 garlic cloves, finely chopped

6 cups (455 grams) black beans, cooked, with their liquid (see page 118 or 119)

1 bay leaf

1 teaspoon fine sea salt, or more to taste

Pinch of freshly ground black pepper, or more to taste

Heat the oil over medium-high heat in a medium heavy-bottomed pot; add the bacon and cook, while stirring, for 1 minute or until it renders its fat. Add the onions and garlic and continue cooking, while stirring, for 2 to 3 minutes or until just softened. Add the beans and their cooking liquid, the bay leaf, salt, and pepper. Bring to a simmer; cover, lower the heat, and simmer for 20 minutes. Remove the lid, stir, and continue cooking for 10 more minutes or until the liquid is slightly thickened. Discard the bay leaf. Serve hot.

Frijoles Blancos con Costilla de Cerdo

White Beans with Achiote-Marinated Pork Ribs

Nicaragua | Yield: Serves 4–6 | Difficulty Level: Intermediate | Total Cooking Time: 4 hours

This Nicaraguan version is one of the most famous pork and bean dishes in Central America. Achiote paste tints the stew a golden hue. Few bean dishes are as colorful, especially when served over contrasting white rice, and topped with fresh herbs. Vinegar is often used to marinate meats, particularly pork ribs; marinated in this fashion, the ribs cook quick and tender. Any white bean will do, but I'm partial to larger white ayocote beans (particularly those from Rancho Gordo) because they're meatier and retain their shape. I'll let you in on a little secret: at home, during a busy day, I have been known to make this stew in half the time by using canned white beans—and no one is the wiser.

2 pounds (910 grams) baby pork ribs (about 12 small)

½ cup (120 ml) white vinegar

1 tablespoon achiote paste

1½ cups (170 grams) roughly chopped white or yellow onions

2 garlic cloves, finely chopped

1 tablespoon fine sea salt, divided

1 teaspoon dried thyme

1 bay leaf

2 tablespoons vegetable oil

4 ounces (120 ml/½ cup) Sofrito con Achiote (page 195)

1 pound (455 grams/6 cups) cooked white beans, plus their cooking liquid

Chopped fresh cilantro or parsley, to taste, for garnish (optional)

Cut the baby back ribs into sections of 2 ribs; place them in a large nonreactive bowl. In a small bowl, combine the vinegar and the achiote paste, stirring to dissolve. Add this to the ribs, along with the onions, garlic, 1 teaspoon of the salt, thyme, and bay leaf; marinate for 30 minutes at room temperature (or refrigerate and marinate for up to 8 hours). Heat the oil in a large pot set over medium-high heat; add the sofrito and cook for 1 minute. Add the ribs (with the marinade), stirring them for 2 to 3 minutes or until they are well coated with sofrito on all sides. Add the cooked beans, 4 cups of their cooking liquid (or use water), and the remaining 2 teaspoons of salt. Stir well and bring the liquid to a boil; cover, lower the heat, and simmer for 35 to 40 minutes or until the meat is falling off the bones. Serve topped with cilantro or parsley, if desired.

Note: The broth will be soupy; if you desire a thicker consistency, remove 1½ cups of the beans at the end of the cooking process, mash them, and return them to the pot.

Frijoles Sopeados

Bean Stew with Pork Skins

Nicaragua | Yield: Serves 4–6 | Difficulty Level: Easy | Total Cooking Time: 20 minutes

There are many riffs on pork and bean dishes all over the world, but none taste as rich as this one made with whole pork rinds. This filling stew is first seasoned with aromatics and then mixed with crispy pork skins, called catrachas in Nicaragua (and also known as chicharrones) that transform from crispy to soft as they cook. A slight touch of acidity lent by sour orange (naranja agria), or sometimes lemon, cuts into the fatty, salty flavor of the pork skins. Add salt judiciously; even when I give you a starting amount, always taste and adjust at the end of cooking, since each brand of pork cracklings will vary in sodium content. This is peasant food (cocina tradicional), unassuming and inexpensive to make; yet it's among the most satisfying dishes you will ever eat. Serve with any of the green chile sauces in this book or a hot sauce of your own preference. Traditionally, my Nicaraguan friends (mis amigos nicas) offer this as a hearty breakfast or early lunch, with a side of queso fresco (called cuajada), a drizzle of crema or natilla (similar to crème fraiche), and generous amounts of freshly chopped cilantro. This stew thickens as it cools, so add more liquid when you reheat it until it reaches your preferred consistency.

2 tablespoons vegetable oil

½ cup (60 grams) finely chopped white onions

6 garlic cloves, finely chopped

6 cups (455 grams) cooked red or black beans (or use canned)

1½ cups (360 ml) water, chicken broth, or bean cooking liquid

1 pound (455 grams) plum tomatoes, roughly chopped (about 3 cups)

1¾ cups (170 grams) stemmed, seeded, and roughly chopped green bell peppers

4 ounces (115 grams) small pork rinds or chicharrones

2 tablespoons sour orange juice or a combination of half lemon and half orange juices

1 teaspoon fine sea salt, or more to taste

½ teaspoon freshly ground black pepper

Mexican crema, natilla, or crème fraiche, to taste, for garnish (optional)

4 ounces (115 grams) sliced queso fresco (or cuajada), for garnish (optional)

Chopped fresh cilantro or long-leaf culantro, to taste, for garnish (optional)

Heat the oil in a medium pot set over medium-high heat; add the onions and cook, while stirring, until they're translucent, about 2 minutes; add the garlic and cook for 1 minute or until the onions have begun to turn a golden color. Add the beans, liquid, and tomatoes and cook for 2 minutes or until the mixture comes up to a boil. Stir in the peppers and pork rinds, stirring to combine; lower the heat, add the sour orange juice (or orange and lemon juice mixture), salt, and pepper. Simmer, while stirring, until the pork rinds are softened but the peppers still retain some bite, about 3 to 4 minutes (it should still be loose; add more liquid if needed). Season again with salt and pepper; taste and adjust seasoning, if necessary. Serve immediately, topped with crema, queso fresco, and cilantro or culantro (if using).

Did you know? · You will find pork rinds (known as catrachas or chicharrones) used in many dishes throughout the Latin territory—in Mexico they're usually cooked in a sauce (such as the Recado de Tomatillo o Miltomates on page 160); in Guatemala, they're added to stews or rolled into tortillas; and in Honduras, Costa Rica, and Nicaragua, they're used as a crunchy topping for salads. In Colombia and Venezuela, they are served in long strips, as a garnish on many of their dishes. In Argentina they are called cueritos de chancho and are served in place of bread or as a side dish. In Peru, chicharrones can also be made with fish or chicken skins. All throughout the Americas, you'll find crispy chicharrones sold by street vendors or packaged in bags that are sold in supermarkets. The best way to eat them, in my opinion, is simply sprinkled with fresh lime juice and a dash of hot chile, as a snack.

Habichuelas Guisadas

Pink Bean Stew

Puerto Rico | Yield: Serves 4–6 | Difficulty Level: Easy | Total Cooking Time: 30 minutes

This, to me, is the taste of Puerto Rico. I first sampled this pink bean stew in college, made by my many Boricua friends when we gathered to feed each other the dishes we were most nostalgic for. It's a rendition of pork and beans that features earthy and briny flavors mixed together. None of my friends had exact recipes, yet between the one who added "enough of this" and another who added a "handful of that," it always tasted right. None of their abuelas taught them to measure or write anything down when they cooked, and not surprisingly, each one had a different version. Sometimes we used bacon and other times ham, but most often we made it with frankfurters. There was some consensus: the beans were always canned, the olives plump, and the potatoes creamy. This is a speedy and inexpensive recipe that goes quickly from pot to table, because abuelas know how to feed their grandchildren quickly when they're hungry.

2 tablespoons olive oil

8 ounces (225 grams) boneless pork chops, diced into bite-sized pieces

3 tablespoons (45 ml) Sofrito de Ana Raquel (page 21), or store-bought

1 teaspoon Adobo de Casa (page 6), or store-bought

1 teaspoon Sazón con Achiote y Culantro (page 199), or store-bought

Two 15 ounce (425 gram) cans pink beans (habichuelas rosadas), with liquid

12 pimento-stuffed Spanish olives

1 tablespoon capers

1 medium white potato (6 ounces/170 grams), peeled and cut into bite-sized pieces

Arroz Blanco (page 323) about 1 cup per person

Heat the oil in a medium pot over medium-high heat; add the pork and brown the pieces all over, about 4 minutes. Lower the heat to medium. Add the sofrito, adobo, and sazón; cook for 1 to 2 minutes or until fragrant. Add the beans and their liquid, the olives, and the capers. Bring to a simmer; cover, lower the heat, and cook for 20 minutes. Add the potato and continue cooking, covered, for about 10 minutes or until the potato is fork tender. Serve over rice.

Note: You can use red or pinto beans in a pinch.

Sopa de Riendas

Cranberry Bean and Pasta Soup

Chile | Yield: Serves 4–6 | Difficulty Level: Easy | Total Cooking Time: 45 minutes

This thick cranberry bean and pasta soup is a marriage of the cuisines of the Mapuche people (the largest Indigenous group in Chile) and of the Italian immigrants who came to the Americas. Those familiar with Italy's pasta e fagiole soup will recognize its spirit here. At the base of sopa de riendas is Italian sofrito, a balanced mix of carrots, celery, and onions (known in French as mirepoix). Chileans love their beans, which they call porotos; hundreds of traditional Indigenous varieties, lost in the years of colonialism, are today being rescued in Chile by the group Biodiversidad Alimentaria. Cranberry beans are a mottled pink and red bean that cooks a reddish color; use cannellini beans if you can't find them. The long strands of pasta symbolize a horse's reins (riendas), and represent the cowboy or huaso culture of the region of central Chile that this dish comes from. This soup is meant to be a full meal.

2 teaspoons extra-virgin olive oil

4 ounces (115 grams) pancetta or bacon, roughly chopped

¼ cup (30 grams) finely chopped shallots

½ cup (85 grams) peeled and finely chopped carrots

½ cup (60 grams) finely chopped celery

3 garlic cloves, finely chopped

½ cup (120 ml) full-bodied red wine, such as Merlot

Two 15 ounce (425 gram) cans cannellini beans, rinsed, drained, and divided

4 cups (680 grams) peeled and seeded butternut squash, diced into ½ inch (12 mm) cubes

One 14.5 ounce (411 gram) can diced tomatoes with juices (about 1½ cups)

6 cups (1.4 liters) chicken broth, plus more to taste

1½ teaspoons dried oregano

1 teaspoon dried thyme

1 teaspoon ground cumin

½ teaspoon ají molido or smoked Spanish paprika

1½ teaspoon fine sea salt, or to taste

½ teaspoon freshly ground black pepper

½ pound (255 grams) spaghetti, cooked al dente (follow package directions)

¼ cup (20 grams) finely chopped fresh Italian or flat-leaf parsley (leaves and tender stems)

½ heaping cup (40 grams) grated Parmesan cheese

In a large soup pot (at least 6 quarts/5.7 liters), heat the oil over medium-high heat; add the pancetta or bacon and cook until it has rendered its fat and is beginning to crisp, about 4 minutes. Remove the pancetta from the pot and set on paper towels to drain. Discard all but 2 teaspoons of the rendered fat from the pot. Return the pot to medium-high heat and add the shallots, carrots, and celery; sauté until they have begun to soften, about 2 to 3 minutes. Add the garlic and sauté until fragrant, about 30 seconds. Pour in the red wine and deglaze the pot, stirring up the brown bits stuck to the bottom. Set aside 1 cup of the cooked beans and add the rest to the pot, along with the butternut squash. Add the tomatoes (with their juices) and the cooked pancetta; simmer for 5 minutes. Add the broth, oregano, thyme, cumin, paprika, salt, and pepper. Bring the soup to a boil; cover, lower the heat, and simmer for 15 to 20 minutes or until the squash is fork tender. Mash the reserved cup of beans and stir them into the soup. Drop the cooked spaghetti into the soup and stir well. Bring the soup back up to a simmer and cook for 5 minutes or until the pasta is warmed through. Ladle the soup into bowls; sprinkle it with parsley and cheese.

A Spanish Lesson · *Sopa* means "soup"; *sopeado* means "soupy." There's more: *asopao* means a "soupy stew." Oh, and a *locro* is a creamy soup in South America, while *lagua* (or *l'agua*) means "soup" in Bolivia.

Frijoles Fritos, Refritos o Volteados

Refried Beans

Various Countries | Yield: Makes 3½–4 cups (840–960 ml) | Difficulty Level: Intermediate |
Total Cooking Time: 30–35 minutes

Any kind of bean can be refried. Peruvians refry canary beans, while Belizeans love to use small red beans. Mexicans prefer to use pinto beans, but Central Americans often use black beans. If you're in a hurry, use a well-drained can or two of cooked beans. During my catering days long ago, I loved refrying white beans, spreading them on tiny tostadas and topping them with assorted salsas—they were always a hit. Refried beans freeze beautifully, are easily reheated in the microwave, and taste ever so good when homemade.

¼ cup (60 ml) melted lard or vegetable oil (more if making them volteados, see variation)

½ cup (115 grams) finely chopped white onions

6 cups (455 grams) cooked pinto, black, red, or white beans, with their cooking liquid

1½ teaspoons fine sea salt, or to taste

Heat the lard or oil in a large frying pan set over medium-high heat. Add the onions and cook until they begin to turn golden, about 2 minutes. Drain the beans over a bowl, reserving the cooking liquid. Add the beans to the frying pan and season with salt. Use a potato masher to mash the beans, adding some of the reserved cooking liquid a little at a time, until they reach the desired consistency. If you like your beans a bit looser, add more liquid while they cook; if you like them a bit drier, cook them a little longer. If making the beans a day ahead of time, reserve an additional cup (240 ml) of cooking liquid to thin out the beans when you reheat them, or use water.

Note: If you want a smooth paste, process or blend the cooked beans with some of the cooking liquid before you refry them. Strain the beans through a sieve if you want to remove the skins (optional).

VARIATIONS: To make frijoles volteados (beans shaped into a loaf), you'll have to cook the beans to a thick paste, similar to the texture of playdough. Process or blend the cooked beans with some of the cooking liquid until they are completely smooth. In a large nonstick pan set over medium heat, add 2 tablespoons of vegetable oil and the processed beans; stir, cooking over medium heat anywhere from 5 to 10 minutes or until they slide from the bottom of the pan. Hold the pan from the handle with both hands. Flip the beans over a few times in the pan—much in the same manner that you would flip a pancake—until they form an oblong loaf. Slide the bean loaf onto a plate and serve. If flipping the beans is too hard for you, press them together against the pan and form them into a loaf using a rubber spatula.

Depending on the country, different aromatics, spices, and oils may be added to the beans. In Mexico, cumin, oregano, epazote, and cilantro are popular, while in Guatemala bay leaves, thyme, cilantro, and epazote (called apazote there) are commonly used. In Peru, ají pastes, huacatay, and cumin are the go-tos, while in Cuba and the Carribean, ají dulce, onions, garlic, and culantro are favored. Venezuelans like to add cumin, while in Belize, achiote, coconut milk, basil, and hot sauce are preferred.

Empanadas Dulces de Plátanos y Frijoles

Sweet Plantain and Bean Empanadas

Guatemala | Yield: Makes 12–14 empanadas | Difficulty Level: Intermediate | Total Cooking Time: 1 hour

These empanadas are made with plantain dough and sweetened beans. As soon as the skins split while boiling, the plantains are ready to transform into dough. I prefer wide plantains—those that measure about 2 inches (5 cm) in diameter—because thinner ones take much longer to ripen and sometimes don't soften quite enough to use for this dough. Purchase the plantains when they have golden skins with a few black spots (or purchase them green and place them in a paper bag to ripen for a few days). The dough is easy to make but will burn quickly if you're not careful when frying it, as the sugar in the plantains will go from caramelized to scorched in no time. Dredging the empanadas in flour lightly before frying them prevents them from sticking to the bottom of the pan as they cook. The bean paste is easily made with black refried beans (recipe on page 131 or use canned beans, see Note).

FOR THE BEAN FILLING

1 cup (240 grams) black frijoles volteados (page 131) or canned refried black beans

¾ cup (150 grams) white granulated sugar, plus more for sprinkling

1 tablespoon cocoa powder

1 teaspoon pure vanilla extract

½ teaspoon ground cinnamon

FOR THE DOUGH

4 large yellow plantains (about 2½ pounds/1.2 kilogram total)

1 tablespoon fine sea salt

⅓ cup (40 grams) all-purpose flour

Vegetable oil, for frying

Line two baking sheets with parchment paper and set them aside. To make the filling: In a medium bowl, combine the beans, sugar, cocoa, vanilla, and cinnamon; pour the mixture into a medium skillet set over medium heat. Stir until the beans are completely smooth (they will be the texture of thick sauce and will look shiny), about 45 seconds to 1 minute, being careful not to burn them. Remove from heat and set aside to cool. To make the dough: Cut off the tips of the plantains with a sharp knife and then slice the plantains in half, crosswise. Place them in a large pot, cover with water, and add the salt. Bring the pot to a boil over high heat; boil the plantains for 10 to 12 minutes or until they are fork tender and their skins split open. Reserve ½ cup (120 ml) of the cooking liquid and set aside. Drain the plantains and transfer them to a large bowl; allow them to cool completely (about 15 minutes). Peel and mash them very well with a fork or potato masher, until smooth. If the dough is too loose and not holding together when you press it between your fingers, take a bit of flour (a tablespoon at a time) and stir it into the dough until it holds together. If the dough is too dry and not holding together when you press it between your fingers, stir in some of the reserved water, one tablespoon at a time until it does. Divide the dough into 12 equal portions (about ⅓ cup/2.5 ounces/70 grams each). With moistened hands, roll each into a ball, keeping them covered with plastic wrap as you work. Line a tortilla press with a plastic bag that has been cut open on three sides (so it opens like a book). Brush the interior of the bag with water so the dough doesn't stick. Working with one portion of dough at a time, place a ball in the middle of the tortilla press and flatten it into a 4 inch (10 cm) disc, about ¼ inch (6 mm) thick. If you don't have a tortilla press, use a flat-bottomed heavy skillet to press them down between the plastic bag. Place 2 tablespoons of the filling in the middle of the disc, leaving a ½ inch (12 mm) rim; use the bag to fold the dough over the filling, forming a half-moon. Press the edges together with your fingers to seal well. Place the empanadas on the prepared baking sheets; set them aside until all are filled and shaped, keeping them covered as you go.

To fry the empanadas: Fit a large baking sheet with a metal cooling rack and set aside. In a large skillet with high sides (or in a Dutch oven), heat ½–1 inch (12 mm–2.5 cm) of oil to 360°F (180°C) or use a deep fryer according to the manufacturer's directions. Working in batches, dredge the empanadas in the flour and slide them into the oil. Fry them until they are golden and crispy, 3 to 4 minutes, turning them over halfway through. If the oil gets too hot as you fry and they're browning too quickly, lower the temperature and cool the oil slightly before frying more. Use a spatula to transfer them to the prepared rack to drain. Let them rest for 1 to 2 minutes before sprinkling them with sugar. Serve them hot or at room temperature.

Note: My favorite brands of refried black beans are Ducal (by Goya) or Natura because they're made in Guatemala and have the right consistency and seasonings for this recipe. They are widely available in Latin American grocery stores and online (see Sources).

SQUASH

There are round squashes, long squashes, hard squashes, thin-skinned squashes, orange squashes, gray squashes, yellow squashes, green squashes, and variegated squashes. All squashes are gourds, members of the Cucurbitae family, which is made up of similarly composed plants that grow on vines, curling themselves around anything they can grab. There are three main species within the family: *Curcubita*, *Sechium*, and *Cyclanthera*.

If I had to choose one squash species to highlight at the beginning of the story of the Americas, I would choose *Cucurbita*. Part of the early trinity known as "the Three Sisters," the members of *C. pepo*, native to Mexico and Guatemala, played a starring role, providing ground protection that helped the roots of corn and beans grow beneath them.

Domesticated more than ten thousand years ago, by the time that the Spanish colonizers descended on the American continent *Curcubita* squashes had traveled and cross-pollinated with other squash varieties, setting their fruits from coast to coast across the entire region—quite the family saga, if you ask me! Members of the squash family include long, round zucchini (which the Maya call güicoyes), pattypan squashes, straightneck squashes, yellow squashes, summer squashes, and acorn squashes.

Cinderella's beloved orange pumpkin belongs to the *C. maxima* species. So does the giant, white-fleshed zapallo or ayote (the size of a watermelon), as well as all other smaller specimens like buttercup and butternut squashes. These most probably originated in South America, in an area that is now Peru, Argentina, Chile, and part of Bolivia. It merits mentioning that the word *zapallo* is used interchangeably for many types of pumpkins in South America.

Secondary, though by no means inferior, are the members of the *Sechium* species, native to the Caribbean and Mesoamerica.

These include *S. edule*, known as chayotes (from the Nahuatl word *chayotl*), and also called güisquiles, chuchu, papa del aire ("air potato"), Chinese potato, or guatilla, among many other names. They also include the white variety known as perulero. All of these are thin-skinned gourds, with a very watery flesh that tastes like a mild potato. Some are larger than others, covered with prickly needles that are quite sharp and that protect their dark green and pebbly skins. Most familiar are the thin-skinned, light green varieties that are smooth to the touch. The difference in their flesh is subtle, but the latter is waterier than the former. Their roots, called ichintal, are also eaten. Their tender shoots are known as puntas de güisquil or quiletes and are rich in protein and vitamin A.

Lastly, playing the best supporting role are the members of the *Cyclanthera* species. *Cyclanthera* includes the chaigua squash, which is beloved in Ecuador and Bolivia and looks like a banana pepper. (It is delicious when stuffed with rice or picadillos and covered in tomato sauce.)

Squashes are divided into summer and winter varieties, which is confusing for gardeners who don't realize that all are sowed and harvested in the summer and fall, depending on where you live. The difference is that thin-skinned gourds must be eaten fresh, while hard-skinned ones can be preserved for longer periods and usually last way into winter (and some even up to two years).

Since ancient times, the people of Latin America have enjoyed the seeds of many squashes roasted or toasted, sometimes peeled and sometimes used whole. These are often added to stews and sauces, as a thickening agent and for their nutty flavor. The flowers of many squashes are also edible, and are sometimes served stuffed with cheese. Since all squashes are fruits, they are used in both sweet and savory recipes. Some are baked into cakes, pies, and puddings, some are turned into jams and jellies, and others are added to savory soups and side dishes.

Here, you will find a small but representative collection of some of the most popular everyday squash recipes. New varieties of squashes are still being born today, the results of the cross-pollination that naturally occurs when two or more varieties are planted near each other. So, the family saga continues.

Calabaza con Mantequilla

Buttered Squash

Various Countries | Yield: Serves 4–6 | Difficulty Level: Easy | Total Cooking Time: 30 minutes

Few things are more comforting than the soft, tender flesh of fresh winter squash, perfectly sauced with creamy butter. This is one of the simplest recipes, yet one that allows the fruit's flavor to soar (yes, squashes are fruits). Use any variety you have on hand: butternut, acorn, sugar pumpkin, and kabocha all work deliciously here. Don't bother peeling it—the flesh is easy to scoop out after it cooks and the squash looks beautiful if served with skin, too. Many Latin American babies cut their teeth with purees like this one—perhaps this is why so many adults consider it comfort food.

One 2 pound (910 gram) butternut, acorn, sugar pumpkin, or kabocha

2 tablespoons melted butter

½ teaspoons fine sea salt, or more to taste

Pinch of freshly ground black pepper, or more to taste

With a sharp knife, carefully cut the squash into quarters; remove the seeds (see the box on roasting seeds, below) and the stringy inner pulp that surrounds them. Place the squash in a medium pot and cover completely with cold water. Set over medium-high heat and bring to a boil; cover, lower the heat, and simmer for 15 to 25 minutes (the exact time will depend on the kind of squash used) or until the flesh is fork tender. Remove the squash pieces and place them on a cutting board. Use a spoon to scrape the flesh out of the skins and transfer the flesh to a bowl. Drizzle with the butter and sprinkle with salt and pepper. Serve immediately.

Roasting Squash and Pumpkin Seeds · Save the seeds. Wash them well to remove any of the flesh attached to them by rinsing them under cold water. Set them out in one layer on paper towels to dry. Once dried, you can coat them with oil and spices (such as salt, pepper, smoked paprika, cumin, or chile powders) and roast them to eat whole; or you can dry-roast them (without oil) and grind them into powder to make polvo de ayote to thicken sauces. Do not confuse squash seeds with pepitas, which are the seeds of Styrian or oilseed pumpkins.

Calabacitas

Summer Squash and Zucchini Toss

Mexico | Yield: Serves 4–6 | Difficulty Level: Easy | Total Cooking Time: 20 minutes

For this recipe, you'll want the best zucchini you can find. They can be round or long; green or variegated. The bright yellow summer squashes also called for are favorites of contemporary Mexican home cooks. This recipe can also be made with just zucchini or just summer squash, if you can only find one or the other. Colorful, vibrant, and quick to make, I like to prepare this vegetable mélange at the very last moment, right before serving. The fact that every ingredient can be readied well in advance, saving me time to cook other things in the meantime, has made it one of the side dishes I serve often.

2 tablespoons vegetable oil or melted lard

1 cup (120 grams) finely chopped yellow onions

1 garlic clove, finely chopped

2½ cups (340 grams) zucchini, chopped into bite-sized pieces

2½ cups (340 grams) yellow summer squash, chopped into bite-sized pieces

1 cup (225 grams) finely chopped plum tomatoes

1 roasted poblano pepper, stemmed, seeded, and finely chopped (about ¼ cup) (see box on page 182)

1 cup (140 grams) corn kernels (fresh or frozen and thawed)

½ teaspoon dried oregano (preferably Mexican)

½ teaspoon fine sea salt, or more to taste

Pinch of freshly ground black pepper, or more to taste

1 cup (60 grams) Cotija cheese

Heat the oil or lard in a large skillet set over medium-high heat. Add the onions and garlic and sauté for 2 minutes. Add the zucchini, summer squash, tomatoes, poblano, corn, and oregano; continue cooking for 5 to 6 minutes or until the squash is just tender. Add the salt, pepper, and cheese; stir and remove from the heat. Serve immediately.

Pastel Salado de Güicoy

Savory Zucchini Tart

Various Countries | Yield: Serves 6 | Difficulty Level: Easy | Total Cooking Time: 1 hour

Pastel salado de güicoy is not a quiche, nor a tart, nor a custard, but rather a mixture of all three. I grew up eating tiny, round zucchini squash in Guatemala, called güicoyitos (pronounced *wee-ko-yee-tohs*). In fact, I never saw a long zucchini until the 1980s, when they became the little darlings in most markets (although they have always been favored in Mexico and in South America). There are many varieties of zucchini, from the short and fat, variegated Mexican version, to the dark green and round eight-ball, to the light green globe zucchini that I love the most. These days, I plant my own güicoyitos in my summer garden; seeds are not hard to come by now that everyone seems to be planting their own vegetable patches again. However, any kind of green, soft-skinned zucchini (or summer squash) you can find will work in this recipe. My grandmother Mita learned to cook it when she lived in Mexico City (although similar versions can be found throughout Latin America) and loved to serve it when she entertained family and friends. This is her recipe, and a favorite of my cousin Vivian de Solís, who saved it and gave it to me so I could share it with you.

3 cups (340 grams) thinly sliced zucchini

1 cup (140 grams) all-purpose flour

1½ teaspoon baking powder

1 teaspoon fine sea salt

½ teaspoon freshly ground black pepper

4 eggs

½ cup (120 ml) whole milk

¼ cup (60 ml) melted butter

¼ cup (60 ml) extra-virgin olive oil

½ cup (85 grams) finely chopped white onions

¼ cup (20 grams) chopped fresh Italian parsley

½ cup (70 grams) grated Parmesan cheese

Preheat the oven to 350°F (180°C). Layer the zucchini slices in an ungreased 8 x 8 inch (20 x 20 cm) baking dish. In a medium bowl, whisk together the flour, baking powder, salt, and pepper; set aside. In another bowl, stir together the eggs, milk, butter, oil, onions, and parsley; pour this into the flour mixture and stir to combine well. Pour the batter over the top of the layered zucchini and sprinkle all over with cheese. Bake for 40 to 50 minutes or until the casserole is puffy and set in the middle, and the cheese is golden. Let it rest for 10 minutes before cutting into slices and serving.

Chayotes Rellenos de Queso

Cheese-Stuffed Chayotes

Various Countries | Yield: Serves 4–6 | Difficulty Level: Easy | Total Cooking Time: 1 hour

If you love vegetables stuffed with creamy melted cheese and covered in sauce, you'll love this Mesoamerican rendition. It can be made ahead of time and reheated just before serving. Pear-shaped chayote squashes (*Sechium edule*) are starchy—albeit watery—gourds, native to Mexico. You are probably familiar with the smooth, light green variety cultivated widely for shipping today, but fewer people are acquainted with the dark green chayote, covered in tiny spines, that is my favorite because its flesh is less watery than the former. Of course, the smooth chayote is much easier to handle and to find in stores, and either one will work here. Chayotes come in varying sizes and weigh anywhere from ¾ to 1 pound (340 to 455 grams) each. I gravitate toward the smaller ones, as I find them to have sweeter flesh than the larger ones. Here, three cheeses with different textures make a toothsome filling for the delicate gourd. The sauce is meant to be light and chunky, although if you want to really impress, I highly recommend serving the squash on a pool of Salsa Santa Rosa (page 163). Offer plenty of hot, crusty bread on the side, to sop up the juices.

Three 11 ounce (310 gram) chayotes

2 teaspoons vegetable oil

2 tablespoons finely chopped white onions

3 garlic cloves, finely chopped

½ cup (145 grams) finely chopped plum tomatoes

¼ teaspoon thyme

¼ teaspoon fine sea salt

Pinch of freshly ground black pepper

¾ cup (200 grams) drained whole-milk ricotta cheese

⅓ cup (45 grams) Cotija cheese or grated Parmesan cheese

½ cup (120 grams) finely diced fresh mozzarella cheese

Wash and dry the chayotes, cut them lengthwise in half, place them in a large pot, and cover them with water by 2 inches (5 cm). Bring to a boil over high heat, then cover, lower the heat, and cook at a low boil for 20 to 25 minutes or until fork tender. Drain and set aside. Preheat the oven to 400°F (200°C). In a medium skillet, heat the oil over medium-high heat. Add the onions and cook for 30 seconds, then add the garlic, tomatoes, thyme, salt, and pepper. Continue cooking for 2 to 3 minutes or until all vegetables have softened; transfer to a bowl and set aside to cool slightly. Once cool, stir in the ricotta and Cotija or Parmesan and set aside. Carefully remove the seed and white fiber in the center of each chayote squash; discard. With a spoon, scoop as much of the flesh from each squash as you can, leaving a rim of about ¼ inch (6 mm) of flesh intact, so as not to tear the skins; place the skins in a large oven-safe baking dish and set aside. You should have about ¾ cup of chayote flesh. Pat the flesh dry with paper towels or a clean kitchen towel, chop it, and add it to the tomato-cheese mixture. Divide this mixture into the chayote skins, filling the cavities generously. Top each with mozzarella cheese and bake for 25 to 30 minutes or until the cheese is melted, bubbly, and slightly golden.

VARIATION: Stuff chayotes with any of the picadillo recipes in this book and top with cheese before baking to make chayotes rellenos de carne.

On Stuffing Vegetables · The tradition of stuffed vegetables (called *mahshi* in Arabic) is one that dates back to ancient Persia. The Moors had already introduced this preparation to the Spanish before the conquistadores set out for the New World. In fact, Europeans brought with them recipes for many stuffed vegetables featuring fillings that combined meats, raisins, olives, nuts, and eggs, much in the Persian manner. From this tradition came dishes like the many empanadas of Latin America that feature such fillings, and other festive food such as Mexican chiles in Nogada (poblano chiles stuffed with beef and topped with almond sauce and pomegranate seeds, typically served in September during the national independence holidays). However, Sephardic Jews who escaped the Spanish Inquisition by trekking to the Americas, and the Lebanese who later settled there in the mid-nineteenth century, deserve most of the credit for popularizing stuffed vegetables throughout the continent, adapting and creating many new renditions that include cheese, rice, onions, sweet spices, and all kinds of meat (particularly lamb and goat).

Gratinado de Chayote

Chayote Gratin

Various Countries | Yield: Serves 4–6 | Difficulty Level: Easy | Total Cooking Time: 1 hour (includes resting time)

Delicately flavored chayote is also known as chaya, güisquil, xuxu, and machuchu, depending on what country you are in. Raw chayote flesh has the texture and appearance of a green apple; it takes about the same time to bake as an apple, too. I have a deep fondness for this dish because my children loved it when they were little.

Vegetable oil, for greasing the pan

1½ pounds (700 grams) chayote squash (about 3–4)

1 teaspoon fine sea salt

1 cup (240 ml) crema, natilla, or crème fraiche

½ cup (120 ml) half and half (or nata criolla)

2 tablespoons unsalted butter, melted

¼ cup (45 grams) dried bread crumbs

¼ cup (45 grams) grated Parmesan cheese

Preheat the oven to 400°F (200°C). Grease an 8 x 8 inch (23 x 23 cm) baking dish. Peel the chayotes using a potato peeler. Slice them lengthwise in half; scoop out the seeds and the inner white core using a spoon and discard. Slice the chayotes very thinly and sprinkle with salt. Arrange the slices in two or three layers in the prepared baking dish. In a medium bowl, combine the crema and half and half; pour this evenly over the slices. Cover the dish tightly with foil and bake for 30 to 35 minutes. In a medium bowl, stir together the butter, bread crumbs, and Parmesan. Remove the dish from the oven, uncover, and sprinkle evenly with this mixture. Return to the oven and continue baking, uncovered, until the top is golden and the chayotes are fork tender, about 15 to 20 minutes (the casserole will be bubbly and the crust will be crispy and a beautiful golden color). Remove from the oven and let rest for 10 minutes before slicing and serving.

Güisquiles con Mantequilla

Buttered Chayotes

Central America | Yield: Serves 4 | Difficulty Level: Easy | Total Cooking Time: 30 minutes

In Guatemala, where I grew up, güisquiles (pronounced *wheez-kee-lehs*) were considered very healthy. Their flavor and mild starchiness reminds many of potatoes, but they have a lower carbohydrate content. Texturally, especially when cooked this way, they are more similar to turnips. Chayotes do not become creamy when mashed, unless they're mixed with emulsifiers or with a custard base (see Las Chancletas de Antonieta, page 147). Use any chayote you can find; as long as they're firm and unblemished, they will produce exquisitely delicate flavor.

2 chayote squashes (approximately 10–12 ounces/290–350 grams each)

2 tablespoons unsalted butter

1 teaspoon fine sea salt, or more to taste

Peel the chayotes with a potato peeler (if they have spiky skins, make sure to hold them in a clean kitchen towel to protect your hands). Quarter them and remove the seed and white pith inside. Place the chayotes in a medium pot and cover with cold water. Set over medium-high heat and bring to a boil; lower the heat and simmer for 20 to 25 minutes or until fork tender. Drain the chayotes and place them on a serving platter; toss with butter and salt. Serve hot.

Las Chancletas de Antonieta

Sweet, Twice-Baked Chayotes

Guatemala | Yield: Serves 4 | Difficulty Level: Intermediate | Total Cooking Time: 1½ hours

If you love puddings, you'll be seduced by the custardy texture of this dessert—its name derived from its shape, said to resemble chancletas (flip-flops)—that reminds me a little bit of pumpkin pie. My grandmother used to make this sweet cinnamon-scented pudding on rainy days. Sometimes she'd stud them with raisins, other times with almonds; on other days, she spiked them with rum. In Guatemala, the spiny chayote is preferred for this recipe; it is larger, meatier, and holds on to its shape when stuffed. However, smooth chayotes are easier to handle. If you can find the former, always hold them in a folded kitchen towel or with tongs or the needles will prick your fingers. If you can only find smooth chayotes, know that when the flesh is removed, their skins will break easily, making them harder to stuff. If the skins break or if you find it too cumbersome to stuff each chayote, bake the prepared custard directly in an oven-safe dish (see Note). This recipe is adapted from one taught to me by Antonieta, a home cook who would make them for me when I visited my beloved Tía Roky's home. The crispy crust is traditionally made with champurradas, a type of cookie; I have substituted Maria cookies (widely available online and in Latin American stores), but vanilla wafers or animal crackers will also yield great results.

2 chayote squashes (approximately 12 ounces/350 grams each)

One 5 inch (12 cm) piece of Mexican cinnamon bark (canela)

4 ounces (115 grams) Maria cookies (or vanilla wafers or animal crackers)

5 tablespoons (72 grams) softened unsalted butter, divided

1 egg

¼ cup (55 grams) dark brown sugar (grated piloncillo or panela work, too)

½ teaspoon ground cinnamon

Pinch of fine sea salt

1–2 tablespoons dark rum (optional)

2 tablespoons raisins or slivered almonds (optional)

Slice each chayote in half lengthwise; place them in a large pot with the piece of cinnamon bark and cover with cold water. Set the pot over high heat and bring to a boil; partially cover, lower the heat, and continue cooking at a soft boil for 25 to 30 minutes or until the flesh of the chayotes is easily pierced with a fork (fork tender). Remove the chayotes and place them on a large plate until cool enough to handle. Preheat the oven to 350°F (180°C); line a large baking pan with parchment paper and set aside. Using a spoon, remove the white pit and white fiber in the center of each chayote half; discard. Use a spoon to remove most of the flesh of each chayote half, leaving about ¼ inch (6 mm) of flesh still attached to the skins, to help them hold their shape. Place the scooped-out flesh in a small bowl and set aside (you should have about 1½ cups of cooked flesh). Crush the cookies slightly and place them in the bowl of a food processor fitted with a metal blade; process them until they are finely ground (like bread crumbs); remove about ⅓ cup (30 grams) of crumbs and set aside for the topping. Add 3 tablespoons (45 grams) of the butter, the egg, brown sugar, ground cinnamon, pinch of salt, and the reserved chayote flesh to the food processor; pulse until the mixture resembles scrambled eggs or loosely cooked oatmeal. If using, stir in the rum and the raisins or almonds. Spoon as much of the mixture into each chayote shell as it will hold (or pour directly onto a baking dish; see Note). Top each chayote half with the remaining cookie crumbs and dot with the rest of the butter. Bake for 40 to 50 minutes or until the tops are beautifully golden and crispy and the custard is set.

Note: Periodically check the flesh of the chayotes as they boil by piercing them with a fork—it should go in easily, as into a cooked potato, with no resistance. Start checking on the lower end of the time frame given. If you prefer to use a baking dish instead of the chayote shells, grease an 8 x 8 inch (20 x 20 cm) baking dish and bake for 35 to 40 minutes or until the top is beautifully golden and crispy and the custard is set.

TOMATOES

Although at the first mention of tomatoes, most cooks think of Italy, these fruits are actually native to Peru. Nomadic tribes took tomatoes from South America to Mesoamerica, where the Aztecs domesticated them first, making them fit to eat (as they weren't edible). By the time Spanish conquistadores traveled to Mexico, they found that tomatoes were already an important part of the Aztec and Mayan diets. Mostly, they were used to make mollis or salsas.

According to Fray Bernardino de Sahagún's *General History of the Things of New Spain* (also known as *The Florentine Codex*), published in 1577, there were many chile and tomato sauces in Mesoamerica. At least two of these still exist today, one made with yellow chiles and the other with red ones. Known as chilemollis, chirmoles, or chilmoles, these are fresh, liquid salsas; after the Columbian exchange, alliums (like onions and garlic) and herbs (like cilantro and mint) were added.

The Spaniards were the first ones to take tomatoes back to Europe. However, tomatoes, which are members of the nightshade or Solanaceae family (as are eggplants and potatoes), were not quickly embraced. Since Europeans recognized many of the nightshades as poisonous (the most familiar poison at the time was belladonna, also known as deadly nightshade and famously written about much later in the book *My Cousin Rachel*, by Daphne du Maurier), tomatoes were erroneously regarded as poisonous too. It took three hundred years for tomatoes to go from ornamental plants to edibles at the table. The first tomatoes to make it to Europe were probably yellow and not red, as Italians named them *pomo d'oro*, or golden apple. The ever-romantic French followed, calling them *pommes d'amour*—love apples.

The first written recipes for cooking with tomatoes come from Spain and Naples (back then its own country, before it became a part of Italy). In my opinion, the fact that tomatoes were first written about in European books (and not Latin American cookbooks) is the main reason most people think they're Italian. Antonio Latini, author of *Lo scalco alla moderna* (*The Modern Kitchen*, 1696), was the first person to publish a recipe for a sauce made with roasted tomatoes, onions, chiles, and vinegar. Although the dish was popular throughout Latin America when he wrote about it, he did not give any credit to the cuisines that inspired it. This has perpetuated the myth that tomatoes are Italian. Once Latini's book was published, myriad variations on tomato sauces became popular in Italy, but to this day, similar salsas from Mesoamerica to Peru are still made in exactly the same manner and served with simply prepared meats, just as Latini suggested.

Salsa, as we know it today—a mixture of tomatoes, onions, cilantro, and citrus—is only one sort of tomato sauce, formally known as pico de gallo. By definition, the word *salsa* just means "sauce," and can refer to any kind of sauce, raw or cooked, tomato based or not. Salsas are extremely important in the cuisines of Latin America—the recipes are never-ending, as you'll see from the examples I've included here.

However, sauces are, of course, not the only foods to be prepared with tomatoes in Latin America. You'll also find them transformed into soups, used in salads, stirred into egg dishes, stuffed with grains, and tossed into stir-fries.

I am always in search of rare seeds so I can grow many varieties of heirloom tomatoes in my garden. I plant them in all sorts of reds, golds, purples, oranges, and greens and in different sizes, so I can enjoy them, fresh or preserved, all year round.

Chirmol de la Mari

Oven-Roasted Tomato Sauce

Guatemala | Yield: Makes 1 cup (240 ml) | Difficulty Level: Easy | Total Cooking Time: 50 minutes

In the town of San Martín Jilotepeque, smack in the middle of Guatemala, people have been making this simple tomato mixture since the beginning of the Mayan civilization. Chirmoles are salsas from Guatemala and El Salvador, made with charred ingredients, mashed into loose sauces. At the base are charred tomatoes or tomatillos. This chirmol is as rustic—and probably as close to the original tomato "molli," or "mixture," from pre-Columbian America—as it gets. Although cilantro is widely used in Latin America, it was the Europeans who introduced the herb, which, based on Sanskrit and biblical references, can be traced back thousands of years to the Middle East. Roasting vegetables is an Indigenous cooking technique still used to prepare sauces in Mesoamerica today. The beauty of roasting plum tomatoes in the oven is that they require little attention. Plus, as they char, their skins inflate and separate from the flesh of the fruit, which makes them easy to peel.

1½ pounds (680 grams) plum tomatoes, sliced lengthwise in half

2 tablespoons finely chopped cilantro (leaves and tender stems)

¼ teaspoon fine sea salt, or to taste

Preheat the oven to 425°F (220°C). Line a large baking sheet with a high rim with parchment paper. Place the tomato halves, cut side down, on the prepared sheet and roast for 35 to 40 minutes or until the skins have blackened, blistered, and puffed up. Remove from the oven and peel the tomatoes by pulling off the skins with tongs (they should come off easily in one piece). Transfer the tomatoes to a large bowl, and using a fork (or potato masher), mash them into a sauce, leaving some small chunks for texture. Add the cilantro and salt and mix well.

Pico de Gallo

Chopped Salsa

Mexico | Yield: Serves 4–6 | Difficulty Level: Easy | Total Cooking Time: 15 minutes

This is undoubtedly the most recognized version of the Mexican chopped sauce. *Pico de gallo* literally translates as "rooster's beak." Why the name, you ask? There are three theories. Perhaps it is because *picar* in Spanish means "to chop," and all of the ingredients are prepared thusly. Or that roosters can only grab small pieces of grain at a time, an action described as picando el suelo, or pecking the ground. The third theory says that the colors of this vibrantly fresh dipping sauce represent all the hues that can be found on a rooster's beak. Regardless, this sauce is sometimes also called salsa de mesa (table salsa) or salsa fresca (fresh sauce) and is super easy to make. I love to serve it tableside to top steaks and fish, as a garnish for tacos, as an accoutrement for ceviches, or as a dipping sauce for totopos (tortilla chips). This salsa tastes best made right before serving.

2 cups (340 grams) finely chopped plum tomatoes

1 cup (115 grams) finely chopped white onions

1–2 jalapeño or serrano peppers, finely chopped (seeded and deveined if less heat is desired)

1 cup (85 grams) finely chopped cilantro (leaves and tender stems)

¼ cup (60 ml/¼ cup) freshly squeezed lime or lemon juice

½ teaspoon fine sea salt, or more to taste

Pinch of freshly ground black pepper, or more to taste

In a large, nonreactive bowl, combine the tomatoes, onions, peppers, cilantro, and lime juice; season with salt and pepper. Let the salsa rest at room temperature for 15 to 20 minutes in order for the flavors to blend. Serve at room temperature or chilled. This will keep, if well covered and refrigerated, for up to 24 hours.

Salsas were originally prepared by grinding ingredients in stone basins known as molcajetes, batánes, or metates. Today, food processors and blenders are used for expediency in Latin American kitchens, just as they are around the world.

In the land of the Maya that spanned from the Yucatán Peninsula through Guatemala, Belize, Honduras, and El Salvador, tomato-based sauces are often referred to as recados, simple mixtures of roasted tomatoes (or tomatillos), salt, and water. Some recados are further thickened with masa, toasted corn, pulverized seeds, burned bread, or bread crumbs. Recados are mostly distinguished by their seasonings, such as herbs, cinnamon, anise, alliums, or spices.

Chirmol o Chilmol Típico

Traditional Roasted Tomato Sauce

El Salvador and Guatemala | Yield: Makes 2 cups (480 ml) | Difficulty Level: Easy | Total Cooking Time: 30 minutes

Chirmoles, of which there are many, are pre-Columbian salsas made with a base of charred tomatoes that are mashed in a molcajete until very smooth. Usually flavored with alliums (garlic, onion, leeks, or shallots) and different herbs, some are made with hot chiles, but this one, typically found as an everyday condiment, is not. I find that the easiest way to char or roast vegetables is to cook them in a nonreactive, heavy-bottomed skillet, set directly over the heat, or to broil them in the oven. I recommend using a dark skillet because charring will blacken the finish, ruining shiny pans. If you don't have a molcajete or a mortar and pestle, use a potato masher and a bowl to make the sauce.

1 pound (455 grams) whole plum tomatoes

1 medium (4 ounces/115 grams) green bell pepper, halved and seeded

2 garlic cloves, unpeeled and left whole

½ cup (115 grams) finely chopped white onions

3 tablespoons (45 ml) freshly squeezed lime juice, or more to taste

¾ teaspoon fine sea salt, or more to taste

½ teaspoon dried Mexican oregano (optional)

¼ cup (20 grams) finely chopped fresh Italian parsley (leaves and tender stems)

¼ cup (20 grams) finely chopped fresh mint

Set a dark, heavy-bottomed skillet over medium-high heat. Once hot, place the whole tomatoes, peppers, and garlic cloves in the skillet, turning them over as their skin blackens and chars, about 5 minutes total. Place the tomatoes in a molcajete (or a medium bowl). Place the unpeeled, charred garlic and the pepper aside on a cutting board. Remove the charred peel of each garlic clove and discard; add the garlic cloves to the tomatoes. Using a pestle, a potato masher, or a sturdy fork, mash the tomatoes and garlic. Leave some texture; don't puree it completely. Use a knife to chop the roasted pepper and add it to the tomato mixture, along with the onions, lime juice, salt, and oregano. Just before serving, stir in the parsley and mint.

VARIATIONS: For a completely different, albeit traditional chirmol, substitute the parsley and mint with ½ cup (40 grams) long-leaf culantro, or double the amount of cilantro. For a spicy chirmol, add chopped chiltepines, serranos, or jalapeños, to taste. For a more acidic chirmol, roast 3 to 4 tomatillos along with the other vegetables and mash them with the tomatoes.

Ensalada de Tomate de Diario

Everyday Tomato Salad

Various Countries | Yield: Varies | Difficulty Level: Intermediate | Total Cooking Time: 20–30 minutes

This is a recipe in which measurements have little place, because most of us who learned to cook from our grandmothers, no matter where we're from, learned to do so by feel. So, I will not give you exact measurements, because none are needed. You can't go wrong. Use as many tomatoes as you like and season with as much oil and vinegar as you desire. The same blanching technique used to peel tomatoes can be used to peel peaches.

Tomatoes (your favorite variety as long as they are large)

Vinegar (any kind you like)

Olive oil

Salt, to taste

Freshly ground black pepper, to taste

Finely chopped fresh chives, or chervil, or cilantro

Bring a large pot filled with water to a rolling boil. Fill a large bowl with iced water and set aside. With a knife, make an X on the skin on the bottom of each tomato. Carefully plunge each tomato into the boiling water and let it blanch for 40 seconds to 1 minute (depending on the size). Immediately remove it from the water and plunge it into the iced water. Do the same with the remaining tomatoes. Remove the tomatoes from the iced water. Notice that the skins are beginning to pull back at the X. With your fingers, pull back the rest of the skin. If they don't peel off easily, repeat the process of boiling and cooling. Slice the peeled tomatoes crosswise (as thinly as you can) and place them attractively on a platter. In a small bowl, combine one part vinegar to three parts olive oil; season with as much salt and pepper as you wish, whisking together. Pour the dressing over the tomatoes, sprinkle with the herbs, and serve.

Ensalada de Tomate y Cebolla

Tomato and Onion Salad

Chile | Yield: Serves 4–6 | Difficulty Level: Easy | Total Cooking Time: 20 minutes

This is the ubiquitous salad found in every Chilean home, so simple to make that calling it a recipe feels almost like cheating. The one thing that is common to most recipes that use raw onions in this South American country is the fact that they are blanched in boiling water, to decrease their pungency. You can skip this step and use sweet onions instead, but I rather like following the method exactly. Use the freshest heirloom tomatoes you can find. I grow my own and have also started to grow my own banana peppers, just for the purpose of making this salad.

1 cup (115 grams) very thinly sliced yellow onions

1 pound (455 grams) round tomatoes, sliced into wedges

1 banana pepper (sweet or medium), stemmed, seeded, and finely chopped

3 tablespoons (45 ml) red wine vinegar

¾ teaspoon fine sea salt

½ teaspoon freshly ground black pepper

¼ cup (60 ml) vegetable oil

2 tablespoons (10 grams) finely chopped fresh Italian parsley (optional)

Place the sliced onions in a medium heat-resistant bowl and pour over enough boiling water to cover; let sit for 8 minutes. Fill a medium bowl with iced water. Drain the onions and immediately plunge them into the iced water; let cool completely. Drain well and place in a large salad bowl; add the tomatoes and the banana peppers and set aside. In a medium bowl, whisk together the vinegar, salt, pepper, and oil; drizzle the dressing over the salad, tossing well. Garnish with parsley. Serve at room temperature (or chill until ready to serve).

Hogado Casero

Cooked Tomato Sauce

Colombia | Yield: Makes 1½ cups (360 ml) | Difficulty Level: Easy | Total Cooking Time: 20 minutes

My friend Luisa Fernanda Ríos is a well-known private chef in Vancouver and an expert on the cuisine of her native Colombia. As she wrote to me, most of her family's recipes exist only "en las cabezas de las dos tías mayores que ya casi llegan a sus 90s—afortunadamente, con una memoria extraordinaria"—inside the head of the two oldest aunts, who fortunately have extraordinary memories! I hope that this rendition, which Luisa based on their shared recollections and is at the base of so many home-cooked meals in her family—and of Colombian recipes in general—makes them proud, even though I'm told they seldom agree on anything.

2 tablespoons vegetable oil

1 cup (170 grams) finely chopped white onions

2 cups (340 grams) roughly chopped vine-ripened tomatoes

2 large green onions, finely sliced (about ⅓ cup/30 grams)

1½ teaspoons fine sea salt

1½ teaspoons ground cumin

½ teaspoon garlic powder

½ teaspoon freshly ground black pepper

Heat the oil in a medium skillet set over medium heat; add the onions and sauté until transparent, about 2 minutes. Add the tomatoes, green onions, salt, cumin, garlic powder, and pepper; sauté, stirring occasionally, until thickened, about 8 minutes. Remove from heat; allow to cool and store in a covered jar for up to 1 week in the refrigerator. If you want to keep the sauce longer, freeze it in ice cube trays; once solid, transfer the cubes into freezer-safe containers or bags. They will last in the freezer for up to 6 months.

Luisa's Aliño Crudo

Fresh Tomato Sauce

Colombia | Yield: Makes 1½ cups (360 ml) | Difficulty Level: Easy | Total Cooking Time: 10 minutes

This is a raw version of the hogado casero sauce (the base for many cooked recipes) used in Colombia that features the addition of sweet peppers. It's particularly delicious when used as a topping for soup, such as a sancocho from the region of Antioquía, similar to the Cocido on page 462 but made with chicken. It's a spectacular topping for leftover boiled beef that is chopped very finely in a food processor, known by Colombians as carne en polvo (pulverized beef).

2 tablespoons vegetable oil

2 cups (340 grams) roughly chopped vine-ripened tomatoes

1 cup (170 grams) finely chopped white onions

1 cup (115 grams) stemmed, seeded, and roughly chopped red bell peppers

2 large green onions, debearded and finely sliced (about ⅓ cup/30 grams)

1½ teaspoons fine sea salt

1½ teaspoons ground cumin

½ teaspoon garlic powder

½ teaspoon freshly ground black pepper

Place all ingredients in a blender and blend until smooth. It keeps in the refrigerator for up to 2 weeks or frozen for up to 6 months; freeze in ice cube trays, then transfer to a freezer-safe container to use as needed.

Molho Campeiro

"Country Sauce"

Brazil | Yield: Makes 2¾ cups (690 ml) | Difficulty Level: Easy |
Total Cooking Time: 1 hour 15 minutes (includes time to marinate)

This is the classic accompaniment to grilled meats in Brazil. Make it one hour before you serve it, so it can marinate and the flavors can blend.

1½ cups (225 grams) seeded and chopped plum tomatoes

½ cup (55 grams) finely chopped white onions

¾ cup (140 grams) finely chopped red or green bell peppers

2 tablespoons finely chopped fresh Italian parsley

½ cup (120 ml) white vinegar

2 teaspoons dried oregano

2 teaspoons fine sea salt, or more to taste

½ teaspoon freshly ground black pepper

½ cup (120 ml) avocado oil

Combine all the ingredients in a large bowl with ¼ cup (60 ml) water and stir well to combine. Let marinate at room temperature for 1 hour. Serve.

Note: If you wish to keep this sauce longer, cover and chill for up to 2 days. Bring it back to room temperature before serving.

Recado de Tomatillo o Miltomates

Classic Cooked Tomatillo Sauce

Mesoamerica | Yield: Makes 1 quart (960 ml) | Difficulty Level: Easy | Total Cooking Time: 1 hour

Tomatillos (*Physalis ixocarpa*) are members of the gooseberry family. As the fruits mature into small green to purplish tomato-like berries, the outer calyxes of their flowers enlarge and inflate, becoming papery casings that enclose them. Where I grew up in Guatemala, tomatillos are known as miltomates or "a thousand tomatoes" because the plants are so prolific that they produce thousands. Tomatillos vary greatly in size, from tiny ones the size of small blueberries, to giant tomato-like fruits. Over the years, I was honored to host the author Diana Kennedy on her visits to North Carolina, trekking along with her during ingredient scouting trips. We became friends and we'd go to out to lunch, to museums, or to my lake house. Diana taught me that the bigger tomatillos are always bitter and that most grocery stores carry gigantic ones, so I started growing my own. If you shop for them, opt for the smallest in the bins (usually medium in size). This is one of my go-to sauces during the week because it can be used as a base for many different dishes such as chicken stews and enchiladas, or simply spooned over fried eggs. I make it in large batches in the early autumn when I harvest my own tomatillo plants, and then freeze it to use over the winter months. It's cooked twice: first to cook the tomatillos, then a second time to thicken it to the desired consistency.

1½ pounds (680 grams) tomatillos, husks removed, and washed (about 20 medium/12 large)

2 cups (280 grams) roughly chopped white onions

3 garlic cloves, halved

3 serrano peppers, roughly chopped (or 1 large jalapeño)

1 large bunch cilantro (leaves and tender stems) (about 2½ packed cups)

1 teaspoon fine sea salt, or to taste

¼ teaspoon freshly ground black pepper, or to taste

In a large Dutch oven set over medium-high heat, add the tomatillos, onions, garlic cloves, serrano peppers, and 1¾ cups (420 ml) water. Bring to a boil; lower the heat to medium, and cook until all the tomatillos have popped, about 15 to 20 minutes. Let this mixture cool enough to handle (about 20 minutes). Working in batches, place half the tomatillo mixture and half the cilantro in the jar of a blender; blend until smooth; repeat with the remaining tomatillo mixture and cilantro. Season with salt and pepper. Return the sauce to the pot, and simmer, uncovered, until it has thickened, about 20 minutes. Use immediately or cool and refrigerate.

Note: If well covered, this sauce will last in the refrigerator for up to 2 days. You may also freeze it for up to 4 months; reheat well before using. If the sauce is too bitter (because you could only find giant tomatillos), add a bit of honey, a teaspoon at a time, just to tame the bitterness.

VARIATIONS: For a great salsa cruda verde, blend all of the ingredients in this recado without cooking them and without the water. You'll end up with a refreshing salsa, perfect to top tacos, enchiladas, and tostadas, or to use as a dip for chips. For a creamy salsa de aguacate y tomatillo, add an avocado to the blender. Just make sure to eat these raw sauces within three days of making them.

Salsa de Tomate Preparada

Tomato Sauce

Various Countries | Yield: Makes 4 cups (960 ml) | Difficulty Level: Easy | Total Cooking Time: 20 minutes

This sauce, which I learned to make in Mexico, is one that I have been making for decades, great for ladling over fried eggs to make huevos rancheros or on fried tortilla strips to make chilaquiles. It features a whisper of heat and a hint of smoky flavor. Refrigerate it for up to one week or freeze for up to three months. Canned chipotles are mixed with a vinegary sauce called adobo, which you will also use in this sauce.

One 28 ounce can (or two 14.5 ounce cans) diced tomatoes

2 large green onions (white and light green parts only), debearded and halved

1 garlic clove, roughly chopped

1 chipotle pepper from can of chipotles in adobo sauce, plus 2 teaspoons of the adobo sauce

1 teaspoon fine sea salt

1 teaspoon Mexican oregano

½ teaspoon dried thyme

½ teaspoon freshly ground black pepper

¼ cup (60 ml) vegetable oil

In a blender, combine the tomatoes, green onions, garlic, chipotle, adobo sauce, salt, oregano, thyme, and pepper; blend until smooth. Heat the oil in a medium saucepan set over medium-high heat until it shimmers. Carefully, standing back, add the blended sauce (it will splatter). Lower the heat to medium and stir with a long wooden spatula. Cover, lower the heat to low, and simmer for 10 minutes.

VARIATIONS: Salsa de tomate preparada showcases traditionally Mesoamerican flavors. For a South American version, replace the chipotle and the adobo sauce with two sweet ají peppers. To give it a Peruvian accent, use 2 tablespoons ají panca paste. Finally, to give it a Latin Caribbean taste, skip the chipotle and the adobo sauce and instead add a teaspoon of ground cumin.

Frying Sauces · Maya and Aztecs share a cooking technique in which sauces are "fried" in lard (or any other fat). To do this, the fat is heated well before adding the raw sauce—which always splatters. You can shield yourself from the splashing liquid with the lid of a large pot; always stand back a little and use a large spoon to stir. As the sauce first sizzles, its vibrant colors are set and its flavors deepen.

Salsita Casera de Tomate

Everyday Tomato Sauce

Guatemala | Yield: Makes 3 cups (720 ml) | Difficulty Level: Easy | Total Cooking Time: 30 minutes

This was my grandmother's tomato sauce recipe and the one I taught my children to make. Use this classic sauce to pour over rolled and fried taquitos, flautas, or eggs.

1 pound (455 grams) plum tomatoes, very roughly chopped (about 3 cups)

2 cups (280 grams) very roughly chopped white onions

½ cup (115 grams) stemmed, seeded, and roughly chopped red bell peppers

5 garlic cloves

¼ cup (60 ml) vegetable oil

2 tablespoons tomato paste

1 teaspoon dried thyme

1 large bay leaf

1 teaspoon fine sea salt

Pinch of freshly ground black pepper, or more to taste

Place the tomatoes, onions, peppers, and garlic in the jar of a blender and blend until liquified. Heat the oil in a medium pot set over medium-high heat; add the tomato paste, thyme, and bay leaf and cook for 30 seconds, stirring well to dissolve the paste in the oil. Add the blended ingredients, salt, and pepper. Stir and cook over medium-high heat for 4 minutes; cover, lower the heat to low, and continue cooking, stirring occasionally, for about 20 minutes or until the mixture is thickened. Remove from the heat and discard the bay leaf. Use at once or cool and freeze in freezer-safe containers. Keeps for up to 1 week if refrigerated; 8 months, if frozen.

Salsa para Envueltos

Tomato Sauce for Egg-Battered Food

Mesoamerica | Yield: Makes 2 cups (480 ml) | Difficulty Level: Easy | Total Cooking Time: 20 minutes

This tomato sauce is a cinch to make and gives a flavor profile that is a mix of acidic, smoky, and sweet. Not only is this the ideal topping for any fried food, but it also makes a great dipping sauce for tortilla chips. The use of canned fire-roasted tomatoes will save you some time in the kitchen that can be better used for battering and frying. If you can't find fire-roasted tomatoes, use regular tomatoes instead.

One 28 ounce (840 ml) can (or two 14.5 ounce/411 ml cans) fire-roasted tomatoes

3–4 green onions (white and light green parts only), debearded and halved

1 garlic clove, peeled and cut in half

1 bay leaf

1 teaspoon fine sea salt, or more to taste

½ teaspoon ground thyme

½ teaspoon freshly ground black pepper

In a blender, combine the tomatoes, green onions, and garlic; blend until smooth. Transfer the sauce to a saucepan; cover, set over medium-high heat, and bring to a simmer. Add the bay leaf, salt, thyme, and pepper, and lower the heat to low; cover and simmer the sauce for 10 minutes. Discard the bay leaf.

Note: You can make this sauce a day in advance and keep it well covered and chilled in the refrigerator; reheat when ready to use. Or you can freeze it for up to 4 months.

Salsa Santa Rosa

Tomato Sauce "Santa Rosa"

Guatemala | Yield: Makes 1¾ cups (420 ml) | Difficulty Level: Easy | Total Cooking Time: 35 minutes

Back when my dad was a little boy in the 1940s, there was a restaurant called Santa Rosa in the old part of Guatemala City (known as "el Centro"), by the La Merced church. It was mostly famous for its enchiladas (which in Guatemala are crispy tostadas topped with beet salad), but it was the tomato sauce that covered them that became legendary, for its particularly smooth texture and slight sweetness. The restaurant closed its doors before I was born, but my father used to rave about this sauce. My mother spent decades trying to figure out the recipe, interviewing people who remembered the restaurant and collecting myriad formulas claiming to be "the one." To this day, many cooks proclaim that they have the only "real" recipe for this sauce. After studying many of these recipes, I finally came up with my own version. Not having ever tasted the original myself, I am not one to judge—who knows how time shifts taste memories?—but this one is delicious. My secret addition? A handful of fresh green beans, which lends a velvety texture and brings out the sweetness of the tomatoes. I sometimes like to triple this recipe and freeze it; it lasts for up to four months and allows me to have some on hand whenever I need a prepared tomato sauce. Try it slathered over a plain tostada and topped with queso seco; pour over eggs for breakfast; or eat it straight from the pot with a spoon.

1 pound (455 grams) plum tomatoes

2 ounces (55 grams) green beans, tips removed

2 tablespoons olive or vegetable oil

2 tablespoons finely chopped white onions

1 tablespoon finely chopped fresh Italian parsley (leaves and tender stems)

2 teaspoons ground achiote (see Sources)

2–3 green onions (1 ounce/30 grams), debearded and roughly chopped

2 tablespoons all-purpose flour, toasted (see Note)

1½ teaspoons (9 grams) fine sea salt

Place the tomatoes and the green beans in a medium pot and cover them with water by 1 inch (2.5 cm); set them over medium-high heat and bring to a boil. Cover and lower the heat; simmer for 10 minutes or until the skins of the tomatoes have split and the tomatoes have softened slightly (they will retain their shape). Remove the tomatoes and beans with a slotted spoon into a bowl; reserve the cooking liquid and allow it to cool in a separate bowl. Peel the tomatoes and transfer them, along with the green beans, to a blender; blend until smooth and set aside. Heat the oil in the same pot used for cooking the vegetables over medium-high heat; add the onions and sauté for 1 minute or until they start to change to a light golden color. Add the blended tomato mixture (careful, it will splatter, so stand back and stir with a long-handled spatula; it should stop sputtering in a few seconds). Stir in the parsley, achiote, and green onions; lower the heat and simmer for 5 minutes. In the meantime, combine the toasted flour with ¾ cup (180 ml) of the reserved cooking liquid; pass it through a fine sieve directly into the sauce and stir well. Continue simmering the sauce for about 5 minutes or until it's thickened to a smooth, pourable consistency (if it thickens too much, add more of the reserved cooking liquid). Use immediately or cool and refrigerate, well covered, for up to 3 days.

Tip: Rather than making a roux, Latin cooks like to use toasted flour to thicken sauces because it lends a nutty flavor and a bit of color. Put the flour in a small nonstick pan and set over medium heat. Cook, stirring constantly, for 1 to 1½ minutes or until the flour has changed to a light golden color (be careful not to let it burn). Transfer the toasted flour immediately to a plate (or it will continue cooking and burn). Set aside. You can toast large amounts of flour at once (although recipes typically call for only a few tablespoons at a time); it lasts stored in a jar for up to 2 months. Keep in mind that the capacity of flour to thicken a sauce diminishes when it is toasted.

Tuco

Italo-Argentinean Tomato Sauce

Argentina | Yield: Makes about 5 cups (1.2 liters) | Difficulty Level: Easy | Total Cooking Time: 30 minutes

As tomato sauces go, this is perhaps the most basic of them all. Italians call it sugo, but Argentineans favor the term tuco. You'll find it generously spooned over pasta, poured over stuffed vegetables, stirred into gnocchi, and served with polenta. Argentineans often joke that the way to tell Italians and Argentineans apart is that the latter will always follow a bite of pasta with one of bread. So go ahead, do as they do in Argentina and add a bit more sauce to pasta than is the norm—then sop it up with crusty bread.

Two 28 ounce (796 ml) cans crushed tomatoes

¼ cup (60 ml) extra-virgin olive oil

3 garlic cloves, finely chopped

1 tablespoon balsamic vinegar

1½ teaspoons fine sea salt

Pinch of red pepper flakes, or more to taste

1 large bunch basil leaves, divided (about 1½ cups)

1 tablespoon unsalted butter (optional)

In a large pot set over medium-high heat, stir together the tomatoes, oil, garlic, vinegar, salt, and red pepper flakes. Bring the sauce to a boil; cover, lower the heat to low, and simmer for 20 minutes. Remove from the heat; tear half of the basil leaves and stir them into the sauce. Return the sauce to medium-high heat and, if using, stir in the butter until melted. Tear and add the remaining basil leaves. If not using immediately, cool the sauce to room temperature; cover and chill for up to 1 week or freeze for up to 6 months.

Quimbombó con Tomate

Okra with Tomatoes

Brazil, Cuba, and Puerto Rico | Yield: Serves 4–6 | Difficulty Level: Easy | Total Cooking Time: 25 minutes

Okra and tomatoes are a marriage made in the Americas—a product of the creolization of foods and cultures. Here, both take on the smoky flavor of ham. The word *okra* evolved from the African word *gumbo*. In English it became *quick-gumbo*, and in Latin America it turned into *quimbombó* (pronounced *keem-bohm-boh*) or *guingambo* (*gueen-gahm-boh*). The Afro-Latino culinary movement is an important piece of the Latin American cultural quilt. Africans imprinted their flavors throughout the Latin Caribbean, in Panama, Colombia, Venezuela, Nicaragua, Belize, Ecuador, and Brazil. Okra is one of those vegetables that you either love or hate—and it can be slimy, stringy, and bitter if picked too late in the season. For this reason, select the smallest okra pods, usually available at the start of the hot summer months. Some cooks add bell peppers, squash (calabaza), or potatoes to this dish. In Cuba, green plantain balls are stewed in the broth; sometimes, dried shrimp are also added. Serve over white rice, with a side of fried, sweet plantains.

¼ cup (60 ml) olive oil

1 cup (115 grams) finely chopped white onions

2 garlic cloves, finely chopped

2 ounces (60 grams) smoked ham or Spanish chorizo, chopped

1½ pounds (680 grams) okra, trimmed of stems and cut into ½ inch (1.25 cm) slices

1½ pounds (680 grams) plum tomatoes, cored, seeded, and chopped (about 4½ cups)

1 bay leaf

½ teaspoon fine sea salt, or more to taste

Pinch of freshly ground black pepper, or more to taste

Heat the oil in a large nonreactive skillet (preferably nonstick) set over medium-high heat. Add the onions and garlic and cook, while stirring, for 2 minutes or until the onions are translucent. Add the ham or chorizo and cook for 2 minutes. Add the okra, tomatoes, bay leaf, salt, pepper, and 1 cup (240 ml) water. Cover, decrease the heat to low, and simmer, stirring occasionally, until the okra is just tender, about 15 minutes. Discard the bay leaf and serve hot.

Huevos a la Ranchera

Rancher-Style Eggs

Central America | Yield: Serves 4–6 | Difficulty Level: Easy | Total Cooking Time: 20 minutes (if the sauce is already prepared)

Every birthday celebration in my house started with our entire family entering the celebrant's bedroom before sunrise, singing "Las Mañanitas" (a traditional birthday song) and carrying gifts. After the presents were opened, a breakfast composed of these eggs drenched in tomato sauce, French bread, and black beans always followed. Today, I still make huevos rancheros for special occasions in my home.

6 tablespoons (90 grams) unsalted butter or lard, divided

12 eggs, divided

1 recipe Salsita Casera de Tomate (page 162), kept warm

Warm French bread (for sopping up the sauce)

In a large nonstick pan set over medium heat, melt half of the butter or lard. Crack 6 eggs into the pan. Cover the pan and cook just until the eggs are set, about 3 to 4 minutes. Transfer the eggs to a platter and repeat with the rest of the butter and eggs, until all are cooked; transfer all the eggs to the platter and cover with ample amounts of sauce. Serve with the bread on the side.

VARIATION: To make Mexican huevos rancheros, instead of using bread place the cooked eggs on a tostada base and then cover with the sauce; garnish with crema, Cotija cheese, and cilantro.

Huevos Perico

Scrambled Eggs with Onions and Tomatoes

Various Countries | Yield: Serves 4 | Difficulty Level: Easy | Total Cooking Time: 15 minutes

These deliciously moist scrambled eggs are mixed with tomatoes in what is a very common breakfast item throughout Latin America. In Venezuela, they're stuffed into arepas; in Guatemala, they are used to top pirujos (crusty, torpedo-shaped bread rolls) and drenched in hot sauce; in Honduras, they are rolled into hot flour tortillas, with beans and cheese; and in Mexico, they are used to fill tortas.

2 tablespoons (30 grams) unsalted butter

1 cup (115 grams) finely chopped white onions

1 cup (170 grams) chopped plum tomatoes

1 jalapeño pepper, finely chopped (seeded and deveined if less heat is desired)

8 eggs

½ teaspoon fine sea salt, or more to taste

Pinch of freshly ground black pepper

In a large nonstick skillet set over medium-high heat, melt the butter. Add the onions and sauté until soft, about 3 minutes (don't let them take any color). Add the tomatoes and jalapeño; cook until the peppers are soft, about 2 minutes. In a medium bowl, beat the eggs and season them with salt and pepper; pour them directly into the skillet, stirring. Cook until the eggs are set, about 3 minutes. Remove from the heat and enjoy.

CHILES

When I was growing up, there was a tiny garden in our home in Guatemala City with three peach trees that never gave much fruit, a navel orange tree for breakfast orange juice, and a lemon tree that gifted me pink-fleshed, variegated fruits I ate sprinkled with salt, despite my father's admonitions to protect my tooth enamel (he was also my dentist). Alongside the wall, directly under the kitchen windows and beside the door for easy access, our cook planted bitter lettuces, endive, parsley, long-leaf culantro, thyme, a bay leaf tree, and four chiltepe (bird's-eye pepper) bushes. The first time I tasted the tingling heat of a pepper was as a deterrent for biting my nails—little did anyone know that in the process of leaving my nails alone, I would also begin a life-long love affair with capsaicin, the oily, alkaloid substance that contains the phenolic compounds (called capscaicinoids) that define the level of heat of each pepper.

Chiles (and ajíes, as they're known in South America and the Latin Caribbean) are fruits. Like tomatoes and potatoes, they belong to the Solanaceae family of plants, but are members of the *Capsicum* genus branch. The word *chile* is Nahuatl, the word *ají* is Taíno; and the word *pimiento* is Spanish and refers to the sweet varietals such as bell peppers. There are thirty-one species of chiles, but of these, only five have been domesticated. It is mind-boggling to think that from these, hundreds of peppers have been developed (and continue to be developed).

The *Capsicum annuum* species was domesticated in Mesoamerica and includes jalapeños, serranos, chiltepes, poblanos, padrones, costeños, guajillos, mulatos, pimientos, cobaneros, cayennes, congos, zambos, and chiles de árbol. The *C. chinense*
species, domesticated in the Andes (most probably in Bolivia and Peru), are known as ajíes (as previously noted, the South American word for chiles). They include the ají cachucha, ají limo, ají dulce (ajicito), ají panca, and the chiles habanero and petenero. *C. baccatum*, probably domesticated in Brazil, includes ají amarillo, ají limón, and ají mirasol. *C. frutescens*, from Bolivia and Peru, includes the malagueta and the chocolate chiles. Finally, the *C. pubescens* of Brazil includes the round and red rocotos and manzanos.

Today, it is possible to find many varieties harvested by farmers all over the world. They're also among the easiest plants to grow from seed. I recently planted my first pepper garden, a beautiful array of cayenne, jalapeños, serranos, yellow and green bell peppers, and ajicitos of different colors that resemble Christmas lights. My peppers thrived to the point that I decided to expand my seed collection. One of the most meaningful gifts I've ever received was a box of seeds from three South American cultivars (ají amarillo, ají dulce, and ají limo rojo) from my Venezuelan friend Chef Lis Hernández. Now I save precious seeds and propagate my plants every year in an effort to grow the spicy-hot fruits so I can cook Latin American recipes with the appropriate peppers. And yes, I grow plenty of the chiltepe chiles I fell in love with as a child, too.

Luckily for those who lack a green thumb, all the chiles used in my recipes can be easily sourced online or bought in grocery stores, so you too will be able to make plump chiles rellenos, escabeches with sweet pimientos, and spicy salsas to serve over steaks, tacos, and soups.

Ají Crema

Spicy Yellow Aioli

Peru | Yield: Makes 1¼ cups (300 ml) | Difficulty Level: Easy | Total Cooking Time: 10 minutes

This creamy sauce is the favored condiment in many Peruvian homes, where garlicky and spicy-hot flavors are heartily embraced. Ají amarillos can be found already seeded, deveined, and processed; they are also available as a paste. You'll find them packed into jars and sold in most Latin American stores, or you can order them online (see Sources). Ají amarillos are both spicy and fruity, and when preserved in brine, they're easy to peel. Use this crema as a spread for sandwiches, to top grilled fish and rotisserie chicken, or on potatoes.

1 cup (240 ml) mayonnaise

4 whole ají amarillos, peeled, seeded, deveined; or 3 tablespoons (45 ml) ají amarillo paste

3 large garlic cloves, minced

1 tablespoon freshly squeezed lime juice, or to taste

½ teaspoon fine sea salt, or to taste

¼ teaspoon ground cumin

In a blender, combine all the ingredients and blend until smooth. Transfer the crema to a bowl; cover and chill for at least 1 hour or up to 4 days.

Ají Verde de Pollería

Spicy Green Aioli

Peru | Yield: Makes 2 cups (480 ml) | Difficulty Level: Easy | Total Cooking Time: 10 minutes

This is the one hot sauce I can't live without: citrusy, super spicy, and addictive as can be. It's a classic accompaniment to Peruvian chicken (like the one on page 388), but I use it to dip Tostones (page 305), Papitas Fritas (page 292), or simple boiled potatoes. Huacatay is a South American mint; you can find it frozen or jarred in Latin American stores and online (see Sources). This sauce will keep in your refrigerator for up to one week.

1 large bunch cilantro (leaves and tender stems) (1 packed cup/70 grams)

4 large jalapeño peppers, stemmed and sliced (do not remove the seeds)

2 green onions (white and green parts), sliced

½ cup crumbled (85 grams) queso fresco or feta cheese

2 large garlic cloves, roughly chopped

¼ cup (75 ml) ají amarillo paste

¼ cup (75 ml) freshly squeezed lime juice, or more to taste

2 teaspoons chopped huacatay leaves or paste (frozen or from a jar)

2 teaspoons honey

1 teaspoon ground cumin

1 teaspoon fine sea salt

4 tablespoons (60 ml) cold water

½ cup (120 ml) vegetable or avocado oil

Place the cilantro, jalapeños, green onions, cheese, garlic, ají paste, lime juice, huacatay, honey, cumin, salt, and water in a blender; blend until smooth. With the motor running, add the oil in a thin stream until the sauce is creamy.

La Huancaína

Spicy Yellow Pepper Sauce for Salads

Peru | Yield: Makes 2 cups (480 ml) | Difficulty Level: Easy | Total Cooking Time: 10 minutes

This is the classic yellow, citrusy, spicy, and creamy sauce from Peru. Peruvians use it on boiled potatoes, stirred into hot pasta, or as a dip. Jarred or canned ají amarillos are easy to find or order online (see Sources); their skins are easy to peel, and leftovers can be stored in the refrigerator for months. If you only find fresh ajíes, blanch them briefly to separate their skins and then peel them. Evaporated milk is a must in this recipe, so don't use any other kind. Use a flavorless oil (never olive oil!) to avoid overpowering the other ingredients.

4 ají amarillos, peeled, seeded, and deveined, or 3 tablespoons (45 ml) ají amarillo paste

1 garlic clove

1 cup (140 grams) crumbled queso fresco

3 saltine crackers

⅓ cup (75 ml) evaporated milk, or more to taste

2 tablespoons vegetable oil

¼ teaspoon fine sea salt, or more to taste

Pinch of freshly ground black pepper, or more to taste

2–3 tablespoons freshly squeezed lime juice, or more to taste

Place the ajíes, garlic, cheese, saltines, evaporated milk, and oil in a blender; blend until smooth. Transfer to a bowl and season with salt, pepper, and lime juice.

Note: This sauce will last in the refrigerator for up to 1 week and will thicken as it chills; to make it creamy again, let it sit at room temperature for a few minutes, or stir in a bit more evaporated milk.

Tip: Animal crackers, saltines, and day-old bread are often used to thicken sauces like this one in Peru. I prefer the clean taste of square saltines (the ones wrapped in sleeves); crumble a couple at a time in your hands and blend them into the sauce until it has thickened, to taste.

Crema Fría de Chile Poblano

Poblano Cream

Mexico | Yield: Serves 4–6 | Difficulty Level: Easy | Total Cooking Time: 5 minutes (30 minutes if you have to roast the chiles)

This crema is green and smoky from the roasted poblano chiles, but it is not spicy and is used to serve as a garnish or dipping sauce for tacos, flautas, and doraditos. I particularly love it paired with my Salmón al Tequila (page 363). I like to roast several dozen poblano peppers at a time; then seed, devein, and either leave them whole (to make chiles rellenos) or cut them into strips (called rajas), which I freeze portioned out, in little baggies. That way I can easily retrieve them for use in a recipe, such as this easy sweet and tangy cream sauce, anytime I want.

2 poblano chile peppers, roasted, peeled, seeded, and deveined (page 182)

½ cup (120 ml) Mexican crema or crème fraiche

Pinch of ground cumin, or more to taste

Pinch of fine sea salt, or more to taste

Place all ingredients in a blender and puree until smooth. Adjust seasoning. Cover and refrigerate until ready to use (up to 3 days).

Pebre

Red Pepper Salsa

Chile | Yield: Makes about 2 cups (480 ml) | Difficulty Level: Easy | Total Cooking Time: 40 minutes

Pebre is the ubiquitous red and spicy salsa of Chile. According to *The Book of Sent Soví* (one of the oldest culinary manuscripts of Europe), the earliest-known sauces date back to the Middle Ages, when mixtures of onions, garlic, and vinegar similar to this were used to season dishes in Spain. Once the technique came to the Americas, native sweet and spicy peppers were added to the formula. There are many recipes for pebre, and while some cooks add cilantro or parsley and others add a touch of tomato, I'm partial to my version. If you prefer it sweet, use ají molido dulce or paprika instead of the hot pepper flakes this recipe calls for.

1 cup (120 grams) finely chopped white onions

½ cup (85 grams) stemmed, seeded, and finely chopped red bell peppers

4 garlic cloves, finely minced

1 tablespoon ají molido picante (hot pepper flakes) (or use paprika, for less heat)

¼ cup (60 ml) red wine vinegar

½ cup (120 ml) extra-virgin olive oil

1 teaspoon dried oregano

1½ teaspoons of Aliño Completo (page 7)

In a medium bowl, stir together the onions, bell peppers, and garlic. In a small bowl, combine the hot pepper flakes (or paprika) and the vinegar, stirring well. Whisk in the oil until emulsified; add the oregano and the aliño completo, stirring well. Combine the contents of the two bowls. Cover and let the pebre sit at room temperature for 30 minutes, or chill it for up to 2 days. Bring it back to room temperature before serving.

Note: If you don't have any aliño completo, then season to taste with salt and pepper.

La Salsa Picada de Jalapeños de Flor Roldán

Chunky Jalapeño Salsa

Guatemala, Nicaragua | Yield: Makes 3 cups (720 ml) | Difficulty Level: Easy | Total Cooking Time: 10 minutes

This deliciously crunchy, tangy, and spicy (but not too spicy) salsa was created by my friend Flor to satisfy the palates of both my Guatemalan brother, Juan Pablo, and his Nicaraguan wife, Tey. It goes with everything and it's an ever-present accoutrement in their home and so widely requested that a family gathering is not complete without it. It's crucial to chop the ingredients finely by hand in order to keep textural structure and retain a subtle crunch. If processed or blended, the texture becomes watered down and the flavor of each individual component is lost. Do not even consider removing the seeds from the jalapeños! It simply won't taste the same. The secret to this salsa, according to Tey, is to "use coarse salt only, and enough to get the right punch." My daughter, Alessandra, eats it by the spoonful; my husband ladles it on fried eggs in the morning.

2 cups (285 grams) finely chopped white onions

2 cups (150 grams) jalapeños, stemmed and finely chopped

¾ cup (60 grams) fresh cilantro (leaves and tender stems), finely chopped

⅔ cup (165 ml) freshly squeezed lime juice

2 teaspoons coarse sea salt, or more to taste

Combine all of the ingredients together in a medium, nonreactive bowl, along with ¾ cup (180 ml) water. Allow it to marinate at room temperature for 20 minutes. Taste, and adjust the salt as desired. Chill until ready to use.

Note: This salsa lasts up to 1 week in the refrigerator but is best the day it's made, when its color is vibrant and green.

Tip: The best way to wash cilantro is to fill your sink with cold water and swish the entire bunch in it (make sure to remove any ties or rubber bands), so any sand stuck to the leaves will be dislodged. Lift the cilantro out of the water and dry it between paper towels or in a kitchen towel. (A salad spinner also works!)

Salsa de Chile Verde de Maris

Serrano and Tomatillo Hot Sauce

Mexico | Yield: Makes 2½ cups (600 ml) | Difficulty Level: Easy | Total Cooking Time: 10 minutes

My niece, Marissa de Alfaro, is from Tijuana, Mexico; her family owns one of the most famous resorts, La Escondida, on the carretera Mexico-Toluca. This is a raw version of the hot sauce they serve there—a truly kick-in-the-pants salsa! Marissa puts it on anything and everything from beans, tortas (sandwiches), and eggs to rice dishes, tacos, and avocado. I like to use small, long-stemmed white onions (cebolla de tallo grande or cebolla del país) because their taste is more robust. You can find these bunching onions in organic markets or you can grow your own, like I do. If you can't find them, use regular white onions. Do not even think of removing the seeds or veins from the chiles for this sauce—it's all about the heat! This salsa lasts, refrigerated, for two weeks if kept in a glass jar fitted with a tight lid or in an airtight container.

10–12 medium tomatillos, husks removed, quartered

1 small bunch fresh cilantro, chopped

2½ ounces (70 grams) white onions, sliced

1 garlic clove

2 serrano chile peppers (1 if less heat is desired)

4 tablespoons freshly squeezed lime juice

1 tablespoon vegetable oil

1 teaspoon fine sea salt

½ cup (120 ml) cold water

Place all of the ingredients in a blender and blend until smooth.

Salsa de Chiltepe

Very Hot Bird's-Eye Chile Pepper Relish

Guatemala | Yield: Makes 1 cup (240 ml) | Difficulty Level: Easy | Total Cooking Time: 20 minutes

This is the table salsa I grew up with in Guatemala. Chiltepes or chiltepines, also known as bird's-eye peppers, are among the smallest and hottest chiles you'll find. As a rule of thumb, the smaller the chiles, the hotter they are. Capsaicin is found in the veins of the chiles; the seeds are hot because they're attached to the veins (and not the other way around, as is often believed). The smaller the chiles, the harder it is to remove the seeds and veins (in the case of tiny ones like chiltepes, they're impossible to remove). Therefore, be warned that this is a very spicy-hot relish that will make your tongue burn and your lips tingle. Whether you use fresh or jarred chiltepes, always remove their stems before using. Use gloves if you're sensitive to chiles. Freshly grown chiltepes freeze well; my harvests last me all winter long. This salsa will keep for up to a week in your refrigerator.

2 ounces (60 grams) white onions, roughly chopped

½ ounce (15 grams) chiltepines, stemmed (see Note)

1 small bunch fresh parsley (leaves and tender stems), finely chopped

½ cup (120 ml) freshly squeezed lime or lemon juice

2 tablespoons water

1 teaspoon fine sea salt

Place the onions, chiltepines, and parsley in the bowl of a food processor, fitted with a metal blade, and pulse until the mixture is very finely chopped (about 1 minute), stopping to scrape down the sides of the bowl. Transfer to a nonreactive bowl (or a glass jar); stir in the lime juice, water, and salt.

Note: If using jarred chiltepines packed in brine, rinse them under cold running water and remove the stems. If you don't have a food processor, chop the ingredients with a knife.

Did you know? · Putting a few grains of coarse salt on your tongue is supposed to make your eyes water enough to wash out any capsaicin. I don't know if this old wives' tale really works, but I wish I'd been warned as a child that the pretty flowers of chile plants are as hot as their fruit, before I touched my eyes. Be careful not to touch your face after you handle any hot chiles.

Escabeche de Pimientos

Marinated Red Peppers

Various Countries | Yield: Serves 8 | Difficulty Level: Easy

Escabeches are found throughout Latin America and are descended from the Arab technique of preserving food in vinegar. Fish, meats, poultry, vegetables, and seafood can all be preserved in "escabeche." You can use bell peppers of any color for this recipe: red, green, yellow, orange—a combination can be nice. If you can find jarred, roasted peppers, use those instead—it'll make this even easier to prepare. In Uruguay and Argentina, these are usually served alongside grilled meats and sausages. In Guatemala and Costa Rica and in other South American countries, they serve as an appetizer, usually paired with cheese, sliced charcuterie, and crusty bread.

⅔ cup (165 ml) extra-virgin olive oil

1 small (about 4 ounces/115 grams) white or yellow onion, thinly sliced

5 large roasted bell peppers, cut into strips ½ inches (12 mm) wide and 3 inches (7.5 cm) long (see box on page 185)

8 sprigs fresh thyme (or 1 teaspoon dried)

1 bay leaf

6 whole black peppercorns

6 garlic cloves, sliced thinly

½ cup (120 ml) good-quality red wine vinegar

1 tablespoon sugar

1 teaspoon fine sea salt, or more to taste

½ teaspoon freshly ground pepper, or more to taste

Crusty bread

In a medium stainless steel or enamel-coated saucepan with high sides set over medium heat, combine the oil, onions, peppers, thyme, bay leaf, and peppercorns; cook, while stirring, for 4 to 5 minutes or until the onions have softened (don't let them take any color; lower the heat to medium-low if necessary and stir often). Add the garlic and cook for 1 minute or just until fragrant. In a small bowl, combine the vinegar and sugar with ¼ cup (60 ml) water; add this to the peppers and simmer, uncovered, for 5 minutes. Remove the escabeche from the heat and bring it to room temperature; taste, and season with salt and pepper. Serve at room temperature with crusty bread to sop up the juices.

Note: This escabeche keeps in the refrigerator (if properly covered) for up to 2 weeks; bring it back to room temperature before serving.

What's in a Name? · When is a bell pepper a chile, a pimiento, a morrón, an ají, or a chiltoma? All bell peppers are chiles, as are all hot chiles; bell peppers of any color can be called pimientos, but only red bell peppers are known as morrones. Ají refers to any pepper—hot or not—as long as you're in South America or the Latin Caribbean. Finally, a chiltoma is a green bell pepper, but only in Nicaragua. Confused yet? That's okay, you're not alone.

Escabeche de Chile Ancho

Preserved Dried Chiles

Mexico | Yield: Serves 10–12 | Difficulty Level: Easy | Total Cooking Time: 3 hours (includes cooling)

Escabeche is a cooking method by which ingredients are conserved in vinegar, and which the Spaniards first learned from the Ottomans and then introduced to Latin America. As opposed to other traditional ways of pickling, in which acidified boiling liquid is added to raw ingredients, escabeches call for cooking the ingredients in the vinegar marinade itself, and then letting them cool. In Latin America, this method is used to preserve everything from vegetables to meats, fish, chicken, and, of course, chiles. These preserved chiles are a little bit spicy, a little bit sour, and a little bit sweet. I learned to make them from my grandmother, who lived for several years in Mexico City. Ancho chiles are dried poblano peppers; they have a rich, chocolatey flavor with a hint of raisin. Whenever you purchase dried chiles, make sure that they are still pliable—a sign of freshness. If they're brittle, they're old. This escabeche keeps for up to six months in the refrigerator.

1 cup (240 ml) white vinegar

½ cup (120 ml) avocado or vegetable oil

4 ounces (120 grams) grated piloncillo or muscovado sugar

1½ teaspoons fine sea salt

¼ teaspoon dried thyme

1 bay leaf

4 ounces (120 grams) shallots, finely chopped

2 garlic cloves

4 ounces (120 grams) dried ancho chile peppers, stemmed, seeded, deveined, and cut into strips (about 2 cups)

Combine the vinegar, oil, piloncillo (or sugar), salt, thyme, and bay leaf in a small pot set over medium heat; bring to a simmer. Add the shallots and garlic and remove from the heat; stir well, until the sugar is dissolved. Add the chiles to the pot and stir well for 2 minutes so the residual heat can cook them; transfer them to a medium glass bowl. Let them sit at room temperature for 2 hours; transfer to a glass jar with a tight-fitting lid and chill until ready to use.

> **Tip** · Scissors are your best tools for seeding, deveining, and cutting dried chiles. Make a slit in the bottom tip of the chile and insert the point of the scissors. Cut the chile from the tip to the base of the stem. Open the chile up like a book; remove the stem and the ovary (the mound of seeds) by cutting it off with the scissors. With your fingers, remove the veins (they pull out easily). Cut or slice the chiles with the scissors.

Jalea de Chiles Secos y Ron Añejo

Rum and Dried Chile Jam

Guatemala and Mexico | Yield: 1 cup (240 ml) | Difficulty Level: Easy | Total Cooking Time: 15 minutes

Sweet and spicy, this is another recipe that I learned to make from my grandmother. Ancho chiles are rich in pectin, which helps to thicken this chunky jam. Don't skip the dried chicken bouillon—it's a classic ingredient in the Latin American kitchen—but if you have to omit it, make sure to add more salt. Serve this as part of a cheese course or on grilled meats.

2 dried ancho chile peppers, sliced

2 dried guajillo chile peppers, sliced

4 dried chiles de arbol or crushed red pepper flakes, about ½ teaspoon

½ cup (120 ml) vegetable oil

¼ cup (60 ml) dark rum, brandy, or whiskey

⅓ cup (75 ml) sherry vinegar

½ cup (115 grams) packed grated piloncillo or muscovado sugar

1 tablespoon chicken bouillon powder

With sharp scissors, stem, seed, devein, and slice all of the chile peppers into thin strips (see page 182). Heat the oil in a medium pot set over medium heat. Add the chiles and fry them for 15 to 20 seconds. Transfer them immediately (along with the oil) to a bowl and set aside. In the same pot, combine the rum and vinegar with ¼ cup (30 ml) water over medium heat, until heated through. Add the sugar, bouillon, and reserved chiles, cooking until the mixture thickens to a caramel (it will bubble and froth). Set aside and cool completely (the mixture will continue to thicken as it cools). Transfer to a blender and blend on high speed until it's as smooth as you like it (it will retain some texture from the dried chiles that will soften as time goes by). Transfer to a jar with a tight-fitting lid. This will last indefinitely in your refrigerator.

Note: Try this as a topping for vanilla ice cream; sprinkle crispy rice cereal and chopped peanuts over the top (trust me, it works)!

How to Fry Any Dried Chiles · Set the chiles in a dry skillet over medium-high heat; heat for 15 seconds on each side, just to make them pliable. Remove them from the heat; using scissors, cut off the stems. Seed and devein the chiles; use the scissors to cut them into rings or strips. Heat 1 inch (2.5 cm) of oil in a small pot; fry the chiles for 15 to 20 seconds or until just toasted (be careful not to burn them). Remove with a slotted spoon and let them drain on a plate lined with paper towels. The leftover oil can be used to flavor other dishes, in vinaigrettes, soups, or stews. Fried chiles make a great garnish for Mexican dishes where a little smokiness is desired.

How to Reconstitute Any Dried Chiles · Place the chiles in a large bowl and cover with boiling water. Place a heavy plate on top of the chiles to keep them submerged and soak them for 10 to 20 minutes. Drain the chiles over a bowl; reserve the soaking liquid for use in soups or sauces (or discard).

Geo's Crema de Chile Poblano

Creamed Poblano Soup

Mexico | Yield: Serves 4–6 | Difficulty Level: Easy | Total Cooking Time: 1 hour (includes roasting chiles)

Years ago, my dear friend Georgina and I would drop off our kids at school and head back home to cook together. This is one of the soups she taught me to make. The simplicity of this recipe does not hint at its smooth and elegant flavor, which, surprisingly, is not that spicy. The most time-consuming part is roasting and peeling the poblano peppers (see box below). I keep roasted poblano peppers in bulk in my freezer just so I can make this soup whenever I need lunch ready in minutes. The powdered chicken bouillon is important in this recipe, as it provides the exact degree of saltiness you want—substitute it only with bouillon cubes, if you must.

2 cups (480 ml) chicken broth

2 cups (480 ml) heavy whipping cream

1 cup (240 ml) whole milk

4 poblano peppers, roasted, stemmed, seeded, and deveined

2 tablespoons chicken bouillon powder

2 tablespoons (30 grams) butter, cut into small cubes

6 ounces (170 grams) cubed panela (or fresh mozzarella) cheese (optional)

Place the chicken broth, cream, milk, poblanos, and bouillon in a blender; blend until smooth, about 1 minute. Transfer mixture to a medium pot set over medium-high heat; bring to a simmer, keeping an eye on the soup so it doesn't boil over. As soon as it comes to a boil, lower the heat and simmer slowly for 10 to 15 minutes or until slightly reduced. Slowly, stir in pieces of butter (a few at a time), until melted. Serve the soup hot, topped with cheese, if using.

Note: If you like a thicker soup, make a Salsa Blanca Sencilla (page 24) and add it to the soup a little at a time, until it's thickened to your liking; or add 1 tablespoon of cornstarch to the blender at the start of the recipe.

How to Roast Peppers · Place whole peppers directly over the flame of a gas stove, turning them as their skins blacken. Alternatively, slice the peppers in half and place them on a baking sheet cut-side-down. Broil them for 5 to 7 minutes or until soft and charred. Resist the temptation to rinse roasted peppers while peeling them as you will wash their flavor off.

Sopa Seca de Fideos con Chipotle

Spicy Pasta Casserole

Mexico | Yield: Serves 4–6 | Difficulty Level: Intermediate | Total Cooking Time: 40–45 minutes

Here is a weekday pasta casserole that the whole family will enjoy: tomatoey, cheesy, and comforting, with a crunchy top and a creamy texture within. To tell you the truth, I found it funny when "one pot" pasta dishes started appearing all over the internet, as if they were a new invention, when both Peruvians and Mexicans have been doing it for more than a century. Latin American one-pot pastas are first sautéed (a Persian culinary influence) before they're plunged into bubbling sauces, where they cook until they're tender and have absorbed all of the juices. We call them sopas secas, which means "dried soups"; rice is also given the same treatment and name. My grandmother, who lived in Mexico in the 1950s, had a wide compendium of these kinds of sopas, which she made with differently shaped pastas and cooked entirely on the stovetop. However, it was my friend Diana Kennedy who first taught me to bake the pasta in a casserole dish for a few minutes before serving it, when I assisted as her sous chef in several of her classes. Here, I combine both methods. Fideos are very thin strands of pasta that are either cut into tiny pieces or wound into the shape of coils that resemble bird's nests; this recipe calls for the latter. Angel-hair pasta and vermicelli nests (such as those made by De Cecco) can be substituted easily. Don't skimp on the creamy toppings—they make the dish come alive.

One 28 ounce can (or two 14.5 ounce cans) diced tomatoes (regular or fire roasted)

1 cup (120 grams) roughly chopped white onions

2 garlic cloves, finely chopped

1–2 teaspoons of Pasta de Chipotle (page 12), or to taste

1 teaspoon dried Mexican oregano

½ cup (120 ml) vegetable oil

12 ounces (360 grams) fideos, vermicelli, or angel-hair pasta nests (coils)

1 cup (240 ml) chicken broth

1 teaspoon fine sea salt, or more to taste

½ teaspoon freshly ground black pepper, or more to taste

6 ounces (170 grams) shredded Muenster or chihuahua cheese

1–2 Hass avocados

1 cup (240 ml) Mexican crema or crème fraiche, or more to taste

2 tablespoons finely chopped fresh parsley, mint, or cilantro, for garnish (optional)

Grease a 9 x 13 inch (23 x 33 cm) casserole dish. Preheat the oven to 350°F (180°C). In a blender, combine the tomatoes, onions, garlic, chipotle paste, and oregano; blend until smooth. In a large pot, heat the vegetable oil and sauté the pasta until lightly toasted, about 1 minute or until it starts to turn golden, tossing constantly so it doesn't burn. Add the tomato sauce and stir, to prevent it from sticking. Add the broth, salt, and pepper; cover the pot, and cook over medium heat for 8 to 10 minutes or until the pasta has absorbed half of the liquid (the sauce will have thickened and the pasta will have softened; if using pasta "nests," they will still be al dente). Spread the pasta into the prepared casserole dish in one layer and cover it loosely with aluminum foil. Bake for 15 to 20 minutes or until the casserole is bubbly. Remove the foil, sprinkle the cheese over the top, and place it back in the oven for 5 to 8 minutes or until all of the cheese has melted. Halve, seed, peel, and slice the avocados; arrange them over the top of the casserole. Serve with crema and herbs, if using.

Note: Chipotle (or chilpotle) chiles are smoked, dried jalapeños. If canned, they're preserved in an "adobo" or marinade made with tomatoes, onions, vinegar, and spices. The sauce itself is spicy and smoky—absolutely delicious on its own, and usually added to recipes to enhance flavor. If you open a can and only use a few chiles, line a baking sheet with parchment paper and place each of the unused chiles, topped with some of the sauce, on it, keeping them separate from each other by about an inch. Freeze in one layer until solid. Transfer the solid portions to a freezer-safe bag or container; remove only those you need when a recipe calls for them. They last indefinitely in the freezer. Or make my Pasta de Chipotle on page 12.

Chiles Rellenos

Stuffed and Battered Peppers

El Salvador, Guatemala, Honduras, and Mexico | Yield: Serves 4–8 | Difficulty Level: High |
Total Cooking Time: 2 hours (includes roasting peppers)

Chiles rellenos, or stuffed chiles, are among the most beloved and popular recipes in the Latin repertoire. This is the classic Mexican version, covered in crispy batter and stuffed with cheese. If you stuff them with any of the picadillo recipes in this book, you'll have an example of the kind that most Central Americans serve in their homes. Making chiles rellenos takes a little bit of effort, but the technique is an easy one to master. These are best eaten right after frying but they can be frozen and reheated in the oven. They are traditionally served alongside refried pinto beans and rice, or stuffed into bread rolls with tomato sauce.

8 poblano peppers, roasted and peeled (see box on page 185)

15 ounces (430 grams) shredded chichuahua, blanco, or Muenster cheese

6 eggs, separated

Vegetable oil, for frying

Flour, for dredging

1 recipe Salsa para Envueltos (page 162)

Fit a cookie sheet with a cooling rack and set aside. Working with one poblano at a time, carefully make a slit in the side of each (from the top of the chile to the base, being careful not to tear it). Using scissors or kitchen shears, remove as much of the seeds and pod as you can, leaving the stem attached. Fill each chile with about ⅔ ounce (25 grams) of the cheese, until all the chiles have been stuffed. Place the egg whites in a large bowl (or in the bowl of an electric mixer) and whisk or beat until they form soft peaks; add the egg yolks, one at a time, beating well after each addition. The mixture should be very foamy and of a mousse-like consistency. Heat 2 inches (5 cm) of oil in a sauté pan with high sides, set over medium-high heat until it reaches 350°F (180°C) or a wooden spoon sizzles when it comes in contact with the hot oil. Working quickly, dredge each chile in the flour. Drop each chile into the egg mixture, turning with a large spoon to coat on all sides, and carefully slide them into the hot oil. Fry the chiles in batches of 3 or 4 until they're lightly browned on all sides. Drain on the prepared rack. To serve, plate each chile and cover with tomato sauce.

Cook's Tip: Divide and conquer! When it comes to cooking recipes that have several steps, it is sometimes smart to divide the tasks across two different days. For example, make fillings a day in advance and finish the recipes on the second day. If you've ever wondered how so many cooks who work all day have time to make sophisticated meals during the week, it's precisely because they follow this suggestion. I use this rule when I make tamales, empanadas, pies, rolls, or tarts, if the recipe allows.

ACHIOTE

When the conquistadores settled in the Americas, they brought with them the tradition of coloring their food, particularly rice dishes, with saffron, an idea inherited from the Arabs. However, saffron, the stigma of the *Crocus sativus* flower, was (and still is) the most expensive spice in the whole world, and did not exist in Latin America. What the Spaniards found when they arrived in the Americas, though, was that the Indigenous people dyed masa for tamales, broths for soups, and potato-based dishes a golden color with a seed they referred to as "onoto," "urucu," and "bija." The conquistadores must have felt as if they had struck gold.

Native to South America, the *Bixa orellana* bush is a perennial that produces flowers that go from white to pink to deep red. The red-ochre seeds, contained within the fruits, are called achiote, or annatto. To this day, there is no consensus about the name; depending on the country and the Indigenous group that controlled each area, it was known by different terms. Although most every Latin American speaks Spanish, we don't necessarily speak the same Spanish!

It is believed that achiote originated in the subtropical zone of Brazil, deep in the southwestern Amazon region. However, anthropologists and biologists have also discovered signs of its domestication throughout other areas of the Americas, all around the same time. Therefore, some believe that it's native to Mexico, while others adjudicate its origin to Peru. What we know for sure is that it was being cultivated and cooked with long before Europeans ever thought of circumnavigating the world.

Wherever they went, European conquistadores found achiote—whether as a condiment, mixed with other flavors such as sour orange, as the Maya did, or mixed with the leaves of the coca plant for medicinal purposes, as was done in areas of ancient Peru. Throughout the Latin territories, Indigenous peoples used the deep red seeds in different ways.

Achiote seeds were ground and made into pastes to use in food and color textiles, and to paint clay and ceramic vessels, as well as faces and bodies for different religious ceremonies. Achiote was one of the first spices transported from the Americas to Europe, where it was adopted as a colorant for fabrics and textiles, as an ingredient in charcuterie, as a pigment used in cosmetics, and as a new tint that artists could mix into their paint palettes. From there, it quickly made its way to Asia and was so widely adopted, that today, the Asian production of achiote is only second to that of Peru.

When it comes to its culinary uses, achiote lends different tones to dishes, turning them from pale yellow to dark red and vibrant orange. It is what makes margarine and butter golden, and what gives cheddar cheese, which is naturally white, its orange color.

In the contemporary Latin American kitchen, achiote is widely used for color in yellow rice; as a base color and flavoring for some kinds of seasoning bases, such as sofritos and recados; as a flavor additive in soups and stews; and as the main spice in classic dishes such as Cochinita Pibil (page 196).

Its taste is subtle. In fact, when it's used in small quantities, it is almost imperceptible. But when it's used in larger amounts, it imparts a slightly nutty, acrid, and acidic flavor that I can only describe as deliciously "rusty." Achiote is easy to find both in stores and online (see Sources), either in seed form, already ground into powder, or mixed with other spices into thick pastes (that are shaped into bricks). Be aware that achiote will stain your clothes (sometimes permanently), so use an apron to protect them. It will also stain your skin, so I recommend using gloves if you don't want to tint your fingers (I don't mind, and it washes off in a few days).

Achiote is a key ingredient in the food of most Latin American countries, including all of Mesoamerica, Cuba, Puerto Rico, the Dominican Republic, Brazil, Ecuador, Colombia, Venezuela, and Peru. Here I share a handful of the hundreds of recipes that incorporate achiote that you will find in Latin American kitchens.

Aceite de Achiote

Achiote Oil

Various Countries | Yield: Makes 1 cup (240 ml) | Difficulty Level: Easy | Total Cooking Time: 25 minutes

Achiote is the seed of the *Bixa orellana* plant, native to Latin America. The rust-colored seeds, found within brilliantly purple and fuchsia pods, are dried before their color can be extracted. Since ancient times, Indigenous peoples have used it not only for flavoring, but also to color textiles used to weave clothes, and as ink for manuscripts. The golden hue lent by this red oil, also known as aceite de color, is what distinguishes Latin American rice dishes from those that hail from Spain, where saffron is used instead. Many say that achiote doesn't taste of anything, but I disagree; to me, it carries a nutty, acidic, and almost "rusty" flavor in a balance that makes it very agreeable to the palate. This is the most basic of oils but one that distinguishes the dishes of many Latin American countries. Use it to start a pot of rice, to incorporate into sofritos, to give color to masa and other doughs, and to impart flavor to stews.

1 cup (240 ml) olive oil
or vegetable oil

2–3 tablespoons whole
achiote seeds

Heat the oil in a small pot over medium-low heat; add the achiote seeds and heat for 1 minute from when you first see small bubbles forming around the edges of the oil. Remove the pot from the heat (any longer and the seeds will burn). Let the oil steep for 10 to 15 minutes, then strain the seeds through a sieve set over a glass bowl or jar. Discard the seeds. The oil is now ready to use; if stored in an airtight glass container, it will keep at room temperature for 2 weeks.

Sofrito con Achiote

Achiote, Onion, and Tomato Sofrito

Various Countries | Yield: Makes 3 cups (720 ml) | Difficulty Level: Easy | Total Cooking Time: 30 minutes

This is a classic sofrito that the Latin Caribbean and Central America have in common. It's at the base of sauces for tamales, potato stews, and yellow rice dishes, such as the classic Arroz con Pollo (page 332). The combination of achiote and tomatoes gives the sofrito a deep red color; the addition of cumin gives it its signature taste.

1 pound (455 grams) plum tomatoes, very roughly chopped

2 cups (280 grams) very roughly chopped white onions

1 cup (115 grams) stemmed, seeded, and roughly chopped red bell peppers

5 garlic cloves

¼ cup (60 ml) vegetable oil

2 teaspoons ground achiote

1 teaspoon ground cumin

1 teaspoon fine sea salt

¼ teaspoon freshly ground black pepper

Place the tomatoes, onions, bell peppers, and garlic in the bowl of a food processor fitted with a metal blade; pulse until finely chopped (about ten to fifteen 1-second pulses), stopping occasionally to scrape down the sides of the bowl (or chop them very finely by hand). Heat the oil in a large skillet set over medium-high heat; add the achiote and cumin and cook for 30 seconds. Add the processed ingredients (being careful not to cut yourself with the blade), along with the salt and pepper. Stir and cook over medium-high heat for 4 minutes; lower the heat to low and continue cooking, stirring occasionally, for about 10 minutes or until the mixture is thickened. Remove from the heat. Use at once or freeze in ice cube trays (about 2 tablespoonfuls each) until solid, then transfer to freezer-safe containers. Keeps for up to 1 week if refrigerated or 8 months if frozen.

Cochinita Pibil

Cochinita Pibil

Yucatán Peninsula | Yield: Serves 8–10 | Difficulty Level: Easy | Total Cooking Time: 24 hours (includes marinating time)

This vibrantly rusty-red pulled pork stew is perhaps the most recognized dish from the entire Yucatán Peninsula. Pibil is traditionally cooked outdoors, in an earth oven called a "pib." I have always prepared it in a pot in my kitchen. It's a dish that is perfect for a weekend project. The secret to its deep flavor is the sour marinade, tinted and flavored with achiote, that also serves as the braising liquid. The banana leaves that cover the meat as it cooks also lend tropical flavor. This braise cooks slowly, lazily simmering over the stove, without any effort from the cook. Most of the time needed to make it is spent marinating the meat. Sour oranges (known also as Seville orange or naranja agria) are not easy to purchase fresh, but their juice is readily available in bottles, both online and in supermarkets (see Sources). At home, we eat this pulled pork with rice and beans, and I suggest you also try it as a filling for tacos, a topping for nachos, a stuffing for empanadas, and mixed with melting cheese to fill quesadillas. This recipe calls for achiote paste; the seasoned paste is shaped into bars that are easy to slice with a knife.

One 4 pound (1.8 kilogram) pork butt or shoulder, bone in

3 ounces (85 grams) achiote paste

2½ cups (600 ml) sour orange juice or a combination of half lemon and half orange juices

½ cup (120 ml) white vinegar

¼ ounce (8 grams) piece of Mexican cinnamon (canela) or one 4 inch (10 cm) stick

1 large bay leaf, cut into tiny pieces with scissors

2½ teaspoons fine sea salt

2½ teaspoons ground cumin

1½ teaspoon dried Mexican oregano

1 teaspoon freshly ground black pepper

½ teaspoon ground cloves

4 whole allspice berries

4 large banana leaves (available frozen in most supermarkets)

½ cup (120 ml) melted lard or vegetable oil

Place the pork in a large, resealable plastic bag. In a blender, combine the achiote paste, orange juice, vinegar, Mexican cinnamon, bay leaf, salt, cumin, oregano, pepper, and cloves; blend them until the mixture is completely smooth. Pour the marinade and the allspice berries over the pork in the bag; seal well and make sure to coat all the pork, turning the bag over several times. Place the bag in a large bowl and marinate the pork in the refrigerator for at least 8 hours, but preferably overnight (up to 24 hours), turning the bag occasionally to redistribute the marinade. When ready to cook, line a large Dutch oven with the banana leaves, making sure to leave a generous overhang. Remove the pork from the bag and place it in the Dutch oven; pour the marinade over the pork. Pour the lard and ½ cup (120 ml) water over the pork; cover it well with the banana leaves. Set the pan over high heat and bring the liquid to a boil. Cover the pan with a tight-fitting lid, reduce the heat to low, and simmer for 2½ to 3 hours or until the pork shreds easily with a fork and falls away from the bone. Remove the pork from the heat; transfer the meat to a separate bowl, leaving the sauce and the banana leaves in the Dutch oven. Using two forks, shred the pork and return it to the sauce; stir to coat.

Note: Mexican cinnamon is actually from Sri Lanka; known as canela de Celaya (Ceylon cinnamon), it is sweeter than the cassia cinnamon often used in baking, which is spicy and hard. By contrast, Ceylon cinnamon is soft and brittle, and can be blended without ruining the motor of a home blender. Do not try to substitute one for the other; if you can't find it, use ground cinnamon instead.

Pollo Guisado con Achiote

Chicken and Achiote Stew

Belize | Yield: Serves 4–6 | Difficulty Level: Easy | Total Cooking Time: 12 hours (include marinating time)

This saucy, piquant—albeit not spicy-hot—red chicken is a typical everyday stew in the homes of mis amigos Beliceños. Living in Guatemala for years afforded me the opportunity to taste many dishes from neighboring Belize. In my opinion, the tomato and achiote sauce in this recipe best captures the many flavors of the area where British, Maya, and Garifuna collided near the Yucatán Peninsula to create a vibrant culture. The simplicity of this recipe is beguiling to any home cook who wishes to deliver lots of flavor with ease. The key here is to give the marinade ample time to penetrate the chicken all the way to the bone—overnight is best. You could make this with deboned chicken, but then you'd lose the rich flavor and the collagen imparted by the bones. People unfamiliar with achiote may perceive it only as a food coloring, but it actually has an acidic, earthy flavor; in this recipe, where it is used in both the marinade and the sauce used to cook the chicken, it shines through clearly.

1½ cups (360 ml) Sofrito Rojo (page 21), divided

2½ teaspoons fine sea salt, divided

1 teaspoon freshly ground black pepper

1 teaspoon ground achiote

1 teaspoon cumin

½ teaspoon ground garlic powder

2 bay leaves

One 4 pound (1.8 kilogram) chicken, cut into 4 to 6 portions

1 pound (455 grams) white potatoes

2 tablespoons vegetable oil

Place ½ cup (120 ml) of the sofrito in a large resealable plastic bag (or in a bowl); add 1 teaspoon of the salt, the pepper, achiote, cumin, garlic powder, and bay leaves. Add the chicken pieces and stir well. Refrigerate and marinate for at least 8 hours (or overnight), stirring once or twice to make sure all of the chicken is coated. When ready to cook: Peel the potatoes and cut them into 4-6 large (2 inch/5 cm) slices each; set aside. Heat the oil in a large pot set over medium-high heat. Remove the pieces of chicken (discard the marinade) and brown them in the oil, turning until they're golden on all sides, about 4 to 6 minutes. Add the potatoes, the rest of the salt, the remaining sofrito, and 1½ cups (360 ml) water; bring to a boil. Cover, lower the heat to low, and simmer the chicken for 40 to 45 minutes or until cooked through (you'll know it's ready when the juices from the thickest part of the chicken run clear when pierced with a knife). Serve hot.

Note: If the sauce is too loose for your liking, remove the chicken and potatoes to a large, deep, serving platter and tent with foil. Raise the heat to medium-high and boil the sauce until thickened (being careful not to burn it). Return the chicken and potatoes (and any reserved juices) back into the pot; stir and serve.

How Achiote Is Sold · You will find achiote sold as whole seeds, ground into a powder, or pre-seasoned and mixed with oil before it's shaped into bars. Each has its own different use in the Latin kitchen; make sure to use the type of achiote specified in each recipe for best success.

Recado Chapín

Mayan Tomato and Seed Recado

Belize and Guatemala | Yield: 3 cups (720 ml) | Difficulty Level: Intermediate | Total Cooking Time: 40–45 minutes

Recados are pre-Columbian mixtures of tomatoes or tomatillos, dried chiles (usually, the guajillo, also known as chile guaque), and achiote. Alliums such as onions and garlic and sweet spices were added as seasonings shortly after the conquista and remain an integral part of the formula. Recados are usually thickened with pumpkin (known as calabaza or ayote) seeds, native to the Americas, or with sesame seeds, a later addition brought from Africa. Both are used in this version. The vegetables and the seeds are ground (or blended) into a loose sauce and cooked until thickened. Sometimes, recados are thickened further with a paste made with masa or masa harina, or by adding a bit of charred bread or corn tortilla to the mix, after which the sauce is blended a second time, until smooth. It sounds much harder than it actually is, especially if you use my quick blender method. Once made, this recado can be divided into individual portions, refrigerated for up to one week, or frozen for up to six months.

1½ pounds (680 grams) plum tomatoes, roughly chopped

1½ cups (170 grams) roughly chopped white onions

1 guajillo chile, seeded, deveined, and roughly chopped

2 garlic cloves, chopped

¼ cup (30 grams) toasted hulled green pumpkin seeds (see box on page 224)

¼ cup (30 grams) toasted sesame seeds (see box below)

1 tablespoon achiote paste (see Sources)

1½ teaspoons fine sea salt, or to taste

½ teaspoon ground cloves

¼ teaspoon ground allspice

¼ cup (60 ml) lard or vegetable oil

Place the tomatoes, onions, chile, garlic, pumpkin seeds, sesame seeds, achiote paste, salt, cloves, and allspice in a blender and blend on the highest speed until smooth (you may have to add a bit of water to get the motor running; if so, start with ¼ cup/60 ml at a time). Heat the lard or oil in a medium, high-sided pot over medium-high heat, then add the blended sauce. (Careful, it will splatter for the first 30 seconds, so stand back and use a long-handled wooden spoon to stir. Once you stir, it will stop sputtering.) Cover, lower the heat, and simmer the sauce for 15 to 20 minutes or until it thickens enough to coat the back of a spoon.

Uses for Recado · Wrap a piece of firm white fish (like cod or halibut), topped with recado and a few green olives, inside a large piece of parchment paper or aluminum foil, or in a banana leaf; bake it at 400°F (200°C) (or grill it over indirect heat) for 25 to 30 minutes or until the fish is flaky.

You can also use recado to top shredded poached chicken and serve over rice, or mix it into a pot of beans and make a stew. Mixed with a little chicken broth and cooked hominy, it makes an instant "posol," similar to the pozoles of Mexico but traditionally Guatemalan.

How to Toast Sesame Seeds · Place the sesame seeds in a dry skillet over medium heat, stirring until golden (I prefer a nonstick skillet, but any will work). Cooking time will vary depending on how many seeds you have to toast, so check constantly. A half cup (60 grams) of sesame seeds will take 2 to 4 minutes. Remove to a plate and let them cool completely before using.

Sazón con Achiote y Culantro

Achiote and Coriander Spice Mix

Puerto Rico | Yield: ½ cup (115 grams) | Difficulty Level: Easy | Total Cooking Time: 5 minutes

This is my go-to seasoning when I want to make a quick yellow rice. Mass-produced sazón (which means "flavoring") mixtures abound in supermarkets, but I am partial to this version, made without the addition of MSG and rich with the taste of coriander and achiote. I use it to add flavor to rice-and-beans recipes and to season meats, casseroles, and soups. The achiote lends a golden hue to all foods; feel free to substitute bijol, a Cuban condiment made of ground achiote, cornmeal, and cumin that is free of both MSG and gluten. I make my own achiote powder by grinding the seeds in a spice grinder until pulverized, but you can purchase it already ground.

1½ tablespoons ground cumin

1½ tablespoons garlic powder

2½ teaspoons ground achiote (or bijol)

2 teaspoons ground coriander

1½ teaspoons fine sea salt

½ teaspoon freshly ground black pepper

Combine all of the ingredients in a bowl and stir together well; transfer to a jar with a tight-fitting lid. Store for up to 6 months in a cool, dark place.

Tip: Help your spice mixes last longer by storing them in glass jars; add a food-grade desiccant silica gel pack, and they will keep without clumping.

Sopa Seca con Albahaca a la Chinchana

One-Pot Spaghetti with Achiote and Basil

Peru | Yield: Serves 4–6 | Difficulty Level: Easy | Total Cooking Time: 30 minutes

A quick meal, if there was ever one, here is a Peruvian version of one-pot spaghetti, like those that have become all the rage in the past decade. This is the way it's been made for more than a century in the Chincha province of Ica, in Peru. The ingredients may change slightly depending on the cook. Some use granular chicken bouillon in place of stock; others include a spicy touch of ají amarillo. Other recipes call for chopped vegetables, such as broccoli or carrots. What is de rigeur is the use of deep ochre oil made with achiote seeds (see page 194) and a hefty amount of fresh basil leaves—nothing else will do. If anyone ever tells you that Latin American food is complicated, make them this—it couldn't be simpler. It's traditionally served with the pork stew called carapulcra or as a side dish to Milanesas (page 42). Turn it into an easy main meal by adding cooked chicken or sautéed mushrooms at the end.

½ packed cup (15 grams) fresh basil leaves

4½ cups (1 liter) chicken stock (or broth), divided

3 tablespoons (45 ml) Aceite de Achiote (page 194), or vegetable oil

½ cup (60 grams) finely chopped red onions

1 tablespoon Pasta de Ajo (page 12) or 2 garlic cloves, very finely chopped

1 tablespoon ají panca paste

1 pound (455 grams) spaghetti, broken in half (to make into smaller strands)

½ teaspoon fine sea salt, or more to taste

Place the basil and 1 cup of the chicken stock in a blender; blend until it's completely smooth (about 1 minute) and set aside. Heat the aceite de achiote or oil in a large pot and set over medium-high heat; add the onions and cook, while stirring, for 2 minutes or until softened. Add the pasta de ajo or chopped garlic and cook for 20 seconds. Add the ají panca paste and the reserved basil sauce, mixing well; cook for 2 minutes. Add the spaghetti and the remaining broth; cook uncovered, stirring often, until the pasta is cooked through but still al dente, about 12 to 15 minutes (most of the sauce will be absorbed by the pasta). Season with salt and serve immediately.

Note: If you like your pasta more saucy, simply incorporate a bit more stock (or water) at the end, and stir until the sauce reaches your desired consistency. The amount of salt you need to season will depend on how much sodium is in your chicken stock to begin with; always taste and adjust at the end of cooking.

AVOCADOS

When was the first time you ate avocado toast? The craze that seduced the world in the early twenty-first century actually began in the Americas, millennia earlier.

Cultivated since 7000 BC, the avocado is native to Mexico, Guatemala, and the Antilles. Known as aguacate in Mesoamerica, its name is derived from the Nahuatl word *ahuacatl*, which meant "testicle," because of the way the oblong fruits hang in pairs. It is not hard to understand why avocados were once considered aphrodisiacs by the Indigenous peoples of the ancient American world.

Not all Latin Americans have the same words to describe ingredients. Once you cross over into South America, the avocado is known as *palta*, a Quechua word. The Palta peoples, who lived in the Andean highlands of Ecuador before the European conquest, spoke a language that developed from Arawakan. Although there is little that remains from this ancient civilization, the name for avocado pays homage to them.

There are more than five hundred varieties of avocados today; native avocados are still classified in varieties called "races." All avocados derive from the *Persea americana* family. Mexican avocados belong to the *drymifolia* variety; Guatemalan avocados, to the *guatemalensis* variety; and the Antillan to the *americana* variety.

Most of the avocados we eat today are hybrids. The most renowned is the popular Hass avocado, which has a pebbly, dark green skin. This is the one you find most often in grocery stores. Nevertheless, there are many other interesting varieties out there. These include the Criollo, with skin so thin, it can be eaten, and the Fuerte, which is almost as delicate. There is the Zutano, a smooth-skinned variety with a mild flavor (a Mexican-Guatemalan hybrid). The Guatemalan Reed is a large round avocado, easy to peel and very creamy. The Palta Edranol has a big pit, less flesh, and a very green skin. The Negra de la Cruz is a Chilean variety with purple-black skin; the Torres of Argentina is famously creamy, as is the Carmero, a Colombian avocado from the area of El Carmen de Bolivia. There is one called Bacon, with light green skin that is easy to peel off with your fingers. The Pinkerton has a longer, more oblong shape; the Carmen is pear shaped and similar to Hass, but its skin turns purple and black as it ripens. The Lamb Hass is like the Hass but with black skin. Israel has become a huge exporter of avocados, particularly of the Wurt and Nabal varieties, the latter with hard skin and flesh that sticks to the shell, making it perfect for stuffing. Among the largest are the Choquette avocados grown in Florida, which have flesh that is more watery than oily.

The pulpy flesh of avocados has long been used to make mollis (which mean "mixtures," also known as moles). The word *guacamole* actually means "avocado mixture"—so please don't make dips with green peas or sweet potatoes and call them guacamole! And since ancient times, Mexicans and Guatemalans have used avocado leaves—hojas de aguacate—as seasoning for beans, soups, and stews. The leaves have a mildly licorice flavor.

I always buy my avocados green, with sturdy stems still attached. I like to buy them a couple of days ahead of their intended use and place them on a sunny windowsill to ripen. Avocados ripen best at room temperature; if you wrap them in paper bags or newspaper you will speed up the process. Once ripe, avocados can be kept in the refrigerator for up to a couple of days.

Ancient lore has it that keeping the seed inside the avocado or putting it in the middle of a bowl of guacamole keeps the avocado from turning brown, but I don't believe that's true. When it comes to avocados, what helps to prevent them from oxidizing is the addition of an acid in the form of citrus juice or vinegar. Still, Guatemalan "guacamol" is traditionally served with the pits as garnish.

Leftover avocados can be stored in an airtight bag or container with a cut piece of onion (the gasses from the onion will prevent the avocado from turning brown) for 24 hours.

Some believe that the best way to eat an avocado is to wrap pieces in a freshly made corn tortilla. But I find nothing more delicious than to eat them like I did as a little girl: picked from the ground where they fell by the roots of the tree, sprinkled with sea salt (that I carried with me specially in a plastic bag), and squeezed right out of the skin. Think of this the next time you have avocado toast for breakfast.

How to Find a Ripe Avocado · Do you know how to truly know when an avocado is ripe? Yes, pressing slightly on the flesh to make sure it yields is a good start, but that alone doesn't work. I have a method that I call the "belly button test."

Avocados have belly buttons—the place where the stems meet the flesh. If you pull gently on the stem and it stays in place, the avocado is unripe. If when you tug at the stem it comes out easily, the avocado is ripe. But there is ripe, and then there is rotten, and when it comes to avocados this is a very fine line indeed. Here is where the belly button comes in: check the color of the flesh that peeks out at you from the indentation left by the stem. If it's yellow or bright green, your avocado is perfectly ripe. If it's brown, your avocado is overripe and growing roots inside. If you've ever made stringy guacamole, your avocados were overly ripe and past their prime. It only takes a day to go from a flawless avocado to a spoiled one.

Guacamol

Guacamol

Guatemala | Yield: Makes 1½ cups (360 ml) | Difficulty Level: Easy | Total Cooking Time: 20 minutes

You say "guacamole" and I say "guacamol." The different pronunciation is the first sign that this is the Guatemalan and not the Mexican version. Despite sometimes having the same meaning, Maya and Nahuátl words vary slightly. Such is the case of *mole* or *moli*, which mean "mixture." With time, *ahuacátl mole* became *ahuacamolli*; in modern times, it became *guacamole* in Mexico and *guacamol* in Guatemala. This is the Mayan version, much more acidic than the one from Mexico and made without tomatoes or chiles. Guatemalans like their guacamol smooth and simply garnished with a bit of oregano and, sometimes, cheese—it's all about the avocado. Some versions have onions, but garlic is almost never used.

3 Hass avocados

3 tablespoons (45 ml) freshly squeezed lime juice, or to taste

2 tablespoons finely chopped white onions

½ teaspoon dried Mexican oregano, divided

½ teaspoon fine sea salt, or more to taste

¼ teaspoon white pepper

Queso seco (feta is a good substitute), crumbled, for garnish

Split the avocados in half, and, using a spoon, remove the flesh—and save the pits. Place the avocado flesh in a large bowl. Mash the avocado finely with a fork until it's smooth. Add the lime juice, onions, half of the oregano, salt, and pepper; mix thoroughly. Place the pits of the avocados decoratively in the center of the guacamol. Sprinkle with fresh cheese and the remaining oregano.

El Guacamole de Don Mariano

Guacamole

Mexico | Yield: 2½ cups (600 ml) | Difficulty Level: Easy | Total Cooking Time: 15 minutes

Here it is: the classic guacamole recipe you are looking for. It was taught to me by Don Mariano Patiño Gonzales, the late father of my friend Georgina. He taught me that Mexican guacamole only has a hint of lime, that cilantro is best added at the end, and, most importantly, that no one should even bother adding chiles to the mixture if they can't take the heat; better to leave them out entirely than be stingy with them. There isn't a time when I make true Mexican guacamole that I don't think of Don Mariano. There may be plenty of other recipes for guacamole, but I never vary from the one he taught me.

3 ripe Hass avocados

½ cup (55 grams) finely chopped white onions

2–3 minced serrano peppers, finely chopped (see Note)

1 cup (170 grams) cored, seeded, and finely chopped plum tomatoes

⅓ cup (30 grams) chopped fresh cilantro , or more to taste(optional)

Freshly squeezed lime juice, to taste (just a smidgen!)

Fine sea salt, to taste

Freshly ground black pepper, to taste

Slice the avocados in half, remove and discard the pits, and scrape the flesh into a small bowl; mash it, leaving some chunks for texture. (Mexican guacamole always has some texture, according to Don Mariano!) Add the onions, chiles, tomatoes, and cilantro (if using) and mix well. Season with a few drops of lime juice, salt, and pepper to taste.

Note: Although Don Mariano insisted that guacamole should be spicy, you can remove the seeds and veins of the chiles and still get delicious flavor and crunch. That'll stay our secret!

Guasacaca

Venezuelan Avocado Salsa

Venezuela | Yield: Makes about 1½ cups (360 ml) (serves 4–6) | Difficulty Level: Easy | Total Cooking Time: 10 minutes

Here is the version of avocado sauce most beloved in Venezuela. It's made with vinegar in place of citrus, and although it's only a small change, the flavor profile of this salsa is completely different from the Mesoamerican renditions. This is more of a sauce than a dip, so make sure to add enough vinegar (or even a tablespoon or two of water) to thin it out to the right consistency. Caribbean sweet peppers (known as ajíes dulces) resemble habanero peppers, but without any of the fiery heat; I grow my own and keep them in my freezer so I can reach for them whenever I need them. They are not that hard to find in supermarkets nowadays, especially during the summer. However, if you have a difficult time finding them you may substitute them with a deveined and seeded jalapeño pepper, a sweet banana pepper, or more bell pepper.

2 ripe Hass avocados

2 tablespoons red wine vinegar, or more to taste

1 green onion, thinly sliced (white and light green parts only), about 2 tablespoons

2 tablespoons very finely chopped red onions

2 tablespoons stemmed, seeded, and very finely chopped red bell peppers

2 tablespoons seeded and finely chopped plum tomatoes

2 tablespoons minced fresh Italian parsley (leaves and tender stems)

1 ají dulce, seeded and minced or a seeded and deveined jalapeño pepper (for less heat)

½ teaspoon fine sea salt, or to taste

Pinch of freshly ground black pepper, or to taste

Slice the avocados in half; remove the pits and discard them. With a spoon, scoop out the flesh of the avocados into a medium bowl. Mash with the tines of a fork (it should retain very little texture, although some cooks like to leave a few tiny chunks). Add the vinegar, green onions, red onions, bell peppers, tomatoes, parsley, ají, salt, and pepper. Stir well. If it's too thick, add a bit of water or vinegar and stir well. Serve immediately.

Salsa de Aguacate

Avocado Salsa

Costa Rica | Yield: Makes 1¾–2 cups (420–480 ml), depending on the size of your avocados | Difficulty Level: Easy | Total Cooking Time: 10 minutes

This creamy sauce is the perfect accoutrement for ceviches, tacos, flautas, chips, and grilled fish, and can even be used as a salad dressing. Put it on all kinds of dishes, especially if they're spicy, as it'll tame the heat.

2 Hass avocados

¼ cup (60 grams) finely grated white onions

1 large garlic clove, finely chopped

Pinch of dried oregano (preferably Mexican)

2 tablespoons sour cream

Juice of 1 lime, or more to taste

½ teaspoon fine sea salt

Pinch of freshly ground black pepper

Slice the avocados in half; remove and discard the pits. Scoop out the flesh of each avocado using a spoon into a medium bowl. Mash the avocados. Add the onions, garlic, and oregano, sour cream, lime juice, salt, and pepper; stir well. Cover with plastic wrap and chill until ready to use.

Palta Reina de Atún

Tuna-Stuffed Avocadoes

Chile | Yield: Serves 3–6 | Difficulty Level: Easy | Total Cooking Time: 20 minutes

This elegant main course salad of tuna-filled avocados is a classic in Chilean homes, where avocados are known as paltas. The avocados are usually served in their skins, which act like bowls. Tuna is just one of the ingredients that can be transformed into a creamy, mayonnaise-laden filling, as it is in this recipe. Cooked chicken, seafood, and even potatoes are frequently substituted, which makes the versatility of these stuffed avocados ideal for everyday cooking. Stuffed avocados were all the rage in the 1970s country club scene throughout the Americas, and I recall eating them for lunch at the Mayan Golf Club in the outskirts of Guatemala City. In Chile, you are most likely to find them in homes, where cooks go all-out and decorate them with all sorts of garnishes: chopped roasted peppers or hard-boiled eggs, sliced olives, curly parsley, and capers are just some of the versions I've seen.

One 6 ounce (170 gram) can tuna packed in water, drained well and flaked

2 tablespoons finely chopped celery

2 tablespoons finely chopped onions (any color)

2 tablespoons seeded and finely chopped tomatoes

3 tablespoons (45 ml) mayonnaise

¼ teaspoon fine sea salt, or more to taste

Pinch of freshly ground black pepper, or more to taste

2–4 tablespoons freshly squeezed lemon juice, or more to taste

3 large Hass avocados

In a medium bowl, combine the tuna, celery, onions, tomatoes, mayonnaise, salt, pepper, and lemon juice; mix well. Halve and pit the avocados. Divide the tuna salad into 6 equal portions and scoop it into the avocados (mounding it where the pit used to be). Serve immediately.

VARIATIONS: Don't like mayonnaise? No problem; fill the avocados with freshly made ceviches, egg salad, or cooked shrimp dressed with Salsa de Country Club (page 31) instead.

Did you know? · Chileans eat the most mayonnaise per capita in Latin America.

Ensalada de Pollo y la Reina Pepiada

Chicken, Avocado, and Green Pea Salad

Venezuela | Yield: Serves 4–6 | Difficulty Level: Easy | Total Cooking Time: 15 minutes

This classic interpretation of chicken salad, a mixture of chicken and green peas in a creamy avocado dressing, is one that you'll find all over Caracas, the Venezuelan capital. In homes, it's served on lettuce leaves, but in the streets, it's offered as a filling for thick arepas (see recipe on page 104).

6 cups (680 grams) cooked and shredded chicken (page 27), or rotisserie chicken

2 Hass avocados

2 large garlic cloves, minced

1 cup (240 ml) mayonnaise

¼ cup (30 grams) chopped white onions

¼ cup freshly squeezed lime juice, or more to taste

1 cup (170 grams) green peas (fresh or frozen and thawed)

½ teaspoon fine sea salt, or more to taste

Pinch of freshly ground black pepper, or more to taste

Place the shredded chicken in a large bowl. Peel, pit, and slice the avocados; transfer them to the jar of a blender; add the garlic, mayonnaise, onions, and lime juice. Blend until smooth. Combine the sauce with the chicken, stir in the peas, and season with salt and pepper.

VARIATION: To make reina pepiada, a beloved arepa named after a 1950s beauty queen, and the most famous variation on this salad: Prepare 6 freshly made corn arepas as per the recipe on page 104. Place the arepas on a baking sheet and keep them warm in an oven preheated to 250°F (120°C) (they keep well for 30 minutes without drying out). Once the chicken salad is ready, slice each arepa lengthwise in half. Fill with a generous amount of the chicken salad on the bottom halves of the arepas; cover with the tops to make a sandwich and serve immediately.

Ensalada de Aguacate

Avocado Salad

Cuba | Yield: Serves 4–6 | Difficulty Level: Easy | Total Cooking Time: 20 minutes

This is an everyday salad on Cuban tables. The success of a salad—of any recipe, in fact—with so few elements relies on the quality of the ingredients you use. Perfectly ripened avocados have flesh that yields slightly when pressed; the tomatoes must be firm but juicy. I much prefer the creamy Hass avocados, but my Cuban-born and raised consuegra (my daughter's mother-in-law), Deysi Aguilera, always uses much larger Florida avocados such as the Pollock, Donnie, Lula, and Choquette varieties. Florida avocados have a meaty rather than creamy texture that makes them ideal to slice and chop; they also have less fat content and a milder flavor than the Hass. Use whichever you can find.

- ⅓ cup (75 ml) freshly squeezed lime juice
- ½ teaspoon ground cumin
- ¼ teaspoon garlic powder
- ¾ teaspoon fine sea salt, or more to taste
- Freshly ground black pepper, or more to taste
- ½ cup (120 ml) extra-virgin olive oil
- 2 large tomatoes (heirloom preferred), peeled and sliced
- 2 Hass avocados (or one Florida avocado), pitted, peeled, and sliced
- ½ cup (55 grams) very thinly sliced white onions

In a medium bowl, whisk together the lime juice, cumin, garlic powder, salt, and pepper. Slowly whisk in the olive oil. Place the tomatoes, avocados, and onions on a large platter; drizzle with the dressing and serve immediately.

Sopa de Aguacate

Cold Avocado Soup

Costa Rica | Yield: Serves 4–6 | Difficulty Level: Easy | Total Cooking Time: 75 minutes (includes chilling time)

Here is a cold and creamy avocado soup you can make in a matter of minutes. Avocados abound in Costa Rica all year round, and, in combination with a few other ingredients, they make a terrific first course. Incredibly refreshing, sopa de aguacate is ideal to serve on very hot days. To make it into a whole meal, serve the soup topped with tiny cooked shrimp or with poached or smoked salmon. If you want a soup with a thinner consistency, simply add a bit more broth. I like to top mine with homemade croutons or crumbled tortilla chips.

- 2 Hass avocados
- 2 cups (480 ml) chicken or vegetable broth
- 1 cup (240 ml) heavy whipping cream
- ¼ cup (60 ml) dry sherry
- ¾ cup (55 grams) very thinly sliced leek, white part only
- 2 tablespoons finely chopped white onions
- 1 garlic clove, finely chopped
- 1 teaspoon fine sea salt, or more to taste
- Pinch of white pepper, or more to taste
- 2–3 tablespoons freshly squeezed lime juice, or to taste

Halve and pit the avocados; scoop out the flesh with a spoon into a blender. Add the broth, whipping cream, sherry, leeks, onions, garlic, salt, and pepper; blend until smooth. Transfer the soup to a nonreactive bowl; season with lime juice, to taste. Cover well with plastic wrap and chill for at least 1 hour (and up to 6 hours).

VARIATION: Cut the broth and cream by half and add a pinch of cumin to transform this into a delicious dip for chips or boiled seafood (think crab legs, lobster, and scallops).

Pasta con Palta

Pasta with Avocado Pesto

Chile | Yield: Serves 4–6 | Difficulty Level: Easy | Total Cooking Time: 20 minutes

If you like pesto, just wait until you try this version made entirely with avocados. A no-cook sauce that's a cinch to make, this is one of my favorite recipes to teach in my cooking classes because it always delights and surprises with its creamy and subtle taste. In Chile, avocados come in all different sizes—from miniature one-serving fruits to some that are as big as my head. Some are watery, while some are as buttery as fresh lard. Make sure to cook the spaghetti before you make the sauce, which takes only a couple of minutes to assemble. Once prepared, this superb (and vegan!) sauce must be enjoyed immediately, as it will not keep for long.

1 pound (455 grams) spaghetti or fettucine

2 Hass avocados

½ cup (2 ounces/60 grams) walnut pieces

2 garlic cloves, chopped

2 tablespoons olive oil

1½ teaspoons fine sea salt, or more to taste

½ teaspoon freshly ground black pepper, or more to taste

Cook the pasta in a large pot of salted, boiling water, according to the package directions, until al dente. In the meantime, halve, seed, and remove the flesh from the avocados; place the flesh in the bowl of a food processor or in a blender. Add the walnuts, garlic, and oil; process or blend until smooth. As soon as the pasta is ready, reserve a cup of the cooking water; drain the pasta and place it in a large bowl. Toss it with the avocado sauce; season with salt and pepper, and serve. If the sauce is too thick, drizzle some of the hot cooking water that you reserved and toss again, until it reaches your preferred level of creaminess.

LA HORTALIZA

(THE VEGETABLE

When I was a little girl growing up in Guatemala City, there wasn't a single meal that didn't include loads of vegetables. Platters of buttered güicoyitos (round zucchini), creamed carrots, battered green beans, or steamed cauliflower were always present and, indeed, abundant. Despite stereotypes that have labeled Latin American food as unhealthy, the endless number of vegetarian and vegetable-based recipes says otherwise. In Latin America, they are always on the table. The array of seasonal vegetables is mind-boggling.

In Latin America, vegetable gardens are called hortalizas, huertos, or huertas. These are small parcels, usually in a home's backyard or adjacent lot, that are used to grow produce for a family or small community. And these gardens are not only for vegetables. Like a French potager, an hortaliza will often feature fruits, herbs, and flowers.

These include foods the Indigenous peoples of the Americas ate before they were conquered: wild greens, like chipilines, quelites, and verdolagas, that foreigners didn't recognize, and mushrooms, such as chanterelles, were also consumed in areas like Mesoamerica.

One of the greatest contributions that the Europeans brought to the American continents was the vast array of vegetables from the other side of the world: brassicas, which include broccoli, cauliflower, Brussels sprouts, and kale, that had been grown by Etruscans since the times of the Roman Empire, were introduced in the 1500s; and asparagus, native to Egypt and widely consumed by the ancient Greeks, and carrots, native to Europe and Southwest Asia. We know also that beets were brought over on Christopher Columbus's second voyage to the Americas. Fennel, salsify, spinach, lettuces, cabbages, onions, garlics, leeks, and so many more found their way onto the Latin American table toward the start of the 1500s. However, others, like radishes, cardoons, artichokes, capers, and cucumbers (really a fruit but widely accepted as a vegetable), made it to Latin America at the end of the sixteenth century. Other vegetables like broccolini, endives, and radicchio came later, during the European migration at the start of the 1900s. Hortalizas feature different selections of produce, depending on the country, and even neighbor to neighbor.

Truth be told, modern-day Latin foodways are made up of a vast number of vegan and vegetarian recipes. In fact, before the colonization, meat was only used as a condiment, much in the same manner as it is used in many Asian cuisines, where vegetables take precedence at the table. The diet of the Indigenous peoples included animals like deer, duck, fish, protein-rich insects, rodents such as tacuazines (possums) and cuy (guinea pig), as well as some reptiles (among them iguanas and turtles), but the mainstay of their diets remained squash, beans, corn, and wild greens.

These Novo American cuisines developed from a culture tied to the land; many Indigenous peoples, and many Latin Americans who live outside of metropolitan areas today, still grow their own food, whether in terraced gardens or in small vegetable patches, not only as a means to feed their families, but also as a way to make a living. Because of its vast size, the Latin terrain encompasses an area with a wide array of microclimates and soil microbiomes that make it possible to grow abundant flora.

In societies where beef and poultry can be expensive, protein- and vitamin-rich vegetables are an important source of nutrients. The fact that animal protein is more costly than vegetables also means that the majority of dishes that Latin American families consume are vegetable-centric, with protein coming mostly from beans and other legumes to which small portions of meat are added, when possible, for additional flavor.

In general, salads in Latin America are

very simple fare: a mix of lettuce greens, a handful of chopped vegetables, a mound of quickly pickled cabbage (curtidos), or a mixture of sliced tomatoes, onions, and avocado. We generally dress salads lightly with oil and vinegar and avoid gloppy, creamy dressings. Simple salads make frequent appearances on menus, especially during the lunch hour, as a side to asados or churrascos (centered around grilled meats, usually served outdoors, but not always), and in more recent years, as a meal in themselves (a North American influence).

Our salads may be plain, but when it comes to vegetables more broadly, the cornucopia of existing recipes is endless and terribly exciting. Vegetables are boiled, fried, sautéed, baked, stir-fried, braised, and stewed. While you may find eggplant breaded and fried in Argentina, you will encounter it sautéed and sauced in Chile, and roasted and pureed in Brazil. You'll find vegetarian noodle stir-fries in Peru, pasta dishes stuffed with vegetables in Uruguay, creamy vegetable soups in Ecuador, and delicate gratins in Costa Rica.

Mashed vegetables abound, as do mashed potatoes, on Argentinean, Peruvian, Guatemalan, and Chilean tables (see page 294), as well as the African-inspired fufús found on Cuban and Dominican menus. We douse vegetables in peanut, tomato, and cream-based sauces, depending on what is seasonal at the market, or we boil them (to death sometimes, which derives from the fact that it wasn't considered healthy to eat undercooked vegetables way back, and that way of cooking them remained ingrained in the tradition of many countries. Latin Americans love to transform vegetables into pickled delicacies called escabeches (see page 180) that can be made with peppers, fennel, mushrooms, cauliflower, and carrots (sometimes together, but often not). So if at any point you hear the stereotype that Latin food is all cheese laden and fried, you can now set the record straight and point out that many of the everyday dishes served in most Latin American homes are, in fact, vegetable based and healthy.

A visit to any marketplace on any given day in any Latin American town or city will prove my point. You'll find stall after stall mounded high with seasonal and local varieties of vegetable offerings: eggplants, lettuces, onions, leeks, purslane (verdolagas), spinach, kales, carrots, radishes, beets, peas, runner beans, turnips, kohlrabi, Swiss chard, celery, broad beans, green beans, arugula, cabbages, tubers, and more. This is nothing new. Markets date back to pre-Columbian times. In his *Letters from Mexico*, written to King Charles II, Hernán Cortés described "all kinds of green vegetables" sold in Mexican markets. Before the colonization of the Americas (and immediately after), tomatoes, sweet peppers and spicy chiles, squash, corn, cacao, quelites (wild leaves), and peanuts made up the vast majority of produce sold. With the arrival of the Europeans came the myriad vegetables they brought with them; however, the tradition of selling and going to market was already deeply ingrained long before the conquest. Today, modern grocery stores and state-of-the-art supermarkets with fancy produce sections can be found in large metropolitan areas throughout Latin America. However, they haven't replaced going to the market (mercado), which still remains a popular way to purchase fresh vegetables.

Among my first memories growing up in Latin America were visits to the Mercado Central in Guatemala City (which, sadly, burned down and no longer exists), where I was taught to barter with vendors for better prices, a tradition that is slowly disappearing but that was part of a ritual for shoppers throughout the Americas for generations. Both performed and encouraged by vendors, bartering was like a courtship dance, and allowed for a free market negotiation that satisfied everyone. Not participating meant offending the sellers. It went something like this:

"A cuánto la docena de tomates?" (How much for a dozen tomatoes?)

"A treinta centavos, para usted, mi reina." (Thirty cents, just for you, my dear.)

"Me llevo la docena si me la deja a veinte centavos, seño." (I'll take a dozen for 20 cents, ma'am.)

"No, muy poco. Te doy un tomate más,

si me das veinticinco." (No, too cheap, I'll give you one more tomato, if you give me twenty-five.)

"Vaya pues, me los llevo." (Okay, then, I'll take them.)

"Son los mejores tomates del mercado!" (They're the best tomatoes in the entire market!)

"A ver, si es cierto!" (We'll see if it's true!)

Traditions like this one are on their way to disappearing as modern-day grocery stores take over Latin American cities. However, the rich tradition of cooking vegetable-laden recipes will never disappear. Here is a collection of vegetable-centric recipes—recipes that celebrate the bounty of la hortaliza—found every day in the kitchens of people from Mexico all the way to Brazil.

A Land of Plenty · Just imagine how Europeans (and immediately after them, Africans brought by force) must have felt when, after weeks of journeying, hungry and exhausted, they finally set foot on land on which they couldn't recognize a single plant. Of the giant leaves and all of the wild vegetation they could see, which were safe to eat? Which were a source of nutrients and which were a death sentence? Starvation was at their heels, and yet, a single bite of the wrong thing could spell the permanent end to their journey on Earth.

They looked around, hungry, and yet they were not aware that they were staring at nature's succulence, a buffet of corn, beans, squash, pineapples, prickly pears (known as tunas), zapotes, guavas, jícamas, anonas, avocados, cacao, tomatoes, potatoes, papayas, peanuts, quelites (edible leaves), mushrooms, chiles, and so much more.

The conquistadores (and the people they enslaved) owed their survival to the generosity of the Indigenous people they were conquering, who showed them what was edible and what was not. This was particularly true during the first voyages to the Americas. After that, Europeans began to bring flora and fauna from their own lands: wheat, cilantro, citrus fruits, and many vegetables, as well as cattle and poultry, were introduced to Latin America from other countries.

The richness of what Latin America had to offer in terms of edible ingredients was vast, particularly when it came to agricultural products. Not only did the Mesoamericans domesticate corn, but as Charles Mann wrote in his book *1941*, "the inhabitants of Mexico and northern Central America also developed tomatoes, now basic to Italian cuisine; peppers, essential to Thai and Indian food; all the world's squashes (except for a few domesticated in the United States); and many of the beans on dinner plates around the world."

The Inca were great farmers. In fact, they were called "farmer-soldiers," because they would only leave their land to fight wars and then would return to continue their agricultural tasks. Spanish texts depict them as soldiers who were known to abandon a battle to go farm their lands. The Inca were renowned for their irrigation and terracing systems, still used today. In fact, it is estimated that before the colonization of the Americas, no other world civilization cultivated more varieties of plants. Vegetables were as prized then as they are now in Latin American foodways.

Cebollitas Curtidas

Pickled Onions

Mexico | Yield: Serves 4–6 | Difficulty Level: Easy | Total Cooking Time: 12 hours (includes pickling time)

These pickled red onions are beloved in the Yucatán Peninsula and throughout Central America, prized for their bright pink color, crunchy texture, and refreshingly sour flavor that cuts through the oil in fried foods and complements highly spiced dishes. Make them often—if you're like me, you'll develop a craving for them and will use them in sandwiches, salads, and on eggs. Make this recipe at least one day prior to serving it. I add garlic cloves to my version; you may remove them if you please but they are delicious sliced thinly after pickling and used as a topping for grilled meats.

3 cups (400 grams) very thinly sliced red onions

2 large garlic cloves, peeled and left whole

1 cup (240 ml) freshly squeezed orange juice

1 cup (240 ml) apple cider, pineapple, or banana vinegar

¼ cup (60 ml) freshly squeezed lime juice

1 teaspoon fine sea salt

2 sprigs fresh thyme (or ½ teaspoon dried thyme)

1 teaspoon dried Mexican oregano

5 allspice berries

5 whole black peppercorns

Set the onions and garlic in a large, nonreactive bowl (heatproof glass preferred). In a medium saucepan set over medium-high heat, heat the orange juice, vinegar, lime juice, salt, thyme, oregano, allspice, and peppercorns; as soon as the mixture comes to a boil, remove it from the heat and pour it directly over the onions and garlic. Cool completely to room temperature, stirring occasionally so all the onions and garlic are submerged; cover well and chill in the refrigerator for at least 8 hours or overnight.

Note: Keep these onions in a glass jar or in a plastic container; well sealed, they should last 2 weeks in the refrigerator.

Ceviche de Mango Verde con "Pepitoria"

Mango Ceviche with Pumpkin Seed Powder

Central America | Yield: Serves 4–6 | Difficulty Level: Easy | Total Cooking Time: 1–2 hours (includes marinating time)

In Guatemala and El Salvador, the season for mangos criollos, or small, green mangoes, starts in January and runs all the way into May. Street vendors sell chopped mango salad in plastic bags with toppings on the side, but I love this version, found all over Costa Rica, which is made with very thinly sliced mango (use a mandoline or a potato peeler to make the slices paper thin). If you don't live in Latin America, fresh green mangoes are available at Latin or Asian grocery stores. Sometimes you can also find them frozen or jarred.

1 pound (455 grams) small green mangoes (as green and hard as possible)

1 cup (60 grams) very thinly sliced red onions, soaked in cold water for 20 minutes

1 cup (240 ml) freshly squeezed lime juice

1 teaspoon fine sea salt, or more to taste

½ cup (90 grams) hulled green pumpkin seeds

Pinch of chile de arbol powder, or to taste

Peel the mangoes; use a potato peeler to remove the outer skin and discard, then continue peeling the flesh in long strips, working around the seed until it is all that remains (discard the seed). Place the mango strips in a large bowl; drain the onions and add them to the bowl. Add the lime juice and season with salt, to taste. Cover and chill in the refrigerator for at least 1 hour (up to 4 hours). In the meantime, place the pumpkin seeds in a dry, nonstick pan set over medium heat; toast the seeds, stirring constantly for 2 to 3 minutes or until they begin to puff up and develop a golden hue. Remove from the heat immediately and transfer to a plate, to cool completely; transfer them to a food processor (or spice grinder) and pulse them a few times until they are ground to a fine powder. Right before serving, toss the ground pumpkin seeds with the mango, sprinkle chile powder over the top, and serve at once.

How to Toast Pumpkin Seeds · Place the seeds in a dry skillet set over medium heat and toast until golden and puffed. Cooking time will vary depending on how many you have to toast, so check constantly. One-half cup (75 grams) of pumpkin seeds will take about 2 to 4 minutes. Remove to a plate and let them cool completely before using.

Ceviche de Palmito

Hearts of Palm Ceviche

Costa Rica | Yield: Serves 4–6 | Difficulty Level: Easy | Total Cooking Time: 1 hour (includes chilling time)

This is a completely vegan recipe that features the ubiquitous palmito (heart of palm), widely cultivated throughout Costa Rica. Ceviche doesn't have to be made with fish or seafood—the denaturation process caused by marinating in citrus can be applied to other ingredients, as with this variation found in homes throughout San José. Served as a salad, this refreshing, no-cook recipe is particularly prized during the hot summer season. Whenever I make it, it's gobbled up quickly, but you'll be happy to know that it will keep in the refrigerator for up to two days. Lizano sauce is a beloved Costa Rican condiment, similar to Worcestershire sauce; it can be found in Latin American stores (see Sources). Serve this ceviche with Plataninas (page 308) or with soda crackers.

5 cups (25 ounces/710 grams) jarred hearts of palm, drained well and sliced thinly

1 cup (115 grams) finely sliced red onions

1 jalapeño pepper, thinly sliced (seeded and deveined if less heat is desired)

1 cup (80 grams) finely chopped fresh cilantro

½ cup (120 ml) freshly squeezed orange juice

½ cup (120 ml) freshly squeezed lemon or lime juice

2 tablespoons ketchup

1 tablespoon Lizano or Worcestershire sauce

1 teaspoon fine sea salt, or to taste

¼ teaspoon freshly ground black pepper, or to taste

In a large bowl, combine the hearts of palm, onions, jalapeño, and cilantro. In a small bowl, whisk together the citrus juices, ketchup, Lizano or Worcestershire sauce, salt, and pepper. Add the marinade to the vegetables and stir well. Cover and chill for at least 1 hour (or overnight). Serve cold.

Curtido de Repollo

Pickled Cabbage Slow

Central America | Yield: Serves 6 | Difficulty Level: Easy | Total Cooking Time: 90 minutes (includes cooling time)

This healthy, tangy, crunchy, and very refreshing vegetable slaw is beloved in many countries and is to Latin cooks what sauerkraut is to German ones. *Curtido* means "pickled," and you'll find many variations throughout the Americas, from the onions of the Yucatán Peninsula (see page 223) to the spicy vegetables found on most Mesoamerican tables, to the beets of South America. More than a salad, this is an accompaniment to spicy or fried dishes such as doraditos, molotes, and chicharrones. In fact, it's so common in the coastal towns of Latin America that you will be pressed not to find a jar or two in every refrigerator. The basic ingredients of curtidos remain the same; the variations are found mostly in whether or not a recipe includes chiles, or on the type of vinegar used. Dark (negro) vinegar is preferred in Nicaragua, while banana vinegar is prized in Belize and Honduras. In the northernmost departamentos or states of Guatemala and in the Yucatán Peninsula, pineapple vinegar is valued. Other cooks will only use white vinegar. In other words, your favorite kind of vinegar (with the exception of balsamic, which is too sweet and way too dark) will work. If you love fermented foods such as kimchi, I suggest you try this and add a hefty amount of spicy chiles for a kick.

6 cups (800 grams) finely shredded green cabbage

1½ cups (115 grams) finely shredded carrots

¾ cups (115 grams) finely chopped white onions

½ cup (115 grams) stemmed, seeded, and finely chopped green bell peppers

1½ cups (360 ml) vinegar of your choice (see headnote)

2 tablespoons white granulated sugar

2 teaspoons fine sea salt, or to taste

5 whole black peppercorns

1 teaspoon dried oregano (Mexican oregano, preferred)

Combine the cabbage, carrots, onions, and bell peppers in a large glass (or nonreactive) and heatproof bowl. In a small pot set over medium-high heat, combine the vinegar, sugar, salt, and peppercorns with about ½ cup (120 ml) water, stirring until the sugar is dissolved. As soon as it comes to a boil, remove it from the heat and pour it over the vegetables, stirring well; set aside for 1 hour or until cooled completely. Stir in the oregano and combine. At this point, refrigerate, well covered, for at least 30 minutes or up to 2 weeks.

Curtido de Remolacha y Repollo

Pickled Beets and Cabbage

Guatemala | Yield: Serves 4–6 | Difficulty Level: Intermediate | Total Cooking Time: 2 hours (includes chilling time)

This sweet-and-sour slaw takes on a vibrant fuchsia hue from beets, making it one of the most colorful salads in the Latin repertoire. Guatemalans celebrate the Day of the Dead on November 1 with a composed salad called fiambre. This slaw often serves as a base for the red version of fiambre (there is a white version too), topped with myriad cold cuts, individually pickled vegetables of every kind, assorted cheeses, olives, sardines, and whatever else the cook has on hand. However, this slaw is also traditionally eaten as an everyday salad, on its own, or as a topping for tostadas embellished with pulled pork, cheese, and hard-boiled eggs, called enchiladas (for the chile sauce used to crown them).

2 pounds (906 grams) red beets, peeled and diced into tiny cubes

4 tablespoons (60 ml) vegetable oil

6 cups (540 grams) finely shredded green cabbage

1 cup (115 grams) finely sliced white onions

1 cup (170 grams) green peas (fresh or frozen and thawed)

½ cup (120 ml) distilled white vinegar

2 tablespoons white granulated sugar

1 large bay leaf

1 teaspoon oregano (Mexican preferred)

1½ teaspoons fine sea salt, or to taste

½ teaspoons freshly ground black pepper, or to taste

Place the beets in a medium pot; cover with cold water and set over medium-high heat. Bring to a boil, then reduce the heat slightly and boil until the beets are fork tender, about 6 to 8 minutes; drain and set aside. Heat the oil in a large Dutch oven set over medium-high heat; add the cabbage and onions and cook for 2 minutes or until the onions are translucent. Add the cooked beets, peas, vinegar, sugar, bay leaf, and oregano; simmer for 5 minutes or until the cabbage is soft, stirring often. Season with salt and pepper. Cool completely; remove the bay leaf and discard. Transfer the curtido to a nonreactive bowl; chill for at least 2 hours (and up to 1 week).

Note: You will need 2 pounds of raw beets to get 6 cups diced. When working with beets, I use disposable plastic gloves or a plastic bag to protect my skin from staining. It's much neater to cut the beets before cooking them than the other way around; plus, chopped beets cook much faster than whole ones. Use canned beets, if desired.

Did you know? · In Guatemala, the word *fiambre* refers to composed salads served only for Day of the Dead celebrations. However, in Argentina, the term means cold cuts such as ham, mortadella, sausages, paté, charcuterie, and salami—all of which can also be found in a Guatemalan fiambre.

Rábanos en Curtido

Quick Pickled Radishes

Various Countries | Yield: Serves 4–6 | Difficulty Level: Easy | Total Cooking Time 2 hours (includes cooling time)

There are many types of quick pickles, called curtidos, in the Latin repertoire that do not require great planning or any special equipment; this is one of them. You can eat these radishes after a couple of hours, but they will last up to one week in the refrigerator. Big radishes tend to be fibrous and bitter; tiny radishes are sweet and smooth. Thus, the only important rule to keep in mind is to always use the freshest radishes when they're still small. I grow my own every year in my garden, but if you purchase them, make sure to select radishes that are vibrantly colored (with so many varieties you can pick any color you wish, although traditionally, we use the red ones) and smooth skinned, with perfectly crunchy flesh. These pickles are normally prepared with white distilled vinegar, but over the years I have come to love the more nuanced flavor of other types of vinegar such as rice, apple cider, white balsamic, or wine vinegars; use whichever one you prefer (except dark balsamic vinegar, which is too dark and will stain the radishes an off-color).

1 pound (455 grams) small radishes, washed, debearded, and thinly sliced (about 4½ cups)

1 cup (240 ml) rice wine vinegar (or white wine, white balsamic, or apple cider vinegar)

¼ cup (50 grams) white granulated sugar

1 tablespoon fine sea salt

1 teaspoon anise seeds

Place the sliced radishes in a nonreactive bowl or glass jar and press them down tightly. In a small pot, combine the vinegar, sugar, salt, and anise seeds; place over low heat, and stir until all of the sugar and salt are dissolved and the vinegar is warm to the touch (but not boiling). Pour this over the radishes and cover tightly with plastic wrap (or with the lid of the jar, if using). Let them sit at room temperature for 1 hour. Transfer to the refrigerator and chill for at least 1 hour or up to 1 week.

Encurtido Nikkei

Nikkei Pickled Slaw

Peru | Yield: Serves 4–6 | Difficulty Level: Easy | Total Cooking Time: 1 hour

Crunchy, sweet, salty, sour, and spicy flavors intermingle in this classic red cabbage slaw. *Nikkei* is the term given to the culinary fusion of Peruvian and Japanese flavors. Japanese laborers arrived in Peru in the late 1880s to work on sugar and cotton farms. By the 1930s, more than 30,000 Japanese nationals had settled in Peru. Japanese ingredients such as soy sauce (sillao or shoyu), garlic, and ginger (kion) are pantry essentials in Peruvian homes and are often married with Incan ingredients like ajíes such as amarillo, rocoto, and limo, and with potatoes. This is a recipe born from this culinary movement, easy to re-create at home.

- 3 cups (910 grams) thinly sliced red cabbage
- 3 cups (910 grams) thinly sliced green cabbage
- 3 cups (455 grams) finely shredded carrots
- 3 tablespoons (45 ml) rice wine vinegar
- 2 tablespoons vegetable oil

- 1 tablespoon soy sauce
- 1 tablespoon toasted sesame seed oil
- 2 teaspoons white granulated sugar
- One ½ inch (12 mm) piece fresh ginger root, peeled and grated
- 1 teaspoon ají amarillo paste (optional)

- Pinch of fine sea salt, or to taste
- Pinch of freshly ground black pepper, or to taste
- ⅓ cup (40 grams) chopped unsalted roasted peanuts
- ½ cup (60 grams) chopped unsalted cashew nuts
- ¾ cup (50 grams) sliced green onions, about

In a nonreactive bowl, toss together the red cabbage, green cabbage, and carrots. In a separate bowl, combine the vinegar, vegetable oil, soy sauce, sesame seed oil, sugar, ginger root, and ají amarillo paste (if using), whisking well; taste and season with salt and pepper. Add the vinaigrette to the slaw and toss well. Let the slaw sit at room temperature for 15 minutes, before covering with plastic wrap and chilling (for at least 30 minutes or up to 24 hours). Right before serving, stir in the peanuts and cashews; toss to combine, sprinkle with the green onions, and serve.

Salpicón de Jícama, Pepino y Aguacate

Jícama, Cucumber, and Avocado Salad

Mexico | Yield: Serves 4–6 | Difficulty Level: Easy | Total Cooking Time: 20 minutes

Salpicones are thirst-quenching chopped salads made from leftover boiled meats, potatoes, or a mix of fruits and vegetables that are marinated in bitter orange or other citrus, or vinaigrettes, as in this version from Mérida. I have always favored those made with crunchy jícama (pronounced *hee-kah-mah*), a tuberous root, also called Mexican turnip, with a texture similar to a pear but with a milder flavor that takes on any seasoning. You could dress this salpicón with any citrus juice, but in my home, I like it with my Vinagreta de Albahaca (page 33), which brings out the natural sugars in the vegetables. Try to chop all of the ingredients the same size so as to make a visually appealing salad. Always select firm, unblemished jícamas that are smooth and a light tan color so when you cut into the flesh you find it white, and crisp. The easiest way to peel a jícama is to use a sharp knife; remove both top and bottom to flatten, and then peel the sides as you would an orange, moving the knife from top to bottom. The skin is thin, so be careful not to peel off too much flesh as you go; a potato peeler works well, if sharp. Once peeled and cut into pieces, submerge the jícama in water; kept well chilled, in a covered container, jícama should last up to 4 days, retaining its color and crunch.

1 large jícama (1 pound/455 grams), peeled and cut into small cubes

1 cucumber (8 ounces/225 grams), cut into small cubes

1½ cups (170 grams) stemmed, cored, seeded, and diced sweet bell peppers (any color)

1–2 Hass avocados, halved, seeded, peeled, and cut into small cubes

1 small serrano chile, finely chopped

1 recipe Vinagreta de Albahaca or 1 cup (240 ml) freshly squeezed lime juice

Salt, to taste

Place the jícama, cucumbers, peppers, avocado, and chile in a large bowl; dress liberally with the vinaigrette or lime juice. Season with salt, to taste. Chill well before serving.

Note: This keeps in the refrigerator for up to 2 days. If you think you'll keep it for longer (up to a week), then add the avocado only before you serve it or omit it altogether.

Ensalada de Verdes y Palta con Vinagreta Nikkei

Greens Salad with Avocado and Nikkei Vinaigrette

Peru | Yield: Serves 4–6 | Difficulty Level: Easy | Total Cooking Time: 20 minutes

This is one of my favorite salads to serve when I have company, because of its colorful appearance. The dressing combines Japanese, African, and Peruvian ingredients that collided over time to produce Nikkei, one of the most exciting cuisines in Latin America. To make it a main meal, I recommend adding grilled shrimp, chicken, or tofu.

1 pound (455 grams) washed mixed lettuces or greens

1 cup (145 grams) grape tomatoes, each sliced in half

½ cup (115 grams) thinly sliced red onions

¼ cup (60 ml) white vinegar

½ cup (120 ml) olive oil

2 teaspoons soy sauce

½ cup (55 grams) toasted sesame seeds (see box on page 198)

⅓ cup (75 ml) freshly squeezed lemon or lime juice

½ cup (115 grams) roughly chopped yellow onions

1 teaspoon fine sea salt, or to taste

½ teaspoon freshly ground black pepper, or to taste

1–2 Hass avocados

1 recipe Canchita (page 50) (optional)

Place the greens, tomatoes, and red onions in a large salad bowl and set aside. In the jar of an electric blender, place the vinegar, oil, soy sauce, and sesame seeds; blend on high for 30 seconds. Add the lemon juice and white onions, and blend on high for 1 to 2 minutes or until the mixture is smooth. Taste and add salt and pepper as needed. Halve, pit, and scoop out the flesh of the avocados; dice and add them to the salad. Drizzle the salad with dressing, toss, and serve immediately. Garnish with the canchita corn nuts, if using, for a touch of crunch.

Ensalada Completa

Composed Salad

Argentina | Yield: Serves 4–6 | Difficulty Level: Easy | Total Cooking Time: 20 minutes

This is my version of the salad commonly enjoyed by many Argentineans, typically served individually plated. It usually comes together serendipitously, with whatever ingredients are on hand. It's what most salads look like in Latin America. Not including it would be like forgetting to add a garden salad or a Caesar salad in an American cookbook. Some cooks add marinated mushrooms, roasted peppers, or a bit of tuna (the kind packed in oil). The vinaigrette is usually offered in a carafe, on the side. At home, I like to place all the ingredients in separate little dishes and let guests serve themselves salad bar style, as everyone pleases. You'll notice that the amounts I give you here are not precise; use it as a template to make your own. Think of including watercress, slices of fresh leeks, onions of any color, chunks of hearts of palm, cooked beets, cubed provolone, or whatever else suits your fancy.

1 washed and torn head of lettuce (iceberg, romaine, or any fresh, local variety)

Hard-boiled eggs, quartered (one half per person)

2 small new potatoes, boiled and halved, per person

Shredded carrots

Thinly sliced shallots or sweet onions

English cucumber, seeded and sliced thinly

Grape tomatoes

Green or black olives

Canned or marinated artichoke hearts, halved (two halves per person)

Freshly ground black pepper, to taste

Vinaigreta Básica (page 32), or any dressing of your choice

Arrange all of the ingredients attractively on a platter or on individual plates. Dress liberally with vinaigrette and serve immediately.

Ensalada de Coditos

Macaroni Salad

Various Countries | Yield: Serves 6–8 | Difficulty Level: Easy | Total Cooking Time: 2 hours (includes chilling time)

It may seem like a stretch to include this as part of a chapter on vegetables, but coditos—which means "elbows"—and macaroni salads are a mainstay in the kitchens of Guatemalan, Salvadorian, and Honduran cooks, and this book would be incomplete without them. As pasta salads go, creamy and citrusy versions like this one can be truly considered Latin American; children carry it in their lunchboxes, and cafeterias that specialize in home-style food feature it on their menus. Mayonnaise has been a key ingredient in Latin America since the 1700s, when homemade versions were the norm. Once factory-made mayonnaise arrived on the scene in the 1930s, it became the rage; cooked meats, potatoes, and pasta became a canvas for mayonnaise-based dressings. Use bell peppers of any color—have fun playing with red, yellow, orange, or green varieties. Other traditional additions include cubed ham, flaked tuna, green peas, sliced green onions, olives, and chopped eggs.

1 cup (240 ml) mayonnaise

¼ cup (60 ml) crema, crème fraiche, or sour cream

¼ cup (30 grams) finely chopped onions (any color)

1 garlic clove, finely chopped (or ¼ teaspoon garlic powder)

¼ cup (60 ml) freshly squeezed lime juice, or to taste

1 teaspoon fine sea salt, or to taste

½ teaspoon freshly ground black pepper, or to taste

1 pound (455 grams) elbow-shaped pasta (macaroni), cooked, rinsed under cold water, and drained

¾ cup (145 grams) stemmed, seeded, and finely chopped bell peppers

1 cup (145 grams) thinly sliced celery

¼ cup (20 grams) finely chopped fresh Italian parsley

Paprika or pimentón, for garnish (optional)

In a large bowl, whisk together the mayonnaise, crema, onions, garlic, lime juice, salt, and pepper, until thoroughly combined. Stir in the cooked macaroni, peppers, celery, and parsley. Cover and chill for at least 30 minutes (or overnight). Right before serving, sprinkle with paprika, if using.

Note: Cold foods benefit from having their seasonings adjusted right before serving, as the cold suppresses our perception of salty and sour flavors. For this reason, I always recommend that you taste cold, mayonnaise-based salads before serving them and adjust the salt and lime juice, to taste.

Salada de Cuscuz e Verduras

Vegetable and Couscous Salad

Brazil | Number of Servings: 4–6 | Difficulty Level: Easy | Total Cooking Time: 45 minutes (includes chilling time)

Couscous is a tiny North African semolina granule (from the Berbere peoples) that cooks like pasta and makes a great backdrop to many vegetables. In São Paolo, this is a classic pasta-style salad, full of vegetables, and in most Brazilian churrascarías (steakhouses) it is often part of the offerings in enormous salad bars. Couscous made its way to Brazil with enslaved Africans and later again with the Lebanese that settled in large numbers in the late 1800s and early 1900s. It's no wonder that it's imprinted on the cuisine of this South American country—the largest in the entire territory. Couscous has been precooked, so it only needs to be steamed in very hot liquid in order to be reconstituted, making this a superb, no-cook recipe. Plan to give this salad some time to chill before serving it. To make it vegan, omit the chicken broth and use water instead.

½ cup (120 ml) extra-virgin olive oil

¼ cup (60 ml) freshly squeezed lemon juice, or more to taste

2 large garlic cloves, very finely chopped

1 teaspoon fine sea salt, or to taste

½ teaspoon freshly ground black pepper, or to taste

2 cups (310 grams) couscous

3 cups (720 ml) boiling chicken stock (or water)

1½ cups (225 grams) chopped and seeded plum tomatoes

Half of a seedless English cucumber, unpeeled and chopped (about 1¼ cups) (see Note)

½ cup (35 grams) sliced green onions (white and green parts)

⅓ cup (30 grams) chopped fresh mint leaves

2 tablespoons drained capers

10 pitted black olives, sliced or chopped

In a small, nonreactive bowl, whisk together the olive oil, lemon juice, garlic, salt, and pepper; set aside. Place the couscous in a large bowl and pour the stock (or water) over it; cover the bowl with a plate (or plastic wrap) and let it stand until all of the stock has been absorbed (about 10 minutes). Fluff the couscous with a fork; set aside to cool, about 20 minutes. In a large bowl, combine the tomatoes, cucumber, green onions, mint, capers, and olives. Add the cooled couscous to the vegetable mixture. Drizzle the entire salad with the dressing, mixing to combine it thoroughly. Cover and chill the salad in the refrigerator for at least 30 minutes (and up to 24 hours) before serving.

Note: Any type of cucumber will work in this recipe, as long as you remove the seeds (where the bitterness is hidden). I prefer English cucumbers because their seeds are sweet and almost nonexistent, making it unnecessary to remove them.

Ensalada de Coliflor

Cauliflower Salad

Various Countries | Yield: Serves 4–6 | Difficulty Level: Easy | Total Cooking Time: 30 minutes

This is a perfect example of how a few ingredients tossed together can create formidable flavor. Each bite is an explosion of juxtaposing tastes and textures: sour, piquant, smooth, creamy, and crunchy. I prefer to let it marinate overnight and allow the flavors to blend, but it can be enjoyed shortly after mixing. Tear the cauliflower florets with your fingers and make them as small as you can by cutting off the cores—you want them to be bite-sized.

3 cups (680 grams) cauliflower cut into tiny florets

2 green onions, thinly sliced (about ½ cup/35 grams)

1 cup (170 grams) stemmed, seeded, and finely chopped red bell peppers

½ cup (120 ml) mayonnaise

2 tablespoons white wine vinegar

1 large garlic clove, finely chopped

¼ cup (20 grams) finely chopped fresh parsley, or to taste

½ teaspoon fine sea salt, or to taste

½ teaspoon freshly ground black pepper, or to taste

Wash the cauliflower florets in a fine strainer under cold running water; drain very well and place them in a large bowl with the green onions and bell peppers. In a medium bowl, whisk together the mayonnaise, vinegar, garlic, parsley, salt, and pepper until combined. Pour the dressing over the cauliflower and stir to coat; chill for at least 20 minutes (or up to overnight) to allow the flavors to blend.

Ensalada de Pepinos en Anillos y Perejil

Parsleyed Cucumber Salad

Various Countries | Yield: Serves 4–6 | Difficulty Level: Easy | Total Cooking Time: 1 hour (includes marinating time)

This is a refreshing, crunchy, and flavorful salad that goes well with any meal. Fermented or long-pickled cucumbers are not traditional in Latin America, but we do love them quickly marinated in vinaigrettes. Some cucumber seeds can be bitter, especially if they are large; for this reason, I prefer to remove them entirely. I love English cucumbers, because the seeds are not bitter. This salad, however, is prettier when the cucumbers are seeded so use an apple corer or a small spoon to help you do so.

¼ cup (60 ml) freshly squeezed lime or lemon juice

1 tablespoon red wine vinegar

1 teaspoon white granulated sugar

1 teaspoon fine sea salt, or to taste

¼ teaspoon white pepper, or to taste

2 tablespoons extra-virgin olive oil

2 large (620 grams) English cucumbers, peeled, seeded, and sliced

¼ cup (60 grams) finely chopped red onions

⅓ cup (30 grams) finely chopped fresh Italian parsley (leaves and tender stems), or more to taste

In a large bowl, combine the lime or lemon juice, vinegar, sugar, salt, and pepper; stir well. Slowly, whisk in the olive oil. Toss the sliced cucumbers, onions, and parsley with the vinaigrette; let the salad sit at room temperature for at least 20 minutes (and up to 1 hour), stirring occasionally. Chill until ready to serve.

Ejotes Verdes

The Greenest of Green Beans

Various Countries | Yield: Serves 4–6 | Difficulty Level: Easy | Total Cooking Time: 8–10 minutes

Guatemala is one of the largest producers of pencil-thin green beans, known in French as haricot verts, and I grew up eating them. Green beans are beans with edible pods native to Mexico, Central America, and South America. Here is the way I was taught to cook them long ago by Felipa, my grandmother's home chef, so the beans preserve their brilliant verdant hue instead of turning a grayish color. The secret is a pinch of baking soda added to the water. It seems like such a simple recipe to give you, but it is a classic vegetable served throughout the Americas that every cook should learn to cook well. You can use other green beans, and adapt the cooking time depending on how thick they are. I opt to leave the green beans whole; if cut into juliennes, they will be ready on the shorter end of the time frame noted above. Latin Americans like their beans to be tender—not soft, mushy, nor al dente, but somewhere in the middle. Throughout the region, green beans are also known as vainas, vainitas, judías verdes, habichuelas verdes, porotos verdes, vainicas, and alubias. In Guatemala they're called ejotes (not to be confused with elotes, which are corncobs).

2 pounds (890 grams) green beans, preferably haricot verts

¼ teaspoon baking soda

2 tablespoons unsalted butter

½ teaspoon fine sea salt

Place the green beans in a medium pot; cover with cold water and stir in the baking soda. Bring the pot to a boil over medium-high heat; cook the beans, uncovered, at a rolling boil, until they are tender, about 8 to 10 minutes. Strain the beans and transfer them to a platter; toss them with butter and salt and serve immediately.

Vainas Guisadas

Green Bean Stew

Dominican Republic | Yield: Serves 4–6 | Difficulty Level: Easy | Total Cooking Time: 15 minutes

Green beans swim in a light and slightly tangy red sauce in this typical everyday side dish. All you need to know is that the best green beans to use for this recipe are thin, stringless varieties and that any color will do. Since these are meant to cook rapidly, avoid the long-cooking types or flatter green beans such as romanos. I prefer to select the pencil-thin haricot verts, which I grew up with in Central America, but really, use what you know will cook quickly. In a pinch, since these are stewed, use frozen; no one will know and I won't tell. This dish can be prepared ahead of time and reheated right before serving, served at room temperature, or eaten cold.

2 tablespoons vegetable oil

1 cup (120 grams) finely chopped yellow onions

1 garlic clove, finely minced

3 tablespoons (45 ml) tomato paste

1 pound (455 grams) green beans such as haricot verts, washed, trimmed, and julienned

1 teaspoon fine sea salt

2 teaspoons white vinegar

Heat the oil in a large skillet over medium-high heat; add the onions and garlic and cook, while stirring, for 1 to 2 minutes or until softened, but don't let them take on any color; if necessary, lower the heat. Add the tomato paste and ½ cup (120 ml) water and stir until dissolved. Add the green beans, salt, and vinegar; cover, lower the heat to low, and simmer for 8 to 10 minutes or until the beans are tender.

Note: If the beans are too soupy for your taste, just uncover and increase the heat until the sauce has thickened slightly. If the sauce is too thick, add a couple more tablespoons of water and stir.

Zanahorias con Crema

Creamed Carrots

Various Countries | Yield: Serves 4–6 | Difficulty Level: Easy | Total Cooking Time: 20 minutes

Simple flavors are sometimes the most elegant, as is the case of this side dish in which sweet carrots are coated in a golden sauce. Many of the home cooks I've talked to mentioned recipes similar to this one; it is a favorite in Guatemala, Honduras, El Salvador, and Chile. Some cooks finish it with grated orange zest, Parmesan cheese, or freshly grated nutmeg at the very end. This is best served immediately after adding the cream (the sauce breaks when reheated). If you prefer, the carrots may be cooked in advance and heated through when you add the cream.

3¼ cups (455 grams) carrots, peeled and cut into ¼ inch (12 mm) slices

2 tablespoons unsalted butter

¾ cup (180 ml) heavy whipping cream

½ teaspoon fine sea salt, or to taste

¼ teaspoon white pepper, or to taste

2 tablespoons finely chopped fresh parsley (optional)

Place the carrots in a medium pot and fill it with cold water; set over medium-high heat. Bring to a boil; lower the heat and simmer, uncovered, for 6 to 7 minutes or until the carrots are just fork tender but still have a little bite. Drain the carrots in a colander and return them to the pot; set the heat back to medium-high. Add the butter, cream, salt, and pepper. Bring back to a boil and cook for 3 to 4 minutes or until the cream has thickened. Sprinkle with parsley (or with any other garnish you want), and serve immediately.

Anacates con Crema

Chanterelles in Cream Sauce

Guatemala | Yield: Serves 4–6 | Difficulty Level: Easy | Total Cooking Time: 20 minutes

Many of my friends, some of them world-renowned chefs, are surprised when I tell them that chanterelles (*Cantharelus cibarius*) are very popular in Guatemala and that I grew up eating them regularly. They assume that they are a uniquely French ingredient and a bit upscale; however, they are abundant in Mesoamerican areas that are rich in oak tree forests. The Maya know them as K'anxul or Xuul, and these mushrooms have been part of their diet since at least Columbian times (and perhaps before, based on hieroglyphs that depict people eating similarly elongated mushrooms). Visit Guatemala City during the rainy season (July through October) and you'll find street vendors moving through crowded streets, weaving between cars stopped at red lights, selling plastic baggies filled with chanterelles, for less than a dollar per pound. The classic way to cook them is in this cream sauce, almost always served atop a piece of perfectly grilled beef tenderloin or filet. I also love them over lightly sautéed chicken or pork medallions or with pasta.

3 tablespoons (45 ml) vegetable oil

2 tablespoons ghee or clarified butter

2 garlic cloves, finely chopped

4 cups (455 grams) fresh chanterelles, cleaned, split in half lengthwise, washed, patted dry between clean kitchen towels, and chopped (see Note)

2 tablespoons dry sherry

¾ cup (180 ml) heavy whipping cream

2 tablespoons finely chopped fresh parsley, or more to taste

1 teaspoon fine sea salt, or to taste

¼ teaspoon freshly ground black pepper, or to taste

Heat the oil and ghee in a large skillet set over medium-high heat; add the garlic and cook for 30 seconds or until just fragrant. Add the chanterelles and toss while cooking for 2 to 3 minutes. Add the sherry and toss the mushrooms until it has evaporated, about 2 minutes. Add the cream and parsley; cook, while stirring, until the sauce comes up to a boil; stir for 2 to 3 minutes or until slightly thickened. Add the salt and pepper and stir well. Remove from the heat immediately and serve.

Note: Wild chanterelles are a bit trickier to clean than farmed ones. In a bunch of fresh chanterelles, some will have to be thrown away, which is why it's important to always buy a few more than you'll need and to wash them after checking them well. It is important to split them in half before washing—if there are any worms hiding within, toss the chanterelle out, as it will be bitter (this is not necessary with farmed chanterelles). The inner flesh of these elongated cêpes or mushrooms should be perfectly firm and white. Once you've weeded out any bad ones, wash the mushrooms quickly under running water. If possible, use fresh chanterelles, preferably the day you purchase them. But if needed, you can also substitute 6–8 ounces (160–225 grams) of dehydrated chanterelles and rehydrate them in boiling water until plump.

Berenjenas Empanizadas al Horno
Oven-Fried Breaded Eggplant

Argentina | Yield: Serves 4–6 | Difficulty Level: Easy | Total Cooking Time: 45–50 minutes

My dear friends Frank and Elena Fumagalli are of Italian heritage. He is from Argentina, and she is from Venezuela. Breaded eggplant is typically fried, but they taught me to bake it instead, which ensures that the breading becomes perfectly crispy, instead of a soggy mess. These eggplant rounds are scrumptious on their own, but allow me to suggest that you stuff them into sandwiches—cold, with mayonnaise and lots of lettuce, or hot, topped with tomatoes and fresh mozzarella. Or portion the eggplant into individual ramekins, sauce lightly with the Tuco on page 165, and sprinkle with a good melting cheese, before broiling until hot and bubbly so you can enjoy eggplant "a la parmigiana," Argentine style.

4 tablespoons (60 ml) olive oil, plus more if needed

½ cup (85 grams) all-purpose flour

1¾ cups (200 grams) fine bread crumbs

1 teaspoon fine sea salt

½ teaspoon freshly ground black pepper

3–4 eggs, beaten well

1 tablespoon water

1 large eggplant (about 1 pound 3 ounces/555 grams), stemmed and sliced into thin rounds

Line two baking sheets with parchment paper; brush each with 1 tablespoon of the oil. Preheat the oven to 400°F (200°C). Place the flour in a shallow dish. Place the bread crumbs in another shallow dish and season with salt and pepper; place the eggs and water in a large bowl and whisk. Working with one eggplant slice at a time, coat each in flour, dip it in the egg, and turn it over to coat well on both sides before dipping it into the bread crumbs, pressing down to ensure that they stick to both sides. Place each breaded eggplant slice on the prepared sheets and continue until all are breaded. Drizzle the remaining oil over the breaded eggplant slices, trying to get some oil on all of them (it's okay not to soak them in oil, but try to divide it evenly among them). Bake them for 25 to 35 minutes or until the slices are golden and have crispy exteriors but creamy interiors (being careful not to overbake them). Remove from the oven and serve hot or at room temperature.

Note: If the egg mixture begins to get a bit thick (due to the flour that falls into it), whisk in another tablespoon of water. To slice an eggplant: Cut off both the stem end and the bottom end; then slice thinly. How thinly? The thinner the slices, the crunchier they'll be; if, like me, you like them a bit creamy in the center, slice them ¼ inch (6 mm) thick. Of course, if you prefer, fry the breaded eggplant in oil, until golden and crispy, about 1 to 2 minutes per side.

Caserola de Berenjenas al Horno

Eggplant Casserole

Argentina | Yield: Serves 6 | Difficulty Level: Easy | Total Cooking Time: 1 hour

If you love eggplant Parmesan, you'll enjoy this easier version, popular throughout Argentina. This is one of my practical casseroles to make on busy weekdays, as it takes only minutes to put together. There is no breading of the eggplant involved and everything is cooked quickly in a skillet before being baked briefly in the oven. The sauce itself cooks as it bakes, so the entire recipe comes together in a cinch. Serve it on its own with crusty bread, over cooked pasta, as a side dish, or as a topping for polenta or rice.

½ cup (120 ml) olive oil

1 cup (120 grams) finely chopped white onions

4 large garlic cloves, finely chopped

2 large globe eggplants, diced into ½ inch (12 mm) cubes (about 14 cups)

One 16 ounce (480 ml) can crushed tomatoes

1½ teaspoons fine sea salt

1 teaspoon dried oregano

½ teaspoon freshly ground black pepper

2 cups (225 grams) sliced or shredded fresh mozzarella cheese

½ cup (40 grams) finely chopped fresh flat Italian parsley

Preheat the oven to 400°F (200°C). Grease a 9 x 13 inch (23 x 33 cm) ovenproof casserole dish. Heat 2 tablespoons of the oil in a large skillet over medium-high heat. Sauté the onions and garlic together for 2 minutes; remove them to a separate plate. Add half of the remaining oil to the pan and, working in batches, sauté the eggplant for 4 minutes or until lightly golden, adding more oil as needed, about 8 to 10 minutes; remove from heat. Combine all of the cooked eggplant, onion mixture, tomatoes, salt, oregano, and pepper in the pan and stir together well. Pour the eggplant into the prepared casserole dish and top evenly with the cheese; bake for 20 to 22 minutes or until the cheese has melted. Sprinkle with parsley and serve.

Couve Refogada

Quick-Braised Collard Greens

Brazil | Yield: Serves 4–6 | Difficulty Level: Easy | Total Cooking Time: 20 minutes

Here collard greens (called couve in Brazil) are quickly sautéed before they're braised in liquid for a brief moment, rendering them vibrantly green and utterly delectable. Collards are perfectly simple and unassuming, yet their bright color and deep flavor carries through and enhances the dishes they're served with, whether it's a grilled rib eye steak, called picanha (pronounced *pee-kahn-yah*), or a plate of black beans such as the Feijoada Todo Dia do Janine on page 125.

2½ pounds (1.1 kilograms) collard greens

4 tablespoons (60 ml) olive oil, divided

2 tablespoons finely chopped white onions

2 garlic cloves, finely chopped

1 teaspoon fine sea salt, or to taste

Remove the stems and the thick center ribs of the collard greens by pulling the leaves in an upward motion while holding the stems (or use a knife to cut them off); discard the stems. Working in batches, stack the leaves one on top of the other; roll them tightly into a cigar and slice them very thinly across, into thin ribbons. Repeat until all are sliced and set them aside. Heat half of the oil in a large nonstick skillet set over medium-high heat; add the onions and garlic and cook, while stirring, for 1 minute or until fragrant. Add the collard greens (start with a few at a time, they will all fit as they cook down), stirring them well. Add 1½ cups (260 ml) water and salt, then cover and reduce the heat to low. Simmer for 8 to 10 minutes or until the collards are soft; drain them in a colander. Transfer them to a platter, drizzle with the remaining oil, and serve.

VARIATION: Sometimes, Brazilian cooks will add a bit of cubed Calabrese sausage (pancetta, bacon, or mortadella also work) and sauté it in the oil before adding the other ingredients. The sausage gives this dish a completely different flavor. Serve this version with plenty of white rice and beans for a complete meal.

Overcooking · The tradition of overcooking vegetables can be traced back to the colonial period, when eating undercooked vegetables wasn't considered healthy. This has lasted through the centuries and, now, vegetables are not only thoroughly washed (sometimes with special cleansers) to remove pathogens and insecticides, but also cooked to death in order to ensure that they are safe to eat. Thankfully, this way of cooking vegetables is somewhat in decline, as more people return to organic gardening.

Canelones de Espinaca con Queso

Spinach and Cheese Cannelloni

Uruguay | Yield: Serves 6–8 | Difficulty Level: Intermediate | Total Cooking Time: 3 hours (includes chilling time)

This bubbly, cheesy, spinach casserole makes for a delightful lunch or light dinner. Like neighboring Argentina, Uruguay is home to many Italian-inspired recipes, and the use of crespelle (thin crepes) in place of fresh pasta is commonplace. The delicate filling benefits from a period of chilling that helps the cheeses set up, making it much easier to handle. At home, I'll frequently divide the canelones into individual portions (usually two or three each) and bake them in small dishes, so everyone can get their own little casserole. Once assembled, canelones freeze beautifully; simply fill, roll, and place them on a baking sheet; freeze until solid and transfer them to freezer-safe containers. Thaw them on a baking dish before saucing and baking. Or prepare them entirely ahead of time with the sauce and freeze them in a freezer-to-oven-safe baking dish; then bake (you'll have to add a few extra minutes of baking time).

8 packed cups (680 grams) spinach leaves

½ cup (120 ml) water

2 tablespoons finely chopped white onions

½ cup (115 grams) cream cheese

½ cup (115 grams) ricotta cheese

1½ cups (100 grams) grated Parmesan cheese, divided

1 tablespoon unsalted butter

¼ teaspoon fine sea salt, or to taste

¼ teaspoon ground nutmeg

1 recipe Crepas Básicas (page 40) or Crepas de Hierbas (page 41)

1 recipe Salsa Blanca Sencilla (page 24)

Chopped fresh chives, for garnish (optional)

Wash the spinach well, but don't drain it. Place the spinach and the water in a large skillet set over medium-high heat. Cook until the spinach is soft and most of the water has evaporated, stirring often (it may seem like too much spinach to fit in the skillet, but it will reduce in volume as it cooks). Place a sieve over a bowl; drain the spinach well, reserving any liquid that remains. Transfer the spinach to the jar of an electric blender, along with a couple of tablespoons of the reserved liquid (if you don't have enough, use water). Add the onions, cream cheese, ricotta, 1 cup (50 grams) of the Parmesan, the butter, salt, and nutmeg; blend until smooth. Transfer the spinach mixture to a bowl, cover with plastic wrap, and refrigerate for at least 2 hours (or overnight). Grease a 9 x 13 inch (23 x 30 cm) baking dish and preheat the oven to 375°F (190°C). Working with one crepe at a time, lay on a clean surface. Place about 3 tablespoons (45 ml) of the filling in the bottom center of each crepe. Fold the bottom overhang of the crepe over the filling. Then fold over both sides of the crepe to enclose the edges of the filling (it should look like a rectangle). Continue tightly rolling the crepe from bottom to top. Place the rolled crepe, seam side down, in the baking dish. Continue with the rest, making sure to place them closely together in the dish. Top them with the salsa blanca sencilla, spreading it evenly over the top of the crepes. Sprinkle with the remaining ½ cup (50 grams) Parmesan and bake for 20 to 25 minutes or until the sauce is bubbly and the top becomes golden. Sprinkle with chives, if desired, and serve.

Tip: When I don't have time to make my own pasta or crepes for canelones, I use store-bought sheets of fresh pasta, premade crepes, or large egg roll wrappers.

Tostaditas con Espinaca

Spinach Toasts

Guatemala | Yield: Serves 4–6 | Difficulty Level: Easy | Total Cooking Time: 25–30 minutes

Most Guatemalan children, going back a few generations, grew up eating crusty bread, topped with vibrantly green puree, adorned with slices of hard-boiled egg, just like these. This is how I learned to eat spinach and why I never understood why some people turn up their noses up at the very mention of it. To me, the secret lies in seasoning the spinach with plenty of butter and salt so it tastes divine. The fact that these little toasts are so pretty helps to tempt even the finickiest eater. Traditionally, pan de miga or pain de mie (fancy terms for sandwich bread) are used; brioche and sliced baguette are wonderful too. Still popular today, this is a recipe worth saving for future generations of children everywhere.

6 packed cups (340 grams) spinach leaves

2 tablespoons unsalted butter

½ teaspoon fine sea salt

6 slices white bread, halved and toasted

⅓ cup (30 grams) grated queso seco or Parmesan cheese

2 hard-boiled eggs, peeled and sliced thinly

Wash the spinach well but don't drain it. Place the spinach and ½ cup (120 ml) water in a large skillet set over medium-high heat. Cook until the spinach is soft. Transfer the spinach (and any residual liquid) to the jar of an electric blender; add the butter and blend until smooth (if the motor won't start, add a few tablespoons of water to get it going). Return to the skillet and set over medium heat, stirring until it's the consistency of soft mashed potatoes, about 15 minutes. You should have 1 cup (240 ml) of spinach puree; season with salt and keep warm until ready to use. Spread the warm spinach puree evenly onto each piece of toast (a generous tablespoon each), sprinkle generously with cheese, and top with a slice of hard-boiled egg. Serve immediately.

Pascualina

Swiss Chard, Egg, and Ricotta Pie

Argentina and Uruguay | Yield: One 10 inch (25 cm) tart | Difficulty Level: Advanced | Total Cooking Time: 2 hours

Visit Argentina and Uruguay around Easter time (época de Pascua) and you'll find that everyone is making or eating this rustic greens, egg, and ricotta cheese pie, a gigantic and very filling culinary tradition inherited from Italian immigrants of Umbrian descent. It is usually served warm or at room temperature, but is also delicious cold; leftovers make for a luxurious snack.

- 4 tablespoons (60 grams) unsalted butter or vegetable oil
- 1¾ cups (280 grams) finely chopped white onions
- 2 garlic cloves, finely chopped
- 6 cups (455 grams) Swiss chard or kale, washed and thinly sliced into strips

- 1¼ cups (280 grams) whole-milk ricotta (drained in a sieve for 30 minutes if watery)
- 2 cups (170 grams) grated Parmesan cheese
- 7 eggs, divided
- ⅓ cup (40 grams) dried bread crumbs
- ¼ teaspoon ground nutmeg

- ½ teaspoon fine sea salt
- ½ teaspoon ground white pepper
- 1 recipe Pasta para Tarta Salada (page 38)
- All-purpose flour for rolling out pastry, if using
- Egg wash made with 1 egg and 2 tablespoons water (optional)

Melt the butter in a large skillet set over medium-high heat. Add the onions and garlic and cook, stirring constantly for 3 minutes or until the onions are soft. Add the chard or kale and, stirring constantly, cook for 6 to 8 minutes or until soft and most of the liquid has evaporated. (If at first you can't fit all of the chard into the pan, add it bit by bit; it will all fit as it cooks.) Remove from the heat and allow to cool at room temperature for 20 minutes. In the meantime, in a large bowl, combine the ricotta, Parmesan, 2 eggs, bread crumbs, nutmeg, salt, and pepper. When cool, add the chard to the mixture and stir well to combine. Chill for 30 minutes (or up to overnight). Preheat the oven to 350°F (180°C). Cut out a 10½ inch (27 cm) circle of parchment paper for the bottom of a 10 inch (25 cm) springform pan. Spray the bottom and sides of the pan with cooking spray (or butter it generously); place the circle of parchment paper in the bottom of the pan; secure the ring of the pan in place. On a well-floured surface (or over a large sheet of parchment paper), roll out two-thirds of the pastry into a 15 inch (38 cm) circle so it will cover the bottom and sides of the pan. It should be about ¼ inch (6 mm) thick. Carefully, using the rolling pin to aid you, transfer the pastry into the pan, sliding it into place to fit the bottom and up the sides, making sure to leave an overhang. Spoon the filling into the pastry and level it evenly. Using a large spoon (a large ice cream scoop, or ½ cup/120 ml measuring cup also work), make 5 indentations in the filling (one in the middle and four around the edges). Each one should be large enough to hold an egg inside. Break each of the remaining eggs, one at a time, and slide each into a hole; set aside. Roll out the remaining pastry into a 12 inch (30 cm) circle, about ⅛ inch (4 mm) thin, and carefully drape it over the pie, making sure to cover the entire surface. Press both the top and bottom overhangs together and fold the excess under the edge, sealing them together (this should be folded under the rim, as you will remove the tart from the pan after it's baked). Use a fork or your fingers to crimp the edges of the pie shell. With a sharp knife, cut 4 vents in the center of the top crust—be careful not to cut too deep, or you'll burst the egg yolks. Place the pie on a large baking sheet (this is to help you move it). If using, brush the top with the egg wash. Bake the pie for 1 hour and 20 minutes or until the pastry is golden and has pulled away from the sides of the pan. Cool for 15 minutes in the pan. Remove the ring and cool completely before transferring to a serving platter.

Note: If you only have an 8 inch (20 cm) springform pan, use only 6 eggs: 4 for inside the tart and 2 for the filling. You'll have to bake the smaller tart for 1 hour and 40 minutes.

Coliflor Envuelta en Huevo

Battered Cauliflower with Tomato Sauce

Guatemala | Yield: Serves 4 | Difficulty Level: Intermediate | Total Cooking Time: 35 minutes

My first memories of eating cauliflower involve these crispy and pillowy batter-coated florets, called envueltos, bathed in tomato sauce. Make a light tomato sauce right before you start cooking the cauliflower and it should be ready just as you finish frying the florets (or use the Salsa para Envueltos on page 162 if you prefer; just be sure to make it ahead of time). Batter and fry the cauliflower right before serving so it retains some crunch. Serve the sauce on the side so the crispy vegetables don't get soggy and so everyone can enjoy as much or as little tomato flavor as they like.

FOR THE SAUCE

One 14.5 ounce (411 gram) can whole tomatoes

2 garlic cloves, roughly chopped

1 teaspoon fine sea salt

¼ teaspoon freshly ground black pepper

2 tablespoons vegetable oil

FOR THE CAULIFLOWER

1 cauliflower head (about 1½ pounds/680 grams), trimmed and cut into 8–10 large florets

3 large eggs, separated

¼ cup (30 grams) all-purpose flour

Vegetable oil, for frying

¼ cup (20 grams) finely chopped fresh parsley, for garnish (optional)

To make the sauce, in a blender, combine the tomatoes, garlic, salt, pepper, and oil; blend until smooth. Transfer to a medium saucepan and bring to a boil over medium-high heat. Cover, reduce the heat, and simmer for 15 minutes. (If you prefer a thicker sauce, remove the lid and cook for a few minutes more or until it has reduced to your liking.) Keep warm and covered until ready to use or refrigerate for up to 4 days; reheat before serving.

To make the cauliflower, place the florets in a medium pot and cover with cold water. Bring to a boil, cover, lower the heat, and simmer for 5 to 7 minutes or until the florets are just barely fork tender. Immediately drain them in a colander and rinse them under cold running water until cool to the touch. Drain well and place them in a single layer on a clean kitchen towel. In the meantime, place the egg whites in a large bowl and whisk until they form soft peaks, about 1 minute (or use an electric mixer on medium speed); add the egg yolks, one at a time, beating well with each addition. Whisk in the flour until foamy. Fit a large baking pan with a metal cooling rack and set aside. In a large skillet with high sides, heat 2 inches (5 cm) of oil to 360°F (180°C) (or use a deep fryer according to the manufacturer's directions). Working with one cauliflower floret at a time, drop it in the batter, turning it with a large spoon to coat all sides. Use the spoon to carefully transfer the floret to the oil. Repeat the process with each floret, making sure to batter them only when you are ready to drop them in the oil, and avoid crowding them in the pan. Fry them until golden, about 3 to 4 minutes, turning them over halfway through. Using a slotted spoon, transfer them to the prepared rack to drain (see Note). Since the cauliflower florets must go directly from batter to the frying pan, fry them in small batches. Set the fried cauliflower on a plate, cover with the sauce (or make a pool of sauce on the plate and top it with the cauliflower), and serve immediately, sprinkled with parsley, if desired.

Note: Keep the battered cauliflower warm by setting it on the prepared sheet with the rack in a 250°F (120°C) oven for up to 30 minutes. Leftovers are best refrigerated for up to 24 hours; reheat them in the same manner, in a 350°F (180°C) oven for 15 to 20 minutes.

VARIATIONS: Many vegetables are given this treatment in the Latin kitchen. Simply blanch whatever vegetable you are using, until just tender, then lightly batter and fry it. Slices of celery root, chayotes (called güisquiles) and sliced chayote roots (called ichintal), potatoes, bundles of green beans tied with chives, salsify roots, and, of course, stuffed chiles (rellenos) all work.

Lentejas con Tomates y Hierbas

Lentils with Tomatoes and Herbs

Chile | Yield: Serves 4–6 | Difficulty Level: Easy | Total Cooking Time: 40 minutes

Brought over by Europeans, lentils or lentejas (pronounced *lehn-teh-haws*) became a mainstay of everyday cooking in Latin American countries with deep Spanish culinary roots, such as Cuba, Argentina, and, especially, in Chile, where brown lentils are preferred. Lentils cook quickly— a bonus for the busy cook. Serve these with white rice and crusty bread.

1½ cups (280 grams) brown lentils, picked over for debris

1 bay leaf

1 teaspoon olive oil

3 ounces (85 grams) bacon or pancetta, sliced or cubed

1 cup (115 grams) chopped white or yellow onions

1 garlic clove, finely chopped

One 14.5 ounce (411 gram) can diced tomatoes with juices

2 tablespoons chopped fresh Italian parsley

¼ cup (60 ml) white wine (optional)

1½ teaspoons fine sea salt, or more to taste

½ teaspoon freshly ground black pepper, or more to taste

Place the cleaned lentils and the bay leaf in a medium pot and cover with water by at least 2 inches (5 cm); bring to a boil over medium-high heat. Lower the heat slightly (you'll want the lentils to remain at a healthy boil without letting the water boil over), and cook, uncovered, for 15 to 20 minutes or until the lentils are al dente (tender with toothsome centers); remove 1 cup (240 ml) of liquid and reserve. Drain the lentils and discard the rest of the liquid. Return the lentils and the cup of reserved liquid to the pot and set them aside. Heat the oil in a large nonstick skillet over medium-high heat. Add the bacon, onions, and garlic, cooking, while stirring, for 2 to 3 minutes or until the onions begin to soften. Add the tomatoes and parsley and continue cooking for 5 to 6 minutes or until slightly thickened. Add the wine, cook for 2 minutes, and stir the sauce into the lentils; season with salt and pepper. Bring to a simmer, cover the pot, and lower the heat to medium-low. Cook for 10 to 12 minutes or until all of the liquid has been absorbed. Serve hot.

Niños Envueltos

Stuffed Beef and Rice Cabbage Rolls

Dominican Republic and Ecuador | Yield: Serves 6–8 | Difficulty Level: Intermediate | Total Cooking Time: 3½ hours

The Arabic influence on the cuisine of the Dominican Republic can be found in the myriad recipes that feature Middle Eastern ingredients and culinary techniques, such as this ancient version of stuffed leaves—in which tasty meat-filled cabbage rolls are simmered in a light tomato sauce—that still endures today. The Spaniards and Jews (known as conversos because they had converted to Catholicism) who arrived during the colonization brought with them many recipes that they had inherited from the Moors. In the latter part of the eighteenth century, Lebanese merchants made their way to the Americas, and many of them settled in new countries, such as Ecuador, Brazil, and Mexico, further popularizing stuffed leaves and vegetables of all types—eggplants, peppers, tomatoes, and onions among them. As you can imagine, there are many, many versions, depending on where the recipe is from: Egypt, Syria, and others. This is my interpretation. It is a weekend meal; most of the time is inactive, as this casserole cooks long and slow in the oven.

2 tablespoons plus 1 teaspoon fine sea salt, divided

1 large (3 pound/1.35 kilogram) green cabbage, outer leaves removed, cored, and left whole

⅔ cup (145 grams) medium-grain white rice

3 tablespoons (45 ml) olive oil

½ cup (60 grams) finely chopped yellow onions

½ cup (60 grams) finely chopped green onions

1 garlic clove, finely chopped

1 pound (455 grams) lean ground beef

One 28 ounce can (or two 14.5 ounce cans) diced tomatoes with juices, divided

¾ cup (140 grams) finely chopped carrots

1 cup (140 grams) stemmed, seeded, and finely chopped red bell peppers

¼ cup (60 ml) chicken broth or water

2 tablespoons tomato paste

2 teaspoons white granulated sugar

½ teaspoon dried oregano

¼ teaspoon freshly ground black pepper

¼ cup (20 grams) finely chopped fresh Italian parsley

1 tablespoon unsalted butter at room temperature

Bring a large pot filled with water to a full boil; add 1 tablespoon of the salt. Carefully immerse the cabbage; when the water returns to a boil, cook uncovered for 10 to 11 minutes, or just until the leaves can be separated and the cabbage is tender but not cooked through (be careful not to fully cook the cabbage). Fill a very large bowl with iced water and carefully transfer the whole cabbage head into the bowl; spoon the iced water all over, until the cabbage cools completely, about 12 to 15 minutes. Drain the cabbage; carefully pull the outer leaves off, keeping them as intact as you possibly can (they will break a little bit). You should have 12 to 16 large leaves (see Note below); reserve the remaining leaves to line the baking dish. Set aside. Place the rice in a bowl, soak it with hot water (110°F/40°C), and let it sit for 10 minutes. Drain and set aside.

Make the filling: Heat the oil in a large skillet set over medium-high heat; add the chopped white and green onions and garlic, cooking, while stirring, for 3 to 4 minutes or until softened; set aside to cool slightly. In a large bowl, stir the beef, rice, one of the cans of tomatoes (or half of the larger can) (with juices reserved; add the juices to the remaining tomatoes), and 1 teaspoon of salt together, until well mixed; set aside. Lay a few cabbage leaves at a time on a clean work surface with the outer sides of the leaves facing down. With a knife, carefully cut off the thick part of the center stem at the bases of the leaves. Place 3 tablespoons (45 ml) of the filling in the middle of each leaf; fold the sides of the leaf inward over the filling (like an eggroll) and roll the leaf up into a cigar (not too tightly but taut enough that the filling won't escape). Repeat with all the leaves until all of the filling is used. Preheat the oven to 350°F (180°C). Chop the remaining cabbage leaves with the leaves you reserved earlier, and set aside. Grease a 9 x 13 inch (23 x 33 cm) baking pan. Line the pan with the chopped cabbage leaves; top with the carrots and peppers. →

Snuggle the filled cabbage rolls, sides touching, in the pan, over the vegetables, until all are packed in one single layer (it will be tight). In a medium bowl, combine the remaining tomatoes (and all the juices), broth or water, tomato paste, sugar, remaining salt, oregano, pepper, and parsley; pour this directly over the rolls. Dot with the butter. Place a piece of parchment paper directly over the cabbage; cover the dish tightly with aluminum foil and place it on a baking sheet with a rim (some juices will boil over). Bake for 2 hours or until the beef is cooked and the rice is tender (you'll have to cut into a roll to find this out). Wait 10 minutes before serving.

Note: The pot must be large enough to submerge the entire cabbage. The biggest outer leaves may be cut in half, after the stem is cut off, for a total of 16 leaves.

A Name with Different Meanings · *Niños envueltos* translates literally to "blanketed children." There are many versions of stuffed rolls with the same name found in different countries but that are made with completely different ingredients. In Venezuela, niños envueltos refers to rolled plantains stuffed with cheese; in Chile, to meat rolls stuffed with vegetables; and in Mexico, to spiral sandwiches sometimes stuffed with ham and cheese. Although we all speak Spanish in Latin America, what means one thing in one country can refer to a completely different thing in another.

Sopa Juliana

Soup of Julienned Vegetables

Central America | Yield: Serves 4–6 | Difficulty Level: Easy | Total Cooking Time: 30 minutes

Julienne is a French term used to describe food cut into small, thin matchsticks, and it gives its name to this soup filled with colorful strips of vegetables that swim in clear beef broth. Throughout Central America, soups such as this one, which are inexpensive to make, often use broth leftover from boiling beef, although many modern-day cooks use store-bought broth, for convenience. For a heartier meal, I'll sometimes add a cupful of cooked white beans and a handful of small pasta shapes; then, pair it with a simple salad and warm tortillas. Use any vegetables you have on hand: celery, fennel, leeks, squash, and fresh green beans are also delicious when added to this recipe.

1 tablespoon vegetable oil

½ cup (85 grams) thinly sliced white onions

1–2 chayote squashes (280–340 grams), peeled, cored, seeded, and thinly julienned

2 cups (140 grams) peeled and thinly julienned carrots

2 cups (160 grams) stemmed, seeded, and julienned red bell peppers

2 cups (225 grams) peeled and thinly julienned russet potatoes

8 cups (2 liters) Caldo de Res (page 29) or canned beef broth

½ teaspoon fine sea salt, or more to taste

1 small sprig fresh mint

Heat the oil in a medium pot set over medium-high heat. Add the onions, chayote, carrots, and bell peppers; cook for 3 to 4 minutes or until the vegetables start to soften (they shouldn't take any color). Add the potatoes and the broth; taste the liquid and add salt to taste. Increase the heat and bring to a boil; cover, lower the heat, and simmer the soup for 15 to 20 minutes or until all of the vegetables are fork tender. Add the mint sprig and turn off the heat; let the mint steep for 5 minutes, then remove and discard. Serve the soup hot.

Tallarines Verdes

Pasta with Basil and Arugula Sauce

Peru | Yield: Serves 4–6 | Difficulty Level: Easy | Total Cooking Time: 20 minutes (includes cooking the pasta)

Let me introduce you to the velvety Peruvian version of pesto, with a twist. Basil provides the base for the Italian classic, but in Peru the sweet herb simply enhances the taste of other greens (usually spinach, although I prefer the more peppery flavor of arugula). The Peruvian version is also made with nuts and turns a vibrant green color. However, that's where the similarities end, because this sauce is made with pecans, not with pine nuts, and with evaporated milk and creamy queso fresco in place of oil. The result, although completely different from pesto, is just as delicious when mixed with hot and perfectly al dente pasta. Most of the time it's served on linguine or fettucine, but in Peruvian homes, any shaped pasta goes. Pair this pasta with Milanesas (page 42) or with any grilled meat.

4 cups (85 grams) fresh baby spinach or arugula

1 cup (20 grams) fresh basil leaves

½ cup (60 grams) finely chopped shallots

2 garlic cloves, finely chopped

One 12 ounce (354 ml) can evaporated milk

1½ cups (170 grams) crumbled queso fresco (or feta)

½ cup (55 grams) pecans or walnuts

2 tablespoons olive oil

1 cup (55 grams/1 cup) grated Parmesan cheese

1 teaspoon fine sea salt, or more to taste

½ teaspoon freshly ground black pepper, or more to taste

1 pound (455 grams) linguine or fettucine (or any pasta of your choice)

In a blender, combine the arugula, basil, shallots, garlic, evaporated milk, queso fresco, and pecans; start the motor and blend. Slowly, with the motor running, add the oil through the feeding tube, until emulsified. Transfer the mixture to a bowl and stir in the Parmesan, salt, and pepper; set aside. Cook the pasta according to the package directions; drain well and transfer to a large bowl. Stir in as much of the sauce as you like.

Note: Feta cheese is saltier than queso fresco; if using, add the salt after tasting the sauce. You may not need to add any.

YUCA

Yuca (pronounced *yoo-kah*) is the long root of the plant known botanically as *Manihot esculenta*.

Before we continue, I beg you not be confused by the plant of similar name, spelled "yucca." That single extra consonant yields a completely different meaning. One is a starchy food, the other is a succulent ornamental plant. I so often see them confused in cookbooks that it merits mentioning here.

Yuca root has proved to be one of humanity's most valuable crops, easy to grow and rich in nutrients. It can last under the ground for several years after it's ready to harvest, preserved for long seasons. It's easily propagated by planting stem cuttings into the ground (like potatoes) and has fed civilizations around the world for centuries. It has been food for peoples on the Amazonian riverbanks for more than seven thousand years and grew beneath the American soil long before Christopher Columbus landed.

Yuca is native to South America, first domesticated in Brazil. It is often associated with Africa, due to the fact that yuca is the principal starch in the Latin American countries where the numbers of enslaved Africans were largest. The culinary exchange that brought coffee, plantains, and okra from Africa took yuca in the opposite direction. The popularity of yuca extends throughout the entire Latin American territory; you'll find it in recipes from Central America through the Latin Caribbean and deep into South America. Yuca is mashed, stewed, fried, and used to make bread—sticky and chewy or thin and crispy. It's eaten in both savory and sweet dishes.

Yuca is so rich in cyanide that it's highly poisonous if eaten raw. (Someone had to figure that out!) Don't worry, though. The poisonous juices are removed by boiling the roots until they're softened, or by grating them and pressing the juices out, drying it, and pulverizing it. Pulverized yuca is called tapioca; mixed with water and shaped into tiny spheres, it becomes boba, also known as tapioca pearls.

There are different ways to purchase yuca. If you have a grocery store nearby that caters to Latin American, African, or Caribbean customers, you'll find fresh yuca roots; these will always have a coating of wax on their skins, needed to preserve them, as yuca rots quickly after it's harvested. Sometimes you'll find canned yuca; stay away from that unless you plan to use it in a puree, because it's soft and mushy. If you're really fortunate, you'll find yuca in the frozen section of your grocery store, already peeled, sectioned, and ready to cook.

To cook yuca, peel them with a knife or potato peeler, cut them into large sections, place them in a pot, and cover them entirely with cold water. Bring to a boil; lower the heat slightly (so that it stays at a slow boil but doesn't boil over) and cook until the yuca is fork tender, anywhere from 20 to 35 minutes. How long the yuca will cook will depend on how thick it is, how old or young it is, and how thick its skin is. My trick for discerning how long a particular root will take to cook is to try to peel off some skin with my thumbnail—if it comes off easily, it will cook in less time than if it is hard to peel. Before you can use cooked yuca in a recipe you must first split it in half lengthwise and remove the hard, inner fiber (it looks like a thin piece of rope) that is in the middle of every tuber.

Various kinds of flours made with the yuca root are used in the cuisines of South America. Polvihlo doce (also called almidón) is the finest of these flours, made by cooking the yuca and straining the liquid left behind. It's a snowy-white color with the texture of cornstarch. This is what you will use for most baking recipes, including the Mbejú (page 270) and Chipá o Pão de Queijo (page 276) in this book. White yuca flour (harina de yuca blanca or farinha de mandioca branca) is obtained by finely grinding the yuca root. It's thicker than polvihlo doce, with the texture of wheat flour. Toasted yuca flour is called farofa; its texture is like that of whole-wheat flour with a golden color and toasted aroma. It's usually served as a condiment to top grilled meats called churrasco. And then there is the massa para tapioca: the hydrated yuca flour that is used to make the cracker-like flatbread known as Tapioca or Casabe (page 273). All you have to do is to sprinkle it directly into a skillet (panela) and watch it come together into a cracker right before your eyes. For where to find these flours, see Sources.

Yuquitas Fritas

Yuca Fries

Various Countries | Yield: Serves 4–6 | Difficulty Level: Easy | Total Cooking Time: 40 minutes

Yuca root is a favored starchy vegetable all over Latin America, particularly in countries with a strong Afro-Latino heritage. From Cuba to Peru, all the way to Brazil, you will find that these crispy and toothsome fries make a frequent appearance on menus, either as an appetizer before a meal or as a side dish in place of (and sometimes together with) potato fries. What I love most about yuca is that they are even starchier than potatoes, with a sweeter flavor, too. My family request these whenever we have Peruvian-style chicken. If you use frozen yuca, it'll be easier to cut into fries when it has thawed almost completely.

3 pounds (1.4 kilograms) yuca root, peeled and sliced into thick fries (about 3½ inches long by ½ inch thick/9 cm long by 1.2 cm thick).

2 tablespoons fine sea salt, divided

Vegetable oil, for frying

Place two large, clean kitchen towels on your counter. Place a metal cooling rack over a large baking sheet and set aside. In a large pot, bring 4 quarts (3.8 liters) of water to a rolling boil; add 1½ tablespoons salt. When the water returns to a rolling boil, add the yuca and cook until fork tender, about 8 minutes. Remove the yuca with a slotted spoon and place on the clean towels to dry for at least 20 minutes (up to 1 hour). In a large Dutch oven set over medium-high heat, heat 2 inches of oil to 360°F (180°C). Working in batches, fry the yuca until it's golden and crispy, about 5 minutes. With a slotted spoon, transfer the fried yuca onto the baking sheet to drain. Sprinkle the remaining salt all over the fried yuca and serve immediately.

Note: To keep the yuca fries warm for longer, preheat the oven to 250°F (125°C) and place them on the rack-lined baking sheet for up to 30 minutes. This will prevent them from cooling and from getting soggy.

Bolitas de Yuca y Queso

Yuca and Cheese Puffs

El Salvador | Yield: Makes 24–26 bolitas (serves 4–6) | Difficulty Level: Easy |
Total Cooking Time: 1 hour (includes cooking the yuca; 20 minutes if yuca is already cooked)

These light, fluffy, and crispy little croquettes filled with cheese (or sometimes minced shrimp, flaked crabmeat, or chopped langoustines) are so dainty that you'll think they were made by a chef in a fancy restaurant. Yet they are part of the everyday menu in the homes of many Salvadorians, including that of my friend Maria del Pilar de Fernandez, who makes them for her family. Although yuca is easy to mash with a fork, I find that these take on a lighter texture when the yuca is run through a food processor, so I offer you both methods here. As long as the yuca is combined with some liquid (in this case, eggs), it will not become gummy when processed. Once the balls are assembled, they can be frozen in a single layer on cookie sheets, then transferred to a freezer-safe container. Those made with cheese can be stored in the freezer for up to 4 months; if you stuff them with cooked shrimp, they'll only last for 2 months. When you wish to eat them, there is no need to defrost; they can go directly from the freezer into hot oil until they fry up crispy. If you need to keep them warm after frying, do so in a 250°F (120°C) oven; they'll hold for up to 1 hour.

1 pound (455 grams) cooked yuca root (see page 263)

2 eggs

½ teaspoon fine sea salt, more for sprinkling

1 cup (115 grams) mozzarella cheese, diced into ½ inch (12 mm) cubes

½ cup (60 grams) dried bread crumbs

Oil, for frying

Line a large baking sheet with parchment paper and fit it with a cooling rack. If mashing the yuca by hand: place the cooked and deveined root in a large bowl and use a fork to mash it as finely as you can (you don't want large pieces left); stir in the eggs and salt until combined. If using a food processor: Place the cooked and deveined yuca in the bowl of a food processor; add the eggs and salt, and pulse until you have a smooth puree. With moistened hands, take tablespoonfuls of the mixture and shape them into balls; place a cube of cheese (or a piece of cooked shrimp, see Note) in the center and press the yuca around it. Roll them back into balls and then immediately roll them in the bread crumbs. Place on the prepared baking sheet and repeat until all are done. Line another baking sheet with a metal cooling rack and set aside. Heat 2 inches of oil in a medium pot set over medium-high heat. It will be ready when it reaches 350°F (180°C) on a thermometer or when the end of a wooden spoon sizzles when it comes into contact with the oil. Working in batches, lower the yuca balls with a slotted spoon or a spider into the oil and fry them until golden and crispy, about 1 to 1½ minutes. If the balls are browning too quickly, lower the heat and wait for the oil to cool slightly before continuing to fry. When golden, transfer them with a slotted metal spoon onto the sheet with the cooling rack; sprinkle with salt as soon as you set them on the rack (the hot oil will help the salt stick). Continue frying until all are done.

Note: For an even crispier crust, use Japanese-style bread crumbs, known as panko. If you're are stuffing these with shrimp, you'll need 1 cup (100 grams) of cooked and chopped shrimp.

Empanadas de Yuca

Yuca Turnovers

Various Countries | Yield: Makes 12–14 empanadas | Difficulty Level: Intermediate | Total Cooking Time: 1½ hours

The word *empanada* derives from the Latin term *in panis*, for "inside bread." However, Latin American turnovers are not always made with wheat-based dough. In Brazil, Nicaragua, the Dominican Republic, Panama, Cuba, and Puerto Rico, you'll find yuca empanadas, also called catibias or pasteles. Because this dough is very sticky, I prefer to use a food processor to make it; however, a potato masher will also work well. To work the dough into a disc, I press it between pieces of plastic wrap and keep my hands moist while working with it so it doesn't stick. Here I offer you my absolute favorite cheese version, popular with kids and adults alike.

1½ pounds (680 grams) frozen, peeled yuca

10 ounces (280 grams) melting cheese, like queso blanco, mozzarella, or Monterey Jack, cut into slices measuring about 1½ by 2½ inches (4 x 6 cm) and ¼ inch (6 mm) thick

Vegetable oil, for frying

Salt, for sprinkling

Place the yuca in a large pot and cover it with cold water. Bring it up to a boil over medium-high heat and boil it for 15 to 20 minutes or until the yuca is just fork tender (enough that a fork can be easily inserted in the flesh but the middle still has a bit of resistance). Drain it and cool it slightly and slice the pieces in half lengthwise; remove and discard the tough fiber found in the middle. Chop the flesh of the yuca and let it cool completely. Transfer it to the bowl of a large food processor fitted with a metal blade, and pulse until it comes together into a ball (about 25 to 30 one-second intervals). Turn the dough onto a sheet of plastic wrap and, using the wrap, shape it into a ball. Cover it with the plastic wrap and let it rest at room temperature for 30 minutes. Line a large baking sheet with parchment paper and set aside. With moistened hands, divide the dough into 12 to 14 portions (about 2 ounces/55 grams each). Moisten your hands again and shape the pieces of dough into small balls. Cut a ziplock bag open on three sides, like a book. Place a ball of dough in the middle of the bag; fold the bag over and with the palm of your hand flatten it slightly. Use a flat-bottomed plate (or skillet) to flatten the ball into a 4½ inch (11 cm) disc. Place one slice of cheese in the middle of the disc, leaving a small rim; use the bag to fold the dough over the filling, forming a half-moon. Press the edges together with your fingers to seal well. Transfer the empanada to the prepared sheet. Repeat with the rest of the dough and filling, keeping the empanadas covered with a sheet of plastic or a clean kitchen towel as you work. Fit a large baking sheet with a metal cooling rack and set it aside. In a large skillet with high sides, heat 1½ inches (4 cm) of oil to 360°F (180°C). Working in batches, carefully slide the empanadas into the oil and fry them until they are golden, about 4 minutes, turning them over halfway through. If the oil gets too hot as you fry and they're browning too quickly, lower the heat and cool the oil slightly before frying any more. Use a slotted spoon to transfer the fried empanadas to the prepared rack to drain. Sprinkle them with salt, let them rest for a couple of minutes, and serve.

VARIATIONS: There are many fillings that can be used to make these empanadas. Make only the dough portion of this recipe, then fill with any of the picadillo or shredded beef recipes in this book. Leftover shredded cooked or rotisserie chicken or tuna work well too.

Tortitas de Yuca con Miel y Crema

Yuca Pancakes

Central America | Yield: Makes 14–16 (serves 4–6) | Difficulty Level: Intermediate | Total Cooking Time: 1 hour

I vividly remember eating yuca cakes as a child—the contrast between the sticky, sweet honey and the tart and velvety crema, which coated my palate with each bite. In my mother's house, they were served with white corn syrup; my grandmother preferred the lightest honeys she could find. I learned to add the crema from my Nicaraguan and Salvadorian friends. If you are able to purchase yuca that has already been cleaned and cut (find it in the frozen section of many supermarkets and in Latin grocery stores), it will save you time in the kitchen. I like to use a small ice cream scoop to drop the batter into the skillet; I then press down on it with an oiled spatula to flatten slightly. These are not thin pancakes, but rather about ½ inch (12 mm) thick.

1¼ pound (570 grams) yuca, peeled and sectioned

¾ cup (75 grams) all-purpose flour

1 teaspoon fine sea salt

½ teaspoon baking soda

3 eggs

¼ cup (60 ml) vegetable oil, divided (or more as needed), plus more for dipping the spatula

2 tablespoons unsalted butter, divided (or more as needed)

Honey or white corn syrup, for serving

Crema or crème fraiche, for serving

Fit two large rimmed baking sheets with metal cooling racks and set them aside. Place the yuca into a large pot, cover with cold water, and set over medium-high heat. Bring to a boil; lower the heat slightly and cook at a slow boil until the yuca is fork tender (about 20 to 25 minutes). Drain in a colander, rinse under cold water, and set aside to cool completely, about 15 minutes. In a large bowl, stir together the flour, salt, and baking soda; set aside. When the yuca is cool, transfer it to a large bowl and mash it with a fork as smoothly as possible (a few small chunks will remain; you should have about 4 cups/520 grams of mashed yuca). Whisk the eggs into the flour mixture and add the yuca; stir to combine. Heat half of the oil and half of the butter in a nonstick skillet set over medium-high heat. Fill a semi-shallow dish with a couple of tablespoons of oil (this is to grease the spatula) and set aside. Working in two or three batches, drop the yuca batter into the skillet in generous ¼ cup (60 ml) scoops. Dip the bottom of the spatula into the dish with the oil just to coat the bottom and then use it to push down on the yuca balls slightly to form small pancakes. Cook for 3 minutes on the first side or until they're golden; turn over to the second side and cook for 1½ to 2 more minutes. Remove the pancakes with the spatula and place them on the prepared racks as they are finished. Add more oil and butter to the pan, as needed, to finish cooking all of the pancakes. If the pan is getting too hot (you'll know because the pancakes will brown too quickly), remove the pan from the heat and let it cool completely before placing it back on the heat. Once all the pancakes are made, serve warm, with honey and crema.

Note: Once cooked, the pancakes may be kept warm in a 250°F (125°C) oven for up to 30 minutes. They can also be frozen after they're cooked, for up to 3 months, and reheated in a 350°F (180°C) oven for 10 to 12 minutes.

Mbejú

Cheese and Yuca Flatbread

Argentina, Brazil, and Paraguay | Yield: Serves 4–6 | Difficulty Level: High | Total Cooking Time: 30 minutes

This rich, gluten-free, cheesy, chewy bread from Paraguay is hard to resist when it's freshly made and is traditionally served alongside a cup of yerba mate or coffee. It can also be found in Argentina and Brazil and provides a filling start to the day for people who do heavy labor, in the fields, and in the mountains. Its name is Guaraní for "pan aplastado" or "flatbread," and is pronounced *beh-joo*. Queso criollo is typically used, but a good quality melting cheese such as block mozzarella, queso chihuahua, or Monterey Jack will work well too. Mbejú is traditionally cooked over coals in a cast-iron skillet, but modern-day home cooks use their stoves and cook it in nonstick pans instead. At first, the dough is very crumbly; it is essential to cook it at a very low heat so the cheese can melt slowly and evenly without burning—for this, you'll have to be patient. As you press down on the mbejú over the heat, the melting cheese provides the moisture needed to make the dough, magically forming bread.

It is imperative not to stop pressing it down as it cooks; you should begin to see the strands of cheese peek through the powdery surface. Once the top begins to moisten, it is time to turn it over and cook the other side. Here is where most cooks run into trouble: you'll need to use a large platter to flip the bread over before you slide the flatbread back into the pan to cook the other side. Eat immediately after cooking.

2 cups plus 2 tablespoons (225 grams) yuca flour (also called polvilho doce)

½ teaspoon fine sea salt

3¼ cups (400 grams) grated queso criollo, mozzarella, chihuahua, or Monterey Jack cheese

6 tablespoons (90 ml) whole milk

In a large bowl, whisk together the flour and salt. Add the cheese and work it with your fingers, rubbing it with the flour until the mixture resembles very coarse sand. Add the milk and stir to combine—the mixture will still be very sandy and will look like very crumbly streusel topping. Preheat a 12 inch (30 cm) nonstick pan over medium-low heat. Place the mixture in the skillet, making sure it covers the entire skillet evenly throughout. Using a small spatula (or flat metal spoon), press the dough down, constantly, as it cooks. Cook on the first side for 12 to 15 minutes or until the cheese strands melt (they should be visible). The top of the dough will change from powdery to moist, and come together to form bread. You should at this point be able to slide the bread in the pan when you shake it. The bottom will become golden brown. Set a large plate directly over the top of the skillet and place the entire palm of your hand over the bottom of the plate. Lift the pan, holding on to the plate. In one quick move, flip the pan over onto the plate. Remove the pan (the cooked side of the bread will be on top). Carefully, using the plate, slide the bread (uncooked side down) back into the skillet; cook the second side, pressing with a spatula constantly, for another 8 to 10 minutes or until set—the bottom should be a nice golden color. Transfer to a cutting board and cut into portions. Eat immediately.

Tapioca or Casabe

Yuca Crisps

Brazil | Yield: Serves | Difficulty Level: Easy | Total Cooking Time: 25 minutes

The gluten-free craze may have driven these crêpe-like yuca crackers to the zenith of their popularity in the past decade, but they have been made by the Indigenous Amazonians for centuries. Some cooks use polvihlo doce (see Sources) and rehydrate it at home—but it's not an easy task, and if you've ever made a cornstarch slurry, you'll know that mixing starch and water can be a feat, since no sooner has the starch settled than it repels the water and becomes hard as a brick. For this reason, you will want to look for massa para tapioca or prepared fécula de mandioca hidratada (almidón de yuca hidratado) online or in Brazilian food stores. This powder is pre-hydrated and ready to use. Just sprinkle it over a warm skillet, cook, flip, fill, and fold. You will find similar flatbreads in Venezuela, larger, chewier, and sold from street vendors. I'm eternally thankful to my friend David Perry, whose love of Brazilian food has kept us connected over the years and who introduced me to this magic ingredient, forever changing the way I make these for my family and friends. A one-ingredient recipe, mi gente (my people)!

1 pound (455 grams) massa para
tapioca hidratada (see Sources)

Set a small (8 inch/20 cm) skillet over medium heat. Sprinkle a generous ¼ cup (30 grams) of the powdered dough directly onto the base of the skillet, making sure to coat it all (I like to spoon it into a sieve and shake it over the pan). If the cracker looks too lacey, sprinkle a bit more of the powder to cover the holes. Cook without touching for 1 minute (at this point, you will see the flour turn transparent in parts, with crackly edges, and the middle will set slightly). Once the cracker starts to set, use a large soup spoon or an offset spatula to pat it down, just to help it cook in the middle (be careful not to drag the spoon or the cracker will break) and continue cooking for 30 seconds. Flip or use a spatula to turn the cracker over to the other side (it will look powdery and very white—that's the way it should be). Cook for 1 to 1½ minutes on this second side and remove to a plate. Wipe off any excess flour left in the skillet before you make the next one. Repeat until all are done, placing the crackers over each other as you finish them.

VARIATIONS: For filled tapioca, don't remove the finished cracker from the skillet. Place the filling of your choice on one half and fold the other half over the filling to form a half-moon; cook on each side for 20 seconds and serve. My favorite fillings include dulce de leche and sliced bananas; Nutella and sliced strawberries; melting cheese; a mixture of ham and cheese; scrambled eggs; and cream cheese with smoked salmon. For gluten-free pizza: Transfer the crackers onto a baking sheet as you finish them. Top them very lightly with tomato sauce and toppings of your choice (spinach or other vegetables, sun-dried tomatoes, olives, basil or other herbs, and cheese, for example), and bake in a preheated oven at 350°F (180°C) until the cheese is melted.

Nhoque de Mandioca

Yuca Gnocchi

Brazil | Yield: Serves 6 | Difficulty Level: Intermediate | Total Cooking Time: 1½ hours (includes resting)

These gnocchi are light and slightly sweet. Yuca (known in Brazil as cassava or mandioca) is a pivotal ingredient in Afro-Latino cookery, often replacing potatoes. In Brazil, where yuca is particularly popular, gnocchi such as these are a trendy convenience food, found in the frozen section of most supermarkets. Luckily, they are quite easy and fun to make and freeze rather brilliantly, for convenient use whenever you want them. The dough is extremely easy to handle thanks to the starchiness of the yuca root. I prefer to buy frozen yuca because it's been peeled and cut, which greatly reduces the time and effort needed to make these little pillows. If you can only purchase raw yuca, peel it and cut it into pieces before cooking it. Cooked yuca is sticky and only needs a small amount of flour to make a dough, but no matter how smoothly you try to mash it, it'll always retain a bit of texture. Therefore, I suggest using a potato masher, rather than a fork, to puree it. Most nights, I'll simply dress these gnocchi with butter and cheese, but in Brazil, you'll also find them sauced with cream-, coconut-, or tomato-based sauces.

1½ pounds (680 grams) peeled yuca, cut into large chunks	1½ cups (170 grams) all-purpose flour, plus more, as needed	Pinch of freshly ground black pepper
2 eggs, well beaten	½ teaspoon fine sea salt	¼ teaspoon grated nutmeg

Line a baking sheet with parchment paper (or flour the sheet well) and set aside. Place the yuca in a medium pot and cover with water; bring the water to a boil. Lower the heat slightly and continue boiling for 20 to 25 minutes or until the yuca is soft. Drain and cool for 25 minutes or until cool enough to handle. If needed, remove the fiber in the middle of each piece of yuca and discard. Use a potato masher to mash the yuca until it is smooth (it will retain some texture). On a clean surface, mound the mashed yuca; make a well in the center. Surround the yuca with the flour, forming a ring. Pour the eggs, salt, pepper, and nutmeg into the middle of the well and slowly, with the aid of a fork, begin to incorporate the yuca into the eggs. Once the eggs are mixed, slowly incorporate the flour into the yuca mixture; switch to using your hands and knead the mixture together until it forms a smooth dough. Do the gnocchi test by rolling a teaspoon of dough into a ball and plunging it into a small pot of boiling water. If it stays together and holds its shape, the dough is ready to use; otherwise, knead in a bit more flour and test again. Cover the dough with a clean kitchen towel and let it rest for 10 minutes. Divide the dough into 8 to 10 pieces and, on a floured board, roll each piece into a rope, about 1 inch (2.5 cm) thick. Cut each rope into 2 inch (5 cm) pieces. Use a fork to make a slight indentation on top of each gnocchi, placing the finished dumplings on the prepared baking sheet. Bring a large pot of water to a boil; add the gnocchi and cook until they rise to the surface, about 2 to 3 minutes. Drain well and serve them on a platter, topped with the sauce of your choice.

Note: These will keep, uncooked, in the refrigerator for up to 24 hours. They freeze beautifully, uncooked, when placed on a floured baking sheet in a single layer. Freeze them solid before transferring them into freezer bags; they'll keep for up to 6 months. Drop directly from the freezer into boiling water and add a few minutes to the cooking time for a convenient meal whenever you're in a hurry.

Chipá o Pão de Queijo

Cheese and Yuca Rolls

Brazil and Paraguay | Yield: Makes 24–30 rolls | Difficulty Level: Easy | Total Cooking Time: 30 minutes

Envision a toothsome, cheesy, chewy, warm roll and you'll begin to get an idea of what these tiny little balls of dough taste like. Flatter versions of yuca breads existed long before Europeans arrived in the Americas, but the first versions of these sweet and savory rolls can be traced back to the eighteenth century and the Indigenous Guaraní people. I haven't been to a meal at a Brazilian friend's home where these little gluten-free bites are not offered, either as part of the repast or as appetizers. My Paraguayan friends make theirs a bit larger and serve them for breakfast (simply adjust the baking time if you make them this way, by adding a few more minutes in the oven). These rolls are best enjoyed fresh out of the oven. The good news is that you can make and shape them a couple of hours ahead of time and refrigerate them, lightly covered with plastic wrap, until you're ready to bake them. They also reheat beautifully in a toaster oven at moderate heat (350°F/180°C) in just a few minutes. Most cooks make these by hand, but I cut corners and make them entirely in a food processor (you'll need a large one or the blade will stop running). Here, I'll give you both methods. Look for yuca flour (called polvilho doce or mandioca in Brazil) in most grocery stores that sell gluten-free products.

3¼ cups (400 grams) yuca flour, plus more for kneading

½ teaspoon fine sea salt

½ teaspoon baking powder

3 eggs

10 tablespoons (400 grams) butter, at room temperature

3 cups (340 grams) grated Parmesan cheese

2 cups (200 grams) shredded mozzarella cheese

½ cup (120 ml) whole milk

Line a baking sheet with parchment paper and set aside. Preheat the oven to 400°F (200°C). If making the rolls by hand: In a large bowl, whisk together the flour, salt, and baking powder. Use a wooden spoon to incorporate the eggs and butter. Use your hands to knead in the cheeses and milk, until you end up with a dough that holds together (if the dough is too loose, add a bit more yuca flour, one tablespoon at a time). Turn the dough onto a clean surface that has been lightly dusted with yuca flour, and knead until smooth. If making in the food processor: Place all of the ingredients in the bowl of a large food processor fitted with a metal blade and pulse until the dough comes together into a ball, about 40 one-second pulses or about 2 minutes (if the dough is too loose, add a bit more yuca flour, one tablespoon at a time). Cover and let it rest for 10 minutes, so all the moisture is absorbed by the flour.

Once you've made your dough, roll it into 3 inch (7.5 cm) balls and place them about 2 inches apart. Bake them for 20 to 22 minutes (longer, if you make them bigger) or until they're a nice golden color all around.

Note: I am pretty finicky when it comes to my rolls being the exact same size. For this reason, I shape them using an ice cream scoop. I don't even roll them into balls, just let them take the shape of the scooper and drop them onto the baking sheet. They have a rugged exterior that I love, rather than a smooth appearance—either way, though, they're delicious!

Enyucado de Coco

Yuca and Coconut Cake with Syrup

Colombia and Venezuela | Yield: Makes one 8 x 8 inch (20 x 20 cm) cake |
Difficulty Level: Easy | Total Cooking Time: 1 hour 30 minutes

Typical of many coastal desserts, this cake gets its delicious sweetness from a bath of sugary syrup. The texture is somewhere between a pudding and a cake—toothsome, yet a bit creamy. Syrups made from unrefined sugar (called papelón, panela, or piloncillo) are very common throughout Latin America—dating back to the 1600s, when white sugar was prohibitively expensive for the populace—and they have remained popular ever since. They are either served on the side, as in this recipe, so everyone can add to taste, or used as a base for fruit bars (ates), jams (jaleas), or candies (dulces).

FOR THE CAKE

Butter for greasing the pan

1 pound (455 grams) peeled yuca root, cut into large pieces

One 13.5 ounce (398 ml) can unsweetened coconut milk

1 cup (60 grams) unsweetened shredded coconut

3 large eggs

¼ cup (60 grams) white granulated sugar

1 teaspoon pure vanilla extract

½ teaspoon anise seeds

Pinch of fine sea salt

FOR THE SYRUP

1 cup (150 grams) grated piloncillo (or unrefined brown sugar)

1½ cups (360 ml) water

Place the yuca root in a large pot; cover with water. Bring to a boil over medium-high heat and boil the yuca until fork tender, about 20 minutes (don't let it get mushy). Remove from the water and let it cool completely. Once cool, slice it in half and remove the tough fiber in the center. Preheat the oven to 350°F (180°C). Grease an 8 x 8 inch (20 x 20 cm) square pan (a Pyrex pan works great too) and set aside. Carefully grate the yuca, using the larger holes on a box grater; set aside (if it's too soft to grate, mash it well with a fork but leave a bit of texture). In a bowl, mix together the coconut milk, shredded coconut, eggs, sugar, vanilla, anise seeds, and salt. Add the yuca and combine well. Pour this mixture into the prepared pan and bake for 1 hour and 15 minutes or until a toothpick inserted into the center comes out clean and the top is golden. Cool the cake to room temperature. In the meantime, to make the syrup, place the piloncillo and water in a small saucepan over medium heat; cook until the syrup has thickened slightly (about 10 minutes), stirring often; keep warm. Cut the cake into portions and top each serving with syrup.

POTATOES

nvariably, the first image that comes to mind for most people at the mention of potatoes is that of a mound of French fries. Although I can think of other more delectable dishes, such as puffy croquettes, perfectly whipped mash, and creamy salads, I am accepting of this reality. That is, as long as everyone understands that the humble potato is not native to France or Belgium, but actually to the Andean region.

Peruvians first domesticated potatoes back in the year 2000 BC—not an easy task, given the toxic nature of the plant and the fact that it cannot be eaten raw. The Inca, who did everything well, are said to have cultivated about 3,800 different varieties of potatoes, not including the countless natural and wild hybrids. Picture an ancient Incan marketplace in Cuzco, where mounds of round, oblong, fat, finger-thin, and long potatoes vied for space with others shaped like pine cones, snakes, and grape clusters. Some potatoes were red, while others were blue, yellow, black, purple, white, brown, gold, and orange. What a sight that must have been to the Spanish conquistadores!

Potatoes love to grow at very high altitudes and can withstand freezing temperatures, which made them an ideal crop for the Inca. In addition to this, potatoes can be harvested up to a year after they have matured. Invaders, who ignored the flora and fauna of the New World, didn't know about the existence of the roots—the part of the plant that we eat mashed, fried, and baked—beneath the soil, and so were denied precious sustenance as they tried to take over Incan territories. In fact, it is believed that as part of the domestication process (a term I use here to describe the human intervention by which an indigenous or wild plant goes from inedible to safe to consume or to be used medicinally), ancient Andeans used to eat potatoes as part of a soup made with clay. The clay that leached into the water had enough minerals to offset the poisonous solanine and

tomatine elements that make all members of the nightshade or Solanaceae family famously toxic to humans (just like their cousins, the first tomatoes and eggplants). The Inca also developed a method to freeze-dry potatoes, called chuño. Today, chuño is still found on Peruvian menus. You can find them packed into bags in grocery stores that cater to Latin American cooks. They only need to cook in liquid to become soft again. Thus, it's not far-fetched to say that the Inca invented the first instant potatoes. Misjudged as ignorant by the conquistadores, the Inca, like all of their Amerindian counterparts, were actually a very advanced society.

Not surprisingly, the potato went the same way as the tomato when it came to traveling the world. When they were first introduced to Europe by the conquistadores, potatoes were received only as ornamental plants to be exhibited as curiosities on the tables of the wealthy. Granted, Europeans were particularly wary of green potatoes, those that developed solanine, which are the most toxic to humans. If you've ever been warned not to eat green potato chips, it is because too much solanine can indeed make you sick; throw green potatoes out or let them take root and plant them in the garden.

It wasn't until the 1800s that the potato became popular on European tables. At first, it was relegated to being a food for the poor. But in 1772, Antoine de Parmentier, a French pharmacist and former prisoner of war, discovered the nutritious power stored in the potato. He opened the first soup kitchens in the world, and is credited with saving the French from starvation. Other nations followed suit: the Polish, Norwegian, Swiss, and, most famously, Irish, who were saved from starvation by these "soil's apples" (pommes de terre). The name was coined in France, as were the potato recipes that carry Parmentier's name, like the leek and potato soup known as potage Parmentier, and the ground beef and potato casserole known as hachis a la Parmentier. These and other famous European recipes such as rösti, a Swiss potato pancake, British fish and chips, the French cold potato soup vichyssoise, and, of course, French fries or frites, led to the mistaken belief that these Andean roots are European.

Of course, nutritional value was not enough to make a food trendy back in the eighteenth century—there needed to be some added lore, for excitement. Thus, potatoes were advertised as an aphrodisiac, as were many other plants from the New World.

There is so much more to the humble potato than just the three or four selections you find today in grocery stores. Demand more varieties of diverse colors and shapes from your vendors, and let's bring the potato back to its former glory. Plant them in your gardens once more! Long ago, in a faraway land atop the mountainous Andes, the potato reigned supreme among the tubers of the Americas; it has fed millions of people around the world and saved generations from starvation. It's high time that we give it its rightful place on our plates!

Ensalada Rusa

Russian Potato Salad

Various Countries | Yield: Serves 6–8 | Difficulty Level: Easy | Total Cooking Time: 2 hours (includes chilling)

This is the classic potato salad that you will find all over Latin America. Although true Russian salad includes beets, most Latin cooks omit them because they tint the dressing a pink color. When beets are added, this potato salad becomes an "ensalada rosada." Any starchy kind of potato works well here; try russets or Yukon golds. There are two ways to cook potatoes: one calls for boiling them with the skins on (my preferred way to cook potatoes when I will mash them); the second is to peel, cube, and boil them, and this is my choice when making potato salads such as this one, because they cook and cool quickly, keep their shape perfectly, and any waterlogged pieces ultimately help to thin the dressing and keep it loose. To cook the carrots, simply place them in a pot of cold water and bring them to a boil; cook for 5 to 6 minutes or just until tender. As a shortcut, I use the frozen mélanges of carrots and peas that you can find at most supermarkets and simply thaw them (since they're already blanched, there's no need to cook them) and add them straight to the salad.

2 pounds (910 grams) cooked, peeled, and cubed potatoes (any starchy kind)

1 cup (155 grams) green peas (fresh or frozen and thawed)

1 cup (170 grams) cubed and cooked carrots

1 cup (240 ml) mayonnaise

¼ cup (60 ml) sour cream, crème fraiche, or crema

2 tablespoons finely chopped white onions, or more to taste

¼ cup (60 ml) freshly squeezed lime juice, or more to taste

1 teaspoon fine sea salt, or more to taste

½ teaspoon freshly ground black pepper, or more to taste

2 hard-boiled eggs, peeled and sliced

2 tablespoons finely chopped fresh Italian parsley, for garnish (optional)

½ teaspoon paprika or pimentón dulce, for garnish (optional)

In a large bowl, combine the cooked potatoes, peas, and carrots. In medium bowl, whisk together the mayonnaise, sour cream, onions, lime juice, salt, and pepper. Pour the dressing over the potato mixture and combine well; chill for at least 30 minutes (and up to overnight). Before serving, adorn the top with the hard-boiled eggs; sprinkle with parsley and paprika, if desired.

VARIATION: To make this into an ensalada rosada, add 1 or 2 large cooked, peeled, and cubed beets to this salad.

How to Boil Potatoes · Place the desired number of potatoes inside a pot large enough to give them room to move as they boil. Cover completely in cold water. Set the pot over medium-high heat and bring to a rolling boil; keep uncovered and lower the heat slightly in order to keep the water boiling but not boiling over (about medium to medium-low heat). Boil continuously, adding more boiling water as needed so the potatoes are always covered completely (at this point, the water you add must be boiling, so as not to bring down the temperature). Start checking the potatoes for doneness after 20 to 25 minutes by piercing the flesh with a fork. Depending on how large and/or waxy they are, the cooking time will vary. When the tines of a fork go through easily all the way to the center of the potatoes, they are ready. Don't overcook them, or they will fall apart.

Papas a La Huancaína

Huancaína Potato Salad

Peru | Yield: Serves 4–6 | Difficulty Level: Easy | Total Cooking Time: 45 minutes

This salad of perfectly boiled potatoes is dressed with a spicy, cold, and creamy dressing and is traditionally made with waxy potatoes, but in Peruvian homes it lends itself to many interpretations in which sweet, purple, and speckled potatoes are used. After all, there are more than three thousand varieties of potatoes in this South American country. At home, I keep a jar of beautiful bright yellow Huancaína sauce (La Huancaína, page 175) on hand during the summertime, so I can whip this salad together whenever I want. Black olives and hard-boiled eggs are traditional accoutrements, but contemporary home cooks often also serve it with tuna, green beans, and tomatoes, in the style of a salade Niçoise.

2 pounds (910 grams) yellow potatoes

1 recipe La Huancaína (page 175)

12 black olives, sliced, or to taste

2 hard-boiled eggs, peeled and sliced

¼ cup (20 grams) finely chopped fresh chives

Place the potatoes in a large pot and cover them with water. Bring them to a boil over medium-high heat; lower the heat slightly and continue boiling the potatoes for 25 to 30 minutes or until they are fork tender. Drain the potatoes in a colander and let them cool (for a quicker route, submerge them in iced water until they're cooled through). Peel the potatoes and slice them into thick rounds; place them attractively on a platter. Dress with as much sauce as you want and garnish with the olives, eggs, and chives. Chill until ready to serve.

Note: This salad will last, covered, in the refrigerator for up to 3 days.

Causa de Atún

Layered Potato and Tuna Salad

Peru | Yield: Serves 6 | Difficulty Level: Easy | Total Cooking Time: 2 hours

If you think potato salads are humdrum, you have not visited Peru, where they are anything but ordinary. A causa is a potato salad with three layers: the top and bottom layers are composed of spicy, sour potatoes; the middle layer is always creamy and made with anything from tuna, chicken, or seafood to crabmeat, eggs, or vegetables that have been coated in mayonnaise. Vibrantly golden ají amarillo adds unmistakable heat (but don't use too much to begin with, as you can always add more on the side). Citrus livens the flavors with a kick of sour tang. In addition, causas are embellished with all sorts of colorful and textural garnishes: olives, avocado, peas, and corn are just some options. In restaurants, causas are presented like little works of art, usually made to order and served in miniature portions (some almost too pretty to eat). At home, however, causas are much more informal. They can be shaped in a regular bowl and unmolded at the table, served and sliced casserole style, or even shaped into roulades to slice into pinwheels. Depending on the potato used, causas can come in a tremendous array of colors. I tend to use Yukon gold potatoes because they remind me of Peruvian papas criollas, with their yellow and creamy flesh that's easy to mold. But use any kind of waxy potato you love. Russets, purple potatoes, and sweet potatoes will all work in this recipe, adding color and sweet tones to the dish. The most important thing is to mash the potatoes thoroughly so the causa will slice evenly, without falling apart. This tuna variation is a favorite with my kids and a good one to start with. More than a recipe, what I offer here are a few suggestions so you can find your own favorite combo. Have fun with the garnishes. Olives, avocado, hard-boiled eggs, bacon crisps, roasted red peppers, hearts of palm, capers, sliced tomatoes, and herbs are just some of my favorites. Causas last for up to three days, covered with plastic wrap and in the refrigerator.

FOR THE POTATO LAYERS

2½ pounds (1.2 kilograms) potatoes (see headnote)

⅓ cup (75 ml) freshly squeezed lime or lemon juice, or more to taste

¼ cup (60 ml) extra-virgin olive oil

3–4 tablespoons ají amarillo paste, or to taste

¼ cup (115 grams) very finely chopped onions (any color)

2 teaspoons fine sea salt, or more to taste

¼ teaspoon freshly ground black pepper, or more to taste

FOR THE TUNA LAYER

15 ounces (430 grams) canned white tuna, drained and mashed well

½ cup (120 ml) mayonnaise

1 tablespoon freshly squeezed lime or lemon juice, or more to taste

½ cup (40 grams) finely chopped celery

½ teaspoon fine sea salt

¼ teaspoon freshly ground black pepper

To make the potato layers: Place the potatoes in a large pot filled with cold water; boil the potatoes until tender (about 20 to 30 minutes); drain, peel, and mash them until smooth (use a potato ricer, if you have one). You should have about 5 cups of mashed potatoes. In a large bowl, combine the mashed potatoes, ⅓ cup (75 ml) of the lime juice, the oil, ají paste, onions, salt, and pepper; stir well and set aside to cool. To make the tuna layer: In a large bowl, gently stir together the tuna, mayonnaise, lemon juice, and celery, and season with salt and pepper, to taste; set aside.

How to Mold a Causa   Here are three different ways to mold causas easily at home:

- Brush a large loaf pan with oil and line the inside with a couple of layers of plastic wrap, leaving an overhang over the sides. Pour half of the potato mixture into the bottom; top with the tuna and spread the remaining potato mixture over the top, forming three layers. →

- Brush an 8 x 3 inch (20 x 8 cm) round pan with oil (or use cooking spray) and line the inside with a couple of layers of plastic wrap, leaving an overhang all around; use a large rubber band to secure the overhanging plastic wrap to the outside of the pan to keep it in place. Pour half of the potato mixture into the pan and spread it evenly to form one layer; top with the tuna, followed by the remaining potato mixture, spreading it evenly with a spatula.
- Use six individual (8 ounce/240 ml) ramekins, or baking rings. Oil them (or use cooking spray); layer a portion of the potato mixture in the bottom of each and pat it evenly to form a flat layer. Top with the tuna, followed by another layer of the potato mixture, spreading it evenly with a spatula.
- Cover the top of the causas with plastic wrap and chill for at least one hour (or up to 4 hours). Carefully invert the molds or ramekins onto plates (or lift the baking rings) and unmold; remove the plastic wrap. Decorate the top with any garnishes of your choice. To serve, slice into thick wedges; serve cold.

VARIATIONS: In place of the tuna, substitute 1 pound (455 grams) cooked lump or claw crabmeat, picked over for shells; cooked and finely chopped chicken meat; or cooked ham, finely chopped. Or substitute 1 pound (455 grams) cooked chopped shrimp and add 2 tablespoons ketchup and 1 tablespoon cognac or brandy to the mayonnaise.

For a vegetarian causa, replace the tuna with 8 hard-boiled eggs, 10 pitted olives, and a few gherkins (or sweet pickles), all of them finely chopped.

Papas Asadas

Oven-Roasted Potatoes

Various Countries | Yield: Serves 4–6 | Difficulty Level: Easy | Total Cooking Time: 1 hour 40 minutes (includes brining time)

Perfectly roasted potatoes with a crispy crust and creamy interior are a joy to eat. When most cooks think of brining, they think of turkeys or tough cuts of meat. However, in Latin America, we sometimes brine root vegetables before roasting. The world has the Incas to thank for potatoes, but it owes the invention of the oven to Europeans. Without the horno, as it is called in Spanish, Latin Americans wouldn't have created this scrumptious techinique for "steam-roasting" potatoes, which gives them a creamy interior while still developing a crisp and crusty skin. I think the world can agree that this was a win-win culinary exchange.

1 tablespoon plus ¾ teaspoon fine sea salt, divided

8 cups (2 liters) cold water

2½ pounds (1.2 kilograms) russet potatoes, scrubbed, peeled, and halved lengthwise

⅓ cup (75 ml) Aceite de Achiote (page 194), or vegetable oil

Pinch of ground white pepper

In a large bowl, combine 1 tablespoon of the salt with the water; place the potatoes in the brine and let them sit at room temperature for 1 hour. Line a large baking sheet (or two smaller ones) with parchment paper; preheat the oven to 425°F (220°C). Brush half of the oil all over the parchment paper. Remove the potatoes from the brine and pat them dry with paper towels. Place the potatoes, cut side down, directly onto the oiled paper. Brush the remaining oil over the potatoes and sprinkle with the remaining salt and pepper. Roast the potatoes for 32 to 35 minutes or until they are crispy and golden on the outside and fork tender.

Papas Doradas al Sartén

Skillet Potatoes

Various Countries | Yield: Serves 4–6 | Difficulty Level: Easy | Total Cooking Time: 1 hour (includes brining time)

These crispy potato bites are cooked in a mixture of fats: the butter adds a lovely flavor, while the oil prevents the former from burning. I prefer to use a nonstick skillet to cook these potatoes so they don't stick at all; however, after steaming, they will release from a regular skillet.

1½ pounds (680 grams) potatoes, such as Yukon gold, carola, or German butterball, peeled and cubed into ½ inch (12 mm) cubes

¼ cup (60 grams) vegetable oil

2 tablespoons (30 grams) unsalted butter

1 teaspoon fine sea salt

¼ teaspoon garlic powder

¼ teaspoon smoked Spanish paprika or pimentón dulce

Place the diced potatoes in a large bowl and cover with cold water; let them sit for 30 minutes or up to 4 hours (any longer and they will discolor). Drain the potatoes in a colander and dry them thoroughly with clean kitchen towels (it is imperative that you dry them very well, so they don't splatter when cooked). Heat the oil in a large skillet set over medium-high heat. Add the butter (it should instantly sizzle and melt). Add the potatoes, salt, garlic powder, and paprika; cook, stirring constantly, until the potatoes are lightly browned, about 6 to 8 minutes. Cover the skillet; lower the heat to medium-low and cook, to steam the potatoes for 8 to 10 minutes or until they are fork tender.

Papitas Fritas

Fries

Various Countries | Yield: Serves 4–6 | Difficulty Level: Intermediate | Total Cooking Time: 45 minutes

Crispy potato fries are a very typical accompaniment to many homemade dishes throughout Latin America and not relegated to fast food alone. We eat them not only with ketchup, but also with chimichurri, Peruvian cremas, mayonnaise-based sauces, and chile relishes.

4 pounds (1.8 kilogram) starchy potatoes, such as russet, peeled

Vegetable oil, for frying

Salt

Fit two large rimmed baking sheets with metal cooling racks and set aside. Using a sharp knife, slice the potatoes into fries that measure approximately 4 to 5 inches (10 to 12 cm) long and ¼ inch (6 mm) thick. Immerse the potatoes in a bowl of iced water for 15 minutes. Drain the potatoes and lay them flat on clean kitchen towels, patting them until they're dry; transfer them to dry kitchen towels and arrange them in one layer; let them air-dry for another 10 minutes (it is imperative that you dry them very well, so they don't splatter when fried). Heat 1½–2 inches (4–5 cm) of oil in a large pot set over medium heat until it reaches 250°F (120°C) (or use a deep fryer according to the manufacturer's instructions). Working in batches, fry the potatoes in the oil until they're soft, about 4 minutes (at this point they will not brown). Use a slotted spoon to transfer them to the prepared baking sheets. When all of the fries have been cooked, increase the oil temperature to 360°F (180°C). Again, working in batches, slide the fries back into the oil and fry them until they're golden and crispy, about 5 minutes. Transfer them back onto the cooling racks and sprinkle them with salt. Serve immediately.

Note: If you wish to keep the fries warm for a while, preheat the oven to 250°F (120°C) and transfer the baking sheets to the oven; they'll stay crispy for up to 30 minutes.

A Note on Fried Foods · When the conquistadores took over the Americas they introduced lard, tallow, butter, oils, and the techniques that made it possible to fry food. (Before they arrived, native Americans boiled or cooked their food directly over fire.) Whether you're frying fish, potatoes, plantains, yuca, or buñuelos (fried dough), you'll be more successful if you follow a few very important rules:

- First, the oil must always be between 360°F and 375°F (180–190°C). The proper temperature will ensure that you form a crust that will stop oil from seeping into the food. If the temperature is too low, the food will absorb the oil like a sponge before it begins to crisp and it will become greasy; if the temperature is too high, the food will burn quickly without cooking through.
- Never fry any food if there are children or pets around; instead, fry before you're ready to serve the meal (see final bullet point below on how to keep fried foods warm).
- It is imperative that the food you are going to fry is completely dry before it comes into contact with the hot oil; this is so you can prevent dangerous splatters. For this reason, most fried foods are coated in crumbs or thick batter. However, when frying something that has no coating, please follow my drying instructions within each recipe.
- If you don't have a deep fryer, do as I do and fry in either a large skillet with high sides (when shallow-frying) or in a deep cast-iron pot when deep-frying.
- Here are two ways to know when your oil is hot enough to fry in:
    1. Use a deep-frying thermometer that can gauge the exact temperature of the oil (they are easy to find online and in kitchen stores).
    2. Dip a wooden spoon into the oil (do not use bamboo or any other kind of spoon). If the spoon bubbles on contact, the oil is ready for frying.
- After all that work making sure the oil is at the right temperature in order to get the perfect crust, nothing is worse than placing the food on paper towels. When hot food comes into contact with paper towels, it produces steam, which invariably turns the crispy texture into a soggy mess. For this reason, always fit rimmed baking sheets with metal (oven-safe) cooling racks. Place the fried food on the racks, allowing excess oil to drain through.
- To keep fried food warm for up to an hour, preheat the oven to 250°F (120°C) and transfer the food on the prepared racks (in the baking pans). This will keep the food elevated and create an airflow that will keep fried foods crispy all around.

Puré de Papas de Mita

My Grandmother's Potato Mash

Guatemala | Yield: Serves 4–6 | Difficulty Level: Easy | Total Cooking Time: 30 minutes

Nobody made creamier or more velvety mashed potatoes than my Mita, my grandmother, Roksanda de Prem. Long before entertaining became a trend, Mita was famous for her parties (some casual and some elaborate), showstopping tablescapes, and majestic flower arrangements. Her manicured estate, Nahoa, features a stately home flanked by four gigantic hexagonal pyramids, and still stands on the outskirts of Guatemala City. On the grounds was an organic farm that grew everything from loquats and pineapple-guavas to heirloom corn varieties of all colors, oranges, and pecans. She raised cattle, chickens, ducks, and pigs. I spent most of my weekends growing up there, and learning to cook with her staff. Regardless of the help she had in the kitchen, not a single meal went out without Mita's final blessing. This is one of the earliest recipes she taught me. Mita would always crown mashed vegetables with butter and plenty of fresh parsley; you should too.

3 large or 5 medium white potatoes, such as russets (about 2½ pounds/1.2 kilogram), peeled and cubed into 2 inch (5 cm) pieces

1 tablespoon plus 1 teaspoon fine sea salt, divided

1 cup (240 ml) whole milk

8 tablespoons (115 grams/1 stick) unsalted butter, diced and divided

Pinch of ground white pepper

2 tablespoons chopped fresh Italian parsley (optional)

Place the potatoes in a large pot and cover them with cold water by 1 inch (2.5 cm); set over medium-high heat and bring to a simmer. Add 1 tablespoon of salt, lower the heat as needed to keep the potatoes at a good simmer, and cook, uncovered, until tender, about 18 to 20 minutes. Shortly before the potatoes are ready, place the milk in a small saucepan over medium heat and bring it to a simmer; remove from heat. Drain the potatoes well in a colander and pass them through a ricer until smooth (see tip below). Once mashed—and while still very hot—add 6 tablespoons (90 grams) of the butter, the milk, the remaining salt, and pepper; stir until well combined. Transfer the mashed potatoes to a serving platter, top with the remaining butter, and sprinkle with the parsley, if using.

Tip: My favorite kitchen tool for mashing tubers is a ricer with adjustable-size holes that works like a giant garlic masher; one push and the potatoes are pureed without any danger of turning them gluey. However, a potato masher or a fork—and plenty of muscle—will do.

Papas Chorreadas

Potatoes with Tomato and Cheese Sauce

Colombia | Yield: Serves 4–6 | Difficulty Level: Easy | Total Cooking Time: 35 minutes

These messy but delectable potatoes are a signature of cooks from Bogotá. They come together very quickly if you have a batch of Hogado Casero (page 158) made in advance; otherwise, the hogado can be easily made in minutes while the potatoes boil. It is traditional to leave the potatoes whole and unpeeled for this dish but I prefer to quarter them before adding the sauce so they can absorb more flavor.

2 pounds (910 grams) white potatoes, unpeeled

2 tablespoons unsalted butter

1 teaspoon all-purpose flour

1 recipe Hogado Casero (page 158)

½ cup (120 ml) whole milk

4 ounces (115 grams) mozzarella cheese, diced into ½ inch (12 mm) cubes

1 teaspoon fine sea salt, or more to taste

¼ teaspoon freshly ground black pepper, or to taste

Chives, for garnish (optional)

Place the potatoes in a large pot and cover with cold water; bring to a boil, uncovered. Continue boiling (lower the heat if the water is boiling over) for 25 minutes or until the potatoes are fork tender. Cool them slightly, then cut each potato into quarters and set them on a platter (keep them tented or lightly covered with foil while you finish the sauce). Set a medium pot over medium heat; melt the butter and stir in the flour, cooking for 1 minute. Add the hogado casero and the milk, cooking until heated through, about 3 to 4 minutes. Add the cheese in batches, stirring until it melts; season with salt and pepper. Pour this sauce directly over the potatoes; sprinkle with chives, if using, and serve immediately.

Ñoquis de La Nona con Mantequilla Negra

Potato Gnocchi with Brown Butter

Various Countries | Yield: Serves 6 | Difficulty Level: Intermediate | Total Cooking Time: 2 hours

As the numbers of Italian immigrants arriving to "make the Americas" increased during the start of the nineteenth century, their culinary influence put down deep roots that remain entrenched to this day. Gnocchi are a long-standing tradition in Latin America, but nowhere are they more revered than in Argentina and Uruguay, where they are served on the twenty-ninth day of each month, a custom that dates back more than a hundred years. By month's end, money could be scarce for the Argentinean-Italian working class. Inexpensive potatoes and a handful of wheat flour were made into dumplings that were filling enough to delay hunger one more day. Home cooks who could afford to would add cheese or eggs to the dough to make it richer. The last day of the month was "payday," and meat again made an appearance on the table. This tradition has stuck over the years, and now you'll find "Gnocchi del 29" not only in homes but also on restaurant menus. My dear friend Irene de Delprée hails from an Italian family that settled in Guatemala City, and still makes her mom's traditional ñoquis for her grandchildren today. The trick to her lighter-than-air dumplings is to mix the mashed potatoes directly into the flour while they're still hot, which makes for a more malleable dough. Because potatoes vary in starch content, I always do a test run with one piece of dough before I shape it all. To do this, simply roll a teaspoon of dough into a ball and place it into a pot of boiling water. The dumpling will fall to the bottom of the pot and rise to the top in a few seconds. If it doesn't fall apart, the rest of the dough is ready to shape and cook; if it disintegrates, add a bit more flour (add ¼ cup/30 grams at a time) until you get the desired results. Gnocchi can also be dressed in rich meat ragù or simple tomato sauces called tuco, but I highly recommend you try Irene's version and serve it alongside a crisp green salad with a simple vinaigrette.

When not serving them immediately, Irene covers the baking dish with the gnocchi with aluminum foil and puts it in a larger pan halfway filled with hot water (a technique called baño María, or bain-marie) and places it in the oven at 250°F (120°C) for up to an hour.

2 pounds (910 grams) russet potatoes

1 tablespoon fine sea salt, divided

2½ cups (345 grams) all-purpose flour, plus more as needed and for dusting

½ teaspoon freshly ground black pepper

8 tablespoons (115 grams/1 stick) unsalted butter, diced

Plenty of grated Parmesan cheese (preferably Parmigiano Reggiano or Reggianito)

Generously flour two large baking sheets and set aside. Grease a 9 x 13 inch (23 x 33 cm) baking pan. Peel and quarter the potatoes and place them in a large pot; cover them with cold water and add 2 teaspoons salt. Bring to a rolling boil over medium-high heat and cook, uncovered, until fork tender, about 15 to 20 minutes. In the meantime, heat a small pot of water until boiling; keep it covered. Drain the potatoes and pass them through a food mill or a ricer to mash them (if mashing them by hand, make sure they are completely smooth). Place them in a large bowl and add the remaining salt and the pepper; mix well with a wooden spoon. While the potatoes are still hot, add all of the flour at once and mix thoroughly with the wooden spoon until combined. As soon as you can, switch to your hands and knead the dough for a couple of minutes, until it comes together into a ball. Do the gnocchi test by rolling a teaspoon of dough into a ball and plunging it into the small pot of boiling water. If it stays together and holds its shape, the dough is ready to use; otherwise, knead in a bit more flour and test again. While the dough is still warm, cut pieces of dough and roll them into ropes about 12 inches (30 cm) long. Cut each rope into 1 inch (2.5 cm) pieces. Roll these pieces into balls; use your thumb to make a slight indentation in the middle of each one and place them in one row on the prepared, floured sheets.

Once all the gnocchi are shaped, fill a large pot with water and bring it to a rolling boil. In the meantime, make the butter sauce: Set a small, heavy-bottomed skillet over medium-high heat. Add the butter and whisk until melted. Continue to cook the butter until it begins to foam up. As soon as the foam subsides (anywhere from 2 to 4 minutes), you'll see brown bits form at the bottom of the pan and the butter will smell nutty. Remove it immediately from the heat and pour it into a medium bowl; set aside to cool while you cook the gnocchi. Add the gnocchi to the boiling water—they'll fall to the bottom of the pot and then, shortly after, float back to the top. Cook them for 30 seconds to 1 minute after they rise to the top and use a strainer to remove them and place them in the prepared baking pan, layering them with some of the browned butter and cheese as you take them out of the pot. Sprinkle with more cheese on top and serve immediately.

A note on shaping gnocchi: Irene's way is to simply push your thumb lightly over the top of each ball of dough to make an indentation. But how you shape them doesn't really matter, and you can even leave them rolled into balls or cut into pillows. The little indentations are just to help sauces and cheese cling to them when cooked.

A Cheesy Secret · It's not unusual to find Latin American cheeses made "in the style of" Italian cheeses. Such is the case with Reggianito, sold in both Argentina and Uruguay; it's made in the style of Parmigiano-Reggiano and is a perfect substitute in recipes that call for the latter. When I can't find either, I use local Parmesan cheese or a nutty, hard cheese such as Romano or Manchego. Reggianito can be found in many grocery stores with high-end cheese sections and in many Latin American grocery stores.

Saice Tarijeño

Beef and Potato Mince

Bolivia | Yield: 4–6 | Difficulty Level: Easy | Total Cooking Time: 30 minutes

Beef and potatoes are at their best in this emblematic picadillo from Tarija, near the Guadalquivir River in Bolivia. This is the kind of recipe you'll want to prepare on a busy night, as it takes only minutes to make but delivers rich and homey flavor. Saice (pronounced *sigh-seh*) became popular in the 1930s, when soldiers on their way to war during the Battle del Chaco were fed this dish by locals; it provided them with the sustenance they needed for the fight. It remains a staple of Bolivian food, no doubt due to its comforting properties, and it reheats beautifully and tastes even better a day after it's made.

2 tablespoons (30 ml) vegetable oil

1½ cups (170 grams) finely chopped red onions

2 garlic cloves, finely chopped

¾ cup (115 grams) finely chopped plum tomatoes

2 tablespoons ají panca paste

1 pound (455 grams) ground beef

1½ teaspoons ground cumin

1 teaspoon ground oregano

1 teaspoon fine sea salt, or more to taste

½ teaspoon freshly ground black pepper, or more to taste

1 pound (455 grams) boiled potatoes, peeled and diced into bite-sized cubes (see how to boil potatoes on page 283)

1½ cups (255 grams) green peas (fresh or frozen and thawed)

Heat the oil in a large skillet set over medium-high heat; add the onions, garlic, and tomatoes. Cook for 2 to 3 minutes or until softened. Add the ají panca and cook for 2 minutes. Add the beef, stirring and breaking it up with a wooden spoon; cook for 2 minutes. Add the cumin, oregano, salt, and pepper and keep on cooking until the meat is no longer pink, stirring often (about 3 minutes). Add ½ cup (120 ml) water and stir well; let the beef simmer, uncovered, for 2 to 3 minutes or until the sauce thickens slightly. (Don't let all of the sauce absorb, as you'll want it to coat the potatoes.) Stir in the cooked potatoes and the peas; heat through and serve.

Soufflé de Papa y Ñame

Potato and Yam Casserole

Panama | Yield: Serves 4–6 | Difficulty Level: Intermediate | Total Cooking Time: 1½ hours

Latin Americans often combine root vegetables in the same recipe. If you love potato casseroles, you'll enjoy this light Panamanian version. Since ñames (white yams) have a higher water content than potatoes, they lighten the overall texture of what is a favorite side dish in my home. This is a light casserole, rich with cheese, and the perfect accoutrement for any kind of roast. Leftover ñame—which has to be used quickly after cutting or it will spoil—is ideal here, because the mashed base can be prepared a day in advance and mixed with the remaining ingredients right before baking. This also makes a fabulous brunch offering to serve alongside egg dishes.

1¼ pounds (600 grams) white potatoes, peeled and cubed

2 pounds (910 grams) ñame, peeled and cubed

1 tablespoon plus 1 teaspoon fine sea salt, divided

4 tablespoons (55 grams) unsalted butter, divided

3 eggs plus 1 egg white

1 cup (115 grams) grated Parmesan cheese

½ cup (120 ml) whole milk

Place the potatoes and ñame in a large pot and cover them with water; add 1 tablespoon of the salt and bring to a boil; lower the heat and simmer, uncovered, for 20 to 25 minutes or until fork tender. Drain well and return the potatoes and ñame to the pot. Use a potato masher to mash the vegetables until smooth—if you have a potato ricer, pass them once through to ensure that no lumps remain and transfer to a bowl. Add 2 tablespoons of the butter and the remaining tablespoon of salt; stir well and let cool for 20 to 30 minutes (or chill, up to overnight). In the meantime, preheat the oven to 400°F (200°C) and grease a 9 x 13 inch (23 x 33 cm) dish. Separate the eggs, placing the egg yolks into a small bowl and the egg whites into the large bowl of a mixer. Beat the egg whites (on high speed, if using an electric mixer) until they form soft peaks, about 1 minute (if using a whisk, about 3 minutes). Add the egg yolks and beat them for 15 seconds or until just combined. Stir the cheese and milk into the potato mixture and carefully fold in the whipped eggs until just combined. Pour into the prepared pan and bake for 30 minutes or until the top is golden.

PLANTAINS

You say "banana," but I say "plátano," because although we eat bananas like everyone else, what really distinguishes Latin American cuisines from most others are the large, starchy fruits of the *Musa paradisiaca* plant. The bananas you slice onto your cereal are from a different plant, *Musa sapientum*. Related, yes, and both delicious, but one is unlike the other because plantains cannot be eaten raw and must always be cooked, while bananas can be enjoyed right from the tree. Like tomatoes, plantains are used both as a vegetable and as a fruit in Latin American recipes. Confused? Let me explain.

Plantains were brought to the Americas from Africa, and although all research points to East Asia as their place of origin, the way Latin Americans cook plantains most certainly resembles African culinary traditions the most. This fruit takes on different properties depending on what stage of ripeness it's at when used.

When plantains are first cut from the tree, they are hard and very green; this is when their starch content is at its highest. At this stage, they are best treated as a vegetable. The flesh of a green plantain is white, and it behaves in the same manner as most tubers, like potatoes and yuca. It can be boiled and mashed into fluffy purees or fried until crispy. This is when it's best suited for soups or stews, where it can cook for a long time and hold its shape. This is also the ideal point to use it in recipes that require "double-frying," such as Puerto Rican tostones and mofongo that are fried first, then mashed or shaped, only to be fried a second time. It's also the best time to use plantains to make thin, crispy chips such as the mariquitas and plataninas that you will find in Guatemala, El Salvador, Panama, and all the way down to Colombia and Ecuador.

As plantains mature, their skin begins to turn yellow. While the plantain is still variegated with greens and yellows, its flesh begins to soften a little bit; only a hint of sweetness is detectable. This is when a plantain is at its best for turning into dough for empanadas and grating for use in cakes and fritters, such as the ones found in Belize, Nicaragua, and Venezuela.

As it continues to ripen, the skin turns a deep golden color and develops mottled brown spots. At this point, the magic begins to happen! This is when the starch commences its transformation into sugars that will turn the flesh a bit yellow, softer, and sweeter. At this point, plantains are still typically treated like a vegetable; they're ideal to mash, but the result will be much sweeter tasting—this is the best time to transform them into fufús, directly inherited from western Africa and popular in Cuba, Puerto Rico, and the Dominican Republic (where it is called mangú). Shallow-fried at this point, the sliced plantains will still be on the savory side, but that hint of sweetness will be more accentuated, ideal for making the famous Honduran iteration of fried plantains called tajadas, served with a dollop of crema and a good slice of queso fresco.

Then, as the sugars caramelize within the flesh of the plantain, it becomes a deep golden color and the skins turn brown—their mottled spots develop to a deep brown and then black color. Now, treat them like fruits. The darker the skin, the sweeter the flesh. When plantains become mostly dotted with brown spots, they are perfect for making maduros or platanitos fritos, the sticky and caramelized slices of softened plantains that taste like candy and that accompany dishes of eggs and beans for breakfast in Central America and Venezuela, or lunch plates of carne asada and gallo pinto in Nicaragua. Bake them with a touch of rum to serve over ice cream as is customary all over the Latin continents. Add them mashed into batters for pancakes, waffles, and muffins.

Right when you think the plantains are past their prime, because their skins turn black as ebony and white mold forms at the tips, is when they are at their sweetest. At this point, cook them and turn them into jams and sauces.

Fufú de Plátano

Plantain Mash with Pork Rinds

Cuba | Yield: Serves 4–6 | Difficulty Level: Easy | Total Cooking Time: 40–45 minutes

This traditional Cuban mash is both sweet and savory, with the ideal combination of soft and crunchy in every bite. In western Africa, fufú (pronounced *foo-foo*) is a mash made with yams, plantains, or yuca, pounded in a large pilón or mortero (mortar) made of wood. In Latin America, fufú can be made from tuberous vegetables such as malanga, potatoes, or yautía, mashed, usually with the addition of chicharrones (pork rinds), which are either crushed or crumbled into the mix. In Puerto Rico, it's known as mofongo. Before the colonization of America, the Siboney, the Amerindian, and the Taíno peoples inhabited the Latin Caribbean. The cuisines of these island nations are, not surprisingly, based on a melding of all of these cultures. The western African culinary influence in this recipe is clear and worthy of celebration. Boiling the plantains with their skins on will save you from the tedious work of trying to peel them when they're raw (when the fruit sticks to the skin). The skins will automatically split as they boil, making them a cinch to remove. Make sure that the plantains are always covered in water; it may be necessary to add boiling water to keep them covered as the water evaporates.

3 large green plantains (about 2 pounds/910 grams)

3 tablespoons (45 ml) olive oil or melted butter

1 teaspoon fine sea salt, or more to taste

½ teaspoon freshly ground black pepper, or more to taste

4 ounces (115 grams) crushed pork rinds (optional, but recommended)

Cut off the ends of the plantains with a sharp knife; place the plantains in a large pot. Fill the pot with enough cold water to cover the plantains; set the pot over medium-high heat and bring to a boil. Simmer the plantains until they are easily pierced with a fork, about 30 to 35 minutes. Reserve 1 cup of the water in which you cooked the plantains and set aside. Drain the plantains in a colander and let them cool enough to handle. Peel the plantains, then slice them into small pieces and transfer to a large bowl. Use a potato masher or a fork to mash the plantains, adding some of the reserved water to help the mash soften to the desired consistency. Stir in the olive oil, salt, and pepper. Sprinkle with the pork rinds, if using, and serve immediately.

Note: Pork rinds can be easily found in most grocery stores around the world. I prefer to use plain ones, not any of the flavored kinds. Place them inside a bag and use a rolling pin or heavy skillet to crush them; alternatively, pulse them in a food processor, until pulverized to your desired texture.

Tostones

Twice-Fried Plantain Coins

Latin Caribbean | Yield: Serves 4–6 | Difficulty Level: Intermediate | Total Cooking Time: 50–55 minutes

These thick chips, also known as patacones, are made to dunk into thick salsas or dips. Select green plantains that don't have any yellow marks on them. You'll want the fattest, thickest plantains possible because they're easier to handle than thin ones (which tend to break when you peel them). You'll have to cut the plantains into thick chunks (at least 1 inch/2.5 cm thick) because after frying them to soften them, you'll flatten them down until they form coins; then, you'll fry them a second time, to crisp them. Although most Latin cooks who make tostones own "tostoneras" (wooden presses with slight indentations to fit the plantain chips), you really don't need one; a mallet or a heavy skillet and a plastic bag will suffice—even a tortilla press will work. Pair them with Aji-li-mójili (page 9), Guacamol (page 207), Guasacaca (page 209), Chimichurri al Cuchillo (page 13), or any of the Peruvian cream sauces. Serve them in place of potato fries and as a side to sandwiches or bistecs (beefsteaks).

2 tablespoons fine sea salt, plus more for sprinkling at the end

1 pound (455 grams) very green plantains (about 3–4 large)

Vegetable oil, for frying (peanut oil works great)

Fill a large bowl with cold water; stir in 2 tablespoons of salt and set aside. Fit two large rimmed baking pans with metal (oven-safe) cooling racks and set aside. Cut off both ends of the plantains with a sharp knife. Score the skin lengthwise (but don't score the flesh). Slide your thumb up and down under the skin, until it comes off. Slice each of the plantains into 1 inch (2.5 cm) slices (you'll get anywhere from 8 to 10 per plantain), and immerse them in the salted water; allow them to brine for 20 minutes (this is to remove the extra starch). Drain the plantains and lay them flat on clean kitchen towels, patting them until they're completely dry; transfer them to dry kitchen towels and arrange them in one layer. Heat 1½-2 inches (4-5 cm) of oil in a large pot set over medium heat until it reaches 250°F (120°C) (or use a deep fryer according to the manufacturer's instructions). Working in batches, slide the plantain slices into the oil and fry them until halfway cooked through, about 1 to 2 minutes. (If they're browning too quickly, remove the pot from the stove and allow the oil to cool down a bit.) Using a slotted spoon, transfer the plantains to the prepared racks and cool for 10 minutes. Working with one at time, transfer each slice to a cutting board and use a mallet or a skillet (or a tostonera) to flatten them down until they are ½ inch (12 mm) thick; repeat until all are flattened. (You can prepare them up to this point and let them sit at room temperature for up to 1 hour before proceeding with the recipe. If you choose to do this, remove the oil from the heat until you're ready to continue.) Heat the oil to 360°F (180°C); working in batches, return the plantain slices to the oil and fry them until they're crispy and a deep golden color, about 2 to 3 minutes. Transfer to the prepared racks to drain, and sprinkle with salt while hot.

Note: You can keep the tostones warm in a 250°F (120°C) oven for up to 1 hour.

VARIATION: To make jibaritos, the famous Puerto Rican sandwiches, slice the plantains in half, not into coins. Fry the halves in the oil as you would for the tostones, until they're slightly golden all over, 2 to 3 minutes. Use tongs to transfer them to the prepared metal racks; remove the oil from the heat. Working with one piece of plantain at a time, flatten them between two pieces of parchment paper with a heavy skillet (or a mallet) to ¼ inch (6 mm) thick (they'll be about the size of a small slice of bread). When all of the pieces are flattened (you should have 6 or 8 total), set the oil back on medium-high heat; when the oil is hot, fry the plantain slices about 1-2 more minutes or until golden brown and crispy. →

Drain them. To make the sandwiches, layer a piece of lettuce on half of the plantain slices; top each with a generous amount of Carne Mechada (page 461, or see the variation for Ropa Vieja). Top this with a slice of queso blanco or a good melting cheese and drizzle with mayonnaise and hot sauce, before topping it with another plantain slice. I bet you can't eat one without making a delicious mess!

Platanitos Fritos

Fried Sweet Plantains

Various Countries | Yield: Serves 6–8 | Difficulty Level: Easy | Total Cooking Time: 20 minutes

Sweet, sticky, caramelized plantains are part of the Latin trinity along with beans and rice, and are the ever-present accompaniments to daily meals in many countries. Perfectly cooked, they develop a crispy and chewy exterior while remaining creamy inside. Some people call them maduros, machos, or plátanos dulces. I call them decadently delectable, because that's what they are when made well. They go magnificently with both savory and sweet dishes. Sometimes, they're stuffed into sandwiches—like in the famous arepas pabellón, which combine shredded beef, beans, cheese, and plantains. When I was little, I ate them as an after-school snack, sprinkled with sugar and doused with crema. In my husband's childhood home, they were often served as dessert, alongside mashed black beans and a giant bowl of sugar. Make sure the plantains you use for this recipe have almost completely blackened skins; their flesh should be soft but not mushy. The trick here is to cook them in oil that is hot but not too hot, so you don't burn the natural sugars in the plantains, which will make them bitter. Turn them over only when the bottoms are caramelized, and they won't stick to your pan.

1½ pounds (680 grams) very ripe plantains (about 4–5), with fully blackened skins

Vegetable oil, for frying

Fit a baking pan with a metal cooling rack and set aside. Using a sharp knife, cut off the ends of the plantains; slit the skins lengthwise (being careful not to cut through the flesh) and peel the plantains. Heat ½ inch (12 mm) of oil in a large pan to 325°F (160°C), set over medium heat. Add the plantains and fry them slowly, letting them turn golden on the first side before turning them over to the second (about 3 minutes per side). Don't let the oil get too hot; lower the heat if necessary. Use two forks to lift the plantains and place them onto the prepared cooling rack; drain. Serve immediately or keep them warm in a 250°F (120°C) oven for up to 1 hour.

Note: Freeze the plantains in a container, layering them between parchment paper, and cover tightly. They keep frozen for up to 2 months. When ready to use, thaw them in the refrigerator for a couple of hours before transferring them to a parchment paper–lined baking sheet. Reheat in a 300°F (150°C) oven until warm, about 10 minutes.

VARIATION: To make pabellón, a traditional Venezuelan dish, serve a portion of these plantains with a mound of white rice, a good portion of Frijoles de Olla (page 118) and Carne Mechada (page 461). You can also add plantains and shredded beef to the filling for Arepas Dominó (page 109) and the Arepas Pabellón (page 109).

How to Peel a Plantain · Always begin by cutting off the top and bottom tips. If the plantain is hard and green, the skin will be firmly attached to the flesh, making it hard to peel. Use a sharp knife to slice through the skin from top to bottom, being careful not to cut through the flesh. Slip your thumb through the open slit and slide it up and down, all the while turning the plantain as the skin releases. Your thumbs will turn black with the resin that seeps from the skins. You can also use a potato peeler to remove tough sections of skin. If the plantain is ripe, you'll cut through the skin in exactly the same way, but the skin will peel off like that of a banana.

Plataninas

Plantain Chips

Various Countries | Yield: Serves 4–6 | Difficulty Level: Intermediate | Total Cooking Time: 20 minutes

Crunchy, salty, thin plantain chips—also known as mariquitas or chifles, depending on the country—are among Latin Americans' favorite foods to serve as an accompaniment to soups, as a topping for salads, or to dunk in guacamoles, salsas, ceviches, and cremas. Make them up to two days ahead and keep them in paper bags so they remain crunchy. These can be served as a side dish to many of the recipes in this book; they are particularly delicious when dipped into Aji-li-mójili (page 9) or any chimichurri, or alongside a ceviche of your choice.

1 pound (455 grams) very green plantains (about 3–4 large)

Vegetable oil, for frying (peanut oil works great)

Salt, to taste

Fit two large-rimmed baking sheets with metal cooling racks and set them aside. Using a sharp knife, cut off both ends of each plantain; score the skin lengthwise (but don't score the flesh). Slide your thumb up and down under the skin until it comes off. Slice the plantains with a mandolin or a sharp knife into thin strips (here, you can choose to cut them on the bias for long chips, or across for tiny, circular chips). Heat 1½–2 inches (4–5 cm) of oil in a large pot set over medium heat until it reaches 360°F (180°C) (or use a deep fryer according to the manufacturer's instructions). Working in batches, fry the plantains for 1½ minutes or until they're golden and crispy (depending on how thick they are, they'll take more or less time to crisp). Use a slotted spoon to transfer them to the prepared racks to drain and sprinkle them with salt immediately.

Note: Plantains can be slippery, so be very careful when using a mandoline to slice them; always use the finger guard (the protective tool with grips in the bottom) to hold the plantains as you slice, following the guide wall on the side as you push into the slicing blade. Or use cut-resistant gloves (available online and in kitchenware stores).

Mofongo

Plantain and Pork Rind Cups

Puerto Rico | Yield: Serves 8 | Difficulty Level: Intermediate | Total Cooking Time: 1 hour

Say it three times—"Mofongo, mofongo, mofongo!"—and celebrate these crispy cups of delight that combine the sweet flesh of plantains with the meaty flavor of pork. Most Puerto Rican cooks own at least one pilón (a Taíno wooden mortar and pestle, shaped like a deep cup), necessary to pound ingredients together; a food processor will do the job well, too. Expert cooks shape the mofongo cups in the pilones and bang them upside down to slide them out. You can press individual portions in ramekins or use a handheld metal citrus juicer and obtain the same result. Fill mofongo with Mojito Isleño (page 10), seafood salads, or ceviches. This version is simple to make at home, even if you don't have a mortar and pestle.

Vegetable oil, for frying

3 green plantains (about 1 pound/790 grams), peeled and cut into 1 inch (2.5 cm) slices

3½ cups (170 grams) coarsely chopped fried pork rinds

1 recipe Mojito Isleño (page 10)

Fit a large baking pan with a metal rack. In a large skillet with high sides, heat 2 inches (5 cm) of oil to 360°F (180°C) (or use a deep fryer according to the manufacturer's instructions); working in batches, slide the plantains into the oil and fry until golden, about 5 to 6 minutes total, turning to cook on all sides. Remove them with a slotted spoon and place them on the prepared baking pan to drain.

Oil eight ½ cup (120 ml) ramekins and set aside. Working in batches, pound together a third of the plantains, a third of the pork rinds, and a quarter of the mojito in a large, sturdy bowl or a mortar and pestle (or use a food processor and pulse them together) until the mixture holds together when pressed between two fingers; repeat with another third of the ingredients and then the rest. Divide the pounded mixture into eight ⅓ cup (75 ml) portions and press each into the bottom and sides of the prepared ramekins; shape them into cups; turn them over and unmold. Turn the cups over and fill them with the remaining mojito and serve, filled with seafood salads or ceviches.

Empanadas de Maduros

Ripe Plantain and Beef Turnovers

Central America and Latin Caribbean | Yield: Makes 12 empanadas |
Difficulty Level: Intermediate | Total Cooking Time: 1 hour

Not all empanadas are made with bread dough. Here, beef picadillo is stuffed into a gluten-free plantain dough in order to create the sweet and savory version of empanadas loved throughout the Latin Caribbean. Plantains were brought to the Americas from Africa, and today, there is not a single Latin country where they are not included as part of a trinity completed by rice and beans. In Guatemala, plantain empanadas are filled with refried beans; in Nicaragua, they are filled with cheese and sprinkled with sugar after frying; and in the Latin Caribbean, they are stuffed with myriad picadillo recipes, such as those found in this book. The marriage of sweet and savory flavors is one we inherited from Middle Eastern cuisine. Enjoy these empanadas for breakfast, paired with eggs, or for dinner, alongside a salad.

4 large yellow plantains (about 2½ pounds/1.2 kilograms)

1 tablespoon fine sea salt

⅓ cup (40 grams) all-purpose flour (rice or yuca flour work well for gluten-free cooking), as needed

1 recipe Picadillo Sencillo (page 449), chilled

Vegetable oil, for frying

With a sharp knife, cut off the tips of the plantains; slice the plantains in half, crosswise. Place them in a large pot; cover with water and add the salt. Bring to a boil over high heat; boil the plantains until fork tender (their skins will split open), about 20 to 22 minutes. Drain the plantains well and transfer them to a large bowl; let cool for 15 minutes. Peel the plantains (discard the peels) and mash them well with a fork or a potato masher, until very smooth. If the dough is too loose, chances are that your plantains were too ripe; to solve this, you can add flour, one tablespoon at a time, until the dough holds when pressed together. Divide the dough into 12 equal portions (about 2 ounces/55 grams each). Moisten your hands and shape the dough into small balls. Cut a ziplock bag open on three sides, like a book. Place a ball in the middle of the bag and flatten it slightly. Use a flat-bottomed plate (or skillet) to flatten the ball into a 5½ inch (14 cm) disc. Place 2 heaping tablespoons of picadillo (or any other filling) in the middle of the disc, leaving a small rim; use the bag to fold the dough over the filling, forming a half-moon. Press the edges together with your fingers to seal well. Transfer the empanada to the prepared sheet. Repeat with the rest of the dough and filling, keeping the empanadas covered with a sheet of plastic or a clean kitchen towel as you work. Fit a large baking sheet with a metal cooling rack and set it aside. In a large skillet with high sides, heat 1½ inches (4 cm) of oil to 360°F (180°C). Working in batches, carefully slide the empanadas into the oil and fry them until they are golden, about 3 to 4 minutes, turning them over halfway through. If the oil gets too hot as you fry and the empanadas are browning too quickly, lower the heat and cool the oil slightly before frying any more. Use a slotted spoon to transfer the fried empanadas to the prepared rack to drain. Sprinkle with salt, let rest for a couple of minutes, and serve.

VARIATIONS: For vegetarian and vegan options: In place of picadillo, fill with a shredded melting cheese, such as mozzarella, or with refried beans (canned are fine). For a truly decadent empanada, fill each with a piece of queso blanco and a spoonful of guava jelly.

Pastelón de Plátano Maduro y Carne

Plantain and Beef Casserole

Dominican Republic and Puerto Rico | Yield: Serves 6–8 | Difficulty Level: Easy | Total Cooking Time: 1½ hours

This is one of the most iconic family meals in the Latin Caribbean: sweet, savory, filling, and oh, so rich in Creole flavor. Think of this as a gluten-free lasagna (with attitude!), in which layers of mashed plantain envelop tangy meat, seasoned with sofrito. Every bite is an explosion of juxtaposed flavors—a little sweetness interspersed with a lot of piquant zing but without any hint of spicy heat. My version is similar to one made by my friend Maria Isabel, from Santo Domingo. Depending on the household, you'll find variations that include raisins, olives, capers, or all of the above, as part of the filling; feel free to make your own mélange. Use ripe plantains; the more specks of black in the yellow peel and the sweeter the flesh inside, the quicker they'll cook in the water, and the easier they'll be to spread. The herb of choice in the Latin Caribbean is long-leaf culantro, also known as sawtooth coriander (*Eryngium foetidum*), which to me tastes like über cilantro, with a stronger, grassier taste than regular cilantro. If you can't find it, simply double the amount of the latter. Like many casseroles, this one is even better the day after it's made so I always plan to have leftovers. It also freezes well and reheats beautifully in the microwave.

6 large, ripe plantains (about 4 pounds /1.8 kilograms)

1 tablespoon fine sea salt, divided

2 tablespoons vegetable oil

1¼ cups (175 grams) roughly chopped white or yellow onions

1 cup (175 grams) stemmed, seeded, and finely chopped green bell peppers

1 cup (175 grams) stemmed, seeded, and finely chopped red bell peppers

2 cups (200–225 grams) finely chopped plum tomatoes

½ cup (30 grams) long-leaf fresh culantro, finely chopped (or double the amount of cilantro)

2 large garlic cloves, finely chopped

1 pound (455 grams) lean ground beef

¼ cup (60 ml) tomato paste

½ cup (120 ml) white wine

½ cup (70 grams) raisins (optional)

4 tablespoons (60 grams) unsalted butter

½ teaspoon white pepper

2 cups (225 grams) shredded queso blanco, mozzarella, Muenster, or other good melting cheese

Grease a 19 x 13 inch (23 x 33 cm) baking pan and set aside. With a sharp knife, cut off the tips of the plantains, then slice the plantains in half crosswise. Place them in a large pot and cover them with water; add 1 teaspoon fine sea salt. Bring the pot to a boil over high heat; boil the plantains until they're fork tender and their skins split, about 20 to 22 minutes. Preheat the oven to 350°F (180°C). Heat the oil in a large nonstick skillet set over medium-high heat; add the onions, peppers, tomatoes, culantro, and garlic, cooking, while stirring, until the vegetables are soft, about 4 to 5 minutes. Add the beef and cook until the beef is no longer pink, making sure to break it up with a spoon as it cooks (about 4 minutes). Add the tomato paste, wine, raisins, and 2 teaspoons of salt. Continue cooking until most of the liquid has evaporated, about 4 minutes. Set aside while you prepare the plantain layer.

Transfer the plantains to a large bowl; reserve ½ cup (120 ml) of the cooking liquid and set aside. Drain the plantains well and allow them to cool slightly, about 5 minutes. With a knife, slice the peel lengthwise, and slide the flesh into a bowl (discarding the skins); mash the plantains well with a fork or a potato masher until smooth (using some of the reserved liquid, to make it more spreadable and the consistency of soft mashed potatoes). Add the butter and the white pepper and stir until melted. Spread half of the plantains onto the prepared baking pan in an even layer; top with half of the cheese and all of the meat mixture. Layer the remaining plantain mixture on top, making sure to spread it evenly; top with the rest of the cheese. Bake the casserole in the oven for 30 to 35 minutes or until it's bubbly and the cheese has melted thoroughly and begins to turn a golden color. →

Note: If you wish to give this dish a Puerto Rican flavor, add 1 tablespoon of the Sazón con Achiote y Culantro on page 199 and 1 teaspoon fine sea salt.

VARIATIONS: For a vegetarian alternative, skip the beef filling and instead layer a mixture of good melting cheese, sliced green onions, and red bell peppers to make a pastelón de queso.

Cilantro: You Either Love It or You Hate It · If you lack a "cilantro gene" (as did Julia Child, who just couldn't stand the flavor), this herb probably tastes bitter and soapy, instead of lemony. Try culantro before you completely give up—it's a different herb, and some people who can't stand one do well with the other. However, if your palate truly rejects it, know that you are not alone. If you really can't eat cilantro, substitute with equal parts parsley and fresh mint—the flavor is not the same, but the combination offers a similar punch with a lovely aroma.

Plátanos con Tocino

Plantain and Bacon Hash

Honduras | Yield: Serves 4–6 | Difficulty Level: Easy | Total Cooking Time: 20 minutes

If you like the combination of savory and sweet flavors, you'll swoon over this golden plantain hash. Eat it for breakfast, lunch, or dinner. At home, I serve it with black beans, fluffy flour tortillas, and plenty of tangy crema (preferably Honduran, which is rich and higher in acidity than other Central American varieties) or sour cream. If you like crispy bacon, then use thin slices; but if, like many Hondurans, you prefer it meatier, then use thick-cut rashers, if you can find them. I prefer to use a nonstick pan to cook this because it prevents the plantains from sticking, helping them to retain their shape and stay intact.

3 large ripe plantains (about 1½ pounds/680 grams)

6 ounces (170 grams) sliced bacon

4 to 6 eggs, scrambled or fried (optional)

Peel and cut the plantains into bite-sized cubes and set aside. Cut the bacon into bite-sized pieces and place in a nonstick skillet, set over medium-high heat. Cook the bacon until it has rendered its fat but still retains some chewiness, about 2 to 3 minutes. Remove the bacon with a slotted spoon and set aside in a bowl. Add the plantains to the pan and cook, while stirring, until they're browned all over, about 5 to 6 minutes. Return the bacon to the skillet and stir, cooking for 1 to 2 minutes or until the bacon is a bit crispier (being careful not to let it burn). Serve immediately and top with an egg, if using.

Plátanos en Gloria

Plantains in Rum and Butter Sauce

Various Countries | Yield: Serves 4–6 | Difficulty Level: Easy | Total Cooking Time: 1 hour

Here the beloved plantain is transformed into a syrupy and sweet dessert easy enough to make on a weekday, yet elegant enough to serve on your finest china. This is a common dessert all over the Latin Caribbean, where rum and sugar abound. When I was a child, this was always served with a generous portion of velvety crema or vanilla ice cream, which would melt delicately into the sauce. Use the darkest rum you can find for a rich flavor. You'll want to use very yellow plantains with black spots on the skin that are starting to soften. Move over, bananas Foster!

2 pounds (910 grams) ripe plantains (about 4 large)

1 cup (240 ml) freshly squeezed orange juice

¼ cup (60 grams) dark rum

1 packed cup (170 grams) brown sugar

4 tablespoons (30 grams) unsalted butter, melted

One ¼ ounce (10 gram) stick of Mexican cinnamon (canela)

4 whole cloves

Pinch of fine sea salt

Crema or vanilla ice cream (optional)

Preheat the oven to 375°F (190°C). Grease a 9 x 13 inch (23 x 33 cm) baking dish and set aside. Peel the plantains with a knife and cut them across in half; set them in the dish. In a medium bowl, whisk together the orange juice, rum, brown sugar, butter, cinnamon, cloves, and salt. Pour mixture over the plantains and cover the entire dish with aluminum foil. Bake for 1 hour (stopping to baste the plantains with the juices a couple of times during the cooking process) or until the plantains are soft and the sauce is syrupy. Serve hot or warm.

RICE

Rice arrived in the Americas with the second Spanish expedition, when the conquistadores once more crossed the ocean. This time, however, they knew which familiar ingredients they would need to bring with them to survive in the New World. Ironically, and in the same year that Queen Isabel de Castilla and King Fernando de Aragón paid the Genovese explorer Christopher Columbus to voyage the seas, Spain had only just reconquered their own land from the Arabs who had ruled it for seven hundred years. By the time Spaniards arrived in the Americas, they had already inherited a passion for rice dishes from the Ottomans, who popularized them in Spain during their rule. The Spanish had high hopes that rice would be as easy to grow in the New World as sugar had proved to be on the first voyage. By 1512, rice had become popular with the inhabitants of the conquered lands, but the first agricultural results proved a dismal failure.

Even though Indigenous peoples, European conquistadores, and African workers (both enslaved and free) coexisted from the very onset of the conquista, the marriage (or mestizaje) of their food came long before the legalized union of their peoples. In 1514, by legal decree Spain proclaimed the lifting of these impediments; interracial marriages were not only allowed but encouraged. In contrast to the British colonizers, who believed mixed unions produced "impure" races, the Spaniards believed that interracial marriages provided stability to their governments and further allowed for the religious conversion of the colonized natives.

Rice became a key element in the culinary commingling that ultimately gave us present-day Latin American cuisines. What would these be without the iconic rice and beans, which represent the marriage of Spanish, African, and Indigenous tastes?

I like to think that the whole of Latin America was shaped in the kitchen and seasoned on the metaphorical table of history. Looking back, it was inevitable. Looking forward, it is unstoppable. The colonial period (*época colonial*) that spanned from 1521 to 1821 (the year when Latin American countries began to gain their independence from Spain) solidified the creolized cuisines of these twenty-one countries, with a combination of classic European techniques, Spanish baroque elements, African touches, and Persian influences, all of them sustained by those of the Amerindians.

It was during this time that the pilaf method (in which grains are first toasted in fat before any liquid is added) became the favorite of Latin American kitchens, as it has continued to be up to modern times. The paellas that peasants created in Spanish fields translated into all sorts of mixed rice dishes like the arroces atollados of Colombia and the rice and seafood delicacies of Belize. Arroz con pollo in all its iterations—whether a Puerto Rican sofrito-laden version, or a Peruvian arroz con pato—became emblematic of the food of abuelas everywhere. Crispy rice croquetas and rice casseroles—creamy or layered—were cemented into everyday repertoires, as were sweet rice puddings, studded with dried fruits, seeds, and nuts.

The rice that originated in Asia became a key ingredient in almost every national dish in the Americas. And African traditions of mixing rice and peas allowed for the creation of many new dishes that featured American beans. By the time new immigrants arrived in Latin America at the turn of the nineteenth century, palates were ready to welcome the risottos of Italy, which became the arroz quesú of Paraguay; the fried rice concoctions of Asia, which translated into the chaufas of Peru and the chaulafanes of Ecuador; the rice and pasta mixtures of the Middle East, which became the arroz con fideos of Argentina;

and the one-pot rice meals or sopas secas of Mexico.

You can taste that history in these recipes. Some of these dishes were created in ancient times, some were passed down from mothers and grandmothers, and some are modern inventions by busy cooks who need a quick meal that can feed an entire family. This is by no means an all-inclusive list; for every one of these recipes, there are thousands more in the Latin territory.

Arroz Blanco

Basic White Rice Pilaf

Various Countries | Yield: Serves 4–6 | Difficulty Level: Easy | Total Cooking Time: 30 minutes

Many cooks are intimidated by cooking rice. This is my dependable method that takes away any guesswork. I was taught to wash rice to rinse off any excess starch that causes the grains to stick together; most Latin cooks still do the same thing. This is the easiest way I know to make rice that's perfectly fluffy and with grains that stay separate, without clumping.

1¼ cups (250 grams) long-grain white rice

2 tablespoons vegetable oil, butter, or lard

1 teaspoon fine sea salt

Place the rice in a fine colander and rinse for 1 minute under cold water, rubbing the grains with your fingers to rid them of excess starch; drain the rice well and let it dry slightly for about 5 minutes. Heat the oil in a medium pot set over medium-high heat; add the rice, stirring to coat well with the oil, for about 1 to 2 minutes (the grains will become translucent). Stir in 2½ cups (600 ml) water and the salt. Bring the liquid to a rolling boil; cover, lower the heat to low, and simmer, undisturbed for 18 minutes (no peeking!). Uncover and continue cooking until the rice is dry (all liquid has evaporated), about 2 more minutes. Remove from the heat, fluff with a fork, and serve.

VARIATION: Easy yellow rice pilaf: Dissolve 1½ teaspoons of Bijol or Badia food coloring powder and 2 teaspoons of chicken bouillon granules in the cooking liquid; continue with the recipe.

Arroz Amarillo

Yellow Rice

Cuba | Yield: Serves 6 | Difficulty Level: Easy | Total Cooking Time: 30 minutes

You'll find that this classic golden rice makes a frequent appearance on Cuban tables. It gets its vibrant color from the rust-colored seed of the achiote tree (*Bixa orellana*). The hard seeds, found in the international aisle of most supermarkets, are steeped in oil until they release their reddish color; then they are discarded. In order for the rice to grab on to the color, you must sauté it for at least two minutes; skipping this step will give you unevenly colored rice.

¼ cup (60 ml) Aceite de Achiote (page 194)

1 cup (170 grams) stemmed, seeded, and finely chopped green bell peppers

½ cup (115 grams) very finely chopped white onions

2 cups (400 grams) long-grain white rice

3 garlic cloves, minced finely

3¾ cup (900 ml) chicken stock or water

2 teaspoons fine sea salt

½ teaspoon freshly ground black pepper

Heat the oil in a medium Dutch oven set over medium-high heat. Add the bell peppers and onions and cook until softened, making sure to stir often, about 4 minutes. Add the rice and cook, while stirring, for 2 minutes, making sure to coat all of the grains well with the oil; add the garlic and cook for 30 seconds. Add the stock (or water), salt, and pepper, stirring the mixture well. Bring the liquid to a boil; cover the pot, lower the heat to a simmer, and let the rice cook undisturbed for 20 minutes. Fluff the rice with a fork and stir to combine the ingredients well.

VARIATION: Add a few sliced green olives, a handful of capers, and chopped roasted red peppers to make this into an arroz criollo. Add some chopped bacon, carrots, tomatoes, and peas to make a Dominican arroz con vegetales. Add ½ cup (120 ml) of Aliño (page 9) when you sauté the rice and 1 pound (455 grams) of cooked and chopped shrimp in the last 2 minutes of cooking time to make an Ecuadorian arroz con camarones.

Seasoning Rice · Nothing is worse than rice that needs more salt after it's been cooked. Salt won't dissolve into a pot of cooked rice. The easiest way to control the final flavor is to taste the cooking liquid at the start of the process. Adjust it (and other flavorings) as soon as liquid is added. Remember to taste, taste, taste!

Arroz Pegao

Crispy White Rice

Various Countries | Yield: Serves 6 | Difficulty Level: Intermediate

Spaniards call it socarrat, Persians (who taught the Spanish how to make it) call it tahdig (literally, "bottom of the pot"), and Latin Americans call it arroz pegao, concón, concolón, pegado, or rapita (among other names). All refer to the crispy, golden crust left in the bottom of a pot of cooked rice. You'll also find this technique in recipes such as the jollofs of West Africa. It comes as no surprise that toasted rice dishes are favorites, particularly in countries like Brazil, Panama, Colombia, and Ecuador, where these cultures collided. This is a recipe to cook using all of your senses: as the heat is increased toward the end of the cooking process, you should be able to smell the rice toasting, and if you listen carefully, a gentle crackling sound. Only then should you reach into the bottom of the pot with a spoon to check if the rice has formed a base that gives a little bit of resistance when prodded. This is not the kind of rice you invert beautifully onto a platter with a perfect golden crust on top. Rather, the crust that remains stuck to the bottom of the pot when the rice is removed is broken off in pieces and scattered over the top. This is my cousin Lucrecia de Aguiar's recipe. I don't know anyone who makes it better.

4 tablespoons (60 ml) vegetable or olive oil, or melted unsalted butter or lard, divided

½ cup (60 grams) finely chopped white onions

3 garlic cloves, finely chopped

1½ cups (325 grams) medium-grain rice

2 teaspoons fine sea salt

Heat half of the oil in a medium pot, set over medium heat. Add the onions, garlic, and rice and toss constantly until the grains begin to toast (they'll change color slightly), about 3 to 4 minutes. Add 3¼ cups (780 ml) water and the salt; taste and adjust the seasoning to your liking; increase the heat to medium-high. Bring the liquid to a boil; cover, reduce the heat to low, and simmer for 20 to 22 minutes, undisturbed (do not peak under the lid during this time; it's imperative that the steam remain trapped inside the pot). Remove the lid (small holes or craters should have formed in the rice); drizzle the remaining oil and 2 tablespoons of water all over the top of the rice. Cover again and increase the heat to medium; continue cooking, undisturbed, until you can smell the rice toasting or hear it crackling slightly, about 5 to 8 minutes. To gauge if it's ready, remove the lid and bury the back of a wooden spoon into the rice until it reaches the bottom of the pot, then take a peek. If you see that the crust has stuck to the bottom, it's ready. If the rice still moves freely at the bottom of the pot, keep on cooking, uncovered, checking it every couple of minutes (be careful not to let it burn). Remove the pot from the heat and cool slightly, about 5 minutes. To serve, place the rice (without the crust) on a serving platter, remove the crust from the pot by scraping it off (it will break), and place it over the top of the rice. Serve hot.

VARIATION: Even if you can make arroz pegao perfectly, the crust is not always enough to go around (lucky are the ones who get to it first!). To make a "falso pegao" (a "fake it till you make it" crispy rice layer), place 2 tablespoons of fat (lard, oil, butter, bacon renderings, duck fat, etc.) in a nonstick pan; add a layer of cooked rice (about ½ inch/12 mm thick) and pat it down with a spatula to cover the entire base of the skillet. Cook it over medium heat until you can easily slide it around the pan, a sign that the base is crisping. At this point it should be easy to lift one side and check the color; it's ready when it is golden and crispy.

Arroz Tostado con Lorocos

Toasted Rice with Loroco Buds

El Salvador | Yield: Serves 4–6 | Difficulty Level: Easy | Total Cooking Time: 30 minutes

This toasted rice dish is typical in Salvadorian homes, where it is often served with grilled beef (carne asada) or chicken (pollo a la plancha) and a simple salad of lettuce and tomatoes. Here, rice is toasted in two different steps. First, it's toasted dry. Toasting dry rice before cooking adds a nutty flavor and has been done for centuries in Asia (to make Thai khao-khua, or toasted rice powder). Then it's toasted a second time, in fat (known as the pilaf method). These techniques—which arrived with the Spaniard colonizers during the fifteenth century—are frequently used in combination in Central American countries. The term *arroz tostado*—toasted rice—became embedded in the Latin culinary lexicon when Asian immigrants settled in the Americas. Loroco are the buds of a wild flower that grows throughout Mesoamerica. They grow in clusters held together by edible stamens; they must be chopped before cooking. Their taste falls somewhere between asparagus and spinach—since many people assume they're eating asparagus tips, you can substitute them here. You can buy loroco frozen in Latin American stores or in jars (see Sources).

10 ounces (280 grams) plum tomatoes

1 very small (about 2 ounces/ 55 grams) white or yellow onion, peeled and left whole

2 whole garlic cloves, unpeeled and left whole

1 red or green bell pepper (roughly 6–7 ounces/170–200 grams), stemmed, seeded, and cut in half

1 cup (185 grams) long-grain white rice

1 tablespoon vegetable oil

1 tablespoon unsalted butter

1 cup (240 ml) vegetable or chicken broth (or water)

1½ cups (115 grams) chopped loroco buds (or asparagus tips, see headnote)

1 teaspoon fine sea salt, or more to taste

¼ teaspoon freshly ground black pepper, or more to taste

Place the tomatoes, onion, garlic cloves, and bell peppers (cut side up) in a dry skillet and roast them for about 6 to 7 minutes, turning them often until they are charred on all sides. Peel the onion and garlic and transfer them to a blender; chop the tomatoes and the pepper and add them to the blender. Blend until completely smooth, about 1 minute and set aside. Toast the rice by placing it in a large skillet with high sides set over medium-high heat and stirring constantly for 2 to 3 minutes or until it turns a light golden color. Add the oil and butter and continue toasting for 1 to 2 more minutes or until the rice is a rich golden color (be careful not to let it burn). Immediately add the entire blended mixture and stir for 1 minute (be careful, as it will splatter at first). Add the broth, loroco buds, salt, and pepper. Bring to a boil; cover, lower the heat, and simmer the rice for 18 to 20 minutes or until all of the liquid has evaporated. Serve hot.

Arroz con Fideos

Rice and Vermicelli Pilaf

Various Countries | Yield: Serves 4–6 | Difficulty Level: Easy | Total Cooking Time: 25 minutes

White rice is speckled with strands of toasted fideos (vermicelli) in this dish representative of the Arab-Latino culinary movement. All of the pilaf-style rice recipes prevalent in Latin American cuisines originated in the Middle East and in northern Africa. This side dish, commonly found in the recipe cards of cooks in the Dominican Republic, Colombia, Venezuela, Argentina, Mexico, and Brazil, hasn't changed in centuries, and is identical to ones you will find in Egypt, Syria, and Lebanon. To make a pilaf, grains are first toasted or lightly fried in fat; only when they have begun to change color is liquid added and the grains allowed to steam. My Venezuelan-born friend Elena Fumagalli taught me to make this decades ago. The secret lies in making sure that the fideos (or broken strands of angel-hair pasta) are perfectly golden before the rice joins them in the pot. You may cook this with water, but I prefer the taste lent by chicken broth (vegetable broth also works wonders here).

3 tablespoons (45 ml) vegetable oil

2½ ounces (70 grams) fideos or broken strands of vermicelli or angel-hair pasta

1¼ cups (255 grams) long-grain white rice

2⅓ cups (550 ml) chicken or vegetable broth or water

½ teaspoon fine sea salt, or more to taste

1 tablespoon unsalted butter (optional)

Heat the oil in a medium pot set over medium-high heat; add the fideos and cook, while tossing, until they are a deep golden color (being careful not to burn them), about 1 to 1½ minutes. Stir in the rice and cook for 1 minute, making sure to coat all of the grains with the oil. Add the chicken broth and salt (the liquid will sizzle on contact—this is what you want to hear!). Bring to a rolling boil; cover, lower the heat to low, and simmer, undisturbed, for 18 to 20 minutes or until all of the liquid has been absorbed. Remove from the heat. If using, dot the top of the rice with the butter and let it sit, covered, for 5 minutes. Fluff with a fork, and serve.

Arroz con Pato

Rice and Duck

Peru | Yield: Serves 8 | Difficulty Level: Intermediate | Total Cooking Time: 1 hour

This deeply comforting rice is soupy and very creamy—almost like risotto. Spaniards brought composed rice dishes from the Old World, including paella. Today, every country in Latin America features its own version of arroz con pollo, or rice with chicken. However, Peruvians make this magnificent version with duck. The rice takes on a green color from the addition of culantro (*Eryngium foetidum*), an herb that I describe as the flamboyant cousin of cilantro. (If you can't find it, simply use double the amount of cilantro.) Use a meat cleaver or have your butcher chop the duck (through the bone) into small pieces so it can cook through in the same time that it takes the rice to cook. This makes a big pot—enough for a crowd or for leftovers.

1 cup (115 grams) coarsely chopped white onions

1 packed cup (85 grams) culantro (leaves and tender stems) (or double the amount of cilantro)

1 packed cup (85 grams) fresh Italian parsley (leaves and tender stems)

6 green onions (100 grams), coarsely chopped

3 large garlic cloves, coarsely chopped

1 ají amarillo (or 1 serrano pepper), peeled, seeded, and finely chopped

2 tablespoons vegetable oil

4 pounds (1.8 kilograms) duck, cut into 10–12 small pieces

1 cup (200 grams) peeled and crushed canned tomatoes

1 teaspoon dried oregano

2 cups (480 ml) dark beer

2½ cups (570 grams) long-grain white rice

4 cups (960 ml) chicken broth

2 cups (340 grams) green peas (fresh or frozen and thawed)

1½ cups (200 grams) peeled and finely diced carrots

Half a small butternut squash, peeled, seeded, and finely diced into ¼ inch (6 mm) cubes (about 1 pound/455 grams)

2 teaspoons fine sea salt, or more to taste

¾ teaspoons freshly ground black pepper, or more to taste

In the bowl of a food processor fitted with a metal blade (or in a blender with a good motor), combine the white onions, culantro (or cilantro), parsley, green onions, garlic, and ajíes. Pulse until they form a paste, stopping to scrape down the sides of the bowl as needed; set aside. Heat 2 tablespoons of the oil in a 6 quart Dutch oven set over medium-high heat. Pat the duck dry well with paper towels. Working in batches, brown the duck pieces on all sides, about 8 to 10 minutes total. Remove them with a slotted spoon to a platter and set aside. Remove all but 2 tablespoons of the remaining fat from the pot (save it for other uses or discard). Add the processed mixture; sauté for 2 to 3 minutes or until it has thickened. Add the tomatoes, oregano, and beer; cook for 5 minutes or until reduced by half. Add the rice and cook, while stirring, for 2 minutes. Add the broth, peas, carrots, squash, salt, and pepper; stir well. Nestle the duck pieces into the rice, and bring the liquid to a simmer. Cover the pot and simmer for 25 to 30 minutes or until almost all of the liquid has been absorbed and the rice is fluffy.

Note: Rendered duck fat is prized like gold in the Latin American kitchen. Use it to start other rice dishes or to make scrambled eggs. Well covered and refrigerated, it will harden and last well for 2 weeks.

Arroz con Pollo

Chicken and Rice, My Way

Various Countries | Yield: Serves 4–8 | Difficulty Level: Easy | Total Cooking Time: 40 minutes

Yellow rice and chicken cooked together and studded with colorful vegetables is a dish that families are built on and that abuelas pass down. Virtually every family has their own rendition, some soupy, some that are more chicken than rice. Some cooks add capers, others add leeks, and yet others use saffron. This is my recipe.

¼ cup (60 ml) Aceite de Achiote (page 194)

4 pounds (1.8 kilograms) bone-in chicken thighs (about 8)

1 cup (225 grams) finely chopped Spanish chorizo (spicy or regular)

1 cup (115 grams) finely chopped white onions

1 cup (185 grams) finely chopped plum tomatoes

One 4 ounce (115 gram/½ cup) jar chopped pimentos or roasted red peppers

3 garlic cloves, finely chopped

2 bay leaves

2 teaspoons dried thyme

2¼ cups (455 grams) converted long-grain white rice

1 cup (150 grams) finely chopped carrots

5 cups (1.2 liters) chicken broth

1 teaspoon fine sea salt

½ teaspoon freshly ground black pepper, or more to taste

1½ cups (225 grams) green peas, frozen and thawed

1 cup (110 grams) sliced green olives

2 hard-boiled eggs, sliced

½ cup (40 grams) grated queso seco (or Pecorino)

¼ cup (20 grams) chopped fresh Italian parsley

Heat the oil in a large Dutch oven set over medium-high heat. Brown the chicken pieces for about 4 minutes, then transfer them to a plate; sauté the chorizo in the same pan until it has rendered its fat, about 1 minute. Add the onions, tomatoes, pimentos, and garlic, sautéing for 5 to 6 minutes or until thickened. Stir in the bay leaves, thyme, rice, and carrots; cook, while stirring, for 2 minutes. Add the chicken broth, salt, and pepper; bring the mixture to a boil. Return the chicken pieces (and any juices) back to the pot; cover, reduce the heat, and simmer for 15 minutes. Stir in the peas and olives, cover, and continue cooking for 8 to 10 minutes or until all of the liquid has been absorbed. Transfer to a large platter. Decorate with the sliced eggs, sprinkle with the cheese and parsley, and serve immediately.

Arroz con Vino

Brown Rice with Red Wine, Pine Nuts, and Raisins

Chile | Yield: Serves 6–8 | Difficulty Level: Easy | Total Cooking Time: 1 hour

Here is a recipe with European undertones but that perfectly exemplifies the technique for making the pilaf that is preferred through Latin America. Here, toothsome brown rice is paired with sweet and nutty elements. For this dish, I prefer Chilean wines made with medium-bodied Carmenere grapes, with similar flavor notes to Merlot; stay away from full-bodied wines such as Bordeaux, which can impart a slight bitterness. If you like even lighter flavors, use white wine or skip altogether and use water or more stock. I love serving this as a side dish to roast chicken or baked fish.

2 tablespoons vegetable oil

¼ cup (30 grams) finely chopped shallots

2 cups (375 grams) long-grain brown rice

2 cups (480 ml) red wine (such as Merlot, see headnote)

2 cups (480 ml) chicken stock

1½ teaspoons fine sea salt

½ teaspoon ground white pepper

⅓ cup (50 grams) raisins

⅓ cup (50 grams) pine nuts, lightly toasted

½ cup (20 grams) finely chopped fresh flat-leaf parsley (leaves and tender stems)

Heat the oil in a medium Dutch oven set over medium-high heat; add the shallots and cook, while stirring, until softened, about 1 minute. Add the rice and stir constantly until it's lightly toasted and fragrant, about 2 to 3 minutes. Add the wine, chicken stock, salt, and pepper; stir and bring the liquid to a boil. Cover, reduce the heat to low, and simmer for 40 minutes. Add the raisins; cover and cook for an additional 5 minutes or until all of the liquid has evaporated. Uncover the rice and stir in the pine nuts and parsley.

Arroz Quesú

Cheesy Rice

Paraguay | Yield: Serves 4–6 | Difficulty Level: Easy | Total Cooking Time: 20–22 minutes

If you love cheese-laden risottos, you'll love this decadent, soupy rice. This is a recipe that my Paraguayan friends yearn for when they miss home; it is the national comfort food of Paraguay. Use medium-grain rice, starchier than long-grain, because this dish is meant to be velvety and will require the extra amylopectin that coats the grains and makes them sticky. You can find medium-grain rice online and in Latin stores; if you must, use short-grain rice. Paraguayan cheese, queso paraguayo, is semi-hard; if you can't find it, substitute Gouda, Havarti, or a neutral melting cheese. The rice should be soupy, creamy, and al dente. Pair it with Guiso de Cordero (page 436) and a glass of red wine. This is food for days when you're feeling like you need a hug.

4 tablespoons unsalted butter

¾ cup (118 grams) very finely chopped yellow onions

½ teaspoon fine sea salt

1 tablespoon granulated chicken bouillon

1½ cups (315 grams) medium-grain white rice

1½ cups (360 ml) whole milk

¼ cup (60 grams) cream cheese, softened to room temperature

8 ounces (230 grams) Paraguayan, Gouda, or Havarti cheese, cubed into small pieces

Melt the butter in a medium pot set over medium heat; add the onions and the salt. Cook, while stirring, until the onions soften, about 2 minutes (they shouldn't take any color); add the chicken bouillon and the rice; stir together, coating the grains with the butter and onion juices. Add 3 cups (720 ml) water and bring to a boil; lower the heat to medium and let cook, uncovered (stirring occasionally so the rice doesn't stick to the bottom and burn), for 8 to 10 minutes or until the liquid has been almost completely absorbed. Stir in the milk and the cheeses. Lower the heat slightly and continue stirring until the cheese is melted and the rice comes back to a boil, about 2 minutes. Cover, lower the heat to low, and cook for 10 minutes, stopping to stir once midway through cooking. If it's still too soupy, uncover and let it cook, undisturbed, for 2 to 4 more minutes or until there is only a film of creamy liquid on the top of the rice. Cover, turn off the heat, and let sit for 5 minutes before serving (this will thicken it a bit more).

Granulated Bouillon · Latin American home cooks love their cubed or powdered bouillon because it adds great umami flavor to anything it comes into contact with—seriously, dust some of it on one of your fingers; then tell me it's not the best-tasting finger on your whole hand! Like other condiments, such as Maggi and Worcestershire sauces, granular bouillon is an ingredient that is almost always found in recipes dating back to the early 1900s, when these ingredients were invented in Europe. Serious Latin home cooks often have a variety of beef, chicken, vegetable, and other flavored bouillon in their pantries—I certainly can't live without them. Even though some cooks turn up their noses at those of us who still use them, they are part of our culture and I don't see us stopping.

Arroz con Maiz y Crema

Rice and Corn Casserole

Guatemala | Yield: Serves 8 | Difficulty Level: Easy | Total Cooking Time: 40 minutes

This is a classic recipe from Guatemala City, one of those dishes that has been made since the 1950s, especially to quedar bien—impress—family and friends

6 cups (800 grams) cooked white rice

1¾ cups (280 grams) corn kernels (fresh or frozen and thawed)

1½ cups (340 grams) sour cream

1 cup (225 grams) mayonnaise

1 cup (100 grams) grated Cotija, queso seco, or Parmesan cheese

1 cup (85 grams) finely chopped fresh parsley (leaves and tender stems)

½ cup (40 grams) finely chopped green onions

One 6 ounce (170 grams) roasted red pepper (drained, if jarred), sliced thinly

1 teaspoon fine sea salt

¼ teaspoon freshly ground black pepper

1½ cups (115 grams) shredded chihuahua, Monterey Jack, or other melting cheese

Preheat the oven to 350°F (180°C). Butter a 9 x 13 inch (23 x 33 cm) baking dish. In a large bowl, combine the rice, corn, sour cream, mayonnaise, Cotija cheese, parsley, green onions, roasted pepper, salt, and pepper; mix well. Spread the rice mixture into the prepared baking dish, sprinkle with the shredded cheese, and bake for 30 to 35 minutes or until the casserole is bubbly, the cheese has melted, and the top is golden.

VARIATIONS: Instead of corn, use canned, drained, and chopped asparagus, hearts of palm, loroco buds, or artichoke hearts. Or stir in a little bit of chopped ham.

Note: Although different types of rice will vary slightly in weight after they are cooked, I typically go with this formula: 1 cup of cooked white rice = 250 grams. Although most Latin American cooks will use either long-grain or medium-grain white rice, whenever you are using leftover rice in the recipes of this book you can use any cooked rice you have on hand (except wild rice, which is actually a type of grass and not a grain).

Arroz Tapado

Layered Rice Casserole

Peru | Yield: Serves 4–6 | Difficulty Level: Easy | Total Cooking Time: 30 minutes

Peruvians have such an intense love for rice that they'll even eat it alongside potatoes! So it's no coincidence that they have many everyday meals that feature leftover rice as a main component. *Tapado* means "covered," and in Peru, the term is used to describe rice timbales, stuffed with saucy, spicy stews. Any leftover stews or stir-fries can be used, and this is an ideal way to stretch one meal into another. I favor this rendition because it showcases the Persian elements so often found in Latin food; here, the combination of beef (I use hand-chopped tenderloin or ground beef) with sweet spices and dried fruits. However, you can use any leftover stew that you may have from a previous meal, leftover chicken, seafood stir-fries, or cooked ground meats—as long as they have a little bit of sauce to hold everything together. This recipe makes one large casserole, but feel free to divide it into smaller ramekins for individual portions. Individually portioned tapados are often served topped with a fried egg and a side of fried ripe plantains.

2 tablespoons vegetable oil, divided, plus more for greasing the baking dish

1 pound (455 grams) ground beef

1 cup (115 grams) finely chopped red onions

2 garlic cloves, finely chopped

2 tablespoons ají panca paste

1¼ cups (225 grams) finely chopped plum tomatoes

1 teaspoon ground cumin

2 tablespoons finely chopped fresh Italian parsley

2 tablespoons raisins

1 teaspoon fine sea salt

½ teaspoon freshly ground black pepper

4 cups (455 grams) hot cooked white rice

Heat 1 tablespoon of the oil in a medium skillet set over medium-high heat. Add the beef and cook until it has browned, about 6 to 8 minutes. Add the remaining tablespoon oil and the onions; sauté for 2 minutes, stirring well or until the mixture begins to turn golden. Add the garlic and ají paste and cook for 30 seconds. Add the tomatoes and cumin; cook, while stirring, for 1 minute, then lower the heat to medium and cook until it thickens, about 3 to 4 minutes. Add the parsley, raisins, salt, and pepper; stir to combine. Oil one 2 quart (8 cup) round mold (or a bowl). Layer half of the rice on the bottom of the mold or bowl. Top with all of the beef mixture; spread evenly, pressing it down with a spoon to compress. Top it with the remaining rice. Use a plate to press it down. Turn the mold over onto a platter and unmold. Serve immediately.

Arroz Seco Verde

Green Rice

Mexico | Yield: Serves 6–8 | Difficulty Level: Intermediate | Total Cooking Time: 1 hour 15 minutes

A classic recipe that falls into the category known as sopas secas ("dry soups"), this rice gets its color from spinach, herbs, and poblano chiles. You can serve it directly from the pot, but I prefer to bake it as a casserole, topped with cheese, because it makes for a prettier presentation at the table. Some cooks will add corn, chopped pimentos, and even cooked and shredded chicken to make it into an entire meal.

8 cups (165 grams) fresh spinach leaves, trimmed and rinsed but not dried

1 cup (80 grams) finely chopped fresh Italian parsley (leaves and tender stems)

2 tablespoons chopped onions

2 garlic cloves

3½ cups (840 ml) chicken broth (or water), divided

¼ cup (60 ml) vegetable oil

2 cups (360 grams) long-grain white rice

1 teaspoon fine sea salt

½ teaspoon freshly ground black pepper

2 roasted, peeled, seeded, and chopped poblano peppers, cut into ½ inch (12 mm) dice (see Note on page 182)

2 tablespoons unsalted butter, cut into small pieces

1 cup (85 grams) shredded Monterey Jack cheese

Grease a 9 x 13 inch (23 x 33 cm) baking dish and set aside. Preheat the oven to 350°F (180°C). Place the spinach in a saucepan with no added water, cover, and cook at low heat for 5 to 6 minutes or until softened. Transfer to a blender and add the parsley, onions, garlic, and ½ cup (120 ml) of broth; puree until smooth. Heat the oil in a medium skillet set over medium-high heat; add the rice and sauté for 3 to 4 minutes or until lightly golden. Add the spinach puree (careful, it will splatter) and cook, while stirring with a long wooden spatula, 2 minutes or until thickened. Add the rest of the broth, salt, and pepper; bring rice to a boil. Cover the rice and lower the heat to medium-low; simmer for 20 minutes or until the rice is tender and the liquid has been absorbed. Place half of the rice in the bottom of the baking dish and spread it out evenly. Layer the poblano peppers over the rice, and top with the remaining rice. Dot the top of the casserole with the butter. Cover the dish with foil and bake for 10 minutes; uncover the dish, top the rice with the grated cheese and bake, uncovered, until cheese is melted, about 8 minutes. Serve immediately.

Arroz con Langosta

Rice with Lobster

Belize | Yield: Serves 4–6 | Difficulty Level: Easy | Total Cooking Time: 25 minutes

One of the most delicate mariscos (shellfish) to find its way onto the Belizean everyday table is lobster, which is so abundant between February and June—the months known for their yearly Lobsterfests—that I like to say it jumps from ocean to plate almost by itself. By far, the preparation that has most enamored my palate is this easy and homey delicacy that rivals any other lobster I've ever eaten, even those at some of the world's best restaurants. I like to purchase lobster tails when they're on sale at my local market (see the note below on how to cook them). In lieu of lobster, use langoustines instead; not only are they less expensive, but they're easily available year-round, peeled, frozen, and ready to cook. If you happen to have any leftover lobster meat from other meals, you can use it to make this recipe.

2 tablespoons coconut or vegetable oil

½ cup (60 grams) finely chopped white onions

½ cup (60 grams) thinly sliced celery

1 garlic clove, finely chopped

1½ cups (325 grams) medium-grain rice

1 cup (225 grams) seeded and finely chopped plum tomatoes

½ teaspoon dried oregano

Pinch of ground allspice

One 13.5 ounce (398 ml) can unsweetened coconut milk

1½ cups (360 ml) Caldo de Pescado (page 31) or water

1½ teaspoons fine sea salt, or more to taste

1 bay leaf

1 pound (455 grams) cooked and chopped lobster meat or langoustines (thawed, if frozen)

Chopped fresh parsley, for garnish (optional)

Heat the oil in a large pot set over medium-high heat. Add the onions, celery, and garlic; cook, while stirring, for 1 minute. Add the rice and toast slightly for 2 minutes (the center of the grains will turn bright white). Add the tomatoes, oregano, and allspice; cook for 1 minute. Add the coconut milk, fish stock (or water), salt, and bay leaf, making sure to stir the bottom of the pot well. Bring the liquid to a boil; cover the pot, lower the heat, and simmer for 18 minutes. Uncover the rice, stir in the cooked lobster meat, and cook, while stirring, until the lobster is warmed through, about 2 minutes. Discard the bay leaf and serve hot, sprinkled with parsley, if desired.

Note: How to cook lobster tails: If the lobster tails are frozen, thaw in the refrigerator for several hours or overnight—they will cook more evenly this way. Use scissors to cut through the shells (at the top of the lobster tails), from top to bottom all the way to the fin. Bring salted water to a boil in a large pot. Fill a large bowl with iced water and set aside. Carefully slide the lobster tails into the pot and boil for 1 minute per ounce (or until the lobster meat is firm and white, and the shells are bright red). Remove the tails with tongs and place them into the iced water to cool. Now they are ready for you to pull the meat out of the shells; chop it and continue with the recipe.

Chaulafán o Arroz Chaufa

Fried Rice

Ecuador and Peru | Yield: Serves 4–6 | Difficulty Level: Easy | Total Cooking Time: 30 minutes

When Chinese immigrants first came to Peru during the nineteenth century, they brought their culinary traditions along with them. The word *fàn* means "rice" in Chinese, and in Peru, Chinese-style dishes (and the restaurants that serve them) are known as chifas (in Cantonese, *chifa* means "to eat"). Fried rice is called chaufa in Peru and chaulafán in neighboring Ecuador and is the perfect way to use up all that leftover rice that home cooks often find themselves with. More than a recipe, this is a technique. I'm giving you a canvas on which you can add any protein to transform it into a filling main dish. Cooked duck, chicken, shrimp, bacon, fish, pork, ham, or beef can all be added. Vary the vegetables: think celery, broccoli, carrots, mushrooms, zucchini, and so on. Just remember to chop them into little bite-sized pieces all about the same size, so they cook quickly and evenly. Worcestershire sauce (often known as "English sauce," because nobody can pronounce it!) adds a bit of pungency and balances the saltiness of the soy sauce with a touch of sweetness.

2½–3 cups (400–480 grams) leftover cooked white rice (cold)

3 tablespoons (45 ml) vegetable or peanut oil

⅓ cup (20 grams) green onions, sliced on the bias

2 garlic cloves, finely chopped

¾ cup (140 grams) stemmed, seeded, and finely chopped red bell peppers

¾ cup (140 grams) stemmed, seeded, and finely chopped green bell peppers

½ cup (60 grams) green peas (fresh or frozen and thawed)

1 tablespoon Worcestershire sauce

3 tablespoons (45 ml) dark soy sauce

1 tablespoon toasted sesame oil

Break up the rice into small clumps with a wooden spoon and set aside. Heat a wok or large nonstick skillet over medium-high heat. When hot, add the vegetable or peanut oil and swirl the pan to coat. Add the green onions and garlic and cook for 20 seconds or until fragrant. Add the bell peppers and peas (if using, include any cooked protein at this time) and stir-fry for 1 to 2 minutes. Add the rice, stirring well with a wooden spoon to break up the clumps completely. Drizzle the Worcestershire sauce, soy sauce, and sesame oil over the rice, stirring constantly, until the rice starts to turn evenly golden, about 2 to 3 minutes. Serve immediately.

Note: Eggs are often added to fried rice as an inexpensive and delicious way of adding protein. However, adding the egg directly into the rice before cooking it makes it gummy; for this reason the egg is first cooked into a thin omelet, called a tortilla de huevo, which is then sliced and stirred into fried rice. Here's how to make it: Before you make the rice, beat 4 eggs lightly in a bowl. Heat 1 tablespoon of oil (preferably peanut or vegetable) in a large nonstick pan set over medium heat. Add the eggs and swirl them around the pan to form a thin omelet. Cook for 3 to 4 minutes or just until set. Slide the omelet onto a cutting board and let it come to room temperature. Roll the omelet and cut it into strips. Make your fried rice as directed above, then add these egg ribbons right before you serve it.

Croquetas de Arroz

Rice Fritters

Various Countries | Yield: Serves 6 | Difficulty Level: Easy | Total Cooking Time: 45 minutes

Latin Americans have a knack for using up every last bit of leftovers, and one of our favorite ingredients to repurpose is rice. You will find it recycled in dishes such as the Cantonese-style fried rice wonders of Peru and Ecuador, myriad Afro-Latino versions of rice and bean dishes in the Latin Caribbean, and innumerable casseroles. However, my personal favorites are these cheese-laden torpedo-shaped morsels, called croquetas (pronounced *kroh-keh-tahs*), that juxtapose crispy crusts with creamy interiors. You can use any rice leftover from another meal, but I favor yellow or white rice. When my daughters were little, I would add pureed vegetables into the mix; they unsuspectingly ate their peas and carrots without a problem. Feel free to change the type of cheese (Cotija, Manchego, and Pecorino are my other favorites) to suit your taste. If you wish to make the croquetas entirely gluten free, use gluten-free bread crumbs and rice flour in place of the wheat flour. I make them in a food processor so all of the ingredients can be blended into dough, but if you don't have one, just mix the ingredients by hand (the grains of rice will stay whole).

2½–3 cups (400–480 grams) cooked white rice (any that you have leftover)

1 cup (115 grams) grated Parmesan cheese

2 eggs

½ cup (65 grams) dried bread crumbs, or more, if needed

1–2 tablespoons milk or cream (optional, only if needed)

2 tablespoons all-purpose flour, for dredging

Vegetable oil, for frying

Fit a baking pan with a metal cooling rack and set aside. Place the rice, Parmesan, eggs, and bread crumbs in the bowl of a large food processor fitted with a metal blade (or do it in two batches, if you have a smaller one). Process all until thoroughly combined (it will resemble dough or a thick paste). Take a portion and press it between your fingers; if it holds together, it is ready. If it's too wet to hold together, add a bit more bread crumbs (one tablespoon at a time); if it's too dry, add a bit of milk or cream (one tablespoon at a time). Transfer the mixture into a bowl, cover with plastic wrap, and allow to rest for 10 minutes at room temperature (or refrigerate for up to 3 hours) so the rice can absorb all of the liquid. When ready to fry, measure 2 tablespoons of the mixture and shape it into a torpedo (a long cylinder or a ball also works). Repeat with the remaining mixture. Lightly dredge the croquetas in flour, shaking off the excess to ensure that they won't splatter when fried. In a large skillet with high sides, heat 1-2 inches (2.5-5 cm) of oil to 360°F (180°C) (or use a deep fryer according to the manufacturer's directions); carefully slide the croquetas into the oil, one at a time. Fry them for 4 to 5 minutes or until golden, using two forks to turn them over on all sides so they're evenly cooked. Use the forks to transfer them to the prepared rack to drain. Serve while hot.

Keeping Fried Food Crispy · Placing fried foods on baking sheets fitted with metal cooling racks allows excess oil to drain while keeping your food crispy. Transferring this setup into a warm oven you will create "convection" air that is able to circulate around the fried food, keeping it even crispier. Don't drain fried foods on paper towels—it will cause their crusts to steam and thus destroys the crisp coating you worked so hard to achieve.

El Asopao de Mita

My Grandmother's Soupy Rice Stew

Cuba and Puerto Rico | Yield: Serves 8–10 | Difficulty Level: Intermediate |
Total Cooking Time: 1½ hours (includes cooking the giblets)

Several generations of children in my family grew up eating bowls of this rice dish, not thick enough to be called a stew but too thick to be a soup. This recipe is based on one my grandmother taught me that she developed after extensive travels to the Latin Caribbean. Asopaos ("soupy rices") are thick, stick-to-your-ribs dishes—a meal in and of themselves—like a more viscous arroz con pollo. Some cooks in Cuba like it on the thicker side, and eat it with a fork; not so my Puerto Rican friends, who like it soupy and eat it with a spoon (or my grandmother, who would thin it out with more broth, depending on how many people she was feeding at any given point). This recipe will thicken further as it sits, so keep extra broth on hand to thin it out to taste. Always taste soups before serving and adjust the salt; the amount of sodium in the starting stock will dictate how much salt you will ultimately need. Although this is usually made with poached chicken, I have found it a brilliant way to use up leftover rotisserie chicken.

8–12 cups (2–2.8 liters) chicken stock

1¼ cups (310 grams) short-grain rice, such as arborio

2 cups (270 grams) cooked and shredded chicken

¼ teaspoon ground cloves

¼ teaspoon ground allspice

2 cups (140 grams) finely chopped carrots

½ cup (115 grams) very thinly sliced green beans

1 cup (140 grams) green peas (fresh or frozen and thawed)

1 cup (225 grams) cooked and chopped chicken giblets (see Note)

2 ounces (60 grams) drained and chopped jarred pimentos

2 tablespoons olive oil

½ cup (115 grams) roughly chopped white onions

¾ cup (140 grams) stemmed, seeded, and chopped red bell peppers

1½ cups (225 grams) roughly chopped plum tomatoes

Pinch of saffron threads

1 teaspoon paprika

2–2½ teaspoons fine sea salt, divided, or more to taste

Heat the chicken stock in a large soup pot; add the rice, cooked chicken, cloves, allspice, carrots, green beans, peas, giblets, and pimento. Simmer for 20 minutes or until the rice is tender. In the meantime, heat the olive oil in a small sauté pan set over medium-high heat; when the oil is hot, add the onions, bell peppers, tomatoes, saffron, paprika, and 1 teaspoon of salt. Sauté for 6 to 8 minutes, transfer the mixture to a blender, and puree until smooth. Add this mixture to the simmering soup. Simmer for 10 more minutes. Add more broth to your liking (it should still be thick); season with the rest of the salt, if needed, and serve hot.

Note: I buy chicken giblets (which include hearts and gizzards but not livers) in bulk, and divide them into portions, which I freeze. To cook them, simmer them in enough water to cover by 2 inches (5 cm); cook, partially covered, for 1 hour, replenishing the water if the level reduces by too much; allow the cooked giblets to cool slightly before chopping them. You can use the resulting broth from the giblets as part of this soup or for other recipes.

Gallo Pinto

Red Beans and Rice

Costa Rica and Nicaragua | Yield: Serves 6 | Difficulty Level: Easy | Total Cooking Time: 30 minutes

There is great debate about where this savory rice and bean dish is really from. I was taught to make the Nicaraguan version by my sister-in-law, Maria Esther de Alfaro (Tey), whose family hails from León; her rendition is made with kidney beans and gets a tangy, even spicy, kick from a hefty amount of Worcestershire sauce. However, those who have tried the Costa Rican version are familiar with a sweeter interpretation made with Lizano sauce, a condiment made with molasses, carrots, and onions, so beloved in the Central American country that it's poured on everything (think of it as a type of ketchup). Lizano is very easy to find online (see Sources), but use whichever you prefer. Here is my recipe, which combines my favorite element of each country. I am partial to the use of cranberry beans, which retain a toothsome texture, but feel free to use dark red kidney or any other kind of red beans (canned work, too). The one thing Tey insists on is toasting the beans in the oil until they split and develop a crust, which helps them add texture to the final dish. This is a fabulous way to use leftover rice. When served topped with a fried egg, it is said to be a caballo—"on horseback."

2½ tablespoons vegetable oil

¾ cup (100 grams) finely chopped white onions

½ cup (140 grams) stemmed, seeded, and finely chopped red bell peppers

½ cup (80 grams) finely chopped fresh long-leaf culantro (or double the amount of cilantro)

2 cups (155 grams) cooked cranberry or dark red kidney beans (may be canned and drained)

2½–3 cups (400–480 grams) cooked white rice

½ cup (120 ml) Lizano sauce (see Sources) or Worcestershire sauce

½ teaspoon fine sea salt

Pinch of freshly ground black pepper

In a large sauté pan with high sides, heat the oil over medium-high heat; add the onions, peppers, and culantro (or cilantro), cooking until the onions have softened, about 2 to 3 minutes. Add the beans, tossing them as they toast for 2 to 3 minutes—some of the beans will develop crusts, some will split open. Add the cooked rice, Lizano or Worcestershire sauce, salt, pepper, and ¼ cup (60 ml) water. Stir well to coat the rice and beans until all of the ingredients are thoroughly combined. Lower the heat to medium-low and allow the mixture to heat through for 5 minutes, then serve.

Rice and Beans

Rice and Red Beans with Coconut

Belize | Yield: Serves 4–6 | Difficulty Level: Easy | Total Cooking Time: 24 minutes (if using cooked beans; longer if using dried)

This creamy rice stew is ubiquitous in Belize, served at homes, in restaurants, and wherever you go. It is a marriage of Garifuna (also known as Afro-Amerindian) and Mayan flavors like no other. Kidney beans and rice meld together with coconut milk into a truly comforting, savory dish. Its telltale pork essence is often lent by pig's feet or ears, or bacon. I do as my many Belizean friends do and use lard instead; if you wish it to remain completely vegetarian, just substitute the lard with oil (coconut oil works best). You may use canned beans; just rinse them well under cold water first. Belizeans serve this with stewed meats or chicken, seafood, fried plantains, and potato salad (yes, really!).

2 tablespoons lard or vegetable oil (coconut oil is best)

1½ cups (255 grams) long-grain white rice

1½ cups (155 grams) finely chopped white onions

3½ cups (225 grams) cooked kidney beans (rinsed, if canned)

1 teaspoon fine sea salt

¼ teaspoon dried thyme

¼ teaspoon freshly ground black pepper

One 13.5 ounce (398 ml) can unsweetened coconut milk

Heat the lard or oil in a medium pot set over medium-high heat. Add the rice and onions and cook for 2 minutes or until the onions are translucent and the center of the grains of rice turns a bright white. Add the beans, salt, thyme, and pepper, and continue cooking for 2 minutes or until the beans are slightly toasted (their skins will split). Add the coconut milk and 1¼ cups (300 ml) water. Bring to a boil; cover, lower the heat, and simmer for 18 to 20 minutes or until the liquid has been absorbed (the rice will be creamy). Stir and serve.

QUINOA

f you were to walk into a quinoa garden filled with tall plants (or panojas) tinted gold, green, purple, pink, gray, black, and white, I wonder if you would recognize them as the flowers that hide the tiny seeds that have fed the Andean civilizations of Bolivia and Peru for centuries. Quinoa grows in tall, beautiful plumes that sit in the middle of huge leaves; each is composed of thousands of tiny flowers, the size of lentils. Each flower houses miniature seeds within. Once dried, it is easy to collect the seeds by shaking the flowers into a drum or a large bowl.

As a food historian, it thrills me to include a chapter on a wonder grain that was first grown in Peru and Bolivia more than five thousand years ago—a grain so small that the conquistadores deemed it "Indian food," inconsequential, and too tiny to even bother growing, and that now, centuries later, is revered by scientists as a supergrain and a whole food. Quinoa is one of the most important ingredients that the Americas gave the world: gluten free and rich in protein, this nutrient bomb with a long shelf life is an ideal staple to keep in your pantry.

Chenopodium quinoa, a close cousin to amaranth, is a flowering species of the Amaranthaceae family, most probably native to the area surrounding Lake Titicaca. Archeologists date its domestication back seven thousand years. In *Comentarios Reales de los Incas* (*Royal Chronicles of the Incas*), the famous Spanish raconteur Garcilaso de la Vega described quinoa as "Segundo lugar de las mieses que se crían sobre la haz de la tierra" ("Second only [to wheat] of the cereal terrains that are harvested on the face of the Earth"). In fact, quinoa was called "the wheat of the Incas" by the conquistadores (even if they weren't impressed enough to cultivate it themselves).

However popular it was with the Incas, Europeans didn't appreciate quinoa and replaced it with wheat and oats as their staple grains. It would be centuries before this beautiful South American seed became popular around the world, due to its protein-laced power.

Known as a pseudo cereal, quinoa cooks like a grain but is really a seed (you can see the germ unfurl from the seed when cooked). Although most of us only eat the seeds, the green leaves are also edible and can be cooked like spinach. Quinoa is very rich in B vitamins, iron, magnesium, and potassium, and is the only seed that contains all eight essential amino acids, as well as protein, vitamins, and unsaturated fats needed by our bodies. It's also super high in omega-6 and omega-3 fatty acids. No wonder it's considered a superfood!

Of course, Bolivians and Peruvians have known this since forever; they also perfected the art of cooking it long ago, transforming quinoa into all sorts of succulent dishes that remain part of their modern-day diet.

The seeds are coated in a bitter-tasting and mildly toxic chemical called saponin that occurs naturally in some plants (some beans contain it too). For this reason, it's important to rinse quinoa seeds well, until the foamy substance is gone and the water runs clear. You can also purchase quinoa already washed, although rinsing quinoa really is an easy procedure done in no time.

Quinoa cooks very similarly to rice; simply boil it in a two-to-one ratio of water to grain and you'll produce fluffy, loose quinoa. It quadruples in volume when cooked, so for every cup of uncooked quinoa, you will end up with four cups cooked. The texture of cooked quinoa is similar to that of couscous (tiny semolina pasta), so once cooked, it can be used in the same way that couscous is used. It's particularly delicious when topped with hot stews, or simply with a dollop of butter and served as a side dish. Quinoa comes in different colors; you'll find golden, black, and red varieties most frequently—sometimes all mixed together into the same bag, which makes for a very colorful presentation at the table.

Its taste is neutral, so it takes on any flavoring you might add, from savory to sweet. Lemon, garlic, and herbs such as basil, chives, and sage are a suitable addition to a bowl of cooked quinoa, as are spoonfuls of honey, maple syrup, or sugar, with a touch of cinnamon and some cut-up dried fruit. Chill it and use it in salads, cook it in soups, or turn it into a casserole. You can also cook it in milk; stir in some fruit and add a touch of agave syrup or grated piloncillo (raw, unrefined sugar) for a comforting breakfast. Use cooked quinoa to top yogurt and serve with berries for a healthy snack.

My favorite use for quinoa is to grind it into flour to use in baked goods. You'll also find quinoa flour in most health-food stores and online (see Sources). It adds loads of protein and a nutty texture to cakes, muffins, and meatloaves.

Quinoa may be tiny, but it is also one of the most nutritious ingredients ever to grow on Earth. It can grow in even the most inhospitable terrains, where the weather can vary from scorching hot to frigid cold and where rainfall is infrequent. The high plains (altiplanos) in the Andes (encompassing Peru, Ecuador, Argentina, Bolivia, and Colombia) have long been the treasure-bearer of this superfood that finally seduced the modern world with its health benefits and versatility and that will undoubtedly feed huge swaths of people in the twenty-first century. Highly lucrative, quinoa has been a source of income for innumerable small, family-owned farmers who would otherwise not be able to feed their own.

Quinoa Simple

Steamed Quinoa

Bolivia, Chile, Ecuador, and Peru | Yield: Serves 4–6 | Difficulty Level: Easy | Total Cooking Time: 30 minutes

This is the simplest way I know to prepare quinoa and the way to begin any recipe that uses cooked quinoa. Always start by washing the quinoa while rubbing the grains between your fingers. This will remove the foamy saponin (the coating that gives quinoa a bitter flavor). Quinoa is done when the little germ separates from each seed. If you eat it as a side dish, consider adding a bit of extra flavor with some butter or flavored oil (such as olive, avocado, or nut oil) and a touch of salt. If you're using it as a base for another recipe, leave it plain.

1 cup (170 grams) quinoa (any color)   2 cups (480 ml) water or chicken broth

Place the quinoa in a fine sieve and wash well under cold water, while rubbing the grains with your fingers, about 1 minute or until the grains stop foaming. Place the quinoa in a medium pot, add the water or broth, and set over medium-high heat. As soon as it comes to a boil, cover, lower the heat to low, and cook, undisturbed, for 18 to 20 minutes (just as you would rice) or until all the liquid is absorbed. Remove from the heat, uncover, and fluff with a fork.

Pilaf de Quinoa con Parmesano

Parmesan Quinoa Pilaf

Peru | Yield: Serves 4–6 | Difficulty Level: Easy | Total Cooking Time: 25 minutes

Quinoa is given the same treatment as rice in this recipe for pilaf, in which the grains are first toasted before any liquid is added. The texture and flavors will be familiar to anyone who loves simple risotto. After washing the quinoa, let it drain very well so it's dry when you add it to the hot oil.

1 tablespoon unsalted butter

1 tablespoon olive oil

½ cup (60 grams) finely chopped white onions

1 cup quinoa (175 grams), washed well under running water until it runs clear

½ teaspoon fine sea salt

2 cups (480 ml) chicken broth or water

½ cup (60 grams) finely grated Parmesan cheese

¼ cup (20 grams) chopped fresh Italian parsley

Heat the butter and the oil in a medium saucepan set over medium-high heat; when the butter is melted, add the onions and cook for 1 minute or until softened. Add the quinoa and salt and stir for 2 minutes; add the broth or water and bring to a boil. Cover; lower the heat and simmer for 18 to 20 minutes or until all of the liquid has been absorbed. Using a fork, fluff up the quinoa; stir in the cheese and parsley. Serve immediately.

VARIATION: Add a handful of toasted almonds and an equal amount of chopped dried fruit (such as figs, apricots, berries, raisins, or apples) at the end of the cooking process for a sweet and savory side dish.

Quinoa con Limón

Chilled Lemony Quinoa

Bolivia and Peru | Yield: Serves 4–6 | Difficulty Level: Easy | Total Cooking Time: 40 minutes

Quinoa lends itself perfectly to being served cold, as in this refreshing and versatile summer salad that I learned to make decades ago in Toronto when my Bolivian girlfriends and I would get together for informal lunches. Sometimes, we'd add cubed ham or smoked turkey; other times, we'd stuff the quinoa into seeded tomatoes or roasted red peppers. I love to top mine with sliced grilled chicken breast, steak, fish, or shrimp.

1 cup (170 grams) uncooked quinoa

2 cups (480 ml) chicken broth or water

¾ cup (85 grams) crumbled queso fresco (or feta)

¾ cup (255 grams) seeded and finely chopped plum tomatoes

¼ cup (15 grams) finely chopped red onions

¼ cup (15 grams) stemmed, seeded, and finely chopped red bell peppers

1 garlic clove, finely chopped

¼ cup (20 grams) finely chopped fresh Italian parsley

⅓ cup (75 ml) freshly squeezed lime juice, or to taste

1 teaspoon fine sea salt, or more to taste

¼ teaspoon ground cumin

¼ teaspoon freshly ground black pepper, or more to taste

2 tablespoons extra-virgin olive oil

Place the quinoa in a fine sieve and wash under cold water, while rubbing the grains with your fingers, about 1 minute (or until the grains stop foaming). Place the quinoa in a medium pot; add the broth or water and set over medium-high heat. As soon as it comes to a boil, cover, lower the heat to low, and cook, undisturbed, for 18 to 20 minutes (just as you would rice) or until all the liquid is absorbed. Remove from the heat; transfer the quinoa to a sieve and rinse under cold running water for 2 minutes, to cool. Set aside to drain completely. In a large bowl, combine the cooled quinoa, cheese, tomatoes, onions, bell peppers, garlic, and parsley, stirring well to combine. In a medium bowl, whisk together the lime juice, salt, cumin, and pepper; slowly whisk in the oil until it is all combined. Pour the dressing over the quinoa and mix well. Chill for 20 minutes and serve.

Did you know? · In Bolivia, quinoa is eaten for breakfast. Cook it in milk and then stir in a few slivered almonds, some raisins or cocoa nibs, and a good spoonful of honey or agave syrup.

"Quinotto" de Camarones y Hongos

Mushroom–Shrimp Quinoa "Risotto"

Peru | Yield: Serves 4–6 | Difficulty Level: Easy | Total Cooking Time: 30 minutes

Quinoa works perfectly as a substitute for rice. By stirring in hot liquid slowly and a bit at a time as it cooks, it takes on a character similar to risotto, making it luscious and velvety. Cooking quinoa this way has come into vogue. This one is creamy, filling, and chock-full of flavor. It is important to wash the quinoa well under running water, while rubbing it with your fingers; this is done to remove the saponin, or bitter coating, around each seed; unless you have a very trusted source, do it even if the package claims to come already prewashed, to avoid a bitter disappointment. Once you learn this technique for preparing quinoa, substitute the mushrooms for any other vegetable such as peas, asparagus, spinach, artichoke hearts, or hearts of palm. Instead of shrimp, try it with lump crabmeat or lobster.

1 cup (170 grams) white quinoa

2 tablespoons olive oil, divided

⅓ cup (85 grams) finely chopped shallots

1½ cups (85 grams) thinly sliced cremini mushrooms

2 garlic cloves, finely chopped

¼ teaspoon red pepper flakes

12 large raw, peeled, and deveined shrimp (about ½ pound/225 grams; 20-25 count), chopped

1½ cups (360 ml) vegetable or chicken broth, divided

½ cup (40 grams) finely chopped fresh Italian parsley (leaves and tender stems)

½ teaspoon fine sea salt, or more to taste

¼ teaspoon freshly ground black pepper, or more to taste

2 cups (170 grams) grated Parmesan cheese, divided

2 limes, quartered (optional)

Place the quinoa in a fine sieve and wash it well under cold running water, rubbing it between your fingers for about 1 minute (or until the grains stop foaming). Place the quinoa in a medium saucepan and cover with 2 cups (480 ml) water; bring to a boil over medium-high heat (watch that it doesn't boil over). Cover, reduce the heat, and cook for 15 minutes or until all of the liquid has been absorbed (the quinoa will be tender). Set aside. In a large saucepan, heat 1 tablespoon of the oil over medium-high heat; add the shallots and cook, stirring often, for 2 minutes or until fragrant. Add the remaining oil and the mushrooms and continue cooking, stirring occasionally, for 2 to 3 minutes or until the mushrooms begin to turn golden. Add the garlic, red pepper flakes, and shrimp; cook for 1 to 2 minutes, stirring well. Add ¾ cup (180 ml) of the broth; using a wooden spoon, scrape up the browned bits at the bottom of the pan, and cook for about 1 minute. Lower the heat to medium, stir in the cooked quinoa and the remaining broth; cook, while stirring, until the liquid has almost evaporated, about 3 minutes. Stir in the parsley, salt, pepper, and 1 cup of the cheese. Serve immediately, sprinkled with the remaining cheese and with the lime quarters on the side.

VARIATIONS: Substitute the shrimp and mushrooms for other ingredients, such as sautéed asparagus, cooked Spanish chorizo, cooked pork (such as the Puerco Asado on page 410), marinated artichoke hearts, green peas, or roasted vegetables. Or steam the quinoa as directed in the recipe and combine it with your favorite vinaigrette or salad dressing (like Vinagreta de Albahaca, page 33) and add some fresh chopped vegetables. Serve well chilled.

Sopa de Quinoa

Quinoa Soup

Bolivia | Yield: Serves 6–8 | Difficulty Level: Intermediate | Total Cooking Time: 1½ hours

This is a hearty meal, with meat and plenty of vegetables. Children in the mountainous areas of Bolivia cut their teeth on similar soups. I just love to serve this in large, deep bowls during the cold winter months because it warms me up to my core. It may be necessary to add more liquid when you reheat leftovers, as the quinoa will continue to absorb liquid as it sits; re-season for salt if you add more broth or water. You may chop the cooked beef into bite-sized pieces or serve it in chunks. If you're serving more people, add a couple more ribs to the pot.

2 tablespoons vegetable oil

1½–2 pounds (680–910 grams) bone-in short ribs

2 cups (280 grams) finely chopped white onions

2 cups (300 grams) peeled and finely chopped carrots

2½ cups (255 grams) thinly sliced celery

2½ teaspoons fine sea salt, divided, or more to taste

2 teaspoons ground cumin

1 teaspoon dried oregano

½ teaspoon freshly ground black pepper, or more to taste

1½ cups (225 grams) washed and drained quinoa

3 cups (455 grams) peeled and finely diced yellow potatoes such as Yukon gold

2½ cups (225 grams) peeled and finely diced butternut squash

1½ cup (225 grams) green peas (fresh or frozen and thawed)

Heat the oil in a large pot set over medium-high heat; add the short ribs and brown on all sides, about 6 to 8 minutes. Add the onions, carrots, and celery; continue cooking, while stirring, for 4 to 5 minutes or until the vegetables have softened. Add half of the salt and all of the cumin, the oregano, and the pepper; stir well. Add enough water to cover (about 10 cups/2.4 liters) and bring to a boil; cover, reduce the heat to low, and simmer for 45 minutes. Add the quinoa, potatoes, squash, peas, and remaining salt. Bring the heat back up until the liquid comes to a boil; cover, lower the heat to medium, and cook, uncovered, for 20 to 25 minutes or until the vegetables are tender and the quinoa is soft. If the soup has thickened too much, add a bit more water and reheat; taste and adjust the salt. Remove the meat from the pot; divide it into portions and discard the bones. Serve hot.

Pastel de Quinoa, Almendra y Zanahoria

Quinoa, Almond, and Carrot Cake

Bolivia | Yield: Makes one 9 inch (23 cm) Bundt cake | Difficulty Level: Intermediate | Total Cooking Time: 1 hour 10 minutes

This afternoon cake with a beautiful dark brown crust is deliciously dense, nutty, and sweet. Before eating gluten-free became a movement—since pre-Columbian days, actually—Latin Americans have been using gluten-free grains. And way before eating quinoa became a health trend in the rest of the world, it was already an everyday ingredient in South America. I first tasted a cake similar to this one at a party of Latin American expats in Canada back in the late 1980s. You can find quinoa and almond flours in some supermarkets and online (see Sources)—or, if you have a food mill, grind it yourself whenever you feel like baking this cake. It mixes like a quick bread, simply by adding the wet ingredients into the dry, and couldn't be easier to make. It's just as good when paired with a cup of hot chocolate, yerba mate, coffee, or tea. Keep it, covered, at room temperature for up to four days—it'll get better and better as it sits.

1½ cups (150 grams) quinoa flour

1½ cups (150 grams) almond flour

2 teaspoons baking powder

2 teaspoons ground cinnamon

1 teaspoon ground ginger

½ teaspoon fine sea salt

3 eggs

4 tablespoons (60 ml) vegetable oil

6 tablespoons (90 ml) honey

⅔ cup (140 ml) whole-milk yogurt

1 teaspoon pure vanilla extract

1 cup (85 grams) shredded carrots

¼ cup (20 grams) shredded coconut

Confectioner's sugar, for garnish (optional)

Set the oven rack in the bottom third of the oven and preheat the oven to 350°F (180°C). Butter or spray with cooking spray a 9 cup (9 x 3 inch/23 x 7.5 cm) Bundt cake pan and set aside. In a large bowl, whisk together the quinoa flour, almond flour, baking powder, cinnamon, ginger, and salt; set aside. In another bowl, whisk together the eggs, oil, honey, yogurt, and vanilla, until combined; pour the wet ingredients into the flour mixture, stirring with a spatula until just combined. Stir in the carrots and coconut. Spoon the batter uniformly into the prepared pan; bake for 40 to 45 minutes or until a toothpick inserted into the center comes out clean. Remove the cake from the oven and let it rest for 15 minutes before unmolding onto a cooling rack (you may have to slide a knife around the pan to help it release). Cool completely; transfer to a serving platter and sprinkle with confectioners' sugar, if desired.

Note: If you don't have a Bundt cake pan, use any other baking pan—just adjust the cooking time until a toothpick inserted in the center comes out clean.

atin America is surrounded by the Atlantic Ocean on one side and the Pacific Ocean on the other. No two parts of its coasts are alike. Visit cities like Cartagena in Colombia and you'll find some of the most beautiful beaches in the world, covered in white sand that stands out against the aquamarine and blue ocean waters; or witness stunningly black volcanic sand that contrasts with the foamy crests of crashing waves and the ochers of a pink sunset in the small town of Monterrico in Guatemala. Only two of the twenty-one countries that make up Latin America (Paraguay and Bolivia) are completely landlocked; the rest are exposed to the majesty of the seas.

It's different to be a tourist in an area for just a few days than it is to live in a place. The food that visitors are exposed to when they travel is not necessarily the same as what is served in locals' homes, and yet the ingredients are often identical—it's all in the interpretation. While professional chefs embellish, home cooks simplify; the former must attract customers, the latter must feed a family. And yet, your chances of tasting the most authentic foods of a country are most likely found along the beaches, because there, food is all about the ingredients, the catch of the day and the freshest produce in the marketplace.

One of the most traditional methods of preparing fish and seafood in Latin America is also one of the easiest. When citrus juice is poured liberally over raw ingredients, it causes a process called denaturation that changes their texture and chemical composition, in essence curing or "cooking" without heat. Ceviches (or seviches or cebiches, depending on the country) have

been made in Latin America for centuries (the ones we know today were made possible only when Europeans introduced citrus to the Americas, but it is believed that the Incas used the acidic juice of the tumbo fruit to denaturate thinly sliced fish). However simple the basic ingredients, the recipes for ceviches go through dramatic transformations depending on which country one is in. Peruvians, for example, garnish them with spicy ajíes, onions, and corn nuts (called cancha); Ecuadorians add ketchup and garnish theirs with popcorn (yes, the kind that you get in movie theaters, but without the butter); Costa Ricans embellish theirs with Lizano (a Worcestershire-style sauce); and Mexicans add cilantro and chiles. Every country has several favorite versions, some even made without fish or seafood.

The oceans may provide the main ingredients, but the cultures that collided in each country to form each diverse cuisine most often provide the supporting elements, such as the particular spices, herbs, vegetables, and aromatics that make each dish—because it is always the people of a place that give food its flavor. For this reason, you'll find plantains, coconut milk, and allspice added to recipes from places where the Garifuna peoples, descendants of Africans, settled. You'll find soy sauce and sesame oil added to recipes where Chinese, Hakka, and Japanese immigrants made their homes. You'll find combinations of seafood and rice in places with a strong Middle Eastern presence and saffron and garlic in towns where Spain left its imprint. And of course, chiles and peanuts, native to the Americas, season all manner of seafood recipes throughout this chapter.

Bacalao con Pan y Vino

Cod with Bread and Wine

Chile | Yield: Serves 4–6 | Difficulty Level: Easy | Total Cooking Time: 1 hour

Here, juicy, flaky fish is topped with a crust that is crispy on the outside and soft on the inside, for an elegant yet super-easy casserole to serve midweek. Both fresh cod and Chilean sea bass are plump and maintain their meaty texture as they bake. This recipe has some Andalusian character, as the crust is reminiscent of the "bread sauces" so prevalent in Arab cuisines during the Moorish conquista of Spain. Fish wrapped in bread is a frequent theme in Latin American cuisine, as witnessed by the first recipes that Europeans brought for making empanadas, which were made with fish encrusted in bread and enjoyed during Lent. If you decide not to use the aliño completo spice mix, just add more salt and pepper.

1¼ pounds (570 grams) fresh cod or Chilean sea bass

½ teaspoon Aliño Completo (page 7)

1 cup (225 grams) roughly chopped plum tomatoes

½ cup (55 grams) finely chopped white or yellow onions

2 garlic cloves, finely chopped

¾ cup (180 ml) dry white wine

2 eggs, beaten

1 cup (115 grams) dry bread crumbs

2 tablespoons finely chopped fresh Italian parsley

¼ teaspoon fine sea salt

2 tablespoons olive oil

Preheat the oven to 400°F (200°C). Butter a 9 x 13 inch (23 x 33 cm) baking dish. Season the fish on both sides with the spice mix and place it in the baking dish in one layer. In a large bowl, combine the tomatoes, onions, garlic, wine, eggs, bread crumbs, parsley, and salt until they come together into a paste. Spread the paste over the fish. Drizzle evenly with the olive oil and bake for 45 to 50 minutes or until the crust is golden (and a bit crispy on top), and the fish is cooked through.

Note: The fish is cooked through when it can be easily flaked with a fork.

Salmón al Tequila

Tequila-Agave Salmon

Mexico | Yield: Serves 4 | Difficulty Level: Easy | Total Cooking Time: 1 hour 15 minutes

This is a contemporary recipe that makes use of two by-products of the agave plant, called maguey: its famous liquor, tequila; and its sugary syrup, agave. Salmon is a newcomer to Mexican tables, a result of open imports from Canada and of modern fish-farming businesses. In addition to being used here, it is also particularly delicious when topped with Pico de Gallo (page 153). In lieu of an outdoor grill, cook the salmon over a hot stovetop in a covered sauté or grill pan.

Four 6 ounce (170 gram) salmon filets, skin on

2 tablespoons agave nectar

2 tablespoons premium tequila

2 tablespoons whole-grain mustard

½ teaspoon fine sea salt

Pinch of freshly ground black pepper

Lime wedges

Place the salmon filets in a large glass baking dish, skin side down. In a small bowl, combine the agave nectar, tequila, and mustard; brush liberally over the top of the salmon. Cover and refrigerate for 1 hour (or up to 3 hours). Heat a grill or indoor grill pan. Season the salmon with salt and pepper and immediately place it skin side down on the grill. Close the grill and cook for 12 to 15 minutes for medium well or 15 to 18 minutes for well done (if you're using an indoor grill pan, simply cover the fish with a lid or with an inverted heatproof metal baking pan to trap the steam while the fish cooks). Using a spatula, remove the fish to a platter, leaving the skin behind (you can scrape it off later) and being careful not to break up the filets. Serve with lime wedges on the side.

Biche (Viche) de Pescado

Fish and Peanut Soup

Ecuador | Yield: Serves 4–6 | Difficulty Level: Intermediate | Total Cooking Time: 1 hour 20 minutes

This hearty fish chowder is typical of the province of Manabí, on the coast of Ecuador. The Afro-Latino culinary vein runs through the Americas, and here, it's apparent in the addition of peanuts. Although most home cooks will use raw maní (peanuts) to make a paste, I find that natural, sugar-free peanut butter—the kind I can grind fresh in the store—saves me precious time in the kitchen. Filled with starchy vegetables, this soup is a meal in itself. Some biches (fish soups and chowders) will include shrimp or mollusks, but the classic version is made with albacore tuna (which abounds in Ecuador). However, in order to preserve this endangered fish, I suggest you use mahi-mahi or halibut instead. Popcorn is often used to top soups and ceviches in Ecuador, and here it provides a crunchy garnish. Serve this with plenty of Garnitura Simple (page 15) or Ensalada de Tomate y Cebolla (page 156).

8 cups (2 quarts) Caldo de Pescado (page 31 or store-bought), clam juice, or water

1 cup (240 ml) Refrito (page 22)

1 cup (240 ml) whole milk

½ cup (115 grams) natural, no-sugar-added peanut butter

1 tablespoon ground cumin, divided

2 tablespoons Aceite de Achiote (page 194) or vegetable oil

¾ cup (115 grams) finely chopped white onions

1 cup (170 grams) stemmed, seeded, and finely chopped green bell peppers

2 garlic cloves, finely chopped

1 teaspoon ground achiote

1 teaspoon dried oregano

2 ears of corn, chopped into 3–4 round slices each

1 pound (455 grams) yuca, peeled and sliced into 2 inch (5 cm) pieces

1–1½ pounds (455–680 grams) ripe plantains, peeled and sliced into 2 inch (5 cm) coins

1½ pounds (680 grams) ahi tuna, mahi mahi, or halibut filets, cut into 2 inch (5 cm) pieces

1–2 teaspoons fine sea salt, or more to taste

Finely chopped fresh parsley or cilantro, for garnish (optional)

Garnitura Simple (page 15) or Ensalada de Tomate y Cebolla (page 156) (optional)

Lime wedges (optional)

Popcorn (optional)

Place all but 2 cups of the fish broth in a large pot. In a blender, combine the remaining 2 cups of the fish broth, the refrito, milk, peanut butter, and 2 teaspoons cumin; blend until completely smooth. Add this directly to the fish stock in the pot and stir. Heat the aceite de achiote or vegetable oil in a medium skillet set over medium-high heat; add the onions, peppers, and garlic, and cook for 3 to 4 minutes or until the onions begin to soften. Add the remaining teaspoon of cumin, the ground achiote, and the oregano and stir for 1 minute. Pour this mixture into the fish and peanut broth and bring it to a boil over medium-high heat, stirring often. Add the corn and yuca and bring back to a boil. Cover, lower the heat to medium, and simmer, stirring occasionally, for 25 to 30 minutes or until the yuca is fork tender. Add the plantains, fish, and 1 teaspoon of salt; bring back to a simmer, cover, and cook for 10 to 15 minutes or until the plantains are fork tender. Taste the broth and add more salt, if needed (this will depend on the salinity of the broth used). Serve, sprinkled with parsley or cilantro, if using. Offer Garnitura Simple or Ensalada de Tomate y Cebolla, lime wedges, and popcorn on the side, if desired.

Note: The blended peanut mixture adds creamy texture to the soup. If you want the broth to be very light, then strain the peanut mixture through a sieve before adding it to the fish and discard the solids; you'll end up with all of the flavor of the peanuts but a much more refined broth.

Encebollado de Pescado

Tuna Fish Soup

Ecuador | Yield: Serves 4–6 | Difficulty Level: Easy |
Total Cooking Time: 40 minutes (if all components are made ahead—1 hour, if not)

Tender chunks of fish and yuca keep their toothsome texture and shape while they simmer together seamlessly in this soup. A flavor base rich in onions and spices makes this the national fish soup of Ecuador, recognizable at first taste. If ever there was a recipe that illustrates the importance of flavor bases in Latin cookery, this is it, as you'll use two: refrito and aliño. I keep my freezer well stocked with a variety of these bases divided into portions, so that I can retrieve them whenever I need to. This saves me time and helps me prepare recipes like this soup very quickly. Ecuador is the second-largest producer of albacore tuna in the world; you'll find an abundance used in many recipes. But because it is a "near threatened" species, I recommend that you use bluefin tuna, yellow-fin tuna, or mahi-mahi, instead. Encebollados are traditionally served with sliced avocado in ceramic bowls. Popcorn—yes, the kind you eat at the movies, but without butter—is a typical garnish in Ecuador, where it is offered as a crunchy topping for soups (and for ceviches).

14 ounces (400 grams) fresh and peeled (or frozen and thawed) yuca

1 tablespoon Aceite de Achiote (page 194) or vegetable oil

½ cup (60 ml) Refrito (page 22)

½ cup (100 grams) very finely chopped plum tomatoes

2 tablespoons Aliño (page 9)

1½ pounds (680 grams) fresh tuna (or mahi-mahi, see headnote) filets, cut into bite-sized pieces

2 teaspoons fine sea salt, or more to taste

1 cup (80 grams) chopped fresh cilantro, divided

2 Hass avocados

1 recipe Garnitura Simple (page 15) (optional)

Popcorn (optional)

Place the yuca in a medium pot filled with water; set over medium-high heat and bring to a boil. Cook until it's barely fork tender, about 15 minutes (it will finish cooking in the soup); drain and set aside to cool. When cool enough to handle, split each yuca in half, remove the tough vein in the middle and discard it, and cut the flesh into bite-sized cubes. Place a large pot over medium-high heat; add the aceite de achiote or vegetable oil, refrito, and tomatoes, stirring for 2 minutes (it will thicken); add the aliño and cook for 1 minute. Add the tuna and 8 cups (2 liters) of water. Bring to a boil; reduce the heat to medium and cook at a simmer, uncovered, for 10 minutes. Add the yuca, salt, and half of the cilantro; continue cooking for 10 minutes. Halve and seed the avocados; scoop out the flesh and slice thinly. Ladle the soup into bowls; top with avocado and sprinkle with a generous amount of cilantro. Serve immediately, with garnitura and popcorn, on the side, if using.

Moqueca do Peixe

Fish Moqueca

Brazil | Yield: Serves 4–6 | Difficulty Level: Easy | Total Cooking Time: 30 minutes

This is a creamy and spicy-hot fish stew from the state of Espirito Santo off Brazil's central coast. Moqueca (pronounced *moh-keh-kah*) is derived from an Indigenous dish called moquém, in which fish is wrapped in banana leaves and steamed slowly over a fire. When the colonizers landed, vegetables were added to the recipe; when enslaved Africans were brought to the Americas in the seventeenth century, the dish evolved further to include coconut and the rich red palm oil known as dendê (pronounced *den-jeh*). Instead of wrapping the fish in leaves, it is now cooked in clay casseroles called panelas; today it is one of the most emblematic fish stews of Brazil. Serve it over white rice or cooked yuca.

1½ pounds (680 grams) grouper, halibut, or other firm white fish, cut into ½ inch (12 mm) strips

2 tablespoons freshly squeezed lemon juice (from 1 large lemon)

1 tablespoon coconut or vegetable oil

2–2½ cups (280–340 grams) thinly sliced red onions

2 cups (185 grams) red bell peppers, stemmed, seeded, and sliced into ¼ inch (6 mm) strips

2 cups (185 grams) green bell pepper, stemmed, seeded, and sliced into ¼ inch (6 mm) strips

1 pound (455 grams) thinly sliced plum tomatoes

2 garlic cloves, finely chopped

⅓ cup (25 grams) finely chopped fresh cilantro, divided

2 teaspoons fine sea salt

1 teaspoon freshly ground black pepper

1 cup (240 ml) coconut milk

1 cup (240 ml) clam juice or Caldo de Pescado (page 31, or store-bought fish stock)

1 tablespoon red palm (dendê) oil

6 cups (680 grams) cooked white rice

Malagueta hot peppers (or hot sauce), to taste (optional)

Place the fish on a large plate in a single layer; sprinkle with lemon juice and let it rest for 20 to 30 minutes. In a large skillet with high sides set over medium-high heat, melt the coconut oil and sauté the onions and peppers for 2 minutes. Add the fish (and any juices on the plate), tomatoes, garlic, half of the cilantro, salt, and pepper. In a small bowl, combine the coconut milk and clam juice or fish stock; top the fish with this mixture. Bring to a simmer over medium-high heat. Partially cover, lower the heat to medium, and simmer for 20 to 22 minutes, uncovering twice to stir the stew (be careful not to break up the fish too much). Stir in the red palm oil and mix until incorporated. Sprinkle with the remaining cilantro and serve immediately, over rice, with the malagueta peppers or hot sauce on the side, if using.

Tapado

Seafood Stew

Belize, Guatemala, and Honduras | Yield: 4–6 | Difficulty Level: Easy | Total Cooking Time: 30 minutes

This soup, a dish of the Garifuna people (who call it tapou), represents a marriage of cultures. It is colored with red achiote seeds from the Caribbean islands, rich with coconut milk from Africa, and flavored with sofrito inherited from Spain. There is no forgetting my first taste of a tapado back in Río Dulce, Izabal (in the northwestern tip of Guatemala), which borders Belize and Honduras. I was exhilarated as I slurped broth to find plump shrimp, tender plantains, and plenty of meaty crab legs. It was like fishing for prizes at the state fair! The seafood that is used varies depending on the catch of the day; while one bowl may feature sweet bay scallops, another will offer spiny lobster (plentiful on the beaches of Belize), mussels, or clams. Ever present are firm white fish (usually cod or halibut), plantains, yuca (or a similar root vegetable), and coconut milk. Use seafood fresh to your area; add it only at the last minute to cook just until done. That is how you'll get the cleanest, purest taste without overcooking. Use firm plantains with yellow skins and only a few brown spots. Use frozen yuca if you can find it: it comes peeled, ready to use.

2 tablespoons Aceite de Achiote (page 194)

⅔ cup (165 ml) Sofrito Rojo (page 21)

6–8 cups (1.4–2 liters) Caldo de Pescado (page 31, or store-bought fish stock), clam juice, water, or a mixture of all three

1 pound (455 grams) plantains (about 2 large), peeled and cut into bite-sized slices

1 pound (455 grams) yuca root (about 1 large), peeled and cut into bite-sized pieces

One 13.5 ounce (398 ml) can unsweetened coconut milk

8 ounces (225 grams) halibut, cut into bite-sized chunks

8 ounces (225 grams) peeled and deveined shrimp (about 12 medium or 6 jumbo)

8 ounces (225 grams) scallops (about 20 medium or 10 large)

1½ teaspoons fine sea salt, or more to taste

½ teaspoon freshly ground black pepper, or more to taste

Chopped fresh cilantro or parsley, for garnish (optional)

Heat the aceite de achiote in a large pot set over medium heat; add the sofrito and cook for 2 minutes or until thickened. Add 6 cups (1.4 liter) of the fish broth or clam juice, the plantains, and the yuca and bring to a boil. Lower the heat slightly and cook, uncovered, for 12 to 15 minutes or until the vegetables are fork tender. Add the remaining liquid and the coconut milk and heat for 2 to 3 minutes. As soon as it comes to a boil, add the fish, shrimp, scallops, salt, and pepper. Lower the heat slightly, and simmer for 4 to 5 minutes or until the seafood is just cooked through. Taste, adjust seasonings to your liking, and divide into bowls. Serve, garnished with cilantro or parsley, if using.

Ceviche de Boca Colorada Tico

Red Snapper Ceviche

Costa Rica | Yield: Serves 4–6 | Difficulty Level: Easy | Total Cooking Time: 30 minutes

Quickly tossed together, ceviches are fast food at their best. This is a good time to make friends with your local fishmonger so you can be guaranteed only the freshest catch of the day. Fish, freshly caught, is preferred for ceviches because there is no actual cooking involved. Once mixed with citrus (lime or lemon, traditionally), it undergoes a chemical process known as denaturation in which the flesh is cured, thus changing its texture from soft to toothsome (the same as when cooked with heat).

1 pound (455 grams) red snapper, fileted and sliced into thin strips

1¼ cups (340 grams) peeled, seeded, and diced firm and semi-ripe mango

1 cup (115 grams) finely chopped red onions

1⅓ cups (140 grams) finely chopped red, orange, or yellow bell peppers

1 cup (80 grams) minced fresh cilantro (leaves and tender stems)

1½ cups (360 ml) freshly squeezed lime or lemon juice

2 teaspoons fine sea salt, or more to taste

½ teaspoon freshly ground black pepper, or more to taste

In a large, nonreactive bowl, combine the snapper, mango, red onions, bell peppers, cilantro, and lime or lemon juice; cover and refrigerate for at least 30 minutes (up to 2 hours). Season with salt and pepper to taste.

VARIATION: Substitute cooked shrimp, langoustines, or lobster for the fish. Shellfish for ceviches must always be cooked in boiling water for a couple of minutes and immediately tossed into ice water to stop the cooking process, to ensure that it's safe to eat.

Camarones al Ajillo

Garlic Shrimp

Various Countries | Yield: 4–6 | Difficulty Level: Easy | Total Cooking Time: 15 minutes

In this dish, shrimp swim in buttery oil that is given a robust flavor by garlic and merkén (a smoky, dried pepper from Chile). You may have come across this dish under different names: Mexicans make it with chile de árbol and lime and call it camarones al mojo de ajo. Cubans skip the chiles but add cumin and call it camarones con mojo; Guatemalans add cobanero chile and beer and call it camarones borrachos. I call them all delicious! Offer this meal with plenty of crusty bread to sop up all of the juices.

½ cup (60 ml) extra-virgin olive oil

2 tablespoons unsalted butter, at room temperature

4 garlic cloves, sliced thinly

1 teaspoon pimentón molido or sweet paprika

½ teaspoon dried merkén chile (or hot pepper flakes)

½ teaspoon fine sea salt, or more to taste

¼ teaspoon freshly ground black pepper, or more to taste

2 pounds (910 grams) large shrimp (31-35 count), peeled and deveined, tails left on

Fresh Italian parsley or cilantro, for garnish (optional)

Place a large sauté pan with high sides over medium-high heat; when it is very hot, add the oil, butter, garlic, paprika, merkén, salt, and pepper. Stir quickly; after about 20 seconds, add the shrimp and toss for 1 to 2 minutes or until they are pink. If using, tear the parsley or cilantro up coarsely with your hands, sprinkle it over the shrimp, and serve immediately.

Camarones Veracruzanos

Veracruz-Style Shrimp

Mexico | Yield: 4–6 | Difficulty Level: Easy | Total Cooking Time: 25 minutes

I was a curious six-year-old the first time I visited the Gulf of Mexico and tasted camarones Veracruzanos. At first, I turned up my nose at the idea of olives and capers. But my father convinced me to try them, and I was pleasantly surprised by the way in which the vinegary brine enhances the sweetness of fresh Gulf shrimp. This was the first of many times that I trusted my dad to help me navigate my way around a menu. It was also the very first time I had the courage to ask a chef for a written recipe, which he sent to me scribbled almost undecipherably (particularly for a little girl just learning to read and write) on a stained piece of paper. Decades later, this recipe, my own re-creation of the flavors imbedded in my taste memory is still one that I love to make. Any size shrimp will work, but I prefer larger specimens, usually 25–30 count per pound; if you make sure to select medium-sized olives and tiny capers, they will not overpower the shrimp. Even if you don't like pickled flavors, be adventurous and trust my dad!

1½ tablespoons olive oil

1 cup (115 grams) chopped yellow onions

2 garlic cloves, finely chopped

One 14.5 ounce (411 gram) can diced tomatoes with juices (about 1½ cups)

1¼ cups (210 grams) Manzanilla olives

¼ cup (40 grams) capers, rinsed under cold water and drained

1½ teaspoons dried oregano (Mexican preferred)

1 bay leaf

½ teaspoon fine sea salt, or more to taste

¼ teaspoon freshly black pepper, or more to taste

1 pound (455 grams) shrimp (25–30 count), peeled and deveined

Heat the oil in a large sauté pan with high sides set over medium-high heat. Add the onions and sauté for 3 to 4 minutes or until softened. Add the garlic and sauté for 30 seconds or until fragrant. Add the tomatoes, olives, capers, oregano, and bay leaf. Bring the mixture to a simmer and season with salt and pepper. Cover, lower the heat, and simmer for 10 minutes. Add the shrimp and cover them with the sauce. Cook, covered, for 3 to 4 minutes or until cooked through; discard the bay leaf. Serve immediately.

Note: Manzanilla olives are green olives that are stuffed with red pimiento peppers.

Ceviche Cartagenense

Shrimp, Coconut, and Mango Ceviche

Colombia | Yield: Serves 4 | Difficulty Level: Easy | Total Cooking Time: 1 hour

I first ate creamy, citrus-marinated shrimp on a recent visit to Cartagena de Indias. For days, my husband and I strolled the cobblestoned streets of this walled city where colonial European and western African cultures collided. We took in the rich history, were fascinated by stories of battles with pirates, breathed the salty coastal air, attended mass in old churches, and found small mom-and-pop restaurants that beckoned us with homey flavors. For a striking presentation, ceviches like this one are served directly on halved coconut shells. I spent much of my time in the National Library doing research, and talking to locals about their home cooking, including their favorite ways to make coconut-based ceviches. As soon as I got back, I made up this rendition. There isn't a time when I eat it that I don't recall the sound of horse-driven carriages rolling over the pebbled streets at dusk in Cartagena.

1 cup (115 grams) finely sliced red onions

1 pound (455 grams) shrimp (21–30 count), peeled and deveined

1¼ cups (340 grams) peeled and seeded ripe mango, chopped into ½ inch (12 mm) cubes

1 garlic clove, finely chopped

1 cup (240 ml) freshly squeezed lemon juice

¼ cup (60 ml) canned unsweetened coconut milk

1 tablespoon ají amarillo paste (or 1 minced serrano chile)

¼ cup (20 grams) finely chopped fresh chives

1 teaspoon fine sea salt, or more to taste

½ teaspoon freshly ground black pepper

Plataninas (page 308), for garnish (optional)

Place the onions in a medium bowl and cover with cold water; let them sit for 15 minutes, drain, and set aside. Fill a medium pot with water and bring to a boil over medium-high heat. Fill a bowl with iced water and set aside. Add the shrimp to the boiling water and cook for 2 to 3 minutes; drain them and immediately plunge them into the iced water; drain after 5 minutes. Chop the shrimp coarsely and place them in a large, nonreactive bowl. Add the onions, mango, and garlic and stir to combine. In a medium bowl, combine the lemon juice, coconut milk, ají amarillo paste, chives, salt, and pepper. Pour this mixture over the shrimp; cover it and chill for 20 minutes or up to 2 hours. Serve cold with plenty of plantain chips, if using.

Mohlo de Bobó de Camarão

Shrimp Chowder

Brazil | Yield: Serves 4–6 | Difficulty Level: Easy | Total Cooking Time: 25 minutes

The cuisine of the city of Salvador in the Brazilian state of Bahia is greatly influenced by that of western Africa. When this creamy shrimp sauce is mixed into mashed yuca (which Brazilians call cassava), the traditional chowder becomes almost identical to seafood recipes still found in Ipete, Africa. Many of my Brazilian friends adapt this recipe by removing the yuca to make it into a lighter chowder, which they serve over rice. To me, there is something particularly comforting when it's paired with Nhoque de Mandioca (page 274), because it brings it back to the original interpretations. Dendê oil lends a rich red color and umami taste; it can be purchased online or in health food stores; omit it if you can't find it.

2 tablespoons vegetable oil

½ cup (115 grams) finely chopped white onions

3 garlic cloves, finely chopped

1 teaspoon ground achiote (optional)

One 14.5 ounce (411 gram) can diced tomatoes with juices (about 1½ cups)

1½ pounds (680 grams) shrimp (25–30 count), peeled and deveined

1½ teaspoons fine sea salt, or more to taste

½ teaspoon freshly ground black pepper, or more to taste

One 13.5 ounce (398 ml) can unsweetened coconut milk

1–2 teaspoons dendê oil (optional)

¼ cup (20 grams) chopped fresh cilantro or parsley, for garnish (optional)

1–2 limes, quartered, to taste (optional)

Heat the oil in a large skillet set over medium heat. Add the onions, garlic, and achiote; cook for 1 minute or until the onions are translucent. Add the tomatoes and lower the heat to medium; cook for 10 to 15 minutes or until slightly thickened. Add the shrimp. As soon as the shrimp start to turn pink, increase the heat to medium-high; add the salt, pepper, and coconut milk and cook until just heated through, about 3 minutes. Right before serving, stir in the dendê oil, garnish with the cilantro or parsley, and serve with lime wedges on the side, if desired.

Xinxim de Galinha

Chicken in Shrimp and Peanut Sauce

Brazil | Yield: Serves 4–6 | Difficulty Level: Intermediate | Total Cooking Time: 1 hour

This is a spicy, creamy chicken stew like no other I've had. The state of Bahia in Brazil is rich with African culinary culture; red palm oil, also known as dendê oil, is used abundantly, whether to fry black-eyed pea cakes (acarás) and croquettes or to finish up sauces, such as in this stew. Dried shrimp is made by salting, drying, and then grinding shrimp, skins and all, which aids in thickening sauces; they also impart a deliciously sweet and savory taste that is commonly found in the food of Latin cultures influenced by western Africa (from Mexico all the way to Brazil). Shrimp powder can be found online and in Latin American, Caribbean, and Asian grocery stores. The combination of poultry and seafood is a classic not only in Afro-Latino cooking but in Spanish food, too (think paellas, fideuas, and arroces).

4 pounds (1.8 kilograms) bone-in chicken thighs (about 8 thighs)

Juice of 2 limes (about 2 tablespoons)

1 cup (170 grams) finely chopped yellow onions

¾ cup (115 grams) roasted peanuts

3 garlic cloves, finely chopped

One 2 inch (5 cm) piece of ginger, peeled and chopped

3 Malagueta peppers (or one small serrano), stemmed and left whole

½ cup (30 grams) shrimp powder or dried ground shrimp, divided

2 cups (480 ml) chicken broth or water, divided

2 tablespoons vegetable oil

1½ teaspoons fine sea salt, or to taste

2 tablespoons red palm (dendê) oil

Place the chicken in a bowl and rub it well with the lime juice; let it marinate at room temperature for 15 minutes. In the meantime, in the bowl of a food processor with a metal blade (or in a blender), combine the onions, peanuts, garlic, ginger, and Malagueta peppers; process or blend for 1 to 2 minutes (stopping a couple of times to scrape down the sides of the bowl) or until the mixture resembles a paste. Add half of the shrimp powder and 1 cup (240 ml) of broth (or water) and process (or blend) until smooth; set aside. Remove the chicken from the lime marinade and dry well. Heat the oil in a large pot set over medium-high heat. Working in batches, add the chicken pieces and brown on all sides, about 8 to 10 minutes (make sure not to overcrowd the pan, so they'll brown evenly). Remove the browned pieces to a bowl until the rest are done. Remove all but 2 tablespoons of the oil in the pot (discard the rest). Return the chicken pieces (and any juices that collected in the bottom of the bowl) to the pot. Add the blended sauce and stir well. Add the remaining shrimp powder, broth (or water), and salt; bring up to a boil. Cover, lower the heat, and simmer for 30 minutes (or until piercing the chicken with a fork yields only clear juices). Stir in the dendê oil and cook for an additional minute—just until it is combined. Serve immediately.

Note: I use jarred Malagueta peppers when I can't grow my own; you can find them in Latin American grocery stores or online.

Ceviche de Cangrejo

Crab Ceviche

Costa Rica and Mexico | Yield: Serves 4–6 | Difficulty Level: Easy | Total Cooking Time: 20 minutes

Crab ceviche is popular throughout Mesoamerica but is particularly at home in the city of Tecate, in the area of Baja California where the United States and Mexico converge. The beauty of crabmeat is that it is already cooked when you purchase it (in plastic tubs or cans); a quick bath in citrus juice marinates it in minutes. In Costa Rica, ceviches are usually served with thin and crispy plantain chips. In Mexican homes, they're sometimes stuffed into avocado halves (or the avocado is stirred in).

1 pound (455 grams) cooked crabmeat (preferably from the claw), picked over for shell fragments

½ cup (85 grams) seeded and finely chopped plum tomatoes

⅓ cup (40 grams) finely chopped red onions

⅓ cup (30 grams) finely chopped fresh cilantro (leaves and tender stems)

⅔ cup (165 ml) freshly squeezed lime or lemon juice, or more to taste

2 tablespoons finely chopped jalapeños (seeded and deveined for less heat), or more to taste

1 teaspoon fine sea salt, or more to taste

¼ teaspoon freshly ground black pepper, or more to taste

3 Hass avocados

In a medium nonreactive bowl, stir together the crabmeat, tomatoes, onions, cilantro, lemon or lime juice, and jalapeños, being careful not to break up the crabmeat too much; season with salt and pepper. Cover and chill until ready to serve (up to 6 hours). Before serving, halve, pit, and peel the avocados. At this point, you can stuff the slices with copious amounts of ceviche or slice the avocado into cubes and stir it into the ceviche.

VARIATION: To make ceviche tostadas, make or purchase 12 tostadas (see my recipe on page 91) and top each with the crab mixture, sliced cabbage, and avocado.

Sopa Seca de Mariscos

Mixed Seafood Pasta

Peru | Yield: Serves 4–6 | Difficulty Level: Intermediate | Total Cooking Time: 1 hour

One-pot pasta is nothing new to Peruvians. Here, the pasta is cooked like risotto, by adding a little bit of hot broth at a time while stirring it until it undulates, like waves, when the pan is shaken (or what Italians call "al onda"). Find ají panca and garlic pastes online; if you can't find them, use my harissa recipe (Harissa de Santo Domingo, page 16) and my garlic paste (Pasta de Ajo, page 12).

2 tablespoons vegetable oil

⅔ cup (115 grams) very finely chopped onions (any color)

2 tablespoons Pasta de Ajo (page 12)

⅓ cup (90 ml) ají panca paste

1 teaspoon ground achiote

One 14.5 ounce (411 gram) can diced tomatoes with juices (about 1½ cups)

½ cup (120 ml) dry white wine

1½ teaspoon fine sea salt, or more to taste

1 teaspoon ground cumin

½ teaspoon freshly ground black pepper

5 cups (1.2 liters) hot chicken broth or clam juice, divided

1 pound (455 grams) spaghetti

6½ ounces (185 grams) sea scallops, chopped

8 ounces (225 grams) peeled and deveined shrimp, chopped

14 ounces (400 grams) halibut or other firm white fish, chopped into bite-sized pieces

2 tablespoons chopped fresh parsley or chives, for garnish (optional)

In a large pot, heat the oil over medium-high heat. Add the onions and garlic paste and cook for 1 minute; add the ají panca paste and lower the heat to medium, cooking and stirring constantly for 5 minutes. Add the achiote, tomatoes, wine, salt, cumin, and pepper; increase the heat to medium-high and cook for 5 more minutes or until the sauce is reduced by half (stirring often). Add 3 cups (720 ml) of the broth (or clam juice) and the spaghetti; bring to a boil over medium-high heat, stirring constantly. As soon as most of the broth has been absorbed (about 6 minutes), add another cup (240 ml) of broth. Keep stirring the pasta; when most of the broth has been absorbed, add the remaining cup (240 ml) of broth and the scallops, shrimp, and fish. Cook, stirring constantly, for about 4 minutes or until the seafood is cooked through, the spaghetti is al dente, and the sauce clings to the pasta. Serve, sprinkled with parsley or chives, if desired.

Note: If the seafood is still uncooked and the sauce is thickening too much, add 1 cup (240 ml) water, broth, or clam juice and cook for a couple more minutes.

POULTRY

No one is certain exactly where in the world chickens (*Gallus domesticus*) first came from, but the consensus is that they were domesticated in the Himalayan region between southern Asia and the easternmost part of India more than four thousand years ago. What we know for sure is that the bird was nowhere to be found in precolonial America.

Or do we?

Absent from American soil were the beloved birds that Europeans craved, chickens among them, so as soon as they could, the colonizers introduced poultry to Latin America. That is, if we are to believe what hundreds of history books have been teaching generations of children.

It may very well be that the Spaniards first introduced chickens into Mesoamerica, but according to studies published in the *Proceedings of the National Academy of Sciences* in 2007, fossilized chicken bones dating back about six hundred years before the Spaniards ever stepped on American soil have been discovered near Arauco, Chile. These genetically dated bones point toward Polynesia as the origin of Novo American chickens.

So, if you've ever wondered which came first (at least in America), the chicken or the egg, you can be assured that it was hens along with enough roosters to help produce both. How and when they arrived is something for scientists to ponder in years to come. Did chickens fly over on their own from the Pacific? Or did Polynesians actually live in the Americas at some point before the conquistadores arrived? No matter who introduced them, when, and how, what we know for certain is that chickens multiplied successfully, to the point where they became a main component of every Latin American cuisine today.

Chicken recipes can be found in old Latin American cookbooks dating back to the sixteenth century. Chickens drenched in nut sauces or boiled in chile or ají sauces clearly reflect Amerindian culinary traditions. In Latin America we love our chickens boiled, broiled, grilled, roasted, stewed, and fried. We like them cooked on their own or mixed with many other ingredients.

There may be mystery surrounding the arrival of the bird to the New World, but perhaps these recipes can help fill in some of that history.

Caldo de Gallina

Hen Bone Broth

Various Countries | Number of Servings: 6 cups (1.4 liters) | Difficulty Level: Easy | Total Cooking Time: 2 hours

Caldo de gallina is a luxurious, golden broth that is made with stewing hens by many Indigenous peoples in the Americas. Hens are much leaner and tougher than roosters, thus their meat is not as prized and is typically discarded. However, few birds produce richer, denser, or more flavorful broth. This broth is traditionally served as clear consommé before a meal. Little children often enjoy miniature pasta shapes (shells, stars, or alphabet letters) boiled in it as one of their first solid foods. I find it extremely comforting—an elixir that revives me when I need something light yet nutritious. This fights a cold better than any other broth I know. You can find stewing hens at most Latin American grocery stores, and this bone broth lasts frozen for up to four months.

1 stewing hen (about 1.8 pounds/820 grams), cleaned and left whole

1 small (about 4 ounces/115 grams) yellow onion, skin on and halved

1 teaspoon fine sea salt

Place the hen in a large pot and cover with 12 cups (3 liters) cold water (it should cover the hen by at least 3 inches; if needed, add more); set over medium-high heat and bring to a boil. During the first 10 minutes, skim off any foam that rises to the top. Add the onion and salt; lower the heat and simmer, partly covered, for 1½ hours, adding more water to the pot if the liquid reduces by more than half. Remove from the heat and let the hen cool in the broth for 30 minutes, then strain out and discard all of the solids. Serve hot (or cool, degrease, and freeze for up to 4 months).

Sopa de Fideos o Sopa Aguada

Chicken Noodle Soup with Sofrito

Mexico | Yield: Serves 4 | Difficulty Level: Easy | Total Cooking Time: 30 minutes

Most lunches at my grandma's house started with soups like this one. *Aguado* means "watery," and in Mexico pasta and rice dishes will be described as aguados if they contain liquid, and as secos when they don't. This is the soup my children asked for when they were under the weather; now that they're all grown up, they still request it whenever they need a comforting dish. At the base of this classic is a sofrito of aromatics, chiles, and tomatoes. Fideos— vermicelli that have been broken into tiny pieces—are sold online and in most supermarkets; if you can't find them, substitute angel-hair pasta or vermicelli and break it into pieces. For a different, but equally classic, rendition, substitute equal amounts of rice in place of the pasta.

One 14.5 ounce (411 gram) can diced tomatoes with juices (about 1½ cups)

1 cup (115 grams) roughly chopped white onions

3 garlic cloves, roughly chopped

¼ cup (15 grams) roughly chopped fresh cilantro (leaves and tender stems)

1 teaspoon ancho chile powder

¾ teaspoon ground cumin

2 tablespoons vegetable oil

1 cup (115 grams) fideos (or thin pasta broken into 1 inch pieces)

8 cups (2 liters) chicken broth

2 teaspoons fine sea salt, or to taste

1 Hass avocado

1 cup (120 ml) crumbled queso fresco (or feta)

Lime wedges

Hot sauce (optional)

Place the tomatoes, onions, garlic, cilantro, ancho chile powder, and cumin in a blender; blend until completely smooth and set aside. Heat the oil in a medium soup pot set over medium-high heat. When the oil is hot, add the pasta and stir constantly, about 1 to 2 minutes or until it begins to toast and turn a light golden color (it will go from golden to brown swiftly, so be careful not to burn it). Quickly pour in the blended tomato mixture all at once (careful, it will splatter). Use a long wooden spatula, and immediately begin to stir (the bubbling will subside), cooking and stirring for 1 to 2 minutes or until thickened. Add the broth and salt. Bring to a boil; cover, reduce the heat, and simmer for 10 minutes or until the pasta is fully cooked. Halve, seed, scoop out, and dice the flesh of the avocado. Divide the soup between 4 bowls; garnish each bowl with avocado and queso fresco. Offer lime wedges on the side and hot sauce, if using.

Note: I loved using different shapes of tiny pasta for this soup when my children were little. Find pastina in Italian markets, or mini shells, alphabet pasta, orzo, and such in Latin American markets. Fry exactly as directed in the recipe.

Ají de Gallina

Chicken in Pecan and Yellow Pepper Sauce

Peru | Yield: Serves 4–6 | Difficulty Level: Easy | Total Cooking Time: 20–25 minutes

This everyday chicken stew is the national chicken dish of Peru. It features a velvety sauce spiced and tinted yellow by ají amarillo chile peppers. The mixture of nuts, chiles, and dairy is a direct result of the blending or mestizaje of traditions during the colonial period of the Americas, when ingredients from all over the world found themselves sharing space for the very first time. Crackers—saltines, in this case, but sometimes animal crackers or other simple cookies—are frequently used as the main thickener in Peruvian sauces; they eliminate the need to make a roux and they thicken almost immediately. Evaporated milk also appears here. First popular in places where refrigeration was scarce, it is now a favorite because it is a pantry-stable ingredient, easy to keep on hand. This chicken dish is traditionally served with rice and boiled potatoes, black olives, and hard-boiled eggs.

1 tablespoon olive oil

1 cup (115 grams) roughly chopped white onions

2 garlic cloves, roughly chopped

10 saltine crackers, coarsely crumbled between your fingers

1 cup (240 ml) chicken broth

One 12 ounce (354 ml) can evaporated milk

⅓ cup (45 grams) pecan halves

3 tablespoons (45 ml) ají amarillo paste

1 pound (455 grams) shredded cooked chicken

½–1 teaspoon fine sea salt, or more to taste

2 hard-boiled eggs (see box on how to boil eggs on page 55), peeled and sliced

10–12 pitted black olives (optional)

Heat the olive oil in a large nonstick skillet set over medium-high heat. Add the onions and garlic and cook until the onions begin to soften and turn slightly golden, about 2 minutes; remove them to a plate and let them cool slightly. Place the cooled mixture in a blender; add the crackers, broth, evaporated milk, pecans, and ají paste. Blend until smooth. Return the sauce to the skillet and set it over medium-high heat, stirring until it thickens, about 4 minutes. Add the chicken and salt and stir until heated through. Serve immediately, topped with eggs and the olives, if using.

Pollo al Horno

My Mother's Lemon or Lime Roast Chicken

Various Countries | Yield: 4–6 | Difficulty Level: Easy | Total Cooking Time: 1½ hours

Every cook should know how to roast a chicken. To roast is to cook with dry heat, at a high temperature. This traps the juices inside the meat, keeping it moist, while crisping the skin. Smaller chickens have more flavor than big ones and are perfectly suited for a small family. If you can only find larger chickens, adjust the cooking time, adding 20 extra minutes per pound. This was the very first recipe that my mother, Sandra de Alfaro, taught me to make.

One 3 pound (1.4 kilogram) chicken

1 tablespoon fine sea salt

2 teaspoons freshly ground black pepper

1 whole lemon or lime

1 sprig fresh rosemary

2 tablespoons unsalted butter, softened

Preheat the oven to 400°F (200°C). Pat the chicken with paper towels so the skin is completely dry. Season the chicken—inside and out—with salt and pepper. Use the tines of a fork to pierce the lemon (or lime) about 3 or 4 times; insert the whole lemon or lime and the rosemary into the cavity of the chicken. Rub the butter over the entire chicken. Place the chicken breast side up in a roasting pan. Roast for 1 hour and 15 minutes; cook until an instant-read thermometer inserted into the thickest part of the thigh registers 185°F (85°C) or a toothpick inserted in the thickest part of the thigh releases clear juices; if the juices are still pink, roast further. The skin should be golden and crispy. Remove the lemon and rosemary from the cavity and discard. Let the chicken sit at room temperature for 15 minutes before carving.

Note: Letting the chicken rest before carving is important so the juices—which always go toward the surface of the meat as it roasts—can travel back throughout the chicken and keep it moist.

Pollo al Estilo Pollada

Restaurant-Style Roasted Chicken

Peru | Yield: Serves 4–6 | Difficulty Level: Easy | Total Cooking Time: 3 hours (or 24 hours for a longer marinating time)

Home-roasted chicken is at its best when it is well seasoned and cooked slowly in the oven until its skin is crispy but its flesh is still juicy. Although one cannot fully mimic the flavor of the wood-smoked chicken of Peruvian pollerías—chicken restaurants—at home, my recipe will get you very close. Butterflying or "spatchcocking" the chicken (opening it up and flattening it) helps it cook much faster (see below for instructions on how to do this easily). Flavored with Andean herbs and dark beer, chicken takes on a deep flavor that "sazona hasta los huesos"— seasons through to the bones. For best results, use the darkest beer you can find and marinate the chicken for up to twenty-four hours before cooking it. Serve with any of the Peruvian cremas in the Basics chapter, with Yuquitas Fritas (page 265), Papitas Fritas (page 292), or hot white rice.

One 4 pound (1.8 kilogram) whole chicken

¼ cup (60 ml) ají panca paste

1 teaspoon ají amarillo paste

2 garlic cloves, finely chopped

1 teaspoon ground cumin

1 teaspoon fine sea salt

2 tablespoons vegetable oil

1 cup (240 ml) dark beer

Remove any giblets from inside the chicken (freeze them for making stock later) and butterfly the chicken (see Note) so it lays flat; transfer the chicken to a large ziplock bag. In a medium bowl, combine the ají panca paste, ají amarillo paste, garlic, cumin, salt, vegetable oil, and beer; pour this marinade all over the chicken. Seal the bag and place it in a large bowl; refrigerate for at least 2 hours or up to 24 hours. Place an oven rack in the center of the oven. Preheat the oven to 450°F (230°C). Fit a large rimmed roasting pan with a metal cooling rack. Remove the chicken from the marinade and transfer it, skin side up, to the prepared roasting pan (discard the marinade). Roast for 45 to 50 minutes or until the juices run clear when pierced with a fork at the thickest part (the chicken should register 185°F/85°C). Remove the chicken and transfer it to a cutting board; let it rest for 10 minutes before cutting into portions.

How to Butterfly or Spatchcock a Chicken · Place the whole chicken on a cutting board, breast side down (the legs should be facing you). Using kitchen scissors or a very sharp knife, cut out the back bone by cutting one side off first, and then the other, all the way up to the neck (I prefer to use kitchens shears or scissors for this). Remove the backbone and set it aside for other uses (it's great for making stocks and sauces; you can freeze it and keep it for up to 3 months, until ready to use). Turn the chicken over so the breast side is up; use the palms of your hands to press in between the breast—this will flatten the chicken and you'll hear a crack. You have just butterflied a chicken; it should lay flat.

Pollo para Tacos

Chicken for Tacos

Mexico | Yield: Serves 4–6 | Difficulty Level: Easy | Total Cooking Time: 30 minutes

This is my favorite way to prepare chicken for tacos because it has a kick and a good dose of flavor that plays well with other ingredients. To transform it into an unforgettable taco experience, you will need a great corn or flour tortilla (depending on who you ask). Think of a taco as a gift: the wrapper is your first impression, but the treat is what is inside. After that, it's all about the toppings: chopped onions, cilantro, avocado, hot sauces, crema, minced chiles, escabeches, lime juice—you name it. The key is to include just the right amount of filling on a tortilla so the taco can journey from plate to mouth without it falling apart in the middle.

6 boneless, skinless chicken breasts (each weighing 6 ounces/170 grams)

1 tablespoon Adobo para Carnes Asadas (page 6)

2 teaspoons Pasta de Chipotle (page 12)

2 tablespoons vegetable oil

In a large bowl, combine the chicken breasts, spice mix, and chipotle paste. Cover with plastic wrap and marinate, at room temperature, for up to 30 minutes (or up to overnight, in the refrigerator). Heat an indoor grill pan or griddle over medium-high heat. When hot, add the oil and spread it around with a brush. Add the chicken breasts, cooking for 4 to 5 minutes on each side (or until the juices run clear when the chicken is pierced with a fork). Set aside for 5 minutes, then slice the chicken on the bias.

Note: Chipotle peppers in adobo are canned smoked jalapeños, marinated in a tomato and vinegar-based sauce. The best way to store them after opening is to freeze them. See page 12 for a simple way to use chipotles.

Muslitos con Mojo

Chicken Thighs in Mojo

Cuba | Yield: Serves 4–6 | Difficulty Level: Easy | Total Cooking Time: 1½–4 hours (depending on marinating time)

Mojos are garlic and citrus marinades. For this one, I use sour orange juice from a bottle when I cannot find it fresh (see Sources). If you've never tasted sour orange (also called Seville orange), you've missed out on a flavor profile that defines the food of the Latin Caribbean (however, using equal parts of orange and lime juice works too). The rum is my addition—a liberty I take because it reminds me of the taste of a mojito cocktail, and no one has complained yet. This is a quickly marinated dish—any longer and the flesh of the chicken will get spongy. This dish also works perfectly well when cooked on the grill (just add the oil to the marinade instead).

1½ pounds (680 grams) boneless, skinless chicken thighs (about 6–8 thighs)

1 cup (240 ml) sour orange juice (see Note)

1 packed cup (30 grams) chopped fresh long-leaf culantro (or double the amount of cilantro)

2 tablespoons finely chopped fresh mint

2 tablespoons dark rum

2 garlic cloves, finely chopped

1½ teaspoons fine sea salt, or more to taste

1 teaspoon ground cumin

1 teaspoon freshly ground black pepper

¼ cup (60 ml) olive oil

Place the chicken in a nonreactive dish. In a medium bowl, combine the sour orange juice, culantro, mint, rum, garlic, salt, cumin, and pepper; pour the marinade over the chicken pieces, turning them so they are coated all over. Marinate in the refrigerator for at least 1 hour and up to 3 hours, turning the chicken pieces occasionally. Heat the oil in a large, nonstick skillet set over medium-high heat. Cook the chicken for 10 to 15 minutes, turning halfway, or until the juices run clear when pierced with a fork and the pieces turn golden-brown.

Note: If you can't find sour orange, combine ½ cup (120 ml) of freshly squeezed orange juice with ½ cup (120 ml) of freshly squeezed lemon juice instead.

Pollo en Cerveza

Chicken with Beer

Central America | Yield: Serves 4–6 | Difficulty Level: Easy | Total Cooking Time: 45 minutes

During my many travels through Central America, I often lunch on stews similar to this one, scented with thyme, mustard, and beer. One of my preferred yearly field trips when I was a child was our visit to the Cervecería Centro Americana, S.A., on the outskirts of Guatemala City. It may not be politically correct these days to take children to a beer-processing plant, but I must say that for me it was a learning opportunity. There we learned the science of fermentation and about the nutritious elements of cebada (barley), and got to witness the intricacies of the bottling process. I particularly remember learning that fermented barley smells terrible to a child. Since it happened to be the same plant where sodas were bottled, at the end of this exciting field trip we were always invited to select a cold bottle of our choice. (It was the real reason I loved this excursion so much! And no, we couldn't select beer.) Latin Americans use beer both to tenderize meats and to impart zing. My beloved late uncle, Mirko Samayoa, would always ask me to make this for him whenever we got together; there isn't a time I make it now that I don't think of him.

One 4 pound (1.8 kilogram) chicken, cut into 8 pieces

2 tablespoons vegetable oil

2 cups (285 grams) thinly sliced yellow onions

½ teaspoon dried thyme

1 bay leaf

2 tablespoons of your favorite mustard

2 tablespoons Worcestershire sauce

1½ cups (360 ml) light beer

1 teaspoon fine sea salt, or more to taste

¼ teaspoon white pepper, or more to taste

1 tablespoon flour or cornstarch

2 tablespoons cold water

¼ cup (30 grams) finely chopped fresh Italian parsley

Pat the chicken pieces dry with a paper towel and set aside. In a large pot with high sides, heat the oil over medium-high heat until it shimmers; add the onions, thyme, and bay leaf and cook, while stirring, until the onions are transparent, about 3 minutes. Transfer the onions to a plate and set aside. Working in two batches, place the chicken pieces (skin side down) in the pot, turning occasionally, just until lightly golden on all sides; remove the browned pieces to a bowl and repeat with the remaining chicken. Return all of the chicken and the onions to the pot (with any collected juices). In a small bowl, combine the mustard and Worcestershire sauce; stir into the pot with the chicken; add the beer and stir in the salt and pepper. Bring to a boil; cover and lower the heat to a simmer; continue simmering for 20 to 25 minutes or until the chicken is cooked through (the juices should run clear when pierced with a fork). Remove the bay leaf and discard. In a small bowl, stir the flour or cornstarch and water together to make a paste; slowly, while stirring, add it to the pot. Let the stew come back to a simmer and cook for 5 minutes, stirring until the sauce thickens slightly. Sprinkle with parsley and serve.

Pollo en Coco

Golden Coconut Chicken

Honduras and Nicaragua | Yield: 4–6 | Difficulty Level: Easy | Total Cooking Time: 45 minutes

The first time I tasted this comforting dish, near Tegucigalpa, in Honduras, it came topped with fresh cilantro leaves. Its deep coconut flavor reminded me of the curries of Thailand, but without the heat. This saucy stew features sweet, savory, and sour undertones, and a subtly fruity taste. Coconut sauces are found throughout the coastal areas of Latin America, but this one is quite unique to both Honduras and Nicaragua (where it's lovingly known as pollo dorado). Although through the years I've eaten renditions made with and without mustard, I prefer to add it for increased piquancy. Pollo en coco is traditionally made with banana vinegar or sour oranges, but white wine vinegar makes a very good substitute. I've always had this stew served in deep bowls over cooked rice, with plenty of French bread to sop up the abundant sauce.

6 boneless and skinless chicken thighs (about 1.25 pounds/ 570 grams total)

1 teaspoon chicken bouillon or consommé powder (optional)

2 teaspoons white wine vinegar

2 teaspoons whole-grain mustard

½ teaspoon fine sea salt

½ teaspoon freshly ground black pepper

2 tablespoons coconut or vegetable oil, divided

1 cup (120 grams) chopped white or yellow onions

1 cup (100 grams) stemmed, seeded, and finely chopped bell peppers (any color)

1 cup (185 grams) chopped plum tomatoes

2 garlic cloves, finely chopped

One 13.5 oz (398 ml) can unsweetened coconut milk

1 cup (85 grams) chopped fresh cilantro (optional)

Place the chicken thighs in a medium bowl, sprinkle with the bouillion or consommé powder (if using), vinegar, mustard, salt, and pepper, coating the pieces well. Marinate at room temperature for 15 minutes. Place a medium pot over medium-high heat. Add 1 tablespoon of the oil, and as soon as it is hot and begins to shimmer add the onions, bell peppers, tomatoes, and garlic, stirring for 6 to 7 minutes or until the vegetables are no longer juicy; remove them with a slotted spoon to a bowl and set aside. Add the remaining oil and the chicken, turning the pieces until they take on a golden color on all sides. Add the coconut milk and the reserved vegetables; stir well, making sure to scrape up the brown bits at the bottom of the pot. Bring to a simmer, cover, and lower the heat to low for a slow simmer. Cook the chicken until cooked through, about 15 minutes or until the juices run clear when pierced with a fork. Uncover, increase the heat to medium, and bring the liquid to a boil; continue cooking for 5 minutes or until the sauce has thickened slightly, stirring constantly. Remove from the heat and serve with cilantro on the side, if desired, for each person to add as they like.

Pollo en Jocón

Chicken Jocón

Guatemala | Yield: 4–6 | Difficulty Level: Intermediate | Total Cooking Time: 1 hour

Dating back to the sixteenth century, tender chicken has been stewed in a slightly corn-thickened green tomatillo sauce to produce one of Guatemala's most traditional chicken comida típica (typical food). Beatriz de Descamps is a well-known food personality in Guatemala City and has been my friend since elementary school. This is her recipe, but I've adapted it to serve a small family. It is particularly delicious when accompanied by the Tamalitos Blancos on page 74.

One 4 pound (1.8 kilogram) whole chicken, cut into 8 pieces

One 10 ounce (280 gram) white onion, peeled and halved

10 ounces (280 grams) whole tomatillos, husks removed and washed

10 ounces (280 grams) green tomatoes (any kind)

3 ounces (85 grams) green onions, debearded and left whole

3 garlic cloves, unpeeled

1½ packed cups (115 grams) fresh cilantro, washed and spun dry

10 chiltepín peppers (fresh or brined), rinsed well under cold water (or 1 serrano)

2 cups (480 ml) chicken broth, divided

2 tablespoons masa harina

2 tablespoons vegetable oil

1½ teaspoons fine sea salt

½ teaspoons freshly ground black pepper

Cooked white rice

Pat the chicken dry with paper towels and set aside. In a dry skillet (preferably cast-iron) heated over medium-high heat, place the onion halves, tomatillos, tomatoes, green onions, and garlic cloves; cook while turning frequently until their skins are charred all over, about 8 minutes. Quarter all of the charred vegetables except the garlic and transfer them to a blender. Peel the garlic cloves and add them to the blender, along with the cilantro, chiltepín peppers, and 1 cup of the broth; blend until you have a smooth sauce. Add the masa harina and blend until smooth. In a large Dutch oven, heat the oil over medium-high heat. Working in batches, brown the chicken pieces on all sides; remove the browned chicken to a platter (this will take about 8 to 10 minutes in total). Remove and discard all but 1 tablespoon of the fat in the pot. Return the pot to the stove and add the blended sauce all at once (careful, it will splatter for a few seconds), stirring with a long wooden spoon. Bring the sauce to a boil while scraping up the brown bits at the bottom of the pot; add the remaining broth, salt, and pepper, stirring well. Lower the heat and simmer for 5 minutes. Return the chicken (and any juices that collected on the platter) to the sauce; bring the liquid back up to a simmer by increasing the heat slightly. Once it returns to a simmer, lower the heat to medium-low and continue simmering, uncovered, for 20 to 25 minutes or until the chicken is cooked through, stirring often so the sauce doesn't burn on the bottom of the pot. Serve hot over rice.

Did you know? · Although all tomatoes are known as tomates throughout Latin America, red plum tomatoes are known as jitomates in Mexico.

Pollo en Loroco

Creamy Chicken with Loroco

Guatemala | Yield: Serves 4–6 | Difficulty Level: Easy | Total Cooking Time: 1 hour

This chicken stew is so deeply flavored that it tastes as though it should take a long time to make, yet it's actually very quick. Its elegant appearance and subtle flavor are fit for a fancy soiree, but it's part of the repertoire of most Guatemalan home cooks. Lorocos are the delicately flavored flower buds of a wild edible herb (*Fernaldia pandurata*) found in Mesoamerica. They are green and taste like a mix between asparagus tips and spinach. They are hard to find fresh outside the areas where they grow in the wild, but they're easy to find brined and jarred in stores and online (see Sources). You can also buy frozen loroco in many stores that sell Central American products. Like the very tips of asparagus spears, loroco cooks quickly, which is why it's used as a last-minute addition in most recipes; in a pinch you can use roughly chopped asparagus tips. Edible herbs that grow in the wild, such as loroco buds, are also known as quelites or quilites.

2 pounds (910 grams) boneless chicken thighs

2 cups (480 ml) chicken broth

2 cups (150 grams) chopped fresh cilantro, divided

4 garlic cloves, one whole, the rest finely chopped, divided

2 tablespoons unsalted butter

¾ cup (115 grams) finely chopped white onions

1 cup (225 grams) finely chopped plum tomatoes

1 cup (240 ml) Mexican crema, heavy whipping cream, or crème fraiche

1 cup (70 grams) loroco buds (if jarred, drained and rinsed)

1¼ teaspoons fine sea salt, or more to taste

½ teaspoon white pepper

Place the chicken in a medium Dutch oven and cover with the broth; bring to a simmer over medium-high heat. Add 1 cup of the cilantro and the whole garlic clove; cover, lower the heat, and cook for 15 minutes, removing (and discarding) the foam that collects at the top of the pot. Remove the chicken from the broth and set aside; strain the broth into a bowl (discard the solids) and reserve 2 cups (240 ml); freeze the rest for another use. Return the Dutch oven to the stovetop and set it over medium-high heat; melt the butter and add the onions, remaining garlic, and tomatoes, stirring while you cook, until thickened, about 5 minutes. Return the chicken to the pot and stir to coat with the vegetables. Add the reserved broth and bring to a boil; cover, lower the heat, and cook for 5 minutes. Add the crema and lower the heat further, stirring well until combined—do not let it boil. Stir in the loroco buds and cook until warmed through, about 5 minutes. Season the chicken with salt and pepper, remove from the heat, and serve immediately with the remaining cilantro sprinkled over the top.

Pimienta Blanca, Pimienta de Castilla, and Pimienta Gorda · Pepper is known as *pimienta* in Spanish—not to be confused with the word *pimiento*, which refers to the fruit pepper. Many cooks in Latin America prefer the subtler taste and light color of white pepper (pimienta blanca) for creamy sauces. Black pepper is known in many Latin countries as pimienta de Castilla, a reference to the fact that the peppercorn was brought to the Americas by the Spaniards (Castellanos/Castilians) back in the fifteenth century. The Spaniards found allspice in the Latin Caribbean; its appearance, round and brown when dried, was the same as that of the black pepper they recognized. Allspice, however, tasted entirely different; it had the flavor of cloves, cinnamon, and nutmeg all mixed together. In Latin America, allspice is better known as pimienta gorda, which means "fat pepper," because it's rounder than its counterpart. I do not recommend substituting one for the other, as they each have their own characteristics.

Pollo Guisado

Stewed Chicken

Panama | Yield: Serves 4–6 | Difficulty Level: Easy | Total Cooking Time: 1 hour

When I asked a Panamanian friend of mine, the well-known chef Francisco Castro, to share his favorite recipe to serve at home on a weekday, he sent me this chicken stew. At first glance, the recipe seems so simple that it is hard to imagine the complexity of flavors that are present in the final dish, and yet every single bite detonates with alliums, herbs, and tomatoes, all seamlessly brought together by the subtle flavor of achiote. Here is an example of how much a well-crafted sofrito can do in terms of flavor, without the need to add lots of spices or heat. Ají criollo is a sweet chile (also known as ají cachucha in Cuba and ajicito dulce in Puerto Rico); it is a member of the *Capsicum chinense* family of chiles that includes the hot habanero. Many online sources carry it, but if you're unable to find it, substitute with any fresh, sweet pepper of your choice. Served over white rice, or with plenty of crusty bread to sop up the sauce, this dish is the epitome of comfort food.

One chicken (3½–4½ pounds/ 1.6–2 kilograms), cut into 8 pieces

2 teaspoons fine sea salt

½ teaspoon freshly ground black pepper

¼ cup (60 ml) Aceite de Achiote (page 194)

¾ cup (115 grams) finely chopped white onions

3 garlic cloves, finely chopped

½ cup (115 grams) stemmed, seeded, and finely chopped ají criollo or other sweet pepper

¼ cup (60 ml) tomato paste

1 cup (240 ml) pureed or strained tomatoes (passata)

3 cups (720 ml) chicken broth

¼ cup (30 grams) finely chopped fresh long-leaf culantro (or double the amount of cilantro)

Pat the chicken dry with paper towels and season liberally with salt and pepper. Heat the aceite de achiote in a large pot or Dutch oven set over medium heat; add the onions, garlic, and ají criollo (or sweet peppers) and cook, stirring occasionally, for 4 to 5 minutes or until vegetables are softened and the base has taken on the rich golden color of the achiote. Add the tomato paste and cook for 1 minute, stirring to dissolve. Add the pureed tomatoes, chicken broth, and culantro and stir well. Carefully add the chicken to the pot. Increase the heat to high and bring to a boil; cover, lower the heat, and simmer for 30 to 40 minutes or until the juices run clear when the chicken is pierced with a fork (the time this takes will depend on the size of the chicken, so start checking at 30 minutes). Serve hot.

Note: Always check for salt after cooking, and remember that it's always best to under-salt than to over-salt a dish, because you can easily correct the former but not the latter.

Sancocho de Domingo

Chicken and Root Vegetable Soup

Panama | Yield: Serves 6 | Difficulty Level: Easy | Total Cooking Time: 5 hours (includes 4 hours marinating time)

When my friend Chef Elena Hernandez invited me to a Zoom class with Chef Francisco Castro, I couldn't pass up the opportunity. I met a couple dozen cooks, all of whom discussed their own ways for making and serving this hearty stew (the word *sancochar* means "to braise"). Some of the cooks I talked with like to mash the ñame (white yam) at the end, to make the liquid creamier. Elena's grandmother grated part of the raw ñame into the soup so it melted and turned the liquid a velvety texture. Some Panamanian cooks serve sancocho on its own, but Francisco likes to serve it with Arroz Pegao (page 325). Platanitos Fritos (page 307) and patacones which are also known as tostones (on page 305) are also popular accompaniments. This is my interpretation of sancocho—a mix of all of the ideas I got that day. Start this recipe a few hours ahead of time in order to give the chicken a chance to marinate.

One 4 pound (1.8 kilogram) chicken, cut into 8–10 pieces

¾ cup (115 grams) chopped white onions

4 garlic cloves, finely chopped

¼ cup (80 grams) finely chopped fresh long-leaf culantro (or double the amount of cilantro)

½ teaspoon dried oregano (preferably Mexican)

1½ tablespoons fine sea salt, divided, or more to taste

½ teaspoon freshly ground black pepper

2 tablespoons vegetable oil

One 3½ pound (1.6 kilogram) ñame root, peeled, cubed into bite-sized pieces, and placed in a bowl of cold water (see Note)

Mix together the chicken pieces, onions, garlic, culantro, oregano, half of the salt, and the pepper in a large nonreactive bowl; cover well and chill in the refrigerator for 4 hours (or up to overnight). Heat the oil in a large, heavy-bottomed soup pot set over medium heat. Add the chicken and all of the marinade to the pot and cook, covered, stopping to stir every 5 minutes, until the chicken has sweated and looks half-cooked, about 10 to 15 minutes. The point here is not to give it color, but rather to cook the chicken slowly in the juices that it releases during this process. Add enough water to cover the chicken completely (about 8 cups/2 liters). Increase the heat to medium-high and bring the liquid up to a boil; cover, lower the heat to medium-low, and simmer for 20 minutes. Drain the ñame and add it to the pot, along with the remaining salt; increase the heat until the liquid comes to a slow boil and cook until the ñame starts to fall apart and the broth becomes cloudy, about 20 minutes. If you wish it to be thicker, remove some of the ñame, mash it, and return it to the pot; if you wish it to be thinner, add more water. Heat and serve.

Ñame · Ñame or white yam is native to Africa; you will find it sold in Latin American markets and stores that cater to Afro-Caribbean populations. Panama's cuisine has been influenced hugely by both African and Afro-Indian cultures (Africans that arrived from the West Indies). In the Fuli language spoken in the Senegambia region of West Africa, and in countries like Jamaica, *ñame* means "to eat." To peel ñame, I cut both ends off with a sharp knife and then use a potato peeler to remove the outer brown skin all over its surface. As soon as it is cut, ñame will begin to oxidize; for this reason, it's important to place the cut pieces into a bowl of cold water, which will prevent discoloration.

Pie de Pollo para Onces

Chicken, Leek, and Mushroom Pie

Chile | Yield: Makes one 9½ inch (24 cm) pie or one 10½ (26.5 cm) pie, depending on your preferred thickness | Difficulty Level: Intermediate | Total Cooking Time: 2 hours

I was a caterer for a brief period, and this was the pie most requested for elegant tea parties (called "elevenses" or "onces") from my Chilean customers. It is an ideal recipe for any leftover cooked chicken (see page 27) or for store-bought rotisserie chicken. Jarred roasted red peppers have made my work much easier, and although as a caterer I was known for my pastry, if you're in a hurry you can use store-bought dough.

8 tablespoons (115 grams/1 stick) unsalted butter

2 cups (170 grams) thinly sliced leeks (white and light green parts only)

2 cups (145 grams) finely chopped cremini mushrooms

½ cup (170 grams) finely chopped roasted red bell peppers

½ cup (120 ml) dry white wine

1½ teaspoons Aliño Completo (page 7)

3 cups (430 grams) shredded cooked chicken

¾ cup (55 grams) grated Parmesan cheese

1 recipe Salsa Blanca Sencilla (page 24)

Cooking spray or butter, for greasing the pan

1 recipe Masa Basica para Pies y Tartas (page 35)

Egg wash made with 1 beaten egg and 1 tablespoon water (optional)

Melt the butter in a large pan set over medium-high heat; add the leeks and cook for 2 minutes or until softened. Add the mushrooms and peppers; continue to cook for 4 to 6 minutes or just until the mushrooms are soft. Add the wine and spice mix; cook until the wine has evaporated, about 2 to 3 minutes. Stir in the chicken, cheese, and béchamel sauce and mix. Remove from the heat, cover, and chill for 30 minutes (or up to overnight). Preheat the oven to 350°F (180°C) and place the rack in the middle of the oven. Use scissors to cut out a piece of parchment paper in a circle to cover the base of a 9½ or 10½ inch (24 cm or 26.5 cm) springform pan. Spray the bottom and sides of the pan with cooking spray or butter it generously; place the circle of parchment paper in the bottom of the pan and secure the ring of the pan in place. On a well-floured surface (or over a large sheet of parchment paper), roll out two-thirds of the pastry into a 15 inch (38 cm) circle so it can cover the bottom and sides of the pan. It should be about ¼ inch (6 mm) thick. Carefully, using the rolling pin to aid you in moving the pastry, transfer it into the pan, sliding it into place to fit the bottom and up the sides. Make sure to leave an overhang (don't cut it). Spoon the filling into the pastry and spread it evenly. Roll out the remaining pastry into a 12 inch (30.5 cm) circle and carefully drape it over the pie, making sure to cover the entire top surface. Press both the top and bottom overhangs together and fold the excess under the edge, sealing them together (this should be under and inside the rim, as you will remove the pie from the pan after it's baked). Use a fork to crimp the edges of the pie shell. With a sharp knife, cut 4 vents in the center of the top crust. Place the pie on a large baking sheet (this is to help you move it). If using, brush the top with the egg wash. Bake the pie for 1 hour and 20 minutes or until the pastry is golden and has pulled away from the sides of the pan. Cool for 15 minutes in the pan, then remove the ring and cool completely before transferring to a platter.

Note: The dough recipe makes two equal-sized disks; make sure to cut one in half and combine it with the other to get the necessary amount to cover the bottom and sides of the pan. This pie reheats well in a 400°F (200°C) oven until it's hot in the middle, about 20 minutes.

VARIATION: If you can get your hands on a few baking-style empanada discs (called pasta hojaldrada, and typically found in the freezer section of Latin stores), you can use this exact filling to make 24 empanadas; just fill, fold, seal, and bake them for 30 to 35 minutes or until golden.

Tallarín Saltado de Pollo y Kion

Stir-Fried Noodles with Chicken and Ginger

Peru | Yield: Serves 6 | Difficulty Level: Intermediate | Total Cooking Time: 45 minutes (includes chopping)

Soft noodles are coated with a spicy-hot sauce and dressed with tender chicken and crispy vegetables in one of the most recognized dishes from Lima, where Chinese and Peruvian flavors coexist deliciously. Toasting the noodles helps them absorb more of the sauce, and tossing the chicken with flour gives it a luxurious coating, while keeping it from clinging to the pasta. The ingredient list may seem long, but this recipe comes together quite quickly once the cooking begins. If you wish to cut down on the heat, omit the rocoto paste (or serve it on the side).

2 tablespoons all-purpose flour

1 teaspoon fine sea salt

½ teaspoon freshly ground black pepper

3 tablespoons (45 ml) dark soy sauce

4 tablespoons (60 ml) oyster sauce

1 teaspoon rocoto paste (optional)

1 cup (240 ml) chicken broth

1½ tablespoons cornstarch

⅓ cup (75 ml) vegetable oil, divided

1 pound (455 grams) cooked Chinese wheat noodles or spaghetti

1 pound (455 grams) boneless, skinless chicken thighs, diced (about 2 cups)

⅓ cup (60 grams) green onions, sliced on the bias

4 garlic cloves, thinly sliced

¼ cup (15 grams) peeled and thinly sliced fresh ginger

1 cup (115 grams) thinly sliced red onions (preferably sliced into strips)

1 cup (170 grams) stemmed, seeded, halved, and thinly sliced bell peppers (any color)

½ cup (70 grams) green peas (fresh or frozen and thawed)

2 cups (140 grams) sliced white mushrooms

1 ají amarillo, stemmed, seeded, peeled, and cut into thin strips (about ¼ cup)

1 tablespoon toasted sesame seed oil

Stir together the flour, salt, and pepper in a bowl and set aside. In another bowl, stir together the soy sauce, oyster sauce, and rocoto paste (if using); set aside. In a small bowl, stir together the broth and the cornstarch; set aside. Add 1 tablespoon of oil in a large nonstick skillet or wok and lightly stir-fry the cooked spaghetti for 1 to 2 minutes or until lightly toasted; remove to a separate plate. Coat the chicken pieces with the flour mixture; heat 2 tablespoons of oil in the same large nonstick skillet (or wok) and cook the chicken for 1 to 2 minutes or until lightly golden. Add the remaining 1 tablespoon of oil, green onions, garlic, ginger, red onions, bell peppers, green peas, mushrooms, and ají amarillo and stir for 2 to 3 minutes. Add the soy sauce mixture, and stir; return the cooked spaghetti and toss to combine, about 2 minutes. Stir the broth mixture again to disperse the cornstarch and add it to the skillet, stirring thoroughly. When all is hot, stir in the toasted sesame oil and serve immediately.

VARIATIONS: Substitute beef, duck, shrimp, or pork in place of the chicken. Don't have mushrooms? Use any vegetable you have on hand: broccoli, carrots, celery, bean sprouts, and bok (pak) choy all work well in this recipe.

The History of Peruvian Chicken · Peruvians actually invented the multi-rotisserie system (called "rotombo") back in the 1950s and first showcased it at the then-famous restaurant La Granja Azul, in the Santa Clara neighborhood of Lima. This way of cooking chickens as they rotate on an axis, basting in turn the other birds above and beneath them, gives a particularly crispy skin and juicy meat. The method was exported into the United States in the 1990s. Traditional accompaniments often include fries (both potato and yuca), rice, salad, and a compendium of spicy sauces.

Panes con Chumpe en Relajo

Turkey Sandwiches

El Salvador | Yield: Makes 8 sandwiches | Difficulty Level: Intermediate | Total Cooking Time: 2 hours

Perfectly roasted turkey, mounded on crusty bread and slathered in red sauce, is here topped with crunchy cabbage slaw and cilantro for one of the most iconic Latin American sandwiches you'll ever taste. As times have gotten busier for modern-day home cooks, roasting an entire turkey is left for special occasions. Make these sandwiches by roasting only the turkey breast (like I do here) or using store-bought roast turkey as a shortcut. *Relajo* means "mess," and the traditional sauce is a mix of spices and tomatoes, almost identical to the Recado Chapín on page 198, so I use that instead. Salvadorian cooks will also add peanuts and spicy chiles to their sauce—I omit them, but feel free to stir a tablespoon of peanut butter into the sauce and offer plenty of hot sauce on the side. Just don't forget to have lots of napkins on hand!

One 5 pound (2.3 kilogram) bone-in, skin-on turkey breast

¼ cup (60 ml) freshly squeezed lime juice

8 tablespoons (115 grams/1 stick) softened, unsalted butter

2 tablespoons brown mustard

2 teaspoons Worcestershire sauce

1 teaspoon ground thyme

1 teaspoon fine sea salt

½ teaspoon freshly ground black pepper

⅔ cup (165 ml) chicken broth

1 recipe Recado Chapín (page 198)

8 large rolls (tortas, bolillos, or crusty French bread rolls)

1 recipe Curtido de Repollo (page 227)

Fresh cilantro, to taste

Pat the turkey breast well dry with paper towels; place it in an oven-safe Dutch oven and rub with the lime juice; let it marinate for 10 minutes. In a bowl, make a paste with the butter, mustard, Worcestershire sauce, thyme, salt, and pepper and spread all over the turkey breast; set aside while the oven preheats (no longer than 30 minutes). Preheat the oven to 400°F (200°C). Pour the broth around the turkey breast, cover it, and roast for 1 to 1½ hours or until the juices run clear when the breast is pierced at its thickest point with a fork (or registers 160°F/70°C with an instant-read thermometer), basting it a few times while it cooks. Uncover and roast for 15 more minutes or just until the skin is a bit browned (it will register about 180°F/80°C). Remove from the oven and allow the turkey to rest for 20 minutes. Remove the breast to a board (reserve the juices for later; see Note) and carve, slicing it uniformly. Reheat the recado sauce and keep it warm. Place the bread in the hot oven and turn the oven off, allowing the residual heat to warm the bread (being careful not to let it burn), about 5 to 8 minutes. To assemble the sandwiches, slice the bread in half and fill with turkey, slaw, and cilantro. Serve with the reserved sauce on the side. Ladle the sauce over as you eat—messily.

Note: The roasting juices are quite delicious; degrease them and use to keep the turkey meat moist, or to make soup or gravy.

Spanish Lesson · Turkey is known by different names throughout Latin America. In ancient Nahúatl, it went by huehxōlōl or cuauhotōtolin (for wild varieties) and tōtolin (for domesticated turkeys). Today, in Mexico, it is known as either totole or Guajolote. In Central America, it takes on a name that resembles the Quechua word *chumpipi* and is called chumpe or chompipe. Other Central American countries know it as piche, which is derived from the ancient Cakchiquel Mayan language. The Spaniard conquistadores were the first ones to call it pavo, from the Latin *pavus* (meaning "peacock"), a word widely used today throughout the entire Latin America territory.

Kak'ik

Mayan Turkey Soup

Guatemala | Yield: Serves 4–6 | Difficulty Level: Intermediate | Total Cooking Time: 2 hours

This turkey soup originated in city of Cobán, in the department of Alta Verapaz in Guatemala (what is known as the altiplanos or high plains, where nights can get pretty cold). In the Q'eqchí language, *kak* means "red," and *'ic* means both "spicy" and "hot." This filling turkey soup is tinted red by tomatoes and achiote and is quite spicy due to the spicy-hot chile cobanero, which you may omit if you prefer. (I suggest you start with the smaller amount of this chile and try it; if you can take more heat, add the rest.) Some cooks make kak'ik with a whole small turkey, but in Cobán it is most traditional to prepare it with dark meat only. For this everyday rendition, I selected only turkey legs, which I can easily find portioned out in pairs at most grocery stores in my area. Feel free to use legs and thighs if you prefer. Although each person is supposed to get a whole turkey leg (in fact, it's typically plated with a leg sticking out from each bowl), you may opt to divide the meat into portions instead; in that case, this soup may feed a couple more people. Serve this soup with steaming hot corn tortillas, cooked white rice, or with the Tamalitos Blancos on page 74. Find dried chiles in Latin American stores or online (see Sources).

6 turkey legs, or a mixture of legs and thighs (about 4½ pounds/2 kilograms total)

2 tablespoons fine sea salt, divided

1 pound 4 ounces (570 grams) plum tomatoes, left whole

10 ounces (280 grams) medium tomatillos, husks removed, washed and left whole

One 10 ounce (280 gram) white onion, peeled, debearded, and halved

One 5 ounce (140 gram) red bell pepper, left whole

4 garlic cloves, unpeeled

1 stick of Mexican (Ceylon) cinnamon (canela)

2 guajillo chiles

2 pasilla chiles

2 packed cups (85 grams) fresh cilantro (leaves and tender stems)

⅓ packed cup (15 grams) fresh mint leaves

5 whole allspice berries

5 whole black peppercorns

2 teaspoons ground achiote

⅓ packed cup (50 grams) masa harina dissolved in ½ cup (120 ml) water

1–2 teaspoons ground cobanero chile (optional)

Place the turkey legs in a large pot and pour enough cold water to cover by 2 inches (5 cm); stir in 1 tablespoon of the salt. Bring to a boil; remove the foam that rises to the top with a slotted spoon and discard. Cover, lower the heat, and simmer for 45 minutes or until the turkey legs are tender (the meat will pull off the end of the bones but will still remain attached). Remove the pot from the heat and set aside while you make the rest of the soup. In a cast-iron skillet set over medium-high heat and working in batches, roast the tomatoes, tomatillos, onion halves, bell pepper, garlic, and cinnamon stick, turning until they are charred all over (about 6 to 8 minutes total). Halve the tomatoes and roughly chop the onion; place them into the jar of a blender. Peel the garlic; stem and seed the bell pepper; transfer them, along with the rest of the charred vegetables and the cinnamon, into the blender. Remove the skillet from the heat and, while still hot, toast the dried chiles for 20 seconds on each side; stem and deseed the chiles and add the chiles to the blender. Add the cilantro, mint, allspice berries, peppercorns, achiote, dissolved masa harina, and cobanero chile (if using) to the blender. Blend it all until smooth and pour it over the pot with the turkey and broth. Return the pot to the heat and bring the soup up to a boil; stir in the remaining salt, lower the heat, and simmer uncovered, stirring occasionally, for 30 minutes or until the broth has slightly reduced and has a velvety consistency. Divide the turkey legs into large soup bowls and top with plenty of broth.

Pavo en Mole

Turkey in Mole

Mexico | Yield: Serves 8–10 | Difficulty Level: Intermediate | Total Cooking Time: 2½ hours

In this dish that epitomizes the way Mesoamericans ate shortly after the colonization of the Americas, boiled turkey is bathed in a chile sauce enhanced with just a hint of chocolate. Turkeys, tomatoes, chocolate, and chiles are all ingredients native to Mexico and Central America; sesame seeds, raisins, and dried fruits were products of both Africa and the Middle East, brought over by the Spaniards. This is a special-occasion dish in Mexico, and it usually takes days to prepare, but armed with my simple recipe for mole poblano (which you can make a couple of days before cooking the turkey), it becomes easy to make any day of the week. I like to serve this with freshly made corn tortillas and cooked rice.

One 4–5 pound (1.8–2.5 kilogram) bone-in turkey breast

1 white onion (about 4 ounces), peeled and halved

2 garlic cloves, peeled and left whole

1 bay leaf

1 tablespoon fine sea salt

1 recipe Mole Poblano para Todos los Días (page 478)

⅓ cup (40 grams) sesame seeds

Place the turkey breast, onion halves, garlic cloves, and bay leaf in a large pot. Pour in enough water to cover it by 2 inches (5 cm). Add the salt and bring the pot slowly to a boil over medium-high heat, spooning off any foam that rises to the surface. When foam no longer rises, reduce the heat to medium or medium-low, just so that the liquid simmers. Simmer, uncovered, for 1 to 1½ hours, turning the turkey breast over once so both sides poach uniformly. Add more boiling water if the liquid evaporates too quickly. Test for doneness by piercing the flesh with a fork. If the juices run clear, the turkey is done; if not, continue simmering and checking every 10 to 15 minutes. Once the turkey is done, remove it from the stock and allow it to cool slightly before deboning, about 20 minutes; slice it neatly. Strain the stock into a large bowl and discard the vegetables and bay leaf; set aside 1½ cups (360 ml) of the broth to use in this recipe and save the rest for another use (see Note). In the same pot, combine the mole and the broth, stirring until well combined; bring up to a nice simmer over medium heat. Place the turkey slices in the mole and cook, uncovered, for 20 minutes. Transfer the turkey to a platter and cover with the mole; sprinkle with sesame seeds and serve.

Note: Leftovers of this turkey and the leftover turkey stock can be frozen for up to 3 months. Use the stock to make soups or gravy.

VARIATION: Make tortas (Mexican sandwiches) by slicing bolillos or ciabatta rolls in half. Spread one half with mashed avocado, mayonnaise, and shredded lettuce or cabbage. Top with the turkey in mole. Spread the other half of the bread with some Pasta de Chipotle (page 12) and place it over the turkey. Leftover turkey never tasted better.

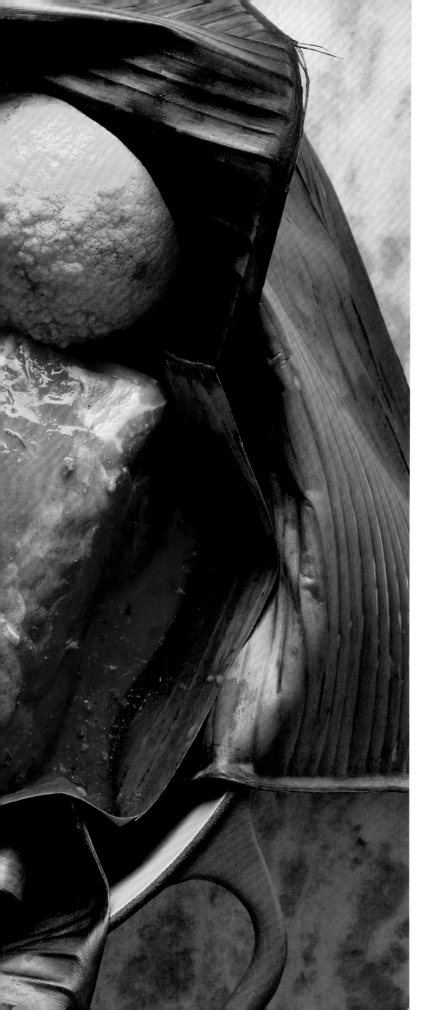

No other animal has made itself more at home in Latin America than the pig. Hardly had pigs been introduced to American soil when they escaped captivity and quickly took over vast swaths of territory. Unstoppable, they roamed freely from Mexico up to North America, and down to the tip of Brazil. I doubt this was the plan when Christopher Columbus brought the first eight Iberian pigs with him; they were probably just meant to feed his soldiers. If historical accounts of the colonization of Latin America are to be believed, from these eight pigs came millions more. To say they multiplied exponentially is to put it mildly!

Europeans brought with them techniques for making charcuterie, and for curing and salting hams. Chorizos and embutidos (sausages, salted and cured meats) still play a huge part in modern Latin cuisines, scrambled into eggs, chopped into salads, layered on pizzas (called cocas in Puerto Rico), and stuffed into empanadas. Spaniards knew the secret of frying. They brought to the Americas the technique for rendering lard (manteca) until crispy skin is left behind (for making chicharrones and charrascas). They knew how to poach pork in its own fat, the French way (confit) that produced carnitas in Mexico, masitas in Puerto Rico, and fritanga in Ecuador.

Boiled pork became the base for recipes, such as the sancochos (pork and vegetable stews) of South America, the secos (pork braised in spicy sauces) of Peru, and the cocidos (meat soups) of El Salvador. Slowly roasted and smoked pork recipes featuring Asian marinades are now mixed into soups, sliced for sandwiches, or stir-fried with rice in Peru. The explosive flavors obtained by the heavenly marriage of pork and beans have created many classic dishes in most Latin American countries, such as the feiojadas (black bean and pork stews) of Brazil and the frijoles con costillas (red beans and pork rib dishes) of Central America.

Lamb (oveja) and goat (chivito) have never enamored Latin American palates to the same degree as pork, perhaps because in some countries they are still expensive. However, every country features a few specialty dishes made with them. The Spanish and Portuguese colonizers imported goat and sheep during the colonial period; they brought with them recipes for stewing and braising their meat and also introduced the French technique of roasting it in ovens, called gigot. Indigenous Americans took to cooking goat and sheep directly on spits, over fire, a technique the Taíno people called barbacoa. Peruvians, Mexicans, and the peoples of the Latin Caribbean would also wrap meats in leaves and cook them in makeshift ovens in the ground, a technique still used today to make recipes such as pibiles (pork braised in citrus and achiote, encased in banana leaves, and cooked in the ground) by the Maya and Pachamanca (a dish of mixed meats and tubers that's cooked in a huatía or earth pot, covered with leaves and hot stones) by the Quechua; pork, goat, and lamb are the preferred meats to cook in this manner (as are llamas and guinea pigs, called cuy).

Although the first Jews to come to the Americas arrived with Columbus, the first major established Jewish communities weren't founded in Brazil, the Dominican Republic, Mexico, Cuba, Puerto Rico, Peru, and Colombia until the end of the sixteenth century. The largest numbers of both Sephardic and Ashkenazi Jews emigrated en masse to Latin America in the nineteenth century, and then again after World War II in the twentieth century, bringing with them a long tradition of cooking sheep and goats. Around half a million Arabs (mostly Morrocan, Lebanese, and Syrian) emigrated to the Americas between 1880 and 1924 (when the so-called French Mandate, which restricted migrants from Syria and Lebanon from moving to Latin America, was signed), and along with them came other ways of preparing these two meats. Countries like the Dominican Republic, Argentina, Uruguay, Mexico, and Brazil, which received the highest numbers of Arab migrants, absorbed and adapted goat and sheep recipes derived from Middle Eastern culinary traditions, including for kebabs called alambres, pinchos, or chuzos and stews spiced with cumin, cinnamon, cloves, and black pepper. Goat and lamb recipes abound in countries where these world influences have been biggest.

Here I have selected an array of everyday dishes for you. Absent are those that require you to roast a whole hog, or spit-cook an entire goat over a fire pit in your backyard, because, although that's still done in many Latin American countries, it is relegated to long weekends or special celebrations. Instead, here are some of the recipes that average cooks turn to at the end of a busy day. Among

my favorites are those that will remind you of the global cultures that helped define the cuisines of a particular country, like the Chinese-inspired lacquered pork ribs, Puerco Asado (page 410), so beloved in Peru.

While many of the dishes in this chapter put meat at the center of the plate, others, like the Pasta con Salsa Caruso (page 427) and the Receta de Domingo de Maruca (page 430), are examples of dishes that stretch just a little bit of meat into a full meal, as many home recipes often do. Some recipes produce elegant results, such as the South American Canelones de Hongos y Jamón (page 426), while others are meant to be enjoyed as informally as you possibly can, as is the case with the Cuban Lechón Asado con Mojo (page 419), which will have you licking your fingers.

Fritanga

Fried Pork Bites

Ecuador | Yield: Serves 6–8 | Difficulty Level: Intermediate | Total Cooking Time: 2–2½ hours

The French influence in Latin cuisine is clear in the many recipes in which meat is cooked slowly in its own fat, a technique called confit (the same one used to make Mexican carnitas and pig skin chicharrones). You'll have to make this recipe if you wish to prepare the Mote Sucio on page 70, because the browned and caramelized rendered fat left in the bottom of the pan (called mantequilla negra or black butter) is the base of that recipe. Whenever I make fritanga, I freeze the rendered lard in a container so I can use it whenever I want to add flavor to other dishes; it's delicious to cook eggs, spread on tortillas, or to flavor beans. Fritanga is usually served with a refreshing crisp and citrusy side dish. I suggest the Garnitura Criolla (on page 14) or the Garnitura Simple (page 15). I love to serve this with peeled orange slices, too, but I leave it up to you. Leftover fritanga freezes well for up to one month.

One 3½ pound (1.6 kilogram) boneless pork butt

¼ cup (120 ml) melted lard or vegetable oil

2 navel oranges, unpeeled and quartered

1 small (about 4 ounces/115 grams) yellow onion, peeled and quartered

8 garlic cloves, peeled and quartered

1 teaspoon fine sea salt

1 teaspoon ground cumin

1 teaspoon ground achiote

¼ teaspoon freshly ground black pepper

Pat the pork dry using paper towels and dice it into 2 inch (5 cm) cubes. Melt the lard or vegetable oil in a large Dutch oven over medium-high heat; cook the pork on all sides, about 8 to 10 minutes (it will not take much color at this stage). Add 3 cups (720 ml) water, the oranges, onions, garlic, salt, cumin, achiote, and pepper. Bring the liquid to a boil; cover, reduce the heat to low, and simmer the pork for 45 minutes or until it is fork tender. Increase the heat to medium-high and bring to a rolling boil; cook, uncovered, stirring occasionally, for 20 minutes. At this point you'll notice that the liquid starts to become viscous; keep it cooking at a boil until it caramelizes and coats the pork. Brown sticky bits will have formed at the bottom of the pot. At this point, begin to stir the pork often (but gently so that the pieces don't fall apart) as you continue cooking for 12 to 15 more minutes until all of the liquid has evaporated and the pork is frying in its own fat. Remove the pork from the heat to a platter (discard the oranges) and cover with aluminum foil to keep it warm. (Reserve all of the fat and the brown bits in the bottom of the pan for use in other recipes.

VARIATIONS: Mexican carnitas are made in exactly the same manner but are cooked in milk. To make carnitas, substitute 3 cups (720 ml) of milk for the water, add 1 teaspoon of dried Mexican oregano, and remove the achiote. Serve with plenty of lemon and warm corn tortillas.

Salvadorian chicharrones de cerdo are also made with the same method but without the oranges, cumin, or achiote. Serve with warm corn Tortillas de Nixtamal (page 83) or Tortillas de Masa Harina (page 84) and with Curtido de Repollo (page 227).

Puerco Asado

Char Siu

Peru | Yield: Serves 4–6 | Difficulty Level: Intermediate | Total Cooking Time: 8 hours (for marinating), 45 minutes to cook

Char siu—Chinese barbecued pork—can be bought prepared in many Peruvian grocery stores in Lima. In the U.S., unless you are lucky enough to live near a place that sells it, you will need to make your own. The good news is that it's super easy to do. In Peru, this pork is eaten alone, served with rice, stuffed into buns, in soups, in fried rice (such as in the Chaulafán on page 340), or as the main ingredient in other stir-fries such as Chancho en Salsa de Tamarindo (page 413). Select pork that has a good amount of fat, as it will render while it cooks, creating flavor and a good texture. For this purpose, I prefer to use country ribs or long strips that are cut near the end of the shoulder, the fattiest part of the pig. This recipe doubles well, in case you want to eat the ribs one day and have leftovers for other dishes.

¼ cup (60 grams) white granulated sugar

2 teaspoons fine sea salt

½ teaspoon Chinese five-spice powder

¼ teaspoon white pepper

1 teaspoon toasted sesame oil

3 tablespoons (45 ml) Shaoxing rice wine, divided

3 tablespoons (45 ml) hoisin sauce, divided

3 tablespoons (45 ml) soy sauce, divided

2 tablespoons unsulfured molasses

4 garlic cloves, finely chopped

2 pounds (910 grams) pork shoulder, cut into pieces (5 inch/12 cm x 3 inches/7.5 cm), or whole country ribs

2 cups (480 ml) plus 1 tablespoon boiling water, plus more as needed

¼ cup (60 ml) honey

Combine the sugar, salt, five-spice powder, white pepper, sesame oil, 2 tablespoons rice wine, 2 tablespoons hoisin sauce, 2 tablespoons soy sauce, the unsulfured molasses, and the garlic in a large bowl; mix well. Add the pork, making sure to turn the pieces so they are coated well on all sides. Cover and refrigerate for at least 8 hours or overnight; turn the pork in the marinade occasionally. In a separate bowl, combine the remaining wine, hoisin sauce, and soy sauce and the honey; cover and set aside. When ready to cook: Preheat the oven to 475°F (240°C). Line a large, deep baking pan with parchment paper and fit it with an oven-safe metal cooling rack. Place the pork pieces on the prepared rack but don't let them touch each other; discard the marinade. Place the pan in the oven and pour 2 cups (600 ml) of boiling water into the bottom of the pan (the rack shouldn't come in contact with the water). Roast the pork for 15 minutes. Reduce the heat to 375°F (190°C) and cook for 20 additional minutes. Turn the pork pieces over (if the water has evaporated, add more boiling water to the bottom of the pan). Roast for 12 to 15 minutes or until the pork reaches 145°F (63°C). In the meantime, add 1 tablespoon boiling water to the reserved wine mixture and stir it until the honey is dissolved. Brush the pork on all sides with half of the honey glaze and continue roasting for 5 to 7 minutes or until the glaze gets sticky and the pork browns well. Remove the pork from the oven and brush it with the remaining honey glaze. Let cool slightly. Serve the pork or cool it to use in another recipe. You can keep leftovers, refrigerated and covered, for up to 3 days.

Chancho en Salsa de Tamarindo

Pork and Tamarind Stir-Fry

Peru | Yield: Serves 4–6 | Difficulty Level: Easy | Total Cooking Time: 15 minutes

This is a classic dish in the chifas—Chinese restaurants—of Lima that is simple to re-create at home. Tamarind sauces are available in Asian and Latin American grocery stores. When I can't find a bottled version, I make my own very simply (see Tip below). In Peru, snow peas are known as holantao; most other Latin countries know them as arvejas chinas—Chinese peas. The amount of salt you will need will depend on how salty the soy sauce is and how sour the tamarind paste you find is—therefore, adjust to taste before serving.

2 tablespoons vegetable oil (peanut oil is best)

2 cups (225 grams) white onions, cut into thin wedges

3 cups (400 grams) red bell peppers, stemmed, seeded, and cut into squares

⅔ cup (140 grams) snow peas, cut into thirds

2 tablespoons grated fresh ginger

1 jalapeño pepper, stemmed, seeded, and thinly sliced (leave seeds if more heat is desired)

3½ cups (475 grams) thinly sliced Puerco Asado (page 410)

2 tablespoons soy sauce

1 cup (240 ml) tamarind sauce (see Tip)

1 teaspoon fine sea salt, or to taste

½ cup (30 grams) green onions (white and green parts), debearded and sliced thinly on the bias

1 tablespoon toasted sesame seeds (see box on page 198)

Heat the oil in a large wok or nonstick skillet with high sides; add the onions, peppers, snow peas, ginger, and jalapeño. Cook, while stirring, for 3 to 4 minutes. Add the puerco asado and cook for 2 minutes or just until heated through. Add the soy sauce and tamarind sauce. Stir for 2 minutes. Season with salt; sprinkle with the green onions and sesame seeds and serve immediately.

Tip: To make tamarind sauce, place 1 cup (225 grams) of tamarind pulp (with seeds) in a medium bowl. Cover with 1 cup (240 ml) of warm water (100°F/40°C). Let it sit for 10 minutes. Press and squeeze the pulp through a sieve set over a bowl, removing the seeds and the fibers (discard them). Scrape the pulp that sticks underneath the sieve and add it to the bowl (it will be watery). You should have 1 cup (240 ml); add more water if needed to reach this amount. This is your sauce. You can also just use prepared salsa de tamarindo (tamarind paste without pulp).

Puerco en Chile Verde

Pork Chile Verde

Mexico | Yield: Serves 6 | Difficulty Level: Easy | Total Cooking time: 2 hours 45 minutes

Moles are special-occasion dishes because they typically require a lot of time to craft. However, rich and comforting stews like this are much quicker to prepare and still deliver deep flavor. This pork stew, redolent with herbs and flavored by tangy tomatillos (related to gooseberries and not to the green tomatoes they resemble), is perhaps one of the most recognizable dishes of contemporary Mexican cuisine. It is a favorite offering at most casual Mexican restaurants around the world, precisely because it's common fare in homes. I've developed this recipe so it falls on the mild side; feel free to add a couple more jalapeños.

1½ pounds (680 grams) fresh tomatillos, husks removed, and rinsed

1 small (about 4 ounces/115 grams) white onion, peeled and quartered

1 large or 2 small jalapeño peppers, stemmed (remove seeds and veins for less heat)

4 garlic cloves

2 teaspoons fine sea salt

1½ teaspoons ground cumin

1 teaspoon Mexican oregano

1 small bunch (3 ounces/85 grams) cilantro (leaves and tender stems) (about 2 packed cups)

2 green onions, debearded and quartered

3 pounds (1.4 kilograms) boneless pork shoulder, cut into 1½ inch (4 cm) pieces

3 tablespoons (45 ml) vegetable oil, divided

In a medium, nonreactive pot set over medium-high heat, combine the tomatillos, onion quarters, jalapeños, and garlic cloves; cover with 5 cups (1.2 liters) of cold water and bring to a simmer. Lower the heat to medium-low, cover, and continue simmering for 10 to 12 minutes or until the tomatillos have turned an olive-green color and have softened but still remain whole (larger tomatillos will take longer to cook than smaller ones). Strain the vegetables over a bowl, reserving the cooking liquid, and place them in a blender. Let the mixture cool for 10 minutes. Add the salt, cumin, oregano, cilantro, and green onions and blend (add a bit of the reserved liquid to help the motor run) until you have a smooth sauce, and set aside. Pat dry the pork with paper towels. Heat 1 tablespoon of the oil in a large pot (or Dutch oven) set over medium-high heat until it begins to shimmer; add half of the pieces of pork (being careful not to crowd the pan) and brown them well on all sides. Transfer them to a bowl; add another tablespoon of oil to the pan and cook the remaining pork pieces, browning until all are done (about 10 to 12 minutes, total). Add the remaining tablespoon of oil and the blended sauce—careful, it will splatter for the first 30 seconds, so stand back—and lower the heat to medium. Make sure to scrape up all of the brown bits that have collected in the bottom of the pot. Return the pork (and any collected juices in the bowl) back to the pot along with 1½ cups (360 ml) of the reserved cooking liquid (discard the rest). Bring the liquid to a boil, cover, lower the heat to low, and simmer for 1½ to 2 hours or until the pork is fork tender.

Note: You can always leave the seeds and veins of the chiles in a recipe if you can withstand their level of heat (or add more chiles) but keep in mind that it's nearly impossible to remove the heat once the recipe is cooked.

Herbs and Their Stems · If there is one thing that makes me smile, it's when students in my cooking classes, faced with having to chop cilantro or parsley, begin to pluck the leaves off their tender stems, as if they are playing "She loves me, she loves me not." I tell them that whoever they're thinking of definitely loves them, so they can stop plucking. After decades of teaching, I have discovered that most home cooks discard the stems of tender herbs, even though they actually contain much of the flavor. Here is my rule of thumb for herbs: If the stems are hard, such as those of rosemary, thyme, mint, and oregano, take off the leaves—but don't pluck them. Simply slide them down the woodsy stems; they will release into a neat pile. But if the stems are soft, like cilantro and parsley, take advantage of their flavor! Remove only the bottom of the stem (often, the least-tender part), and then mound the herbs together and chop them all up, both leaves and stems.

Cañón de Cerdo Entomatado

Pork Tenderloin with Sweet Tomato Sauce

Honduras | Yield: Serves 4–6 | Difficulty Level: Easy | Total Cooking Time: 1½ hours

If you love sweet and savory flavor combinations, you'll enjoy this pork, which is covered in rich tomato sauce with a hint of sugar. Usually served with flour tortillas, white rice, and a salad, this recipe is adapted from one I remember childhood friends from San Pedro Sula making whenever we got together at the beach. Quick to prepare, it is ideal for everyday cooking, and any leftovers make absolutely delicious panitos (sandwiches)—simply stuff crusty rolls with the sauced pork, lots of mayonnaise, hot sauce, and shredded lettuce or cabbage.

2 pork tenderloins (1½–2 pounds/ 680–910 grams total), cleaned and silver skins removed

1 pound (455 grams) plum tomatoes (about 5 large), quartered

1 large green or red bell pepper, stemmed, seeded, and cut into 6 pieces

1 cup (115 grams) very roughly chopped white onions

2 garlic cloves, quartered

⅓ cup (30 grams) chopped fresh cilantro (leaves and tender stems)

3 tablespoons (45 ml) tomato paste

2 tablespoons packed brown sugar (piloncillo or panela)

1 tablespoon of any kind of mustard

1 teaspoon fine sea salt, or more to taste

½ teaspoon freshly ground black pepper

Preheat the oven to 350°F (180°C). Lightly grease a 9 x 13 inch (23 x 33 cm) baking dish and set the pork in it; set aside. In a large blender, combine the tomatoes, bell peppers, onions, garlic, cilantro, tomato paste, brown sugar, mustard, salt, and pepper with ½ cup (120 ml) water; blend until smooth (it may be necessary to stop the blender and scrape down the sides a couple of times to help it blend). Pour this all over the pork and bake for 1 hour, basting on occasion, until the pork reaches an internal temperature of 180°F (80°C) or the juices run clear when pierced with a fork and the surface of the sauce has thickened somewhat (the bottom will still be liquid). Remove the pork from the oven and let it rest for 10 minutes; transfer to a cutting board and slice thinly; return the pork to the sauce and serve.

Note: For an elegant presentation, spoon the tomato sauce into a bowl and serve alongside the sliced pork. If you want a thicker sauce, transfer the pork to a platter; keep it covered. Place the sauce into a small pot and cook it over medium-high heat until it's thickened to the desired consistency.

Chuletas de Diario

Everyday Pork Chops

Mexico | Yield: Serves 4–6 | Difficulty Level: Easy | Total Cooking Time: 1 hour

I'm keen on destroying the stereotypes that surround Latin cooking, and one of those is that all of our dishes—especially those hailing from Mexico—are spicy-hot. Chiles can also be used for their fruity flavor and not for heat. Here, chocolatey dried poblano chiles, also called chiles anchos, provide both a fruity, raisin-like essence and an earthy taste, without imparting any heat. The longer you marinate the pork chops, the deeper the flavor will be. Offer these with sides of Elotes con Rajas on page 51 or with the Calabacitas on page 140, and with rice, such as the Arroz Seco Verde on page 338 or the Arroz Blanco on page 323.

Six 6 ounce (170 gram) pork chops, with or without bone

2 tablespoons avocado or vegetable oil

1 teaspoon ancho chile powder

1½ teaspoons fine sea salt

½ teaspoon freshly ground black pepper

½ teaspoon garlic powder

¼ cup (20 grams) finely chopped fresh parsley or cilantro (leaves and tender stems)

Brush the pork chops with the avocado oil and set aside. In a bowl, combine the chile powder, salt, pepper, garlic powder, and parsley. Rub the pork chops with this mixture and refrigerate for at least 30 minutes (or up to overnight). Remove the chops from the refrigerator 20 minutes before cooking and let them come to room temperature. Heat an outdoor grill (or indoor grill pan) until very hot. Cook the pork chops until they register 145°F (63°C) on an instant-read thermometer, or about 4 to 5 minutes per side (they will be slightly pink in the middle). Cook them more, if you prefer them well done, about 2 minutes more per side per degree of doneness.

Chuletas Fritas

Breaded, Pan-Fried Pork Chops with Lime and Parsley

Honduras | Yield: Serves 4 | Difficulty Level: Easy | Total Cooking Time: 35–40 minutes

Breaded pork chops are found in many cultures around the world, including in Honduras, where they are a regular feature on menus. Bone-in pork chops have more flavor and tend to remain juicier than boneless ones. I will often make two or three batches of these and fry and freeze them in a single layer; once frozen solid, I transfer them to freezer bins or bags. That way, whenever I need a quick dinner, I simply preheat the oven to 400°F (200°C) and bake the desired number of pork chops, without thawing, until heated through, about 20 to 25 minutes. That gives me just enough time to whip up a salad to serve on the side.

Four 8 ounce (225 gram) bone-in pork chops, pounded to ¼ inch (6 mm thick)

½ cup (60 grams) all-purpose flour

½ teaspoon fine sea salt

3 whole eggs, well beaten with 2 tablespoons cold water

1½ cups (170 grams) dried bread crumbs

Vegetable oil for frying, about ½ cup (120 ml) or as needed

3–4 tablespoons (15–20 grams) finely chopped fresh parsley

1–2 limes or lemons, sliced in half

Line a baking sheet with parchment paper and preheat the oven to 400°F (200°C). Pat dry the pork chops well with a paper towel. On a shallow plate, stir together the flour and salt and set aside. Place the beaten egg mixture in a bowl; place the bread crumbs on a plate. Dredge each pork chop in the flour; dip in the egg, coating well on both sides before dipping in the bread crumbs and pressing them well so they stick to all sides. Heat the oil in a large skillet set over medium-high heat. Cook the chops until the breading is golden, about 3 to 4 minutes on each side (they will not cook through at this stage). Place each fried chop on the prepared baking sheet. Transfer the sheet to the oven and finish cooking for 8 to 12 minutes or until the meat is cooked through. Transfer to a platter, sprinkle with parsley, and serve with lime or lemon wedges on the side.

Note: To pound the pork chops thinly, work with one at a time. Place a pork chop inside a ziplock bag and, using a heavy mallet (or skillet), pound the meat where there is no bone, starting from the middle of the chop and moving outward, pressing and pounding the meat until it reaches the desired thickness.

Lechón Asado con Mojo

Citrus and Cumin Pork Roast

Cuba | Yield: Serves 8 | Difficulty Level: Easy | Total Cooking Time: 5 hours (includes marinating time)

This citrus- and garlic-infused pork is one of the most recognized Cuban recipes. Parties with friends almost always include a whole pig (lechón) that is cooked on a spit and mopped with marinade as it roasts lazily, directly over the embers, while revelers converse, have a few drinks, and nosh on tostones. Luckily, you don't have to wait for an invitation, nor will you need to purchase an entire pig to make this during the week. Mojo (pronounced *mo-ho*) is the name of an acidic marinade made with garlic and spices. I prefer to marinate the pork loin overnight; however, a few hours will suffice. You will notice that Latin Americans often use the "steam-roast" method, in which meats are both steamed and roasted in the oven until their surfaces caramelize. If you were to leave this roast uncovered the entire time, the marinade would reduce and burn; remove the foil at the end so the marinade can reduce into a light sauce with concentrated citrus flavor.

⅓ cup (75 ml) olive oil

¾ cup (115 grams) roughly chopped white onions

3 garlic cloves, thinly sliced

1½ cups (300 ml) sour orange juice (see Note)

1 teaspoon dried oregano

1½ teaspoon fine sea salt, divided

1 teaspoon ground cumin

½ teaspoon freshly ground black pepper

2 tablespoons water

One 2 pound (910 gram) pork loin

Heat the oil in a small saucepan set over medium heat; add the onions and garlic. Cook for 3 minutes, making sure not to burn the garlic. Add the sour orange juice, oregano, salt, cumin, pepper, and water; simmer for 5 minutes. Remove from the heat and let cool to room temperature. Place the pork loin inside a large, resealable plastic bag. Pour in the mojo marinade and close the bag. Marinate the pork in the refrigerator for at least 3 hours (or up to 24 hours), shaking occasionally to redistribute the marinade. Preheat the oven to 400°F (200°C). Line a 9 x 13 inch (23 x 33 cm) roasting pan with a piece of parchment paper. Place the pork in the prepared pan and pour the marinade around it. Cover the roast with a piece of aluminum foil, sealing well, and roast for 40 minutes; remove the aluminum foil and continue roasting until the pork reaches an internal temperature of 150°F (65°C) and the top begins to turn golden (about 30 to 35 minutes). Let the pork rest for 10 minutes before slicing; strain the sauce into a serving bowl and offer it on the side.

Note: Sour orange juice can be found, bottled, in the Latin section of most supermarkets and online (see Sources), or substitute with a mixture of equal halves orange and lemon juice.

VARIATION: The Cuban Sandwich, or "Media Noche"

Cuban bread, a mix between a brioche and a baguette, is the ideal loaf to make a Cuban sandwich—a media noche—as it collapses on the grill, producing a crispy crust. When not available, substitute high-quality sub rolls. Layer the bread with slices of the pork loin, ham, Swiss cheese, and pickles; slather the top with mustard and cook it on a panini grill (weighed down on a grill or griddle works too) until flattened and warmed through.

Pamplonitas de Cerdo

Stuffed Pork Rolls

Uruguay | Yield: Serves 4–6 | Difficulty Level: Intermediate | Total Cooking Time: 1 hour

In Uruguay, a pamplona is a large piece of meat that has been flattened, stuffed, wrapped in bacon, rolled, and then grilled to perfection. These smaller versions are very popular and can be cooked indoors. Once assembled, the rolls can be chilled (for up to twenty-four hours) and cooked to order. Pamplonitas—small pamplonas—are easy enough to make for an everyday meal; however, I suggest you do as the Uruguayans do and cook them on a leisurely weekend; slice them very thinly, and enjoy them with bread and a bottle of good wine, over a long conversation—a sobremesa (see box on page 423). Just don't forget to remove the toothpicks before serving!

Four 6 ounce (170 gram) boneless center pork chops, about ½ inch (12 mm) thick

4 slices cooked ham

4 slices provolone cheese

12 large or 16 small manzanilla olives

12 thin slices bacon (about 1 pound/455 grams)

1 teaspoon vegetable oil

Preheat the oven to 400°F (200°C). Line a baking sheet with parchment paper and set aside. Working with one chop at a time, place each chop on a clean chopping board lined with plastic wrap and cover it with another piece of plastic wrap (this will keep the pork from sticking to your mallet or your board). Use a mallet or heavy skillet to pound the pork chop until it is ¼ inch (6 mm) thick, making sure that it's evenly flattened. Repeat with the remaining chops, setting them aside on a plate. Place three slightly overlapped bacon slices horizontally on the board and set one chop in the middle of the bacon (see photos on facing page). Place one slice of ham in the center of each chop, then top each with one slice of the cheese. Place the olives in a row over the cheese. Starting at the bottom end (the one closest to you), roll the pork chop upward, making sure that the bacon is rolled up along with it, until you have a tight cylinder (if an olive escapes, push it back into the center). Continue rolling the chop until it's wrapped with the bacon; use 3 or 4 toothpicks to secure. Repeat until all of the pork chops are wrapped in bacon. Heat the oil in a large grill pan set over medium-high heat; as soon as it's hot, place the pork rolls seam side down—you should hear them sizzle. Cook, turning often, until golden on all sides, about 5 to 6 minutes (the cheese will melt a bit, and if an olive escapes, just reinsert it). Transfer the pork rolls onto the prepared sheet; bake for 25 to 30 minutes or until the internal temperature reaches 185°F (85°C) and the juices run clear when pierced with a fork. Remove from the heat and let rest for 10 minutes before slicing across and serving.

VARIATIONS: Here, I use pork, but you can make pamplonitas with chicken, beef, veal, or lamb. Let your imagination soar and change up the fillings: artichoke hearts, roasted peppers, eggplant, salami, spinach, mushroom paste, and sun-dried tomatoes are just some of the many possibilities. Just always include a good melting cheese to serve as the "glue" to hold everything together. Prosciutto can be used in place of the bacon—you just want a salty, meaty crust to form around each pamplonita. Manzanilla olives are green olives stuffed with pimiento peppers—but use any olives you like, as long as they are pitted.

La Sobremesa · Perhaps one of the warmest rituals in Latin America is the sobremesa, the conversation that follows a meal. It's during sobremesas that politics are discussed, religion is debated, philosophy is introduced, daily problems are solved, morals are taught, and friendships are forged. It is a time for families to catch up in the most intimate and safe of spaces. It's also the time in which relationships are solidified through free and frank discourse, where people either agree or agree to disagree. This is one of the most important culinary traditions that Latin Americans take with us whenever we move somewhere else—the reason we insist on sitting together at the table at least once a day. Over the centuries, many future sons-in-law have been interrogated (sometimes subtly; other times not so much) over the dinner table, pregnancies have been announced, serious illnesses have been revealed, and love matches have been made. It is a tradition that is sure to continue as long as there are Latin American families eating together.

Subanik

Hot and Spicy Pork and Chicken Stew

Guatemala | Yield: Serves 4–6 | Difficulty Level: Intermediate | Total Cooking Time: 2½ hours

Subanik (pronounced *soo-bah-neek*) is a traditional Mayan stew, often called the "food of the gods." Usually served for special occasions in the city of San Martín Jilotepeque, it's cooked in huge clay cauldrons lined with leaves of the heliconia plant—called mashán or nijao—that are tied on the top, like a giant present to be opened at the start of a feast (comensales). The leaves can be found frozen in Latin American grocery stores and online; banana leaves can be substituted in their place (and are what I use most frequently). Traditionally, three meats are used—beef, pork, and chicken—and several days go into making the sauce. My friend Mirciny Moliviatis, chef-author and television star, shared this easier version with me. Prepare the meats and the sauce a day in advance and put the stew together a couple of hours before serving. The resulting flavors are well worth the effort. Dried chiles vary in intensity, heat, and fruity flavor depending on the variety that you use. Subanik makes good use of long, green cobanero chiles (used, if possible, when they are still fresh, but here, like most cooks, I use them dried and ground into a red powder). The teardrop-shaped sun dried zambo chile is common, too. Use whichever you can find. I have adapted this recipe to be on the spicy-hot side but not overwhelmingly so. Leftovers freeze beautifully.

1 pound (455 grams) plum tomatoes, halved

6 ounces (170 grams) tomatillos, husks removed, washed and halved

1 large red bell pepper, seeded, cored, and halved

2–3 pasilla chiles, seeded, cored, deveined, and cut into pieces

2–4 guajillo chiles, seeded, cored, deveined, and cut into pieces

1–2 teaspoons cobanero or zambo chiles, whole (or red pepper flakes)

1 pound 8 ounces (700 grams) bone-in chicken breasts, cut into 10 small portions

1 pound 8 ounces (700 grams) boneless center pork chops, cut into 1 inch (2.5 cm) cubes

4 large banana leaves (fresh or frozen)

1½ teaspoons fine sea salt, or more to taste

In a large pot, place the tomatoes, tomatillos, bell peppers, and dried chiles; cover with 4 cups (1 liter) water. Bring to a boil over medium-high heat, uncovered, then lower the heat and simmer for 30 minutes. Remove from the heat and let cool. Transfer the tomatoes, tomatillos, peppers, and chiles to the jar of a blender with a slotted spoon; add enough of the cooking water to help the motor start and blend until perfectly smooth. Set the sauce aside (it can be made two days ahead and refrigerated); discard the remaining cooking liquid. In a medium pot, place the chicken and just enough water to cover; bring to a boil over medium-high heat. As soon as it reaches a boil, lower the heat so it remains at a simmer, removing and discarding the foam that rises to the top during the first 10 minutes; keep simmering, partly covered, for 25 minutes. Cool the chicken in the broth for 30 minutes. In the meantime, in a medium pot, place the pork and enough water to cover; bring to a boil, lower the heat slightly, and continue simmering, uncovered, for 30 minutes. Remove the chicken with a slotted spoon and set aside; reserve the broth for another use (see Note). Remove the pork and set aside; reserve the broth. Line a large Dutch oven with the banana leaves, making sure to leave a generous overhang. Add the chicken and pork and pour the sauce over the top; add enough of the reserved pork broth to cover the meats. Fold the ends of the banana leaves over the top to cover the stew. Set the Dutch oven over high heat and bring the liquid to a boil. Cover it with a tight-fitting lid; reduce the heat to low and simmer for 30 to 40 minutes. Season with salt and serve.

Note: Don't throw the chicken broth away; it is delicious in other recipes. If you can't find whole Cobanero or zambo chiles, use only 1 teaspoon of their ground versions.

Canelones de Hongos y Jamón

Mushroom and Ham Cannelloni

Chile | Yield: Serves 4–6 | Difficulty Level: Intermediate |
Total Cooking Time: 1½–2 hours (including preparing the crepes and béchamel sauce)

Over my decades teaching home cooks how to simplify their cooking, I have stressed that deconstructing what seem like complicated recipes by breaking them into steps makes them doable and relatively unintimidating. Such is the case with this dish. Make the crepes a day in advance (or a month ahead and keep them frozen; just thaw before using). Make the béchamel next and keep it covered with a piece of parchment paper set directly over its surface (to prevent it from forming a skin) until ready to use; you can make it as early as a day ahead of time and refrigerate it until you need to use it. The filling, too, can be prepared in advance, chilled, and finished before assembling the finished cannelloni. Planned this way, you can have dinner on the table in less than an hour. Serve with a salad and a nice glass of chilled white Chilean wine.

2 tablespoons unsalted butter

⅓ cup (60 grams) finely chopped shallots or yellow onions

3 garlic cloves, finely chopped

8 cups (680 grams) chopped white button mushrooms

1 cup (130 grams) finely chopped cooked ham

1 recipe Salsa Blanca Sencilla (page 24), divided

1 recipe Crepas Básicas (page 40)

2 tablespoons grated Parmesan cheese, or more to taste

2–3 tablespoons chopped fresh chives or parsley, for garnish (optional)

Heat the butter in a large skillet set over medium-high heat. Add the shallots or onions and garlic; cook, while stirring, for 1 minute or until fragrant. Add the mushrooms and cook, stirring often, until the mixture is almost dry (the mushrooms will release their juices as they cook, then will reabsorb them), about 10 minutes. Add the ham and ½ cup (120 ml) of the béchamel sauce and stir well to form a paste; set aside to cool slightly. Grease a 9 x 13 inch (23 x 30 cm) baking dish and preheat the oven to 400°F (200°C). Working with one crepe at a time, lay the crepes on a clean surface. Place about 3 tablespoons (50 grams) of the filling in the bottom center of each crepe. Fold the bottom overhang of the crepe over the filling. Then fold over both sides of the crepe to enclose the edges of the filling (it should look like a rectangle). Continue tightly rolling the crepe from bottom to top. Place the rolled crepe, seam side down, on the baking dish. Continue with the remaining crepes, making sure to place them closely together in the dish. Top them with the remaining béchamel sauce, spreading it evenly over the top. Sprinkle with the Parmesan cheese and bake for 12 to 15 minutes or until the sauce is bubbly and the top becomes golden. Sprinkle with chives or parsley, if desired, and serve.

Tip: Too busy to roll? No worries. If you don't have the time to fill and shape cannelloni, layer the crepes and filling instead; top them with the sauce and proceed as directed above. Cut it into squares to serve. Purchase already-prepared crepes if you can find them; you can also use uncooked egg roll wrappers or cooked sheets of fresh pasta.

Pasta con Salsa Caruso

Pasta Caruso

Uruguay | Yield: Serves 4–6 | Difficulty Level: Intermediate | Total Cooking Time: 30 minutes

This creamy pasta is among my daughter Alessandra's all-time favorite dishes. Named after the famous tenor Enrico Caruso, it was created in Montevideo, Uruguay, and is believed to have first been served in the restaurant Mario and Alberto back in the 1950s—more evidence of the Italian influence in this South American country. Some cooks make the sauce with all milk, some with half milk and half cream, and others entirely with evaporated milk; even though all work well, I prefer to use heavy cream to make mine. Bouillon is a must-have ingredient in many Latin American kitchens, and Uruguayans make good use of it to give richness and additional flavor to pasta sauces such as this one. Don't skimp on it here, because it's a classic component in this recipe; keep some in your pantry, as it'll come in handy each time you want to make this recipe—and chances are that you'll want to make it often. Traditionally made with cavatelli, any shaped pastas that can grab on to the sauce will work.

1 pound (455 grams) cavatelli, farfalle, or other shaped pasta

4 tablespoons (50 grams) unsalted butter

½ cup (115 grams) finely chopped white onions

½ cup (90 grams) finely chopped red bell peppers

3¼ cups (285 grams) chopped button mushrooms

¼ cup (30 grams) all-purpose flour

1 tablespoon beef bouillon

2 cups (480 ml) heavy whipping cream

1¼ cups (140 grams) cooked ham, cut into ¼ inch (6 mm) cubes

1 cup (115 grams) fresh mozzarella cheese, cut into ½ inch (12 mm) cubes

½ cup (30 grams) freshly grated Parmesan cheese

¼ teaspoon fine sea salt

½ teaspoon freshly ground black pepper

¼ teaspoon freshly grated nutmeg

Chopped fresh parsley, for garnish (optional)

Fill a large pot with water and bring it to a rolling boil; cook the pasta according to the directions on the package. While the pasta cooks, melt the butter in a large, nonstick pan set over medium-high heat. Add the onions and peppers and cook, while stirring, for 2 minutes or until softened (but don't let the onions take any color). Add the mushrooms and cook for 3 to 4 minutes or until softened. Add the flour and bouillon, stirring well to combine; cook for 1 minute. Add the cream and ham, stirring well; cook until the sauce has thickened, about 3 minutes. Drain the pasta (reserving 1 cup/240 ml of pasta water). Add the cooked pasta, mozzarella, Parmesan, salt, pepper, and nutmeg to the sauce, stirring well; if the sauce is too thick, add a bit of the reserved pasta water, a couple of tablespoons at a time, until it reaches a creamy consistency. Serve the pasta, sprinkled with parsley, if using.

Fougazza Rellena

Stuffed Ham and Cheese Focaccia with Onions

Argentina | Yield: Makes 1 large or 6 smaller pies (serves 6–8) | Difficulty Level: High |
Total Cooking Time: 2½ hours (includes making the dough)

As a child, I was a guest at several family lunches at the embassy of Argentina in Guatemala, where this part focaccia, part pizza dish was served. The dough is divided and rolled separately into one large and one smaller round. The bottom piece is covered with ham and cheese, then it's topped with the small one. But wait—there's more. This stuffed pizza is further crowned with a layer of onions before it goes into a very hot oven.

2 tablespoons olive oil, plus more for greasing the baking sheet

3½ cups (560 grams) thinly sliced yellow onions

1 teaspoon ground oregano

½ teaspoon ají molido or red pepper flakes

½ teaspoon fine sea salt

¼ teaspoon freshly ground black pepper

1 recipe Masa para Pizzas (page 39)

8 ounces (225 grams) cooked ham, thinly sliced

8 ounces (225 grams) provolone cheese, thinly sliced

8 ounces (225 grams) mozzarella cheese, thinly sliced

½ cup (55 grams) finely grated Parmesan cheese

Heat the 2 tablespoons of oil in a large skillet set over medium-high heat; add the onions and cook, while stirring, until they begin to soften, about 3 minutes. Lower the heat to medium; add the oregano, ají molido, salt, and pepper and keep cooking for 2 to 3 more minutes or just until the onions begin to turn golden (don't let them brown). Preheat the oven to 450°F (230°C). Brush a large baking sheet (preferably without a rim) lightly with olive oil (or spray with cooking spray) and set aside. Divide the pizza dough into two unequal halves: pull off a third of the dough and shape it into a disc, then shape the remaining dough into a disc. Set both discs aside, covered with a clean towel, for 10 minutes. On a clean and floured surface, roll out the larger piece of the dough into a circle that measures 15 inches (38 cm) in diameter; transfer it to the prepared baking sheet. Making sure to leave a ¼ inch (6 mm) rim around the edges of the dough, layer the ham, slightly overlapping the slices in the center; top the ham with the provolone cheese slices, slightly overlapping; repeat with the mozzarella cheese and sprinkle with Parmesan. On a clean and floured surface, roll out the smaller piece of dough into a circle measuring 12 inches (30 cm) in diameter. Lift the dough and place it over the top of the pizza, centering it so it covers all of the filling. Fold the rim of the bottom crust over the top and seal it well (you can use the tines of a fork or simply pinch it together with your fingers). Top with the cooked onions and bake for 40 to 50 minutes or until the rim of the dough is nicely browned and the onions have begun to caramelize (some of the onions will be crispy). Remove to a large cutting board. Let sit for 5 to 10 minutes before slicing.

VARIATIONS: This recipe is just the beginning. Switch the fillings: artichoke hearts, roasted peppers, sautéed mushrooms, olives, tuna, cooked chicken, and any array of good melting cheeses can be substituted for the ham and cheese. If it can go on a pizza, it can go in a fougazza. Just don't skimp on the onions.

Receta de Domingo de Maruca

Linguine with Ham and Cream

Guatemala | Yield: Serves 4–6 | Difficulty Level: Easy | Total Cooking Time: 20 minutes

I come from a family of great cooks. My cousin Carmen María de Alejos owns food businesses in Guatemala City. Her grandmother, my adored Tía María de Montenegro, was a famous caterer for many years. On weekends, after fulfilling catering orders, she still had to prepare dinner for her family. This recipe saved her every single time. Don't let the simple ingredients fool you. The flavors will wow anyone who tries it—they're elegant and comforting all at the same time. It wasn't until I actually got the recipe that I realized how easy it is to make. Tía Maria taught my cousins and me the basics of French cooking when we assisted her in her kitchen as teens; she always served this with a side of cooked green peas, which she lovingly called petite pois.

1 pound (455 grams) linguine or fettuccine pasta

4 tablespoons (60 grams) unsalted butter

2 tablespoons finely chopped onions (any color)

3 cups (720 ml) heavy whipping cream

2 cups (170 grams) grated Parmesan cheese, divided

¼ teaspoon freshly grated nutmeg

12 ounces (340 grams) DAK canned ham, cut into bite-sized cubes

Chopped fresh parsley, for garnish

Cook the pasta according to the package directions. In the meantime, make the sauce. Melt the butter in a large pot set over medium-high heat; add the onions. As soon as the onions are translucent, about 30 seconds, add the heavy cream and lower the heat to medium so the cream doesn't separate. Cook for 6 to 7 minutes or until the sauce is thickened slightly. Add 1½ cups (130 grams) of the Parmesan cheese and the nutmeg, stirring well. Drain the pasta and add it to the sauce, stirring well. Add the diced ham and stir to combine. Transfer to a large platter and top with the remaining cheese and the parsley, if desired.

Canned Foods in Latin America · Canned foods, from tuna to devilled ham (jamón del Diablo), have been popular in Latin America since the 1950s. Cheap and easy to store in the pantry, these goods became a main ingredient in myriad recipes for croquetas, ham loaves, and sandwiches. Each cook has their particular favorite brands. My Tía Maria swore by DAK canned ham, a brand still available today pretty much all around the world (and one that became popular again during the pandemic of 2020, when people sought safe foods to keep in their pantry in case of emergencies).

Tarta de Cebollas y Tocino

Bacon and Onion Tart

Chile | Yield: Makes one 10 inch (25 cm) tart | Difficulty Level: Intermediate | Total Cooking Time: 1 hour

A mix between a quiche and a pie, this is the kind of snack you will find served at an once— a Chilean teatime where midday snacks are enjoyed (called elevenses in English)—in Santiago but that also makes for an elegant first course. It features flavor profiles similar to those found in Alsace-Lorraine and Germany (ever-present cultural influences in the cuisine of Chile). It is traditionally crafted with a good melting cheese, such as buttery queso chanco, which is characterized by its sweet, nutty, and salty taste with a slightly acidic aftertaste. It is hard (although not impossible) to find queso chanco outside of Chile; I find Muenster cheese to be a great substitute. Serve warm or at room temperature.

2 tablespoons unsalted butter

2 cups (255 grams) thinly sliced yellow onions

1 partially baked Masa Básica para Pies y Tartas (page 35)

1 cup (280 grams) cooked and chopped smoked bacon

1 cup (85 grams) shredded queso chanco or Muenster cheese

½ cup (30 grams) thinly sliced green onions (white and light green parts only)

4 eggs

1¼ cups (300 ml) heavy whipping cream

½ teaspoon fine sea salt

½ teaspoon freshly ground black pepper

In a large skillet set over medium-high heat, melt the butter and add the onions, cooking and tossing until the onions are lightly golden, about 6 to 8 minutes. Set aside and cool completely. In the meantime, preheat the oven to 375°F (190°C). Spread the onions in a layer over the bottom of the partially baked tart shell and top with bacon, cheese, and green onions. In a large bowl, whisk the eggs together with the cream, salt, and pepper; pour over the filling in the tart shell. Bake for 40 to 45 minutes or until the center is almost set. Remove from the oven and let stand at room temperature, on a cooling rack, for at least 10 minutes (or up to 2 hours) before serving. To serve, carefully lift the tart from the pan and slice into portions.

Chuletas de Cordero Asadas o a la Plancha

Grilled or Griddled Lamb Chops

Bolivia | Yield: Serves 4–6 | Difficulty Level: Easy | Total Cooking Time: 1 hour 15 minutes (includes marinating time)

Bolivians allow the flavor of the cuts of meat they cook to come through without much embellishment (what there is is most often provided by a sauce served on the side, like chimichurri). Meats are seasoned lightly—some salt and pepper but few other ingredients. However, when it comes to lamb, a brief period in a simple marinade is all it needs in order to be cooked quickly without sacrificing any flavor. No gamey taste is left, thanks to the citrus that cuts through the fat and allows the taste of young lamb to shine. I prefer to use bone-in lamb chops cut from the loin, which are thicker, larger, and juicier than those cut from the rib; however, the latter will work just fine. Don't panic if you don't own an outdoor grill; a well-seasoned cast-iron skillet or an indoor grilling pan will do the job. Just make sure that you have a good ventilation system and that your skillet is nice and hot before you add the lamb; you'll want it to sizzle on contact in order to caramelize the surface of the meat.

2 garlic cloves, finely chopped

½ cup (40 grams) finely chopped fresh Italian parsley

½ teaspoon dried thyme

¼ cup (60 ml) freshly squeezed lime juice

2 tablespoons olive oil, plus more for rubbing on the grill or griddle

2 pounds (910 grams) bone-in lamb chops, preferably from the loin (about 6–8 pieces)

1 teaspoon fine sea salt, or more to taste

1 teaspoon freshly ground black pepper, or more to taste

Use a mortar and pestle (or a food processor) to make a paste with the garlic, parsley, and thyme; transfer it to a small bowl. Add the lime juice and oil, stirring well. Place the lamb chops in a resealable plastic bag or a nonreactive glass bowl and toss them with the marinade; let marinate in the refrigerator for 30 minutes to 1 hour (not much longer, or the lime will make the chops soft). Preheat an outdoor grill for direct grilling (or an indoor grill pan, see headnote) until very hot. Remove the chops from the marinade (discarding the marinade) and season well on both sides with salt and pepper. Lightly brush the cooking grills or griddle with a bit of oil. Cook the chops for 3 to 4 minutes per side, for medium rare (add 2 more minutes for each extra degree of doneness). Transfer the chops to a platter, and let them rest for 5 minutes before serving.

Cordero con Salsa Málaga

Lamb Chops with Almond Sauce

Dominican Republic | Yield: Serves 4–6 | Difficulty Level: Intermediate |
Total Cooking Time: 1½ hours (longer if marinated overnight)

Almond and bread sauces are remnants of the Spanish colonizing influences left in the cuisines of most of the countries in the Americas. Cordero—lamb—is favored in many of the regions where Arab-Latino culinary traditions are strong. Here, the ancient flavors that first met in Europe during the heights of the Ottoman Empire still survive in a new form halfway around the world and centuries later. History may be rife with pain; however, food serves as testimony to the fact that flavors can evolve and bring people together across space and time.

2 racks of lamb (each about 1¼ pounds/570 grams) or 16 single lamb chops

2 teaspoons fine sea salt, divided

¼ cup (60 ml) Harissa de Santo Domingo (page 16)

2 ounces (60 grams) stale white bread soaked in ¼ cup (60 ml) water

2 tablespoons red wine vinegar, or to taste

⅔ cup (70 grams) slivered almonds

2 garlic cloves, quartered

¼ cup (60 ml) extra-virgin olive oil

¼ cup (20 grams) chopped fresh parsley (leaves and tender stems)

¼ teaspoon freshly ground black pepper, or more to taste

Lime wedges (optional)

Begin by trimming off the sheaths of fat (the silvery skin) that cover each rack of lamb (this is easily done by holding one end of the rack with paper towels and pulling the skin off). Slice individual lamb chops off the rack and season them with 1 teaspoon of the salt (reserve the rest for later). Place the chops in a nonreactive dish and rub them with the harissa on all sides. Cover with plastic wrap and chill in the refrigerator for at least 1 hour (or up to overnight). In the meantime, make the almond sauce: Squeeze the bread dry; sprinkle it with the vinegar and let it sit on a plate for 2 minutes. Place the bread (and liquid left on the plate), almonds, and garlic in the bowl of a food processor fitted with a metal blade (or a powerful blender). Pulse for 30 seconds or until smooth. With the motor running, drizzle the olive oil in a thin stream through the feeding tube until you have a thin paste. Carefully transfer the paste to a bowl. If it's too thick, thin it with a little bit of water; stir in the parsley, salt, and pepper. Heat a grill (or use an indoor grill pan) until very hot. Grill the chops for 4 minutes per side (for medium). Let them rest for 2 minutes before serving with dollops of the sauce. Offer lime wedges on the side, if using.

Note: If you're marinating the lamb overnight, you'll have to chill the almond sauce until it's ready to use. Cover it and refrigerate for up to 12 hours; bring it to room temperature before using. If it's too thick, thin it out with a bit of water and a splash of vinegar, to taste.

Pinchos Asados con Chimichurri

Broiled Lamb Skewers with Chimichurri

Uruguay | Yield: 20–24 small skewers (to make 6 servings) | Difficulty Level: Easy |
Total Cooking Time: 2½–8 hours (depending on marinating time)

Savory, richly seasoned lamb is succulent any day of the week. When it's rubbed with adobo, all gaminess is removed and the sweet flavor of the meat comes through clearly. Here is a terrific way to cook lamb under the broiler. Select the youngest lamb you can find and have your butcher bone it for you (where I live, I can find it sold boneless). Cooking an entire leg of lamb can prove onerous during the week; using it cubed this way reduces the cooking time by a lot. Start the marinating process early in the morning, and it will be ready by the time you get back home from work. It is best to soak the wooden skewers in cold water for at least a couple of hours before you plan to broil, so they don't burn and fall apart from the heat.

One 3 pound (1.4 kilogram) boneless leg of lamb, cut into 1 inch (2.5 cm) cubes

1 tablespoon Adobo Uruguayo (page 7)

1 recipe Chimichurri al Cuchillo (page 13), divided

2 tablespoons red wine vinegar

Twenty to twenty-four 6 inch (15 cm) wooden skewers, soaked in water

Salt, to taste

Sprinkle the lamb cubes with the adobo spice mix, making sure to coat them well on all sides; let them marinate at room temperature for 10 minutes. In a small bowl, combine half of the chimichurri with the vinegar and stir well. Place the lamb cubes in a nonreactive dish; pour the chimichurri marinade over the lamb and turn the pieces to coat well. Cover with plastic wrap and chill in the refrigerator for at least 2 hours (or up to overnight), remembering to toss occasionally so the lamb is coated evenly with the marinade. Thread 2 to 3 lamb cubes onto each wooden skewer, leaving a bit of space between them. Preheat the broiler and transfer the skewers onto baking pans or cookie sheets. Place them under the broiler, turning occasionally, until they are done to your liking (about 10 minutes for medium). Transfer them to a platter and sprinkle with salt, to taste. Serve with the remaining chimichurri sauce on the side.

Guiso de Cordero

Lamb Stew

Bolivia | Yield: Serves 4–6 | Difficulty Level: Easy | Total Cooking Time: 1 hour and 30 minutes (includes prep)

A comforting stew is perfect any day of the week, but especially on cold evenings. Even though beef is revered in South America, lamb is popular in Bolivia. Most renditions of this very casual dish are made using neck bones, but when I make it, I prefer using boneless leg of lamb, which is full of flavor and cooks faster. If you wish, add a couple of neck bones as well. The longer you let this stew cook, the better it will taste.

¼ cup (60 ml) vegetable oil

3½ cups (340 grams) thinly sliced yellow onions

2 large garlic cloves, finely chopped

One 2 pound (910 gram) boneless leg of lamb, cut into 12–16 serving pieces

2 tablespoons sweet paprika

1 cup (215 grams) peeled and finely chopped plum tomatoes

1½ cups (250 grams) peeled and sliced carrots

2 teaspoons fine sea salt, or more to taste

2 large white potatoes (20 ounces/570 grams total), peeled and cut into 12 pieces

2 tablespoons finely chopped fresh Italian parsley

Heat the oil in a large pot set over medium-high heat. Add the onions and coat well with the oil; cook, stirring occasionally, until the onions begin to turn golden, about 5 minutes; add the garlic and cook for 30 seconds or until fragrant. Add the lamb and cook, stirring often, until the lamb begins to brown, about 5 minutes (at this time, the onions will have taken on a beautiful, deep golden hue). Add the paprika, tomatoes, carrots, salt, and 2 cups (480 ml) water. Bring to a boil, while scraping the pan with a wooden spoon in order to dislodge all of the brown bits at the bottom; cover, lower the heat to low, and simmer for 35 to 40 minutes. Then add the potatoes and increase the heat to medium; partially cover and cook until the potatoes are fork tender, about 25 minutes. Add the parsley and serve.

Carbonada Criolla

Goat and Vegetable Stew

Chile | Yield: Serves 4–6 | Difficulty Level: Intermediate | Total Cooking Time: 1 hour 25 minutes

As with most Latin American recipes, carbonadas (stews) take on different characteristics depending on what region you are in, who is cooking, and what ingredients happen to be available at the time. When it comes to what kind of meat is used, beef, chicken, pork, goat, lamb, or even seafood are all good candidates—just not all at once. This recipe calls for goat meat. Some carbonadas are made with corn, fava beans (habas), leeks, or cabbage. They always include a base of sofrito, a hint of paprika, lots of potatoes, squash, and zucchini. Traditional carbonadas will always include rice as one of the ingredients (rice and potatoes often meet on the plate in South America). Resist the urge to cover the pot while it is cooking! Carbonada is always cooked slowly and uncovered, in order for the broth to reduce and concentrate its flavor.

4 tablespoons olive oil

2 cups (280 grams) finely chopped white onions

3 garlic cloves, finely chopped

1 tablespoon sweet paprika

2 teaspoons dried oregano

1 teaspoon ground cumin

4 tablespoons cold water

1 pound (455 grams) lean goat meat, chopped into bite-sized pieces, about ½ inch (1 cm) each

1¼ cups (170 grams) peeled and finely chopped carrots

1 cup (140 grams) stemmed, seeded, and chopped red bell peppers

1 cup (140 grams) chopped celery

4 cups (570 grams) yellow potatoes, peeled and cut into ½ inch (1 cm) cubes

One 1 pound (455 gram) winter squash (such as butternut or buttercup), peeled, seeded, and cut into 1 inch (2.5 cm) cubes (about 2 cups)

2 cups (340–400 grams) zucchini, cut into ½ inch (1 cm) cubes

1 tablespoon fine sea salt, or to taste

½ cup (155 grams) long-grain white rice

½ cup (40 grams) chopped fresh Italian parsley

1¼ cup (140 grams) green peas (fresh or frozen and thawed)

Heat the oil in a large pot set over medium-high heat; add the onions, garlic, paprika, oregano, and cumin; cook for 2 minutes, while stirring, or until the onions have begun to soften. Add the water and lower the heat to medium; continue cooking and stirring for 5 more minutes (this will soften the onions completely). Add the meat and cook for 2 to 3 minutes or until no longer pink. Add the carrots, bell peppers, and celery; continue cooking and stirring for 4 minutes. Add the potatoes, winter squash, zucchini, and salt, stirring well; add enough water to barely cover all of the ingredients by ½ inch (1 cm), about 6 cups (1½ liters). Increase the heat to medium-high and bring to a boil, then lower the heat and simmer, uncovered, for 10 minutes. Add the rice and the parsley, stir well, and continue cooking, uncovered, for 15 minutes. Finish by adding the peas and cooking for 5 minutes (this gives the rice enough time to soften—but any longer, and the vegetables will start to fall apart). Serve in deep bowls.

Kippe

Baked Kibbeh

Brazil and Dominican Republic | Yield: Serves 6–8 | Difficulty Level: Easy |
Total Cooking Time: 1 hour and 30 minutes (includes prepping time)

Here, sweet spices and garlic season lamb before it's shaped into a flat loaf. Then it's stuffed with a filling made of nuts and more lamb, cut into triangles (or diamond shapes), and baked until the top is crisp. A Lebanese-influenced recipe found in several countries throughout Latin America, this lamb and bulghur (cracked wheat) classic is also enjoyed in both raw and fried forms; however, baked into a casserole it becomes easy everyday food that can be assembled quickly. Serve it with plenty of yogurt and with quartered limes or lemons.

2 cups (340 grams) bulgur wheat

2 tablespoons olive oil, divided

1 cup (115 grams) finely chopped white onions

2 pounds (910 grams) ground lamb, divided

2 large garlic cloves, finely chopped

1 tablespoon ground cumin

2½ teaspoons fine sea salt, divided

1 teaspoon ground cinnamon, divided

½ teaspoon freshly ground black pepper

½ teaspoon ground allspice

½ cup (70 grams) lightly toasted pine nuts (see Note)

Place the bulgur in a large bowl and cover with 2½ cups (600 ml) cold water; stir and set it aside at room temperature, covered, for 30 minutes. In the meantime, heat half of the oil in a medium skillet set over medium-high heat; add the onions and cook until softened, about 2 to 2½ minutes; remove from the heat and let cool slightly. By now, the bulgur will have absorbed most of the water; drain it through a sieve and place it in a large bowl. Add half of the lamb, the sautéed onions, garlic, cumin, 1½ teaspoons of salt, and ½ teaspoon of cinnamon and mix with your hands until the mixture becomes like a paste. (You may do it in a food processor fitted with a metal blade, but will have to work in batches; pulse for 5-second intervals until bits of the mixture pressed between your fingers hold together. If the mixture is too mealy, add some water, a couple of tablespoons at a time.) Set aside. In the meantime, heat the remaining oil in the skillet and brown the remaining lamb until it is no longer pink, about 3 to 4 minutes. Season it with the remaining salt, cinnamon, black pepper, and allspice; let cool slightly and stir in the pine nuts. Preheat the oven to 350°F (180°C). Grease a 9 x 13 inch (23 x 33 cm) baking dish. Place half of the lamb and bulghur mixture on the bottom of the dish, spreading it evenly and patting it down with your fingers (or with a spatula). Layer the lamb and pine nut filling over it; then, top with the remaining bulgur mixture, smoothing out the surface with a spatula, to even it out and cover the filling completely (I find that patting the mixture with my fingers works best). Use a sharp knife to cut the kippes into triangles (or diamonds), making sure to cut down all the way to the bottom of the loaf. Loosen the sides of the loaf with the knife by going around the edges (this will keep it from sticking and cracking). Bake until the top is golden and crisp, about 50 to 55 minutes. Serve hot or warm.

Note: To toast pine nuts, place them in a nonstick pan set over medium-high heat; stir and shake the pan until they're toasted, about 2 to 2½ minutes. Transfer them to a bowl or plate to cool.

BEEF

Go back in time to the year 1492, when the first Europeans landed in the Americas. They found that Indigenous people ate iguanas, rabbits, duck, deer, cuy (guinea pigs), jaguars, crabs, fish, snakes, birds, turkeys, a variety of dogs known as mudo or mute, and insects. But where was the beef? Nowhere. Cows had never set their hooves on American soil; cattle simply did not exist in the Americas.

So on the second voyage from Spain to La Española (the Dominican Republic) in 1493, the Spaniards made sure to correct that. Along with enough soldiers to conquer the friendly people who had saved them from starvation by showing them what to eat, they brought their favorite comestibles. Soon, cows roamed freely on the valleys and prairies of the Americas, and beef became as popular among the Native peoples as it was with their invaders.

Along with beef, Europeans brought the first ovens to Latin America. The Indigenous peoples in the Americas used fire pits (some still do). However, with the later waves of immigrants, ovens began to replace the fire pits and wooden stoves used in colonial-period homes. Before ovens crossed the seas, cooks in the Americas "baked" over wooden stovetops. They would invert a clay or metal cover over casseroles that contained the food to be cooked; then, they would top it with hot wood ashes or coals, in order to create heat from below and above at the same time, the way ovens do.

At first, not many kitchens featured ovens—in fact, by the mid-twentieth century, it was still common for neighborhoods in some countries (such as Argentina) to have communal ones, where people would take their food to bake, networking as they waited. These ovens provided cooks with time to exchange many of the recipes that later generations still make today. But by the end of the twentieth century, most modern kitchens included gas or electric ovens and stoves.

Before Europeans arrived, Amerindians boiled meats and, most famously, cooked them directly over fire pits on wooden sticks, using the technique that the Taíno named barbacoa. For their part, Europeans also brought new cooking techniques, such as the French way of roasting meats in ovens, called gigot (a term still used today to describe roasts in some Latin American countries), and picadillos (see box on page 448 and recipes on 449 and 450), made with ground beef and any other ingredient that can be chopped and mixed into it, from raisins and olives to potatoes and cabbage.

Beef is consumed all through Latin America, but the epicenter of its popularity is undoubtedly found in Argentina, Uruguay, Paraguay, and Brazil, where beef is king. South American beef is cooked in all kinds of permutations: stuffed, rolled, and boiled; boiled and stewed; breaded and fried; and, of course, grilled to juicy perfection over a live fire. If there is one thing at which Latin American cooks excel, it is the preparation of myriad sauces and condiments that can be served with beef, from fiery chile and tomato mollis (mixtures that can be used as either marinades or sauces) to cream-based sauces, piquant vinaigrettes, and herbal concoctions (most famously, chimichurris).

Modern-day Latin American cooks know how to make every single part of the cow tasty. Lower cuts of beef—those that are the toughest—are tenderized in long braises and stews; offal and ground meat are chopped finely and transformed into pâtés and fillings for empanadas and pastries (such as volovanes or vol-au-vents). To make beef go further, it is sliced thinly, pounded, and used to make bistec a lo pobre ("poor-man's steak") or milanesas (breaded cutlets).

Here is a small collection of dependable, everyday beef recipes from throughout Latin America. Some have Indigenous roots, while others pull from European culinary traditions. Some of them go way back in history to a time when new cuisines started to emerge from the blending of world cultures; others are inventions of creative cooks in more recent years.

Albóndigas en Salsa

Sherried Meatballs

Uruguay | Yield: Serves 4–6 | Difficulty Level: Easy | Total Cooking Time: 1 hour

This Uruguayan meatball recipe features a sweet and savory combination of ingredients inherited from ancient Persia and modern-day Italy. In other countries, such as Mexico and Chile, cooks will add raisins and almonds to the meat—feel free to add a handful of each here, if you'd like. This recipe gets its sweetness from sweet liquor and a kiss of sugar. Notice that there are no hot peppers to make your tongue burn—because not every Latin American country features spicy food! I make double batches of these albóndigas and freeze them to defrost quickly for sandwiches. The sauce is perfect to crown a bowl of simply boiled pasta, white rice, or perfectly mashed potatoes; crusty bread will also help you sop up the juices.

1 pound (455 grams) ground beef

1 pound (455 grams) ground pork

1½ cups (280 grams) finely chopped yellow onions, divided

2 garlic cloves, finely chopped

½ cup (60 grams) dried bread crumbs

1 egg

2 tablespoons minced parsley

1 teaspoon fine sea salt

¼ teaspoon freshly ground black pepper

¼ cup (30 grams) all-purpose flour, for dredging

3 tablespoons (45 ml) olive oil

1 tablespoon tomato paste

1 teaspoon white granulated sugar

1 bay leaf

¾ cup (180 ml) dry sherry

One 14.5 ounce (411 gram) can diced tomatoes with juices

In a large bowl, combine the beef, pork, ½ cup (60 grams) of the onions, the garlic, bread crumbs, egg, parsley, salt, and black pepper. Mix well and form into 16 meatballs, each weighing about 2 ounces (60 grams). Dredge the meatballs lightly in flour (just to coat them). Heat the oil in a large nonstick pan with high sides and a tight-fitting lid, set over medium-high heat. Working in batches, sauté the meatballs on all sides until they are nicely browned, about 6 to 8 minutes. Remove the meatballs to a bowl as they cook and set aside. Add the rest of the onions and sauté for 3 to 4 minutes or until softened (they will take on a deep golden color). Add the tomato paste and sugar, cooking for 30 seconds before adding the bay leaf, sherry, and tomatoes with their juices; stir well. Bring to a simmer and return the meatballs (plus any juices that collected in the bottom of the bowl) to the sauce. Cover the pan, lower the heat to low, and simmer for 20 minutes. Uncover and keep on simmering until the sauce has thickened, about 3 to 4 minutes. Discard the bay leaf and serve.

Asado Alemán

Stuffed Meatloaf

Chile | Yield: Serves 6 | Difficulty Level: Easy | Total Cooking Time: 1 hour 30 minutes

When sliced, this homey meatloaf looks like an impressive mosaic. Ground beef dishes are very popular throughout Latin America; they're inexpensive to make and feed many. This Chilean recipe with German culinary influences—it's very similar to hackbraten—offers comforting flavors that will please a wide variety of tastes. I keep a small bottle of Aliño Completo spice mix (page 7) in my pantry at all times, and use it whenever I need to add depth of flavor to ground beef dishes without imparting any heat. I highly recommend that you make some for your own use. As every home cook knows, there's power in learning how to stretch a meal; leftovers of this meatloaf are particularly scrumptious when slathered with grainy mustard, sandwiched between two slices of white bread, and garnished with lettuce and tomatoes.

2 teaspoons vegetable oil

1 cup (150 grams) peeled and finely chopped carrots

One 1¾ ounce (50 gram) piece of white bread

½ cup (120 ml) whole milk

6 eggs, 4 of them hard-boiled and peeled

1¾ pound (800 grams) ground beef

1 cup (185 grams) seeded and finely chopped plum tomatoes

½ cup (115 grams) stemmed, seeded, and finely chopped red bell peppers

¼ cup (30 grams) finely chopped shallots

2 garlic cloves, finely chopped

½ cup (115 grams) grated Parmesan cheese

2 tablespoons finely chopped fresh Italian parsley (leaves and tender stems)

2 teaspoons Aliño Completo (see page 7 or Note below) (optional)

1½ teaspoons fine sea salt

Preheat the oven to 400°F (200°C). Heat the oil in a small skillet set over medium-high heat; add the carrots and cook, while stirring, for 2 to 3 minutes or until slightly softened; set aside to cool. On a small plate moisten the bread with the milk; after 5 minutes, press the bread between your fingers to remove excess liquid and place it in a large bowl. Crack the 2 fresh eggs into the bowl. Add the beef, the reserved carrots, and the tomatoes, bell peppers, shallots, garlic, cheese, parsley, spices (if using), and salt; mix lightly until it holds together (don't overwork the meat, or it will become tough). Place half of the beef mixture in the bottom of a 5 x 9 inch (13 x 23 cm) loaf pan, making a slight indentation in the middle. Lay the hard-boiled eggs in a row in the indentation, on their sides, touching each other. Cover with the remaining beef mixture and press down slightly. Bake for 50 to 60 minutes or until the juices run clear when pierced with a fork (the internal temperature must register 155°F/68°C). Remove from the oven and let sit for 10 minutes for easier unmolding. Drain and discard any juices; unmold, slice, and serve hot or warm.

Note: If you're not using the aliño completo, add ½ teaspoon freshly ground black pepper and ½ teaspoon paprika to the mix. If you're short on time, chop all of the vegetables in the food processor.

Tip: If you don't have a loaf pan, simply shape half of the meat mixture into a rectangle directly on a piece of plastic wrap; place the eggs on top and top with the remaining meat. Roll into the shape of a loaf. Carefully transfer onto a rimmed baking sheet lined with parchment paper, then remove the plastic and bake as instructed.

Tortitas de Carne

Beef Patties

Colombia | Yield: Serves 4-6 | Difficulty Level: Easy |
Total Cooking Time: 1-12 hours (if chilled overnight. Includes making aliño.)

Tortitas are little patties and they are a common staple in the everyday cooking of most Latin American cultures, where they are often paired with mashed potatoes, rice, or plantain mash. This recipe is from Bogotá and it produces particularly tender, juicy, and perfectly seasoned beef that kids and adults love. The key ingredient is the aliño (flavor base), rich in tomatoes and aromatics, that is essential in Colombian cuisine. Most Latin Americans cook their meat through (this comes from years of fearing foodborne illnesses caused by undercooked meats); you will want to make sure these are not pink in the middle when you serve them, because only then will all of the ingredients blend seamlessly. Put away the ketchup bottle—you won't be needing it for these!

1 pound (455 grams) lean ground beef (80/20)

½ cup (120 grams) Aliño Crudo (see page 158)

2 tablespoons finely chopped parsley

1 tablespoon finely chopped mint

1 teaspoon ground cumin

1 teaspoon salt

½ teaspoon freshly ground black pepper

2 teaspoons vegetable oil

Pat the beef dry with paper towels and place it in a medium bowl. Add the Aliño crudo, parsley, mint, cumin, salt, and pepper and, using your hands, stir it well, to combine. Do not overwork it or the patties will be tough. (If not cooking them immediately, cover the bowl with plastic wrap and let the beef mixture rest in the refrigerator for up to 10 hours—perfect for making before going to work in the morning! When ready to cook, continue with the recipe.) Divide this mixture into eight equal parts (about 3 ounces/85 gram each). Shape each into a ball, and then pat into a patty about 3-inches (8 cm) in diameter and about ½ inch (1.25 cm.) thick. Heat the oil in a non-stick pan set over medium-high heat. Cook the patties for 4 minutes on each side or until cooked completely through. Serve hot.

Picadillos · "Picar" means "to mince." Picadillos are mixtures of minced meats (usually beef, lamb, or goat, but they can also be made with poultry, seafood, and pork) cooked and flavored with onions, spices, and fruits that date back to ancient Persia. Back in the tenth century, Arabs in the Courts of the Caliph were known for combining all sorts of chopped meats with eggs, dried fruits, vegetables, and nuts in one dish. *The Annals of the Caliphs' Kitchen: Ibn Sayyar al-Warraq's Tenth-Century Cookbook* included a recipe by a thirteenth-century man known as "al-Baghdadi" (his full name was Muhammad ibn al-Hasan ibn Muhammad ibn al-Karim al-Katib al-Baghdadi) for a dish called makhfiya, which involves combining chopped, cooked red meat with hard-boiled eggs, cumin, and ginger that he further shapes into balls. *The Book of Sent Soví*, the treatise of medieval recipes from Catalonia, is filled with picadillo recipes referred to as stuffings or farcies. Not surprisingly, the culinary traditions that the conquistadores brought along with them included plenty of examples of different picadillos, many of which they used to stuff empanadas (hand-held pies), but also to stuff birds and roasts before cooking. In modern Latin America, picadillos are their own category of food by themselves; they can be served alone, on top of rice, or with a tuber pureé, not necessarily as a stuffing. Every single Latin American country features some kind of chopped meat dish, some that still include olives, capers, hard-boiled eggs, and sweet spices in the Persian tradition. Others, such as the picadillos of Guatemala, can include shredded cabbage, while the picadillos of Nicaragua can be made with chicken, and those of Costa Rica are often fashioned with pork and chayote squash.

Picadillo Sencillo

Everyday Picadillo

Central America | Yield: Serves 4–6 | Difficulty Level: Easy | Total Cooking Time: 20 minutes

This is the simple, savory picadillo I grew up with. At home, I serve it over steamed rice and top it with shredded raw cabbage or lettuce. I also love it wrapped in tortillas and fried into tacos. This is what I recommend you use to stuff Molotes (page 87) or to make beef flautas (filled and rolled flour tortillas, fried until crispy). Many Central Americans will choose this over a bowl of chili con carne any day; it's great on homemade tostadas or to fill empanadas.

2 tablespoons vegetable oil

¾ cup (115 grams) finely chopped white onions

½ cup (115 grams) stemmed, seeded, and finely chopped green bell peppers

¾ cup (115 grams) peeled and finely chopped carrots

2 large garlic cloves, finely chopped

1 pound (455 grams) lean ground beef

3 tablespoons (45 ml) tomato paste

1 teaspoon dried oregano

1 teaspoon dried thyme

1 teaspoon fine sea salt

½ teaspoon freshly ground black pepper

Heat the oil in a large nonstick pan. Add the chopped vegetables and the garlic; cook, while stirring, until all are soft, about 4 minutes. Add the beef and cook, while breaking it up with the back of a wooden spoon, until it is no longer pink, about 3 to 4 minutes. Stir in the tomato paste, oregano, thyme, salt, and pepper; continue cooking for 2 more minutes or until the mixture has thickened. Serve hot.

Note: If using as a filling for other recipes, let cool completely before covering and refrigerating. It lasts for up to 2 days in the refrigerator or up to 3 months if frozen (thaw in the refrigerator overnight before using).

El Picadillo de Nikki

Ground Beef with Olives and Capers

Cuba | Yield: Serves 4–6 | Difficulty Level: Easy | Total Cooking Time: 30 minutes

This is a Cuban-inspired picadillo that features the grassy flavor of cumin, brininess from salty olives, and a touch of piquancy from capers. *Picadillo* literally means "minced," and ever since the Spanish colonizers arrived with recipes for ground beef dishes, Latin Americans have been adapting them to suit each country's culinary traditions. There are so many versions of picadillos in Latin America that it's hard to keep them straight. In Chile and in Argentina, they include hard-boiled eggs; in Guatemala, they include carrots; in Costa Rica, you'll find them with potatoes, chayotes, and green beans. I developed this recipe (which tastes even better the next day) for my daughter Nikki so she could make it for her Cuban husband, who especially loves it ladled over Fufú de Plátano (page 304). I based it on several traditional Cuban recipes I inherited from my grandmother's old recipe collections.

2 tablespoons olive oil

1 cup (115 grams) finely chopped yellow onions

½ cup (140 grams) stemmed, cored, seeded, and finely chopped red or green bell peppers

2 garlic cloves, finely chopped

2 tablespoons tomato paste

1½ pounds (680 grams) lean ground beef

1 cup (280 grams) peeled, seeded, and finely chopped plum tomatoes

1½ teaspoons ground cumin

20–25 (60 grams) manzanilla olives

1 tablespoon capers, drained

1 teaspoon fine sea salt, or to taste

½ teaspoon freshly ground black pepper

Heat the oil in a large nonstick skillet set over medium-high heat. Add the onions, bell peppers, and garlic; cook, stirring often until they are softened, about 3 minutes. Add the tomato paste and stir for 30 seconds. Add the beef and cook until it's no longer pink, about 5 minutes (all the while making sure to break it up with a wooden spoon). Add the tomatoes, cumin, olives, capers, salt, and pepper. Cover the skillet and lower the heat to low; simmer for 10 to 12 minutes or until all the flavors have melded together.

VARIATION: To make Cuban empanadas, place 1-2 tablespoons of chilled picadillo in the middle of a store-bought empanada wrapper (find them in the frozen section of any Latin grocery store). Bake or fry them according to the directions on the package.

Bistec a lo Pobre

Poor Man's Steak

Peru | Yield: Serves 4–6 | Difficulty Level: Easy | Total Cooking Time: 20 minutes

Although you'll find thin steaks in every Latin American country, this version, enhanced with garlic, vinegar, and soy sauce, is typically Peruvian. If you want a super-easy, inexpensive, yet amazingly flavorful dish that can be ready in minutes, this is it. Serve over white rice and with a side of French fries (because in Peru, rice and potatoes are most often served together on the same plate).

2 teaspoons Pasta de Ajo (page 12)

½ teaspoon fine sea salt, or more to taste

1 teaspoon ground cumin

2 tablespoons red wine vinegar

1 tablespoon soy sauce

6 thinly cut bottom round steaks (1 pound/455 grams total) (see Note)

2 teaspoons vegetable oil

1 tablespoon unsalted butter

In a small bowl, combine the garlic paste, salt, cumin, vinegar, and soy sauce; season the steaks on both sides with this mixture and let marinate at room temperature for 10 minutes (or up to 4 hours in the refrigerator). Heat the oil in a large skillet set over medium-high heat and cook the steaks for 2 minutes on each side or until browned; add the butter and swirl the pan, coating the steaks with the resulting glaze. Serve the steaks immediately.

Note: Steaks cut from the round tip, called round tip steaks, bottom round steaks, breakfast steaks, sirloin tip steaks, or tip center steaks, are both inexpensive and tender, perfectly suited for this recipe. If you don't have a large skillet, cook the steaks in two batches—the point is to allow them to brown, as opposed to steaming them. Once all the steaks are browned, return them in batches to the skillet and coat them lightly with the butter glaze.

Bistec con Tomates y Cebollas

Beefsteaks with Tomatoes and Onions

Central America | Yield: Serves 4–6 | Difficulty Level: Easy | Total Cooking Time: 30 minutes

Thick slabs of meat have their place on the Latin table, but for economical, quick cooking, thin steaks are preferred. This is a very common lunch recipe because it can be whipped together in no time; just make sure to have all of your ingredients at the ready before you start cooking. At home, I like to serve these steaks with sides of white rice, fried plantains, and black beans.

1 pound (455 grams) thinly cut bottom round steaks (¼ inch/6 mm thick)

2 teaspoons fine sea salt, or to taste

½ teaspoon ground black pepper

2½ tablespoons vegetable oil, divided

2½ cups (340 grams) thinly sliced white onions

1 teaspoon dried thyme

1 large bay leaf

1¾ cups (280 grams) thinly sliced plum tomatoes

3 tablespoons (45 ml) Worcestershire sauce

Season the steaks with salt and pepper and set aside. Heat 1 tablespoon of the oil in a large skillet set over medium-high heat. Add the onions, thyme, and bay leaf; cook for 4 to 5 minutes or until the onions begin to turn golden brown; remove the onions to a separate plate. In the same skillet, add the rest of the oil and cook the steaks for 2 to 3 minutes per side or until just cooked through. Return the onions to the skillet, spreading them over the steaks and topping them with the tomatoes, Worcestershire sauce, and ½ cup (120 ml) water. Cover, lower the heat to medium-low, and cook for 5 minutes. Remove the lid and continue cooking until the sauce thickens slightly, about 3 minutes. Serve.

Bistec Encebollado

Cube Steak and Onions

Puerto Rico | Yield: Serves 4–6 | Difficulty Level: Easy | Total Cooking Time: 30 minutes

Cubed and tenderized sirloin top steaks and similar thin cuts are called bistecs (a word derived from the English term *beefsteaks*). When it comes to quotidian meals, thin, inexpensive cuts of meat are preferred by home cooks. Three reasons make them ideal everyday fare: first, pounded even thinner, they seem larger than they really are, making it look like there's more on your plate; second, they have a lot of flavor; and, lastly, they take very little time to cook. My Puerto Rican friend Ana Raquel Morales, a respected food expert and self-proclaimed "culinary bibliophile" (for her gargantuan cookbook collection), makes this flavorful version of bistec, perfectly seasoned with her classic sofrito. The resulting dish provides enough loose gravy to drizzle deliciously over the steaks, on mashed plantains, on white rice, or on a baked potato (you get the idea).

1½ pounds (680 grams) cube steak

1 teaspoon fine sea salt

1 teaspoon Sazón con Achiote y Culantro (page 199)

½ teaspoon freshly ground black pepper

1 tablespoon vegetable oil

2½ cups (285 grams) thinly sliced white onions

2 tablespoons (2 cubes) El Sofrito de Ana Raquel (page 21, or see Note)

Season the steaks on both sides with salt, sazón, and pepper; set them aside on a plate and allow them to marinate for 10 minutes (and up to overnight, if covered and refrigerated). Heat the oil in a large, nonstick pan over medium-high heat. Add the onions and sauté them for 2 to 3 minutes or until just softened; transfer them to a bowl. Add the steaks to the pan and cook them until they are nicely golden on both sides (about 2 minutes per side). Return the onions to the pan and stir in the sofrito. Cover the pan and reduce the heat to low; braise the beef for 12 to 15 minutes or until tender.

Note: You can purchase premade sofrito in most grocery stores, either jarred or frozen. Likewise, you can find different kinds of sazón spice mixes in the Latin American section of most grocery stores and online.

Carne Asada o a la Plancha

Grilled or Griddled Steaks

Central America | Yield: Serves 4–6 | Difficulty Level: Easy | Total Cooking Time: 30–40 minutes

Sundays at my grandmother's house in the outskirts of Guatemala City were legendary for their huge parties. Sometimes only family would gather, but most of the time no one knew how many guests would show up. My grandmother extended an open invitation that meant artists, priests, philosophers, diplomats, and politicians of all kinds would end up mingling with our family (kids included). The grill was lit early in the morning so the coals could turn into hot embers over which fresh tortillas would be griddled, and meats of all kinds cooked. Lunch was a casual affair served on a long outdoor table. My grandmother would set huge terracotta bowls filled to the brim with guacamol, salsas, salads, escabeches, side dishes, and, of course, mounds and mounds of grilled meats. There was little ceremony; people assembled their own soft tacos by filling them with carne asada and toppings galore. This was my favorite of all the meats served on those occasions, made with a cut we called puyaso (known as picanha in Brazil) that consists of the top cap of the sirloin with a generous bit of fat attached. Use tri-tip, hanger, or flat-iron steak if you can't find this cut in your market. Here's my interpretation, made using an indoor griddle or griddle pan; it makes a good amount of smoke, but as long as you have a robust indoor fan, you'll be fine (otherwise, open the windows!).

2 pounds (910 grams) top cap sirloin steaks, sliced into ½ inch (12 mm) steaks

½ cup (120 ml) fresh or bottled sour orange juice (naranja agria) or a combination of half lemon and half orange juices

2 tablespoons Adobo para Carnes Asadas (page 6)

1 tablespoon vegetable oil

1¼ cups (115 grams) sliced white onions

2 bay leaves

Place the meat in a bowl and sprinkle with the sour orange juice; rub with the spice mix and the oil until all pieces are coated well. Add the onions and the bay leaves, and let marinate at room temperature for 30 minutes (or in the refrigerator for up to 4 hours). Heat an indoor grill pan or skillet over medium-high heat. Cook the steak for 2 to 3 minutes on each side for medium rare (add an extra minute per side per added degree of doneness). Allow it to rest for 5 minutes before slicing it thinly on the bias (against the grain).

Note: If you like, cook the onions after you cook the steak, for 2 minutes or until softened (they are delicious, wrapped in a tortilla or as a side to the beef); otherwise, discard, along with the bay leaf and the remaining marinade.

Falda o Entraña Asada

Grilled Skirt Steak

Various Countries | Yield: Serves 4–6 | Difficulty Level: Easy | Total Cooking Time: 15 minutes

Grilling meat doesn't have to be a big production, particularly when you can use quick-cooking skirt steak, which is ready in minutes. It is a cut meant to be enjoyed medium to medium rare and never well done (unless you're my mother, who says she won't eat beef that can still "moo" at her!). Never overcook skirt steak or it will become stringy. Slice it, wrap it in a warm tortilla, top it with fresh salsas, and call it a taco. Or do what many cooks do today and serve it with whole grains and a salad on the side (such as the Quinoa con Limón on page 352). I love it between sliced bolillos, ciabattas, or baguette, slathered in guacamole, mayonnaise, beans, and hot sauce.

2 pounds (910 grams) skirt steak, cleaned of sinew and cut into 4–6 pieces

2 teaspoons olive or vegetable oil

1 teaspoon fine sea salt

½ teaspoon garlic powder

¼ teaspoon ancho chile powder

¼ teaspoon freshly ground black pepper

Juice of 1 lemon

Rub the steaks well with oil; in a small bowl, mix together the salt, garlic powder, ancho chile powder, and black pepper. Rub the steak with this dry mixture on all sides; then sprinkle with the lemon juice and rub again. Let the steak sit at room temperature for 10 minutes. Grill the steak over very hot coals (or use an indoor grill pan) for 1 to 2 minutes per side or until medium rare (add a minute per side for each level of doneness); allow the beef to rest for 10 minutes before slicing on the bias, then serve.

Vaca Frita

Shredded Beef with Onions and Sour Orange

Cuba | Yield: Serves 4–6 | Difficulty Level: Easy | Total Cooking Time: 20 minutes
(if the steak is cooked ahead—see page 30); 2 hours if starting from scratch

I am extremely proud of my son-in-law, Alex, who moved from Cuba as a young child and grew up to become a pediatrician in the United States. He has a good palate and particularly enjoys it when I make this crispy and caramelized beef that reminds him of his childhood in Holguín. Given that I can't grow sour oranges in my garden or find them easily in stores, I resort to the bottled juice sold everywhere (it's very easily sourced online) or combine equal parts of orange and lemon juice—the taste is almost identical. Make sure to let the bits of beef crisp at the end of cooking—that's part of the charm of this dish. Alex likes to squeeze lime juice and sprinkle salt over the finished dish before eating it.

1 recipe Carne Cocida (page 30)

3 tablespoons (40 grams) lard (or vegetable oil), divided

2½ cups (340 grams) thinly sliced yellow onions

3 garlic cloves, finely chopped

½ cup (120 ml) sour orange juice (from one sour orange) or a combination of half lemon and half orange juices

1½ teaspoons fine sea salt

¼ teaspoons freshly ground black pepper

1–2 limes, quartered

Shred the cooked flank steak into thin strands (like pulled pork), using your fingers or two forks. Heat a large skillet over medium-high heat and melt 1 tablespoon of the lard. Add the onions and garlic and cook for 6 to 8 minutes or until they are golden brown; remove them to a plate and set aside. Lower the heat to medium; add the remaining lard and the shredded meat, being sure to spread it evenly over the entire surface of the skillet, to ensure that most of it is in direct contact with the heat. Cook, without stirring, for 3 minutes or until the meat has browned well on the bottom; use a spatula to flip it over to the other side. Cook for 3 to 4 minutes or until well browned. Stir the meat well and flip it over again; cook for 2 to 3 minutes. Flip it one more time and cook for 2 to 3 more minutes. The beef should be browned and have some crispy bits. Return the onion mixture to the skillet and add the sour orange juice, salt, and pepper. Cook, while stirring, until all of the juices have evaporated, about 8 minutes. Serve at once, with the lime quarters on the side.

Asado Peruano de Luz

Pot Roast

Peru | Yield: Serves 8 | Difficulty Level: Easy | Total Cooking Time: 3½–4 hours

Food can break down barriers. This recipe is from a woman named Luz I met in the lobby of a village inn. We never saw each other again, but during a rainy afternoon, we exchanged recipes. While Luz related memories of her mamita's kitchen in Lima, I recorded recipes she wanted me to try. I jotted them down as fast as I could, on whatever I could. Often, my notebook is my only travel companion, and my research has me frequently deciphering recipes that include directives such as "add a handful of this" or "cook enough." This is one such recipe. Over the years I have tasted similar dishes in the homes of Peruvian friends. Surprisingly, I find very few variations between them—more garlic in one, huacatay (a type of mint) in another, a touch of paprika, a good dark beer or broth in place of water. Yet, the ever-present sillao (soy sauce) and sweet carrots remind me of Luz's directions to simmer it gently because "ese sabor será tu recompensa"—you will be rewarded with deep flavor.

One 3½ pound (1.6 kilogram) eye of round roast, trimmed of all fat

1–2 carrots, peeled and cut into 4 inch (10 cm) long strips, ¼ inch (6 mm) thick (about 12–14 pieces)

4 tablespoons (60 ml) vegetable oil

6 garlic cloves, finely chopped (or ¼ cup/60 ml Pasta de Ajo, page 12)

½ cup (120 ml) aji panca paste

2 teaspoons ground cumin

2 tablespoons dark soy sauce

1 bay leaf

1 medium red onion, peeled and quartered

2 teaspoons fine sea salt, or more to taste

¼ teaspoon freshly ground black pepper, or more to taste

1 tablespoon cornstarch, diluted in 3 tablespoons (45 ml) cold water

Pat-dry the roast with paper towels. With a sharp knife, cut 12 to 14 deep incisions in the meat, and insert one carrot strip into each incision. Heat the oil in a large Dutch oven set over medium-high heat. Add the roast and brown it well on all sides, a total of 4 to 5 minutes. Remove the roast to a plate. In the same pot, add the garlic, ají paste, cumin, soy sauce, and bay leaf; cook for 1 minute, stirring to get the brown bits at the bottom of the pan. Return the roast (and any of the juices collected on the plate) to the pot and add the onion quarters, salt, pepper, and 4 cups (960 ml) water. Bring the liquid up to a boil; cover the pot, lower the heat to medium-low, and cook, undisturbed, for 1½ hours. Uncover, turn the roast over to the other side. Bring the liquid back to a boil by increasing the heat; cover, and lower the heat to low. Continue simmering for 1 hour. Discard the bay leaf; remove the cooked roast to a large platter and let it sit while you make the sauce. Place a large sieve with fine holes over a large bowl and strain the juices left in the pot (you'll end up with all of the solids in the strainer). Return the juices to the pot. Transfer all of the solids to a blender and blend until smooth; add these to the pot and stir well. Stir the cornstarch and the water to dissolve well and add it to the sauce; cook over medium heat, while stirring, until the sauce has thickened slightly. Thinly slice the roast and return the slices to the sauce; simmer for 10 to 15 minutes. Serve.

Note: Like most roasts, this reheats beautifully. It will keep in the refrigerator for up to 3 days (or freeze leftovers for up to 2 months); just reheat and serve.

Carne Guisada

Stewed Beef with Carrots and Potatoes

Guatemala | Yield: Serves 4–6 | Difficulty Level: Intermediate | Total Cooking Time: 2 hours

Tomatoes from the Americas, sweet spices from the Silk Road, beef from Europe, and sesame seeds from Africa meld together into one of the tastiest homemade stews from the land of the Maya. My children grew up hearing me say that if they paid attention, they would be able to taste world history on their spoons. Kitchens are filled with the aromas of global culinary mergers every time someone stirs a pot of this guiso. The beef, slow-cooked in a velvety sauce, cuts easily without need of a knife, and the root vegetables add a comforting creaminess to each bite. Dry-roasting the onions and garlic in their skins renders them sweet (it's akin to roasting them in foil packets), while charring the vegetables imparts a smoky flavor.

1 pound (455 grams) plum tomatoes

1 small (6 ounces / 170 grams) white onion, unpeeled and sliced crosswise in half

4 large garlic cloves, unpeeled and left whole

2 large red bell peppers, stemmed, seeded, and halved

3 tablespoons (25 grams) toasted sesame seeds (see box on page 198)

2 cups (480 ml) beef broth

2 pounds (910 grams) stewing beef

3 tablespoons (45 ml) vegetable oil

One 4 inch (10 cm) piece Mexican (Ceylon) cinnamon (canela), left whole

8 sprigs fresh thyme

½ teaspoon ground cloves

2 bay leaves

1½ teaspoons fine sea salt

½ teaspoon freshly ground black pepper

1½ pounds (680 grams) white potatoes, peeled and cubed

1 pound (455 grams) carrots, peeled and sliced into ½ inch/12 mm slices

Heat a griddle (or cast-iron skillet) over medium-high heat; working in batches, place the tomatoes, onions (cut side down), garlic, and peppers (cut side up) on the griddle; roast them, turning them over as their skins char, 8 to 10 minutes total. Transfer the roasted vegetables into a bowl as they are charred. Peel and chop the onions and garlic cloves; add to the vegetables. Working in two batches, transfer half of the roasted vegetables, half of the toasted sesame seeds, and ½ cup (120 ml) of the broth to a blender; blend until smooth and repeat with the rest, setting it aside. Pat the beef dry with paper towels. In a large Dutch oven, heat half of the oil over medium-high heat until it shimmers; sauté half of the beef pieces until browned on all sides, about 8 minutes total. Remove the browned pieces to a bowl and repeat with the remaining oil and beef, setting the browned pieces aside as they are ready. Working quickly, add the blended mixture to the Dutch oven (careful, it will splatter); reduce the heat to medium and simmer for 2 minutes, stirring well, to scrape up the brown bits on the bottom of the pan. Return the browned beef (and any juices that collected in the bowl) to the pot; stir in the cinnamon stick, thyme, cloves, bay leaves, the remaining broth, salt, and pepper. Increase the heat and bring the stew to a boil; cover, lower the heat and simmer gently for 1 hour. Remove the lid, add the potatoes and carrots, bring back to a boil, and cook, uncovered, for 30 to 35 minutes or until the vegetables are fork tender and the sauce has reduced slightly. Remove the bay leaves and cinnamon stick. Serve.

Note: This stew tastes even better the next day, so make it a day ahead, or plan to have leftovers.

Carne Mechada

Shredded Beef Stew

Venezuela | Yield: Serves 4–6 | Difficulty Level: Easy |
Total Cooking Time: 30 minutes (if the beef is cooked ahead, 2 hours if it's not)

A juicy sauce scented with the aromas of onions and tomatoes bathes shredded beef in this classic Venezuelan dish. Almost every Latin American cuisine inherited one such beef stew from the Spanish colonizers, each one distinguished by the spices used to flavor it. This is a very simple rendition that works perfectly as a filling for arepas. Combined with fried plantains, black beans, and rice, carne mechada makes up the traditional Venezuelan dish pabellón nacional.

1 recipe Carne Cocida (page 30)

¼ cup (60 ml) extra-virgin olive oil

1 cup (115 grams) finely chopped yellow onions

1 cup (185 grams) stemmed, seeded, and finely chopped red bell peppers

1½ cups (225 grams) seeded and minced plum tomatoes

2 large garlic cloves, finely chopped

1½ teaspoon ground cumin

1 teaspoon fine sea salt

½ teaspoon freshly ground black pepper

2–3 cups (480–720 ml) reserved broth from cooking the steak, or low-sodium beef broth

Slice the cooked beef across into three pieces. Use your fingers (or two forks) to shred each piece into thin strands, by pulling the meat in the direction of the grain (like pulled pork); set aside. Place the oil into a large (5-6 quart) Dutch oven and set it over medium-high heat. Add the onions and bell peppers; cook for 2 minutes or until softened. Add the tomatoes, garlic, cumin, salt, and pepper; cook for 3 to 4 minutes or until the mixture begins to thicken. Add the shredded beef, and enough broth to cover it. Bring the stew to a boil, lower the heat to low, and simmer for 15 to 20 minutes to allow the flavors to blend. Taste and adjust seasoning. Remove from the heat and serve.

VARIATION: To make this dish into a Cuban Ropa Vieja, add a handful of pimiento-stuffed green olives and a couple of tablespoons of capers during the last 20 minutes of simmering.

Cocido

Boiled Beef Pot

Various Countries | Yield: Serves 4–6 | Difficulty Level: Easy | Total Cooking Time: 1½–2 hours

Latin Americans inherited recipes for boiled pots of meats and vegetables from the Spaniards; you'll find versions using different ingredients and going by different names, such as puchero, sancocho, or carbonada. This is one of those recipes that cooks itself with little intervention. It's a favorite of modern cooks for the inexpensive ingredients that can be stretched to make more than one meal. Leftovers are used to make Salpicón (see the variation below) or cold beef salads, and the broth is often used as a base for Sopa de Tartaritas (page 463) or other soups. Any leftover vegetables can be mixed with a little milk and blended together to make a quick cream of vegetable soup. The possible additions to these pots abound. In the Latin Caribbean you'll find yuca, ñame, or malanga (also known as yautía) and otóe (taro root); in Argentina, celery; in Chile, leeks; and in Mesoamerica, chayotes and different kinds of winter squash. This was one of my dad's favorite meals. He liked the broth served separately from the rest of the ingredients and he would always eat the cabbage with a lot of grainy mustard. I prefer to have it all served together in a bowl, and to dress it with lime juice, hot sauce, or Chimichurri (see pages 13-14). Growing up, cocido was always served with white rice and corn tortillas.

2 pounds (910 grams) beef shoulder roast (or chuck, shoulder steak, bottom round, or rump)

1 sprig fresh mint (optional)

1 bay leaf

½ small (6 ounces/170 grams) white onion, peeled and halved

2 garlic cloves

2 teaspoons fine sea salt

5 whole peppercorns

½ head cabbage, quartered (about 2 pounds/910 grams)

4 large carrots, peeled and halved across (about 12 ounces/340 grams)

2 large potatoes, peeled and halved (about 1 pound/455 grams)

2 large ears of corn, halved or sliced across into 2 inch (5 cm) slices (about 1 pound/455 grams)

1 chayote squash, peeled, seeded, and quartered (about 7 ounces/200 grams)

In a large stock pot, combine the beef, 12 cups (3 liters) water, mint, bay leaf, onions, and garlic; bring to a boil over medium-high heat. Lower the heat to medium, and during the first 15 minutes, collect all of the foam that rises to the top with a spoon; discard. Add the salt and peppercorns. Increase the heat and bring the liquid back to a boil; cover, reduce the heat to low, and simmer for 1 hour or until the beef is easily pierced with a fork. Add the cabbage, carrots, potatoes, corn, and chayote; cover and simmer until the vegetables are tender, about 20 to 25 minutes. Remove the beef to a cutting board and place the cooked vegetables on a platter, covering them so they'll retain their heat. Allow the beef to rest for 10 minutes, before slicing thinly. Strain the broth through a strainer into a large bowl and discard any solids trapped in the strainer. Return the broth to the pot; add the beef and vegetables, heat thoroughly, and serve in bowls. (Or place the sliced beef on a platter surrounded by the cooked vegetables and serve the broth on the side.)

VARIATIONS: Leftover meat from cocido is often chopped very finely to make salpicón or carne en polvo (beef salad). Typically, it will be mixed with chopped onions and herbs (culantro in Cuba, cilantro in Mexico, mint or hierbabuena in Guatemala). It is then dressed with liberal amounts of sour orange in countries like Guatemala, El Salvador, and Nicaragua or with lime or vinegar in South America. I once had a conversation with Marcella Hazan, the queen of Italian cooking, who was fascinated by the fact that Latin Americans ate salpicón, because at home, she told me, she made an Italian version with the addition of capers, parsley, garlic, and vinegar.

My uncle Mirko Samayoa was partial to a salad made by combining equal parts of leftover meat from cocido with boiled potatoes. He would slice them and dress them with a mixture of mayonnaise and lemon, with a touch of mustard and mint, and would eat the dish cold.

Sopa de Tartaritas

Guatemalan Tiny Crêpe Soup

Guatemala | Yield: Serves 4 | Difficulty Level: Easy | Total Cooking Time: 20 minutes (if broth is made beforehand)

This is a very light starter soup, usually made with the leftover broth from a pot of boiled beef (called cocido, sancocho, or puchero, depending on the country). Tiny, fried crêpes are offered on the side so that each person can float as few or as many as they want on the clear broth. The more oil you use, the crispier the crepes will be; in Guatemala, this varies by each cook's preference. As with any time you fry, the oil will heat up slightly above temperature at times; simply lower the heat accordingly and continue frying. Using a small skillet is key because you can't fry many of these at the same time (by the time some are ready to be turned, others may be burning). It's easiest to manage batches of 8 crepes at a time. These crepes are meant to be tiny—one bite-full each. About 1.25 inches (3 cm) in diameter each. I keep beef stock in my freezer for occasions when I just want to make this quick soup.

FOR THE TARTARITAS

¾ cup (105 grams) all-purpose flour

¼ teaspoon fine sea salt

½ cup (120 ml) whole milk

1 egg

2 tablespoons chopped fresh Italian parsley

¼ cup (60 ml.) vegetable oil

FOR THE SOUP

6 cups (1.4 liters) beef broth (on page 29 or from the Cocido on page 462)

2 teaspoons fine sea salt, or more, to taste

¼ teaspoon white pepper

2 large sprigs of fresh mint

To make the tartaritas, in a medium bowl, whisk together the flour and salt; set aside. In a small bowl, whisk together the milk and egg until combined; stir into the flour mixture and whisk together until the batter is smooth. Let the batter rest for 10 minutes, then stir in the parsley. Line a plate with paper towels and set aside. Heat half of the oil in a small non-stick skillet, set over medium-high heat. When the oil is hot (and working in batches), add the batter by the teaspoonful to form miniature crêpes. Cook for 30-35 seconds or until the bottom of the crepes begins to turn golden. Using two forks, flip the crepes over and cook for 20 seconds or until golden. Transfer the finished crepes to the paper-lined plate, until all are cooked. Continue cooking crepes until all the batter is finished (adding more oil a little at a time, as needed). If the crepes are browning too quickly, lower the heat accordingly, wait for the oil to cool, then start frying them again. To make the soup, heat the broth in a large pot, over medium-high heat; as soon as it comes to a boil, stir in the salt, pepper and the sprigs of mint. Boil for 2 minutes; remove from heat and discard the mint. Ladle the broth onto 4 bowls and top each with a few crepes (offer the rest on the side for each person to add as they please). Serve immediately.

Sancocho de Raquel y Hugo

Beef, Pumpkin, and Root Vegetable Hot Pot

Venezuela | Yield: Serves 6–8 | Difficulty Level: Easy | Total Cooking Time: 2½ hours

This iconic Venezuelan soup is both hearty and healthy—one of the many renditions of boiled beef stews or cocidos that Latin America is known for. Bones and lesser cuts of beef are essential here, for flavor. My dear friends Raquel Parra and Hugo Gimeno gave me their recipe; they use shank meat because the bone and marrow lend deeper flavor to the broth. I add a couple of short ribs to increase the amount of meat. Root vegetables take center stage; use whatever you can find. Look for yuca root, malanga, and white yam (ñame) in either the fresh or freezer sections of Latin grocery stores. This recipe is very easy to make; just pay attention to the fact that the ingredients are added at different times, so as not to overcook some and undercook others. The meat will need the most time to cook to become tender. The pumpkin and ñame will require the least. Don't be intimidated by the amount of salt in this recipe—tubers require that you use plenty. Raquel suggests serving this with your favorite hot sauce or with lime juice.

2 small onions (about 4 ounces/115 grams each), peeled and divided

1 medium red bell pepper, stemmed, seeded, and halved, divided

1 medium leek, divided into light and green parts

8 garlic cloves, peeled and divided

2 pounds (910 grams) beef shank, beef short ribs, or a combination of the two

3 quarts (2.8 liters) beef or vegetable broth, or water

½ cup (60 grams) sliced green onions (white and green parts)

2 ears of corn, sliced across into 10 slices or rounds

2 cups (255 grams) yuca root, peeled and diced into bite-sized pieces

2 cups (255 grams) yautia (or malanga), peeled and diced into bite-sized pieces

2 cups (255 grams) ñame or white yam, diced into bite-sized pieces

½ pound (255 grams) auyama or crookneck squash, peeled, seeded, and diced into bite-sized pieces (about 2 cups)

2 tablespoons fine sea salt, or to taste

½ teaspoon freshly ground black pepper, or to taste

2–3 tablespoons chopped fresh cilantro, stems and leaves, to taste (optional)

Slice one of the onions in half and place it in a large Dutch oven or soup pot; finely chop the remaining one and set aside. Add half of the bell pepper to the pot and finely chop the remaining half; set it aside. Add the green leaves of the leek to the pot; slice the white part of the leek and set it aside. Add 4 whole garlic cloves to the pot; finely chop the remaining garlic and set aside. Add the meat to the pot and cover it with the broth or water. Bring the liquid to a boil over high heat; cover, reduce the heat, and simmer for 1 hour or until meat is tender. Use tongs to remove all of the large vegetable pieces in the pot (and discard them), leaving only the garlic and beef. Now, add the reserved onions, bell peppers, leeks, and remaining garlic, along with the green onions, corn, and yuca root to the pot. Bring back to a boil over high heat; cover, lower the heat, and cook for 10 to 12 minutes or until the yuca root is fork tender. Add the yautia, ñame, and squash and bring to a boil over high heat; cover, lower the heat, and cook for 6 to 8 minutes or until they are fork tender (much longer, and they'll fall apart in the broth). Remove any large pieces of meat and cut into smaller pieces; return to the pot. Add salt, pepper, and cilantro (if using). Stir and let it simmer for 2 more minutes. Serve in large bowls, dividing meat and vegetables between the bowls before adding the broth.

Note: If you can't find white yams, substitute with sweet potatoes (camote). One-half pound (255 grams) of tubers is enough to yield 2 cups, when cooked and diced.

Pepián de Res

Mayan Beef Stew

Guatemala | Yield: Serves 6 | Difficulty Level: Intermediate | Total Cooking Time: 3 hours

This beef and vegetable stew drenched in a rich brown sauce is a regular in Guatemalan households. Pepianes are the moles of the Maya, rich with charred tomatoes, tomatillos, dried chiles, seeds, and herbs. They include at least one type of sweet spice, such as cinnamon, allspice, or cloves; they can be red (rojo), green (verde), or dark like this one, called pepián negro. Some pepianes use plantain peels as a thickener, others corn masa or charred corn tortillas. This one is traditionally thickened with French bread; the burned bread also adds smoky umami and intensifies the dark color of the sauce. Different cuts of meat can be used, but I usually splurge on bone-in short ribs; feel free to use stewing beef if you like. This stew is not spicy-hot, and although it takes hours to cook, most of the time is inactive. As with any recipe in which a blender is required to pulverize spices, use only Mexican or brittle Ceylon cinnamon; hard cassia cinnamon will break the motor. Pepianes are abundantly soupy and are best served over plenty of rice or plain tamales. Leftovers freeze for up to three months.

3 pounds (910 grams) short ribs (half with bones, half without)

2 pounds (910 grams) Roma tomatoes (about 6 large)

1 pound (455 grams) tomatillos, husks removed and washed (about 16 medium)

1 medium (8 ounces/225 grams) white onion, halved (skin on)

3 large garlic cloves, unpeeled

1 stick Ceylon cinnamon (about 2 inches/5 cm long) or 1 teaspoon ground cinnamon

1 ounce (30 grams/3 tablespoons) raw, hulled pumpkin seeds (pepitas)

1 ounce (30 grams/3 tablespoons) raw sesame seeds

½ teaspoon whole coriander seeds

1½ ounces (40 grams) white bread, sliced and toasted until slightly blackened

1 guajillo chile, stemmed, cored, seeded, and deveined

1 pasilla chile, stemmed, cored, seeded, and deveined

2 tablespoons vegetable oil

2 chayote squashes (about 9 ounces/255 grams each)

3–4 large white potatoes

3 cups (455 grams) green beans, sliced crosswise in half

1½ tablespoons fine sea salt, or more to taste

1 teaspoon freshly ground black pepper

Place the ribs in a large pot and cover them with water by 1 inch (2.5 cm); bring to a boil. Remove the foam that rises to the top in the first 10 minutes; cover, lower the heat, and continue simmering for 1½ to 2 hours or until the meat is tender. In the meantime, in a large, dark skillet set over medium-high heat, and working in batches, roast the tomatoes, tomatillos, onions, and garlic. Peel the onions and garlic and add them to the jar of a blender. Add the rest of the roasted vegetables to the blender. Remove the skillet from the heat (careful, it will still be very hot); add the cinnamon stick and toast until you can see some browned bits on it; transfer to the blender. Add the pumpkin seeds to the skillet and toast for 1 minute; transfer them to the blender. Add the sesame and coriander seeds to the skillet; toast for 1 minute with the residual heat or until golden, then transfer them to the blender. Break the bread into chunks and add it to the blender along with the dried chiles. (If you can't fit all of the ingredients in your blender at the same time, blend them in two batches.) Blend all of the ingredients until smooth, and if necessary, add a bit of water to help the motor run (a few tablespoons at a time); set aside. Once the meat has cooked, strain the broth into a large bowl, reserving it, and set the beef aside. Set the same large pot used to cook the beef over medium-high heat; add the oil, and as soon as it begins to shimmer, add all of the blended sauce at once (careful, it will splatter for a few seconds, so stand back and use a long spoon). Immediately lower the heat to medium, while stirring. Add the beef to the sauce and cook for 20 minutes. Peel, halve, and core the chayotes; cut them into bite-sized pieces and add them to the pot. Peel and halve the potatoes; cut them into bite-sized pieces and add them to the pot, along with the green beans. →

Add the salt, pepper, and 2 cups (480 ml) of the reserved broth to the pot (the remaining broth can be frozen for up to 3 months or used in other recipes). Bring to a boil, cover, lower the heat to medium-low, and cook until the vegetables are fork tender, about 30 minutes. Serve hot.

Note: Charring the ingredients for the sauce can be done a day in advance; the sauce itself can be blended ahead and refrigerated until ready to use once the meat is cooked. If you wish to prepare the chayotes and potatoes ahead of time, keep them submerged in cold water after peeling and chopping so they don't oxidize. They can be kept this way for up to 2 hours before cooking them.

A Note on Charring Vegetables · A comal (a flat cooking utensil made out of steel or heat-resistant clay) is traditionally used in many Mesoamerican homes to char vegetables. One of my own comales is housed in the Food Exhibit at the National Museum of American History at the Smithsonian; therefore, I have reserved an old cast-iron skillet for the purpose of charring vegetables, because they invariably stain skillets black. For this reason, cast iron is ideal. The vegetables should be turned often as they roast in the skillet, until most of their skins are charred. Adding charred vegetables adds a smoky umami flavor and a darker color to sauces; in addition, the flesh of the vegetables becomes sweet. If the vegetables are large, cut them into smaller chunks before you place them in the blender.

Seco de Carne de Res

Beef and Beer Stew

Peru | Yield: Serves 4–6 | Difficulty Level: Intermediate | Total Cooking Time: 1 hour 30 minutes

This hearty beef stew is filled with herbs and heat that awaken the palate. The word *seco* means "dry," but in Peru, ironically, it refers to stews containing a lot of liquid. This recipe calls for long-leaf culantro (*Eryngium foetidum*), a tropical herb with serrated leaves that looks like lettuce and tastes like über cilantro; here, it lends its vibrantly grassy flavor and lively green color to the stew, setting it apart from all others. If you can't find it where you live, use double the amount of cilantro. There isn't a clear consensus as to what kind of beer Peruvian home cooks prefer—usually it's whatever is around; some opt for light beer, while others swear by dark lager. I find that a dark, caramel-colored beer lends deeper flavor to the final gravy, but by all means, use your favorite. For this dish, the Peruvian cooks I know rely solely on the heat lent by fruity ají amarillo, but I love the additional heat of spicier marisol peppers and use them, as well; both are widely available as jarred pastes in Latin American markets and are easy to find online (see Sources). Yellow Peruvian potatoes are now found peeled and ready to use in the frozen section of many Latin stores, however, any golden and creamy variety—such as Yukon gold—makes a nice substitute.

3 large garlic cloves, roughly chopped

½ cup (120 ml) ají amarillo paste

¼ cup (60 ml) ají mirasol paste (optional) for extra heat

3 packed cups (117 grams) whole culantro leaves (or double the amount of cilantro)

1½ cups (360 ml) dark beer

2 teaspoons ground cumin

2 teaspoons fine sea salt

½ teaspoon freshly ground black pepper

3 tablespoons (45 ml) vegetable oil, divided

2 pounds (910 grams) cubed stew meat

2½ cups (228 grams) thinly sliced red onions

3 cups (455 grams) peeled and cubed papas amarillas or Yukon gold potatoes

1½ cups (225 grams) green peas (fresh or frozen and thawed)

Cooked white rice

In a blender, combine the garlic, ají pastes, culantro, beer, cumin, salt, and pepper with 2 cups (480 ml) water; blend until smooth and set aside (you may have to work in batches if your blender is small). Heat half of the oil in a large Dutch oven or pot, set over medium-high heat. Working in two batches, brown the beef (add the remaining oil before browning the second batch), removing the pieces to a separate bowl, until all is done browning, about 8 to 10 minutes total. Add the onions to the pot and cook, stirring well with a wooden spoon in order to scrape up the brown bits collected at the bottom, until the onions are soft, about 1½ minutes. Return the beef (and any juices that collected in the bowl) to the pot; pour the blended sauce over the top and stir well. Bring the mixture to a boil over medium-high heat; cover, lower the heat to low, and simmer until the beef is fork tender, about 45 minutes. Add the potatoes, cover, and continue cooking, until they are tender, about 20 minutes. Add the green peas; cover and cook just until they are warmed through, about 5 minutes. Serve over cooked white rice.

Note: Ají mirasol is much spicier than ají amarillo, so if you're not a fan of hot flavors, skip it, or serve it on the side.

Falso Conejo

Fake Rabbit

Bolivia | Yield: Serves 6 | Difficulty Level: Intermediate | Total Cooking Time: 35 minutes

Nobody really knows why this spicy-hot stew is called fake rabbit, but the popular theories are too good not to share. One hypothesis is that it is most similar to a stew from the Middle Ages made with rabbit "in the style of Castille," which was brought over by Spanish colonizers; since rabbits were scarce in the Americas, beef was substituted and locals added the hot peppers. Or so the story goes. That one doesn't make sense to me, because there were no cows in Bolivia when the Europeans arrived! Another hypothesis is that the finished dish resembled a stew made with cuy—guinea pig—considered a delicacy in the Andes (the stew is still popular today, called conejo lambreado). The name was switched in order to calm any queasy stomachs, since it was much easier to digest when people thought they were eating rabbit and not a large rodent. This argument is a bit more plausible, if you ask me. Most probably, though, the name hails from the traditional Spanish way of cooking rabbit, first tenderizing it by pounding, then breading, frying, and smothering it in sauce. No matter the origin of the name, this is one of Bolivia's comfort foods, a weekday stew most popular in the Altiplano region. It is traditionally served with white rice, boiled potatoes, and Garnitura Criolla (page 14) to offset the spiciness. Ají amarillo paste and ají colorado (or ají panca) are easy to find (see Sources). If you can't get them, use plenty of any hot peppers you can. I've tamed this dish a bit, but always offer hot sauce on the side. This can be made ahead of time and refrigerated for up to one day; reheat gently over low heat and serve.

1 pound (455 grams) bottom round steaks, pounded to ⅛ inch (3 mm) thin

1¼ cups (300 ml) vegetable oil, plus more for brushing on the beef

2 teaspoons fine sea salt, divided

1 teaspoon freshly ground black pepper, divided

¾ cup (20 grams) dried bread crumbs

1 cup (170 grams) chopped yellow onions

2 large garlic cloves, finely chopped

1½ cups (255 grams) chopped plum tomatoes

2 cups (340 grams) carrots, peeled and thinly sliced into matchsticks

2 tablespoons ají amarillo paste

1 tablespoon ají panca paste (optional)

2 teaspoons ground cumin

1 teaspoon dried oregano

2 cups (480 ml) beef broth or water

2 cups (170 grams) green peas (fresh or frozen and thawed)

2 tablespoons chopped fresh parsley (leaves and tender stems)

1 recipe Garnitura Criolla (page 14)

Brush the beef slices on both sides with a bit of oil; season both sides with a pinch of salt and a pinch of pepper. Place the bread crumbs on a large plate; coat both sides of each slice of beef with crumbs, pressing the beef into the bread crumbs so they adhere (the coating should be very light). Heat 1 cup (240 ml) of the oil in a large sauté pan set over medium-high heat. Working in batches, add the breaded beef and cook until it is lightly golden on one side, about 1 minute; turn over and cook until it's also lightly golden, about another minute. Set the cooked beef aside on a plate. In a large pot, heat the remaining oil over medium-high heat. Add the onions, garlic, tomatoes, and carrots, stirring often, until softened, about 6 to 8 minutes. Add the ají amarillo and the ají panca paste (if using), and the cumin and oregano; stir for 1 minute. Add the broth or water; as soon as it comes to a boil, cover and lower the heat; simmer for 5 minutes. Add the peas and parsley; cover, and continue simmering for 5 minutes. Transfer the beef to the sauce, coating it well; cover and simmer for 10 minutes. Serve the beef stew with garnitura criolla on the side.

Note: If you wish to thicken the sauce, simply remove the lid and continue simmering for a few extra minutes or until it has thickened to your liking. As opposed to traditional milanesas, which have thick crusts, the breading of the beef here should be thin. Additionally, the browned bread crumbs add nutty flavor and will thicken the sauce.

Lomo Saltado

Stir-Fried Beef

Peru | Yield: Serves 4–6 | Difficulty Level: Intermediate | Total Cooking Time: 30 minutes

Chinese-style stir-fries are often served in Peruvian homes, where they are called saltados (literally, "tossed"). This is true fusion food: beef tenderloin (lomo) brought over by Europeans; soy sauce (known as sillao) from Asia; and tomatoes and potatoes native to the Inca. Tossed together in a hot skillet, they become the national stir-fry of Peru. Believe it or not, the addition of fries is authentic! Incorporate them into the stir-fry or serve them on the side—just don't skip them.

1½ pounds (680 grams) beef tenderloin or flat-iron steak, sliced into thin strips

4 tablespoons (60 ml) vegetable or peanut oil, divided

3 cups (325 grams) white onions, sliced into fine strips

2 cups (200 grams) stemmed and seeded bell peppers (any color), sliced into fine strips

1½ cups (225 grams) plum tomatoes, seeded and sliced into fine strips

3 tablespoons (45 ml) soy sauce

2 tablespoons oyster sauce

2 tablespoons red wine vinegar

2 teaspoons fine sea salt

1 teaspoon freshly ground black pepper

1 recipe Papitas Fritas (page 292)

½ cup (40 grams) finely chopped fresh cilantro (leaves and tender stems)

2–3 large green onions, sliced on the bias (about ⅓ cup/20 grams)

Cooked white rice

Pat the beef dry with paper towels. Heat 1 tablespoon of the oil in a large nonstick skillet set over medium-high heat. Add half of the beef and cook, while stirring, for 2 to 3 minutes or until it's seared; remove it to a plate. Add another tablespoon of the oil to the pan and the remaining beef, cooking, while stirring, until seared, about 2 to 3 minutes; transfer to the plate and set aside. Heat the remaining oil and add the onions and bell peppers; cook, while stirring, until they've cooked some but are still crisp, about 3 minutes. Add the tomatoes, soy sauce, oyster sauce, and vinegar, and cook for about 2 minutes or until most of the liquid has been absorbed. Return the beef to the skillet and add the salt, pepper, fries, cilantro, and green onions, tossing to combine. Serve alongside a scoop of rice.

Note: If you're in a real bind, use frozen potato fries. Follow the package directions and keep them warm in a 250°F (120°C) oven for up to 30 minutes while you cook the beef.

Lomito en Trozo con Salsa de Chiles Secos y Cognac

Filet Mignon with Chile-Cognac Sauce

Central America | Yield: Serves 8 | Difficulty Level: Intermediate | Total Cooking Time: 1 hour (plus chilling time)

Everything, even beef, tastes better with bacon! Back in the 1950s, when everything French was the rage, beef medallions wrapped in bacon were known as filet mignons, and chefs were setting dishes aflame tableside (flambéing) on a regular basis. By the time the 1990s arrived, these recipes had traveled from fancy restaurants into Latin American homes. This elegant dish is ideal for when your boss or an important guest comes over for a meal and you need to impress. Serve with white rice or mashed potatoes.

FOR THE STEAK

Eight 6 ounce (170 gram) filets cut from a beef tenderloin

16 bacon strips

1 teaspoon fine sea salt

1 teaspoon freshly ground black pepper

FOR THE SAUCE

1 cup (230 grams) unsalted butter

2 cups (280 grams) finely chopped yellow onions

3 garlic cloves, finely chopped

4 ancho chiles, reconstituted, seeded, deveined, and chopped (see page 184 on how to reconstitute chiles)

1–2 cups (240–475 ml) chicken broth

2 tablespoons cognac or brandy

1 teaspoon fine sea salt

¼ teaspoon freshly ground black pepper, or to taste

1 cup (240 ml) Mexican crema or crème fraîche

Chopped fresh parsley or cilantro, for garnish

Prepare the steak: Wrap two strips of bacon around each beef filet and secure well with kitchen twine or toothpicks; season the beef with salt and pepper. Place the beef in a covered dish in the refrigerator for 30 minutes (or up to 4 hours).

Make the sauce: In a large nonstick pan set over medium-high heat, melt the butter. Sauté the onions for 10 to 15 minutes or until they start to caramelize to a deep golden color; add the garlic and cook for 1 minute or until fragrant. Add the ancho chiles; cook, while stirring, for 1 minute. Add 1 cup (240 ml) of the chicken broth and bring the sauce to a simmer; lower the heat and let simmer uncovered for 10 minutes or until the sauce is reduced by half; add more broth if it's reducing too quickly. Cool the sauce for 10 to 15 minutes; transfer it to a blender and puree until smooth, adding more chicken broth if needed. Return the sauce to the pan, add the cognac, and set it over medium-high heat. Carefully light a long match or wooden skewer and bring it close to the sauce to set it aflame. Once the flames subside, stir in half of the cream and season with salt and pepper; keep warm until ready to serve. Grill the steaks on a very hot grill (or cook on a nonstick skillet that has been lightly brushed with vegetable oil) for 4 to 6 minutes per side and 2 minutes on the edges to crisp the bacon, for medium rare (add 2 minutes for each extra degree of doneness). Let the steaks rest for 5 minutes before serving. To plate, make a pool of sauce in the middle of each plate, place the beef in the center and a spoonful of crema or crème fraîche on the side, and sprinkle everything with parsley or cilantro, if desired.

Note: If not serving immediately, you can refrigerate the sauce overnight after the flame has subsided, and reheat it over low heat right before serving. Don't let it come to a boil or the sauce will break.

Warning: Never, ever pour alcohol into a hot pan near a flame directly from the bottle because it can cause the bottle to explode; use my method of adding the liquor away from the heat first, and then lighting it separately.

Matambre

Stuffed Beef Roll

Argentina | Yield: Serves 6–8 | Difficulty Level: High | Total Cooking Time: 2½ hours

This is one of the most well-known Argentinean family meals. Translated, it literally means "to kill hunger" (matar el hambre), no doubt because it can feed a crowd. Matambres are beautiful once they're cut into slices—they look like mosaics. This may seem hard to make the first time, but once you conquer your fear of pounding and rolling the steak over so many ingredients, it will become second nature. Fillings vary, and you can substitute spinach leaves (or any green, for that matter) for the herbs, ground beef or pork for the vegetables, and deli meats and sliced cheese (such as provolone) in place of the eggs. Some cooks will add bread crumbs or even gelatin to help looser fillings hold together inside the steak; olives, capers, pickles (gherkins), potatoes, and raisins are fair game. I've eaten enough styles of matambres in my lifetime to learn that there is no "one" recipe that tops another. Make it this way, then play with the fillings as you wish. Matambres are meant to be eaten at room temperature and sliced thinly; cold, they are incredibly sumptuous in sandwiches.

One 2½ pound flank steak, butterflied and pounded thin into a 12 x 13 x 12 inch (30 x 33 x 30 cm) rectangle, about ¼ inch (6 mm) thick

2 tablespoons white wine vinegar

1 tablespoon plus 2 teaspoons fine sea salt, divided

2 teaspoons dried oregano

1 teaspoon garlic powder

1 teaspoon freshly ground black pepper

½ teaspoon ají molido or smoked Spanish paprika

6 garlic cloves, finely chopped

1½ cups (120 grams) finely chopped fresh Italian parsley

4 canned roasted red peppers, drained, seeded, each sliced open like a book in one piece

4 hard-boiled eggs, peeled and sliced lengthwise in half

2 medium carrots, peeled and sliced into 4 inch (10 cm) sticks

1½ cups (115 grams) grated Parmesan cheese (or Reggianito)

1 small white onion, quartered

1 whole garlic clove

1 bay leaf

4 whole black peppercorns

1 cup (240 ml) white wine, such as Chardonnay

Place the flank steak in a nonreactive baking dish; rub it well with the vinegar on all sides. Cover and refrigerate for 2 hours (or up to overnight) to tenderize the meat. Remove the steak from the refrigerator and season on all sides with 1 tablespoon salt, oregano, garlic powder, pepper, and ají. Place the steak on a clean cutting board and spread with the chopped garlic and parsley on the butterflied side (this will be the inside of the matambre). Layer the roasted peppers over the herbs, covering as much of the surface of the steak as you can. Place the hard-boiled eggs in the middle, in one straight line, over the peppers. Place the carrots in one row on each side of the eggs (they should be touching). Sprinkle all liberally with the cheese. Turn the steak so that the long end is toward you; roll it up tightly and tie the stuffed flank at ½ inch (12 mm) intervals with kitchen twine. Place the matambre in the bottom of a large, heavy-bottomed Dutch oven (an 8 quart/7.5 liter one is a good size for this); add the onion quarters, whole garlic clove, bay leaf, peppercorns, and salt. Pour the wine over the steak and add enough cold water to cover the steak completely. Set the Dutch oven over medium-high heat and bring the liquid to a boil; immediately cover the pot and lower the heat to medium-low; simmer the meat, undisturbed, for 2 hours (checking to make sure that it remains at a simmer; reduce the heat if it's boiling too rapidly). Remove the Dutch oven from the heat and allow the beef to cool in the liquid for 30 minutes; use tongs to remove the beef to a cutting board; allow it to cool for another 20 to 30 minutes before slicing it thinly.

Note: The matambre can be refrigerated until cold before slicing; if serving chilled, accompany it with a potato salad.

CACAO

The history of cacao is as rich as chocolate itself. The journey from bean to bitter paste to melt-in-your-mouth candy bar took centuries to unfold and is full of legend and lore.

In the Mayan language, *cacao* means "food of the gods." Native to Mexico and Guatemala, records date its domestication back to the year 200 BC. When the Aztecs started their domination of Mayan territories around the 1400s, they advanced the dissemination of cacao by ways of trade. Cacao seeds were used as the first form of currency in ancient America, replacing bartering for the first time. They were used to pay tribute to kings and, later, taxes.

Cacao is the seed of the fruit (cherelles) of a flowering tropical evergreen tree that belongs to the Malvaceae family. The fruits are long pods that range from purple to yellow and orange in color. Within the pods grow dozens of seeds (up to sixty) that are covered in a sticky and sweet substance. The meaty pulp can be eaten, but it's the seeds (and the liquor that is extracted from them) that are most valued. Cacao takes time to develop; the seeds can only be cultivated every four to five years. There are many varieties, but they are typically divided into three categories: the forastero, the criollo, and the trinitario.

The Maya were the first to devise methods to grow, mature, ripen, ferment, dry, toast, clean (descascarar), grind, and mold chocolate into round, rustic tablets. The fact that it took all those steps to make a simple cup of drinkable liquor explains, in part, why it was considered food for the elite and for ancient kings—it took a long time and a huge production to make it.

Ancient chocolate drinks served to royalty by Maya and Aztecs featured achiote, which colored it red, and chiles, which added heat—it was bitter and thick. When the Spanish conqueror Hernán Cortés arrived in Mexico, he found that Emperor Montezuma drank a thick potion said to have aphrodisiac powers, called "chocolatl."

Cacao wasn't sweetened with sugar until after the colonization. According to Fray Bernardino de Sahagún, a Franciscan missionary who wrote *General History of the Things of New Spain* in 1877 (also called *The Florentine Codex*), the Aztecs were the first ones to combine cacao and vanilla. Mexican nuns are said to have been the first to add flavorings like sugar, almonds, and seeds (such as pumpkin) to cacao. It has been widely claimed that Cortés introduced cacao to Europe, but according to Dave DeWitt, author of *Precious Cargo: How Food from the Americas Changed the World*, it wasn't until 1544, when Dominican friars took members of the Guatemalan Kekchi tribe to Spain, that Europeans were taught the technique for making beaten chocolate drinks (early forms of chocolate were always liquids). The first shipment of cacao beans for trade arrived in Seville from Veracruz, Mexico, in 1585. The rest, as they say, is history.

According to the documents left by Juan de Cárdenas in his work *Las cosas de La Nueva España*, chocolate tablets were first produced by Guatemalan women of high society, looking for a hot and sweetened drink that was convenient to make. He also credits Guatemalan cooks with first inventing chocolate "masa" that could be mixed with cold water and frothed until it became thick atole, known today as champurrado in Mexico and pinol in Guatemala. It took until 1828 for chocolate to be turned into cocoa powder by the Dutch chemist Coenraad Johannes van Houten; chocolate bars as we know them today weren't invented until 1847 by the British chocolatier J. S. Fry and Sons.

Today, chocolate is often referred to as a "sinful" treat, but originally priests and monks were largely responsible for disseminating it throughout Europe.

Chocolate was mostly reserved for drinking in the Americas until the end of the nineteenth century, when it began to be used in baked goods—a tradition that was brought over by European immigrants. Don't be surprised to find savory recipes in this chapter, which are just as delicious as the sweet concoctions.

Mole Poblano para Todos los Días

Everyday Mole Poblano

Mexico | Yield: Makes 4 cups (960 ml) | Difficulty Level: Easy | Total Cooking Time: 50 minutes

Of all of the mollis in Latin America, the most famous, without a doubt, is mole poblano, the traditional chocolate sauce from Puebla. Moles such as this one are not Indigenous dishes, but a result of the mestizaje or blending of the cultures of Arabs, Spaniards, and Mesoamericans. Mole poblano is said to have been invented by nuns in a convent to celebrate a very important patron; it adds traditional baroque elements like dried fruits and nuts to ingredients native to the Americas, such as tomatoes and chiles. Instead of making the classic sauce, which takes a long time to prepare (sometimes days), I use this quick, everyday version. Many modern-day Mexican cooks will use mole poblano from a jar, but I think it's worth making it my way—even though it cuts corners and uses molasses in place of raisins and dried fruits. Use it to top the chicken enchiladas on page 483 or to pour over roast turkey, or add more broth and use it to sauce chilaquiles.

3 tablespoons (40 grams) unsalted butter, divided

2 cups (170 grams) sliced white onions

3 garlic cloves

1½ cups (225 grams) roughly chopped plum tomatoes

3–4 pasilla peppers, stemmed, seeded, toasted, and reconstituted (see Tip)

3–4 guajillo peppers, stemmed, seeded, toasted, and reconstituted (see Tip)

¼ cup (30 grams) toasted sesame seeds (see box on page 198)

¼ cup (40 grams) hulled and raw pumpkin seeds (see Note)

One 2 inch (5 cm) piece Mexican cinnamon (canela)

3 cups (720 ml) chicken broth, divided

½ cup (120 ml) unsulfured molasses

1 teaspoon fine sea salt, or more to taste

Pinch of freshly ground black pepper, or more to taste

One 3 ounce (85 gram) piece dark chocolate, chopped

1 tablespoon dark cocoa powder (not Dutch processed)

Melt half of the butter in a medium saucepan set over medium-high heat; add the onions and cook, while stirring, for 10 to 15 minutes or until golden. Add the garlic and cook for 30 seconds or until fragrant; add the tomatoes, cook for 5 minutes, and remove from the heat. Transfer the onion mixture to a blender. Add the chiles, sesame seeds, pumpkin seeds, cinnamon, half of the broth, the molasses, and the salt and pepper. Blend, using more broth as needed, to make a smooth sauce. Melt the remaining butter in the same medium saucepan set over medium-high heat; add the blended sauce (careful, it will splatter) and bring it to a boil, stirring often. Lower the heat to medium-low and cook, stirring often, for 15 minutes. Add the chocolate and cocoa powder and stir until fully incorporated; continue cooking until the mole is thickened slightly (add more broth if you want to thin it out). Taste and season with more salt and pepper, if desired.

Note: This mole keeps, if well covered in the fridge, for up to 3 days; it also freezes beautifully for up to 3 months.

Tip: To seed a dried chile, use scissors to cut a slit in one side from bottom to top; remove the stems and shake out the seeds. Never wash chiles, or you'll remove flavor—if they are a bit dusty, wipe them with a damp paper towel before you cut them. To toast dried chiles, heat a dry skillet over medium-high heat and roast them for 20 seconds on each side or until softened, being careful not to burn them. To reconstitute chiles, cover them in boiling water for 10 minutes.

Recipe Rescue · Food is always in flux, particularly in Latin America, where so many cultural elements have clashed together throughout history, creating different culinary trends that often disappear with the next. I feel very strongly that many important, classic Latin American recipes have been lost because there are few people to save them for posterity. Such is the fate of many Cuban and Venezuelan recipes, which have been decimated from the daily repertoire of most of their citizens. These directions have disappeared along with the ingredients that can no longer be found. Few Cubans can now afford red meat; there is very little cattle left on the island and what is left for sale is too expensive for the average person. Venezuela went from being the richest economic power in Latin America to a country in which grocery store shelves are empty; even basic ingredients like corn flour for making arepas is now rationed. As for the rest of Latin America, the art of home cooking has been one mostly transferred through oral history from generation to generation. Recipes, if written down, are still more like sketches than formulas. A cup of flour may vary in size from one grandmother's kitchen to another's. In my research into thousands of old recipes, I've uncovered instructions such as "cook until it looks ready" (cocer hasta que se mire listo), "stir until it looks like baby food" (mesclar hasta que parezca compota de bebé), and "prepare the chicken as usual" (prepare el pollo en el modo usual). Most of these recipes assume that the person reading them already knows how to cook and therefore needs only minor direction. This book, the result of countless hours of recipe research and interviewing many, many home cooks, is an attempt to save some of these recipes from disappearing There is so much more left in danger of being forgotten in Latin American cuisines. My hope is that you will continue my quest and save more recipes.

Carne en Salsa de Chocolate

Beef Tenderloin with Savory Chocolate Sauce

Venezuela | Yield: Serves 4–6 | Difficulty Level: Intermediate | Total Cooking Time: 1½ hours

Chocolate, tomatoes, and brown sugar combine flawlessly in this recipe, which was one of the most sophisticated dishes in the Venezuelan everyday cooking repertoire until the Chavista populist revolution destroyed the country's soaring economy in the twentieth century. Today, mostly only expats living abroad can still afford to eat beef, but this recipe is so important to the history of chocolate in the Americas that it's worth keeping alive for generations to come. I have seen grown-ups lick this sauce off their plates—it's that good!

One 2 pound (910 gram) section trimmed beef tenderloin

1½ teaspoons fine sea salt, divided

½ teaspoon freshly ground black pepper, divided

2 tablespoons vegetable oil

¼ cup (60 grams) packed dark brown sugar

1 cup (115 grams) finely chopped white onions

One 8 ounce (240 ml) can crushed tomatoes with juices

¾ cup (180 ml) beef broth

One 2½ ounce (70 gram) piece unsweetened dark chocolate

1 tablespoon extra-dark cocoa powder (not Dutch processed)

Rub the tenderloin with 1 teaspoon of the salt and ¼ teaspoon of the pepper; let it sit at room temperature for 20 minutes. Heat the oil in a large Dutch oven set over medium-high heat; add the brown sugar and melt it as you stir, about 1 minute (it will get clumpy; be careful not to let it burn). Add the beef; brown it in the sugar mixture, turning to brown on all sides and swirling it around in the pan, about 2 to 3 minutes (use tongs to swirl the beef; it's important to keep moving it so the sugar doesn't burn). Remove the beef to a platter. Quickly, add the onions to the pot; cook for 2 minutes. Add the tomatoes, broth, and remaining salt and pepper. Return the beef (and any juices that have collected at the bottom of the platter) back to the pot. Bring to a boil; cover, lower the heat, and simmer for 20 to 25 minutes or until an instant-read thermometer inserted into the meat registers 135°F (60°C) for medium rare (add 3 to 4 more minutes for each additional degree of doneness). Remove the beef from the pot and set it on a cutting board; tent it with aluminum foil while you finish the sauce. Stir the chocolate and cocoa into the sauce, and stir just until melted; simmer slowly, until the sauce thickens slightly. Slice the beef thinly and serve, covered in the sauce.

Note: If you wish to make this for a larger crowd, double all of the ingredients. Just be sure to carefully measure the temperature of the beef so you don't overcook it (a 5 pound/2.3 kilogram beef tenderloin should take about 30 to 35 minutes to cook, for medium rare).

Enchiladas de Pollo y Mole de Chocolate

Easy Chicken Enchiladas with Mole

Mexico | Number of Servings: 6–8 | Difficulty Level: Easy | Total Cooking Time: 25 minutes (if mole sauce made ahead)

Years ago, my husband, Luis, and I hosted our friend Diana Kennedy, a respected authority on Mexican cuisine, at our lake house. We had spent the day with her, shopping for ingredients for one of her classes, trekking far and wide to get everything she needed, so after a light lunch, we took a few hours to relax lakeside. Years earlier, Diana had given me exclusive permission to teach her recipe for mole poblano, but on that day, she talked me through the best ways to use it for weekday meals. This is the recipe I based on our conversation and that I quickly jotted down in my notebook (although I use my quick version of a mole poblano, and not her exhaustively researched recipe).

½ cup (120 ml) vegetable oil

Sixteen 6 inch (15 cm) store-bought corn tortillas

1 recipe Mole Poblano para Todos los Dias (page 478)

8 cups (910 grams) shredded cooked chicken (page 27) or rotisserie chicken

1½ cups (140 grams) crumbled goat cheese

½ cup (40 grams) Cotija cheese

2–3 large green onions, sliced

Preheat the oven to 450°F (230°C). Grease a large baking pan. Line a baking sheet with a metal cooling rack and set aside. Heat the vegetable oil in a skillet set over medium heat. Working with one tortilla at a time, dip each tortilla in the hot oil and heat it for about 10 to 15 seconds, just to soften it; remove it from the oil and place it on the prepared rack. Again working with one tortilla at a time, dip each tortilla in the mole sauce; place the tortilla on a large plate; fill with ½ cup (115 grams) of the shredded chicken, placing it across the center of the tortilla. Fold the tortilla in half and place it on the baking pan. Repeat with all of the tortillas. Ladle as much of the mole as you like over the tortillas; sprinkle with the cheeses and bake for 8 to 10 minutes or until bubbly. Sprinkle with the green onions and serve.

Ensalada Verde con Naranja y Puntas de Cacao

Green Salad with Orange and Cacao Nibs

Uruguay | Yield: Serves 6 | Difficulty Level: Easy | Total Cooking Time: 15 minutes

Cacao nibs are pieces of crushed cacao beans; they are crispy, bitter, and very chocolatey. They make a succulent addition to salads, where they provide crunch and a depth of flavor that enhances the taste of citrus. Uruguay is among the largest producers of cocoa nibs in Latin America. This salad is a great side dish to a perfectly seasoned steak (asado). Or, to turn it into a whole meal in itself, I often top it with grilled chicken or salmon.

1 pound (455 grams) mixed salad greens

Zest of 3 navel oranges

3 navel oranges, peeled and sectioned (juices reserved)

1 cup (115 grams) thinly sliced red onions

¼ cup (60 ml) white wine vinegar

2 tablespoons freshly squeezed orange juice (in addition to the reserved juices from the oranges, above)

2 teaspoons Dijon mustard

½ teaspoon fine sea salt, or more to taste

½ teaspoon freshly ground black pepper, or more to taste

1 cup (240 ml) extra-virgin olive oil

2 tablespoons cacao nibs (raw or toasted)

In a large bowl, toss the greens, zest, orange sections, and onions together. In a small bowl, whisk together the vinegar, orange juice, mustard, salt, and pepper. Slowly whisk in the oil until the dressing is creamy and emulsified. Toss the salad with the dressing and sprinkle with the cacao nibs; toss again and serve immediately.

Mole de Plátano de la Casa de Lito

Plantains in Chocolate-Chile Sauce

Guatemala | Yield: Serves 6–8 | Difficulty Level: Intermediate | Total Cooking Time: 40–45 minutes

Growing up, I never passed up an invitation to join my dad for breakfast at my grandfather's house. This meant waking up very early on weekend mornings and listening to long conversations on medical studies (both of them were renowned doctors). But the promise of hearty breakfasts made by my grandfather's cook was all the prodding I needed to jump out of bed. Breakfast included hearty huevos rancheros, café de esencia (old-fashioned coffee made from distilled coffee bean liquor), and this dessert, in which sweet plantains are bathed in spicy sauce made with chocolate and tropical fruits (yes, tomatoes, chiles, and bell peppers are all fruits!) and thickened with cookie crumbs. Most people think that chocolate-based moles only exist in Mexico, but historical evidence suggests that both the Aztecs and the Maya made similar concoctions (known as mollis) in pre-Columbian times. Sugar and sesame seeds (ajonjolí) native to Africa were imported as a result of the diaspora. Here is an example of how Indigenous Mesoamerican, African, and European culinary traditions have combined over time.

4 ripe plantains (about 2 pounds/910 grams)

Oil, for frying

4 large and very ripe plum tomatoes, sliced in half

2–3 pasilla chiles, rehydrated, stemmed, seeded, deveined, and chopped

One 4 inch (10 cm) piece of Mexican cinnamon (Ceylon)

4 tablespoons (45 grams) hulled pumpkin seeds (pepitas)

10 tablespoons (85 grams) sesame seeds, divided

1 ounce (30 grams) Maria cookies (or animal crackers), crushed into fine crumbs

One 10 ounce (280 gram) disc of Mexican chocolate, like Abuelita (see Note)

Fit a large baking pan with a metal cooling rack and set aside. Cut off both ends of the plantains with a sharp knife. Score the skin lengthwise (but don't score the flesh) and slide your thumb up and down under the peel until it comes off. With a knife, slice the plantains on the bias (about ½ inch/1 cm thick). In a large skillet, heat 1 to 2 inches of oil to 350°F (180°C) (or use a deep fryer according to the manufacturer's instructions). Working in batches, fry the plantains until golden, about 3 to 4 minutes (they will finish cooking in the sauce). Using a slotted spoon, transfer them to the prepared rack to drain. In a medium pot set over medium-high heat, combine the tomatoes, pasilla chiles, and cinnamon; add 4 cups (1 liter) cold water and bring to a boil. Lower the heat to medium and cook for 5 to 7 minutes or until the skins of the tomatoes have all split; remove from the heat and cool slightly. Strain the tomatoes through a sieve and into a large bowl; save the liquid for later and place all of the solids left in the strainer into the jar of a large blender to cool slightly. Toast the pumpkin seeds in a small nonstick skillet set over medium heat, stirring often, for 2 to 3 minutes (they will turn golden and puff up a bit); remove them to a plate to cool. In the same skillet, add all of the sesame seeds, and toast, for 1 to 2 minutes (careful, they will jump out at you) or just until fragrant; transfer to a plate to cool. Transfer half of the reserved liquid to the blender with the tomato mixture; add all of the pumpkin seeds, half of the sesame seeds (reserve the other half for garnish), and the crushed cookies. Blend until the mixture is completely smooth. Place the sauce in a medium nonstick pot set over medium-high heat; use the rest of the reserved liquid to rinse out the blender, and pour into the pot. Stir constantly as the sauce comes to a boil; reduce the heat, add the chocolate, and cook for 5 to 6 minutes, stirring constantly and keeping the sauce at a constant simmer, until the chocolate has melted completely. Add the fried plantains and continue cooking for 20 to 22 minutes or until the mole is thickened and hot.

Serve in bowls, topped with a generous amount of sauce, and sprinkle with the reserved toasted sesame seeds.

Note: Artisanal chocolate in Latin America is made with cacao liquor mixed with granulated sugar and shaped into tablets (traditionally round, but now found in different shapes). The most common brand is Abuelita, but there are many others. The discs come in a variety of sizes, so when measuring it's best to go entirely by their weight.

Note: To rehydrate the dried chiles, simply cover them in boiling water for 10 minutes; drain, cool, and use as the recipe directs.

Galletas de Chocolate Sencillas

Chocolate Cookies

Panama | Yield: Makes 18–20 cookies | Difficulty Level: Intermediate | Total Cooking Time: 1½ hours

North America has deep culinary ties to Panama due to the long-term business relationship between the countries forged by the building and governing of the Panama Canal. I have fond memories of my Panamanian school buddies sharing cookies like these when they carried extras in their lunchboxes. Pair them with a cup of steaming café con leche (coffee with milk), and enjoy a leisurely break.

12 ounces (340 grams) semisweet chocolate, finely chopped

2 cups (225 grams) all-purpose flour

¾ cup (70 grams) unsweetened cocoa powder

1 teaspoon baking soda

¼ teaspoon fine sea salt

1 cup (225 grams) unsalted butter, at room temperature

1½ cups (300 grams) packed brown sugar

3 large eggs, at room temperature

2 teaspoons pure vanilla extract

Before starting, line two large baking pans with parchment paper and preheat the oven to 300°F (150°C). Place the chopped chocolate in a bowl over a double boiler set over barely simmering water and melt it (do not let any water fall into the chocolate and do not let the water touch the bottom of the double boiler or the chocolate will seize). Set the melted chocolate aside and let it cool slightly, for 3 to 5 minutes. In the meantime, in a separate bowl, whisk together the flour, cocoa powder, baking soda, and salt. In the bowl of an electric mixer, cream the butter and the brown sugar to the consistency of peanut butter. Mix in the eggs, one at a time, and add the vanilla; incorporate the melted, cooled chocolate and mix well. Add the flour mixture a little at a time, beating well—you may have to finish it with a spatula if your mixer is not powerful enough. Chill the dough for 30 minutes. Use a large #16 (4 tablespoon) ice cream scoop to scoop batter onto the prepared pans, leaving 3 inches (7.5 cm) of room between each scoop so the cookies don't stick together as they bake. Bake for 18 to 20 minutes or until their surfaces look cracked. Cool the cookies on the baking pans for 1 minute; then transfer to a wire rack to cool completely.

VARIATION: Ice cream sandwiches, anyone? Do as I do, and sandwich two of these cookies together with a generous scoop of ice cream in between; freeze them until solid. Try filling them with dulce de leche, chocolate, coffee, coconut, corn, avocado or vanilla ice cream—all popular flavors throughout Latin America.

Pudín (Budín) de Pan con Chocolate

Chocolate Bread Pudding

Costa Rica | Yield: Serves 8 | Difficulty Level: Easy | Total Cooking Time: 1½–8 hours (includes soaking time)

Latin cooks have a long tradition of using every last bit of food in the kitchen as part of what I call a "waste not" cuisine. Whatever odds and ends of fruits (dried or fresh), milks or creams, sugar, and sweet spices you have on hand can make it into one of these bread puddings.

8 cups day-old crusty white bread (such as baguette), cut into 1 inch (2.5 cm) pieces

4 ounces (115 grams) semisweet chocolate, chopped

1½ cups (360 ml) heavy whipping cream

2 cups (480 ml) whole milk

4 eggs

½ cup (100 grams) white granulated sugar

¼ teaspoon fine sea salt

1 teaspoon pure vanilla extract

1 tablespoon unsalted butter

Confectioner's sugar, for garnish

Place the bread and chocolate in a large bowl. In a medium bowl, beat together the cream, milk, eggs, sugar, salt, and vanilla. Pour the mixture over the bread and chocolate, stirring well to combine. Cover and refrigerate for 30 minutes (or up to 8 hours). Preheat the oven to 350°F (180°C). Grease a 9 x 13 inch (23 x 33 cm) baking dish with the butter. Pour the bread mixture into the dish and distribute evenly. Bake the pudding for 50 to 55 minutes or until it's set in the middle and the top is golden brown. Allow to cool for 10 minutes before serving. Cut into squares, dust with confectioner's sugar, and serve.

Bolo Brigadeiro

Chocolate Cake

Brazil | Yield: Makes one 10 inch (25 cm) cake | Difficulty Level: Intermediate | Total Cooking Time: 2 hours (includes cooling)

Brigadeiros are the gooey, chocolatey national candy of Brazil. Here, they inspire the filling and icing for a decadent chocolate cake, a favorite for birthday parties. I suggest you place the cake on a large platter with sides, because the topping is messy—it's a casual dessert, after all—and will drip down, pooling around the base. Serve with milk, coffee, tea, or sherry; this cake also goes magnificently well with vanilla ice cream.

FOR THE CAKE

2 cups (260 grams) all-purpose flour

1 cup (80 grams) unsweetened cocoa powder

2 teaspoons baking powder

1 teaspoon baking soda

½ teaspoon fine sea salt

1 cup (225 grams) unsalted butter, at room temperature

2 cups (425 grams) white granulated sugar

4 large eggs

2 teaspoons pure vanilla extract

1⅜ cups (330 ml) whole milk

FOR THE TOPPING

Two 14 ounce (396 gram) cans sweetened condensed milk

¾ cup (115 grams) cocoa powder

1 tablespoon unsalted butter, at room temperature, divided

¾ cup (15 grams) unsweetened shredded coconut

¾ cup (115 grams) chocolate sprinkles (see Note)

To make the cake, preheat the oven to 350°F (180°C). Grease two 10 x 2 inch (25 x 5 cm) round cake pans and fit the bottoms with parchment paper. In a medium bowl, whisk together the flour, cocoa, baking powder, baking soda, and salt. In a large bowl, using an electric mixer, beat together the butter and sugar until it's light and fluffy, about 4 minutes. Reduce the speed of the mixer to low; slowly add the eggs, one at a time, beating well after each addition. Add the vanilla and beat until combined. Add a third of the flour mixture and half of the milk, beating well; follow with another third of the flour mixture, then add the rest of the milk; finish by adding the remaining third of the flour mixture (scrape down the sides of the bowl as needed until the batter is smooth). Pour the batter into the prepared pans. Bake for 40 to 45 minutes or until a toothpick inserted into the center comes out clean and the cake bounces back when pressed lightly. Cool the cakes in the pan for 10 to 15 minutes before unmolding onto a cooling rack; cool completely before icing.

To make the icing: Place the condensed milk in a medium saucepan over low heat and stir to loosen, about 1 minute. Gradually sift the cocoa powder into the condensed milk, stirring well between additions (it will take about 5 minutes to incorporate it all); add the butter, stirring until smooth. Increase the heat to medium and continue cooking, stirring constantly and making sure to scrape down the bottom and sides of the saucepan, until the mixture begins to bubble, about 2 to 3 minutes (be careful not to burn it). Immediately remove from the heat. Remove ½ cup (60 ml) of the chocolate icing to a medium bowl and combine it with the coconut to make the filling for the cake. Place one of the cakes on a large platter, top side down (flat side up). Spread all of the coconut filling over the top. Top with the second cake, in order to form two layers. Frost the entire cake with the remaining chocolate icing, making sure to spread it to cover the sides of the cake. Sprinkle the cake with the sprinkles.

Note: Chocolate sprinkles are also known as jimmies and can be found in the baking section of most grocery stores. Work quickly after the frosting is made or it will solidify before it goes onto the cake. This cake can sit at room temperature, but it can also be refrigerated for longer storage (up to 1 week).

Chocolate Caliente

Hot Chocolate

Mexico | Yield: Serves 6 | Difficulty Level: Easy | Total Cooking Time: 15 minutes

When they arrived in the sixteenth century, Spanish conquistadores found that Aztec and Mayan royalty enjoyed a cold, bitter, and foamy chocolate concoction seasoned with plenty of spicy chiles. When Europeans removed the heat and instead introduced sugar into the equation, chocolate became a world sensation. In Mexico, the cloistered nuns of the colonial period are credited with flavoring chocolate tablets with sugar, almonds, vanilla, and canela (Ceylon cinnamon), in the same way it's still made today. However, while some nuns (like the Carmelites) considered drinking chocolate to be sinful, others, like the Jerónimas, thought it the ideal beverage for days of fasting. Thankfully, modern-day Latin Americans do not require a religious absolution or a special occasion to drink cups of steamy hot chocolate. We drink it on rainy days, on birthdays, at breakfast or at the merienda (coffee break), during the advent season; for many of us, this hot, thick, invigorating, and rich beverage is an everyday indulgence.

6 cups (1.4 liters) whole milk, plus more if needed	6 ounces (170 grams) Mexican chocolate such as Abuelita (3 discs), roughly chopped	1 vanilla bean, split in half lengthwise

Pour the milk into a large pot and add the chocolate and vanilla bean. Heat, over medium-high heat, stirring until the chocolate has dissolved completely. Use a wire whisk or a molinillo (the traditional turned wood whisk used in Latin America) to whisk until the drink comes to a boil and becomes frothy; if it's too thick for your taste, add more milk. Remove the vanilla bean and divide the hot chocolate between six mugs. Serve immediately.

Note: If you can't find Mexican chocolate discs, use 4 ounces (115 grams) bittersweet chocolate instead and add sugar, to taste. If you don't have vanilla beans, substitute 2 teaspoons pure vanilla extract.

COCONUT

The coconut is the largest nut in the world. Native to Asia (although some say they are also indigenous to the Caribbean), coconuts started their world travels with Arabs, who were the first to take them to Europe. The Portuguese actually gave them the name *coco*, which means "head," as the round shape and the three eyes of each coconut reminded them of a skull. To this day, many Latin Americans refer to their heads as "cocos."

European elites became enamored of the exotic nut, not only for its flavorful water or creamy flesh but also for its shell. No matter how hard Europeans tried to grow coconuts, the climate prevented it. That didn't stop the wealthy class from vying to collect them; so coconuts began to be imported from afar. As coconuts gained value, they also became a status symbol. Their brown shells were buffed and polished, shaped into fancy goblets, adorned with jewels, and even mounted on gold pedestals.

The Iberian colonizers (those from Portugal and Spain) were responsible for importing the first coconuts to the Americas, and coconut began to appear in dessert recipes during the colonial period. As the decades rolled by and coconut became ubiquitous in coastal cooking, its milk found its way into rice preparations, stews, and soups.

When it comes to cooking with coconut in the Americas, the most palpable influence comes from Africa, specifically from the Garifuna, the Afro-Caribbean descendants of Garinagu Africans, who resisted the British colonialists. In 1797 they were expelled from Saint Vincent (an island in the Minor Antilles) and exiled to the islands off the coast of Honduras. Garifunas made their home in Belize, Honduras, Guatemala, and Nicaragua. It is believed that they established their first settlement somewhere in Livingston, Puerto Barrios (Guatemala), around 1820 (just a year before Guatemala gained its own independence).

The Garifuna gave us many recipes that use coconut as a main ingredient. I can best describe theirs as a cuisine that blends African, Caribbean, Spanish, Arab, and pre-Hispanic cultures into one. Their close ties to coastal Latin America have given their cuisine a great array of seafood dishes as well. Perhaps the most famous is rice and beans: a mixture of red beans and white rice cooked with red bell peppers, sofrito, and coconut milk (see my version from Belize on page 344). You'll find it served alongside cabbage slaw, beet salad, and fried plantains in all of the towns and countries where African influences are most strongly felt.

You'll find lots of coconut recipes scattered throughout this book, but these are the essential—historically grounded—ones every cook must try.

Panes de Coco

Coconut Bread Rolls

Honduras | Yield: Makes 12 rolls | Difficulty Level: Intermediate | Total Cooking Time: 3–3½ hours

These dense, semisweet bread rolls are the perfect accompaniment to many dishes from Latin America. They are particularly delicious for breakfast, or served alongside other recipes that have coconut-y notes, such as Tapado (page 369). I know many people are intimidated by yeast and the mystery of rising dough. I developed this recipe years ago, precisely so I could teach students how to bake fearlessly. Believe me, once you master it, you'll be baking these rolls on a regular basis. They are my favorite to toast in the morning, topped with mashed avocado and scrambled eggs. Buen provecho!

½ cup (120 ml) warm water (90–100°F/32–37°C)

3 tablespoons (40 grams) granulated sugar

1 package active dry yeast (¼ ounce/7 grams/2¼ teaspoons)

½ cup (40 grams) unsweetened shredded coconut

3½ cups (400 grams) all-purpose flour, plus extra for dusting and kneading

½ teaspoon fine sea salt

1 cup (240 ml) canned unsweetened coconut milk

3 tablespoons (40 grams) unsalted butter, softened

Line two baking sheets with parchment paper and set aside. Combine the warm water, sugar, and yeast in a large bowl. Stir to dissolve and let sit until foamy, about 10 minutes. Add the shredded coconut and let sit for 5 more minutes. In a large bowl, stir together the flour and salt; make a well in the center. Pour the yeast mixture and coconut milk into the well, stirring until the dough starts to come together. Turn the dough out onto a floured surface and spread it out. Dot the pieces of butter on the surface and knead them into the dough. Continue kneading, sprinkling the surface with more flour, until the dough is no longer sticky but smooth, and indentations made with your finger bounce back, about 4 to 5 minutes. Bring the dough together into a ball; return it to the bowl, and let it rest, covered with a damp kitchen cloth, in a warm place until doubled, about 1½ hours.

Divide the dough into 12 equal parts, about ¼ cup (75 grams) each. Roll each piece into a ball, and place each roll onto the prepared baking sheets (touching sides if you like them to be soft or separate if you like them with crusts). Cover the rolls with a damp towel and let them rise a second time, for 30 minutes, while you preheat the oven to 350°F (180°C). Bake for 25 to 30 minutes or until the tops are a light golden color; they should sound hollow when tapped on the bottom. Transfer to cooling racks and cool slightly before serving:

Note: These freeze beautifully; let them cool completely before transferring them to freezer-safe containers. Freeze for up to 2 months. To thaw, place the buns on cooling racks and let them thaw at room temperature for 1 hour; reheat in a low oven until warm and serve.

Tortillas de Harina y Coco

Wheat Flour and Coconut Tortillas

Honduras | Yield: Makes 12 tortillas | Difficulty Level: Intermediate | Total Cooking Time: 45 minutes

These flour tortillas from Tegucigalpa are as fun to make as they are delicious to eat and very different from others you will taste anywhere else because they represent a unique melding of world cultures. The African culinary traditions present throughout the Latin Caribbean are evident in the widespread use of coconut milk (particularly in the northern part of Honduras). However, what surprises many people is that Middle Eastern culinary influences are also huge. That is because Arab and Palestinian migrants (known as "los Turcos," because their passports were Turkish) began to settle in Honduras during the 1890s. Not surprising, then, is that these tortillas are thicker than the regular flour tortillas you'll find (both in other parts of Honduras and in northern Mexico, the other place where wheat tortillas abound) and that they resemble pita bread. In fact, when you flip them over as they cook, they puff up just like pita do when baked—if they don't do this for you on your first attempt, don't worry, as it takes practice; next time, try rolling them out just a bit thinner and give it another shot.

5½ cups (685 grams) all-purpose flour

2 teaspoons baking powder

1 teaspoon fine sea salt

¼ cup (40 grams) chilled lard or vegetable shortening, cut into dice, plus more for shaping the dough

One 13.5 ounce (398 ml) can unsweetened coconut milk

Place the flour, baking powder, and salt in a large bowl and stir to combine. Add the lard or shortening and, using a pastry cutter, cut it into the flour (or rub it between your fingers) until the mixture resembles coarse sand. Slowly add the coconut milk, stirring the dough with your hand; as soon as it starts coming together, begin to knead it softly, until it comes together into a ball. Turn the dough onto a lightly floured surface and knead it for 2 to 3 minutes or until it's smooth. Shape the dough into a ball; flour your working surface again lightly and invert the bowl over it. Let the dough rest for 10 minutes. Divide the dough into 12 equal pieces (about ⅓ cup/85 grams each). Roll each piece, tucking the dough underneath into a knot, then rolling it under the palm of your hand into a smooth ball the way you'd shape rolls. Rub your hands with some lard and roll each ball to give it a thin film; place on the lightly floured surface and cover them with a clean towel. Let them rest for 20 minutes. Preheat a griddle over medium-high heat, while you shape the tortillas; dampen a clean kitchen towel and set it in a bowl (or basket). Working with one ball at a time, roll each one out with a rolling pin, on a floured surface (see "How to Roll Out Pie and Tart Dough" on page 38), until it is 8 inches (20 cm) in diameter. Working with one tortilla at a time, set it on the griddle and cook for 1½ minutes on the first side or until you can see golden flecks on the bottom (it should form bubbles as it cooks). Flip it over to the other side (use a spatula, if it's easier) and cook for 1½ minutes on the second side or until you can see golden flecks on the bottom (some tortillas may inflate as they cook). Turn it over to the first side again and cook for 20 seconds. Wrap each tortilla in the prepared towel (they will steam, which will keep them soft and warm as you work). Repeat with the remaining tortillas (if, as you cook, the tortillas begin to brown too quickly, lower the heat to medium). Serve hot.

Note: Reheating these tortillas is easiest in the microwave; simply wrap them in a couple of moist paper towels and zap for a few seconds, until hot. They also freeze beautifully, for up to 2 months.

Troubleshooting Your Rolling Skills · Whether you're shaping dough for pizza, fougazza, tarts, pascualinas, empanada discs, or flour tortillas, remember these easy steps:

- Lightly flour a clean surface and the rolling pin you will use.
- Start with your dough rolled into a disc.
- Use your hands to press the disc down lightly to flatten it out and make it easier to roll.
- Draw an "Equator" line (imaginary or lightly with a knife) across the center of the dough. Take a rolling pin and set it on top of the equator line. Press down and let the pin rotate as you push it, rolling the dough away from you to the top of the disc.
- Now, take the rolling pin and set it on top of the equator line again. This time, roll the dough toward the bottom of the disc.
- Give the dough a one-quarter turn, making sure to keep the board lightly floured, and repeat, rolling up, then down.
- Continue turning the dough one quarter of the way at a time, and rolling from the middle upwards and then from the middle downward. As you turn and roll, you'll form a perfect round. Continue until you have a round the size that you need.

Arroz con Coco

Coconut Rice

Various Countries | Yield: Serves 4–6 | Difficulty Level: Easy | Total Cooking Time: 25 minutes

Recipes like this one are popular in most coastal areas of Latin America. From Guatemala, Honduras, Nicaragua, Colombia, and Venezuela all the way down to Brazil, you'll find as many renditions as there are cooks. I learned to make this aromatic version during a recent visit to Cartagena de las Indias in Colombia. It's quick and easy, which makes it particularly suited for everyday meals, and it's my go-to method when I want to dress up rice for a special occasion.

2 cups (455 grams) long-grain white rice

One 13.5 ounce (398 ml) can unsweetened coconut milk

1 teaspoon fine sea salt

½ teaspoon ground coriander

¼ teaspoon freshly ground black pepper

¼ teaspoon ground cumin

1 bay leaf

¼ cup (20 grams) chopped fresh Italian parsley

¼ cup (20 grams) unsweetened coconut flakes

In a medium Dutch oven, combine the rice, coconut milk, and 2 cups (480 ml) water; stir well. Add the salt, coriander, pepper, cumin, and bay leaf. Set over medium-high heat and bring to a boil. Cover immediately, reduce heat to low, and simmer, undisturbed, for 20 minutes. Uncover; remove the bay leaf and fluff the rice with a fork. Serve, topped with the parsley and unsweetened coconut flakes.

Note: As a variation, add some chopped dried fruits and/or chopped nuts right before serving.

Tembleque

Coconut Pudding

Puerto Rico | Yield: Serves 6 | Difficulty Level: Easy | Cooking Time: 3–8 hours (includes chilling time)

Beloved in Puerto Rico, this creamy coconut milk dessert is fragrant with vanilla. It is a very unassuming recipe, a simple ending to any meal. It also makes a filling snack for kids when they get back from school, especially on hot and humid summer days. If you prefer, make it in individual ramekins or serving dishes, which makes for a more elegant presentation, particularly when topped with sliced mangoes, or with an array of mixed berries.

One 13.5 ounce (398 ml) can unsweetened coconut milk

½ cup (120 ml) whole milk

½ cup (70 grams) cornstarch

½ cup (100 grams) white granulated sugar

¼ teaspoon fine sea salt

1 teaspoon pure vanilla extract

1 teaspoon ground cinnamon

2 cups (1 pint) berries (any kind) (optional)

In a medium pot, whisk together the coconut milk, milk, cornstarch, sugar, and salt. Set over medium heat and, using a wooden spoon, stir constantly until it thickens to the consistency of pudding, about 6 to 8 minutes. Remove from the heat and stir in the vanilla. Pour into an 8 x 8 inch (20 x 20 cm) casserole dish. Set an 8 x 8 inch (20 x 20 cm) piece of parchment paper directly over the pudding (to prevent it from forming a skin); cover with plastic wrap. Let it sit at room temperature for 20 to 30 minutes to cool slightly. Refrigerate for at least 2 hours or overnight. When ready to serve, slide a knife around the edges of the casserole dish to loosen the tembleque. Cut it into 6 squares. Use a spatula to place each square onto plates and sprinkle with cinnamon; serve immediately, with berries, if using.

Brigadeiros Brancos

Coconut Milk Candy

Brazil | Yield: Makes 30 candies | Difficulty Level: Intermediate | Total Cooking Time: 1 hour

All I'm going to say about this gooey, sticky, sweet coconut candy is that I bet you won't be able to eat only one.

One 14 ounce (396 gram) can sweetened condensed milk

½ cup (50 grams) confectioners' sugar, plus more for dusting, as desired

⅓ cup (30 grams) powdered whole milk (such as Nido)

3 tablespoons (45 grams) unsalted butter, divided

½ teaspoon pure vanilla extract

Pinch of fine sea salt

1 cup (70 grams) unsweetened coconut flakes

Set a half pan sheet aside. Pour the condensed milk into a small saucepan set over medium heat. Slowly sift in the confectioners' sugar and powdered milk and stir until combined. Add 1 tablespoon of butter, the vanilla, and salt. Stir constantly until the mixture comes to a boil, about 4 to 5 minutes. Immediately lower the heat to low and continue stirring constantly, making sure to scrape down the sides of the pot, and the bottom, too, until the mixture has the texture of pudding and leaves a trail in the bottom of the pot when stirred, about 7 to 8 minutes. Pour the mixture onto the reserved half pan sheet; allow it to cool completely, about 35 to 40 minutes. Place the coconut flakes on a shallow plate. Making sure your hands are well buttered so the coconut can stick to the candy, take spoonfuls of the cooled mixture and roll them into balls; roll each ball in the coconut and set each into a paper (or foil) petit four cup. If desired, dust them with a bit of confectioners' sugar. Store in an airtight container for up to 2 weeks. Serve at room temperature.

Tartas de Coco

Coconut Tarts

Belize | Yield: Makes two 9 inch (23 cm) tarts | Difficulty Level: Intermediate | Total Cooking Time: 1½–2 hours

These tropical tarts are sweet, sticky, and sinfully delicious. You'll find miniature versions served in many restaurants in Belize, but home cooks usually bake it as a whole pie. Coconut candy is popular throughout Latin America, and similar desserts made with coconut and sweetened milk but without a crust are called cocadas. This recipe makes two smaller tarts. Eat one now and save one for later (they last up to 4 days at room temperature) or gift one to a friend. I like to pair these with chopped tropical fruit or berries.

1 recipe Masa Básica para
Pies y Tartas (page 35)

4 eggs, lightly beaten

One 12 ounce (354 ml) can
evaporated milk

One 14 ounce (396 gram) can
sweetened condensed milk

1 teaspoon pure vanilla extract

½ teaspoon freshly grated nutmeg

Pinch of fine sea salt

4 cups (300 grams) unsweetened
shredded or flaked coconut

Confectioners' sugar,
for garnish (optional)

Follow the tart shell recipe and blind-bake two 9 inch (23 cm) pie shells. Preheat the oven to 425°F (220°C) and place a rack in the middle. In a large bowl, stir together the eggs, evaporated milk, sweetened condensed milk, vanilla, nutmeg, and salt; use a spatula to stir in the coconut. Divide the filling between both prepared pie shells. Bake for 20 minutes. Reduce the heat to 350°F (180°C) and continue baking for 15 to 20 minutes or until the tops are a dark golden color and the middle is set completely. Remove from the oven and set on racks to cool completely. Sprinkle with confectioners' sugar, if desired, when ready to serve.

SUGAR AND VANILLA

El que miel da a tus hijos, tu boca endulza.
(He who feeds honey to your children, sweetens your mouth.)

—Old folk proverb

Sugar, not gold, was the main reason that Europeans conquered the American continents. The desire to control the world's sugar production had already transformed men into beasts willing to enslave fellow humans, well before anyone thought that there was land worth exploring on the other side of the Atlantic.

The taste for sugar started a bitter mercantile war between European powers. One of these countries was set to become the world's top producer, but at the cost of countless lives.

Before the foreign invasion, the Indigenous peoples of the Americas used wild honey and corn and maguey syrups to sweeten their foods. Sugar, native to India, was introduced to Europe by the Arabs, who also invented the technique for pressing the sweet juices of sugarcane and processing them into a solid.

Up until the start of the fifteenth century, Venice controlled the European sugar market, but the Portuguese explorer Vasco da Gama erased that advantage by discovering a new route to India, which gave the Iberian country the upper hand. Other European nations did not take this sitting down; thus started a war for control of the sugar route that would ultimately lead the Spanish, Portuguese, French, and British to colonize American lands, to destroy entire ancient civilizations, and to enslave countless human beings, forcefully transporting them to work across the world.

The Spaniards brought sugar and its sweet promise to the Americas, but it was Hernán Cortés, who grew sugarcane on his farms at Tlatenango and Tuxtlas de Veracruz, who first introduced the method for transforming unrefined sugar into cones, called piloncillo, papelón, or panela. This method allowed for the mass production of unrefined sugar and put it in the hands of the populace. To this day, many Latin American recipes are still made with unrefined sugar, and not with the white sugar most other countries depend on.

Even though sugar is not an ingredient native to the Americas, it certainly became the region's most important export during the colonial period. Latin America was prime territory for sugar production, and it became the world epicenter of sugar plantations (called ingenios) and rum distilleries.

White sugar was expensive. At the start of the sixteenth century, most Latin American countries had special guilds that controlled the production of sweets and candies. Called gremios de confiteros or gremios de los dulceros, these groups in essence decided who could make or sell any sweets. At first, only very wealthy people could afford sugar and candies, and nuns and convents that depended on selling whatever they could produce in order to pay for their maintenance (along with the donations of rich patrons) turned to selling food.

As such, some of the most famous Latin American dessert recipes were created in the hidden kitchens of nunneries, where Indigenous women, Andalucian nuns (many of Arab origin), the wealthy daughters of European families, and the enslaved African women in charge of their care melded their cooking traditions. Some of the wealthiest inhabitants of the convents, the daughters of important families who paid for them to be kept "pure" for marriage, had their own kitchens where their food was prepared by servants (not every woman there was wealthy, so not everyone had servants). The culinary exchange that occurred within those small kitchens invariably ended up in the main kitchens, or cocinas centrales.

The candies and sweets from this period were marked by both Spanish and Arab influences, such as the use of dried fruits and nuts. Soon, convents that had already become famous for their comida colonial—recipes of the colonial period—began to compete for business by specializing in sweet confections. Recipes became closely guarded secrets that one group of nuns hid from the others so they could vie for customers. This is how some convents ended up specializing in egg-based sweets like yemitas and huevos chimbo, while others became the favored confectioners of milk candies such as canillitas de leche and yet others became renowned for their fruit jellies and fruit pastes, known as ates.

There was also another plant that seduced the palates of newcomers to the Americas. Vanilla, the fruit of the orchid flour of the *Vanilla planifolia* fragrance plant of Mesoamerica, proved to be the perfect ingredient to pair with sugar. Vanilla added a flowery essence that enhanced the flavor of sugar. The fact that vanilla was not easy to harvest made it even more desirable to the upper classes in Europe. To this day, the flowers of this expensive (second only to saffron) spice must be pollinated on the one day that blooms appear—either by hand, or by the abeja Melipona, a rare bee. The pods that result from pollination (vanilla beans) hold thousands of miniature seeds and sticky vanillin crystals within them. At first, the pods are green; they must be dried in the sun and allowed to turn a deep brown color before they become the fragrantly delicate elixir we have all grown to love.

The recipes in this chapter feature one or both of these prized ingredients as part of their formula. I've even given you an easy recipe to produce your own vanilla extract—something I do whenever I can get my hands on precious dried vanilla beans—so you can always have some ready. Vanilla and sugar are usually paired together in Latin American desserts. If you're ever tempted to lift a glass of milk to new heights, stir in a couple of drops of pure vanilla extract and some sugar; that's all that everyday milk needs to become a decadent indulgence.

Homemade Vanilla Extract · Making vanilla extract is easy as long as you have fresh, pliable, and dark brown vanilla beans to begin with. Of the three major varieties, Madagascar, Tahitian, and Mexican, I prefer Mexican, which offers a spicier flavor than the others. The formula is easy. Split three to four vanilla beans in half lengthwise to expose the seeds, leaving the tops attached; place them inside a clean glass jar with a tight-fitting lid (ideally the jar should have the capacity to hold 2 cups/450 ml of liquid). Fill the jar with enough vodka to cover the beans completely. Cover the jar tightly and let it sit at room temperature, in a cool, dark place for 6 months, shaking it vigorously once a week. Once done infusing, it will keep for a year at full flavor (it will keep longer but begin to lose its potency). If you don't like to see the vanilla seeds, you may strain them through a fine mesh and use only the clear extract. I like mine to retain the seeds so I skip this step altogether. I keep the vanilla beans in the extract for the duration, but you may also remove them, if you prefer. Don't discard the beans. Dry them off on a paper towel for a couple of days and when dried, stir them into a bowl of sugar to infuse it with vanilla flavor.

Los Buñuelos de Leonor

Fried Dough with Syrup

Central America | Yield: Serves 4–6 (makes about 24 pieces) |
Difficulty Level: Intermediate | Total Cooking Time: 30–40 minutes

These small doughnuts are drenched in a syrup that renders them delightfully sweet. Buñuelos (pronounced *boo-nyu-eh-lohs*) are the dessert of choice after a heavy meal throughout Central America. In Mexico, they are flat and crispy, but in most other countries, they are made of choux pastry and puffy and hollow, like these. The Spaniards learned to fry dough from the Ottomans, and Africans and Ashkenazi and Sephardic Jews popularized the technique throughout Latin America. Do not confuse them with churros, which, although also made of choux pastry, are shaped into long cigar forms, which renders them very crispy; buñuelos are much lighter. This recipe is adapted from one by my dear friend Leonor de Minondo, who has made them for me in her home in Guatemala.

FOR THE SYRUP

1 cup (200 grams) white granulated sugar

5 stars of anise

1 Ceylon or Mexican cinnamon (canela) stick

FOR THE BUÑUELOS

One 3 inch (7.5 cm) strip of lemon or orange zest (optional)

Pinch of fine sea salt

⅓ cup (80 grams) unsalted butter, diced

1 cup (115 grams) all-purpose flour

4 eggs

Vegetable oil, for frying

Make the syrup first: In a medium pot set over medium-high heat, combine 3 cups (720 ml) water, the sugar, anise, and cinnamon; bring to a simmer and stir until all of the sugar is dissolved. Lower the heat and continue simmering for 20 minutes, then remove from the heat; keep warm until ready to use.

To make the buñuelos: Fit a large baking sheet with a metal cooling rack and set aside. Place 1 cup (240 ml) water, the lemon zest (if using), and salt in a medium pot set over medium-high heat. As soon as it reaches a simmer, use tongs to remove the zest and add the butter, mixing to dissolve. Add all of the flour at once and mix well with a wooden spoon, stirring until the mixture begins to pull away from the sides and bottom of the pan and forms a ball (about 45 to 50 seconds). Transfer this mixture to a large bowl and let it cool slightly for 2 to 3 minutes. Whisk in one egg at a time, adding the next egg only when the first one has been incorporated (at first, the dough will seem to break down and will become watery, but as each egg is whisked in, it will come together again). Heat 2-3 inches (5-7.5 cm) of oil in a medium pot until it reaches 360°F (180°C). Working in batches, take tablespoonfuls (I use a tiny ice cream scoop) of the dough and carefully drop them into the oil. Fry them, turning with a slotted spoon, until they're puffed up (they will almost double in size) and golden on all sides, about 4 to 5 minutes. Remove the buñuelos from the oil and transfer them to the prepared rack to drain while you finish the rest. Serve them hot in small bowls, with the syrup on the side.

Note: Be careful when you're frying, as the buñuelos will splatter a bit. Stand at a distance and use a medium-sized pot. Work in batches of 4 or 5 only. Halfway through frying, they will inflate and split in the middle; after this, they will continue to grow in size. You can make the syrup ahead; cool it completely, strain it, and refrigerate for up to 3 days. Warm it up in a pot before serving.

Flan

Egg Custard with Caramel Sauce

Various Countries | Yield: Serves 4–6 | Difficulty Level: Intermediate | Total Cooking Time: 2 hours

Much has been written about the painful side of colonization, the sadness- and strife-filled history of the world that was once divided between the conquerors and the conquered. I have spent my entire career exploring the silver lining: the delicious culinary evolution that has resulted. This is a beloved ending to any meal, and there are many interpretations: some of us add chocolate, coffee, or coconut to the custard, and some of us are purists and still make it only with sugar and vanilla. This is my version of flan. I make it in a Savarin pan, which allows it to rise only to ¾ inch (1.90 cm), because it cooks evenly and I like mine to be flat. However, ramekins work for individual portions, as does a square or round Pyrex dish. Flan is best enjoyed the day it's made but can be kept in the refrigerator, lightly covered with plastic wrap, for up to 2 days.

FOR THE CUSTARD

5 eggs, lightly beaten

½ cup (100 grams) white granulated sugar

1½ cups (325 ml) whole milk

½ teaspoon pure vanilla extract

FOR THE CARAMEL

¾ cup (150 grams) white granulated sugar

Boiling water

Place a rack in the middle of the oven and preheat the oven to 325°F (160°C). To make the custard: In a large bowl, use a fork to stir together the eggs, sugar, milk, and vanilla, making sure not to whip too much air into the mixture (or your flan will have holes; for this purpose, make sure it doesn't get frothy). Set aside and make the caramel. Place the sugar in a nonstick skillet set over medium heat. Do not stir—rather, allow the sugar to melt slowly, swirling the pan only occasionally, until the sugar is completely melted and reaches a light amber color, about 6 to 8 minutes. Remove from the heat and pour the caramel onto a metal flan pan or into ramekins (fluted pans work well). Swirl the flan pan around so the caramel covers the entire bottom. Place the flan pan inside a high-sided oven-safe baking dish; slowly, pour the egg mixture through a sieve and into the pan, over the caramel (using a fine sieve ensures a no-lump flan). Cover the flan with foil. Transfer the pan to the oven and carefully fill the bottom baking dish with boiling water; it should come up about 1 inch (2.5 cm) on the sides of the flan pan. Place it in the oven and bake, undisturbed, for 40 to 45 minutes or until it is barely set when you shake it (a knife inserted into the center should come out clean). Remove from the oven and let it cool at room temperature for about 35 minutes. Use a knife to loosen the sides of the flan from the mold, being careful not to break it. Unmold onto a platter (choose one with high sides so the caramel can collect) and chill, until ready to serve, at least 1 hour.

Note: For a taller flan, double the recipe for the custard and bake for 1 full hour or until set in the middle (a knife inserted into the center should come out clean).

Tip: Hot caramel is extremely dangerous and can burn skin easily. It's imperative that you make it away from children and pets. Never touch hot caramel; use oven mitts to swirl the pan, and work gently with it. Let the pan cool fully before letting it soak in water to clean.

Manjar de Leche

Milk Pudding

Central America | Yield: Serves 6–8 | Difficulty Level: Easy | Total Cooking Time: 3 hours (includes chilling time)

This sweet, velvety, eggless pudding is one of the simplest desserts to make; simply stir and heat until it comes together. I love to serve it during the summer months with plenty of fresh fruit. Berries, mangoes, kiwis, carambola fruit, and pineapple pair particularly beautifully with it.

4 cups (960 ml) whole milk, or more as desired

½ cup (60 grams) cornstarch

1½ cups (300 grams) white granulated sugar

¼ teaspoon fine sea salt

One 4 inch (10 cm) stick Mexican cinnamon (canela), tied in a piece of cheesecloth to prevent breaking

½ teaspoon pure vanilla extract

½ teaspoon ground cinnamon

In a large nonstick saucepan, whisk together 4 cups (960 ml) of the milk, the cornstarch, sugar, and salt, until everything is thoroughly dissolved. Place the cinnamon in the cheesecloth in the middle of the pot. Set over medium-high heat and cook, stirring constantly with a wooden spoon, until the mixture comes to a soft boil and thickens to the consistency of soft pudding, about 8 to 10 minutes. Remove from the heat and discard the cinnamon stick; stir in the vanilla. If it's too thick for your liking (I prefer mine thick), add more milk, stirring vigorously until smooth. Transfer the pudding to a clean serving bowl; place a layer of plastic wrap or parchment paper directly on top of it to prevent it from forming a skin, and refrigerate for at least 2 hours or overnight. To serve, remove the pudding from the refrigerator, peel off the plastic or paper, and sift the ground cinnamon evenly over the top.

Arroz con Leche de la Abuela

Rice Pudding with Dulce de Leche

Various Countries | Yield: Serves 8 | Difficulty Level: Easy | Total Cooking Time: 1 hour

Few desserts are homier than creamy rice pudding. This traditional sweet can be traced back to the times of Al-Andalus (the name given to the former Islamic states in Spain and Portugal, when Muslims ruled areas of the Iberian Peninsula) back in the eleventh century. The dessert stuck to Spanish cuisine (no pun intended) and appears in compendiums of written recipes dating back to sixteenth-century Latin America. Today, you'll find interpretations that include dried fruit, nuts, cardamom, and brown sugar. I adapted this version, embellished with creamy dulce de leche, from one given to me by my niece Marcela Jongezoon, one of the most promising chefs and culinary entrepreneurs in Guatemala. Serve this pudding warm or cold, as desired.

1 Mexican cinnamon stick (canela)

2 whole cloves

2 cups (370 grams) uncooked long-grain white rice

One 12 ounce (354 ml) can evaporated milk

½ cup (115 grams) white granulated sugar, or more to taste

1 cup (240 ml) almond, rice, or coconut milk

8 ounces (225 grams) thick Dulce de Leche o Arequipe Casero (about 1 generous cup) (page 516), plus more for serving

Bring the cinnamon stick and cloves to a boil in 4 cups (960 ml) water in a medium pot set over medium-high heat; cover, lower the heat slightly, and simmer for 5 to 8 minutes. Remove the cloves with a slotted spoon and discard. Add the rice and bring it to a simmer, uncovered; continue simmering over medium heat, stirring often, until the rice is softened but still has a little bite, about 10 to 12 minutes (the liquid will have reduced and thickened but will not have evaporated completely; if it's evaporating too quickly, reduce the heat slightly). Stir in the evaporated milk and sugar; bring the liquid back to a simmer over medium heat and continue simmering, stirring often (being careful not to let it burn; you may have to turn down the heat slightly), about 10 to 12 minutes or until thickened to a loose pudding consistency (it will thicken further as it cools). While it's still simmering, remove a bit of liquid with a spoon and taste for sweetness; add more sugar if you like it a bit sweeter, stirring well to dissolve. Remove immediately from the heat. Cool the rice slightly. Stir in the almond, rice, or coconut milk and mix well; serve warm or refrigerate and serve chilled. Before serving, pour a tablespoon or two of the dulce de leche into each serving bowl and top with the rice pudding. Top with more dulce de leche, if desired.

Note: It's imperative to stir this pudding as it cooks to prevent the bottom of the pot from scorching and burning the entire batch. If you decide to add more sugar to the pudding, make sure the rice is still hot, so the sugar will dissolve completely; otherwise, you'll end up with a gritty consistency. This pudding keeps in the refrigerator, if well covered, for up to 1 week. If it sets up too much when refrigerated, simply stir in a bit more milk (or water) until it reaches your desired consistency.

Dulce de Leche o Arequipe Casero

Easy Homemade Dulce de Leche

Various Countries | Yield: Makes 1 cup (225 grams) | Difficulty Level: Easy | Total Cooking Time: 3 hours

Although it is widely available in many grocery stores, dulce de leche is a delicacy that most homemakers in Latin America know how to make themselves. If you do buy it, look for Argentinean and Brazilian brands and avoid any that come in a squeeze bottle—they will be too loose.

One 14 ounce (396 gram) can
sweetened condensed milk

Place the unopened can in a medium-sized pot and cover it completely with cold water. Bring it to a simmer over medium-high heat. As soon as it simmers, lower the heat and keep it at a low simmer for 2 hours, uncovered. Keep refilling the pot with additional boiling water as it evaporates to make sure the can is always submerged. Remove from the heat and let the can cool completely in the water until it is room temperature. Store in the refrigerator, until ready to use. To use, open the can and go for it!

Note: You can boil several cans at the same time, as long as the pot is large enough to hold them and still allow plenty of room for water, to cover the cans.

Alfajores con Baño de Chocolate

Dulce de Leche and Chocolate Sandwich Cookies

Argentina | Yield: Makes about 20 cookies | Difficulty Level: Intermediate |
Total Cooking Time: 4 hours (include chilling and cooling times)

I have tasted many versions of these dainty biscuits, filled with hazelnut-chocolate cream, jams, custards, lemon curd, and nut butters. However, these are the ones my children have come to request over the decades, and thus the one you'll see on our family table come birthday after birthday. Like any good shortbread, the dough is delicate; keep in mind that you'll have to chill it for a while before it's ready to cut. Since it's very high in butter, it will keep its shape when cut and baked if it's still cold by the time it hits the oven. In Mar del Plata, Argentina, you'll find alfajores that are completely covered in chocolate. Rather than letting the chocolate drip down the sides, mine leave a chocolate-free rim that allows you to hold them without making a mess. These keep for up to a week in the refrigerator.

FOR THE COOKIES

2 scant cups (250 grams) cornstarch (see Note)

1 cup (105 grams) all-purpose flour

1 teaspoon baking powder

½ teaspoon baking soda

Pinch of fine sea salt

¾ cup (160 grams) unsalted butter, at room temperature

½ cup (100 grams) white granulated sugar

4 egg yolks

1 teaspoon pure vanilla extract

1 cup (240 ml) Dulce de Leche o Arequipe Casero (page 516) or store-bought (see Note on page 519)

FOR THE CHOCOLATE GANACHE

4 ounces (120 grams) bittersweet chocolate, finely chopped

½ cup (120 ml) heavy whipping cream

2 tablespoons unsalted butter, diced and at room temperature

1 teaspoon cognac, brandy, or rum (optional)

To make the cookies: In a large bowl, whisk together the cornstarch, flour, baking powder, baking soda, and salt; set aside. In a separate large bowl, using an electric beater, cream the butter and sugar until light and fluffy (about 4 minutes), scraping down the sides of the bowl well. With the motor at low speed, add one egg yolk at a time, beating well until each is incorporated; beat until creamy, about 1 minute. Add the vanilla and beat slowly, just until combined. Add a third of the flour mixture and beat on low speed just until combined. On a clean surface, place the remaining flour mixture and make a well in the center; pour the beaten dough into the middle of the well and knead together until the dough comes together into a ball, trying to incorporate all of the dry ingredients. Do not overwork. Wrap the dough in plastic wrap and chill for 1 hour. Preheat the oven to 350°F (180°C). Line several baking sheets with parchment paper and set aside. Turn the dough onto a clean and lightly floured surface. Give it a few pats with the full weight of a rolling pin (this is to help it stretch out before rolling it without breaking it, if it's still too cold). Roll the dough out until it's ⅓ inch (8 mm) thick. With a round cookie cutter, cut out 2 inch (5 cm) rounds of dough, placing them about 2 inches (5 cm) apart on the prepared baking sheets. Carefully knead the dough back together and roll out again, repeating until you have 38 to 40 cookies. If the dough gets too warm, wrap it in plastic and chill it for 20 minutes (repeat the rolling and cutting until all rounds are done). Bake the cookies for 12 to 15 minutes or until the edges and bottoms are only slightly golden (be careful not to burn them—they should remain quite light in color). Let them cool on the sheets for 5 minutes; transfer them to cooling racks and cool completely. Top half of the cookies with approximately 1 tablespoon of dulce de leche each and top each with a second cookie. Press down lightly to stick them together (some dulce will seep down the sides). Put them back on cooling racks and make the ganache. To do so, place the chocolate in a heatproof bowl. Place the cream into a small saucepan and bring it to a boil over medium-high heat. →

Pour the cream over the chocolate and let the mixture sit for 30 seconds; with a spatula, mix it slowly until it comes together (do not whip in any air). Stir in the butter one piece at a time, stirring slowly, until melted. If using, add the liquor and stir well. Let the ganache sit at room temperature for 20 minutes so it can thicken slightly (if it's too loose, place it in the refrigerator for a few minutes; you want it to be of a spreadable consistency). Top each sandwiched cookie with 1 tablespoon of ganache (it shouldn't run down the sides of the cookie) and use an offset spatula (or spoon) to spread it just over the top (leaving the sides uncovered). Let the finished cookies rest for 1 hour before serving or until the ganache has set.

Note: When measuring cornstarch, make sure to spoon it into the measuring cup and lightly level it with the back of a knife; never press it down when leveling. You can bake the cookies a day in advance and store them in a container, then fill and decorate them the next day. Dividing this recipe into steps makes it much easier to handle. To make the ganache set faster, chill the cookies for 20 to 30 minutes after decorating. Once assembled, these are best the day they're made; however, they store well in one layer in a container with a tight-fitting lid (at room temperature or in the refrigerator; if chilled, bring them back to room temperature before serving).

Note on store-bought Dulce de Leche: There are several brands of dulce de leche. Avoid any that come in squeezable bottles—it will be too runny. Instead, purchase the thicker dulce de leche sold in cans and in jars. I tend to favor Argentinean and Brazilian brands.

VARIATIONS: Forgo the dulce de leche altogether; use the ganache to fill the cookies and sprinkle them with confectioners' sugar. Or forgo the ganache and let the excess dulce de leche drip onto the sides of each cookie, then roll them in flaked coconut, chocolate sprinkles, or chopped nuts.

Pionono de Dulce de Leche

Dulce de Leche Rolled Cake

Argentina, Chile, and Uruguay | Yield: Serves 6–8 | Difficulty Level: Intermediate | Total Cooking Time: 2½ hours

The base of this light dessert is a sponge cake known as genoise that is filled with a thick layer of milk caramel. It's a classic cake, perfectly suited for a midafternoon snack or a very South American breakfast, alongside a cup of coffee. This simple version is a favorite in Argentina, Chile, and Uruguay. Rolled cakes can intimidate novice bakers, but in reality, they are quite simple to make. Once you bake the first one, you'll be hooked. They're great to make ahead and chill until ready to serve. Homemade or thicker dulce de leche brands work best. (See Sources, and my recipe on page 516.) Cakes like this one are also known as piononos, brazos de gitano (Gypsy's arms), brazos de reina (queen's arms), or niños envueltos (wrapped babies). In Brazil, they're known as rocamboles (rolls). Recipes for rolled cakes date back to Al-Andalus (the time period in which parts of Spain and Portugal were Islamic states) and are of Arab origin. Different countries feature other fillings in rolled cakes: guava jelly or guava paste are traditional in Brazil, Colombia, and the Latin Caribbean. Any kind of fruit jams and whipped cream are traditional in Guatemala. Pastry cream and fruits are traditional in Venezuela, and cajeta (goat's-milk caramel) is traditional in Mexico.

5 eggs, separated, at room temperature

5 tablespoons (75 grams) white granulated sugar

1 teaspoon pure vanilla extract

⅓ cup (37 grams) all purpose flour

½ cup (45 grams) confectioners' sugar, for dusting

1¾ cups (420 ml) Dulce de Leche o Arequipe Casero (page 516) or store-bought (see Note on page 519)

Preheat the oven to 350°F (180°C); line a 10½ x 15½ inch (27 x 39 cm) jelly roll pan with parchment paper and spray the paper with cooking spray; set aside. Place the egg yolks and sugar in the bowl of a stand mixer; start on slow and increase the speed to high, then beat for 1 minute or until the mixture becomes a light foam; add the vanilla. Using a rubber spatula or a whisk, fold in the flour a bit at a time; set aside. In a separate clean bowl, beat the egg whites on high speed for about 2 minutes or until they form stiff peaks. Using a rubber spatula or a whisk, fold the egg white mixture into the yolk mixture, just to combine. Carefully transfer the cake batter into the prepared pan, using an offset spatula to spread it out as evenly as possible and coat the entire bottom of the pan. Bake for 15 to 18 minutes or until the cake is lightly golden and springs back easily when pressed with your fingertips. Dampen a clean kitchen towel well with cold water (make sure to wring it out so it's damp, not dripping wet). Lay the towel flat on the counter and sprinkle it liberally with confectioners' sugar. Turn the cake pan upside down over the towel so the cake unmolds, and remove the cake pan carefully. While the cake is warm, peel off the parchment paper (if it sticks, dampen the paper with a wet basting brush). Starting from the long side, roll the warm cake in the towel; let it cool completely. When cool, unroll the cake and spread the dulce the leche evenly over the top; roll the cake back up again. Trim the edges and transfer cake to a platter. Sprinkle it with more confectioner's sugar, as desired. (See Note on store-bought dulce de leche on page 519).

Tarta Frola de Dulce de Leche

Dulce de Leche Tart

Argentina and Uruguay | Yield: Serves 6–8 (or fewer, in my house!) |
Difficulty Level: Intermediate | Total Cooking Time: 2 hours (including cooling time)

Here flaky pastry combines with thick, creamy milk caramel in every single bite. The birthplace of dulce de leche (pronounced *dool-zeh-deh-leh-che*)is said to be the central region of Argentina that includes Buenos Aires, Córdoba, and La Pampa. It's made by boiling down milk, sugar, and a touch of baking soda until thick and amber colored, in what is a long process. My recipe for dulce de leche on page 516 is very easy to make. However, if you need to save time and effort, you can use store-bought dulce de leche. Find it in many Latin grocery stores and online as manjar, arequipe, manjar blanco, and doce de leite. My first encounter with this dessert was in an Argentinean bakery; every day, a freshly made tart was showcased in the storefront window. As the day progressed, the tart got smaller and smaller. If you've ever had alfajores, the caramel sandwich cookies of South America (my version of them is on page 517), you'll love this giant version that holds much more of the milky, sticky filling than any cookie ever could. To serve, why gild the lily? But, if you must, a scoop of vanilla ice cream couldn't hurt.

1 recipe Pasta Frola (page 37)

3 cups (720 ml) Dulce de Leche o Arequipe Casero (page 516) or store-bought (see Note on page 519)

Egg wash made with 1 egg mixed with 2 tablespoons water (optional)

Preheat the oven to 350°F (180°C). Roll out half of the pastry into a 12 inch (30.5 cm) circle, approximately ½ inch (12 mm) thick. Line a 9 inch (23 cm) tart pan with a removable bottom with the pastry, making sure to press it to the bottom and up the sides. Trim the edge evenly around the rim of the pan. Fill the tart shell evenly with dulce de leche. Roll the other half of the pastry out into a 12 inch (30.5 cm) circle, until it's ⅓ inch (8 mm) thick. Slice it into long strips, each one measuring about 1 inch (2.5 cm) thick. Arrange half of the strips over the filled pie, directly over the dulce de leche, in parallel lines. Lay the remaining strips of dough across the others (don't worry about making a lattice top—it should be rustic). Trim away any very long pieces that may be hanging over the edge of the pan. Pinch the edges together with a fork or spoon, to seal in a decorative way. If desired, brush the tops of the pastry strips with egg wash. Bake the tart for 30 to 35 minutes or until the top is golden. Allow the tart to cool for one hour before sliding it out of the pan and serving it on a platter.

Note: If you don't have a tart pan with a removable bottom, use a regular pie plate. You'll just have to serve it directly from the pan, instead of presenting it on a separate platter.

Dulce de Lechoza Verde

Candied Green Papaya

Venezuela | Yield: Makes 4 cups (960 ml) | Difficulty Level: Intermediate |
Total Cooking Time: 4 hours (including prepping and cooling times)

Long, sweet strands of candied papaya coated in a syrup enhanced with sweet spices is a beloved Venezuelan delicacy during Christmas. Fruits caramelized in sugar—from figs and guava to nances (a tropical fruit that resembles yellow cherries) and tomatoes—have been traditional on Latin America's religious holidays since the colonial period. But don't wait for a holiday to make this—it's good all year round! My Venezuelan friend Lis Hernándes, a well-known chef in Atlanta, Georgia, shared her family's prized recipe with me. The papaya (or lechoza, as it is called in Venezuela) must be solid and unripe, its flesh still a pale green so it can be julienned. Once cooked into a jam, the papaya strands will become translucent, like bronze-colored glass. Lis serves it with sliced queso fresco on the side; I love to serve it as part of an assorted cheese board. This recipe makes a lot, because it's customary to share it with friends; it also lasts a long time in the refrigerator.

One 2 pound (910 gram) very green papaya, peeled, halved, and seeded

1 tablespoon baking soda

1 pound (455 grams) grated panela, papelón, piloncillo, or muscovado sugar (see Note)

1 cup plus 2 tablespoons (255 grams) white granulated sugar

1 tablespoon whole cloves

4 sticks Ceylon cinnamon (canela)

3 fresh or dried fig leaves (optional)

1 tablespoon pure vanilla extract

Using a very sharp knife, julienne or slice the papaya into long slices ¼ inch (6 mm) thick and anywhere between 4 and 6 inches (10–15 cm) long. Place the sliced papaya in a large nonreactive pot and cover completely with water by 2 inches (5 cm); add the baking soda and bring to a boil over medium-high heat. Boil for 6 minutes. Drain in a sieve over the sink and rinse the papaya well under cold water (this is to rinse off the baking soda); set the papaya aside while you make the syrup. Wash the pot and add the sugars; cover with 12 cups (3 liters) of cold water. Bring to a boil over medium-high heat and stir until all of the sugar has dissolved, about 15 minutes at a rolling boil; stir well and continue cooking at a rolling boil for 30 minutes or until reduced by about a third, stirring often. Add the reserved papaya, cloves, cinnamon sticks, and fig leaves (if using). Bring to a boil over medium-high heat and continue simmering for 25 to 30 minutes, stirring often, or until the papaya looks translucent and the syrup has thickened slightly. It will begin to thicken at the end when it foams up; it's important that you check it often so you don't burn it. Remove the pot from the heat and let it cool completely—the syrup will continue to thicken as it cools. Stir in the vanilla until combined. Store in clean glass jars and refrigerate for up to 3 months.

Note: Find green papayas in stores that cater to Asian or Latin American customers. Piloncillo, panela, or papelón, the hardened cones or discs of unrefined sugar used in traditional Latin American cookery, can be found in any Latin American grocery store or online. I use the large holes of a box grater to grate them.

How to Handle a Papaya · Use a potato peeler to peel the papaya. Cut off both ends with a sharp knife so it doesn't wobble around on the cutting board, then slice lengthwise in half. Use a spoon (or an ice cream scoop) to remove all the seeds, and discard them. Slice or chop the papaya as directed in the recipe.

Kidfores de Pecanas

Pecan Shortbread Cookies

Various Countries | Yield: Makes 32–36 cookies | Difficulty Level: Easy | Total Cooking Time: 1 hour

In Latin America you'll find a sin fin (unending) repertoire of powdery cookies that melt in your mouth, called polvorones. Some are made with almonds, others with walnuts, but I love this recipe made with sweet, meaty pecans. Confectioners' sugar is known as azúcar glass in most Latin countries. You can keep these cookies in a tin for up to 2 weeks.

2 cups (225 grams) unbleached all-purpose flour

1 cup (120 grams) finely chopped pecans

Pinch of fine sea salt

1 cup (225 grams) unsalted butter, at room temperature

½ cup (75 grams) packed dark brown sugar

1 teaspoon pure vanilla extract

½–¾ cup (60–95 grams) confectioners' sugar

In a medium bowl, whisk together the flour, pecans, and salt. In a separate bowl, cream the butter and brown sugar until smooth (do this by hand, with a spatula, or with an electric mixer). Stir in the vanilla and mix well. Add the dry ingredients to the wet ingredients and, using your hands, mix them until they come together into a ball. Wrap the dough in plastic wrap and chill it for at least 2 hours (or overnight). Preheat the oven to 350°F (180°C). Line two cookie sheets with parchment paper. Measure 1 tablespoon of dough and roll it into a cylinder, then bend it into a crescent. Place the cookies 2 inches (5 cm) apart on the prepared cookie sheets. Bake for 12 to 15 minutes or until the bottoms of the cookies begin to turn golden (being careful not to burn them). Remove from the oven and cool for 1 minute. Sift the confectioners' sugar into a medium-sized bowl. Roll the warm cookies gently in the confectioners' sugar to coat. Set them on cooling racks, cool completely, and then roll them again in the sugar.

VARIATIONS: Substitute ground almonds or walnuts for the pecans and you'll have classic polvorones.

Granizada o Raspado de Café

Coffee Granita

Colombia and Panama | Yield: Serves 4–6 | Difficulty Level: Intermediate | Total Cooking Time: 12 hours

Back in the 1600s, chunks of ice were cut and brought down from the highest tips of mountains and sold drenched in syrups. Today, on hot summer days, you can still purchase raspados ("scraped ices") sold in paper cups and flavored with simple syrups. Coastal towns didn't serve ices like this one until refrigeration was invented. You must start this recipe one day before you want to eat it in order to allow enough time for the ice crystals to form. Serve it with the Kidfores de Pecanas on page 527.

3 cups (720 ml) hot brewed coffee

¾ cups (155 grams) white granulated sugar

1 tablespoon Kahlúa or coffee liquor

1 teaspoon pure vanilla extract

In a large bowl, combine all the ingredients and stir until the sugar is completely dissolved. Let sit at room temperature until cool, about 15 minutes. Transfer the mixture to a large metal or glass pan and set it in the freezer for 1 hour. After an hour, scrape the mixture with a fork. Repeat every 30 minutes for 4 to 5 hours. The resulting granita should look like loose brown snow. Cover the pan with plastic wrap and keep it in the freezer for at least 1 hour (and up to overnight). To serve, simply scrape one more time and divide into portions.

VARIATIONS: If you're making this for children, use lemonade, orangeade, or cinnamon tea in place of coffee, and omit the liquor.

Kuchen de Manzana

Apple Cake

Chile | Number of Servings: One 9 x 13 inch (23 x 33 cm) cake | Difficulty Level: Easy | Total Cooking Time: 1 hour 15 minutes

Easy fruit-laden cakes such as this one make frequent appearances on the tables of Chilean cooks, whether it is for dessert or for "once"—a teatime snack. The batter can be easily made by hand, but an electric mixer hastens the process. European-style desserts such as this are very common in Chile, where German settlers arrived in great numbers at the end of the nineteenth century. Sweet spices and apples intermingle in this recipe, but it can just as easily be made with any seasonal fruit, such as peaches, plums, pears, or cherries. The thick batter is easier spread with an offset spatula. This cake lasts, covered, at room temperature for four days, and it gets moister as it sits.

3 cups (375 grams) all-purpose flour

2½ teaspoons baking powder

½ teaspoon fine sea salt

1½–2 pounds (680–910 grams) baking apples, peeled, cored, halved, and thinly sliced into ¼ inch (6 mm) slices

Zest of 1 lemon

2 tablespoons freshly squeezed lemon juice

1¼ teaspoons ground cinnamon

¼ teaspoon freshly ground nutmeg

1¼ cups (240 grams) white granulated sugar, divided

¾ cup (170 grams) unsalted butter, at room temperature

1 teaspoon pure vanilla extract

3 large eggs

½ cup (120 ml) half and half

2–3 tablespoons apple or apricot jelly

2 teaspoons brandy

In a large bowl, whisk together the flour, baking powder, and salt; set aside. In another large bowl, mix together the apple slices, lemon zest, juice, cinnamon, nutmeg, and 3 tablespoons sugar; let this sit at room temperature for 20 minutes, to macerate. Preheat the oven to 350°F (175°C). Grease a 9 x 13 inch (23 x 33 cm) baking dish and set aside. In a mixing bowl, with an electric hand mixer on medium speed, beat together the butter, the rest of the sugar, and the vanilla until creamy, about 2 minutes; add the eggs one at a time, beating after each addition. Lower the speed of the mixer, and incorporate half of the dry ingredients, stopping to scrape down the sides of the bowl with a rubber spatula occasionally, until combined. Add the half and half and beat well. Add the remaining dry mixture, beating and stopping to scrape down the sides of the bowl until the batter is smooth. Use a spatula to spread the batter evenly over the bottom of the prepared pan. Arrange the apple slices, overlapping slightly (like shingles on a roof), in one layer on top of the batter. Bake the cake for 45 to 50 to minutes or until the top is golden and a skewer inserted into the middle comes out clean. Mix the apple jelly with the brandy and brush directly over the top of the cake while it's still warm. Cool before cutting into squares.

Pastel de Tres Leches

Tres Leches Cake

Nicaragua | Number of Servings: One 9 x 13 inch (23 x 33 cm) cake | Difficulty Level: Intermediate | Total Cooking Time: 4–12 hours (includes chilling and time to make turrón)

This dense cake (pastel), drenched in a sweetened triple-milk syrup and topped with meringue, is famous the world over. As much as many other countries like to take credit for this decadent dessert, it is actually native to Nicaragua—the recipe was created for an ad for canned milk back in the late 1800s. This is my adaptation of my "nica" sister-in-law's recipe. The three milks in question are sweetened condensed milk, heavy cream, and evaporated milk. If you are lactose intolerant, don't even try it! The porous cake base comes from adding copious amounts of sugar to the batter. The recipe is composed of three parts: the cake base, the liquid syrup, and the cooked Spanish turrón, or cooked egg white frosting (see page 531). Don't let the turrón intimidate you; by following the directions to the letter, you'll have no trouble with it. Of course, you can also use store-bought whipped marshmallow creme. (Many cooks do, but don't say I told you so!)

FOR THE CAKE

2½ cups (280 grams) all-purpose flour

2 cups (400 grams) white granulated sugar

1 teaspoon baking powder

6 eggs, beaten

¾ cup (180 ml) whole milk

1 teaspoon pure vanilla extract

1 recipe Turrón de Convento (page 531)

FOR THE TRES LECHES MIXTURE

One 14 ounce (396 gram) can sweetened condensed milk

One 12 ounce (354 ml) can evaporated milk

1 cup (240 ml) heavy whipping cream

Begin by making the cake: Preheat the oven to 350°F (180°C). Grease a 9 x 13 inch (23 x 33 cm) glass or ceramic baking dish. In a large bowl, whisk together the flour, sugar, and baking powder. In a separate bowl, whisk together the beaten eggs, milk, and vanilla. Add the wet ingredients to the dry ingredients and combine well. Pour the batter into the prepared baking dish and bake for 40 to 45 minutes or until cake is set in the middle (and lightly golden on top) and a toothpick inserted into the center comes out clean. Cool the cake completely. Using a fork or a skewer, poke holes all over the cake—this will help it absorb the liquid. To make the tres leches mixture: In a medium bowl, whisk together the sweetened condensed milk, the evaporated milk, and the heavy cream. Slowly pour this mixture over the cooled cake, adding it a little at a time, as the cake absorbs it (this will take you about 15 to 20 minutes to achieve—be patient). Cover the cake with plastic wrap and place in the refrigerator; let it chill for at least 1 hour or until all liquid has been absorbed. Uncover the cake, frost it generously with a very thick layer (2-3 inches/5-7.5 cm) of the turrón, and chill until ready to serve. The cake will keep in the refrigerator for 3 days—if it lasts that long!

Turrón de Convento

Spanish Nougat

Mesoamerica | Yield: Makes 10 individual servings (or enough for 1 Pastel de Tres Leches, see page 530) | Difficulty Level: Intermediate | Total Cooking Time: 40 minutes

Sweet, glossy, sticky, and shiny meringue has been a classic dessert in any Latin American country where convents abounded during the colonial period. My own experience with it growing up in Guatemala was eating it in crystal coupes, topped with toasted almonds, or stuffed into ice cream cones that were then dipped into chocolate ganache that hardened—the latter was our melt-proof "ice cream" snack. The trickiest part of making a successful turrón is to get the sugar syrup to the right temperature (238°F/115°C). Since you are working with sugar, be careful. It will be very hot—you are making candy, so watch out and make sure there are no kids around while you make this. Use a candy thermometer if you have one; if you don't own one, do what most Latin cooks do: every few minutes, pour a spoonful of the sugar liquid into a glass of iced water. Collect the candy at the bottom and press it into a ball—you want to form a soft, chewy ball, much like transparent toffee—this is called punto de bolita suave, or soft ball stage. Also, as you heat the sugar in the pan, and in order to prevent the sugar mixture from crystallizing and spoiling, make sure to wash down the sides of the saucepan constantly with a pastry brush dampened with cold water. By adding the very hot sugar syrup to the egg whites, you are, in essence, cooking the egg whites to a safe temperature.

6 egg whites

Pinch of fine sea salt

¼ teaspoon cream of tartar

1½ cups (300 grams) white granulated sugar

After making sure that your bowl and beaters are impeccably clean (see Note), place the egg whites, salt, and cream of tartar in the bowl of an electric mixer. Beat this mixture on high speed until the egg whites form soft peaks (about 4 minutes); set them aside. In the meantime, combine ¾ cup (180 ml) water with the sugar in a heavy-bottomed pot and cook to the soft ball stage or until a candy thermometer registers 238°F (115°C). This will take about 15 to 20 minutes. Do not stir, or you will cause the sugar to crystallize, making for a gritty nougat. Watch out, this mixture will go from soft ball to hard ball in no time, and then to caramel, which will be too hot for the nougat. Once the sugar syrup has reached the right temperature, begin beating the egg whites again on high speed and add the syrup very slowly, in a thin stream, until it has all been incorporated into the whites. Keep on beating until the mixture is cool, stiff, and shiny, about 6 minutes.

Note: Start with clean equipment; to make sure your mixing bowl and beaters are perfectly clean, make a paste with vinegar and salt and use it to clean both the bowl and the beaters; then rinse them well under hot running water. This is done to ensure that there is no fatty residue from previous recipes that will prevent the egg whites from clinging to the bowl and thus from attaining the proper volume.

Quesadilla

Cheese Pound Cake

El Salvador and Guatemala | Yield: One 8 x 1½ inch (20 x 4 cm) or one 9 x 1½ inch (23 x 4 cm) cake | Difficulty Level: Easy | Total Cooking Time: 40–60 minutes

If when you hear the word *quesadilla*, you picture tortillas stuffed with cheese, you are thinking of Mexican food. But where the east of Guatemala collides with the northern part of El Salvador, a quesadilla is a pound cake. It looks like any other pound cake but tastes unapologetically of cheese. Oh, it is sweet—it's a dessert, after all—but it also features the salty, pungent flavors of hard cheese (usually, but not always, queso seco). Like many of the baked goods in this region of Central America, the batter is made with rice flour. Sesame, which makes an appearance here, was introduced by enslaved Africans; they called it benne, and Latin Americans call it ajonjolí. Quesadillas taste better as they age, so leftovers are always appreciated, especially alongside a cup of coffee. This is the ideal end to a meal for anyone who craves a bit of sweetness but doesn't want an overly sweet dessert, or in place of a good cheese plate. I love to serve it with sliced berries, guava paste, or vanilla ice cream.

4 eggs, divided

2 cups (295 grams) rice flour, plus more for dusting the pan

2 cups (230 grams) grated hard cheese (queso seco or Parmesan)

1½ teaspoons baking powder

½ cup (115 grams) unsalted butter, at room temperature

¾ cup (155 grams) white granulated sugar

1 cup (240 ml) heavy whipping cream

2 tablespoons sesame seeds

Confectioners' sugar (optional)

Berries of your choice (optional)

Preheat the oven to 350°F (180°C). Butter either an 8 x 1½ inch (20 x 4 cm) or a 9 x 1½ inch (23 x 4 cm) round cake pan. Line the bottom with parchment paper; butter the paper and sprinkle with rice flour. Separate the eggs, placing the 4 yolks in a bowl and 2 whites in another; set aside (reserve the remaining 2 whites for another recipe). Use a whisk (or electric mixer) to beat the egg whites until they hold stiff peaks; set aside. In a large mixing bowl, whisk together the flour, cheese, and baking powder. In a separate mixing bowl, using an electric mixer, cream the butter and the sugar together until light and fluffy, about 2 to 3 minutes; add the egg yolks one at a time, beating well after each addition. Lower the speed of the mixer and add one third of the flour mixture and half of the whipping cream; beat well. Repeat the process, ending with the last third of the flour (remember to stop the motor each time you add the flour, and restart it slowly so you don't cover yourself in batter); set aside. Using a rubber spatula or a whisk, fold a third of the egg whites into the batter; once combined, add the remaining egg whites and fold until incorporated. Transfer the batter to the prepared pan and use an offset spatula to smooth the top. Sprinkle the top with the sesame seeds and bake for 55 to 60 minutes (if using an 8 inch/20 cm pan) or for 40 to 45 minutes (if using a 9 inch/24 cm pan) or until a toothpick inserted into the middle of the cake comes out clean. Remove the pan from the oven and place it on a cooling rack. Allow the cake to cool for 10 minutes before inverting it onto the cooling rack. Cool completely before moving it to a platter. Serve, dusted with confectioners' sugar, and with fruit, as desired.

Note: This cake likes to stick to the bottom of the pan, so using parchment paper saves you a whole lot of trouble. Don't skip this step. You can also use cooking spray to grease the pan instead of butter.

Recommended Kitchen Equipment

Blender   The most important piece of equipment for convenience in a Latin kitchen, used to puree soups and sofrito bases, emulsify sauces and dressings. Blenders have replaced the old mortars and pestles for ease of preparation since the mid-twentieth century.

Food processor   Since the end of the twentieth century, many busy Latin American cooks have added food processors to their kitchen equipment. They come in handy when a lot of chopping must be done in a hurry. If you don't have one, you can chop ingredients by hand, using a knife.

Cutting boards   Use different cutting boards for meat than you do for produce in order to prevent cross-contamination. I have a series of cutting boards for my needs that come in different colors. Don't ruin your kitchen counters!

Measuring cups and spoons (for dry and wet ingredients)   Not all measuring cups are equal. Some are made to measure out dry ingredients, while others (mostly glass ones) are meant to measure out liquids. Make sure you have both kinds. Measuring flour with a cup meant for milk, for instance, will give you higher amounts of flour than a dry measuring cup—thus ruining the entire recipe. This is particularly important when baking. Also, purchase a set of good measuring spoons (although they vary slightly in volume).

Mortar and pestle   These go by so many different names in Latin America—from molote y tejolote to batán, molcajete, piedra y mano, and pilón—that it's hard to keep up. They are stone or wooden utensils used to process different kinds of food that have been used since pre-Columbian times and are still in use in modern kitchens today. For the most part, these are used to pound spice mixes and chiles, to puree sauces, to make pastes (such as moles or fufús), and to pulverize seeds. Modern cooks have replaced them with blenders and food processors, but I still have several of them in use in my kitchen for recipes that call for just a few ingredients or small amounts of food to be ground.

Pots and pans   Called *una batería de ollas* in Spanish, these come in varying sizes, from very large ones (cauldrons) to tiny ones for making sauces. My own collection includes antique clay pots that belonged to my great-grandmother and grandmother, blackened by use over direct fire.

Sharp knives   When students ask me what kind of knife is the best one to have, my answer is always the same: a sharp one. No matter what kind of knives you use, make sure to have them sharpened once or twice a year for precision in your chopping. Sharp knives are much safer than dull ones; the sharper they are, the better they will cut into the ingredients without slipping off.

Whisks and molinillos   Molinillos are wooden stirrers used to stir liquids, like hot chocolate. Whisks are important to mix dry or wet ingredients such as spice mixes, vinaigrettes, or batters.

Tortilla press or heavy skillet   I use these interchangeably whenever I need to pat something into a disc, whether it is ground beef for Tortitas de Carne (page 447) or to make pupusas, tortillas, and other pastry rounds. They are easily available online and are not expensive.

Outdoor grill or indoor grill pan   Grilling meats "asar" is customary throughout Latin America. However, not every home cook owns an outdoor grill. Most outdoor asaderos, or grills, are rustic, heated with coals or wood; few are gas operated. Some contraptions have grills that can be moved up or down, depending on how hot the fire must be to cook the food in question; others are built entirely out of brick; still others are assembled whenever a fire is required. Indoor grill pans are very commonly used to produce a similar result to what can be done outdoors. The trick for these is that they must be heavily constructed (cast iron is most popular). Some have indentations that mimic the grids of a grill, helping the foods to obtain some charring. Some are completely flat—called planchas—and these vary in shapes and sizes; the most common are squares or rounds. These indoor grills can also be used to cook tortillas, arepas, and other recipes in this book.

Woks and large nonstick skillets   Woks in Latin America? Yes, particularly in Peru and Ecuador, where Chinese immigrants introduced them and they are still used to make saltados or chaufa-style dishes. I have a very old, well-seasoned wok that I bought many decades ago; if you don't have one, a very large, nonstick pan with high sides will fit the bill. You'll also need nonstick skillets to cook tortillas, tapioca cracker breads, arepas, and other foods. I always use nonstick pans whenever I toast seeds or spices, which must be toasted at a moderate (not high) heat.

Wooden spoons and spatulas   These are super important in the Latin American kitchen, where food needs lots of stirring. With truly wood spoons, you can check if oil is hot enough to fry with (when the spoon sizzles on contact with the oil, it's ready), to stir sauces, and to hold down masa as it fries. Long-handled wooden spoons are key to helping you fry sauces (to stir a liquid sauce into hot oil is called "frying a sauce"), and to stir thick porridges and bean dishes. Spatulas of all shapes and sizes will also come in handy in the kitchen; always have a couple of delicate ones that don't scrape pans, in case you need to use them in a wok or a nonstick skillet.

Sieves and colanders   I keep them in all sizes in my kitchen, as they always come in handy. You'll need them to drain and rinse ingredients, to soak grains, to drain pots of broth or to strain liquids. Different fineness of mesh are necessary—for instance, you'll need one with very tiny holes to strain oil used for frying in order to remove its impurities, which will help you use the oil for a second or third fry.

Potato ricer or masher   Either or both of these will come in handy when mashing tubers, starchy vegetables, plantains, and other ingredients.

Food mills   Depending on what you're cooking, one of these is bound to come in very handy. A hand-cranked mill or Moulinex was one of the very first things I bought as a newlywed to help me puree beans, beets, potatoes, and roasted tomatoes. It is still a workhorse in my kitchen.

Grain mills   Electric or hand-cranked grain mills will come in handy if you decide to make your own nixtamalized masa. They're also great to grind your own flour. I use mine to grind quinoa into fine flour, wheat berries to make bulghur, and to grind coffee and cocoa beans. Although not a necessity, I highly recommend one if you find yourself making your own corn tortillas or tamales with fresh masa on a regular basis.

Juicers and reamers   I can't tell you how many times I've kicked myself for not thinking of enameling the metal citrus juicers I brought over from Guatemala decades ago, before they hit the market in the 1990s, because I'd be a millionaire ten times over! You can now find them in all different colors, and they are truly the easiest way to juice citrus in small amounts. For making large pots of juice (you'll need a lot of juice to make a ceviche!), I much prefer my electric juicer because it makes the exercise go by quickly. I also keep a wooden reamer in my kitchen for those times when I just need to juice a lemon quickly.

Pepper mill   There is no comparison between freshly ground pepper and that found in jars. One has flavor and aroma; the other tastes like cardboard. The point of using pepper is indeed to add flavor to your dishes—not just specks of color. Any pepper mill is better than no pepper mill! Please, invest in one.

Rimmed baking sheets (half sheets) and metal cooling racks   These are essential whenever you fry any food using my draining and reheating method. Cooling racks must be heatproof so you can place them in a hot oven.

Parchment paper   Not a piece of equipment, but something I can't live without. Lining baking pans with this paper will save you hours of cleaning in the kitchen, plus it

prevents food from sticking to your pans. Use bleach-free whenever you can.

Rolling pin   A rolling pin will come in handy whenever you have to shape dough or pastry for pizza, tarts, pies, empanadas, or other goodies in this book.

Meat mallet   A must, this instrument will help in thinning out meat for milanesas and rolled beef roasts (such as Matambre, page 473), and to crush seeds or nuts.

Large soup pot   My grandmother taught me that as long as there was a pot of soup or beans on our stove, we could always welcome guests to the table. In Spanish we say that we can always add more water to the soup— "hecharle más agua a la sopa"—to stretch it out. Maybe that's one of the reasons why my soup recipes always serve larger crowds— it's not only because they taste better a day later, or that they freeze easily, but that you can open up your home to more people and break bread together. As my Mita would say, "Aunque solo sean frijoles y tortillas les doy, pero pasen adelante"—even if I can only give you beans and tortillas, please come in.

Mail Order Sources and Popular Brands

One of the good aspects of globalization is that ingredients available only in certain countries can now be found worldwide, and in many cases shipped directly to your door. Although this list is not exhaustive by any means, it includes some of my favorite, tried-and-true sources that I hope will make your culinary journey a much easier one.

Amazon
www.amazon.com and www.amazon.co.uk
For Victoria corn grinder for nixtamalized corn; assorted Latin American products including all sorts of chiles and ajíes, spices, Chilean ají de color (sweet paprika), beans, cacao nibs, etc.

Amigo Foods
www.amigofoods.com
Based in Chicago, USA, this is a very comprehensive site where you'll find all sorts of food products from Mexico, Central America, South America, and the Latin Caribbean. A great source for Peruvian peppers and prepared ají pastes, sour orange juice, huacatay, cancha corn, dried canary beans, quinoa, dried and preserved ready-to-use chochos (lupini) beans, Peruvian potatoes, mote corn (for nixtamal). You'll also find tamarind pulp, dulce de leche, Costa Rican Lizano sauce, Guatemalan chiltepe chiles, hot sauces, coffee, cookies, and guava paste. During the COVID-19 Pandemic I ordered plenty of ingredients from them for myself, for friends, and for family craving comfort food. Purchase Hydrated Manioc Flour to make Tapioca here.

Anson Mills
www.ansonmills.com
An excellent source for grains, quinoa, rice, and culinary lime.

Bob's Red Mill Flour
www.bobsredmill.com
A good source for gluten-free flours such as cassava/yuca flour, tapioca and potato starch, masa harina, almond flour, coconut flour, and quinoa flour. Great all-purpose flour and whole wheat flours.

Hodgson Mill
www.hodgsonmill.com
A terrific source for whole grain, organic flours.

Johnny's Selected Seeds
www.johnnyseeds.com
My favorite source for organic, non-GMO seeds such as epazote, a wide variety of chile peppers (sweet and hot), tomatoes, lettuces, herbs, longleaf culantro, curcubita (round zucchini, called "güicoy" in Guatemala), and many other seeds.

King Arthur Flour
www.kingarthurflour.com
My favorite source for all kinds of flour, including pasta flour, all-purpose, bread, and whole grain flour.

La Tienda

www.latienda.com

Peruvian products such as ají pastes in jar (amarillo, panca), Argentinean sausages, dulce de leche, prepared alfajores, and Spanish chorizo extremeño (the cured and cooked kind that looks like salami and is ready to eat).

Masienda

www.masienda.com

Best source for Chef Grade Cal (culinary lime) for nixtamal and for masa harina, as well as for tortilla presses. The only source for a professional grade "molino" or grinding machine for home use (it's expensive but on my dream list). One of the best prepared masa harina mixes you will find.

Mexgrocer

www.mexgrocer.com and www.mexgrocer .co.uk

Great source for all types of prepared ají pastes including ají amarillo, rocoto, panca, etc. You will also find tortilla presses, arepa flour, masa harina, beans, and other Latin American products.

Native Seeds Search

www.nativeseeds.org

A good source for all kinds of chiles, whether you are looking for seeds to plant, dried chiles, dried chile powders, chile products of all kinds.

Rancho Gordo

www.ranchogordo.com

My favorite source for everything beans (including cranberry beans) and dried hominy, dried chiles, ground dry chile mixes, smoked Spanish paprika (pimentón), black quinoa, dried hibiscus flowers (Jamaican), Mexican oregano, herbs, salt, Mexican vinegar, chocolate, and spices.

Zócalo Foods
Online Latin Food Market

www.zocalofoods.com

Best source for all South American products from the Tradiciones Andinas line, which includes frozen, jarred, canned, pureed, and dried South American chiles (ajíes) of all types; garlic puree; chochos/tarwi (lupini beans); canary beans; cancha serrana (corn nuts); Huacatay (Colombian mint); chuño (dried potatoes); arepa flour; dulce de leche; plantain chips, etc. Also sources Central American and Caribbean ingredients such as Costa Rican salsa Lizano; Cuban guava paste and canned guava shells; coffee, chocolate, flours, and condiments such as hot sauces from many countries. Ships to all fifty USA states and Puerto Rico.

Acknowledgments

First and foremost, my thanks go to my beloved husband, Luis, for supporting my work endeavors and helping me reach for my dreams (no matter how crazy they sounded!), for being with me along this journey called life, for never complaining when he ate the same dish repeatedly through tests, and for dining on leftovers often. Over an entire week he shopped for all of the ingredients needed to photograph the more than 150 recipes in this book.

To my agents: Lisa Ekus, who first took a gamble on an unknown writer years ago and had faith in my work before I did. Your guidance and friendship mean the world to me. To Sally Ekus, for cradling this project from its inception, for finding it the best home, and for following the dream through until we made it a reality. To Jaimee Constantine and Sara Pokorny of the Ekus Group, for all of your behind-the-scenes help.

My special thanks to my incredibly kind and sage editor, Tom Pold, who took this book under his capable wings from the very start, helping me shape my vision: Thank you for understanding the essence of its theme and for keeping me sane and confident throughout the process of writing a cookbook during a global pandemic, when shutdowns often meant not finding ingredients (or finding them at a most inopportune time!). This book is as much yours as it is mine.

To everyone at Knopf and Random House for helping to craft a book we can all be proud of. Special thanks to Anna Knighton for designing such a beautiful cookbook. To Amy Stackhouse, who copy-edited this book with care and a great eye for detail.

To my friend and soul brother Kevin Miyazaki for his majestic photography that brings each of the recipes to life. Working with you was one of the highlights of writing this book.

To Kim Calloway, Ellen Clevenger-Firley, Karin Fitspatrick, Kendra Haden, Debbie Moose, Athina Sgambatti, Regan Stachler, Lynn Wells, and Carol Zimmerman, who so generously volunteered their time to help our team cook, style, photograph, clean, and fix the sets between photos as we shot long days. Everyone should be so blessed to have such a wonderful group of friends. I couldn't have done it without you, and I love you!

Recipes must pass rigorous testing to make it to my books. My thanks to Elizabeth Tarpy (Liz), professional recipe tester per excellence, and the sweetest friend anyone could ask for; her attention to detail is never-failing and I couldn't think of publishing a cookbook without her thorough testing expertise. My gratitude goes also to Ellen Clevenger-Firley, Athina Sgambatti, Linda Cristiana, and Alessandra Gutierrez for helping me test many of the recipes in this book. My gratitude to you all is incalculable. I would also like to add my thanks to six-year-old Liam and ten-year-old Isabella for successfully testing the gnocchi recipe all by themselves and to their mom, Kari Smith, who photographed each step so I could see!

For being wise advisers on everything Mexican, from sources for ingredients to how to make proper nixtamal, and so much more: Cristina Potters, Ruth Alegria. For being my source for everything beans: Steve Sando and Rancho Gordo. To Chef Elena Hernandez (and dear Panamanian friend), for connecting me with Panamanian home cooks.

For sharing their family recipes with me from all over Latin America: Chef Francisco Castro, Sandra de Alfaro, Elizabeth Donoso, Pilar Sugrañes, Deysi Aguilera, Maria Esther de Alfaro, Flor Roldán, Doña Antonieta, Leonor de Minondo, Irene de Delprée, Roksanda de Sandoval, Lis Hernández, Mirciny Moliviatis, Vero Albin, Marcela Jongesoon, Don Mariano Patiño Gonzales, Raquel and Hugo Gimeno, Cristina Potters, Beatriz de Descamps, Carmen de Alejos, Vivian de Solís, Georgina Zuñiga, Elena and Francisco Fumagalli, Ana Raquel Morales, Marissa de Alfaro, Luisa Fernanda Rios, Maria Isabel S., Elizabeth de Hernández, Mari Carmen Schell, Luz, and Doña Felipa. To my dear friend Janine Santos-Hertzog and her children Lorenzo and Valentina, for being my taste testers of Brazilian recipes and for sharing their own special dishes with me.

No author is an island, and I owe a depth of gratitude to my colleagues and dear friends who have cheered me on over the years and encouraged me by word and example: Nathalie Dupree, Bruce Weinstein, Mark Scarborough, Rick Rodgers, Robin Asbell, Virginia Willis, Marcie Cohen-Ferris, David Perry, Toni Tipton-Martin, Ronnie Lundy, Carla Hall, David Joachim, John T. Edge, Joe Yonan, Jill O'Connor, Lauren Lawstoka, Stuart Hall, Lisa Cericola, and Andrea Weigl.

To God, always, for blessings received.

Bibliography

Albala, Ken, ed. *Food Cultures of the World Encyclopedia*. 4 vols. Santa Barbara, CA: Greenwood, 2011.

Benitez, Ana, and Monica Lavin. *Sor Juana en la cocina*. Spanish ed. Mexico: Debolsillo, 2010.

Carrillo, Rubén, Asia Llega a América. *Migración e influencia cultural asiática en Nueva España (1565-1815). Asiadémica Revista Universitaria de Estudios sobre Asia Oriental*. Enero, 2014.

DeWitt, Dave. *Precious Cargo: How Foods from the Americas Changed the World*. Berkeley: Counterpoint, 2014.

Diaz del Castillo, Bernal. *The Conquest of New Spain*. Trans. J. M. Cohen. New York: Penguin Books, 1978.

———. *Historia verdadera de la conquista de la Nueva España*. Texto comparado. 3 vols. Ciudad Real: Universidad de Castilla-La Mancha, 2001.

Doménech, Ignacio. *El cocinero americano*. Spain, 1917.

Finlayson, Judith. *The Chile Pepper Bible: From Sweet to Fiery and Everything in Between*. Toronto: Robert Rose, 2016.

Frías Valenzuela, Marcia Argelia; Malacara Herrera, Maria Elena; Martínez Gallardo Sánchez, Edgard; Sánchez Orozco, Montserrat. *La importancia del rescate de la comida barroca como arte culinario dentro de la gastronomía del Estado de Puebla*. Mexico D.F.: Escuela Superior de Turismo, Instituto Politécnico Nacional, 2001.

Laudan, Rachel. *Cuisine and Empire: Cooking in World History*. Berkeley: University of California Press, 2015.

Mann, Charles C. *1941: New Revelations of the Americas Before Columbus*. 2nd ed. New York: Vintage Books, 2011.

———. *1943: Uncovering the New World Columbus Created*. New York: Alfred A. Knopf, 2011.

Miller, Mark, and John Harrisson. *The Great Chile Book*. Berkeley: Ten Speed Press, 1991.

Presilla, Maricel E. *Peppers of the Americas*. California and New York: Lorena Jones Books, Ten Speed Press, 2017.

Sahagún, Fray Bernardino de. *Historia general de lsa cosas de Nueva España*. 1577. Mexico City: Editorial Porrúa, 1992.

Slack, Edward R. *"Sinifying" New Spain: Cathay's Influence on Colonial Mexico via de Nao de China: The Chinese in Latin America and the Caribbean*. Leiden and Boston: Brill, 2010.

Tannahill, Reay. *Food in History*. London: Eyre Methuen, 1973.

Villar Anleu, Luis. *La cocina popular guatemalteca: mitos, hechos y anécdotas*. 2nd ed. Guatemala: Editorial Universitaria, Universidad San Carlos de Guatemala, 2014.

Index

(Page references in *italics* refer to illustrations.)

I

ice cream sandwiches, 488

Indigenous peoples:

achiote and, 191, 194

chocolate and, 477, 486

colonization and, xxii, 222, 321

cooking methods of, 152, 407, 443

corn and, 47-48, 49, 63, 69

culinary heritage from, xxiv, 63, 65, 205, 222, 349, 361

diet of, 219

of Latin America (list), xxvi

slave trade and, xxiii

sweeteners used by, 509

ingredients sources, 539-40

J

jalapeños, 177, 186, 414

Jalea de Chiles Secos y Ron Añejo (Rum and Dried Chile Jam), 183

Jewish people, culinary influence of, xxiii, xxiv, 144, 255, 407, 511

jibaritos, 305-6

jícama, 232

K

Kak'ik (Mayan Turkey Soup), 402

Kidfores de Pecanas (Pecan Shortbread Cookies), 527

Kippe (Baked Kibbeh), 438

kitchen equipment, 535-37

Kuchen de Manzana (Apple Cake), 529

L

lamb:

chops, 433, 434

cultural signifance of, 407-8

kibbeh, 438

skewers, 435

stew, 436

lard:

as flavoring, 409

for fried sauces, 161

mantequilla negra, 70

for pastry, 37

for refried beans, 115, 116

Spanish introduction of, 293, 407

Latin America:

countries in, xvii, xxi

culinary essentials of, 5

culinary heritage of, xvii-xix, xxii-xxv, 481

culinary influences on, xxii-xxv, 219, 222, 321

Indigenous cultures of (see Indigenous peoples)

markets in, 220-21

Latin Caribbean countries, xxi

Latinismo, defined, 119

leaves:

avocado, 205

in chopping herbs, xxvii, 415

for cooking meat, 196, 407, 424

quelites, 220, 222

quinoa, 349

stuffed, 255-56

Lechón Asado con Mojo (Citrus and Cumin Pork Roast), 419

leeks, 399

lemons:

for ceviche, 370

with roast chicken, 387

Lentejas con Tomates y Hierbas (Lentils with Tomatoes and Herbs), 254

lima beans, 52

lime, culinary (calcium hydroxide):

in nixtamalization, 63, 65, 66, 67, 69

sources for, 539, 540

limes (fruit):

for ceviche, 370

in guacamole, 208

pork chops with, 418

with roast chicken, 387

Lizano sauce, 343, 361

lobster:

in ceviche, 370

cooking tip, 339

rice with, 339

risotto, 354

Lomito en Trozo con Salsa de Chiles Secos y Cognac (Filet Mignon with Chile-Cognac Sauce), 472

Lomo Saltado (Stir-Fried Beef), 470

loroco:

chicken with, 395

in pupusas, 88

toasted rice with, 326

Luisa's Aliño Crudo (Fresh Tomato Sauce), 158

lupini beans, 120

M

macaroni salad, 236

mahi-mahi, 364, 366

maize, 47, 63. See also corn

maíz pilado (maíz pelao), 103

Malagueta peppers, 377

mandioca. See yuca

mangoes, 224, 375

Manjar de Leche (Milk Pudding), 514

mantequilla negra (black butter), 70, 409

marinades:

Aliño, 9

beer as, 388

Chimichurri de Cilantro, 14

Harissa de Santo Domingo, 16

Mojo Cubano, 11

mojos as, 391, 419

Vinagreta Básica, 32

vinegar as, 126

marrones, 180

masa:

consistency of, 75

corn used in, 47, 48, 68

flour for, 64

homemade, 65-67, 83, 536

picadillo-stuffed, 87

uses for, 63, 79, 80

Masa Básica para Pies y Tartas (Classic Pie and Tart Shell), 35

masa harina:

defined, 64

hydrating, 79

purchasing, 65, 540

tortilla recipe for, 84

Masa Nixtamalizada, 65

food processor method, 67

grain mill method, 66

Masa Para Pizzas, Fougazza y Fougazettas (Pizza Dough), 39

masarepa, 64

massa para tapioca, 264, 273

Matambre (Stuffed Beef Roll), 473

mayonnaise:

in Latin American cuisine, 236, 238

pink, 31

spicy, 174

Mbejú (Cheese and Yuca Flatbread), 270

meatballs, 444

meatloaf, stuffed, 446

meats:

breaded cutlets, 42-43

for carbonadas, 437

as condiment, 219

cured, 407

dry rubs for, 6, 7

to flavor beans, 115

grilled, 220, 455, 457, 536

marinades for, 11, 16, 32, 126

A NOTE ABOUT THE AUTHOR

In a career spanning more than two decades, Sandra A. Gutierrez, journalist, food writer, cookbook author, food historian, and professional cooking instructor, has taught thousands how to cook.

Born in the USA, she is a bilingual, award-winning journalist, the author of four other cookbooks, and considered one of the top national experts on Latin American foodways and on the Southern regional cuisine of the United States.

In 2017, she was awarded the Les Dames d'Escoffier M. F. K. Fisher Grand Prize for Excellence in Culinary Writing and her work and life story have been featured in the exhibit *Gateways/Portales* at the Smithsonian Anacostia Community Museum. In 2019, her work was recognized as part of the permanent *FOOD* exhibition at the Smithsonian National Museum of American History. On September 15, 2021, in celebration of Hispanic Heritage Month, Sandra was honored by the Smithsonian Institute as a Woman to Know and one of seven Latinas Who Shaped American Culture.

She lives with her husband, Luis, in North Carolina.

A NOTE ON THE TYPE

This book was set in Galaxie Copernicus, a transitional serif typeface designed by Chester Jenkins and Kris Sowersby in 2009. A reconsideration of Monotype Plantin, Galaxie Copernicus is a versatile typeface with a wide base, thick strokes, and balanced proportions.

Composed by North Market Street Graphics, Lancaster, Pennsylvania
Printed and bound by C&C Offset, China
Designed by Anna B. Knighton